W9-AYN-827

Time Out
London

& Lesbian
Gay
London

timeout.com

Time Out Guides Limited
Universal House
251 Tottenham Court Road
London W1T 7AB
Tel + 44 (0)20 7813 3000
Fax + 44 (0)20 7813 6001
Email guides@timeout.com
www.timeout.com

Editorial
Editors Hugh Graham, John Shandy Watson
Consultant Editor Paul Burston
Listings Editors William Crow, Gemma Pritchard
Indexer William Crow

Managing Director Peter Fiennes
Editorial Director Sarah Guy
Series Editor Cath Phillips
Business Manager Daniel Allen
Editorial Manager Holly Pick
Assistant Management Accountant Ija Krasnikova

Design
Art Director Scott Moore
Art Editor Pinelope Kourmouzoglou
Senior Designer Kei Ishimaru
Guides Commercial Designer Jodi Sher

Picture Desk
Picture Editor Jael Marschner
Acting Deputy Picture Editor Liz Leahy
Picture Desk Assistant/Researcher Ben Rowe

Advertising
New Business & Commercial Director Mark Phillips
Magazine & UK Guides Commercial Director St John Betteridge
Account Manager Charlie Sokol
Production Controller Chris Pastfield
Copy Controller Alison Bourke

Marketing
Sales & Marketing Director, North America & Latin America Lisa Levinson
Group Commercial Art Director Anthony Huggins
Circulation & Distribution Manager Dan Collins
Marketing Co-ordinator Alana Benton

Production
Group Production Director Mark Lamond
Production Manager Brendan McKeown
Production Controller Katie Mulhern

Time Out Group
Director & Founder Tony Elliott
Chief Executive Officer David King
Group Financial Director Paul Rakkar
Group General Manager/Director Nichola Coulthard
Time Out Communications Ltd MD David Pepper
Time Out International Ltd MD Cathy Runciman
Time Out Magazine Ltd Publisher/MD Mark Elliott
Group Commercial Director Graeme Tottle
Group IT Director Simon Chappell

Contributors
Introduction Hugh Graham. **Gay London Today** Rupert Smith (*Two tribes, The bravest man in Britain*? Hugh Graham; *Clubbed to death* Paul Burston). **Gay Nightlife** Paul Burston with additional reviews by Hugh Graham (*My favourite things* interviews Nuala Calvi; *The village people, A boy named Woo, An urban legend* Paul Burston; *Straight up* Sarah Guy; *My heart belongs to daddy* Hugh Graham; *Dude looks like a lady* Rupert Smith; *The cultured club* Ottilie Godfrey). **Lesbian Nightlife** Sarah Garrett (*You shall go to the ball* Ottilie Godfrey; *My favourite things* interview Nuala Calvi). **Where to Stay** Adapted from *Time Out London Guide* with additional reviews by Hugh Graham. **Restaurants & Cafés** Adapted from *Time Out London's Best Restaurants* with additional reviews by Paul Burston. **Shopping** Adapted from *Time Out London's Best Shops* with additional reviews by Ottilie Godfrey, Hugh Graham and David Phelan. **Festivals & Events** Adapted from *Time Out London Guide* with additional reviews by Paul Burston. **Comedy & Cabaret** Paul Burston. **Dance** Ian Knowles. **Film** Antonio Pasolini. **Galleries** Adapted from *Time Out London Guide*. **Theatre** Carl Miller. **Music** Adapted from *Time Out London Guide*. **Sport & Fitness** William Crow (*Playing away* Ottilie Godfrey; *The swimming pool library* Hugh Graham; *Gonna make you sweat* Paul Burston). **History** Carl Miller (*An affair to remember* Hugh Graham). **Around Town** Adapted from *Time Out London Guide* (*My favourite things* interviews Nuala Calvi; *Fast love* Hugh Graham). **Brighton** Richard Smith (*Proud marys* Paul Burston). **Directory** Paul Burston, William Crow, Hugh Graham.

The Editors would like to thank Mansur Bavar, Paul Burston, Lynn Chambers, Simon Coppock, Sarah Guy, Dan Jones, Shaun Kent, Jenni Muir, Anna Norman, Cath Phillips, Holly Pick, Patrick Welch, Eileen Whitfield, Elizabeth Winding.

Maps john@jsgraphics.co.uk. London Underground map supplied by Transport for London.

Cover image David Newton

Photography pages 4 (bottom right), 21, 37, 86, 90, 91, 93, 112, 113 (top), 130, 131, 132 (top), 189 (bottom), 195, 230, 237 Rob Greig; page 4 (top right), 120 Pride London; page 4 (bottom left) Rogan MacDonald; pages 4 (top left), 15, 16, 26 (top), 28, 36 (top and bottom right), 45, 51, 56, 66, 106, 119, 140 (top), 147, 168, 170 (bottom), 181, 183, 192, 197, 203, 204, 212, 225, 235 Jonathan Perugia; pages 5 (left and top right), 8, 13, 24, 27, 31, 43, 47, 53, 121, 132 (bottom), 137, 177, 199, 209, 227 Heloise Bergman; pages 5 (bottom right), 23, 186, 190 Ben Rowe; pages 6, 7 Shutterstock; pages 20, 89, 200 Alys Tomlinson; page 26 (bottom) Thomas Skovsende; pages 36 (bottom left), 81, 94, 108, 113 (bottom), 127, 134, 170 (top), 213 (top), 219 Michelle Grant; page 44 Mike Kear; page 46 Adrian Lourie; page 54 AbsolutQueer Photography; pages 55, 59, 62, 65, 67, 75, 92, 114 (top right and bottom), 125, 126, 138, 142, 162, 164, 184, 205, 215 Britta Jaschinski; page 70 Nerida Howard; pages 71, 175, 194, 201, 210 Andrew Brackenbury; pages 76, 77, 78, 133, 161, 221, 228 Olivia Rutherford; pages 82, 87, 97 Michael Franke; pages 95, 96, 109, 175 Ming Tang-Evans; pages 103, 118 (top), 140 (bottom), 225, 226 Ed Marshall; pages 114 (top left), 213 (bottom), 223 Anthony Webb; page 116 Elisabeth Blanchett; pages 118 (bottom), 214 Nick Ballon; page 123 Belinda Lawley; page 124 Gideon Mendel; page 146 Susie Rea; pages 150, 156, 157 Rex Features; page 153, 158 Getty Images; page 163 Morley Von Sternberg; pages 165, 173 Tove K. Breitstein; page 169 Nigel Tradewell; page 172 www.simonleigh.com; page 180 MJ Brooks; page 185 Gemma Day; page 189 (top) Gordon Rainsford; page 206 Emma Wood; page 207 Duncan McKenzie; page 211 Gavin Jackson; pages 222, 234 www.richardrowland.co.uk; page 229 Scott Wishart; pages 232, 233 www.realbrighton.com. The following images were provided by the featured establishments/artists 11, 17, 30, 35, 38, 42, 57, 58, 145, 191.

Printer St Ives (Web) Ltd, Storeys Bar Road, Eastern Industrial Estate, Peterborough PE1 5YS.
Time Out Group uses paper products that are environmentally friendly, from well managed forests and mills that use certified (PEFC) Chain of Custody pulp in their production.

ISBN 978-1-905042-56-2
Distribution by Comag Specialist (01895 433 800).
For further distribution details, see www.timeout.com.

Introduction

L ondon is the queen of gay cities. San Francisco may be a gay mecca, but it has lost its edge. 'Gay Paree' is too elegant to be flaming. New York has good credentials – the Stonewall riots, for a start – but it's too butch. London, by contrast, is screaming. It boasts a long tradition of gender-bending, from Shakespeare's ambiguous plays at the Globe to bewigged judges, from panto dames to pop stars (Bowie, Boy George). It has men in uniform (bobbies, Beefeaters) and naked lust (Hampstead Heath). Royalty is inherently camp: the pomp and ceremony, the costumes, the bitchy courtiers. London's literature is also tinged with pink, from Oscar Wilde to the Bloomsbury Group. The capital has always been a magnet for eccentrics (Quentin Crisp) and style icons (Leigh Bowery). And underground gay culture enters the mainstream here in a way it doesn't across the pond (think Stock Aitken Waterman records, or comics like Graham Norton and Lily Savage). Even

David Beckham flirts with gay imagery; indeed, the term 'metrosexual' was coined by a London writer. Then there's sex: judging from all the tabloid scandals, English reserve belies a kinky side.

So queerness is in London's DNA. But does the reality live up to the gay fantasy? Yes and no. London's huge population has spawned a diverse club scene. Name your niche – indie kid, club kid, pop tart, muscle boy, lipstick lesbian – and your neighbourhood, and there's a bar to fit the bill. But too much choice can be tricky. It's hard to settle down when there's always a new venue, or lover, around the corner; opportunities for sex are plentiful, but love is elusive. To fill the void, you can shop, eat, sightsee or soak up some culture; we've packaged the highlights with a queer eye. But the scene will keep luring you back. And this guide will help you look for love in all the right – and wrong – places. We hope you find it, or have fun trying.

ABOUT TIME OUT GUIDES

This is the fourth edition of the *Time Out Gay & Lesbian London Guide*, one of the series of guides produced by the team behind the listings magazines in London, New York and Chicago. Our guides are written by resident experts. *Time Out* London magazine won Publication of the Year at the 2008 Stonewall Awards for its gay coverage.

ESSENTIAL INFORMATION

For practical information – including details of local transport, hospitals and emergency numbers – turn to the Directory, starting on page 238.

THE LOWDOWN ON THE LISTINGS

Addresses, phone numbers, transport information, opening times and admission prices are included. Listings have been checked for accuracy, but phone ahead to be sure, in case of venue changes or errors. Map references are included for venues that fall on our street maps (starting on p262).

PRICES AND PAYMENT

We have noted which of the following credit cards are accepted: American Express (AmEx), Diners Club (DC), MasterCard (MC) and Visa (V).

TELEPHONE NUMBERS

The area code for London is 020. All eight-digit phone numbers in this guide take this code unless otherwise stated, so add 020 if calling from outside London. To call from abroad, dial your country's exit code, followed by 44 (the international code for the UK), then 20 for London (dropping the first zero of the area code) and the eight-digit number.

FEEDBACK

To help us improve this guide, we'd like to know who's reading it. Let us know if you're gay, lesbian or otherwise. Are you visiting London or do you live here? Contact guides@timeout.com.

SPONSORS & ADVERTISERS

We would like to thank our sponsor, Gaydar, for its involvement in this guide. However, we would like to stress that sponsors have no control over editorial content. The same applies to advertisers. No venue has been included because its owner has advertised. An advertiser may receive a bad review or no review at all. The opinions in this guide are those of Time Out writers and entirely independent.

Introduction   3
Gay London Today   6

Nightlife   13

Gay Nightlife   15
  Map: Vauxhall   25
Lesbian Nightlife   50

Consume   59

Where to Stay   60
Restaurants & Cafés   82
Shopping   99

Arts & Entertainment   119

Festivals & Events   120
Comedy & Cabaret   121
Dance   122
Film   124
Galleries   127
Theatre   129
Music   133
Sport & Fitness   136

Contents

Around Town 147

History 148
Getting Started 159
South Bank & Bankside 160
The City 167
Holborn & Clerkenwell 171
Bloomsbury & Fitzrovia 174
Marylebone & Oxford Street 179
Mayfair & St James's 182
Soho 186
  Map: Soho 187
Covent Garden 194
Westminster & Victoria 198
Kensington & Chelsea 202
North London 207
East London 211
South London 217
West London 225
Brighton 229

Directory 237

Getting Around 238
Resources A-Z 242
Further Reference 249
Index 251
Advertisers' Index 257

Maps 258

London Overview 258
Central London by Area 260
Street Maps 262
London Underground 272

Gay London Today

London has never been more gay, but are we losing our identity, asks **Rupert Smith**.

London is the best city in the world in which to be homosexual. We have the widest variety of clubs and cultures, a high level of social tolerance and legal equality, and a history that goes back centuries. No wonder gay men and women from around the world want to live here. And beautiful people too. If you have an internet connection, no morals and a high sex drive, you can sleep with men and/or women of all nations without leaving the comfort of your own home.

I've been out and about in London for 30 years, and in that time have seen changes that would have staggered my 18-year-old imagination. On the credit side, we have a huge, wide-open gay scene that can be accessed by just about anyone. We have three distinct gay neighbourhoods: in Soho, Vauxhall and Shoreditch, where we can be ourselves without too much hassle. The police, once our enemy with their raids and arrests, now join us on marches and strive to protect us. And there's a thriving cultural scene bursting out of the ghetto and into the mainstream.

But not every change has been for the better. In the olden days, we were all 'gay' together, male and female, young and old, butch and femme, top and bottom. There were so few places and spaces in which we could be ourselves, that we couldn't afford to fragment. As a result, the genders and the generations mixed, we learned from one another and had a sense of common cause. These days, we don't even have a word that we can use to describe ourselves. 'Gay' is thought to exclude women, and has been stolen to mean 'crap'.

Two tribes

Hugh Graham ponders the great gay divide.

In 1984, Frankie Goes to Hollywood hit number one in the charts with 'Two Tribes', a single that took the gay club scene by storm. Twenty-five years later, life is imitating art as the gay scene splinters into two distinct groups. The geographical split boils down to Shoreditch – an artsy enclave in east London – versus Vauxhall, the so-called gay village in south London. But the divide is not just physical: it's cultural too.

The most obvious difference is fashion. The Shoreditch scene is sprinkled with modern-day dandies: young, waif-like figures who dress up to the nines, posing and preening in the **George & Dragon** pub (see p31) like 21st-century New Romantics. Skinny black jeans are de rigueur; tweed blazers, velvet jackets or trenchcoats add cinematic flair, as do the mad hats: pork pies, flat caps, boaters and trilbies. Geeky tortoiseshell glasses are another accessory, as are gal pals sporting Amy Winehouse hairdos. Flaming dyed hair and multiple piercings add '80s glitter.

The Vauxhall brigade, by contrast, are less Oscar Wilde and more Muscle Mary. Designed to show off beefy bodies, their look is conservative in its uniformity: low-cut jeans or combat trousers paired with tight T-shirts; bald or shaved heads adding to the sea of flesh. The only flamboyance comes in the form of elaborate tattoos, displayed in all their glory as men whip off their tops.

And in Vauxhall, the tops do come off, often as the drugs kick in: this scene is literally a case of substance over style. GHB, ecstasy, crystal meth – you name it, many Vauxhall boys will ingest it in order to fuel a weekend of debauchery and sex.

In Shoreditch, fashion is the drug of choice. If the kids dabble, they are more likely to take speed than GHB. But at the George & Dragon, the crowd drinks lager out of plastic cups and drunkenly sings along to the poptastic tunes – everything from the Bangles to the Feeling.

Indeed, the music scene in Shoreditch is pleasingly eclectic and eccentric. DJs slap on a truly catholic mix of records at bars like the G&D and the **Dalston Superstore** (see p31). The monotonous beats in Vauxhall, by contrast, are tailor-made for the identikit bodies that dance to them, and are made palatable by chemicals.

The great gay divide is not always so clear cut, however. Take the **Royal Vauxhall Tavern** (RVT, see p34): with its avant-garde cabaret and irreverent spirit, it is a fish out of water in 'the village'. Equally, the **Joiners Arms** (see p33) in Shoreditch sometimes feels like a Vauxhall club late on a Saturday night, when the house tunes are pumping and a whiff of sex hangs in the air.

And sex transcends all the divisions. But in hedonistic Vauxhall, cruising is at the top of the agenda, whereas in Shoreditch, style takes centre stage and the mood is more cerebral. Still, all that coolness can be cloying. The Vauxhall knocking shops may be clinical, but their naked honesty is refreshing, if scary (see p12 **Clubbed to death**).

Halfway between Shoreditch and Vauxhall is Soho – the centre of London's gay scene, and literally the middle of the road – where tribalism gives way to tourism, and the scene goes mainstream. Where do you fit in?

'Queer' upsets those old enough to remember the hatred with which is was once used, our equivalent of 'nigger'. 'Homosexual', although accurate, is such a bloody mouthful, and has a distinctly medical whiff. And don't get me started on LGBT, or LGBTICQ. We've deprived ourselves of a name, and thus of any possible solidarity.

That said, the outside world seems not only to tolerate but actually to love us. In the 2008 London mayoral elections, both the major candidates actively courted the gay vote, despite the fact that Boris Johnson was, not so long ago, outspokenly homophobic. Watching him

grovelling for forgiveness was gratifying (although the fact that it worked was a bitter pill to swallow). But at least we now know that even Tories think we matter. Not so very long ago they were trying to legislate us out of existence.

Hand in hand with this political acceptance goes a complacency among gay people – the battles are won, activism bores the pants off the Aussie Bum brigade, history is an irrelevance. One young club DJ recently told me that we should all strive to forget the bad old days of homophobia, illegality and activism, because it was all a bit sad and embarrassing. When

those of us with long memories were celebrating 40 years of decriminalisation in 2007, there were plenty of wide-eyed innocents who knew nothing of their own history, and wondered what the old folk were getting so excited about. It's not entirely their fault. It's not taught in schools, there are few books on the subject, and hardly any places where the gay generations can mix and pass on our lore and traditions.

In this fragmented world, probably the biggest challenge we face is to bridge those divisions. Where, for instance, do lesbians and gay men get a chance to play together? Do we still have any sense of common cause, as we did in the good old, bad old days of gay liberation and the AIDS crisis? And what about trans people – once an essential part of the mix, now increasingly restricted to their own spaces, willingly or otherwise. For gay men, the divisions are just as sharp. Any man over 40 who steps into a Vauxclub invites derision, and would have to be off his head on drugs to deal with the noise, the crowds and his own sagging muscles. Young clubbers, by contrast, are so consumed by the 'lifestyle', to use an old-fashioned euphemism for drug use and casual sex, that they have little time or energy to engage on any other level.

With all these unconnected ghettos, the prospect of any sort of dialogue has always seemed slim – until recently. But things are changing. The balance between those places where you go to get out of your mind, and those where you go to use your mind, is being redressed. We're emerging from a period of dreary butchness, soundtracked by dull house music and fuelled by GHB, into what looks like a gay renaissance. The new young queens about town are fantastically camp little things, plastered with make-up, squeezed into ridiculous 1980s-inspired outfits, much happier to mix with girls – less obsessed, it seems, with pecs-and-sex.

In scene terms, the hub of this brave new gay world is Shoreditch and Hoxton, where the pubs and clubs embrace a healthy balance between getting laid, getting off your tits and consuming a bit of culture. Cabaret is back on the menu. Singers, performance artists and comedians are giving us something to focus on other than beats and tit size. Drag artists nurtured in those clubs are now sprinkling their fairy dust all over London. The whole scene is the spiritual offspring of Duckie (see p39), that Vauxhall stalwart.

Beyond the pub and club circuit, there are new platforms for lesbian and gay culture. After years of the decline of gay theatre, there are several venues addressing queer audiences: the Oval House Theatre (52-54 Kennington Oval, SE11 5SW, 7582 7680, www.ovalhouse.com), the Soho Theatre and the Royal Court (for both, see p132) are putting on shows that mix drama, cabaret and comedy to innovative effect; the King's Head pub (115 Upper Street, 020 7226 1916, N1 1QN) in Islington often shows fringe gay plays. And on the bigger stages, queer culture runs riot – at the time of writing, *Billy Elliot* was still packing 'em in at the Victoria Palace, Alan Bennett's *The Habit of Art* was luring the chattering classes to the South Bank, *Holding the Man* had received raves at the Trafalgar Studios and Jonathan Harvey's new play, *Canary*, was causing a stir at the Hampstead Theatre.

But it's outside the theatrical sphere that the big changes are taking place. Bastions of high culture like the V&A (see p202), the Southbank Centre (see p162) and the National Portrait Gallery (see p198) are embracing the LGBT agenda with an enthusiasm that suggests more than just diversity box-ticking. At the National Portrait Gallery, LGBT guides are taking groups on special tours through the collection, talking about the queer artists and subjects on the walls. The British Museum's Roman exhibition, 'Hadrian: Empire and Conflict', confronted the emperor's homosexuality in a positive, almost confrontational way that would have been unthinkable in the 20th century. And the Southbank Centre is now programming queer events across every area, with a gay strand at the London Literature Festival (www.londonlit fest.com) and Polari, a monthly gay literary salon hosted by Time Out's Paul Burston (www.myspace.com/polarigaysalon).

On the face of it, London has never been more gay. You can't open a free newspaper or a listings magazine without seeing the faces of gay celebrities such as Jodie Harsh staring out at you. Gay men rule Soho to such an extent that gangs of marauding straight provincials now know better than to shout insults. The gay club fashion of today is more than likely to be emulated on the high street tomorrow. We can live, love and even marry openly, with little fear of opposition.

Our challenge, as gay Londoners, is to match the support and acceptance we find in the outside world with a bit more respect for one other. Young LGBT people shouldn't have to go it alone in a world that's fraught with dangers and self-destruction. We should create a city that welcomes, nurtures and educates our 'children' – a city in which we take responsibility as well as demanding rights.

The bravest man in Britain?

Gay-rights activist Peter Tatchell shows no signs of mellowing.

Has the battle for gay rights been won?

There's no guarantee that the gains that we've won will remain forever. Who can say what might happen in 20 or 40 years? Climate chaos and an economic depression could fuel the rise of far-right parties that might scapegoat minorities. In 1930, Berlin was the gay capital of the world. There were gay bars, clubs and associations. Three years later, the Nazis came to power and gays were carted off to concentration camps. It shows how quickly freedoms that were taken for granted can be extinguished. What's the saying? The price of freedom is eternal vigilance.

You do brave things, like tackling Robert Mugabe. Where do you find the guts?

I might be right or I might be wrong, but I follow my conscience. I don't think I'm brave, compared to those who risked their lives to defeat Naziism in World War II, or to human rights campaigners in countries like Zimbabwe, Burma, Iran and Saudi Arabia. Those people risk their lives and freedoms more than I've ever done.

Do you ever get scared?

Always. Whenever I protest, I'm incredibly nervous to the point of feeling physically sick. Before I heckled Prime Minister Gordon Brown about civil liberties, I felt my body temperature plummeting and my stomach churning. Once I'd made my statement, I felt a huge sense of relief. Sickness is a price worth paying to challenge people who are abusing their power to harm others.

What's the worst thing that has ever happened to you?

I was knocked unconscious by Mugabe's bodyguards in Brussels in 2001, and left lying in the gutter. And I was battered by neo-Nazis in Moscow in 2007, which left me with long-term injuries. I have reduced vision in one eye and minor brain damage, which has hurt my memory, concentration, balance and coordination. But, by comparison to campaigners in Iran, or Saudi Arabia, my injuries are nothing. People have been raped with police truncheons or had electric shocks applied to their genitals. I got off lightly.

What has been your favourite protest?

The OutRage! direct action protests in the 1990s, which overturned police homophobia. Police were arresting thousands of gay men for consensual sex and ignoring queer-bashing. OutRage! demanded policing without prejudice,

and protection not persecution. We invaded police stations, disrupted press conferences and exposed agents provocateurs. Within three months, the police were pleading with OutRage! to negotiate. Within a year, they agreed to most of our demands. After three years, the number of gay men convicted of 'gross indecency' fell by two-thirds. We saved thousands from arrest. This proves that direct action protests work.

What advice would you give to gays who want to help but don't have your guts?

My way of campaigning isn't the only way. We also need people to lobby their MPs and government ministers. Writing a letter helps. The big issues are the ban on same-sex marriage, mistreatment of LGBT asylum seekers, and the non-prosecution of Muslim fundamentalist clerics and pop stars who incite anti-gay violence. And the way that the media ignores homophobic violence, as in the case of Michael Causer, 18, who was stabbed to death in Liverpool and barely got a mention. Similar racist murders get headlines for weeks.

● *For more details, see www.petertatchell.net.*

Clubbed to death

HIV is back, fuelled by GHB. Is the party over, asks **Paul Burston**

Something scary is happening in the Vauxhall gay village. Doctors know it. Club promoters know it. Clubbers know it too. But nobody is talking about it. Twenty-five years after AIDS was first identified, much has changed in the fight against the disease. A generation has grown up with the message that safer sex saves lives. So why are new infection rates so high? And why are some gay men hell bent on destroying themselves?

In November 2007, on the day before World AIDS Day, the Royal Vauxhall Tavern hosted a night called 'The Biggest Suicide Cult in History'. Strong words, and no less than you'd expect from the man responsible, performance artist David Hoyle. But the flyer went further. 'All over Vauxhall they are fucking without condoms,' it read. 'All over Vauxhall they are dancing till Tuesday morning. All over Vauxhall they are taking G, K, C, V and E [that's GHB, ketamine, cocaine, Viagra and ecstasy]. All over Vauxhall they are dying.'

'I truly believe that a lot of gay men would prefer to be dead,' says Hoyle. 'They clearly have deep-seated self-esteem issues and they go out seeking oblivion because, deep down, they don't believe their lives are worth living.' You certainly don't have to look too far on the gay scene to find people behaving in a manner you might describe as self-destructive.

In the past eight years, the number of gay men with HIV in the UK has almost doubled. Partly this is due to an increase in the numbers coming forward for testing. But partly it's due to a rise in unsafe sex or 'barebacking'. Dr Sean Cummings of Freedomhealth is an expert on gay male sexual health, and has warned for years of a second epidemic. Today, he confirms that sexual health clinics 'have reached crisis point with rocketing rates of new STD diagnoses'. And where there's syphilis and gonorrhoea, HIV often follows.

'I get offered a lot of unsafe sex,' says Simon Casson, promoter of Duckie. 'I'm completely open about my HIV+ status, and I meet a lot of men who want me to fuck them without condoms. I used to go to gay sex clubs and saunas and there was always a lot of unsafe sex. People in those environments tend to be off their faces on drink and drugs. Unsafe sex is actually not that socially taboo. It's quite accepted. Just look at all the men advertising for bareback sex on Gaydar.'

Alternatively, walk into any gay sex shop and the evidence is all around. Bareback porn is outselling all other forms of gay adult entertainment. For years, the focus was on eroticising safer sex. Now the reverse is true. Barebacking is portrayed as just another gay lifestyle choice, like living in a loft-style apartment or shopping at IKEA. Surely this must be affecting behaviour? As one gay porn producer wrote in a letter to the gay weekly Boyz: 'Porn does influence the kind of sex you have in reality, and bareback porn contradicts all the good work and education on HIV prevention.'

In November 2007, three British porn actors contracted HIV on a gay film shoot. Which begs the question: how many gay men have got off watching the film in which they became infected? And how many will imitate their behaviour? Many young gay men think that HIV is no big deal. They've heard about combination therapy, they've seen the ads with muscle men climbing mountains and they've jumped to the conclusion that life on anti-retrovirals is a picnic. There are even the fatalistic few for whom contracting HIV is some sort of rite of passage, or a stepping stone towards having lots of unprotected sex without having to think about the consequences.

Then of course there's the other kind of 'combination therapy', the cocktail of recreational drugs in common use on the gay club scene. Ecstasy has given way to a combination of drugs including coke, crystal meth and GHB. Clubs in Vauxhall even have 'recovery rooms' where people are left to 'sleep off' the effects of GHB – assuming that they don't develop breathing difficulties or have a cardiac arrest. Several prominent gay DJs have warned that GHB is killing the scene in Vauxhall. It's killing the customers too. In 2007 and 2008, there were several deaths related to GHB on the scene. And to echo that famous AIDS warning from the '80s, that's just the tip of the iceberg.

'GHB is a nasty, poisonous drug that is killing gay men on a regular basis,' says Cummings. 'Death often occurs during or just after sex, so victims are found in humiliating circumstances. There is nothing glamorous about finding a young man dead in a harness, having fallen, struck his head and inhaled his own vomit and suffocated.'

'I understand the connection between sex and drugs,' says Casson. 'I experimented for years, and I ended up HIV+. Do I regret it? Yes, I do. The gay world said that it was OK to live like that. And it's not. You can't go out clubbing for four days at a time, necking every drug in sight, and not expect something bad to happen. Gay men tend to meet each other in drink-fuelled, drug-fuelled environments, and it's killing us. People are dying and there needs to be a wake-up call.'

In the early '80s, before AIDS really hit Britain, there was a HiNRG song played at Heaven called 'So Many Men (So Little Time)'. How prophetic those words were. Twenty-five years on, how many men must contract HIV or die from drug overdoses before we change our behaviour? How long before gay men call time on a lifestyle that's killing us?

Nightlife

Gay Nightlife   **15**
  My favourite things Will Young   17
  The best Nightlife   18
  My favourite things
    Dan Gillespie Sells   21
  The village people   24
  Map Vauxhall   25
  Straight up   26
  My heart belongs to daddy   29
  A boy named Woo   30
  My favourite things
    Mark Ravenhill   37
  Dude looks like a lady   38
  The cultured club   42
  An urban legend   44
  My favourite things Paul Burston 46

Lesbian Nightlife   **50**
  The best Clubs   50
  You shall go to the ball   52
  My favourite things
    Rhona Cameron   57

TONKER

EVERY FRIDAY
AT EAGLE LONDON

Tonker's mantra is

BOOZE · CRUISE · TUNES

and this party aims to bring back
the social side of life with our Blokes
parties around the world.

Tonker started over 6 years ago and has
now found it's home at Eagle London.
Every week 400 of the hottest guys
assemble a great mix of blokes, bears
and guys — a very sexy crowd of
'guy next door' meets your favourite dad
or uncle and rugby player! Whatever
your look or style there's always a warm
welcome for everyone at Tonker.

The music is headlined by international
resident DJ Tim Jones, who has played
parties as far afield as Sydney's famous
"Gay Mardi Gras" plus London and
Brighton's Pride festivals. Alongside Tim
you will regularly find the best in local
and international DJ talent, such as
Danny Rampling, Joey Negro
and Andy Bell from Erasure
to name just a few.

EAGLE
LONDON

349 KENNINGTON LANE, VAUXHALL, LONDON SE11 5QY

VAUXHALLVILLAGE   LONDON'S HOTTEST GAY VILLAGE

Gay Nightlife

So many men, so little time.

Admiral Duncan. *See p18.*

Keeping an ear to the ground, and scanning the pages of various social networking sites, one detects some grumblings on London's gay scene. Critics say that it's going through a bit of a down phase. Could this be true? And if so, why? Is it due to the economic downturn? The fact that there aren't enough Muscle Marys to fill more than one circuit-style dance party in a railway arch in Vauxhall? Or is it simply that we've never have it so good, and being British, we have to find something to grumble about? As one gay New Yorker said on one site: 'You should try living in Chelsea' (Chelsea, New York, that is, not Chelsea, London). The fact is, London's reputation as the gay clubbing capital of Europe, if not the world, is still richly deserved. Our gay scene is bigger and more diverse than any you'll find anywhere. It also runs later – much later. Not for us the 2am closing of many US cities. In London, the clubs never close (at least not at the weekend) and, what's more, they cater to just about everybody.

If funky house and circuit-style dance parties aren't your bag, there are plenty of other options to choose from. There are clubs for bears, clubs for indie kids, clubs for drag queens (and kings) – even clubs for people who choose not to define themselves quite so narrowly, but who also happen to be gay. And that's before we get on to venues that describe themselves as 'polysexual' ('mixed', to you and me). And if it all becomes just too overwhelming – or you've got straight mates in your posse – there's no shortage of hip het bars in the capital (*see p26* **Straight up**).

The main developments over the past few years have been the rapid rise and slow decline of the Vauxhall gay village, and the return of alternative drag and the '80s 'club kid' phenonemon in the smaller venues around Shoreditch. In fact, you could characterise the London club scene as one of two tribes: the Muscle Marys dancing with their shirts off in Vauxhall and the club kids dressed to the nines in the East End. And while the muscle boys favour a steady diet of funky house, the club

Compton's of Soho. *See p20.*

Nightlife

My favourite things
Will Young
singer

I love going out dancing, and **Popstarz** (*see p43*) is great on a Friday night. They've got different rooms – a sort of pop room upstairs and a more indie pop one downstairs.

The **Joiners Arms** (*see p33*) in Hackney is good fun; it's a gay pub but a bit rough around the edges and it has a pool table. **BJ's White Swan** (*see p30*) in Limehouse looks hideous from the outside but on a Wednesday and Friday they do amateur strip nights, and it has a garden.

And I like the gay pub in Hampstead: the **KW4** (*see p29*). There's a pancake place next door, so you can go there beforehand to line your stomach.

For a date, I think the cocktail bar in **Claridge's** (Brook Street, W1K 4HR, 7629 8860, www.claridges.co.uk) is absolutely beautiful, and very romantic. There's also a great place near me, the **Portobello Gold** (95-97 Portobello Road, W11 2QB, 7460 4910, www.portobellogold.com). It's very sweet, like something out of the 1940s: there are lots of pot plants, a big conservatory with a roof that they open in summer – quite kitsch. You feel like you're in a café in Weymouth.

I'm a bit of a collector, and my house is full of old Victorian shoes, top hats and gloves – it's very tragic. A great place to pick up bric-a-brac

is **Lassco** (Brunswick House, 30 Wandsworth Road, SW8 2LG, 7394 2100, www.lassco.co.uk): it's a huge salvage place with everything from old boxes to chimneys.

I also go to **Portobello Market** (Portobello Road, W11 1LU, www.portobelloroad.co.uk), although not on a Saturday because it's too busy, and to **Greenwich Market** (College Approach, SE10 9HZ, 8293 3110, www.greenwich-market.co.uk) for old china, clothes and postcards.

---

kids are into everything from disco to electro. That said, these two tribes do sometimes cross paths at places like Vauxhall's **Horse Meat Disco** (*see p40*) or the **RVT** (the venue formerly known as the Royal Vauxhall Tavern, *see p34*). And then, of course, there's Soho, where gays of all persuasions meet and mingle. **Trannyshack** (*see p47*) at Madame Jo Jo's is a haven for gender-benders and pretty boys alike. And just down the road at Charing Cross, that old warhorse Heaven is still going strong, albeit as the new home of long-running superclub **G-A-Y** (*see p40*).

The indie revolution that began 13 years ago with **Popstarz** (*see p43*) has changed the face of gay clubbing in the capital. It's hard to imagine now, but before Popstarz the gay scene consisted of wall-to-wall house music with a side order of cheese at G-A-Y. Now anything goes. In Vauxhall, the **Duckie** crew (*see p39*) provide post-gay performance art and post-punk pogo-ing, with the best retro set in town, courtesy of DJs the Readers' Wifes. Promoter Simon Casson describes Duckie as 'a nightclub with content', and who are we to

argue? In fact, as people simply looking for sex increasingly turn their attention to the internet, the challenge for many venues is to offer more in the way of content to keep people entertained. Live entertainment has come back in a big way, whether it's burlesque, comedy, performance art or plain old-school drag. And who would have thought that **Polari** (*see p43*), a night dedicated to gay literature, would attract such a following?

But it's not all indie music and arty happenings. In Soho you'll also find the cocktail queen. Such creatures were rumoured to be extinct until a few years ago, when the **Shadow Lounge** (*see p25*) opened its doors and the gay glitterati quickly signed up as members. Often name-checked in celebrity-driven mags like *Heat*, the Shadow Lounge has its critics, but the combination of cute staff, cocktails and celeb-spotting keeps the regulars happy. You don't need to be a member to gain entry, although membership does have certain privileges.

Of course, London's gay scene isn't restricted to Vauxhall, Shoreditch and Soho. Look around and you'll find smaller bars and clubs catering to virtually every taste imaginable. Earl's Court is no longer the gay enclave it was in the 1970s and '80s, but there a few bars left up west. Fumblings in the dark, for instance, can be found at **Ted's Place** (*see p36* – just check it isn't tranny night or you may get more than you bargained for). Similar pleasures can be found at **Eagle London** (*see p33*), the **Hoist** (*see p34*) or almost any of the big Vauxhall clubs. Despite facing stiff competition from London's burgeoning sauna scene, clubs appealing to gay men's baser instincts have never gone out of fashion.

If music matters more than the opportunity to get your rocks off, you've definitely come to the right place. From house music in its many varieties to rock, pop, indie, soul and hip hop, London's gay scene is a melting pot of musical sounds and styles. While disco bunnies dance the night away at **G-A-Y** (*see p40*), soul boys enjoy the urban flavours and racial mix at **Bootylicious** (*see p37*). While indie kids leap about at **Popstarz** (*see p43*), Latin fans rumba the night away at **Exilio** (*see p40*) and Eastern aromas are served up twice a month at **Club Kali** (*see p39*). Whatever your taste, you'll find it catered for in the gay capital.

Pubs & bars

Admission to pubs and bars is free unless indicated otherwise.

Central

Admiral Duncan
54 Old Compton Street, W1V 5PA (7437 5300). Leicester Square or Piccadilly Circus tube. **Open** noon-11pm Mon-Thur; noon-midnight Fri, Sat; noon-10.30pm Sun. **Credit** MC, V. **Map** p267 K6.
A traditional gay pub in the heart of Soho, the Admiral Duncan attracts a slightly older, down-to-earth crowd in the heart of boys' town. Once the target of the most devastating homophobic attack in London's history, when a nail bomb went off one busy bank holiday evening, killing three people and injuring many more, the pub has bounced back stronger than ever. The decor hasn't changed much, perhaps in an act of defiance or maybe because that's just the way the punters like it – the aesthetic is butch, camp and cosy all at once, a bit like the crowd here.

BarCode
3-4 Archer Street, W1D 7AP (7734 3342, www.barcode.co.uk). Piccadilly Circus tube. **Open** 4pm-1am Mon-Sat; 4-11pm Sun. **Admission** £4 after 10pm Fri, Sat. **Credit** AmEx, MC, V. **Map** p269 K7.
This busy men's cruise bar is laid out over two levels, with the bustling main bar at ground level and a second bar and dancefloor downstairs. Recently refurbished, with air-con and a spanking new sound system, it's a far cry from the Soho cruise joints of old, where a coat of black paint was deemed all that was necessary to keep the punters happy. The late licence means that most of gay Soho usually ends up here eventually – unless they've already copped off, of course. There's also Comedy Camp on Tuesdays, billed as London's only gay and straight-friendly comedy club, which attracts some of the biggest names in the business. For BarCode Vauxhall, *see p33.*

Box
Seven Dials, 32-34 Monmouth Street, WC2H 9HA (7240 5828, www.boxbar.com). Leicester Square tube. **Open** noon-11pm Mon-Thur; noon-midnight Fri, sat; noon-10.30pm Sun. **Credit** MC, V. **Map** p267 L6.
For years, the Box was associated with its gregarious owner Geoff Llewellyn. It was he who created the winning formula of cute bar staff, café culture and a clubbier feel at night. When Llewellyn retired to Spain a few years ago, some thought the bar's popularity would go with him. They couldn't have been more wrong. The new owners

The best Nightlife

For muscle mania
SuperMartXé (*see p44*); and the clubs at Fire, notably **Later** (*see p42*) and **Orange** (*see p44*).

For a Studio 54 moment
Horse Meat Disco (*see p40*).

For gender benders
Trannyshack (*see p45*); WayOut Club (*see p45*).

For Shoreditch mayhem
Dalston Superstore (*see p31 and p39*); **George & Dragon** (*see p31*); **Gutterslut** (*see p40*).

For getting down and dirty
Central Station (*see p28*); Eagle London (*see p33*); Fort (*see p33*); Ted's Place (*see p36*).

For playing the fool
Duckie (*see p39*); Shinky Shonky (*see p43*).

For 1980s flashbacks
Carpet Burn (*see p37*); Retro Bar (*see p24*).

For father figures
Quebec (*see p24*).

For Stock, Aitken and Waterman
G-A-Y Camp Attack (*see p40*).

For bear hunting
King's Arms (*see p23*); XXL (*see p45*).

saunabar

CENTRAL LONDON'S PREMIER GAY/BISEXUAL SAUNA

www.thesaunabar.co.uk

29 ENDELL STREET   COVENT GARDEN   WC2H 9BA

t: 020 7836 2236

have built on his success and added a few touches of their own. They've also splashed out on some major refurbishments. No longer do the downstairs toilets smell of damp. There's a brighter, cleaner vibe upstairs too, not to mention an improved menu, which makes this a popular place for lunch. As day turns to evening, the muscle boys move in and the atmosphere becomes a whole lot cruisier. In fact, the Box has gained something a reputation as a stronghold for Muscle Marys (there are even leaflets by the toilets warning about the dangers of steroid use). The addition of DJs means it's a very busy pre-club venue at weekends.

Compton's of Soho

51-53 Old Compton Street, W1D 6HN. (3238 0163, www.comptonsbar.com). Leicester Square or Piccadilly Circus tube. **Open** noon-11pm Mon-Sat; noon-10.30pm Sun. **Credit** AmEx, MC, V. **Map** p267 K6.
Long before Old Compton Street was rechristened 'Queer Street', long before Soho became known as the gay village, long before the Village bar or the Admiral Duncan or Balans or even Clone Zone, there was Compton's. An old-fashioned gay pub that used to have blacked-out windows and sawdust on the floor, the venue has changed with the times and now has two floors instead of one, clear glass windows and far nicer toilets. The crowd here hasn't changed all that much. Compton's is still popular with crowds of beer-drinking, blokey gay men, and is pretty cruisey whatever time you choose to visit. The upstairs lounge is quieter and more traditional, with tables, flock wallpaper and a chandelier – a good place for a date or conversation, with views of the crowds on Old Compton Street below. But the main floor bar is where the action is: it's louder, darker and more clubby. Bomber jackets are, of course, optional.

Duke of Wellington

77 Wardour Street, W1D 6QA (7439 1274). Piccadilly Circus tube. **Open** noon-11pm Mon-Wed; noon-midnight Thur-Sat; noon-10.30pm Sun. **Credit** MC, V. **Map** p269 K7.
Set in the heart of Soho, this former straight pub is now a popular gay bar attracting a slightly older crowd who shout at each other over a soundtrack of loud pop. It's a thoroughly mainstream venue whose cheery ambience and clientele are right down the middle of the road. If you crave quiet conversation, try the upstairs lounge.

Edge

11 Soho Square, W1D 3QE (7439 1313, www.edge soho.co.uk). Tottenham Court Road tube. **Open** noon-1am Mon-Sat; noon-11.30pm Sun. **Credit** MC, V. **Map** p267 K6.
A bustling 'polysexual' bar spread over four floors, with great views of Soho Square. Food is served on the ground floor during the day. Upstairs is a lounge bar, above that the alfresco cocktail bar with piano and live entertainment, and above that a club space complete with light-up dancefloor. DJs play either here or down on the ground floor, which gets very busy at the weekends. After years of poor management, owner Andy Jones took the bull by the horns, took on a new manager and spent a small fortune on refurbishing the place. And it shows. The Edge has finally got its edge back. Great for summer drinking.

Escape Bar

10A Brewer Street, W1F 0SU (07905 144835, www.escapesoho.com). Leicester Square or Piccadilly Circus tube. **Open** 5pm-3am Mon-Sat. **Admission** £5 after 9pm Fri, Sat. **Credit** (bar) MC, V. **Map** p268 J7.

Freedom Bar

An intimate gay dance bar, with a large video screen that plays music videos, and a mixed crowd who mingle happily. Pam Ann used to perform here, back in the days before she went supernova. These days, there's less live performance (hardly surprising, given the size of the venue) and the place has become more of a DJ bar.

First Out

52 St Giles High Street, WC2H 8LH (7240 8042, www.firstoutcafebar.com). Tottenham Court Road tube. **Open** 9am-11pm Mon-Sat; 10am-10.30pm Sun. **Credit** MC, V. **Map** p267 K6.
London's original gay café-bar, popular with a truly mixed crowd of men and women of all ages. The main floor has a relaxed community feel, with lesbians munching on veggie food and gay men perusing the gay press. First Out's basement bar is dominated by lesbians on weekend evenings.

Freedom Bar

66 Wardour Street, W1F 0TA (7734 0071, www. freedombarsoho.com). Leicester Square or Piccadilly Circus tube. **Open** 4pm-3am Mon-Fri; 2pm-3am Sat; 2-11pm Sun. **Admission** £5 after 10pm Fri, Sat. **Credit** MC, V. **Map** p266 J6.
A glitzy cocktail lounge and DJ bar, spread over two floors. Once associated with Marc Almond and entourage, Freedom has been through various incarnations, some more successful than others. Currently managed by Shaun Given, the man who gave the Edge (*see left*) its edge back, things have improved enormously in the past couple of years. The glam ground-floor bar attracts a fashion-conscious crowd, who sip cocktail among chandeliers, zebra-print banquettes and venetian mirrors. A few 'strays' and dolled-up gal pals add colour. If the *Dynasty* decor feels too formal, there's a large basement club and performance space, suitable for cabaret during the week, and far busier at the weekend when the gay party crowd moves in.

Friendly Society

Basement, 79 Wardour Street, W1D 6QB (7434 3804). Leicester Square or Piccadilly Circus tube. **Open** 4-11.30pm Mon-Thur; 4pm-midnight Fri, Sat; 4-10.30pm Sun. **Credit** (over £10) MC, V. **Map** p267 K6.
A hip yet friendly basement bar, hosted by the fabulous Maria. Don't let the seedy alley entrance put you off: inside, the decor is a mix of retro and plastic fantastic, with Barbie dolls and other kitsch paraphernalia. The layout is L-shaped, with a smaller bar tucked around the corner from the main action. Musically, expect to hear everything from Dolly Parton to Diana Ross.

G-A-Y Bar

30 Old Compton Street, W1D 4UR (7494 2756, www.g-a-y.co.uk). Leicester Square or Tottenham Court Road tube. **Open** noon-midnight daily. **Credit** MC, V. **Map** p267 K6.
Jeremy Joseph's G-A-Y Bar has everything you'd expect: cheap drinks offers, a young crowd and plenty of Kylie. It's spread out over three floors, and is always busy. Some love it, others love to hate it, but if you're the kind of person who adores pink whistles and cowboy hats, and likes to party with their gal pals, this is the place to come.

My favourite things
Dan Gillespie Sells
singer, The Feeling

I can't bear gay bars where there are no women at all, because they just become meat markets. I like the **Friendly Society** (*see left*), because it's a bit more mixed. It's in a basement and it's quite camp. The woman who runs it is great fun, and she also owns the **Commercial Tavern** (142 Commercial Street, E1 6NU, 7247 1888) in east London, which is gay-friendly and beautifully decorated.

If you want somewhere with a more definitely gay feel, the **George & Dragon** on Hackney Road (*see p31*) is an excellent place. It's only a small pub, but Sunday nights there in summer are crazy – people spill on to the street and drink. You get the fashion crowd, but it's friendly.

I also like Sunday's **Horse Meat Disco** (*see p40*). It's like the anti-gay club – the opposite of G-A-Y. It's run by bears and they play great music by Kate Bush and artists who are a bit more unusual and sophisticated.

Bar Italia (*see p89*) is a classic people-watching place. It has great coffee and if you get there about 4pm on a Friday you're guaranteed a seat. You can just sit there and have a light-hearted bitch about the queens traipsing up and down Old Compton Street.

THE LEGENDARY
DISCO STALLION
EVERY SUNDAY AT
EAGLE LONDON

HORSE MEAT DISCO

Saddle up!

EVERY SUNDAY AT EAGLE LONDON · 349 KENNINGTON LANE, VAUXHALL, LONDON SE11 5QY

 VAUXHALLVILLAGE.com

LONDON'S HOTTEST GAY VILLAGE

Green Carnation

4-5 Greek Street, W1D 4DB (8123 4267, www. greencarnationsoho.co.uk). Tottenham Court Road tube. **Open** 4pm-2am Mon-Sat; 4pm-12.30am Sun. **Admission** £5 after 11pm Mon-Sat. **Credit** AmEx, MC, V. **Map** p267 K6.

Formerly the Element Bar, and before that Sanctuary, this upmarket three-storey venue has changed its name several times, but the vibe remains the same. It's still a dark, elegant, wood-accented lounge bar, dotted with sofas, tables, nooks and crannies. Under its latest incarnation, however, the decor is dedicated to the spirit of Oscar Wilde, whose quotes adorn the green and gold lacquered walls. It attracts an array of gay and straight punters, depending on which night you go; the crowd is always well heeled, and dotted with smartly dressed gal pals. The ground floor offers the familiar mix of cute Brazilian bar staff and commercial dance music. Upstairs, things get more interesting, with live music, the occasional piano player and a film club on Sundays. Drinks aren't cheap, though.

Halfway to Heaven

7 Duncannon Street, WC2N 4JF (7484 0736). Charing Cross tube/rail. **Open** noon-midnight Mon-Sat; noon-11pm Sun. **Credit** MC, V. **Map** p269 K7.

A traditional gay boozer, situated halfway between gay Soho and Heaven, hence the name. For a change from the central London scene, bone up on your trivia for the Wednesday pub quiz or try your luck at the bingo that takes place later that night. The main floor is cosy and traditional, while the basement is clubbier and cruisier.

King's Arms

23 Poland Street, W1S 8QJ (7734 5907). Oxford Circus or Tottenham Court Road tube. **Open** noon-11pm Mon, Tue; noon-11.30pm Wed, Thur; noon-midnight Fri, Sat; 1-11.30pm Sun. **Credit** AmEx, MC, V. **Map** p266 J6.

This busy bears' pub has been around forever, and attracts a loyal crowd of stocky, hairy, beardy men who like a pint. The aesthetic is traditional and cosy: you could be in a country pub, except it's crammed with gay men. Now that bears have gone more mainstream, the place is busier than ever. Some nights they really pack them in. There's a lot less attitude than you'll find in many Soho venues, though it helps if you have a beard.

Ku

30 Lisle Street, WC2H 7BA (7437 4303, www.ku-bar. co.uk). Leicester Square tube. **Open** *Bar* noon-11.30pm daily. *Club* 10pm-3am daily. **Credit** MC, V. **Map** p269 K6.

Voted London's best central gay bar by the readers of *Boyz* and *Pink Paper*, Ku must be doing something right. Formerly known as West Central, it has morphed from a mediocre space into a popular bar and club that offers everything from film nights to comedy. The sheer variety of club nights (held in the basement) is impressive, from Sandra D's Ruby Tuesdays for lesbians to the poptastic O-Zone on Fridays, hosted by veteran drag DJ Dusty O. The nearest rival to G-A-Y Bar, Ku is the first gay venue you reach after leaving Leicester Square tube, so it benefits from lots of passing trade.

In 2010, a new satellite bar opened around the corner in Frith Street. Owned by Gary Henshawe, who kickstarted the gay Soho scene back in the early '90s with the Village

Edge. *See p20.*

West One, it has three storeys, with a loungey area on top. Afternoon tea is served from noon to five – very civilised. **Other locations** 25 Frith Street, W1D 5LB (7437 4303, 7287 7986).

Kudos

10 Adelaide Street, WC2N 4HZ (7379 4573, www.kudosgroup.com). Charing Cross tube/rail. **Open** 4pm-midnight Mon-Sat; 2-11pm Sun. **Credit** MC, V. **Map** p269 L7.

Totally Soho in spirit, if not location, this men's café/bar is situated close to the Oscar Wilde memorial sculpture and Charing Cross station. The ground floor offers 'light bites' during the day, while downstairs is an intimate club space with video screens set into the walls. The music is mainly commercial pop and dance. Kudos attracts a pretty mix of young scene queens, and is particularly popular with the city's Asian community, having once been the regular meeting place of the Long Yang Club.

Profile

84-86 Wardour Street, W1F 0TQ (7734 8300, www.profilesoho.com). Tottenham Court Road or Leicester Square tube. **Open** 11am-11pm Mon-Sat; 11am-10.30pm Sun. **Credit** MC, V. **Map** p267 K6.

Brought to you by the people behind the Gaydar website, Profile is surprisingly sex-free. Originally a three-storey DJ bar on Frith Street, it has got a new address and a brand new image. Instead of a rampant cruise bar, it is done up like a chic American diner, with cosy booths and slick yellow leather banquettes: the vibe is cocktails and camp, rather than cock and cruise. The menu serves salads and burgers; guest DJs add some musical beef.

The village people

Just south of the river, straddling a busy network of roads and railway crossings known locally as Vauxhall Cross, you will find what is commonly referred to as the 'Vauxhall gay village'. It's a strange sort of village by anyone's standards. There is no village post office, for instance, and no village shop. There is a village green of sorts in the shape of Spring Gardens. And there are a few village idiots (they're the ones you see being carted off in an ambulance after overdosing on GHB). The Vauxhall gay village isn't really a village at all, more a collection of clubs where gay men can party all weekend if they want to, provided the drugs don't bring them down first.

It wasn't always thus. A few years ago the only gay venue to speak of was the **Royal Vauxhall Tavern** (now **RVT**; *see p34 and p44*) – which, although home to the club night **Duckie** (*see p39*), hardly qualified as a club venue. Things changed with the opening of Crash (now Union). Despite warnings that West End boys couldn't be persuaded south of the river, Crash built up

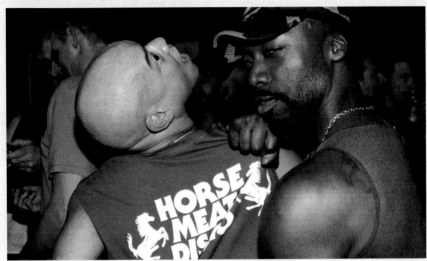

Quebec

12 Old Quebec Street, W1H 7AF (7629 6159). Marble Arch tube. **Open** noon-2am Mon-Thur; noon-3am Fri, Sat; noon-1am Sun. **Credit** MC, V. **Map** p266 G6.
London's oldest gay pub is a busy, down-to-earth West End boozer with a quiet, comfortable main area and disco downstairs. The Quebec is sometimes referred to as the 'elephants' graveyard', on account of its older clientele, though it attracts a good mix of ages – though the younger men are often in search of a daddy. Compared to London's trendier venues, it feels slightly suburban, but this is no bad thing, and it's nice to visit a bar where you don't have to shout. It is certainly a refreshing change from the posey Soho scene. *See p29* **My heart belongs to daddy**.

Retro Bar

2 George Court, off Strand, WC2N 6HH (7839 8760). Charing Cross tube/rail. **Open** noon-11pm Mon-Fri; 2-11pm Sat; 2-10.30pm Sun. **Credit** AmEx, MC, V. **Map** p269 L7.

Tucked away down a little alley, the Retro is one of gay London's secret gems, a small mixed indie bar where eccentrics are welcomed. The music mixes '70s, '80s, New Romantic, goth and alternative, and is reflected in the decor, which features photos of iconic rock and pop figures, from Bolan to Bowie. There's a great jukebox – think Grace Jones, Visage, the Associates – and more women than you'll find in many gay establishments. Manager Wendy knows how to keep her punters happy and they reward her with undying loyalty. If the nostalgic tunes don't leave you with a warm glow, the cosy decor will: red and gold flock wallpaper, creaky wooden floors and red leather love seats. The quieter upstairs bar is a good date spot, though it's not open every night. Themed events include board games night (Sunday) and the poptastic music quiz (Tuesday) – sort of a *Name That Tune* for musos. We once witnessed the entire bar singing the Carpenters' 'Yesterday Once More'.

Rupert Street

50 Rupert Street, W1V 6DR (7494 3059, www.rupertstreet.com). Leicester Square, Piccadilly Circus or Tottenham Court Road tube.

an enormous following. Soon the club's claim
to being 'the underground sound of London'
didn't seem so far-fetched, and other promoters
were sniffing around for a piece of the action.
Competition arrived, appropriately enough, with
the opening of Action. Suddenly there were two
clubs within staggering distance of one another,
both competing for the same demographic:
Muscle Marys with a taste for house music.

Gradually, more clubs moved into the area,
enabling the new village people to spend
the best part of their weekend indoors.
A:M (*see p37*) and **Orange** (*see p43*) opened
as after-hours clubs on Fridays and Sundays,
respectively. Then along came **Beyond** (*see
p37*), aiming for the burgeoning after-hours
Saturday night/Sunday morning market.
It's a measure of Beyond's success that some
people held it responsible for the closure of
Clerkenwell's legendary Trade. With the addition
of after-after-hours clubs like **Later** (*see p42*),
life in the Vauxhall gay village was all sewn up.
It's now possible to go clubbing for the entire
weekend without leaving the area.

There have been a few changes since.
The success of Sunday's **Horse Meat Disco**
(pictured; *see p40*) means that **Eagle London**
(*see p33*) now caters to fashionistas as well
as its traditional audience of bears. **Chariots
Sauna** (*see p49*) has also moved into the area,
providing the perfect place to unwind after all
that dancefloor action. The biggest surprise
of all is that there still seem to be more than
enough punters to go round. Even counting
those who regularly end up in hospital.

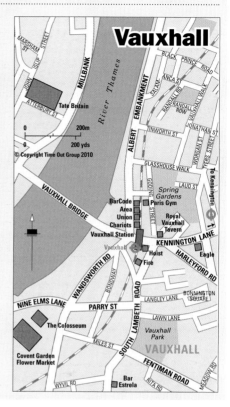

Open noon-11pm Mon-Fri; 11am-midnight Sat; 11am-
10.30pm Sun. **Credit** AmEx, MC, V. **Map** p269 K7.
If your idea of gay life was shaped by TV's *Queer as Folk*,
then Rupert Street is the bar for you. It's a little bit of
Manchester's Canal Street in the heart of London's Soho.
Still trapped in the '90s, the decor is all industrial, boiler-
room chic, with glass wraparound windows and a large
mirror at the back. The staff are beefy and brisk and the
clientele is more smartly dressed than average. Popular
with the after-work crowd, it gets even busier later on –
and also very cruisey. It's quieter during the day, when
there's a decent pub lunch menu available.

79 CXR

*79 Charing Cross Road, WC2H 0NE (7734 0783,
www.79cxr.net). Leicester Square tube.* **Open** 1pm-3am
Mon-Sat; 1-10.30pm Sun. **Admission** £3 after 10.30pm
Mon-Thur; £4 after 10.30pm Fri, Sat. **No credit cards**.
Map p267 K6.
A busy late-night gay men's booze and cruise bar, also
known as 'Chest X Ray' or the 'Last Chance Saloon'.
Sooner or later, everybody ends up here. The customers
are slightly older – the dark lighting camoflauges the
wrinkles – and don't waste time chatting. The decor is
black and nondescript, and a palpable sexual undercurrent
hangs in the air. There's a bird's-eye view of the meat
market from the first-floor balcony.

Shadow Lounge

*5 Brewer Street, W1F 0RF (7287 7988, www.the
shadowlounge.co.uk). Piccadilly Circus or Leicester
Square tube.* **Open** 10pm-3am Mon-Sat. **Admission**
£5 after 11pm Mon-Thur; £10 after 11pm Fri, Sat.
Credit AmEx, DC, MC, V. **Map** p269 K7.
The original lounge bar and gay members' club has had
a bit of a facelift; it's still a hit with bona fide celebrities
and gay wannabes alike (Cilla Black once pole-danced
here with Paul O'Grady, and don't you forget it). In fact,
now that Shaun Given, the original manager, is back on
board, the celeb quotient is higher.

The funky decor, hunky waiters, table service and air-
conditioning all create an atmosphere of urban sophistication, undercut by the suburban antics of some
customers who get carried away on the pole. Earlier in
the week, you'll catch live singers and drag acts. The
weekends are for dancing.

Straight up

Hard to believe when faced with a half of warm lager, some cheese and onion crisps and a carpet that's seen better days, but London has some excellent straight bars. If it's glamour you're after, then hotels are a safe bet: **Claridge's Bar** (*see p69*) is the last word in Mayfair elegance: classy 1930s decor, immaculate cocktails and sophisticated service. The tasteful Lobby Bar at **One Aldwych** (*see p73*), housed in an old Edwardian bank building, is notable for its arched windows and striking modern art. The Long Bar at the **Sanderson** (*see p66*) is a dreamy, Philippe Starck-designed oasis of silver, white and glass. Revamped classics include the Coburg bar at the **Connaught** (*see p69*) and the bar at Dukes Hotel (35 St James's Place, 7491 4840, www.dukeshotel.com) in St James's – both handsomely refurbished and boasting splendid cocktail lists. For wow factor, head to **Galvin at Windows** (London Hilton, 22 Park Lane, 7208 4021, www.galvinatwindows.com), where the view from 28 floors up is hard to beat. Very different, though also in the Hilton, is **Trader Vic's** (7208 4113, www.trad ervics.com), a riot of South Pacific knick-knacks and fruity cocktails.

One neighbourhood over, in Soho, **Floridita** (100 Wardour Street, 7314 4000, www.floridita.co.uk) offers a more tasteful take on Hemingway's Havana, complete with Cuban music, while just north of Soho, across Oxford Street, are two oriental stunners. **Hakkasan** (*see p86*) blends

warehouse chic, Chinese exoticism and LA glam; Shochu Lounge is a 21st-century vision of feudal Japan, downstairs at **Roka** (*see p87*).

Further afield, the kitsch **Trailer Happiness** (177 Portobello Road, 7727 2700, www.trailer happiness.com; *pictured left*) in Notting Hill is known for its killer cocktails. Shoreditch hotspot **Loungelover** (1 Whitby Street, 7012 1234, www.lestroisgarcons.com; *pictured above*) is that rare breed: a camp straight bar, with flamboyant lighting and furniture.

Traditional English pubs are often more conducive to quiet conversation – and often more characterful. Built in 1623, the creaky, atmospheric **Lamb & Flag** (33 Rose Street, 7497 9504) in Covent Garden is one of the city's oldest pubs. The shabby **French House** (49 Dean Street, 7437 2799, www.thefrench housesoho.com) remains a boho Soho legend.

Other olde worlde gems are the tiny, lawyer-filled **Seven Stars** (53 Carey Street, 7242 8521) on the edge of the City; Kensington's rambling **Windsor Castle** (114 Campden Hill Road, 7243 9551, www.thewindsorcastlekensington.co.uk), a country pub in London; and the updated but unspoiled **Fox & Anchor** (115 Charterhouse Street, 7250 1300, www.foxandanchor.com) next to Smithfield meat market.

If you're travelling through St Pancras rail station, take a look at the **Champagne Bar** (7870 9900, www.searcystpancras.co.uk) – the longest one in Europe, with a champagne list to match.

Star at Night

22 Great Chapel Street, W1F 8FR (7494 2488, www.thestaratnight.com). Tottenham Court Road tube. **Open** 6pm-11.30pm Tue-Sat. **Credit** MC, V. **Map** p267 K6.

A characterful Soho haunt, this continental-style bar is mixed, but the emphasis is on the lesbians. Men are welcome as guests on Fridays and Saturdays. Cocktails, wines and food are served in the intimacy of a converted cellar. During the day, it's the Star Café, an old-school Italian caff.

Vault 139

139b-143 Whitfield Street, W1T 5EN (7388 5500, www.vault139.com). Warren Street tube. **Open** 4pm-1am Mon-Sat; 1pm-1am Sun. **No credit cards.**

Just north of Soho, hidden away on a quiet back street – aren't all sex bars? – Vault 139 is London's most central knocking shop. As sex clubs go, Vault 139 is classier than most. The bar area is dark, slick and mellow, with plush sofas, television screens and a DJ booth, and the bartenders seem professional; in short, it doesn't feel seedy and there are few obvious signs of hanky panky. But start wandering the corridors, with their private rooms and furtive men huddled in little groups, and you'll soon realise why this new subterranean venue has quickly amassed such a devoted following. Staff ask you to check your belongings behind the bar when you arrive – as well as your clothes, on certain nights. There are naked sessions on Monday, Wednesday and Thursday, and underwear-only dress codes on Wednesday evenings and Sunday afternoons.

Village

81 Wardour Street, W1D 6QD (7434 2124, www. village-soho.co.uk). Piccadilly Circus or Leicester Square tube. **Open** 4pm-1am Mon-Sat; 4-11.30pm Sun. **Credit** AmEx, MC, V. **Map** p269 K7.

A trendy boys' bar on three floors, the Village was the first venue of its kind to open in Soho, back in 1991. Popular for many years, it fell out of favour and into disrepair at the dawn of the new decade. Now owned by the Soho Bar group, it has been restored to its former glory. The ground-floor café-bar serves food during the day. Downstairs is V Underground, with sleek decor and a DJ booth where you can catch the likes of Dusty O. The upstairs Boudoir offers chaise longues and views of Old Compton Street.

Yard

57 Rupert Street, W1V 7BJ (7437 2652, www. yardbar.co.uk). Piccadilly Circus tube. **Open** 4-11pm Mon-Thur; 11am-11.30pm Fri, Sat; 4-10.30pm. **Credit** AmEx, MC, V. **Map** p269 K7.

A gay men's bar with a spacious courtyard, a loft bar upstairs and food on the menu. The Yard is popular in the summer, when the courtyard comes into its own; it buzzes with a thirtysomething after-work crowd supping pints beneath the evening sky. Drinking in the open air is the big draw, and the new management have spruced up the previously spartan decor. The loft bar is comfy, cosy and convivial. Happy hours operate Monday to Wednesday. It gets busier from Thursday on, with resident DJs playing disco and commercial dance.

Nightlife

Profile. *See p23.*

North

Black Cap

171 Camden High Street, NW1 7JY (7485 0538, www.theblackcap.com). Camden Town tube. **Open** noon-2am Mon-Thur; noon-3am Fri, Sat; noon-1am Sun. **Admission** £2-£4. **Credit** AmEx, MC, V.
This north London institution is famous for its drag shows, and was once second home to Lily Savage and the late Regina Fong, who performed here for 17 years. Once known as 'the Palladium of drag', the Black Cap is keeping the tradition alive with a new generation of show queens, some funnier than others. Lola Lasagne is a regular, as is the legendary Dave Lynn, who actually does his own singing. The upstairs Shufflewick Bar is dedicated to the late, great Mrs Shufflewick, a drag queen who reigned here in the 1970s, while at the back the roof terrace is dubbed Fong Terrace. Never let it be said that the Cap forgets its history. Check the website for a fascinating account of the venue's colourful life and times.

Central Station

37 Wharfdale Road, N1 9SD (7278 3294, www.centralstation.co.uk). King's Cross tube/rail. **Open** noon-1am Mon-Wed; noon-2am Thur; noon-4am Fri, Sat; noon-2am Sun. **Credit** MC, V. **Map** p267 L2.
A gay pub spread over three floors, with male strippers, cabaret, and clubbing and cruising in the basement bar. Name your fetish, they've probably got a club night for it: Scally Ladz (trainers, tracksuits and chavvy fashion), City

Boyz (suits and ties), Pants, SOP (water sports), Shoot (sports clothes), and Butt Naked (self-explanatory). Be warned, though: the dark rooms smell horrible. Dress codes are enforced for the basement, so phone or check the website for details of fetish nights. If you get lucky, but don't want to take your new friend home, you can always check into the B&B upstairs.

Chapel Bar

29A Penton Street, N1 9PX (7833 4090, www.the chapelbar.co.uk). Angel tube. **Open** 5.30pm-1am daily. **Credit** AmEx, MC, V.
Done up with ecclesiastical decorative touches, this hip DJ bar has plenty of disciples: gays, lesbians and strays alike. It's not officially gay, but the recent revamp – complete with chandeliers and elaborate flock wallpaper – certainly adds a note of flamboyance. If the volume gets too loud, escape to the roof terrace. Mediterranean food is served during the week.

Green

74 Upper Street, N1 0NY (7226 8895). Angel tube. **Open** 5pm-midnight Mon-Wed; 5pm-1am Thur; noon-2am Fri, Sat; noon-midnight Sun. **Credit** MC, V.
Now part of the Kudos bar group, and part owned by Andy Jones of the Edge, this chic, modern bar has been totally revamped and much improved. Gone is the narrow bottleneck as you approach the bar. Gone too are the cumbersome dining tables and wobbly DJ decks. Food is still served in the front café and middle bar area, but

Shadow Lounge. *See p25.*

My heart belongs to daddy

The most interesting gay bar in London isn't a steamy Vauxhall bar throbbing with muscle boys, or an edgy Shoreditch venue full of fashionable club kids. No, the most interesting gay bar is the oldest one – in every sense of the word. Opened in 1946, the **Quebec** (see p24) is thought to be London's first gay pub – and it attracts a clientele who are old enough to have drunk there the first time around.

Nicknamed 'the Elephants' Graveyard', it provokes great mirth among younger scene queens for its preponderance of silver-haired daddies. And the contrast with the regular scene is, admittedly, comical. Instead of hearing chiselled models talking about their six-packs, you might overhear pot-bellied blokes discussing their hernias. Instead of talk about Kylie versus Madonna, we recently listened to suited gents debating the merits of Bette Davis and Jean Harlow. Even the drag acts are old school: on one Sunday night, a wrinkled old broad channelled Noël Coward and Vera Lynn to rapturous applause. As for the easy-listening soundtrack, the song titles take on a double meaning here: Cher's 'If I Could Turn back Time', say, or David Soul's 'Don't Give up on Us Baby'.

In a culture obsessed with youth and beauty, the Quebec is an easy target. Young scene queens find it hilarious that old gay men still go to bars – and, shock, horror – are still interested in sex. Sneer if they will, but one day the club kids will grow old, and they too will be grateful that the Quebec exists. It's reassuring to know that gay life doesn't end after 40, and there are plenty of handsome older gents still looking for love. Best of all, they seem to have legions of young admirers. True, some of their biggest fans are

rent boys, a constant presence here. But others have come in search of their elusive daddy or, better yet, a silver fox – if you can't seduce a gorgeous stud your own age, you've got a better chance of snagging a craggy Robert Redford type. And you just can't beat a man in a suit.

Contrary to popular perception, older men know how to have a good time. They certainly outperform the young studs when it comes to conversation. For one thing, they're actually willing to engage in one – a rare treat on the gay scene. And their topics extend beyond Kylie: many can hold forth about politics, and history (not too long ago, you might have bumped into a war veteran here). And the music is soft enough for a conversation – no banging house here. Indeed, the whole atmosphere is soothing. Unlike a slick scene bar, the decor is comfortably suburban, from the patterned carpet and flock wallpaper to the cushy sofas and chairs.

What's more, if the in-your-face gay pride of Soho starts to grate, the Quebec has a deliciously discreet feel – a retro throwback to the days of the gay underground (some people miss the bad old days, when the gay scene was like a secret society). Like the gay bar in Far From Heaven, it's hidden down a dark, alley-like side street. Inside, it's full of men in suits who probably grew up calling themselves 'confirmed bachelors'. The dark basement disco has a vaguely seedy air; there are silent men lurking in the shadows, with naff decor that evokes 1979. For bright young gay things, this might sound like a sad and archaic venue – a reminder of an era we would rather forget. But it feels more real than many a Soho haunt. If you want to escape the chill of the cool crowd, there's warmth to be found in this golden oldie.

the bar has been widened and the rear of the venue turned into a proper club space with a DJ booth, mirror balls and even a light-up dancefloor. The crowd are mainly locals, and come in all shapes and sizes. This is one of the few genuinely mixed bars in town, and it's quite friendly too. Tuesday is quiz night. DJs play Thursday to Sunday; on Sunday, the music is mostly pop with very little house and lounge – which makes a perfect accompaniment to a roast dinner.

King Edward VI

25 Bromfield Street, N1 0PZ (7704 0745). Angel tube. **Open** noon-1am Mon, Tue, Sun; noon-2am Wed-Sat. **Credit** MC, V.
Known as 'the Eddy' to regulars, this is Islington's longest-running gay bar. Tucked away on a backstreet, its secretive location calls to mind the days of the gay underground. It attracts a mixed crowd of locals, some of whom tend to stick together; the ladies usually hang out upstairs. The Eddy is compact, but there's also a lovely beer garden. It gets very busy at the weekend.

KW4 (King William IV)

77 Hampstead High Street, NW3 1RE (7435 5747, www.kingwilliamhampstead.co.uk). Hampstead tube or Hampstead Heath rail. **Open** 11am-11pm Mon-Thur; 11am-midnight Fri-Sun. **Credit** AmEx, MC, V.
This traditional gay local has had a bit of a facelift and, rather like the RVT, or Royal Vauxhall Tavern, has shortened its name to the hipper-sounding KW4. Name change notwithstanding, it's still faintly old-fashioned, though, and relies a lot on drag to draw in the punters. Set in a posh north London neighbourhood, it attracts a more affluent crowd than many gay pubs. In the summer, people spill out into a lovely beer garden. Cruisers stock up on Dutch courage here on their way to Hampstead Heath or come in afterwards for a post-coital drink. Indeed, the pub has attracted a gay crowd since the 1930s (the Heath was a cruising ground even back then). It has even hosted a real queen – Queen Adelaide and King William IV stopped by here in 1835 on their way to Kenwood House, hence the name.

A boy named Woo

London has more than its fair share of alternative drag queens: glittering creatures of the night with an unusual talent for dressing up. Some, like Jodie Harsh, promote clubs and are photographed with famous celebrities. Others, like Le Gateau Chocolat or the Fabulous Russella, sing for their supper or give surreal performances involving pancakes and backing tracks by Christina Aguilera. Then there's Timberlina, hostess with the mostest at the Royal Vauxhall Tavern and a vision in full drag and an even fuller beard.

But ask anyone about London's alternative drag scene and one name crops up time and time again. Jonny Woo is an inspiration to many, and midwife to a number of younger performers including Spanky, Ryan Styles and Russella, each of whom were delivered into the world at Woo's Tranny Talent Contest in Shoreditch.

According to the New York Times, Woo is nothing less than 'Shoreditch's ringmaster'. And his influence doesn't end there. When American performance artist Taylor Mac first hit these shores, it was Woo he paid tribute to. 'I saw Jonny Woo and I realised that drag needn't be just this one thing,' Mac told Time Out. 'It can be anything you want it to be.'

The irony of this is that Woo didn't want to be a drag queen. He wanted to be a contemporary dancer. But when that didn't work out he discovered his true calling, developing a range of looks that include baby doll dresses, Mickey Mouse gloves, tar and feathers, body paint and wigs in every shade including green.

On stage he's a madcap comic performer, whether hosting his riotous Gay Bingo (www.myspace.com/gay_bingo) at venues including **Carpet Burn** (see p37), sizing up the competition

at Tranny Talent at **Bistrotheque** (see p121) or dragging up Bucks Fizz singer Jay Aston in 'Night of 1000 Jay Astons' at the same venue. More recently, he's taken his critically acclaimed one-man show International Woman of Mister E to the Edinburgh Festival. The show was inspired by the night he nearly died from multiple organ failure as result of his 48-hour party lifestyle.

These days Woo is concentrating more on performing and less on getting wasted – good news for his doctor, and his legions of admirers.

● You can catch Jonny Woo regularly at Gutterslut (see p40). See also www.myspace.com/jonnywoouk and www.bistrotheque.com for details of his appearances.

Oak Bar

79 Green Lanes, N16 9BU (7354 2791, www.oak-bar.co.uk). 73, 141, 341 bus. **Open** 5pm-midnight Mon-Wed; 5pm-1am Thur; 5pm-3am Fri, Sat; 4pm-midnight Sun. **Credit** AmEx, MC, V.
A mixed gay local on the western edge of Stoke Newington, the Oak plays host to club nights aimed predominantly at women and attracting all ages and races. Of the mixed nights, Lower the Tone (see p43) offers nostalgic fun as DJs Sadie Lee, Lea Andrews and Dr Kemp play their favourite songs of yesteryear. The Turkish night (second Saturday of the month) attracts plenty of gay Arabic men.

Play Pit

357 Caledonian Road, N7 9DQ (0333 700 1231, www.londonplaypit.co.uk). Caledonian Road & Barnsbury rail. **Open** 8pm-1am Thur; 9pm-2am Fri; 9pm-3am sat; 3pm-1am Sun. **Admission** £9. **Credit** AmEx, MC, V.
Inspired by San Francisco's famous sex clubs like Folsom Prison and Blow Buddies, Play Pit is a North London sleaze

pit where no fantasy is too wild. Sunday afternoons are called Glory Hole, Sunday evenings are for briefs and boxers. You're not in Kansas anymore, Dorothy.

East

Backstreet

Wentworth Mews, off Burdett Road, E3 4UA (8980 8557, 8980 7880, www.thebackstreet.com). Mile End tube. **Open** 10pm-2am Thur; 10pm-3am Fri, Sat; 10pm-1am Sun. **Admission** free-£7. **No credit cards.**
Yes, it really is down a backstreet, and how appropriate: this is a hardcore, underground gay bar. Don't come if you're hoping for Kylie and cosmos. Instead, expect late-night cruising for the dress-code brigade. Don your best leather or rubber gear – and then take it all off again.

BJ's White Swan

556 Commercial Road, E14 7JD (7780 9870, www.bjswhiteswan.com). Limehouse rail/DLR. **Open** 9pm-2am Tue-Thur; 9pm-4am Fri, Sat;

6.30pm-midnight Sun. **Admission**
£5 after 10.30pm Fri, Sat. **Credit** MC, V.
Something of a local legend, the White Swan is the East End's most famous gay boozer. The comedian Michael Barrymore famously came out on stage here. Sir Ian McKellen used to drop in after he came out. And the Sunday Tea Dances are an institution with an older crowd, who waltz and tango the night away. But despite its illustrious history, the pub's decor is not quaint or cosy: on the contrary, it's a rough and soulless space, with a dark warehouse-style aesthetic, enlivened only by the soft-porn videos broadcast from TV screens above the bar (usually naked French rugby players). The crowd, by contrast, is cheerful and rowdy; many Essex lads make the trek here in on the weekend. It is notorious for its amateur strip contests – held on Wednesdays around midnight – in which the young and shameless bare all for cash. On Friday and Saturday nights, there are often strippers or drag queens, who warm up the crowd for a night of dancing to chart tunes and commercial house.

Dalston Superstore

*117 Kingsland High Street, E8 2PB (7254 2273).
Dalston Junction/Dalston Kingsland rail.* **Open** noon-2am Mon-Fri; 11am-2am Sat, Sun. **Admission** varies; phone for details. **Credit** AmEx, MC, V.
The hippest new venue on the scene is not officially gay, more like post-gay. Situated in Dalston, north-east London's most über-arty district, it is suited to its surroundings: a confidently cool and slightly camp New York-style dive bar split between two floors, clad in cement, brick and steel vents. It's enlivened with fluoro flashes, tables for couples, graffiti, art installations and in-the-know aural offerings. The long, wooden bar, manned by approachable and beautiful bar-staff, is top and tailed by a DJ booth and an open-plan kitchen.

Downstairs is where things get louder and larger with regular visits to boogie-town and where the unisex toilets add some extraordinary chat. The drinks are as stripped-back as the decor. With nothing on tap, beer is just bottles courtesy of Asahi and Corona. There's Swedish cider and a cocktail list that doffs its trilby to retro classics. In terms of food, as well as substantially sized, modestly priced sandwiches, burgers and salads, there's also a daily selection of own-made cakes.

Entertainment-wise, there are plenty of ants in these pants with regular DJ showcases, exhibitions, launch parties, barn dances and music nights. While tight denim shorts and pencil moustaches divulge a gay crowd, there's no shortage of daft millinery sported by Dalston dandies and arty locals.

George & Dragon

2 Hackney Road, E2 7NS (7012 1100). Old Street tube/rail or Shoreditch High Street rail. **Open** 6pm-midnight daily. **Credit** MC, V.
This old-fashioned, gay-friendly boozer is the hub of the trendy Shoreditch and Hoxton scene. So naturally it gets busy at the weekends, when 24-hour clubbers pop in for a pint between dance sessions. Much of the clientele comprises budding fashion designers and art students. On some evenings, it's a sea of kids in skinny jeans, black eyeliner and vintage jackets; like them, the bar is scruffy but stylish. It's cosy too. For one thing, it's often crammed. And the crimson walls create a womb-like interior, enlivened by kitsch touches: twinkly lights (it always looks like Christmas here) and knick-knacks galore (pink flamingos, a rhinestone-studded cowboy hat, a stuffed weasel). A cardboard cut-out of Kim Wilde surveys the knowing crowd, who plant tongues firmly in cheek on Saturday nights as they dance to cheesy pop (Kylie, Girls Aloud), vintage gems (Kate Bush, Pulp) and forgotten oddities (Culture Club's

Joiners Arms. *See p33.*

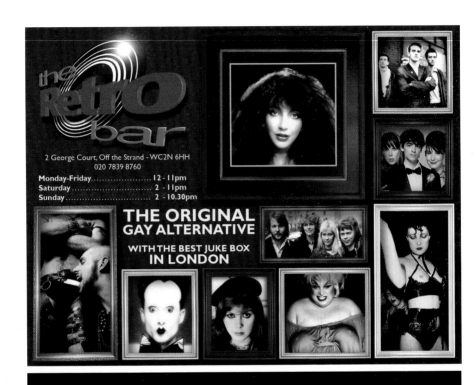

'The Medal Song'). Most punters drink pints from plastic cups. Arrive early at the weekend if you want to snag a table, otherwise it's standing room only.

Joiners Arms

116-118 Hackney Road, E2 7QL (07976 892541). Hoxton rail. **Open** 5pm-2am Mon-Wed, Sun; 5pm-3am Thur; 5pm-4am Fri, Sat. **No credit cards.**
Some of the time, the Joiners Arms is a friendly gay local with regular entertainment and happy hours. On the weekends, however, it pulls a clubby crowd. At times, the atmosphere can get a bit frenetic – in fact, after hours on Saturday night it feels more club than pub, with blaring house beats, wall-to-wall bodies and a hedonistic air. And there's often a queue for the grotty toilets. Though some of the art school crowd from the George & Dragon (*see p30*) end up here, they're mixed in with Muscle Marys, hardcore scenesters and rough boys – the latter are a fixture around the pool table. The vibe is generally friendly, but a few unsavoury characters can spoil the mood.

Nelson's Head

32 Horatio Street, E2 7EH (7729 5595, www. nelsonshead.com). Hoxton rail. **Open** 4-11pm Mon-Wed; 3pm-midnight Thur-Sat; 7am-10.30pm Sun. **Credit** MC, V.
Formerly an East End geezer pub, the Nelson's Head has been tarted up, with rich, dark blue walls, a cosy new carpet, and assorted objets d'art. It's comfortable, a bit eccentric, and attracts an in-the-know Shoreditch crowd: we spotted Dan Gillespie Sells of the Feeling there one night. Not officially gay, it has a loyal queer following. Those with a camp sensibility are attracted to kitsch events like the fancy dress parties, *Jaws* theme nights and the annual dog fancy dress competition, in which owners dress up their pets (held on a Saturday in mid-October). On busy nights, the ratio of gay to straight might be 50:50: the fun part is figuring out which is which. A good pre-drinking venue before hitting the Shoreditch scene, and a good post-clubbing venue: it opens at 7am on Sunday morning.

Old Ship

17 Barnes Street, E14 7NW (7790 4082, www.old ship.net). Limehouse DLR/rail. **Open** 4-11pm Mon; 7pm-12.30am Wed-Sun. **No credit cards.**
A cosy pub on a classic East End square, the Old Ship attracts a mix of geezers and queens. It's full of local characters who tend to know each other. Sometimes heads turn when a stranger walks in, and the regulars like to engage in bouts of bitchy banter around the bar. It's all harmless enough, though, and generally friendly. And on weekends the drag queens break the ice – and lower the tone.

Star of Bethnal Green

359 Bethnal Green Road, E2 6LG (7729 0167, www.starofbethnalgreen.com). Bethnal Green tube. **Open** 11.30am-midnight Mon-Thur, Sun; 11.30am-2am Fri, Sat; noon-midnight Sun. **Admission** free-£5. **Credit** MC, V.
This trendy East End pub is not officially gay, but the hip crowd is polysexual, and there are occasional gay indie nights here like Dick and Fanny and Unskinny Bop, usually on the third Saturday of the month, where kids in skinny jeans who are far too young to remember the 1980s sing along to Echo and the Bunnymen.

South

BarCode Vauxhall

Arch 69, Albert Embankment, SE11 5AW (7582 4180, www.bar-code.co.uk). Vauxhall tube/rail. **Open** 4pm-1am Mon-Thur; 4pm-6am Fri, Sat; 4pm-2am Sun. **Admission** £4 after 10pm Fri, £5 after 10pm Sat. **Credit** MC, V. **Map** p25.
Vauxhall's newest and smartest gay bar boasts sleek pink design and air-conditioning – a luxury for Vauxhall. With its giant BC logo, the front entrance is quite something to behold. Needless to say, the venue attracts a steady stream of punters of all shapes and sizes, with an emphasis on pecs and tight T-shirts. The front DJ bar gets pretty busy most nights of the week, while the rear club space really comes into its own at the weekend. There's also an upstairs lounge area with comfy seating. The terrace at the front gets busy in good weather.

Eagle London

349 Kennington Lane, SE11 5QY (7793 0903, www. eaglelondon.com). Vauxhall tube/rail. **Open** 9pm-2am Mon-Fri; 9pm-4am Sat; 8pm-3am Sun. **Admission** £6. **No credit cards. Map** p25.
What was once a friendly local known as South Central, much loved by the bears brigade, is now a cruise club in the world-famous Eagle tradition. Themed nights include gay wrestling night Grapple 101 on Wednesday and 1980s nostalgia fest Carpet Burn on Saturday. Sunday is the legendary Horse Meat Disco (*see p40*), with its hip soundtrack and heady mix of skinny club kids, scally lads and bears. The venue itself is a traditional boozer, with a pool table, beer garden and barbecues some weekends.

Fort

131 Grange Road, SE1 3AL (7237 7742, www. thefortlondon.com). Bermondsey tube, or Elephant & Castle or London Bridge tube/rail. **Open** 8-11pm Mon, Tue, Thur; Fri; 2-11pm Wed, Sat; 2-10.30pm Sun. **Admission** free-£4. **No credit cards.**
Billed as 'the bar no one admits they visit'. You can say that again. The Fort, an underground cruise bar, is the height – or nadir – of sleaziness and debauchery. Be careful when you go, as there are different themes for different days (these change, so check the website). Currently, customers must wear only boots or shoes – and nothing else – on Monday, Thursday and Saturday, as well as Sunday afternoons (there are lockers available). On Tuesday and Sunday evenings, however, you can wear what you like, so you can cruise away in the dark without fear of baring your bodily flaws. On Wednesday, it's underwear – or less – all day. There are also rubber nights. But whatever you do, don't drop by unprepared on a Friday night, or you might find yourself the recipient of a surprise golden shower. Who said romance was dead?

George & Dragon

2 Blackheath Hill, SE10 8DE (8691 3764, www.george dragon.com). Greenwich DLR/rail. **Open** 8pm-2am Mon-Thur, Sun; 8pm-4am Fri, Sat. **Admission** £3 after 11pm Sat. **Credit** MC, V.
Not to be confused with the George & Dragon in Shoreditch (*see p30*), which is known for its shabby chic, this place is just plain shabby. Though located in Greenwich, it has nothing of the gentility of its neighbour, the Rose & Crown

Nightlife

(*see below*). Its selling point is the late opening hours and, if you like a bit of rough, the raffish air. The staff are friendly, as are most of the punters, including a smattering of lesbians. Despite the bleak surroundings, Kylie et al still get an airing, and drag queens brave the stage on weekends. Dive bars always come with a colourful cast of local characters, but this cast includes a few drunken bores: be careful who you get stuck playing pool with.

Hoist

Arches 47B & 47C, South Lambeth Road, SW8 1RH (7735 9972, www.thehoist.co.uk). Vauxhall tube/rail. **Open** 9pm-2am Wed; 8pm-midnight 3rd Thur of mth; 10pm-3am Fri; 10pm-4am Sat; 2-8pm, 10pm-2am Sun. **Admission** £6 Fri, Sun; £6-£10 Sat; varies Thur. **No credit cards**. **Map** p25.
A popular men's dress-code bar: leather, rubber, uniform and so on. Doormen enforce the dress code, so don't think you can get away with half measures – your suede jacket from Gap just won't cut it. In an emergency, Fetish Freak (*see p110* **Buy sexual**), the shop next door, is open late on weekends. Set in an old railway arch, the decor strikes just the right industrial note for the tough love that occurs here.

Kazbar

50 Clapham High Street, SW4 7UL (7622 0070, www.kazbarclapham.com). Clapham North tube. **Open** 4pm-midnight Mon-Thur; 4pm-1am Fri; 1pm-1am Sat; 1pm-midnight Sun. **Credit** MC, V.
Part of the Kudos bar chain, this venue brings a touch of Soho to south London. Refurbished with wraparound glass windows, it's a lot lighter than it used to be, and slick, if slightly sterile. There's a cosy balcony upstairs with comfy chairs. In the main bar, punters dance in time to the giant video screen, usually blaring with manufactured pop. Warmer weather brings the outdoor tables into demand.

Little Apple

98 Kennington Lane, SE11 4XD (7735 2039). Kennington tube. **Open** noon-11pm Mon-Wed, Sun; noon-midnight Thur; noon-1am Fri; noon-2am Sat. **Credit** MC, V.
Hidden off the main drag in leafy Kennington, the Little Apple is a cosy, if shabby, local pub. There's something slightly shambolic about the whole operation, from the dowdy decor to the sprinkling of local drunks eager to engage in banter. But bar staff are friendly and it's a good place to catch up with friends for a chat or a game of pool (there are a few lesbian regulars too). That said, lately they've been trying to jazz things up by bringing in DJs on weekend evenings, which completely ruins the ambience. People come here for conversation, not hard house.

Rose & Crown

1 Crooms Hill, SE10 8ER (8293 1898). Cutty Sark DLR. **Open** noon-11pm Mon-Thur; noon-midnight Fri, Sat; noon-10.30pm Sun. **Credit** MC, V.
Leafy and genteel Greenwich seems worlds away from London, and so does this elegant Victorian pub. In fact, you feel as if you've walked into a very civilised pub in Bath. The decor is tall, dark and handsome: high ceilings, a sturdy oak bar and tables, with period details such as etched glass, huge picture windows and chandelier. The brown and beige flock wallpaper is tasteful rather than garish, as is the dark green floral carpet. The music is kept at a respectable

volume, in keeping with the respectable crowd, who drop in for a chat rather than a drunken Kylie sing-a-long. If it all starts to feel too polite, lower the tone by moving on to the George & Dragon (*see p33*) down the road.

RVT (Royal Vauxhall Tavern)

372 Kennington Lane, SE11 5HY (7820 1222, www.rvt.org.uk). Vauxhall tube/rail. **Open** 7pm-midnight Mon, Wed, Thur; 6pm-midnight Tue; 7pm-2am Fri; 9pm-2am Sat; 2pm-midnight Sun. **Admission** £5-£7. **Credit** MC, V. **Map** p25.
The venue formerly known as the Royal Vauxhall Tavern is a shabby gay legend. Having survived the Blitz and attempts to bulldoze the place to make way for a shopping centre, the Vauxhall is held in great affection by many gay men and women. Known as the 'Royal Vauxhall Academy of Arts' by those who attend Saturday night's pop and performance club Duckie (*see p39*), it attracts an alternative crowd who wouldn't be caught dead in G-A-Y. They come to watch avant-garde cabaret and mosh to a soundtrack of punk, pop, thrash and trash. Other club nights include Sunday's S.L.A.G.S (*see p46*) and Vauxhall Chill-Out (*see p47*), in which the house tunes come on and the men's tops come off. Weeknights are given over to live entertainment: bingo on Monday, Bar Wotever on Tuesday, cabaret on Thursday, featuring the likes of David Hoyle and Scott Capurro. *See p44* **An urban legend**.

SW9

11 Dorrell Place, SW9 8EG (7738 3116). Brixton tube/rail. **Open** 10am-11pm Mon-Thur, Sun; 10am-1.30am Fri, Sat. **Credit** MC, V.
After the closure of legendary gay superclub the Fridge and the seedy Substation, SW9 is the last gay(ish) stronghold in Brixton. Though hidden down a back alley, this gay-friendly café-bar is far from sleazy. On the contrary, it has a trendy vibe, with gastropubby fare and a unisex bathroom – how *Ally McBeal*.

Two Brewers

114 Clapham High Street, SW4 7UJ (7819 9539, www.the2brewers.com). Clapham Common tube. **Open** 5pm-2am Mon-Thur, Sun; 5pm-4am Fri, Sat. **Admission** free-£5. **Credit** AmEx, MC, V.
Though affectionately nicknamed the 'Two Sewers', this long-established gay pub and club is the opposite of grotty. Indeed, it has had more facelifts than Joan Rivers. Like her, it has been serving the gay community for yonks – 26 years, in fact. Still enormously popular, it's a crowd-pleasing mix of commercial dance music and drag shows (regular performers include Dolly Diamond, Titti La Camp and the ubiquitous Sandra; Dave Lynn, a seasoned veteran who does his own singing, is the best of the bunch). There's lots of local totty on parade too, all in a polished, suburban setting. DJs in the main bar spin pure cheese, while the dark and cavernous back room morphs into a proper club. They do a decent pub lunch too. Very busy at the weekends.

Vauxhall Griffin

8 Wyvil Road, SW8 2TH (7622 0222, www.thevauxhallgriffin.com). Vauxhall tube/rail. **Open** noon-11pm Mon-Thur, Sun; noon-midnight Fri; 6pm-midnight Sun. **Admission** free. **Credit** MC, V.
A bit like gay people who take pride in passing for straight, the Griffin is a 'straight' pub that's very gay-friendly. If the

Carpet Burn. *See p37.*

other Vauxhall venues are too in-your-face gay, then this comfortable pub is a refuge from all the high-NRG tunes and relentless cruising. They do a nice burger, and the pub quiz on Tuesday nights (8pm) is a laugh.

West

Queen's Head

25-27 Tryon Street, SW3 3LG (7589 0262). Sloane Square tube. **Open** noon-11pm Mon-Thur; noon-midnight Fri, Sat; noon-10.30pm Sun. **Credit** AmEx, MC, V. **Map** p265 F11.
This traditional boozer is refreshingly down to earth: steps away from the upmarket King's Road, but miles away in spirit. It's frequented by an older crowd, some of whom have been drinking here for a long time. Split into three rooms, it attracts a lot of straight locals to the front area, and is not particularly cruisy.

Richmond Arms

20 The Square, off Princes Street, Richmond, Surrey TW9 1DZ (8940 2118). Richmond tube/rail. **Open** 1-11pm Mon-Wed; 1-12.30am Thur; 1pm-2am Fri, Sat; 1-11.30pm Sun. **Credit** MC, V.
A friendly local pub, popular with a wide constituency, from students to theatrical types, with the odd straight thrown in. Theme nights range from karaoke to cabaret. There are picnic tables outside for fair-weather drinking.

Stag

15 Bressenden Place, SW1E 5DD (7828 7287). Victoria tube/rail. **Open** 4pm-midnight Mon; 4pm-2am Tue-Fri; 5pm-2am Sat; 5pm-midnight Sun. **Credit** AmEx, MC, V. **Map** p268 H9.

Down a backstreet near Victoria, the Stag is popular with gay civil servants, whose offices are nearby. So there are always a few men in suits. The atmosphere is a curious mix of discreet – it is hidden away and the doormen remind punters they are entering a gay establishment – and positively mainstream, with its karaoke, cabaret and chart DJs getting jiggy at the weekends. The horseshoe-shaped layout ensures you never feel claustrophobic; the tables and banquettes are good for cosy chats. The pub theatre upstairs shows gay plays, old and new.

Ted's Place

305A North End Road, W14 9NS (7385 9359, www.tedsplaceuk.co.uk). West Kensington tube/ West Brompton tube/rail. **Open** 7pm-midnight Mon-Wed, Fri; 8pm-late Thur; 7pm-late Sun. Closed Sat. **Admission** £3-£4; free before 9pm Sun. **No credit cards**. **Map** p264 A12.
Descending the stairs into this cavernous basement bar is like stepping back in time – you half expect to see Quentin Crisp sitting in the corner. Most nights are given over to good old-fashioned cruising. Sunday and Thursday are trannie nights, and Wednesday is underwear night. Curiously, it is closed on Saturday nights.

West 5

Popes Lane, W5 4NB (8579 3266, www.west5ealing. com). South Ealing tube. **Open** 6pm-midnight Mon-Wed; 6pm-1am Thur, Sun; 6pm-2am Fri; 6-3am Sat. **Admission** £4 after 9pm Fri; £6 after 9pm Sat. **Credit** MC, V.
Way out in west London, this venue is a large mixed gay pub/club with a piano bar and a comfortably suburban feel – think Two Brewers but transported to a more leafy setting. Entertainment includes drag, karaoke and

Dalston Superstore. *See p39.*

quizzes. The young crowd comprises flight attendants (Heathrow is not far) and lesbians from nearby Acton (whose presence is harder to explain).

Clubs

A:M

Fire, South Lambeth Road, SW8 1UQ (7582 9890, www.fireclub.co.uk). Vauxhall tube/rail. **Open** 3am-10.30am Sat. **Admission** £12; £8 with flyer before 5.30am. **Credit** (bar) MC, V. **Map** p25.
The long weekend starts here, at the first of several after-hours clubs at Fire. DJs play funky, chunky house for an up-for-it Friday-night party crowd, some of whom will keep going until Monday. (How do they do it? We haven't a clue).

Bar Wotever

RVT, 372 Kennington Lane, SE11 5HY (7820 1222, www.woteverworld.com). Vauxhall tube/rail. **Open** 6pm-midnight Tue. **Admission** free. **Credit** (bar) MC, V. **Map** p268 J7.
Alternative performance art is the draw at this edgy club for underground, alternative, gender-bending 'grrlz and bois' – ie drag kings, cross-dressers, transfolk and, according to club organisers 'freaks, misfits, nerds, beauty queens, jocks and teachers'. A bit like school all over again, then, except with sex and booze. There's a different theme each time, and people are encouraged to dress up.

Beyond

Fire, South Lambeth Road, SW8 1UQ (7582 9890, www.clubtickets.com). Vauxhall tube/rail. **Open** 6am-1pm Sun. **Admission** £12; £12 with flyer before 7am. **No credit cards. Map** p25.
The highlight of many a muscle boy's weekend, this popular Saturday night/Sunday morning after-hours party has settled in at Area. This is where clubbers go when they've failed to pick up at one of Vauxhall's Saturday night superclubs. It's the next logical step. The main floor plays electro grooves, while the Mirror Arch moves to the familiar sound of funky, uplifting house.

Bootylicious

Club Colosseum, 1 Nine Elms Lane, SW8 5NQ (www.bootylicious-club.co.uk). Vauxhall tube/rail. **Open** 11pm-6am 3rd Sat of mth. **Admission** £12; £10 before midnight; £5-£6 reductions. **No credit cards. Map** p25.
It's a sign of how much the gay urban scene has grown that Bootylicious is now on Saturday instead of Friday and has left the old Crash for the far bigger and swankier Club Colosseum. Otherwise, it's the same 'meeting of grinds' it always was, mixing the sounds and sexes of the underground scene: R&B, garage, ragga and party toons. It's also very mixed racially and attracts some big-name PAs.

Carpet Burn

Eagle, 349 Kennington Lane, SE11 5QY (7793 0903, www.carpet-burn.com). Vauxhall tube/rail. **Open** 9pm-4am Sat. **Admission** £3 before 10.30pm, then £6. **No credit cards. Map** p25.
DJs including Mark Moore, Luke Howard, Prince Nelly, Martyn Fitzgerald and our own Paul Burston play a feast of '80s dance, new wave and pop for freaks, geeks, breeders, munchers and moxies. Choose Burn!

My favourite things
Mark Ravenhill
playwright

There isn't a theatre in London any more that's a dedicated gay space like the **Drill Hall** (*see p131*) was 20 years ago, partly because the gay sensibility is more absorbed into the mainstream now. The **Oval House Theatre** (52-54 Kennington Oval, SE11 5SW, 7582 7680, www.ovalhouse.com) in south London is the closest thing, but probably the best work on the fringe can be seen at **Theatre 503** (Latchmere, 503 Battersea Park Road, SW11 3BW, 7978 7040, www.theatre503.com). It's almost exclusively new writing and all on contemporary subjects.

I was asked to write a panto a couple of years ago, so I've done a fair bit of research – I'd say the **Theatre Royal Stratford East** (Gerry Raffles Square, E15 1BN, 8534 0310, www.stratford east.com) is the best place to see panto. They've got good connections with their local community, so you get a totally mixed audience in terms of age, race and class, which is what panto's all about. The upper middle class can't stomach it, but everyone else can.

On a Saturday night, I love going to **Duckie** (*see p39*), the cabaret night at the Vauxhall Tavern. The Tavern has a really good mix of alternative comedy and the guy who programmes it, Simon, has a great eye for new talent. David Hoyle's shows there are also amazing: bizarre performance art meets stand-up meets total surrealism. He's got a great way of presenting an audience with weird material, but somehow keeping them on side.

One Valentine's Day I went to the Skylon restaurant in the **Royal Festival Hall** (Belvedere Road, SE1 8XX, 7654 7800, www.skylonrestaurant.co.uk). It looks out over London and the Thames – perfect for a romantic dinner.

One of my favourite London landmarks is the Maggi Hambling sculpture of **Oscar Wilde** (*see p194*) by Charing Cross station. He's such a magnetic figure, and in terms of his wit, humour and personality and what he means to gay history, it's great that London finally has a memorial of him.

Dude looks like a lady

If you walk down the stairs into Charlie's, a basement club near Aldgate, on a weekday evening, you'll find a bunch of City workers drinking away their office blues. Descend those same stairs on a Saturday night, however, and you'll enter a very different world indeed. Dorothy's emergence into the Technicolor of Munchkinland had nothing on this.

The **WayOut Club** (*pictured; see p45*) as Charlie's becomes for one night a week, is the heart and soul of London's transgender scene, and a more exotic and diverse crowd you will not find. Every shade of the rainbow is here, from the seven-foot glam-queens in showgirl lashes and killer heels, to lumpy civil servants in their wives' dresses. They dance, they pose, they drink (through straws, of course), they cruise – and they have, to all appearances, more fun than at any other club.

The WayOut is at the centre of a scene that's just beginning to dip a varnished toe into the mainstream. Drag is back in Soho, and a new generation of transgender performers rules the Hoxton-Shoreditch-Vauxhall arts/club scene. Scenemakers like Jodie Harsh, Jonny Woo and Yr Mum Ya Dad aren't just stars in the gay clubs, but are flexing some celebrity muscle in the wider media. Drag hasn't been this visible since the gender-bender heyday of the 1980s.

But that's just the attention-grabbing tip of the iceberg; nine-tenths are hidden. The girls that come out to play on the hardcore trannie scene don't want to be famous; many of them lead 'normal' lives, have wives and families and regular jobs, and emerge once a month as exotic flowers. Some of them are gay, but many are bisexual or straight. Some are pre-operative transsexuals; others keep their femme persona in a suitcase, to be let out in spurts. 'Bisexuality is the dominant mode on the trannie scene,' says Tanya Jane Richards, author of *Tranz-Mania*, a fictional account of life on the gender divide. 'Some girls are dressing to attract men, certainly, but many are doing it to unleash the feminine side of their personality. Trannies have moved away from the gay scene, because our needs are different. It's not just about picking up. It's about expressing a hidden part of yourself.'

The trannie scene covers a broad spectrum. At one end, there's **Trannyshack**, the Wednesday night party at Madame JoJo's (*see p45*), run by DJ and promoter Dusty O. 'We're open to anyone,' says Dusty. 'There's no dress code, no elitism, no attitude. All the acts, the pole-dancers and the DJs are trannies, but the audience is a mix. We get club kids, glam couture queens, sex changes and 'manny-trannies', the old men who just put on a dress. And there's a lot of young gay lads, muscle queens, cool straight people – as long as you behave, we won't turn you away.'

In recent years, Trannyshack (which lifted its name from the pioneering San Francisco club) has become such a hit that it's releasing a CD and DVD with in-house stars, such as the glam Lady Lloyd, the trashy Glendora ('the slag in drag') and Dusty O herself. 'We're at the party end of things,' says Dusty. 'We're less hardcore than most of the trannie scene. It can get pretty messy here, but it's more about fun than cruising.'

The WayOut Club, meanwhile, caters to a more grassroots crowd. Founded by Vicky Lee and partner Steffan Whitfield in 1993, it's provided a home and family to generations of girls. 'When we started,' says Lee, 'there was hardly anywhere to go. You could go to Madame JoJo's, but that was more about drag queens entertaining a straight audience. We started at a little wine bar on Goodge Street, we got 100 people on the first night, and the rest is history.'

Over the years, Lee has witnessed some spectacular personal journeys, and has become a mother figure to legions of daughters. 'I've seen guys come down here in drab ['dressed as a boy'] with their wives, then a few months later they appear in drag for the first time. I've seen a successful lawyer who was an occasional transvestite become a transsexual, a prostitute and then work her way back up to the top of her legal career. I've married myself for 30 years – we met when I was 17 and she was 16 – and we've no intention of separating. But my wife has accepted that, given the person I've become, she is almost in a lesbian relationship. There are a thousand stories like that.'

Where the WayOut led, others have followed. There's **Stunners** (www.stunnersstudios.co.uk), the Saturday nighter in Limehouse, which Tanya Jane Richards describes as 'very relaxed, to the point of resembling an orgy sometimes.' Further afield, the **Pink Punters** (www.pinkpunters.com) in Milton Keynes is a hit with 'T-girls' from all over London and the home counties.

And in this strange, glamorous secret world, there's one mystery that's bigger than all the others: the men. Known as 'admirers', they are by no means the 'sleazy raincoat brigade' of old, says Vicky Lee. 'The men on the trannie scene are like regular guys in clubs, and a lot of them are gorgeous. We get all ages, and all races. So what are they doing here? Some of them are taking a look around, and they might be thinking about dressing for the first time. But there's an awful lot of them who are here for the girls. Are they latent homosexuals? I don't know. It's a mystery. But you won't hear anyone down here complaining.'

Circus

Various venues. www.thisiscircus.com **Open** 10.30pm-3.30am Fri. **Admission** £10; £5 with flyer before 11.30pm. **Credit** AmEx, MC, V.
Hostess Jodie Harsh and Knights of Sound play electro, indie, new wave and nu-rave for a hip crowd who love to dress up. Fashion-wise, anything goes. In fact, the more bizarre you look, the better you'll fit in. Guest DJs have included everyone from Sophie Ellis Bextor to Will Young and, yes, Jodie Marsh. Harsh – aka former fashion student Jay Clarke, 24 – describes herself as 'half clown, half Bratz doll'; one scribe called her the Pied Piper, owing to her club kid fans. One of the busiest nights in town, though the venue changes constantly; check the website.

Club Kali

The Dome, 1 Dartmouth Park Hill, N19 5QQ (7272 8153, www.clubkali.com). Tufnell Park tube. **Open** 10pm-3am 3rd Fri of mth. **Admission** £5-£8. **No credit cards**.
The world's largest Asian music lesbian and gay club has been going for aeons and is still as popular as ever. The barn-like venue echoes to the sounds of Bollywood, bhangra and plain old house music. It's a fusion of Eastern and Western aromas guaranteed to whet most appetites.

Cockabilly

Bethnal Green Working Men's Club, 42-46 Pollard Row, E2 6NB (7739 2727, cockabilly.blogspot.com). **Open** 9pm-2am 2nd Fri of mth. **Admission** £6. **No credit cards**.
A rockabilly disco with homosexual tendencies, aimed at juvenile delinquents, homo reprobates, high-school drop-outs and everything in between. Plus live bands.

Dalston Superstore

117 Kingsland High Street, E8 2PB (7254 2273). Dalston Junction/Dalston Kingsland rail. **Open** noon-2am Mon-Fri; 11am-2am Sat, Sun. **Admission** varies; phone for details. **Credit** AmEx, MC, V.
Gay-owned and run, this It Spot attracts a mix of gays and their straight pals, and the atmosphere is hip but attitude free. Nights include Eurotrash, Hot Boy Dancing Spot, Mixtape and Techno In My Fridge. Locals scenesters like JonnyWoo, A Man To Pet and the Lovely JonJo are often found here. The beating heart of Hackney.

Dirtyconverse Disco

Kings Cross Social Club, 2 Britannia Street, WC1X 9JE (www.dirtyconverse.com). King's Cross St Pancras tube/rail. **Open** 9pm-2am 2nd Sat of mth. **Admission** £5 after 10.30pm. **No credit cards.** Map p267 M3.
Gay-friendly disco run by girls and playing serious synth pop to electro and indie. No remixes and no R&B. Plus guest DJs from Scared to Dance.

Duckie

RVT, 372 Kennington Lane, SE11 5HY (7820 1222, www.duckie.co.uk). Vauxhall tube/rail. **Open** 9pm-2am Sat. **Admission** £6. **No credit cards**. **Map** p25.
This legendary, offbeat club features 'post-gay vaudeville and post-punk pogo-ing', and is even funded by the Arts Council. Lesbian New Jerseyite Amy Lamé is your hostess.

Nightlife

DJs the Readers' Wifes play the best retro set in town, effortlessly blending '60s girl groups with '90s indie and everything in between (the set often climaxes with Kate Bush's 'Wuthering Heights', and the crowd goes wild). Some of the performances are off the wall – think sword swallowers, lesbian beauty contests and stripping bears – but the cream of underground performance art has graced the stage here, including the likes of Bette Bourne, David Hoyle, Kiki & Herb and Taylor Mac. The venue is pleasingly shabby, though not for the claustrophobic, and the toilets are abominable. Still, it's a London institution. *See p44* **An urban legend.**

Exilio Latin Dance Club

Guy's Bar, Boland House, St Thomas Street, SE1 9RT (07931 374391, www.exilio.co.uk). London Bridge tube/rail. **Open** 9.30pm-2.30am every other Sat. **Admission** £8. **No credit cards. Map** p267 M6.
Ay, caramba! Held in a student union bar, this casual lesbian and gay Latin club features salsa, merengue and tropical pop, with a bit of Ricky Martin thrown in. Favoured by South American expats — it's a particular favourite of Colombians — and the men who admire them.

Fitladz

Union, 66 Albert Embankment, SE1 7TP (www.club union.co.uk). Vauxhall tube/rail. **Open** 11pm-5am Fri. **Admission** £8; £6 with flyer. **No credit cards.**
As the name suggests, Fitladz attracts randy Scallies and sportswear types – and the men who love them. Held underneath the Arches in the old Crash venue, Fitladz does have DJs, but nobody comes here for the music: it's all about cruising the dark rooms and groping those tracksuits.

G-A-Y

Heaven, Under the Arches, WC2N 6NG (7930 2020, www.g-a-y.co.uk). Embankment tube or Charing Cross tube/rail. **Open** 10.30pm-5am Sat. **Admission** reductions with flyer from G-A-Y Bar; £12 door. **Credit** (bar) MC, V. **Map** p269 L7.
In 2008, mainstream superclub G-A-Y bought legendary club Heaven – and relocated from its long-time home at the Astoria. At least there's a choice of music now: the main floor features the familiar G-A-Y mix of commercial pop and PAs (everyone from boy bands to Madonna has appeared here); the Star Bar plays electro house; and the Island and Pop Rooms feature 1980s and '90s.

G-A-Y Camp Attack

Heaven, Under the Arches, WC2N 6NG (7930 2020, www.g-a-y.co.uk). Embankment tube or Charing Cross tube/rail. **Open** 11pm-4am Fri. **Admission** free with flyer from G-A-Y Bar; £6 door. **Credit** (bar) MC, V. **Map** p269 L7.
London's biggest gay Friday nighter just got even bigger as Camp Attack attacks all that was once held sacred at Heaven. Three rooms play four decades of music. Expect at least one of them to be devoted to a medley of Stock Aitken Waterman: think Bananarama, Dead or Alive, Rick Astley and Scouse belter Sonia. Plus, of course, Kylie.

Gravity

Fire, South Lambeth Road, SW8 1UQ (7582 9890, www.fireclub.co.uk). Vauxhall tube/rail.

Open midnight-8am Thur. **Admission** £12; £5 with flyer. **Credit** (bar) MC, V. **Map** p25.
The Vauxhall after-hours club scene starts its weekend here. DJs from the Orange stable play funky house for people who have better things to do than work on Fridays.

Gutterslut

Various venues (07815 851169, perqx@live.co.uk, www.myspace.com/gutterslutuk). **Open** 10pm-3am, one Saturday a month, call or email for details. **Admission** £5-£8. **No credit cards.**
Boys in frilly white blouses and knickerbockers. Girls with outlandish eye make-up. Gold strappy sandals with three-inch heels – worn by people of both sexes. Shiny disco tops – worn by people of both sexes. Pole-dancing drag queens. Plastic sunglasses. Men in Mexican wrestlers' masks. Geek chic. Lots of androgyny. It could almost be the Blitz or Taboo. But it's not. It's Gutterslut, brought to you by the mischievously named Dalston Gay Mafia. DJs Per QX, Elliot J Brown, Nic Fisher and guests play ghetto electro, facelifting rave and diet techno, with a bit of '80s and disco thrown in; MC Jonny Woo is on the pole. At the time this guide went to press, the club was in search of a new venue, but it will likely be in Dalston or Hoxton. Call for details.

Habibi

Oak Bar, 79 Green Lanes, N16 9BU (7354 2791, www.oak-bar.co.uk). 73, 141, 341 bus. **Open** 9pm-late 2nd Sat of mth. **Admission** £7; £4 before 10pm; £6 before midnight. **Credit** (bar) MC, V.
Green Lanes is a Turkish stronghold, so it's only natural that London's only gay Middle Eastern night is held there. Billed as a 'club without borders', Habibi features DJs spinning Arabic, Turkish, Greek, Balkan and R&B, complete with belly dancer. One of many club nights at the Oak Bar (*see p30*).

Hard On

Hidden, 100 Tinworth Street, SE11 5EQ (07533 402985, www.hardonclub.co.uk). Vauxhall tube/rail. **Open** 10pm-5am last Sat of mth. **Admission** £15 (membership required). **Credit** MC, V. **Map** p25.
This fetish night is as full-on as the event's name suggests. There's hard dance music, regular shows by the more rough-looking variety of porn stars, and a strict dress code: rubber, leather, uniform, skin gear, jocks and boots (no jeans or trainers). The play room boast equipment with which to abuse your fellow clubbers. There is also a viewing gallery in the cruise room. Has amassed an international following. Cabs are available from the club.

Horse Meat Disco

Eagle London, 349 Kennington Lane, SE11 5QY (7793 0903, www.horsemeatdisco.co.uk). Vauxhall tube/rail. **Open** 8pm-3am Sun. **Admission** £6. **No credit cards. Map** p25.
Not your average gay club. Skinny Soho boys and fashionistas rub shoulders with scally lads and bears in a traditional old boozer. The hip soundtrack is an inspired mix of Studio 54, New York punk and new wave. As one *Time Out* critic put it: 'if you ever wished you could hang out in a club like the one in *Beyond the Valley of the Dolls* or *Scarface*, you'll love Horse Meat Disco'. Special events include the 'Vauxhall is Gurning' Vogue Ball. A must.

Nightlife

Ku Bar

30 LISLE STREET + 25 FRITH STREET
LEICESTER SQUARE   SOHO

AWARD WINNING GAY BARS AND CLUB IN THE HEART OF LONDON'S WEST END OPEN LATE 7 DAYS / WEEK

NEAREST TUBE LEICESTER SQUARE

WWW.KU-BAR.COM   facebook : Ku Bar People

Klub Fukk

Central Station, 37 Wharfdale Road, N1 9SD (7278 3294, www.theundergroundclub.net/ klubfukk.html). King's Cross tube/rail. **Admission** £5. **Open** 7pm-midnight, 2nd Sat mth. **Credit** MC, V. **Map** p267 L2
Billed as the world's only radical queer sex club, Klub Fukk is open to all genders and sexualities. Held in the Dungeon of Central Station, it's an evening that's aimed at the open-minded and the polysexual: there might be girl-on-girl action taking place right next to men who are engaging in the love that dare not speak its name. The presence of trannies results in a few Crying Game scenarios.

Later

Fire, South Lambeth Road, SW8 1UQ (7582 9890, www.fireclub.co.uk). Vauxhall tube/rail. **Open** noon-7pm Sun. **Admission** £5. **Credit** (bar) MC, V. **Map** p25.
Sunday morning dance session for insomniacs. This is where all the boys from Beyond end up if they haven't scored. DJs Steve Pitron, the Sharp Boys and Gonzalo keep the clubbers going.

The cultured club

Alright, 28 Shacklewell Lane in Dalston might not be 20 rue Jacob, Paris. But **Tart**, with its strapline 'Where Intelligent Discussion is Expected and Encouraged', is a literary salon event where women meet to rub shoulders and indulge in cultured conversation. Was Tart founder Reina Lewis inspired by the legendary salonista Natalie Barney, nattering to Alice B Toklas, while Gertrude Stein complained to Romaine Brooks about the price of *poissons*? 'We were inspired by the salons of old, both those of the aristocracy, where women who were otherwise excluded from the institutions of art and politics were able to act as patrons and taste-makers, and the bohemian salons of the early 20th century, which have become so iconic in lesbian imagery.'

But does that mean that Lewis hand-picks the invitees from the cream of London lesbian society? Lewis is horrified: 'No! I always imagine that had I been at Natalie Barney's salon it might have been quite horrid to be the not-gorgeous, not-famous one in the corner while the in-crowd was busy being beautiful. We wanted to create a social gathering that focused on the arts, but was friendly and welcoming. We knew that women were craving cultural events and spaces that were not sceney.'

And maybe we're all just getting a bit past it and would rather have a nice sit-down and a chat instead of a drug-fuelled dance. Says Lewis: 'Tart is an antidote to mindless clubbing and noisy bars. Women are entitled to activities with more substance. It is not just that we're getting older, but binge culture has detracted from many queer bar spaces'.

Other soirée-style events, including **Polari** (*see right*) and those hosted by the **House of Homosexual Culture** at the Southbank Centre, suggest that a scene is springing up that is more thinking than drinking. According to Rupert Smith, the foundations for the House of Homosexual Culture were laid 'when a group of thirtysomething friends were moaning about the lack of culture on the gay scene. So we started holding events that focused on a certain issue and mixed expert talk, personal testimony,

performance, discussion and socialising. Obviously it served the needs of an older group, who don't want loud music and drugs. But there are loads of younger people who come and engage very actively, and for them it's an escape from the rigid gay stereotype'.

Meanwhile, *Time Out*'s Paul Burston created his bona night of gay words and music, Polari, in the belief that 'there are people whose idea of gay culture doesn't begin and end with the latest dance remix. What most people refer to as gay culture isn't really culture at all, but a commercial playground. Also, most gay authors don't get opportunities to read in public. I liked the idea of bringing literature to the gay scene, and introducing scene queens to a broader idea of what gay culture means.'

House of Homosexual Culture
www.myspace.com/homoculture.
Polari: An Evening of Gay Words & Music
Southbank Centre (see p134), monthly; free entry. www.myspace.com/polarigaysalon.
Tart
www.tartsalon.co.uk, tartsalon@googlemail.com.

Lower the Tone

Oak Bar, 79 Green Lanes, N16 9BU (7354 2791, www.oak-bar.co.uk). 73, 141, 341 bus. **Open** 9pm-3am last Fri of mth. **Admission** £6. **Credit** (bar) MC, V.

A nostalgic knees-up for the nice, the jaded and the past-it, as DJs Lea Andrews, Sadie Lee and Jonathan Kemp play their favourite tunes of yesteryear. Billed as 'a club for people who hate clubs', it's a fun night out with a different theme each month – and usually quite silly.

Onyx

Area, 67-68 Albert Embankment, SE1 7TP (3242 0040, www.areaclublondon.com). Vauxhall tube/rail. **Open** 10pm-5am Fri. **Admission** £6; £5 reductions. **Credit** AmEx, MC, V (bar). **Map** p25.

New night playing anthemic house, with various themed parties, single launches and guest DJs. Expect a sea of glistening torsos strutting their stuff, both on and off stage.

Orange

Fire, South Lambeth Road, SW8 1UQ (7582 9890, www.fireclub.co.uk). Vauxhall tube/rail. **Open** 11pm-8am Sun. **Admission** £10-12; £5 with flyer before 1am. **Credit** (bar) MC, V. **Map** p25.

The original Sunday after-hours club, and still a popular choice with the Vauxhall gay village people, some of whom have been hard at it since Friday. Two rooms, with lots of funky uplifting house to wash away those Monday blues.

O-Zone

Ku, 30 Lisle Street, WC2H 7BA (7437 4303, www.ku-bar.com). Leicester Square tube. **Open** 9pm-3am Fri. **Admission** £3; free before 11pm. **Credit** (bar) MC, V.

Weekly Friday night club with London's hardest working drag DJ, Dusty O, one of Boy George's old chums. Music is bubblegum pop, crowd tends to be younger.

Polari

Royal Festival Hall, Southbank Centre, SE1 8XX (7960 4200, www.southbankcentre.co.uk, www.myspace.com/polarigaysalon). Waterloo tube. **Open** 6.30-9.30pm monthly. **Admission** free. **Credit** MC, V. **Map** p270 O7.

Dubbed a 'peerless gay literary salon' by *The Independent*, Polari is the brainchild of author and journalist Paul Burston. It has moved from Soho to the South Bank Centre, which is large enough to hold the ever-growing numbers who are turning up to listen to authors and spoken word poets and dance to unexpected musical turns and nostalgic tunes from DJ Burston. The bookshop is provided by Foyles (*see p101*). Reserve tickets in advance. *See also left* **The cultured club**.

Popcorn

Heaven, Under the Arches, WC2N 6NG (7930 2020, www.heaven-london.com). Embankment tube or Charing Cross tube/rail. **Open** 11pm-6am Mon. **Admission** £8 after midnight; £3 reductions. **Credit** (bar) MC, V. **Map** p269 L7.

This mixed mash-up of a club is actually the busiest night at Heaven, despite being on a school night. Sounds are cheesy pop, commercial house, funky house and disco.

Horse Meat Disco. *See p40.*

Popstarz

The Den, 18 West Central Street, WC1A 1JJ (7240 1900, www.popstarz.org) Tottenham Court Road tube. **Open** 10pm-4am Fri. **Admission** £5-£8; free with flyer before 11pm. **No credit cards**. **Map** p267 L5.

The original gay indie night was in a state of flux as this guide went to press, as its old venue, Sin, was under threat. But there are plans to keep this legendary night running, along with its choice of three different rooms: indie, trash and soul. Check the website for details.

Rudeboiz

Fire, South Lambeth Road, SW8 1UQ (7582 9890, www.fireclub.co.uk). Vauxhall tube/rail. **Open** 10.30pm-4.30am Fri. **Admission** £8; £5 with flyer. **Credit** (bar) MC, V. **Map** p25.

This popular cruise night for gay scally lads has returned to Fire. DJs spin the usual Vauxhall floorfillers, but the main attraction isn't the dancing. There's a strip show, a cruise maze, cabins and cinema. Rudeboiz has even inspired its own brand of gay porn – which really tells you all you need to know.

Shinky Shonky

Ku, 30 Lisle Street, WC2H 7BA (7437 4303, www.ku-bar.com). Leicester Square tube. **Open** 10pm-3am Wed. **Admission** free. **Credit** (bar) MC, V. **Map** p269 K7.

Boogaloo Stu, Albert Twatlock and guests play top pop sounds old and new at this unashamedly camp night, where it's cool to act the fool. Twisted cabaret acts include Miss High Leg Kick, the Incredible Tall Lady, Dolly Rocket, Fake Bush and Le Gateau Chocolat.

An urban legend

Standing alone at the bottom of Kennington Lane, surrounded by a small patch of grassland, the Royal Vauxhall Tavern – now the **RVT** (*see p34*) – doesn't look much from the outside. A recent paintjob has smartened up the walls of this old Victorian boozer, but can't hide the fact that this is the last pub standing, the only venue in the area not to be redeveloped or turned into a Starbucks. But behind these doors lies a wealth of gay cultural history. The Vauxhall is London's longest surviving gay venue. It survived the Blitz, and the devastation of AIDS. It even survived the defection of its greatest star, Lily Savage, to television. And like all true survivors, the old

girl is enjoying a comeback. Walk past any night of the week and you'll hear music, laughter and possibly even the sound of a man in a wig singing 'Maybe This Time' by Liza Minnelli.

Performance, and the traditions of camp and drag, have been part of the Vauxhall story from the beginning. Built in 1863, on the site once occupied by the Vauxhall Pleasure Gardens, the pub first became popular as a music hall venue. It wasn't until after the World War II that the cross-dressing performances began to attract a different kind of clientele, as returning servicemen rubbed shoulders with local homosexuals and the flute-like tones of gay slang 'polari' filled the room. One person who remembers gay life at the venue during this period is Bette Bourne, grand dame of the radical drag theatre troupe Bloolips. Bourne first visited the Vauxhall in the 1950s.

'I'd have been about 17, and I was taken there by this guy I was having a scene with, who was a dancer at the Palladium. The layout was different then. The bar came out from the stage. And at a given point the drag queens on stage would holler and run around the counter; you had to pick your drink up quick or it would end up on the floor.'

Not everyone came to watch the show. 'In those days there was another bar that was screened off from the main bar with frosted glass. That was where the straights would go. They might

be builders, or ladies advanced in years, and they'd sit safely in the snug on the other side of the partition. But both bars shared the same loo, which was part of the attraction for both parties.'

For Bourne, the Vauxhall proved a happy hunting ground. 'We were young, and we went there looking for sex. And then, of course, the drag would come on. I hadn't seen much drag before then. There was something wicked and naughty about drag in those days. It was underground, a great naughty secret. Later, I was part of the Gay Liberation Front, and we were all committed to coming out of the closet. But at the time, there was an excitement about leading a double life and being a part of an exclusive club. There was song in the '60s called 'I'm in with the In Crowd', and that's exactly what it felt like.'

In the 1970s, the 'in' crowd came out and the Vauxhall's popularity grew. Hinge & Bracket appeared there, and Diana Dors. By the '80s, the venue was synonymous with Lily Savage, who performed four times a week including Sundays, when the queues would stretch around the block. 'People thought I had shares in the place,' remembers Lily's creator, Paul O'Grady. 'I didn't. I was just the head saloon girl.' And he does mean saloon. 'I used to have a fight in there at least once a week,' he explains. 'It was a cross between the village hall and a wild west saloon. Fabulous! Then there was that night the police came in wearing rubber gloves. The famous police poppers raid. I remember being on stage and shouting at the crowd to riot. The police carted me off in a paddywagon.'

This was in 1988, and the rubber gloves were to protect the police from AIDS. 'When AIDS hit,' remembers O'Grady, 'it devastated the Vauxhall. Every day there'd be someone else who'd got sick. You'd be in the dressing room and someone would announce that they'd tested positive. There was always someone in a black suit and tie. It was all around you. Awful. The place was decimated. I spent three years visiting people in hospitals. There were lots of funerals and endless fundraisers. If AIDS was a war, then the Vauxhall was on the front line.'

By the mid 1990s, the worst of the war was over. But now there was a new threat from a different front as Lambeth Council planned to demolish the historic venue to make way for a shopping centre. The performance club Duckie mounted a vigorous press campaign, protesting outside Lambeth Town Hall and saving the venue from the bulldozers. Still the future remained uncertain.

In 2005, the unlisted building went up for public auction and was saved from the property developers by the intervention of two gay

businessmen, Paul Oxley and James Lindsay. With their investment, the venue is enjoying a level of popularity not seen since Lily Savage left in 1994. Monday night is bingo, Tuesday is **Bar Wotever** (*see p37*), Thursday is cabaret. And with **Duckie** on Saturday (*see p39*) and the DE Experience on Sunday, the emphasis is still on live performance, but with a modern, alternative slant. 'There's a proud legacy at the Vauxhall,' acknowledges Oxley. 'But a legacy won't pay the bills. We have to look to the future.'

Of all the performers to grace the Vauxhall stage, none is more forward-thinking than David Hoyle (the artist formerly known as the Divine David). So the last word should go to him. 'The Royal Vauxhall Tavern is the beating heart of queer London,' declares Hoyle. 'When I'm on stage there, I'm very proud to be part of this incredible history. And it's that legacy that we're all carrying forward. I think that the best nights at the Vauxhall are still ahead.

My favourite things
Paul Burston
author & journalist

I don't go out dancing as much as I used to, but I do love **The Eagle** (*see p33*) in Vauxhall. It's close to where I live and at the weekends they have nights like the legendary **Horse Meat Disco** (*see p40*) and 80s night **Carpet Burn** (*see p37*), where I sometimes DJ. They have a beer garden too; often there's a free barbecue to soak up the booze.

I also enjoy **Gutterslut** (*see p40*) over in Shoreditch. It's like something out of the early 80s, with lots of freaky people, gay and straight, rubbing along together and enjoying the 'ghetto electro' sounds of DJs like Per QX and Elliott J Brown. I still have a soft spot for Duckie too – the Readers Wifes are fantastic.

I tend to prefer venues that offer entertainment – whether it's David Hoyle at the RVT or Jonny Woo or The Fabulous Russella over in the East End. One of the most exciting new venues around is **Dalston Superstore** (*see p31*), which is gay owned and run and attracts a good mix of people, gay and straight. One of my favourite West End bars is **BarCode** (*see p18*), and the **Shadow Lounge** (*see p25*) is back on form now that the original manager Shaun Given is back in charge.

I don't go on dates (I'm a happily married man!) but for a romantic evening we might go for cocktails at **Harvey Nichols** (*see p99*), or for dinner at one of the Portugese places on South Lambeth Road; **Rebato's** (169 South Lambeth Road, 7735 6388, www.rebatos.com) is a favourite.

I'm a shopaholic – suits especially. I usually wait for the sales and pick up Italian designer suits for half price at **Selfridges** (*see p101*)

or at Harvey Nicks. I tell myself that I need them for **Polari** (*see p43*), the gay literary salon that I host at the Southbank Centre. But the reality is that I probably have enough suits to last me a lifetime.

I also love **Closet Case** (47 Brewer Street, 7734 1652) in Soho. The manager, Joey, knows what I like and will often keep things back for me. I've had some great shirts and jackets from there.

As an author, I'm keen to support independent bookshops whether it's **Foyles** (*see p101*) or **Gay's The Word** (*see p102*), or the gay lifestyle store **Prowler** (*see p111* **Buy sexual**), which stocks books as well as saucy underwear and porn. In fact I once had a book launch there. My mum was embarrassed when I said the word 'cock' and walked off into the back of the store, where she found herself surrounded by dildos and images of cocks on porn DVDs!

● *Paul Burston's latest novel is* The Gay Divorcee *(LittleBrown). He recently edited a gay and lesbian short story collection called* Boys and Girls *(Glasshouse Books). For more information, visit www.paulburston.com.*

S.L.A.G.S

RVT, 372 Kennington Lane, SE11 5HY (7820 1222, www.rvt.org.uk). Vauxhall tube/rail. **Open** 2-midnight Sun. **Admission** £8; £5 after 9pm (includes entry to Vauxhall Tavern Chill-out). **No credit cards**. **Map** p25.
DJ Simon Le Vans and the sublime Dame Edna Experience still pack the punters in to this legendary London haunt every Sunday afternoon. The clientele is a mix of hardcore clubbers still partying from the night before, and an alternative crowd who come to watch the genius that is the Dame Edna Experience (her Karen Carpenter is sublime).

SuperMartXé

The Coronet, 28 New Kent Road, SE1 6TJ (7701 1500, www.supermartxelondon.com). Elephant & Castle tube. **Open** 10pm-7am occasional Sat. **Admission** £15 in advance, more on the door. **No credit cards**.

The biggest club success of recent years, SuperMartXé is that rare thing – event clubbing that is throbbingly busy and full-on but with a widespread appeal. The clientele is varied enough to make it friendly, easy-going and almost attitude-free. Music is uplifting and infectious, while the crowd is pumped with fearsome amounts of energy. Stage shows are eye-catching without being so dominating you have to stop dancin' to watch. DJs include Tony English, Jodie Harsh, Fat Tony and Pagano.

Trade

www.tradeuk.net. **Open** 5am-late occasional Sun. **Admission** £15. **Credit** (bar) AmEx, MC, V.
The original after-hours club is no longer a weekly fixture, but still returns for special parties on bank holiday weekends and at other times of the year (Valentine's, Gay Pride). The Fierce Rulin' Trade DJs include some of the biggest names in hard house. Check the website for details.

Trannyshack

*Madame JoJo's, 8-10 Brewer Street, W1F 0SD
(7734 3040, www.trannyshack.co.uk). Leicester Square
tube.* **Open** 10pm-3am Wed. **Admission** free before
midnight, drag queens, trannies, club kids, freaks; £6;
£3 with flyer. **Credit** AmEx, MC, V. **Map** p269 K6.
A night for trannies and friends, hosted by the Very Miss
Dusty O, with DJ Tasty Tim and performers Glendora, Lady
Lloyd, Skinny Marie and more. This cross-dressing extravaganza takes full advantage of the faded glamour of Madame
JoJo's, a glitzy Soho venue that is filled with the ghosts of
burlesque, drag and cabaret performers of decades past.

Vauxhall Tavern Chill-Out

*RVT, 372 Kennington Lane, SE11 5HY (7820
1222, www.rvt.org.uk). Vauxhall tube/rail.* **Open**
6pm-midnight Sun. **Admission** £5; free with entry
to S.L.A.G.S. **No credit cards. Map** p25.
A legendary topless session featuring commercial dance
and a side order of cheese. Arrive early to beat the queues,
and earlier still to catch the divine DE Experience (at
S.L.A.G.S; *see left*), who performs at 5pm.

WayOut Club

*Charlie's, 9 Crosswall, off Minories, EC3N 2JY(07778
157290, www.thewayoutclub.com). Aldgate or Tower
Hill tube.* **Open** 9pm-4am Sat. **Admission** £7-£12.
No credit cards. Map p271 R7.
There's a touch of Vegas glitz about this drag and trannie
nightspot for cross-dressers and their admirers. Changing
facilities and a make-up service are available. The stage
shows are something to behold. Guys dressed as guys also
welcome. *See p38* **Dude looks like a lady**.

Wig Out

*Centro, 16 West Central St, WC1A 1JJ (7287 3726).
Holborn tube.* **Open** 10pm-4am Sat **Admission** £5
before 11pm, then £7. **No credit cards. Map** p267 L5.
Kitschy cool night for the seriously unserious. DJs
include Tommy Turntables, Lady Lloyd, Prince Nelly
and more. Sophie Ellis Bextor's favourite gay club.

Work!

*Hidden, 100 Tinworth Street, SE11 5EQ (7820
6613, www.heaven-london.com). Vauxhall tube/rail.*
Open 11pm-4am Wed. **Admission** £6; £1-£3
reductions or with flyer before 12.30am. **Credit**
(bar) MC, V. **Map** p25.
Patrick Lilley's new night has brought a touch of urban
music to Vauxhall. Hosted by Fredi Dimanche and the
vision of loveliness that is Le Gateau Chocolat, Work offers
music to suit (almost) all tastes. DJs including Big John,
Jeffrey Hinton, Biggy C, Freddie Thomas and Tuomo Fox
play the best in pop, funky bashment and old skool.

XXL

*The Arches, 53 Southwark Street, SE1 1TE (0871
210 0069). London Bridge tube/rail.* **Open** 10pm-3am
Wed; 10pm-6am Sat. **Admission** £3; free members
Wed. £12; £8 members Sat. **No credit cards.
Map** p270 O8.
The biggest bear club in the world. Set underneath three
industrial arches, the club is divided into separate areas,
from a huge dancefloor – full of sweaty grizzlies – to a
dark room where ursine mating rituals occur. Following a
revamp, it doesn't feel as grimy as it once did. Big-name
DJs such as the Freemasons do occasional guest spots.

Popstarz. See p43.

Cutting edge bars

the edge

Soho, W1
Tottenham Court Road
www.edgesoho.co.uk
020 7439 1313

the green.

Islington, N1
Angel
www.thegreenislington.co.uk
020 7226 8895

g-SPOT

Covent Garden, WC2
Charing Cross
www.gspotgirlbar.com
020 7379 4573

KAZBAR

Clapham, SW4
Clapham North
www.kazbarclapham.com
020 7622 0070

The Yard
BAR

Soho, W1
Picadilly Circus
020 7437 2652

KUDOS
Go Go bar

Covent Garden, WC2
Charing Cross
020 7379 4573

Saunas

For gyms and traditional saunas, *see pp143-146.*

Chariots Limehouse

574 Commercial Road, E14 7JD (7791 2808, www. gaysauna.co.uk). Limehouse DLR/rail. **Open** 11am-1am Mon, Tue; 11am Wed-1am Mon. **Admission** £12; £10 reductions. **Credit** MC, V.
Located next to BJ's White Swan (*see p30*) – so if you don't pull at the pub, try your luck here. It's smaller than Chariots Shoreditch, and some say friendlier. In addition to the sauna, there's a large steam room, a cinema room and video cabins, plus a 'huge fun shower'. Start lathering.

Chariots Shoreditch

1 Fairchild Street, EC2A 3NS (7247 5333, www.gay sauna.co.uk). Shoreditch High Street rail. **Open** noon-9am daily (21hrs). **Admission** £15; £13 reductions. **Credit** AmEx, MC, V. **Map** p271 R4.
London's biggest and busiest sauna is decked out like a kitsch Roman bath – and there's plenty of Roman-style debauchery. Search for a gladiator in the indoor pool (no bathing suit required) or in the steam room, sauna, two jacuzzis or cinema room, and then tame him in a private cabin (which feel like a doctor's examination table; some people might like that). Chariots feels a bit like a leisure centre, only with sex. If you don't indulge, recline by the pool and watch the bathing beauties.

Chariots Streatham

292 Streatham High Road, SW16 6HG (8696 0929, www.gaysauna.co.uk). Streatham rail. **Open** noon-1am Mon-Thur; noon Fri-midnight Sun. **Admission** £12; £10 reductions. **Credit** MC, V.
This small venue has themed nights for bears (Tuesday, and the first and third Saturdays of the month) and black men and their admirers (Friday). In addition to the three saunas, two steam rooms, two video rooms and large jacuzzi, there is a sunbed – if you like sex with sizzle.

Chariots Vauxhall

Rail Arches 63-64, Albert Embankment, SE1 7TP (7247 5333, www.gaysauna.co.uk). Vauxhall tube/rail. **Open** noon-9am Mon-Thur; noon Fri-9am Mon. **Admission** £15; £12 reductions. **Credit** MC, V. **Map** p25.
No expense has been spared creating a sauna for the Vauxhall village. With two steam rooms, two saunas, a dark room, two video rooms, a huge café/internet lounge and more private rooms than could surely ever be filled, there is almost too much space. At quiet times the atmosphere can be sterile. Go late on the weekend as the clubs spill out to make the most of the pumped-up muscle crowd.

Chariots Waterloo

101 Lower Marsh, SE1 7AB (7401 8484, www. gaysauna.co.uk). Waterloo tube/rail. **Open** 24hrs daily. **Admission** £12; £10 reductions. **Credit** MC, V. **Map** p269 M9.
Sweat en masse at Chariots Waterloo: it boasts the largest sauna in the UK (with space for 50 guys), a mammoth steam room and a maze of 35 dark rooms. For travellers, there's also a luggage check, so you can get lucky while you wait for your train from Waterloo station.

Locker Room Sauna

8 Cleaver Street, SE11 4DP (7735 6064, www.the-locker room.co.uk). Kennington tube. **Open** 10am-midnight Mon-Thur; 10am Fri-midnight Sun. **Admission** £10.50; £7 before 1pm; £8 reductions. **No credit cards.**
Locker Room is a small, friendly neighbourhood sauna not too far from Vauxhall. There are dark rooms, shower stalls, steam rooms, sunbeds and a sauna.

Pleasuredrome Sauna

Arch 124, Cornwall Road, SE1 8XE (7633 9194, www. pleasuredrome.com). Waterloo tube/rail. **Open** 24hrs daily. **Admission** £15; £10 reductions. **Credit** MC, V. **Map** p270 N8.
A large, popular sauna decorated in an industrial style. Recently renovated, it features two steam rooms, a sauna, a slick maze, private rooms, spa pool, sunbeds and a café.

Portsea Sauna

2 Portsea Place, W2 2BL (7402 3385, www.gaysauna bar.com). Marble Arch tube. **Open** noon-10.30pm daily. **Admission** £13; £10 reductions. **Credit** MC, V. **Map** p263 F6.
In addition to a sauna, there's a steam room, bar, video room and private rooms. Combine with a trip to the Quebec pub (*see p24*); bring a silver fox here for some fun.

Sauna Bar

29 Endell Street, WC2H 9BA (7836 2236, www. thesaunabar.co.uk). Covent Garden tube. **Open** 11.30am-1am Mon-Thur, Sun; 11.30am-7am Fri, Sat. **Admission** £14; £12 reductions. **Credit** MC, V. **Map** p267 L6.
A bar, steam room, splash pool, showers and private rooms have all been crammed into this small sauna. There's also a 35-man jacuzzi – the largest in the UK.

Steamworks

309 New Cross Road, SE14 6AS (8694 0606, www. steamworkslondon.co.uk). New Cross tube/rail. **Open** 11am-midnight Mon-Thur; 11am Fri-11pm Sun. **Admission** £10; £8 reductions. **No credit cards.**
Includes a 20-man sauna, two steam rooms, showers, free refreshments and a free three-day re-entry pass.

Sweatbox Soho

Ramillies House, 1-2 Ramillies Street, W1F 7LN (3214 6014, www.sweatboxsoho.com). Oxford Circus tube. **Open** noon-2am Mon-Thur, Sun; noon-7am Fri, Sat. **Admission** £20 day pass; £15 spa only; £10 under-25s. **Membership** £39-£75/mth; £750/yr. **Credit** MC, V. **Map** p266 J6.
With it's striking black and red design and sleek fittings, this new state-of-the-art gay gym and sauna looks more like a club than a traditional fitness centre. The sauna occupies the lower two floors and features two giant steam rooms, two Turkish hot rooms, a 14-man jacuzzi, large stylish chill-out room with TV and Wi-Fi, two video lounges and a maze of innovative and striking cabins, some with two-way mirrors for the exhibitionists among you. Saturdays are club nights, with promoters including Suzie Krueger of Hard On fame and DJs including Brent Nicholls. Wear a towel, shorts or go naked. For the gym side of things, *see p145* **Gonna make you sweat.**

Nightlife

Lesbian Nightlife

Girls! Girls! Girls!

London may be one of the world's great lesbian cities, but, as with most great cities, the bar scene for women is much smaller than it is for gay men. What there is, however, is immensely varied, in terms of scene and location – and it's constantly changing. These days, there is just as much emphasis on fashion as there is on fun.

Contrary to stereotypes about sensibly shoed lesbians, young gay London women are increasingly fashion-forward and showing off their wardrobe at club nights. You might see dykes decked out in Ted Baker or All Saints clobber on their way to **WiSH** (*see p58*), perhaps, while the grunge gang, in their baggy jeans and T-shirts from Spitalfields market, rub shoulders with the neon-haired club kids at one of the edgier club nights.

The biggest recent local success is WiSH, which attracts a fashionable crowd of media types and slick professionals to Shoreditch. But, thankfully, not everyone on the London lesbian scene is achingly cool.

Alongside these new events are the traditional hangouts for those looking for a good ol' knees up to Kylie or Madonna – places where you can boogie in your comfortable shoes and leave your hair products at home.

Candy Bar (*see right*) is still the place to go in Central London: located in Soho, where strip bars were once ten a penny, it keeps the tradition alive, only this time the exotic dancers are for the eyes of women only.

Just the other side of Charing Cross Road, **First Out** (*see p53*) still reigns supreme as a casual meeting place, with its veggie café and pre-club basement bar; the **Star at Night** (*see p55*), a greasy spoon-cum-cocktail bar, is full of character.

If you shun the mainstream, the capital boasts a burgeoning alternative scene. **Bar Wotever** (*see p55*) attract gender benders and drag kings, and literally gives London's underworld a stage with their cabaret on Tuesdays at the RVT.

Many lesbians don't go out on the scene regularly, so one-off parties hold great appeal. A number of popular, infrequently occurring events have come and gone over the years. **100% Babe** (*see p55*) is an easy one to remember: it's only held on a Sunday night before a bank holiday.

Out in the east end, there are fewer and fewer sapphic strongholds. Once lesbian central, now a yuppie enclave, Stoke Newington nevertheless still draws lesbians to the quirky and laid-back **Oak Bar** (*see p54*).

Pubs & bars

Candy Bar

4 Carlisle Street, W1D 3BJ (7287 5041, www. candybarsoho.com). Tottenham Court Road tube. **Open** 4-11.30pm Mon-Thur; 2pm-2am Fri, Sat; 5-11pm Sun. **Admission** free; £4 after 9pm Fri, Sat. **Credit** MC, V. **Map** p267 K6.
Opened in 1996, the Candy Bar was London's first full-time drinking den for lesbians. It made a splash with its location – in Soho, the heart of boystown – and its enter-tainment: it was the first bar in London to offer female

---

The best Clubs

Classy broads
Green (*see p54*).

Gender benders
Bar Wotever (*see p55*).

Fashion parade
WiSH (*see p58*).

Girls in da hood
Bootylicious (*see p55*).

Pure cheese
Lower the Tone (*see p57*).

Bollywood babes
Club Kali (*see p56*).

Ogling pole dancers
Candy Bar (*see above*).

Candy Bar

strippers and lapdances to lesbians. Naked women are still a draw – there is full-on stripping on the first Friday and the third Saturday of every month – but you can also do your own dancing in the basement club (a cast of DJs spins everything from house and R&B to electro and old school). The crowd varies from lipstick lesbians and butch types to students and professionals.

At the time this guide went to press, the three-storey bar was being refurbished: the owners are promising a cocktail lounge upstairs, complete with sofas for chilling, and a kitchen, though the vital decision on the future of the pool table was still up in the air.

Men are welcome to visit Candy Bar, but they must be accompanied by at least two females, and are not allowed to watch the strip shows.

Central Station

37 Wharfdale Road, N1 9SD (7278 3294, www.centralstation.co.uk). King's Cross tube/rail. **Open** noon-1am Mon-Wed; noon-2am Thur; noon-4am Fri, Sat; noon-2am Sun. **Credit** MC, V. **Map** p267 L2.

On a backstreet near King's Cross, Central Station used to be one of London's shabbier, seedier haunts – a place where randy gay men congregated in a dank cellar to get their end away. Not anymore.

Following a makeover, Central Station now has a roof terrace, a café serving bar snacks and full meals, and a four-room B&B. Though it still hosts a predominantly gay male crowd, there is a mixed vibe, and lesbians do

You shall go to the ball

Ballroom dancing has always been a bit camp, so it seems wholly appropriate that Hilda Ogden, the curlered queen of *Coronation Street*, presides over **Waltzing with Hilda** in the form of a Warhol-esque portrait. Now well into its second decade and increasingly popular thanks to formal dancing being in vogue again, Hilda's is a monthly women-only night specialising in ballroom and Latin partner dancing.

If you don't know your whip from your whisk, arrive early for the beginners' class (45 minutes before the general social dance), and then strut your stuff on the dancefloor. Organiser Wendy Glaze says: 'We concentrate on the six most sociable dances: jive, waltz, rumba, cha cha, quickstep and social foxtrot. Dance etiquette means that new people are never left out. It's a safe environment to make friends.'

As the 'Wild Wild West' (a simple country circle dance that involves partnering everyone in the room) is a popular feature here, it's hard not to make friends. Dancing is also great for your posture and, apparently, better than sex for burning calories. And you can break with the sexist tradition of male leads – you sort of have to here.

The first venue to offer social dancing was men's bar BJ's White Swan, whose famous **Sunday Tea Dance** has been going for more than 20 years. Though it attracts a male crowd, a few women also cut a rug via ballroom, Latin, salsa and disco. For a dance in more salubrious surroundings, **Jacky's Jukebox** is held at the beautiful Rivoli Ballroom, a picture of faded elegance. Proprietor Jacky Appleton has been dancing 'since the Black Bottom' [a flapper dance of the 1920s]. She says: 'In the past few years, the gay dance scene has exploded. Our dancers compete at international level at the Gay Games and other events. Same-sex couples are often seen dancing together at high-profile events like 'Ballroom Blitz' at the Royal Festival Hall. We have yet to appear on *Strictly Come Dancing*, but we keep kicking on that door!'

Promoters are catching on. Past events have included the London Lesbian Ball, a posh black-tie affair hosted by the **Champagne Dining Club** (www.uniquely4girls.co.uk), while **Studio La Danza** organised a queer masked ball in Paris, no less.

And it's not just the ballroom dancers that are coming out of the closet: even the tartan is turning pink. John Tyler runs the **Gay Gordons**, a weekly Scottish country dancing group for gay men, lesbians and their friends, in Islington. Tyler wanted to be a ballet dancer as a child, but 'encountered immovable resistance from the senior male members of my family. However, when I was nine I saw Scottish country dancing on the telly and was hooked. Because we had Scottish ancestry, I was allowed to do this, so ended up in a skirt instead of tights.' Thank goodness he did. Although there is a hardcore of regulars at his event, new people turn up every week and no experience is necessary; you just need soft-soled shoes, enthusiasm and energy. The best part? Kilts are worn by those who have Scottish blood – or just nice legs. But what's underneath?

BJ's White Swan

556 Commercial Road, E14 7JD (7780 9870, www.bjswhiteswan.com). Limehouse rail/DLR. **Open** 9pm-2am Tue-Thur; 9pm-4am Fri, Sat; 6.30pm-midnight Sun. **Admission** £5 after 10.30pm Fri, Sat. **Credit** MC, V.

Ballroom, salsa, jive and disco line-dancing on Sundays.

Exilio Latin Dance Club

Guy's Bar, Boland House, St Thomas Street, SE1 9RT (07956 983230, 07931 374391, www.exilio.co.uk). London Bridge tube/rail. **Open** 9.30pm-2.30am every other Sat. **Admission** £8; £5 before 11pm with flyer from website. **Credit** (website only) AmEx, MC, V. **Map** p271 Q8.

London's long-running queer Latin club plays Latin, salsa, merengue, cumbia, reggaeton and pop.

drop in, particularly on the second Saturday of the month, when the cellar is given over to randy *women* – for the polysexual Klub Fukk (*see p56*).

Drill Hall

16 Chenies Street, WC1E 7EX (7307 5060, www.drillhall.co.uk). Goodge Street tube. **Open** 10am-10pm Mon-Fri; 10am-6pm Sat, Sun. **Credit** AmEx, MC, V. **Map** p267 K5.

If you want to mingle with the lesbian arty crowd, the Drill Hall is crawling with women who are theatrically inclined, plus general culture vultures and studenty types. Note: the bar is attached to the Drill Hall theatre (*see p131*), and is only open on performance nights.

First Out

52 St Giles High Street, WC2H 8LH (7240 8042, www.firstoutcafebar.com). Tottenham Court Road tube. **Open** 9am-11pm Mon-Sat; 10am-10.30pm Sun. **Credit** MC, V. **Map** p267 K6.

By day a relaxed vegetarian café, at night First Out morphs into a buzzing pre-club watering hole. The busiest night is Girl Friday, when female DJs warm up clubbers in the basement bar. It's quieter on the main floor, where a mixed crowd tucks into reasonably priced quiches, homemade soups, pies and jacket potatoes. If you're not a party girl, this long-standing lesbian haunt is also just a good place to grab a beer or coffee with friends, or chill out while reading scene magazines or perusing flyers.

Gay Gordons

Unity Church Hall, 279 Upper Street, N1 2TZ (07752 617708, www.thegaygordons.org). Angel tube. **Open** *Intermediate* 7-9pm Mon. *Beginners* 7-9pm Thur. **Admission** £5-£7. **No credit cards.**

Scottish country dancing for lesbians, gay men and friends. Wear clean soft-soled shoes.

Jacky's Jukebox

Rivoli Ballroom, 350 Brockley Road, SE4 2BY (07715 421349, www.jackysjukebox.com). Crofton Park rail. **Open** 7.30pm-midnight 1st Sat of mth. **Admission** £8. **No credit cards.**

A friendly mixed gay/straight crowd comes for salsa, ballroom, 1970s line-dances, country, Latin and old-time in this classic ballroom.

Kensington Dance Studio

1st floor, Polish Hearth Club, 55 Princes Gate, Exhibition Road, SW7 2PN (07774 443627, www.kensingtondancestudio.co.uk). South Kensington tube. **Open** *Beginners* 7.15-8.15pm. *Intermediate & advanced* 8.30-9.30pm. *Social dancing* 9.30-10.30pm Wed. **Admission** £10; £8 members. **No credit cards.** **Map** p265 D9.

Dance studio hosting gay and lesbian events.

Pink Jukebox

La Cantina, 4 Wild Court, WC2B 4AU (07774 443627, www.pinkjukebox.co.uk). Holborn tube. **Open** 2-7pm 2nd & 4th Sun of mth. *Advanced* 2pm. *Intermediate* 2.30pm. *Beginners* 3.30pm. *Dancing* 4.30-7pm. **Admission** £19; £8 members. **No credit cards.** **Map** p271 Q8.

Jitterbug and jive to music from the past 70 years at these bi-monthly classes.

Salsa Rosada

The Welsh Centre, 157-163 Gray's Inn Road, WC1X 8UE (7813 4831, www.salsa-rosada. co.uk). Chancery Lane or Russell Square tube/ King's Cross tube/rail. **Classes** *Beginners* 7-8pm Wed. *Intermediate* 8-9pm Wed. **Admission** £6 1 class, £9 2 classes. **No credit cards.** **Map** p267 M4.

Salsa classes for gay men and women; *see p137*.

Studio LaDanza

89 Holloway Road, N7 8LT (7700 3770, www. studioladanza.co.uk). Highbury & Islington tube/ rail. **Open** *Classes* 7-8.30pm. *Social dancing* 8.30-10.30pm Wed. **Admission** *Social only* £6. *Classes* £38/4wks. **No credit cards.**

Lesbian-run ballroom and Latin studio; *see p137*.

Waltzing with Hilda

Jacksons Lane Arts Centre, 269A Archway Road, N6 5AA (07939 072958, www.hildas.org.uk). Highgate tube. **Open** *Jan-July, Sept-Dec* 7.45pm-11.30pm 2nd & last Sat of mth. **Admission** £10. **No credit cards.** *See p58.*

Friendly Society

Basement, 79 Wardour Street, W1D 6QB (7434 3804). Leicester Square or Piccadilly Circus tube. **Open** 4-11.30pm Mon-Thur; 4pm-midnight Fri, Sat; 4-10.30pm Sun. **Credit** (over £10) MC, V. **Map** p267 K6.

The futuristic decor alone makes the Friendly Society worth a visit. And though the bar is hidden in a basement on a dark alley, the designers have cheered things up with mirror balls, violet lighting and a sky-blue ceiling; the kitschy decorative touches prevent the modern space from feeling too clinical. The bar attracts a healthy mix of women and men, media luvvies and the odd celeb, especially when DJs visit on Fridays and Saturdays.

G Spot Girl Bar

Kudos, 10 Adelaide Street, WC2N 4HZ (7379 4573, www.www.gspotgirlbar.com). Charing Cross tube/rail. **Open** 5pm-midnight Thur-Sat. **Credit** AmEx, MC, V. **Map** p269 L7.

A sign that Soho's lesbian scene is picking up, G Spot Girl Bar is not quite as steamy as its name suggests, but this dimly lit den of iniquity (they've got a huge lounge bed and intimate booths!) downstairs at Kudos attracts a sophisticated and good-looking crowd

Girls Go Down

G-A-Y Bar, 30 Old Compton Street, W1D 4UR (7494 2756, www.g-a-y.co.uk). Leicester Square or Tottenham Court Road tube. **Open** 7pm-midnight daily. **Credit** MC, V. **Map** p267 K6.

Soho's Girls Go Down has become the forgotten bar of the lesbian scene. Most women over the age of 20 can't stand the place. And no wonder: G-A-Y's sister space is not a very appealing place: it's cramped and hidden in the basement of the popular men's bar – en route to the toilets, no less. The dim lighting, multiple video screens and pumping music (mainly pop, R&B and chart tunes) are not conducive to conversation. Still, the cheap drinks attract a studenty crowd, there's a flirty atmosphere and the bar staff are friendly.

Green

74 Upper Street, N1 0NY (7226 8895). Angel tube. **Open** 5pm-midnight Mon-Wed; 5pm-1am Thur; noon-2am Fri, Sat; noon-midnight Sun. **Credit** MC, V.

For lesbians in fashionable Islington, the choice of gay bars has always been limited. Not many wanted to spend their evenings in the traditional boy bar Edward VI. Then along came the Green, with its Soho swagger: plush decor, cocktails and a sophisticated crowd. Recently refurbished, it now boasts a contemporary aesthetic that still manages to feel warm and cosy, with plenty of sofa seating. The layout is still narrow, and can get a bit congested on weekends – when there are DJs – but you might just bump into a pretty girl; around 20% of the crowd comprises women, most of them older, local professionals. There is a good snack menu, plus a few mains and weekend brunch.

KW4 (King William IV)

77 Hampstead High Street, NW3 1RE (7435 5747, www.kingwilliamhampstead.co.uk). Hampstead tube/Hampstead Heath rail. **Open** 11am-11pm Mon-Thur; 11am-midnight Fri-Sun. **Credit** AmEx, MC, V.

Bar Wotever

Formerly known as the King William IV, this traditional Hampstead pub has long been a favourite of gay men, owing to its proximity to Hampstead Heath. But lesbians like it too, especially during the summer, when they stop in after a dip in the women's bathing pond on the heath. Food is served, including a Sunday roast.

Oak Bar

79 Green Lanes, N16 9BU (7354 2791, www.oak-bar.co.uk). 73, 141, 341 bus. **Open** 5pm-midnight Mon-Thur, Sun; 5pm-4am Fri, Sat. **Credit** MC, V.

A hub for north London lesbians, the Oak Bar is a big and unpretentious queer boozer with a couple of great club nights for women. There's Lower the Tone (*see p57*), a kitsch mixed party held on the last Friday of the month, and Rock the Lezbah, a 'funky and spunky' dance night held every Thursday; soul sisters flock to Soul Naturelle, held on the first Saturday of the month. The rest of the time, a vaguely alternative crowd gathers here to drink beer, cocktails or shooters, or to play pool. There's outside seating in the summer too.

Retro Bar

2 George Court, off Strand, WC2N 6HH (7839 8760). Charing Cross tube/rail. **Open** noon-11pm Mon-Fri; 2-11pm Sat; 2-10.30pm Sun. **Credit** AmEx, MC, V. **Map** p269 L7.

Sister in spirit to the bohemian Royal Vauxhall Tavern, the Retro Bar is the queen of the alternative gay scene for central London. It's hidden down a quaint little alley, so it has a best-kept secret feel. Inside, the ambience is cosy and eccentric, with a jukebox that spins alternative and 1980s music. Although it always draws a mixed crowd, the busiest nights for girls are Monday and Wednesday. The upstairs bar is a great place to chat or have a date – it's a bit quieter – while the ground-floor pub offers a range of themed nights, including a poptastic music quiz (Tuesdays) and karaoke (Wednesday).

Star at Night

22 Great Chapel Street, W1F 8FR (7494 2488, www.thestaratnight.com). Tottenham Court Road tube. **Open** 6pm-11.30pm Tue-Sat. **Credit** MC, V. **Map** p267 K5.

Like many a gay man or lesbian, the Star at Night leads a double life. By day, it's an old greasy spoon, but on a weekend evening – poof! – it is transformed into a lesbian cocktail bar with table service. The retro decor is vintage mom-and-pop Italian (it's been in the same family since 1933) and incorporates red and white checked tablecloths and pre-1950s signs on the walls. After the caff crowd leaves, thirtysomething females gather for a gossip and a cocktail; the occasional DJ or live jazz act makes an appearance in the cosy cellar space.

Clubs

100% Babe

The Roxy, 3-5 Rathbone Place, W1P 1DA (7636 1598, www.theroxy.co.uk). Tottenham Court Road tube. **Open** 8.30pm-3am Sun before bank holiday. **Admission** £6-£7. **Credit** (bar) AmEx, MC, V. **Map** p267 K5.

For London lesbians, bank holiday Mondays can mean only one thing: Sunday nights at 100% Babe. For the last decade, promoters Sue and Sue have staged this occasional club on every Sunday night before a bank holiday. And, despite all the changes in the lesbian club scene, they have stuck to their successful formula: popular house music, feel-good floorfillers and a party mood, all set in a dark and spacious basement club. They must be doing something right, as there are still queues to get in after all these years.

Bar Wotever

RVT, 372 Kennington Lane, SE11 5HY (7820 1222, www.duckie.co.uk). Vauxhall tube/rail. **Open** 6pm-midnight Tue. **Admission** £6. **No credit cards**. **Map** p25.

The Royal Vauxhall Tavern made its name as a divey gay bar, but it has always had an alternative vibe – one that is inclusive of lesbians. Amy Lamé, one of London's most recognisable lesbian faces, hosts the Duckie club night on Saturdays, and Bar Wotever, on Tuesdays (6pm-midnight) has always attracted its fair share of lesbians, particularly drag kings, who complement the gender-bending boys. The atmosphere is arty and flamboyant, but unpretentious. On stage, there is 'talent' of varying degrees – poetry readings, comedy, singing, performance art… wotever. *See also p44* **An urban legend**.

Bird Club

Bethnal Green Working Men's Club, 42-44 Pollard Row, E2 6NB (www.birdclub.org.uk). Bethnal Green tube. **Open** 7pm-2am, days vary. **Admission** £6-£8.

Held, rather incongruously, in the Bethnal Green Working Men's Club. Part rowdy cabaret club, part politically minded butch dyke disco, Bird la Bird and Maria Rosa Young's night celebrates 'queer femininity in all its forms' and ruffles some feathers on the way. Expect satirical skits, neo-burlesque and topical themes, topped off with an indie-electro disco till late.

Bootylicious

Club Colosseum, 1 Nine Elms Lane, SW8 5NQ (www.bootylicious-club.co.uk). Vauxhall tube/rail. **Open** 11pm-6am 3rd Sat of mth. **Admission** £12; £10 before midnight; £5-£6 reductions. **No credit cards**. **Map** p25.

The biggest urban night in London's gay calendar, Bootylicious has also become one of the top underground clubs in the country. After some seven years on the scene, the dancefloor is still filled to capacity with boyz – and girls – from da hood, courtesy of a stellar cast of DJs and MCs, including Biggy C, Jeffrey Hinton, Nikki Lucas, Sugarbear, MC Chickaboo, Miss Bailey and MC Tyron. They play a mix of essential grooves, R&B and urban beats, which draws a multiracial crowd to Club Colosseum in the Vauxhall gay village, on the third Saturday of the month.

Star at Night

Nightlife

City Pink

The Rehearsal Room, Adam Street Club, 9 Adam Street, WC2N 6AA (7379 8000, www.citypink.co.uk). Embankment tube/Charing Cross tube/rail. **Open** 6.30pm-late monthly. **Admission** £10. **Credit** (bar) MC, V. **Map** p269 L7.

City Pink offers gay professional women a place to network in their power suits. Held on a weekday, the events usually bring women who have commuted straight from work in their black trouser-suit combo – there is a strict 'no jeans and trainers' policy. In addition to the white-collar babes, there are lots of old-school lesbians and ambitious wannabes vying for attention. The promoters also arrange a weekend club night, Club Eve. Check the website for details.

Club Kali

The Dome, 1 Dartmouth Park Hill, N19 5QQ (7272 8153, www.clubkali.co.uk). Tufnell Park tube. **Open** 10pm-3am 3rd Fri of mth. **Admission** £5-£8. **Credit** (bar) MC, V.

Billed as the world's largest LGBT Asian nightclub, Club Kali attracts people from all corners of the London scene, along with their admirers. Bollywood, Bhangra and Arabic sounds boom from the speakers, but resident DJs Ritu and Riz & Qurra throw in a sprinkling of chart dance music. Held on the third Friday of the month in the cavernous Dome nightclub, Kali is a fixture on the gay calendar.

Code

Green Carnation, 5 Greek Street, W1D 4DD (07956 529649, www.club-code.net). Tottenham Court Road tube. **Open** 8pm-2.30am last Fri of the month. **Admission** £8; £5 before 10pm. **Credit** MC, V. **Map** p269 K7.

Designer dykes and prim princesses dominate at Code, a monthly one-nighter held in the smart Green Carnation bar. Exclusivity is the watchword – parties are guest list only and you must email a request to info@club-code.net before each event – but the classy ambience makes a nice change from Soho's more raffish venues. You can chat and sip cocktails on the main floor lounge, and dance downstairs to electro and smooth house played by female DJs such as Miss Cupcake and Faye Lanson.

Duckie

RVT, 372 Kennington Lane, SE11 5HY (7820 1222, www.duckie.co.uk). Vauxhall tube/rail. **Open** 9pm-2am Sat. **Admission** £6. **No credit cards.** **Map** p25.

Famous for its camp, hilarious and just plain weird cabaret, this venerable south London knees-up is still a riot. Launched back in the mid 1990s as part of the gay indie movement, Duckie still attracts an alternative crowd, with a thrashy, trashy soundtrack, but longtime host Amy Lamé ensures that nobody takes anything too seriously. Though predominantly a male crowd, the presence of Lamé – New Jersey's most famous lesbian? – pulls in the women too.

Klub Fukk

Central Station, 37 Wharfdale Road, N1 9SD (7278 3294, www.centralstation.co.uk). Kings Cross tube/rail. **Open** 7pm-midnight 2nd Sat of mth. **Credit** (bar) MC, V. **Admission** £5. **Map** p267 L2.

The name says it all. Central Station, that bastion of sleaze, now lends its dungeon to the Wotever crew for their subtly titled Klub Fukk. The basement space is

Duckie

My favourite things
Rhona Cameron
comedian & author

If you fancy comedy, then London is your place. There are a multitude of comedy clubs around these days, and the entire business seems to have trebled in size since I started out in the early '90s. Check the listings but if there's too much to choose from in too little time, head down to the famous **Comedy Store** (1A Oxendon Street, SW1Y 4EE, 7930 2949, www.thecomedy store.co.uk), in the heart of London's West End. Great atmosphere and a fine selection of comics.

There's no choice when it comes to seeing a movie other than the **Curzon Soho** (*see p124*). I'm totally inflexible about that. It's there where you'll find the most intelligent and appreciative audiences, in an environment purely designed for respecting good quality filmmaking. If you're already looking forward to *Sex in the City 3*, then off to the big multiplex for you, full of noisy eaters and people who text during the film.

The **South Bank** (*see pp160-163*) – that whole bit from around the National to the Eye – is pretty interesting. Always a lively mix and fusion of London stuff. Buskers, skateboarders, street performers... A rich tapestry of city life. It's lovely just to walk there, especially at night or at dusk and just watch everyone and everything.

I'm really the wrong person to ask about food and bars as I don't go out into central London as much these days, preferring to stay local in my overpriced and beloved NW3. If I were to eat out in town, though, it would be at the **Ivy** (*see p94*) or **Joe Allen** (13 Exeter Street, WC2E 7DT, 7836 0651, www.joeallen.co.uk). The latter drawing more old-school theatre types, whom I adore, and I always order the chilli con carne. The Ivy, I believe, still has the best-cooked food in London.

By the way, the best Italian restaurant is up the road in Tufnell Park – **Trattoria Nuraghe** (12 Dartmouth Park Hill, NW5 1HL, 7263 4560, www.ristorantenuraghe.co.uk). Outstanding, authentic Italian cooking, in a simple, unpretentious, uncluttered environment, with warm and extremely professional service.

I spend most of the summer's warmest afternoons and evenings on **Hampstead Heath** (*see p209*) – my absolute can't-live-without aspect of London. I run up there in the evenings sometimes and just dive into the women's pond, swim and run home (*see p140* **The swimming pool library**).

If you're not feeling that energetic then just loll around and sunbathe there, cooling off whenever you need. We are so lucky to have a place to swim there. It's full of old Hampstead eccentrics, and most entertaining. The heath is just stunning; it is my garden. Sometimes I meet a friend at **Kenwood House** (*see p210*) in the mornings for a hearty breakfast and a stroll. The air is beautiful there, and we Londoners could all use some of that.

● *For tour dates and news about the author and comedian, visit www.rhonacameron.com.*

sleazy with a capital S, but in addition to the usual rampant men groping in the dark, the playspace is also populated by women and trans folk, who either act out their fantasies or play voyeur. An equal-opportunities orgy.

Lounge

The Penthouse, 1 Leicester Square, WC2H 7NA (07716 335393, www.lounge.uk.net). Leicester Square tube. **Open** 10pm-3am 1st Thur of mth (see website for other dates and venues). **Admission** £8-£10. **Credit** (bar) MC, V. **Map** p269 K7.

Originally established as a professional networking event, Lounge has morphed from an office party into a rather posh do. Held on the second Thursday of the month, it's like frantic than most club nights, but you can still hit the dancefloor in your sexy heels – the dress policy is 'suited and booted, glam and gorgeous, funky and foxy' – and cut a rug to funk, soul, old skool, R&B and

pop. Billing itself as a 'night of tomfoolery for sophisticated metrosexual women', it's the kind of venue where a champagne cocktail goes down a treat.

Lower the Tone

Oak Bar, 79 Green Lanes, N16 9BU (7354 2791, www.oak-bar.co.uk). 73, 141, 341 bus. **Open** 9pm-4am last Fri of mth. **Admission** £6. **Credit** (bar) MC, V.

Never underestimate the power of nostalgia – or cheesy pop. Mixing retro tunes and kitsch classics, the 'club for people who hate clubs' draws a healthy crowd up to Green Lanes on the last Friday of the month; in fact, it has become the busiest night at the Oak Bar. The DJs shamelessly take you down memory lane to the decades that taste forgot – the '70s and '80s – to produce what promoters call 'a Radio 2 extravaganza', with some cool current stuff thrown in. Though mixed, expect to see a large percentage of women in the crowd. A sense of humour is a must.

Popstarz@The Den

The Den, 18 West Central Street, WC1A 1JJ (7240 1900, www.popstarz.org). Tottenham Court Road tube. **Open** 10pm-4am Fri. **Admission** £5-£8; free with flyer before 11pm.
Popstarz, the original and ground-breaking gay indie night, has moved venues a few times over the years, but the successful formula remains the same: a mix of rooms and music genres, from indie to cheesy pop. Check the website for the latest information.

Ruby Tuesdays

Ku Bar, 30 Lisle Street WC2H 7BA (7437 4303, www.ku-bar.co.uk). Leicester Square tube. **Open** 9pm-3am 2nd Tue of mth. **Admission** free. **Credit** MC, V. **Map** p269 K7.
If you want to avoid the weekend crowds of Soho, but still want to dance to DJ Sandra D, Ruby Tuesdays is a lower-key option. Held on the second Tuesday of the month, it is not exactly packed to the rafters, but it has built up a loyal following with students and local office workers. Sandra D spins a mix of current R&B and classic stuff – think Salt 'n' Pepa's 'Push It' or Sister Sledge's 'We Are Family'. But don't expect euphoria on the dancefloor or a hangover on Wednesday; this is simply a good night in which to chill over a bottle of beer and listen to some good tunes.

RuMoUrS

64-73 Minories, EC3N 1DD (07949 477804, www.girl-rumours.co.uk). Tower Hill tube/Tower Gateway DLR. **Open** 8pm-3am last Sat of mth. **Admission** £6. **Credit** (bar) MC, V. **Map** p271 R7.
RuMoUrS has been around for ages, but, strangely, it has experienced a renaissance of late. Its cheesy vibe, which once attracted an older crowd of regulars, now brings in the young things too – they appreciate the novelty value. Nobody gives a damn how you dress or dance, and DJs play trashy pop and R&B hits until the early hours. The

dancefloor is usually rammed with drunken laydeez dancing to 'Tragedy', while the DJ takes endless requests for the remix of 'Total Eclipse of the Heart' – pure class!

Twat Boutique

Dalston Superstore, 117 Kingsland High Road, E8 2PB (7254 2273, www.myspace.com/twatboutique). Dalston Kingland rail. **Open** 9pm-2am 1st Thur of mth. **Admission** free. **Credit** AmEx, MC, V.
Dalston's leftfield gay arts space now has its own eclectronic emporium especially for hipster gay girls. You'll find dance-focused creative types here digging the indie, new wave, electro and disco mash-ups from guest DJs, including Shitdisco and Simian Mobile Disco.

Waltzing with Hilda

Jacksons Lane Arts Centre, 269A Archway Road, N6 5AA (07939 072958, www.hildas.org.uk). Highgate tube. **Open** Jan-July, Sept-Dec 7.45pm-11.30pm 2nd & last Sat of mth. **Admission** £10. **No credit cards**.
This is not a traditional nightclub. It's more like a lesbian social club-cum-dancing school, where women learn ballroom and Latin steps on a real sprung dancefloor. There's a bar too, so you can loosen your inhibitions and strut your stuff. Classes are for beginners and intermediates, singles and couples. *See p52* **You shall go to the ball**.

WiSH

Gramophone, 60-62 Commercial Street, E1 6LT (7377 5332, www.club-wish.co.uk). Liverpool Street tube/rail. **Open** 9pm-3.30am, usually 1st Sat of mth. **Admission** £10; £5 before 10pm. **Credit** (bar) MC, V. **Map** p271 K5.
This supercool monthly event is popular with media luvvies, trendy professionals and young designer gays. Women kick off their Gucci heels to dance to the cream of UK DJs: expect techno and minimalist house booming on the downstairs dancefloor, while upstairs offers an edgy mix of indie, disco and electronica. Call ahead to confirm it's on.

Twat Boutique

Consume

Where to Stay   **60**
   The best Hotels   61
   Homo is where the heart is   74

Restaurants & Cafés   **82**
   The best Restaurants   83
   The best Gay café-bars   85
   Gay dining clubs   88
   How do you take your tea?   93

Shopping   **99**
   The best Shops   99
   Market forces   100
   Buy sexual   110
   Girls aroused   115

Where to Stay

Not a cheap date, but London is good in bed.

London may be a gay hotspot, but as far as specifically gay hotels go, it doesn't exactly rank up there with Key West or Sitges. On the other hand, the lack of ghettoised gay hotels speaks volumes about the city's tolerant culture; you'd be hard pressed to find a hotel desk clerk anywhere in London who raises an eyebrow when you check in with your same-sex partner.

London hotel prices remain obscene, but hoteliers are starting to realise not everybody is travelling on business expenses. As a result, the number of stylish, affordable options is growing. **B&B Belgravia** (*see p73*) and the Mayflower group were the pioneers, but our current favourite is the **Hoxton Hotel** (*see p76*), hopefully a harbinger of things to come.

LOCATION, LOCATION, LOCATION
In terms of gay locations, the old gay village of Earl's Court – still a queer-friendly area – offers several stylish budget hotels, including the **Mayflower** (*see p80*) and **Twenty Nevern Square** (*see p79*). Soho, arguably the gay capital of Europe, only has a couple of hotels, but gay accommodation agency **Outlet** (*see p74* **Homo is where the heart is**) offers a stable of stylish flats to rent in the area. In the gay clubbing district, Vauxhall, leather queens might share a lift with holidaying families at the **Comfort Inn** (*see p77*). And there's a crop of boutique hotels in Clerkenwell, near the edgy Shoreditch scene.

Many of London's swankier hotels are in Mayfair. Bloomsbury is good for mid-priced hotels. For cheaper options, try Ebury Street in Pimlico or Gower Street in Bloomsbury, in addition to Earl's Court. Other areas worth exploring for budget hotels include Bayswater, Paddington and South Kensington.

CLASSIFICATION, PRICES AND BOOKING
Though British hotels are classified according to a star system agreed by the English Tourism Council, the AA and the RAC, we don't list star ratings, which tend to reflect facilities rather than quality; instead, we've classified hotels (within their area headings) according to the price of the cheapest double room per night. Deluxe means a double costs over £300 a night; expensive £200-

£300; moderate £100-£200; budget under £100. Many high-end hotels sneakily quote room prices exclusive of VAT. Always check. We've included this 17.5 per cent tax in prices listed below (due to rise to 20 per cent in January 2011); however, room rates change frequently, so do call and verify costs before you book.

Hotels are constantly offering special deals, particularly for weekends; check websites or ask for a special rate when booking. Also check discount hotel websites for prices that fall well below the rack rates listed here.

If you haven't booked ahead, the obliging staff at the **Visit London Booking Line** (08701 566 366, www.visitlondon.com, open 9am-9pm Mon-Fri; 9am-5pm Sun) will look for a place in your selected area and price range. You can also check availability and reserve rooms on its website.

FACILITIES AND ACCESSIBILITY
We've listed the main services offered by each hotel, but always check before booking if you require a particular service. Rooms in hotels listed as deluxe, expensive or moderate will include a TV and a telephone. Some hotels in the budget bracket have shared bathrooms. Most hotels are now no-smoking throughout, though some do have rooms for smokers (if so, we've noted this). We've also specified if room service is available round the clock. As for internet access, assume the smarter establishments will provide dataport and wireless facilities (often for a hefty price), while budget hotels might just have a public terminal for shared use.

We've tried to indicate which hotels offer rooms adapted for the needs of disabled guests, but check when booking. **Tourism for All** (0845 124 9971, www.tourismforall.org.uk) has details of wheelchair-accessible places.

Gay-friendly hotels

London is a tolerant city, so few hotels feel the need to wave the rainbow flag in their window. However, according to the London Tourist Board, the following hotels are officially gay-friendly – and most cost under £90 for a double room.

Moderate

Church Street Hotel

29-33 Camberwell Church Street, SE5 8TR (7703 5984, www.churchstreethotel.com). Denmark Hill rail or 36, 436 bus. **Rates** (incl breakfast) £120-£180 double. **Rooms** 31. **Credit** AmEx, MC, V.
Craftsman José Raido and his Galician family are behind this attractive hotel near Camberwell Green. It's on the frontier of London's Latin American quarter, reflected in funky bathroom tiles from Guadalajara, imported cinema posters and other Mexicana. The Somerset bed frames in the high-ceilinged bedrooms were forged by José himself. Korres bathroom products are organic, like the pastries and cereals offered for breakfast (even those paying £70-£90 for the shared-bathroom 'Poblito' rooms are entitled to breakfast). The area is up-and-coming and edgy – be careful at night – but there's always lots of street life and buses run all night from nearby Vauxhall and Clapham. *Bar. Business centre. Internet. Parking (£5/day). Restaurant. Room service (24hr). TV.*

Budget

Amsterdam Hotel

7 Trebovir Road, SW5 9LS (0800 279 9132, www. amsterdam-hotel.com). Earl's Court tube. **Rates** £92-£101 double. **Rooms** 27. **Credit** AmEx, DC, MC, V. **Map** p264 B11.
Loyal gay fans return year after year to this smart, discreet B&B on a quiet Earl's Court street. The boutique hotel style of the Amsterdam's refurbished rooms is now extending to the public areas, with pale colours, plain fabrics and good quality fittings creating an upmarket ambience. There's an internet room and free wireless throughout, while in summer the peaceful garden is a big draw. All rooms are en suite; the serviced apartments on the upper floors come complete with kitchenette. The hotel is tolerant of late-night visitors, as long as they are discreet and considerate of other guests. *Internet. TV.*

Central Station

37 Wharfdale Road, N1 9SD (7278 3294, www. centralstation.co.uk). King's Cross tube/rail. **Rates** £40-£95. **Rooms** 4. **Credit** MC, V. **Map** p267 L2.
Not too long ago, Central Station was one of London's seedier pubs. In recent years, it's had a makeover, with the addition of a café, a roof terrace and, now, a B&B. Don't expect too much: a boutique hotel this ain't. Nor is it a particularly salubrious establishment: a cruisy air still dominates, especially in the basement club, with its myriad kinky nights and dark room. But if you need a place to crash after a night on the pull, or pick up a stranger and don't want to bring him home just yet, this is a handy option.

Edward Lear

30 Seymour Street, W1H 7JB (7402 5401, www.edlear. com). Marble Arch tube. **Rates** £117 double. **Rooms** 31. **Credit** AmEx, MC, V. **Map** p263 F6.
Edward Lear, the Victorian artist and poet, was gay. So it's only fitting that this B&B in his former home should be gay-friendly. It's an appealing place: flamboyant floral displays grace the exterior; the interior is bright and cheery, if a little old-fashioned; and the pretty breakfast room makes the most of the Edward Lear connection with poems on the placemats. Rooms are furnished in traditional style and are neither flashy nor luxurious (only four are en suite), but they are comfortable and well proportioned, and the front rooms are gloriously sunny. Oxford Street shopping is close at hand, as is the Quebec pub (*see p24*) – a friendly local for a friendly hotel. *Internet. TV.*

Garth Hotel

69 Gower Street, WC1E 6HJ (0800 634 0294, www.garthhotel-london.com). Russell Square or Tottenham Court Road tube. **Rates** £69-£99 double. **Rooms** 18. **Credit** AmEx, DC, MC, V. **Map** p267 K5.
The owner of this gay-friendly townhouse hotel was in the antiques trade, and it shows: the Garth is decorated in an enjoyably fussy, camp style. The pink lobby walls are lined with framed theatre programmes, vintage fashion ads and

The best Hotels

For Soho action
Outlet (*see p74* **Homo is where the heart is**), **Soho Hotel** (*see p70*).

For flashy fashionistas
Baglioni (*see p74*), **Haymarket Hotel** (*see p69*).

For urban hip
Hoxton Hotel (*see p76*), **Malmaison** (*see p63*), **Zetter** (*see p65*).

For kitsch sake
Pavilion (*see p80*).

For a Vauxhall crash pad
Comfort Inn Vauxhall (*see p77*).

For channelling gay spirits
Edward Lear (*see left*).

For old gold
Claridge's (*see p69*), **Gore** (*see p74*), **Hazlitt's** (*see p70*), **Rookery** (*see p65*).

For budget with beauty
B&B Belgravia (*see p73*), **New Linden** (*see p79*), **22 York Street** (*see p67*), **Vancouver Studios** (*see p79*).

For cruising the night away
Windmill on the Common (*see p77*).

Consume

black and white photos of Hollywood starlets and old London buses. The bedrooms are similarly crammed with interesting pictures, engravings and period prints; they're not luxurious, but the tall ceilings and old fireplaces add period appeal. The verdant garden is delightful. *Internet. TV.*

George

58-60 Cartwright Gardens, WC1H 9EL (7387 8777, www.georgehotel.com). Russell Square tube. **Rates** *£69-£89 double.* **Rooms** 40. **Credit** AmEx, MC, V. **Map** p267 L3.

Yes, it's another 'gay-friendly' hotel, although the George's homely decor doesn't exactly exude gay style. But the hotel occupies a Georgian townhouse on a handsome crescent, so the ceilings are high and public areas spacious. The rooms are fine, with tasteful pine furniture, a pretty blue and yellow colour scheme and new curtains and bedspreads. En suite rooms have minuscule bathrooms; the public loos are perfectly respectable. Guests can use the private tennis courts and garden out front. The location is the George's strong point – Gay's the Word bookshop is around the corner, and the bars of Soho aren't too far away. *Internet. TV (digital).*

Lincoln House Hotel

33 Gloucester Place, W1U 8HY (7486 7630, www. lincoln-house-hotel.co.uk). Marble Arch tube. **Rates** *£89-£119 double.* **Rooms** 27. **Credit** AmEx, MC, V. **Map** p266 G5.

This townhouse hotel sports a nautical motif, the shipping paraphernalia, brass lamps and rich wood panelling of the public areas evoking a cosy old sailing yacht. Though you won't have to scale the rigging, you may have to climb the stairs, for there's no lift. Chandeliers and gaudy floral displays in the lobby add pizzazz. In contrast to the smart public rooms, the bedrooms are plain but they're well equipped, including free wireless internet access. Long-running gay hostelry the Quebec (*see p24*) is a short stroll away. *Internet. Smoking rooms. TV (digital).*

Lynton Hotel

113 Ebury Street, SW1W 9QU (7730 4032, www. lyntonhotel.co.uk). Victoria tube/rail. **Rates** *£75-£95 double.* **Rooms** 13. **Credit** MC, V. **Map** p268 G11.

The Lynton isn't exactly screaming. Its owners, brothers Mark and Simon Connor, aren't even gay. But these cheeky chappies inherited the queer clientele of the defunct Noël Coward Hotel next door (no.111; legend has it that Noël's mum once lived there). The brothers are happy to give gay guests information about the scene, and generally mind their own business about nocturnal guests (just keep the volume down; the hotel's straight guests don't keep Vauxhall hours). The decor is simple, budget Victorian B&B, nicer than the somewhat threadbare halls would suggest; the more attractive rooms are on the upper floors. Some have tiny en suite bathrooms. Soho and Vauxhall are a night bus away, while serious retail therapy is available on the King's Road. *Internet. TV.*

St Alfeges

16 St Alfege Passage, SE10 9JS (8853 4337, www. st-alfeges.co.uk). Cutty Sark DLR/Greenwich DLR/rail. **Rates** *£90 double.* **Rooms** 3. **No credit cards.**

Church Street Hotel. *See p61.*

Consume

'The bright young things will go to Soho, I suppose,' says Robert Gray, co-owner of this diminutive, gay-run B&B in an idyllic corner of Greenwich. So it's left to the over-thirties to enjoy this classy establishment. The decor is tasteful, from the exuberant Victoriana of the three guest bedrooms with their four-poster or cast-iron beds to the bold and eclectic sitting room, complete with mummified cat. Guests are discouraged from bringing 'visitors' home, though a small park nearby provides cruising opportunities. There are a couple of gay pubs in the area, and central London is only 20 minutes away by train. *Internet. TV.*

South Bank & Bankside

The South Bank has much to offer gay visitors. Culture vultures can descend on the **South Bank Centre** (*see p162*), **BFI Southbank** (*see p125*) and **Tate Modern** (*see p165*). Clubbers are close to heaven (literally and metaphorically): famous nightclub Heaven (now home to **G-A-Y**; *see p40*) is just a short walk over the Thames, as is Soho, and Vauxhall isn't that far away either. Cruisers can get action at **Chariots Waterloo** or the **Pleasuredrome Sauna** (for both, *see p49*).

Moderate

Premier Inn London County Hall

County Hall, Belvedere Road, SE1 7PB (0870 238 3300, www.premiertravelinn.com). Waterloo tube/rail. **Rates** £101-£149 double. **Rooms** 316. **Credit** AmEx, DC, MC, V. **Map** p269 M9.
Location, location, location is the USP of this budget chain hotel, housed right next to the London Eye. There may be queue-control barriers in the crammed lobby, but the rooms are as spacious (and well kitted out) as more upmarket gaffs and the restaurant/bar area is a cosy surprise. *Bar. Disabled-adapted rooms. Internet. Restaurant. TV.* **Other locations** throughout the city.

Southwark Rose

47 Southwark Bridge Road, SE1 9HH (7015 1480, www.southwarkrosehotel.co.uk). London Bridge tube/ rail. **Rates** £95-£180 double. **Rooms** 84. **Credit** AmEx, MC, V. **Map** p270 P8.
Perfectly positioned for sampling the South Bank's many delights, the Southwark Rose's interior is sleekly modern, with giant domed, brushed-aluminium lampshades and smart cube chairs in a lobby hung with the work of Japanese photographer Mayumi. The rooms feature dark wood, panelled headboards and the usual crisp white linen. It's fully wired up, and there are electric blackout blinds. Guests can use the next-door Novotel's gym. *Bar. Disabled-adapted rooms. Internet. Parking (£20/day). Restaurant. TV (pay movies).*

The City

During the week, the City is all hustle and bustle. Come the weekend, the place is much quieter. But gay visitors may appreciate its proximity to Shoreditch, which has an increasingly gay

vibe, and the legendary **Chariots Shoreditch** (*see p49*), a huge and rather swinging sauna; and also to the buzzy area around Spitalfields.

Deluxe

Andaz Liverpool Street

40 Liverpool Street, EC2M 7QN (7961 1234, www. andaz.com). Liverpool Street tube/rail. **Rates** £245-£605 double. **Rooms** 267. **Credit** AmEx, DC, MC, V. **Map** p271 R6.
A faded railway hotel until its £70 million overhaul by Conran in 2000, the Great Eastern is now under the ownership of Hyatt's new Andaz portfolio. The new vibe means out with gimmicky menus, closet-sized minibars and even the lobby reception desk, and in with down-to-earth service, eco-friendliness and uncomplicated luxury. Despite the changes, bedrooms still wear the regulation style-mag uniform: Eames chairs, chocolate shagpile rugs and white Frette linens. Eating and drinking options include seafood at Catch, tempura at Miyako and Modern European at 1901, plus a champagne bar, pub and bistro. *Bars/cafés (5). Business centre. Concierge. Disabled-adapted rooms. Gym. Internet. Restaurants (5). Room service (24hr). Smoking rooms. TV.*

Expensive

Threadneedles

5 Threadneedle Street, EC2R 8AY (7657 8080, www.theetoncollection.com). Bank tube/DLR. **Rates** £194-£381 double. **Rooms** 69. **Credit** AmEx, MC, V. **Map** p271 Q6.
Occupying a Victorian banking hall, the former HQ of the Midland Bank, Threadneedles successfully integrates modern design with monumental space. Because of the obvious constraints of developing a listed building, rooms aren't uniform shapes and many of them still have the original windows. The decor is soothingly neutral, with Korres toiletries in the serene limestone bathrooms. Little stress-busting comforts reflect the business-friendly location: fleecy throws, a scented candle lit at turndown, and a 'movie treats' menu of popcorn, ice-cream and Coke. In-house bar/restaurant Bonds offers arguably the best cocktails in London, and one of the finest wine lists. *Bar. Concierge. Disabled-adapted rooms. Internet. Restaurant. Room service (24hr). TV (pay movies).*

Holborn & Clerkenwell

Clerkenwell is one of London's hipper districts. The old warehouses have been converted into stylish lofts and offices; the neighbourhood is brimming with fashionable bars and restaurants. Edgy Shoreditch, nearby, is becoming a fashionable gay area too.

Expensive

Malmaison

Charterhouse Square, EC1M 6AH (7012 3700, www.malmaison.com). Barbican tube/Farringdon tube/rail. **Rates** £276 double. **Rooms** 97. **Credit** AmEx, DC, MC, V. **Map** p270 O5.

Certain touches remind you that this is one of a growing chain, but this hotel has charm. Location is key: it's set in a lovely, leafy, cobblestone square, next to Smithfield Market with its lively restaurants, bars and pubs. The reception is stylishly kitted out with a lilac and cream chequered floor, exotic plants and a petite champagne bar, while purples, dove-grey and black wood dominate the rooms. Rooms are equipped to the standard you'd expect, with nice extra touches including free broadband access and creative lighting. With the City nearby, the clientele is largely businessmen and lawyers during the week, but lower weekend prices attract non-business types. The gym, a subterranean brasserie and a suite of meeting rooms with a rooftop bar complete the picture.
Bar. Disabled-adapted rooms. Gym. Internet. Restaurant. Room service (24hr). TV.

Rookery

12 Peter's Lane, Cowcross Street, EC1M 6DS (7336 0931, www.rookeryhotel.com). Barbican tube/ Farringdon tube/rail. **Rates** £253 double.
Rooms 33. **Credit** AmEx, DC, MC, V. **Map** p270 O5.
Sister hotel to Hazlitt's (*see p70*), the Rookery has long been something of a celebrity hideaway. You'd never guess from the outside that this unassuming row of 18th-century buildings conceals a wonderfully comfortable hotel. Once inside, guests enjoy an atmospheric warren of creaky rooms individually decorated in the style of a Georgian townhouse – huge clawfoot baths, elegant four-posters and an honesty bar in the drawing room – albeit one with free wireless internet. The ground-floor suite has its own hallway, cosy boudoir and subterranean bathroom. Topping it all is the huge split-level Rook's Nest suite, with views of St Paul's.
Bar. Concierge. Internet. Room service (24hr). TV.

Zetter

86-88 Clerkenwell Road, EC1M 5RJ (7324 4444, www.thezetter.com). Farringdon tube/rail. **Rates** £180-£212 double. **Rooms** 59. **Credit** AmEx, MC, V. **Map** p270 O4.
Billing itself as a restaurant with rooms, the Zetter is in fact more than that: it's a fun, laid-back, modern hotel with some interesting design notes. There's a refreshing lack of attitude, and the polyglot staff clearly enjoy their job. The rooms, stacked up on five galleried storeys overlooking the intimate bar area, are sleek and functional, but cosied up with choice home comforts such as hot-water bottles and old Penguin paperbacks, while the walk-in 'raindance' showers are stocked with Elemis products. The top-floor suites have great city views and patios, and the prices beat the West End; it's worth asking about special weekend rates. A bonus: internet access is free. The busy ground floor restaurant – Bistrot Bruno Loubet (*see p85*) – is something special and its wide picture windows make for good people-watching.
Bar. Concierge. Disabled-adapted rooms. Internet. Restaurant. Room service (24hr). TV.

Budget

Clink Hostel

78 King's Cross Road, WC1X 9QG (7183 9400, www.clinkhostel.com). King's Cross tube/rail.
Rates £70 double; from £11 dorm bed. **Beds** 600.
Credit MC, V. **Map** p267 M3.

Rookery

Located in a former courthouse, the awesome Clink sets the bar high for hosteldom. There's the setting: the superb original wood-panelled lobby and courtroom where the Clash once stood before the beak (now filled with backpackers surfing the web). Then there's the urban chic ethos that permeates the whole enterprise, from the streamlined red reception counter to the Japanese-style 'pod' beds and the dining area's chunky wooden tables. If you don't fancy sharing a dorm, there are some single, twin and triple rooms. It's got a happening bar, too. For a cosier option, try Clink 261 (261-265 Gray's Inn Road, WC1X 8QT, 7833 9400, www.ashleehouse.co.uk, £50-£60 double), another design-led hostel with a friendly staff.
Bar. Internet. TV (lounge).

Bloomsbury & Fitzrovia

Bloomsbury, a leafy central district, is handily located within walking distance of the gay nightlife of Soho and King's Cross. It's home to bookshop **Gay's the Word** (*see p102*) and the **Renoir** arthouse cinema (*see p124*).

Expensive

Charlotte Street Hotel

15-17 Charlotte Street, W1T 1RJ (7806 2000, www. firmdale.com). Goodge Street or Tottenham Court Road tube. **Rates** £270-£376 double. **Rooms** 52.
Credit AmEx, DC, MC, V. **Map** p266 J5.
Designer Kit Kemp, doyenne of London's boutique hotels, pioneered the 'modern English' decorative style that has

Connaught. *See p69.*

become one of the capital's dominant design notes. This gorgeous hotel is a fine exponent, fusing traditional English furnishings with avant-garde art. True to the locale, public rooms are adorned with Bloomsbury paintings, by the likes of Duncan Grant and Vanessa Bell. Bedrooms mix English understatement with bold flourishes: soft beiges and greys spiced up with plaid-floral combinations, though management is gradually giving the rooms a style update. The huge, ridiculously comfortable beds and trademark polished granite and oak bathrooms are wonderfully indulgent. The Oscar restaurant and bar is classy and always busy with a media crowd.
Bar. Concierge. Gym. Internet. Restaurant. Room service (24hrs). TV (DVD).

myhotel bloomsbury

11-13 Bayley Street, WC1B 3HD (7667 6000, www. myhotels.co.uk). Goodge Street or Tottenham Court Road tube. **Rates** £245-£260 double. **Rooms** 78. **Credit** AmEx, DC, MC, V. **Map** p267 K5.
It was back in 1999 that this sleek Conran-designed hotel first combined Asian fusion decor and feng shui. Subtle improvements continue to be made, but the essentials remain: an aquarium (with an odd number of fish) and floral arrangements in the calming lobby, strategically placed crystals and scented candles, a wonderfully chilled library in the basement. Rooms are minimalist, but exoticised (think buddha heads and South-east Asian furnishings) and fully accessorised (plasma screens, free Wi-Fi). If you overdo things at the buzzy street-level bar, Jinja ('shrine') offers treatments. The website offers weekend rates, sometimes as low as £125. For a softer, more feminine version and a less urban setting, try myhotel chelsea (35 Ixworth Place, SW3 3QX, 7225 7500, £233-£247).
Bar. Concierge. Gym. Internet. Restaurant. Room service (24hrs). Smoking rooms. TV (DVD/pay movies).

Sanderson

50 Berners Street, W1T 3NG (7300 1400, www. sandersonlondon.com). Oxford Circus tube. **Rates** £235-£470 double. **Rooms** 150. **Credit** AmEx, DC, MC, V. **Map** p266 J5.
No designer flash in the pan, the Sanderson remains one of the city's most stylish hotels. A Schrager/Starck creation, the hotel's sleek design verges on the surreal, starting at the lobby, with its sheer flowing curtains and Dali red-lips sofa. The campery continues as you take the purple lift up to the generously sized guest rooms with their silver-leaf sleigh beds, piled high with cushions, and supermodern glassed-in bathroom areas with powerful steam showers and beautiful stand-alone baths. When it's time to mingle, join the celebs at the Long Bar and Suka restaurant, offering contemporary Malaysian cuisine.
Bars (2). Business services. Concierge. Disabled-adapted rooms. Gym. Internet. Restaurant. Room service (24hr). Spa. TV (DVD).

Moderate

Harlingford Hotel

61-63 Cartwright Gardens, WC1H 9EL (7387 1551, www.harlingfordhotel.com). Russell Square tube/ Euston tube/rail. **Rates** (incl breakfast) £112 double. **Rooms** 43. **Credit** MC, V. **Map** p267 L3.
It's very leafy, and very Bloomsbury, located in a graceful Georgian crescent lined with B&Bs. Despite the rea-

Haymarket. *See p69.*

sonable room rates, the Harlingford has boutique hotel aspirations and leaves other contenders on the block far behind. A stylish redesign has fitted it out with light airy rooms accented with splashes of vibrant turquoise and purple – there's even a Harlingford logo. You can lob a tennis ball in the crescent's private garden or just dream under the trees on a summer's night. *TV.*

Budget

Arosfa

83 Gower Street, WC1E 6HJ (7636 2115, www. arosfalondon.com). Euston Square or Goodge Street tube. **Rates** £95 double. **Rooms** 16. **Credit** MC, V. **Map** p267 K4.

A change of owner and the Arosfa has gone from spartan to Manhattan. Yes, those are Philippe Starck Ghost chairs in the lounge, alongside the mirrored chests and black and white blow-up of the New York skyline. The rest of the hotel is more restrained in style: cappuccino-tinted walls hung with architectural engravings in the halls, neutrally decorated bedrooms decked out with the ubiquitous white linens draped with a silky throw. Those who like elbow room in the shower might find the bathroom units a tad cramped. The wireless internet access is free. *Internet. TV.*

Jenkins Hotel

45 Cartwright Gardens, WC1H 9EH (7387 2067, www.jenkinshotel.demon.co.uk). Russell Square tube/ Euston tube/rail. **Rates** £98 double. **Rooms** 14. **Credit** MC, V. **Map** p267 L3.

Not much has changed at this Bloomsbury favourite since Miss Maggie Jenkins converted the Georgian house into a hotel in the 1920s. There may be TVs and mini-fridges in the rooms, but the decor unconsciously replicates the B&Bs of pre-World War II England – so much so that an episode of *Agatha Christie's Poirot* was filmed here. It's not too chintzy: cream walls, generous floral curtains and pretty bedspreads in the bedrooms, and Nottingham lace table-cloths and Windsor chairs in the breakfast room. *Internet. TV.*

Morgan

24 Bloomsbury Street, WC1B 3QJ (7636 3735, www.morganhotel.co.uk). Tottenham Court Road tube. **Rates** £115 double. **Rooms** 21. **Credit** MC, V. **Map** p267 L5.

Run by the same family since 1978, the guest rooms of this comfortable budget hotel have a distinctly 1970s air – those nifty headboards with built-in bedside tables and reading lamps, the gathered floral bedspreads. But they're well equipped and all geared for the electronic age with free wireless internet access, and voicemail. And the cosy room where the slap-up English breakfast is served is a charmer, with its wood panelling, London prints and blue and white china plates. Their spacious flats are excellent value. *Internet. TV.*

Marylebone

Although there's no specific lure for gay visitors, this upmarket (and central) enclave has a villagey high street with some interesting independents and chain stores. It's also a short walk to the lovely **Wallace Collection** (*see p180*), and Oxford Street.

Moderate

Sumner

54 Upper Berkeley Street, W1H 7QR (7723 2244, www.thesumner.com). Marble Arch tube. **Rates** (incl breakfast) £160-£200 double. **Rooms** 20. **Credit** AmEx, DC, MC, V. **Map** p263 F6.

Sitting on the fringes of Marylebone, this chic boutique hotel is set in a Georgian townhouse. It's all shades of grey in the lounge and halls, and the decor of the custom-designed deluxe rooms may be too hard-edged for some (though they have terrific walk-in showers). Other rooms are softer in tone, and the buttercup-strewn wall and multi-coloured Arne Jacobsen chairs in the breakfast room make for a cheerily elegant start to the day. *Disabled access. Internet. TV.*

22 York Street

22 York Street, W1U 6PX (7224 2990, www.22york street.co.uk). Baker Street tube. **Rates** (incl breakfast) £120 double. **Rooms** 10. **Credit** AmEx, MC, V. **Map** p266 G5.

Imagine one of those bohemian French country houses featured in *Elle Deco* – all pale pink lime-washed walls, wooden floors, sprinklings of quirky antiques and subtly faded textiles. This should give you an idea of the atmosphere of this graceful, unpretentious guesthouse in the heart of Marylebone. There's no sign on the door and the sense

WITH OVER 1 MILLION MEMBERS WORLDWIDE

IT'S TIME TO PLAY

JOIN FOR
FREE

WHATEVER KIND OF GIRL YOU'RE LOOKING FOR YOU CAN FIND HER ON GAYDAR
GIRLS. JUST LOG ON AND GET PLAYING! IT COULDN'T BE EASIER.

gaydargirls.com

WHAT YOU WANT, WHEN YOU WANT IT

of staying in a hospitable home continues when you're offered coffee in the spacious breakfast room/kitchen with its huge, curved communal table. Many of the largely good-sized rooms have baths – a rarity in this price range. *Internet. TV.*

Mayfair & St James's

Mayfair is London's most exclusive address. For gay visitors, the main attraction is the exclusive shopping around Bond Street. Soho is within walking distance, as is Hyde Park, where a certain amount of cruising occurs.

Deluxe

Claridge's

55 Brook Street, W1K 4HR (7629 8860, www. claridges.co.uk). Bond Street tube. **Rates** £700-£830 double. **Rooms** 203. **Credit** AmEx, DC, MC, V. **Map** p266 H6.

Claridge's is synonymous with history and class – and its signature art deco design (the result of an overhaul in the 1920s) still dazzles. Photographs of Churchill and sundry royals grace the grand foyer, as does an absurdly OTT Dale Chihuly chandelier. While remaining traditional, its bars and restaurant are actively fashionable: Gordon Ramsay offers contemporary French cuisine in his restaurant and A-listers gather for champers and sashimi in the Claridge's bar. The rooms divide equally between deco original and Victorian, with period touches such as deco toilet flushes in the swanky marble bathrooms. Bedside panels control the mod con facilities at the touch of a button. If money's no object, opt for one of the Linley suites, tricked out by designer David Linley in gorgeous duck-egg blue and white, or lilac and silver, and with painstaking attention to deco details. One of the most atmospheric hotel stays money can buy.

Bars (2). Business services. Concierge. Gym. Internet. Restaurants (3). Room service (24hr). Smoking rooms. TV (DVD/pay movies).

Connaught

Carlos Place, W1K 2AL (7499 7070, www.the-connaught.co.uk). Bond Street tube. **Rates** £399-£764 double. **Rooms** 121. **Credit** AmEx, DC, MC, V. **Map** p268 H7.

This isn't the only hotel in London to provide butlers, but there can't be many that offer 'a secured gun cabinet room' for hunting season. This is traditional British hospitality for those who love 23-carat gold-leaf trimmings and stern portraits in the halls, but all mod cons in their room. Too lazy to polish your own shoes? The butlers are trained in shoe care by the expert cobblers at John Lobb. Both bars – the gentlemen's club-style Coburg and the cruiseship-sleek, David Collins-designed Connaught – are impressive. *Bars (2). Concierge. Gym. Internet. Restaurants (2). Room service (24hr). Smoking rooms. Spa. TV (DVD).*

Dorchester

53 Park Lane, W1K 1QA (7629 8888, www.the dorchester.com). Hyde Park Corner tube. **Rates** £500-£770 double. **Rooms** 249. **Credit** AmEx, DC, MC, V. **Map** p268 G7.

A glitzy Park Lane fixture since 1931, the Dorchester's interior may be thoroughly, opulently classical, but the hotel is cutting-edge in attitude, providing an unrivalled level of personal service. This opulence is reflected in the grandest lobby in town, complete with Liberace's piano, and a magnificently refurbished spa. The view over Hyde Park from the expansive terrace is the same one Elizabeth Taylor would have seen when she agreed to star in *Cleopatra* – she took the call here. Of the 49 other suites, General Eisenhower planned the D-Day landings in one and Prince Philip held his stag-do in another. The hotel continually upgrades older rooms to the same high standard as the rest, with floral decor, antiques and lavish marble bathrooms; some have park views. The Dorchester employs 90 full-time chefs – both China Tang and the Grill Room live up to their reputations, while the Alain Ducasse team of Nicola Canuti and Bruno Riou launched the master's first London restaurant here.

Bar. Concierge. Disabled-adapted rooms. Gym. Internet. Parking (£30-£40/day). Restaurants (3). Room service (24hr). Smoking rooms. Spa. TV (DVD/pay movies).

Haymarket Hotel

1 Suffolk Place, SW1Y 4HX (7470 4000, www. firmdale.com). Piccadilly Circus tube. **Rates** £294-£535 double. **Rooms** 50. **Credit** AmEx, DC, MC, V. **Map** p269 K7.

The latest opening from decor doyenne Kit Kemp is a perfect vehicle for her trad-mod interiors. The block-size building was designed by John Nash, the architect of Regency London, and Kemp's decor – sinuous sculptures, fuchsia paint and shiny sofas – is a bold complement. Other wow-factors include the basement swimming pool and bar, immortalised by Simon Pegg in *How to Lose Friends and Alienate People* (like Kemp's other hotels, this place is a celebrity magnet). Rooms are generously sized, individually decorated and stuffed with facilities; there are only 50 rooms, so there is a real boutique feel and plenty of attention from staff. An extensive breakfast is served in Brumus restaurant, which is open to non-residents.

Bar. Concierge. Disabled-adapted rooms. Gym. Internet. Restaurant. Room service (24hr). Smoking rooms. Spa. TV (DVD/pay movies).

Metropolitan

19 Old Park Lane, W1K 1LB (7447 1000, www. metropolitan.como.bz). Hyde Park Corner tube. **Rates** £305-£494 double. **Rooms** 150. **Credit** AmEx, DC, MC, V. **Map** p268 H8.

The sassier, younger sister of the more staid Halkin (*see p75*), the Met forms part of a celeb-friendly group of hotels and resorts called COMO, long established in Bali, Bangkok and the Turks & Caicos Islands. Look no further than destination dining spot Nobu or the paparazzi-plagued Met Bar to appreciate its credentials. Designer Christina Ong's background in retail and interior design stand out in the relaxed lobby bar area and throughout the spacious rooms, soundproofed from the regular hum of Mayfair traffic. The gym has been refitted with superior equipment, with personal trainers and massages also available. With its park-view rooms, the hotel that set the standard for modern urban retreats is still a cut above the rest.

Bar. Business centre. Concierge. Gym. Internet. Parking (£45/day). Restaurant. Room service (24hr). Smoking rooms. Spa. TV (DVD/pay movies).

Consume

Covent Garden Hotel

No.5 Maddox Street

5 Maddox Street, W1S 2QD (7647 0200, www.living-rooms.co.uk). Oxford Circus tube. **Rates** £260-£410 one-bed apartment. **Rooms** 12. **Credit** AmEx, DC, MC, V. **Map** p266 J6.

The PR material has it down pat: an inner-city sanctuary. This bolthole off Regent Street is perfect for visitors who want to stay in a chic apartment (one-, two- or three-bedroom, each with a fully equipped kitchen) at a good long-term rate. Here they can shut the discreet brown front door, climb the stairs and flop into a home from home with all mod cons, including flatscreen TVs. The East-meets-West decor – bamboo floors and dark wood furniture mixed with sable throws and the obligatory crisp white sheets – is classic 1990s minimalist. There's no bar, but Patara, a decent Thai restaurant, is on the ground floor.
Business centre. Concierge. Internet. Room service. TV (DVD).

Ritz

150 Piccadilly, W1J 9BR (7493 8181, www.theritz london.com). Green Park tube. **Rates** £470-£646 double. **Rooms** 137. **Credit** AmEx, DC, MC, V. **Map** p268 J8.

Class or snobbery? If you're happy staying in a hotel where jeans and trainers are banned from all public areas, the Ritz may be for you. Founded by hotelier extraordinaire César Ritz, the hotel is deluxe in excelsis. The real show-stopper is the ridiculously ornate, vaulted Long Gallery, an orgy of chandeliers, rococo mirrors and marble columns, but all the high-ceilinged, Louis XVI-style bedrooms are more restrained in pastel colours. Amid this old-world luxury, mod cons include wireless internet, large TVs and a gym. With hotel tours no longer offered, an elegant afternoon tea in the Palm Court (*see p93* **How do you take your tea?**) is the only way in for interlopers.
Bar. Concierge. Gym. Internet. Restaurant. Room service (24hr). TV (DVD/VCR).

Soho

There are few hotels within London's gay mecca. But you can rent a holiday flat from **Outlet** (*see p74* **Homo is where the heart is**).

Deluxe

Soho Hotel

4 Richmond Mews, off Dean Street, W1D 3DH (7559 3000, www.firmdale.com). Tottenham Court Road tube. **Rates** £294-£341 double. **Rooms** 91. **Credit** AmEx, MC, V. **Map** p267 K6.

For her sixth hotel, the queen of English interior design, Kit Kemp, gave her cool country-house style an urban edge. The new-build red-brick structure, tucked down a Soho alleyway, resembles a converted warehouse, while in the drawing room, shocking pink and lime green curtains offset a huge antique dresser. The individually designed bedrooms are classic Kemp – soft neutrals, bold pinstripes, modern florals – but the industrial-style windows and the odd splash of bold colour keep the mood current. In the granite and oak bathrooms, the lotions by Miller Harris are a real treat. Guests hang out in the loungey honesty bar and the buzzy bar/restaurant Refuel. There are also two screening rooms for Hollywood types, and a gym and treatment rooms for stressed execs.
Bar. Business services. Concierge. Disabled-adapted rooms. Gym. Internet. Smoking rooms. Spa. Parking (£48/day). Restaurant. Room service (24hr). TV (DVD).

Expensive

Hazlitt's

6 Frith Street, W1D 3JA (7434 1771, www.hazlittshotel. com). Tottenham Court Road tube. **Rates** £259 double. **Rooms** 30. **Credit** AmEx, DC, MC, V. **Map** p267 K6.

Named after the 18th-century essayist William Hazlitt – just one of the eclectic cast of characters who have resided here – this idiosyncratic Georgian townhouse hotel (sister to the Rookery; *see p65*) has an impressive literary pedigree. Jonathan Swift once slept here (there's a room named after him), it was immortalised in Bill Bryson's *Notes from a Small Island* and the library contains signed first editions from Ted Hughes and JK Rowling. Rooms are true to period, with fireplaces, carefully researched colour schemes, massive carved wooden beds and clawfoot bathtubs. But you'll also find air-conditioning, web TV hidden away in antique cupboards and triple-glazed windows to keep out the sounds of Soho.

Business services. Concierge. Internet. Room service (24hr). Smoking rooms. TV (DVD).

Covent Garden

The heart of Theatreland, Covent Garden is one of the capital's gayest stomping grounds. Gay bars include the **Box** (*see p18*), **First Out** (*see p21*), **Kudos** (*see p23*) and the **Retro Bar** (*see p24*). The swimming pool at the **Oasis Sports Centre** (*see p144*) is a famously gay haunt, and shopping is fantastic. As this guide went to press, the majestic Savoy hotel (Strand, 7836 4343, WC2R OEU, www.the-savoy.com) was closed for a £100 million restoration, but due to reopen imminently.

Deluxe

St Martins Lane Hotel

45 St Martin's Lane, WC2N 4HX (7300 5500, www.stmartinslane.com). Leicester Square tube/

Charing Cross tube/rail. **Rates** £395-£558 double. **Rooms** 204. **Credit** AmEx, DC, MC, V. **Map** p269 L7.

When it opened as a Schrager property a decade ago, the St Martins was the toast of the town. The flamboyant lobby was constantly buzzing, and guests giggled at Philippe Starck's playful decor. Although Starck objects – such as the gold tooth stools in the lobby – have become positively mainstream and the space lacks the impact of its heyday, it's still an exclusive place to stay. The all-white bedrooms have comfortable minimalism down to a T, with floor-to-ceiling windows, gadgetry secreted in sculptural cabinets and sleek limestone bathrooms with toiletries from the Agua spa at sister property Sanderson (*see p66*). Asia de Cuba fusion restaurant is as good-looking as ever, and the Light Bar remains dramatic. To work off the excess, there's the trendy, industrial-look Gymbox next door, to which guests have free access.

Bar. Business services. Concierge. Disabled-adapted rooms. Gym. Internet. Parking (£45/day). Restaurant. Room service (24hr). TV (DVD/pay movies).

Expensive

Covent Garden Hotel

10 Monmouth Street, WC2H 9HB (7806 1000, www.firmdale.com). Covent Garden or Leicester Square tube. **Rates** £276-£388 double. **Rooms** 58. **Credit** AmEx, MC, V. **Map** p267 L6.

Kit Kemp's second hotel has attracted starry custom since it opened in the mid 1990s. Film stars and Hollywood executives attend screenings in the basement cinema (which also shows classics for guests every Saturday night). Brasserie Max, with its retro zinc bar, is a popular meeting spot; you can also snuggle up by the fire in the panelled private library with a drink and – if you're lucky – a Hollywood heart-throb. Kemp's distinctive modern English

Halkin. *See p75.*

Consume

style mixes traditional touches – pinstriped wallpaper, floral upholstery – with bold, contemporary elements and two trademarks: upholstered mannequins and shiny granite and oak bathrooms.
Bar. Business services. Concierge. Disabled-adapted rooms. Gym. Internet. Parking (valet). Restaurant. Room service (24hr). Smoking rooms. TV (DVD).

One Aldwych

1 Aldwych, Strand, WC2B 4RH (7300 1000, www.onealdwych.com). Covent Garden/Temple tube/ Charing Cross tube/rail. **Rates** £276-£465 double. **Rooms** 105. **Credit** AmEx, DC, MC, V. **Map** p269 M7.
Enter via the breathtaking Lobby Bar and you know you're in for a treat. Despite weighty history (the 1907 building was designed by the architects behind the Ritz), One Aldwych is thoroughly modern. Upstairs, everything – from Frette linens and bathroom mini-TVs to the eco-friendly loo-flushing system and REN toiletries – has been chosen with care. The location is perfect for Theatreland, but who wants to leave the building? The hotel's cosy screening room has brunch/dinner-and-movie packages, and Axis restaurant serves upmarket Modern European fare. There are treatments, a gym and a steam room, and a pool where classical music accompanies your laps. If you can, book one of the three round suites that are stacked in the corner tower – they're very romantic.
Bars/cafés (2). Business services. Concierge. Disabled-adapted rooms. Gym. Internet. Parking (£45/day). Restaurants (2). Room service (24hr). Spa. TV (DVD/pay movies).

Westminster & Victoria

If you want to play tourist, this area provides easy access to the postcard sites: Big Ben, Buckingham Palace and Westminster Abbey. The gay nightlife is poor, except for the **Stag** (*see p36*), a local gay pub/club, but it's an easy bus ride to the bars and clubs of Soho and Vauxhall.

Expensive

Trafalgar

2 Spring Gardens, off Trafalgar Square, SW1A 2TS (7870 2900, www.thetrafalgar.com). Embankment tube/Charing Cross tube/rail. **Rates** £235-£294 double. **Rooms** 129. **Credit** AmEx, DC, MC, V. **Map** p269 L7.
The Trafalgar is a Hilton – but you'd hardly notice. It is the chain's first 'concept' hotel. Although it's housed in one of the imposing edifices on the famous square (the former Cunard HQ, in fact, where the ill-fated *Titanic* was conceived), the mood is young and dynamic. The rooms (all of which are a good size) have a masculine feel, with minimalist walnut furniture and white walls. Just to the right of the open reception on the ground floor is the Rockwell Bar, which serves a brilliant selection of bourbon and mixes cocktails for every taste. DJs play Tuesday to Saturday, with things getting pretty fierce of a weekend. Yet it is the location that's the biggest draw: the few corner suites look directly into the square (prices reflect location) and, during summer, those without a view can enjoy themselves on the small rooftop bar.

Bars (2). Concierge. Disabled-adapted rooms. Gym. Internet. Restaurant. Room service (24hr). Smoking rooms. TV (CD/DVD/pay movies/games).

Moderate

B&B Belgravia

64-66 Ebury Street, SW1W 9QD (7259 8570, www.bb-belgravia.com). Sloane Square tube/ Victoria tube/rail. **Rates** (incl breakfast) £125 double. **Rooms** 17. **Credit** AmEx, MC, V. **Map** p268 H10.
How do you make a lounge full of white and black contemporary furnishings seem cosy and welcoming? Hard to achieve, but they've succeeded at B&B Belgravia, which has taken the B&B experience to a new level. It's fresh and sophisticated without being hard-edged: there's nothing to make the design-conscious wince. And there are all kinds of goodies to make you feel at home: a gleaming espresso machine, an open fireplace, newspapers and DVDs.
Disabled-adapted rooms. Internet. TV.

City Inn Westminster

30 John Islip Street, SW1P 4DD (7630 1000, www.cityinn.com). Pimlico, St James's Park or Westminster tube. **Rates** £159-£394 double. **Rooms** 460. **Credit** AmEx, DC, MC, V. **Map** p269 L10.
There's nothing flashy about this new-build hotel, but it is well run, adaptable and neatly designed. The owners have made art a theme, collaborating with the Chelsea College of Art to ensure there are changing art displays in the public areas. The rooms are thoughtfully laid out, with lots of extras (iMacs, CD/DVD library, with players in the rooms, plus free broadband and flatscreen TVs). Service is charming and efficient. On-site facilities include the Millbank Lounge, with its vaunted 75 whiskies and easy-going atmosphere, and the slightly less-convincing City Café, outside which you can sit on a Ron Arad chair on the covered Art Street. All rooms have floor-to-ceiling windows, so river-facing suites on the 12th and 13th floors have superb night views – when the business people go home for the weekend you might grab one at a bargain rate – look online for details.
Bars (2). Business centre. Concierge. Disabled-adapted rooms. Gym. Internet. Parking (£30/day). Restaurant. Room service (24hr). Smoking rooms. TV (CD/DVD/pay movies).

Windermere Hotel

142-144 Warwick Way, SW1V 4JE (7834 5163, www.windermere-hotel.co.uk). Pimlico or Sloane Square tube/Victoria tube/rail. **Rates** (incl breakfast) £129-£165 double. **Rooms** 20. **Credit** AmEx, MC, V. **Map** p268 H11.
Heading the procession of small hotels strung along Warwick Way, the Windermere is a comfortable, traditionally decked-out London hotel with no aspirations to boutique status. The decor may be showing its age a bit in the hall, but you'll receive a warm welcome and excellent service. There's a cosy basement restaurant/bar (the breakfasts here are top-notch) and guests get a discount at the nearby car park.
Bar. Business services. Internet. Restaurant. Room service (until 11pm). TV.

Kensington & Chelsea

South Kensington is famed for its big museums; Knightsbridge is renowned for Harrods and other swanky shops. Both feature countless luxury hotels, and a few cheaper B&Bs. Nearby Chelsea, particularly the King's Road, is another shopping haven. There's not much gay nightlife, unless you count cruising Hyde Park or the old-time gay pub in Chelsea, the **Queen's Head** (see p36).

Deluxe

Baglioni

60 Hyde Park Gate, SW7 5BB (7368 5700, www. baglionihotellondon.com). High Street Kensington or Gloucester Road tube. **Rates** £464 double. **Rooms** 67. **Credit** AmEx, DC, MC, V. **Map** p264 C9.

With an Italian designer vibe and one of the most desirable locations in London, the Baglioni cannot fail to impress. Yet, although occupying a Victorian mansion opposite Kensington Palace and with a butler service on each floor, the Baglioni has none of the snootiness of its English counterparts. The ground-floor Italian restaurant and bar are part baroque, part Donatella Versace: spidery black chandeliers, burnished gold ceilings, gigantic vases and a magnificent Venetian mirror. The chic bedrooms are more subdued: black floorboards, taupe and gold-leaf walls, dark wood furniture enlivened by jewel-coloured cushions and soft throws. Instead of the usual marble, the swanky black-panelled bathrooms have hammered iron sinks imported from Morocco. Health spa treatments range from a four-step anti-ageing itinerary to Botox.

Bar. Business centre. Concierge. Disabled-adapted rooms. Gym. Internet. Parking (£38/day). Restaurant. Room service (24hr). Spa. TV (DVD).

Blakes

33 Roland Gardens, SW7 3PF (7370 6701, www. blakeshotels.com). South Kensington tube. **Rates** £311-£440 double. **Rooms** 41. **Credit** AmEx, DC, MC, V. **Map** p265 D11.

As original as when Anouska Hempel opened it in 1983 – oranges and birdsong fill the dark, oriental lobby – Blakes and its maximalist decor have stood the test of time, a living casebook for interior design students. Each room is in a different style, with influences from Italy, India, Turkey and China. Exotic antiques picked up on the designer's travels – intricately carved beds, battered trunks, Chinese birdcages – are complemented with sweeping drapery and piles of plump cushions. Downstairs is the eclectic, Eastern-style restaurant, complemented by a gym and wireless internet. Celebrities love the discreet vibe.

Bar. Business services. Concierge. Internet. Restaurant. Room service (24hr). TV (DVD).

Gore

190 Queen's Gate, SW7 5EX (7584 6601, www. gorehotel.com). South Kensington tube. **Rates** £170-£423 double. **Rooms** 50. **Credit** AmEx, DC, MC, V. **Map** p265 D9.

Homo is where the heart is

For gay digs, **Outlet** is a poof's best friend. In contrast to many 'gay-friendly' hotels, its stable of Soho holiday flats is stylish – and centrally located. The acclaimed gay accommodation agency rents hip, cheap flats in all the homo haunts: Soho, Covent Garden, Kennington and Fitzrovia. In a cute marketing ploy, they're all named after gay icons: Oprah, Judy, Faith, Dolly, Barbara, Gloria and so on. And, unlike other so-called queer hotels, there's nothing hideous about the decor; the contemporary rooms are kitted out with IKEA furniture; TVs, CD players and modern kitchens complete the picture.

But the real attraction is the low prices. Single rooms in Soho, which come with bathroom and coffee-making facilities or private kitchen, start at a laughable £65 per night (based on a three-night stay; there are no weekly rates, but there's a 25 per cent reduction for continuous stay of one month or more in one location), which wouldn't even get you room service at the nearby Soho Hotel. You can either share a flat with strangers (each bedroom comes with its own lock) or take over an entire apartment with friends. Studio and one-bedroom apartments are a bit pricier, but their starting rate is peanuts for these parts.

Tourists aren't the only lucky ones. For gay residents of London, Outlet's flatshare service is a goldmine. When it started back in 1995, it was a nuts-and-bolts affair operated out of a spare bedroom. But then, in 2001, one of its directors, Josh Rafter, joined the cast of *Big Brother* – and bared his bod for the cameras. Thanks to his chiselled torso, business at Outlet went through the roof. Now they've got a swish office in Soho (you're welcome to drop in), and the website boasts hundreds of flatshare listings in all corners of London; to save you trawling, it matches landlords to prospective tenants. When it's time to rent – or indeed buy – a big gay house, Outlet is also in the know. Their estate agents keep tabs on how gay-friendly the neighbourhood is – top spots include Soho, Islington, Earl's Court, Hackney and Clapham/Brixton.

Outlet

32 Old Compton Street, W1D 4TP (7287 4244, www.outlet.co.uk). Leicester Square tube. **Rates** (holiday lettings, per room) £55-£73 double; £75-£115 studio; £80-£120 1-bed flat; £118-£219 2-bed flat. **Credit** MC, V. **Map** p267 K6.

This fin-de-siècle period piece was founded by descendants of Captain Cook in a couple of grand Victorian town-houses. The lobby and staircase are close hung with old paintings, and the bedrooms have sumptuous drapes, fantastic 19th-century carved oak beds and shelves of old books. The suites are spectacular: the Tudor Room has a huge stone-faced fireplace and a minstrels' gallery, while tragedy queens should plump for the Venus room and Judy Garland's old bed (and replica ruby slippers). Bistrot 190 gets good reviews, and provides a casually elegant setting for great breakfasts, while the warm, wood-panelled 190 bar has a salubrious charm.
Bar. Concierge. Internet. Restaurant. Room service (24hr). TV.

Halkin

Halkin Street, SW1X 7DJ (7333 1000, www.halkin. como.bz). Hyde Park Corner tube. **Rates** £528 double. **Rooms** 41. **Credit** AmEx, MC, V. **Map** p268 G9.
The first hotel of Singaporean fashion magnate Christina Ong (who also brought us the Metropolitan; *see p69*), the Halkin was ahead of the East-meets-West design trend when it opened in 1991. Its subtle decor – a marriage of European luxury and oriental serenity – looks more current than hotels half its age. The 41 rooms mix stylish classical sofas with black lacquer tables and South-east Asian artefacts. A touch-screen bedside console controls everything from the 'do not disturb' sign to the air-con. Gracious and discreet behind a Georgian-style façade, the Halkin is equally renowned for Thai restaurant, Nahm (*see p96*). Success breeds success: repeat custom accounts for more than half the hotel's trade.
Bar. Concierge. Disabled-adapted rooms. Internet. Parking (£45/day). Restaurant. Room service (24hr). TV (DVD/pay movies).

Lanesborough

1 Lanesborough Place, Hyde Park Corner, SW1X 7TA (7259 5599, www.lanesborough.com). Hyde Park Corner tube. **Rates** £581-£699 double. **Rooms** 95. **Credit** AmEx, DC, MC, V. **Map** p268 G8.
Occupying an 1820s Greek Revival building, the lavish Lanesborough feels historic, even though it was only redeveloped in 1991 (it used to be a hospital). The luxurious guest rooms are traditionally decorated with thick fabrics, antique furniture and swish Carrera marble bathrooms. Electronic keypads control everything from the air-con to the superb 24hr room service. As deluxe hotels go, the Lanesborough's rates are unusually inclusive: high-speed internet access, movies and calls within the EU and to the US are complimentary, as are personalised business cards. The Library Bar and modern Italian restaurant Apsleys maintain the high standards.
Bar. Business centre. Concierge. Disabled-adapted rooms. Gym. Internet. Parking (£40/day). Restaurant. Room service (24hr). Spa. TV (DVD/pay movies).

Milestone Hotel & Apartments

1 Kensington Court, W8 5DL (7917 1000, www. milestonehotel.com). High Street Kensington tube. **Rates** £311-£370 double. **Rooms** 56. **Credit** AmEx, DC, MC, V. **Map** p264 C9.
Wealthy visitors are greeted by the comforting, gravel tones of their regular concierge, as English as roast beef, and the glass of sherry in the room. Yet amid old-school luxury, inventive modernity thrives. Rooms overlooking

Hoxton Hotel. *See p76*.

Kensington Gardens feature the inspired decor of South African owner Beatrice Tillman: the Safari suite contains tent-like draperies and leopard-print upholstery; the spectacular Tudor suite has an elaborate inglenook fireplace, minstrels' gallery and a pouffe concealing a pop-up TV. Butlers are on 24hr call. Full-sized Penhaligon's toiletries are offered throughout. House restaurant Cheneston's serves modern British cuisine with a impressive wine list.
Bar. Business services. Concierge. Disabled-adapted rooms. Gym. Internet. Restaurant. Room service (24hr). Smoking rooms. TV (DVD/pay movies).

Expensive

Number Sixteen

16 Sumner Place, SW7 3EG (7589 5232, www. firmdale.com). South Kensington tube. **Rates** £217-£311 double. **Rooms** 42. **Credit** AmEx, DC, MC, V. **Map** p265 D10.
This may be Kit Kemp's most affordable hotel, but there's no slacking in style or comforts. Rooms are generously sized, bright and very light. They are individually decorated with tasteful floral patterns, stripes and muted creams, greens and mauves, making them feminine but far from frilly. In fact, the whole place has an appealing freshness about it, including the drawing room, which is adorned with bird- and butterfly-themed modern art and fresh flowers. Breakfast is served in the cheery conservatory or the garden. It's all utterly relaxing and feels like a real retreat from the city.
Bar. Business centre. Concierge. Internet. Parking (£45/day). Room service (24hr). TV (DVD).

Moderate

Aster House

3 Sumner Place, SW7 3EE (7581 5888, www.aster house.com). South Kensington tube. **Rates** (incl breakfast) £200 double. **Rooms** 13. **Credit** MC, V. **Map** p265 D10.

Although situated in swish Kensington, Aster House is not deluxe. But it has become an award-winner through attention to detail (impeccable housekeeping, the mobile phone guests can use) and the warmth of its managers, Leona and Simon Tan. Decor is low-key: soothing creams with touches of dusty rose and muted green. The lush conservatory serves as a breakfast room and guest lounge. *Internet. TV.*

Budget

Vicarage Hotel

10 Vicarage Gate, W8 4AG (7229 4030, www.london vicaragehotel.com). High Street Kensington or Notting Hill Gate tube. **Rates** (incl breakfast) £85-£125 double. **Rooms** 17. **Credit** AmEx, MC, V. **Map** p262 B8.

Scores of devotees return regularly to this tall Victorian townhouse, tucked in a quiet leafy square just off High Street Ken. It's a comfortable, resolutely old-fashioned establishment. There's a wonderfully grand entrance hall with red and gold striped wallpaper, huge gilt mirror and chandelier, with a sweeping staircase that ascends to an assortment of good-sized rooms furnished in pale florals and nice old pieces of furniture. *TV.*

North

Moderate

York & Albany

127-129 Parkway, NW1 7PS (7387 5700, www. gordonramsay.com/yorkandalbany). Camden Town tube. **Rates** £174 double. **Rooms** 9. **Credit** AmEx, MC, V.

The most recent horse to bolt from the Gordon Ramsay stables, the York & Albany is housed in a grand old John Nash building that was designed as a coaching house, but spent the recent past as a scruffy pub. Downstairs is a restaurant (split over two levels), a bar and a delicatessen; above them sit ten handsome rooms, designed by Russell Sage in pleasingly mellow shades. The decor is an effective mix of ancient and modern, with sturdy and quietly charismatic furniture married to modern technology (including free wireless internet access). Some rooms have views of Regent's Park. *Bar. Disabled-adapted room. Internet. Restaurant. Room service (24hr). TV (DVD).*

Budget

Hampstead Village Guesthouse

2 Kemplay Road, NW3 1SY (7435 8679, www. hampsteadguesthouse.com). Hampstead tube/ Hampstead Heath rail. **Rates** £80-£95 double. **Rooms** 9. **Credit** AmEx, MC, V.

Many a Londoner dreams about living in Hampstead. The leafy northern suburb is achingly picturesque – and

absurdly pricey. But this comfy B&B, in a characterful Victorian pile, makes the fantasy an affordable reality. It's located near Hampstead Heath – a cruising mecca – but the decor is more bohemian than *Country Life*, with an eccentric mix of books, rag dolls, Delftware and other curios in the nine guest rooms. Whether you find it cluttered or charming, it definitely feels like a home: owner Annemarie van der Meer lives on site. Breakfast is served in the garden, weather permitting. There's also a garden studio, which sleeps five. *Internet. TV (DVD).*

East

Moderate

Hoxton Hotel

81 Great Eastern Street, EC2A 3HU (7550 1000, www.hoxtonhotels.com). Old Street tube/rail. **Rates** (incl breakfast) £49-£199 double. **Rooms** 205. **Credit** AmEx, MC, V. **Map** p271 R4.

Ah, the Hoxton… you must have heard about it: winner of this, winner of that, best deal in London. Well, everything you've heard is true: the hip Shoreditch location, the great design values (sort of postmodern country lodge in the foyer), the well-thought out rooms (nice touches include Frette bedlinen, fresh milk in the mini-fridge, free internet access), the budget-airline style pricing (early bird catches very cheap worm – including those £1 a night rooms, still released in small numbers every few months). *Bar. Business centre. Disabled-adapted rooms. Internet. Restaurant. TV.*

Portobello Hotel

Base2stay. *See p79.*

South

Moderate

Windmill on the Common

*Windmill Drive, Clapham Common Southside,
SW4 9DE (8673 4578, www.windmillclapham.co.uk).
Clapham Common or Clapham South tube.* **Rates**
(incl breakfast) £95-£155 double. **Rooms** 29. **Credit**
AmEx, MC, V.
Perched on the edge of Clapham Common, one of London's
loveliest green spaces – and most famous cruising grounds
– the Windmill pub is a pleasant neighbourhood watering
hole (part of the Young's stable). But it also contains one
of the capital's most reasonably priced hotels. In terms of
comfort and decor, the bedrooms, decked out in typical
chain period finery, are superior to most of the city's dowdy
B&Bs. The sights of central London are a short tube ride
away, and Clapham itself is brimming with excellent bars
and restaurants. Ten of the tidy bedrooms are designated
'premium', coming with a stocked fridge and fluffy towels.
A full English breakfast is provided for all guests and there
are some great weekend packages.
*Bar. Disabled-adapted room. Internet. Parking (free).
Restaurant. Room service. TV.*

Budget

Comfort Inn Vauxhall

*87 South Lambeth Road, SW8 1RN (7735 9494,
www.comfortinnvx.co.uk). Vauxhall tube/rail.* **Rates**
£110-£140 double. **Rooms** 115. **Credit** AmEx, MC, V.
Don't be scared off by the bland chain connotations. This
branch of the Comfort Inn has tons going for it. For one
thing, it's smack in the heart of the gay clubbing district.
It's also relatively stylish for the price: there's a modern

lobby bar; the smart, contemporary rooms feature vibrant
colours and crisp white sheets; and the place is decently
equipped, with ceiling fans, TV, modem points and power
showers. There's a small gym, and the coffeeshop out front
has pay internet terminals and a sunny patio garden. Rates
are low – so perhaps it's time to rethink our snobbery
against chains.
*Bar. Business centre. Disabled-adapted rooms. Internet.
Parking (£20/day). TV.*

West

There's not a lot of gay nightlife in this area –
unless you count cruising Hyde Park – but if
you want to spend your holiday shopping and
socialising in Notting Hill, go west. As this guide
went to press, **Miller's Residence** (7243 1024,
www.millershotel.com), a characterful, antique-
filled bed and breakfast in Westbourne Grove,
was closed for a major refurbishment until 2012.

Expensive

Portobello Hotel

*22 Stanley Gardens, W11 2NG (7727 2777, www.
portobello-hotel.co.uk). Holland Park or Notting Hill
Gate tube.* **Rates** (incl breakfast) £223-£353 double.
Rooms 21. **Credit** AmEx, MC, V. **Map** p262 A6.
This decadent Notting Hill mansion has been hosting stars
– from Van Morrison to Kate Moss – for 40 years. And
now it's equipped with a lift, so guests don't have to climb
four sets of stairs after taking advantage of the 24-hour
bar. All rooms come with a large fan and tall house plants,
and most overlook a pretty rose garden. The spectacular
beds range from a Balinese four-poster to a ship's bunk

Pavilion. *See p80.*

and a couple of seductive oriental affairs that resemble Berber tents. In many rooms the Victorian bathtubs take centre stage, including one with a Victorian 'bathing machine'. Other themed pads include the beguiling Moroccan Room, strewn with carpets and cushions, and the serene Japanese Water Garden Room with an elaborate spa bath, buddhas and its own private grotto.
Bar. Internet. Room service (24hr). TV.

Moderate

Base2Stay

25 Courtfield Gardens, SW5 0PG (0845 262 8000, www.base2stay.com). Earl's Court tube. **Rates** £107-£239 double. **Rooms** 67. **Credit** AmEx, MC, V. **Map** p264 B10.
Base2Stay looks good, with its modernist limestone and taupe tones, but keeps prices low by removing the non-essentials: no bar or restaurant, then. Instead, there's the increasingly popular solution of a kitchenette (microwave, sink, mini-fridge, kettle), with all details attended to: not just cutlery and kitchenware, but also a corkscrew and can opener. The rooms, all air-conditioned and en suite (with powerful showers), are carefully thought out, with desks, modem points and flatscreen TVs, but the singles/bunkbed rooms are small. Discount vouchers for nearby chain restaurants are supplied by the friendly duo on 24hr reception.
Disabled-adapted rooms. Internet. TV (pay movies).

Guesthouse West

163-165 Westbourne Grove, W11 2RS (7792 9800, www.guesthousewest.com). Notting Hill Gate tube. **Rates** (incl breakfast) £176-£215 double. **Rooms** 20. **Credit** AmEx, MC, V. **Map** p262 B6.
Set in an impressive three-floor, cream-coloured building, Guesthouse West is a stylish, affordable antidote to exorbitant hotels. It keeps prices down by cutting out room service and offering instead a handy list of local businesses. The look is Notting Hillbilly hip: the retro lobby bar, licensed until 10pm, has a changing art display and the front terrace is perfect for posing. Minimalist bedrooms have enough extras to keep hip young things happy: wireless internet, flatscreen TVs, Molton Brown toiletries.
Bar. Internet. Restaurant. TV (DVD/pay movies).

New Linden

59 Leinster Square, W2 4PS (7221 4321, www.new linden.co.uk). Bayswater tube. **Rates** (incl breakfast) £105-£240 double. **Rooms** 51. **Credit** AmEx, MC, V. **Map** p262 B6.
The Mayflower Group has transformed an indifferent Bayswater hotel into this affordable showstopper. Following a refit, the lobby and lounge are all black and gold glamour, with nods to Asian opulence – a spectacular teak arch, say. The rooms are tranquil havens: creamy walls, low-key colours, gleaming woods and the odd richly coloured accent. The marble bathrooms feature walk-in showers, some with deluge shower heads.
Concierge. Internet. TV.

Rockwell

181-183 Cromwell Road, SW5 0SF (7244 2000, www.therockwell.com). Earl's Court tube. **Rates** £160-£190 double. **Rooms** 40. **Credit** AmEx, MC, V. **Map** p264 B10.

The Rockwell aims for relaxed contemporary elegance – and succeeds magnificently. There are no identikit rooms here; they're all individually designed with gleaming woods and muted glowing colours alongside creams and neutrals. There are power showers, Philippe Starck fittings and bespoke oak cabinets in the bathrooms. Garden rooms have tiny patios complete with garden furniture. There's a welcoming lounge, a bar and the 181 restaurant serving modern British food. Triple-glazing ensures you'll never know you're on roaring Cromwell Road.
Bar. Internet. Restaurant. Room servie (24hr). TV (DVD/pay movies).

Twenty Nevern Square

20 Nevern Square, SW5 9PD (7565 9555, www.twentynevernsquare.co.uk). Earl's Court tube. **Rates** (incl breakfast) £125-£140 double. **Rooms** 20. **Credit** AmEx, MC, V. **Map** p264 A11.
The words 'stylish' and 'Earl's Court' don't usually appear in the same sentence, but this immaculate boutique hotel, tucked away in a secluded garden square, feels far away from its less-than-lovely locale. The modern-colonial style was created by its well-travelled owner. Rooms are clad in a mixture of Eastern and European antique furniture and sumptuous silk curtains; and the beds vary from elaborately carved four-posters to Egyptian sleigh styles. The Far East feel extends to the lounge and airy, conservatory breakfast room. In addition to the group's Mayflower Hotel (*see p80*), there's a sister property in Bayswater, the New Linden (*see left*).
Bar. Internet. Parking (£25/day). Room service (24hr). TV (DVD/satellite).

Vancouver Studios

30 Prince's Square, W2 4NJ (7243 1270, www. vancouverstudios.co.uk). Bayswater or Queensway tube. **Rates** £108-£130 double. **Rooms** 48. **Credit** AmEx, DC, MC, V. **Map** p262 B6.
You'll think you've arrived at an Edwardian bachelor's townhouse when you turn up at this welcoming all-studios hotel in lodging-dense Bayswater – the boots by the stairs, the kilim-effect upholstery in the cosy sitting-room, the resident feline. But just when you think you've got the Vancouver pegged, you're shown into one of their well-equipped studios, which are mainly unfussy contemporary in style, but could equally be drop-dead glamorous or prettily old-fashioned. With sleek kitchenettes, flatscreen TVs and DVD players, they're superb value.
Internet. TV (DVD).

Budget

easyHotel

14 Lexham Gardens, W8 5JE (www.easyhotel.com). Earl's Court tube. **Rates** from £24.50 double. **Rooms** 34. **Credit** MC, V. **Map** p264 B10.
Incorporating the budget airline's no-frills approach to hotels, these rooms are not designed for lingering. Rooms come in three sizes – small, really small and tiny – the last of which is the precise width of the bed. You do get a bed and a pre-fab bathroom unit (toilet, sink and showerhead almost on top of the sink), with no wardrobe, lift or breakfast. Want a window? Pay extra. TV? Housekeeping? Ditto. The rooms, bookable online only, start low – but book well in advance or expect to pay around £40-£50. Beware the cancellation policy: it's not generous.

Housekeeping (£10). Internet (£10). TV (£5).
Other locations 36-40 Belgrave Road, SW1V 1RG; 44-48 West Cromwell Road, SW5 9QL; 10 Norfolk Place, W2 1QL.

Mayflower Hotel

26-28 Trebovir Road, SW5 9NJ (7370 0991, www. mayflowerhotel.co.uk). Earl's Court tube. **Rates** (incl breakfast) £97-£219 double. **Rooms** 50. **Credit** AmEx, MC, V. **Map** p264 B11.
The Mayflower has given Earl's Court – once a boring budget wasteland – a kick up the backside. Following a spectacular makeover a few years back, the hotel proves cheap really can be chic. The minimalist lobby is dominated by a gorgeous teak arch from Jaipur. The wooden-floored rooms are furnished in an Eastern style with hand-carved beds and sumptuous fabrics or sleek modern headboards and units. Ceiling fans add a tropical feel, which extends to the palm trees in the garden. Marble bathrooms, CD players and dataports are nearly unheard-of luxuries for such low rates. And a juice bar in Earl's Court?
Bar. Business services. Internet. Parking (£25/day). TV.

Pavilion

34-36 Sussex Gardens, W2 1UL (7262 0905, www. pavilionhoteluk.com). Edgware Road tube/Marylebone or Paddington tube/rail. **Rates** £85-£100 double.
Rooms 29. **Credit** AmEx, MC, V. **Map** p263 E6.
In a row of dowdy hotels, the Pavilion is a shining star. Or more like a disco ball. When it comes to decor, this hilariously kitsch B&B has tongue firmly planted in cheek. The themed rooms are a riot: Casablanca Nights is a Moorish fantasy complete with Moroccan lanterns; the Highland Fling is a tartan theme park, with plaid bedspreads and stag antlers; Better Red Than Dead is a glam extravaganza of crimson, vermilion and burgundy. Rock stars love the place: a favourite shag pad is Honky Tonk Afro, with its mirror ball, fuzzy dice and heart-shaped mirrored headboards. OK, so the location's not exactly rocking and the bathrooms are small, but the hotel's sheer force of personality makes up for it all.
Internet. Parking (£10/day). Room service. TV (DVD/satellite).

Stylotel

160-162 Sussex Gardens, W2 1UD (7723 1026, www.stylotel.com). Paddington tube/rail. **Rates** (incl breakfast) £89 double. **Rooms** 39. **Credit** AmEx, MC, V. **Map** p263 E6.
This Paddington pad is a retro-futurist dream: metal floors and panelling, lots of royal blue surfaces (the hall walls, the padded headboards) and pod bathrooms. But the real deal at Stylotel is its new bargain-priced studio and apartment (respectively, £120-£150 and £150-£200). This is real minimalist chic: sleek brushed steel or white glass walls panels, and simply styled contemporary furniture upholstered in black or white.
Concierge. Internet. Smoking rooms. TV.

Other options
Apartment rental

The companies listed below specialise in holiday lets, although some of them have minimum stay requirements (making this an affordable option only if you're planning a relatively protracted visit to the city). Typical daily rates on a reasonably central property are around £100-£130 for a studio or one-bed, up to £195 for a two-bed – although, as with any aspect of staying in London, the sky's the limit if you want to pay it. Respected all-rounders include **Astons Apartments** (7590 6000, www.astons-apartments.com), **Holiday Serviced Apartments** (0845 060 4477, www.holidayapartments.co.uk) and **Palace Court Holiday Apartments** (7727 3467, www.palacecourt.co.uk).

See also p74 **Homo is where the heart is**.

Staying with the locals

Several agencies can arrange for individuals and families to stay in Londoners' homes. Prices (including breakfast) are around £37-£85 for a single and £60-£105 for a double, depending on the location and degree of comfort. Agencies include **At Home in London** (8748 1943, www.athomeinlondon.co.uk), **Bed and Breakfast Club** (0870 803 4414, www.the bedandbreakfastclub.co.uk), **Host & Guest Service** (7385 9922, www.host-guest.co.uk), **London Bed & Breakfast Agency** (7586 2768, www.londonbb.com) and **London Homestead Services** (7286 5115, www.lhs london.co.uk). There may be a minimum stay. Alternatively, you can browse around noticeboard-style 'online community' websites such as Gumtree (www.gumtree.com).

University residences

During the university vacations, much of London's dedicated student accommodation is opened up to visitors, providing them with a source of basic but cheap digs.

International Students House
229 Great Portland Street, W1W 5PN (7631 8300, www.ish.org.uk). Great Portland Street tube. **Rates** (per person) £13 dorm; £38 single; £30 twin. **Available** all year. **Map** p266 H4.
King's College Conference & Vacation Bureau
Strand Bridge House, 138-142 Strand, WC2R 1HH (7848 1700, www.kcl.ac.uk/kcvb). Temple tube. **Rates** £20-£40 single; £54-£59 twin. **Available** end June-mid Sept. **Map** p269 L7.
LSE Bankside House
24 Sumner Street, SE1 9JA (7107 5750, www.lse vacations.co.uk). London Bridge tube/rail. **Rates** £43-£55 single; £75 twin/double. **Available** July-Sept. **Map** p271 Q8.
The London School of Economics has vacation rentals across town, but Bankside House (tucked behind Tate Modern) is the best located.

Stylotel

stylotel

YMCAs

It may, as the Village People said, be fun to stay at the YMCA. But you'll need to book months ahead; this Christian organisation is primarily concerned with providing housing for homeless young people. A few of the larger hostels open to all are listed below (all are unisex), but you can get a complete list from the **National Council for YMCAs** (8520 5599, www.ymca.org.uk). Prices are around £30-£35 per night for a single room, £40-£60 for a double.

Barbican YMCA *2 Fann Street, EC2Y 8BR (7628 0697). Barbican tube.* **Map** p270 P5.
London City YMCA *8 Errol Street, EC1Y 8SE (7628 8832). Barbican tube/Old Street tube/rail.* **Map** p270 P5.
Wimbledon YMCA *200 The Broadway, SW19 1RY (8542 9055). South Wimbledon tube/Wimbledon tube/rail.*

Youth hostels

If you're not a member of the International Youth Hostel Federation (IYHF), you'll pay an extra £3 a night, but you can avoid paying this fee by joining the IYHF for £15.95 (£9.95 for under-18s) at any hostel, or through www. yha.org.uk. Of the hostels below, Thameside and Holland Park include breakfast in the price. All under-18s receive a 25 per cent discount. Youth hostel beds are arranged either in twin rooms or in dormitories.

There are also numerous independent hostels in London, including the **Clink Hostel** (*see p65*).

Central *104 Bolsover Street, W1W 5NU (0845 371 9154, www.yha.org.uk). Great Portland Street tube.* **Open** Reception/access 24hrs daily. **Rates** £15-£29. **Map** p266 4H
Earl's Court *38 Bolton Gardens, SW5 0AQ (0845 371 9114, www.yha.org.uk). Earl's Court tube.* **Open** Reception/access 24hrs daily. **Rates** £15-£29. **Map** p264 B11.
Holland Park *Holland Walk, W8 7QU (0845 371 9122, www.yha.org.uk). High Street Kensington tube.* **Open** Reception/access 24hrs daily. **Rates** £16-£27. **Map** p262 A8.
Oxford Street *14 Noel Street, W1F 8GJ (7734 1618, www.yha.org.uk). Oxford Circus tube.* **Open** Reception 7am-11pm daily; access 24hrs daily. **Rates** £18-£24.50. **Map** p266 J6.
St Pancras *79-81 Euston Road, NW1 2QE (0845 371 9344, www.yha.org.uk). King's Cross tube/rail.* **Open** Reception/access 24hrs daily. **Rates** £15-£29. **Map** p267 L3.
St Paul's *36 Carter Lane, EC4V 5AB (7236 4965, www.yha.org.uk). St Paul's tube/Blackfriars tube/rail.* **Open** Reception/access 24hrs daily. **Rates** £14-£29. **Map** p270 O6.
Thameside *20 Salter Road, SE16 5PR (0845 371 9756, www.yha.org.uk). Rotherhithe tube.* **Open** Reception 7am-11pm daily; access 24hrs daily. **Rates** £16-£27.

Consume

Restaurants & Cafés

Everybody's got a hungry heart.

London now ranks as the world's most dynamic and varied culinary destination. You'll find food from every corner of the globe, from Armenia to Vietnam, with some of the more prevalent ethnic cuisines reaching unprecedented heights: **Hakkasan** (*see p86*) was the UK's first Chinese restaurant to be awarded a Michelin star, **Nahm** (*see p96*) the first Thai. And the unthinkable has happened: 'British cuisine' is no longer a contradiction in terms, as illustrated by patriotic critically acclaimed restaurants such as **Hix** (*see p90*), the **National Dining Rooms** (*see p95*) and **Great Queen Street** (*see p94*).

There is even a clutch of 'gay restaurants', which includes **Balans** (*see p91*) and **First Out** (*see p90*), and increasing numbers of gay bars that serve food: the **Edge** (*see p20*); **Profile** (*see p23*); **Rupert Street** (*see p24*); and the **Green** (*see p28*). Still, the concept of gay dining is baffling – are the chefs gay? What makes a menu queer? The term mainly refers to location (Soho) and the sexuality of the clientele and ownership.

Not all London restaurants insist on reservations, but it is advisable to book in advance. Smoking is not allowed in restaurants. Tipping – ten to 15 per cent – is standard practice. Some restaurants add service to the bill, so double-check this or you may end up tipping twice.

We don't have room to explore every cuisine here; for more on eating out in the capital, buy the annual *Time Out London's Best Restaurants* and, for a remarkable range of budget meals, *Time Out Cheap Eats in London*.

South Bank & Bankside

British

Roast

Floral Hall, Borough Market, Stoney Street, SE1 1TL (7940 1300, www.roast-restaurant.com). London Bridge tube/rail. **Open** 7-11am, noon-3pm, 5.30-11pm Mon, Tue; 7-11am, noon-4pm, 5.30-11pm Wed-Fri; 8-11am, noon-4pm, 6-11pm Sat; 11.30am-6pm Sun. **Main courses** £12.50-£28. **Credit** AmEx, MC, V. **Map** p271 P8.
Roast specialises in British food and, as the name suggests, spit-roasts are a forte, from spatchcocked partridge to

Zucca

suckling pig. With its post-industrial setting beneath the railway arches over Borough Market, it feels quintessentially London. The kitchen uses fresh, top-quality produce that is imaginatively prepared, even if the results can be uneven.

Gastropubs

Anchor & Hope

36 The Cut, SE1 8LP (7928 9898). Southwark tube/ Waterloo tube/rail. **Open** 5-11pm Mon; 11am-11pm Tue-Sat; 12.30-5pm Sun (bookings only). **Main courses** £11-£16. **Credit** MC, V. **Map** p270 N8.
A low-key yet deliriously popular gastropub, with an imaginative menu and some great, affordable wines. Its fans know the pleasures of dishes such as cold roast beef on dripping toast, and brawn (pig's head, trotters and herbs). You can't book, so be prepared to wait (in the bar) for a table.

Global

Baltic

74 Blackfriars Road, SE1 8HA (7928 1111, www. balticrestaurant.co.uk). Southwark tube. **Open** noon-3pm, 5.30pm-midnight Mon-Sat; noon-10.30pm Sun. **Main courses** £10-£17. **Credit** AmEx, MC, V. **Map** p270 N8.
Baltic's wow factor never wanes. Its stark whiteness is punctuated by exposed beams, bare red brickwork and a stunning amber chandelier. Baltic remains London's only east European 'destination' restaurant, where traditional ingredients are given a modern twist.

Consume

Italian

Zucca

184 Bermondsey Street, SE1 3TQ (7378 6809, www.zuccalondon.com). Bermondsey tube/London Bridge tube/rail. **Open** 12.30-3pm, 6.30-10pm Tue-Sat; 12.30-3pm Sun. **Main courses** £8.50-£14.50. **Credit** MC, V.

This modern Italian restaurant has a stark, stylish feel, Italian staff and a brief but enticing menu. Tuck into salty focaccia as you choose from dishes such as grilled squid with lemon and chilli dressing or braised pork with sage and garlic. An intelligent all-Italian wine list, delectable puddings and pasta made on the premises complete a pleasing picture.

The City

Cafés, bars & brasseries

Café Below

St Mary-le-Bow Church, Cheapside, EC2V 6AU (7329 0789, www.cafebelow.co.uk). St Paul's tube or Bank tube/DLR. **Open** 7.30am-9pm Mon-Fri. **Main courses** £6.20-£7.75. **Credit** MC, V. **Map** p270 P6.

The Place Below has renamed itself and, even more radically, added meat to the menu and started opening for dinner. We heartily approve – the crypt premises are lovely, but best suited to the evening (or winter), and all the meat dishes we tried were top-notch (this a commitment to well-sourced ingredients here). Portions are generous (the Spanish plate of Serrano ham, chorizo, roast peppers, gordal olives, habas fritas and foccacia defeated us) and prices fair. Coffee, cakes and sandwiches are served all day, or pop in for a bacon butty or Bircher muesli at breakfast. A wonderful contrast to nearby expense-account eateries.

Caravan

11-13 Exmouth Market, EC1R 4QD (7833 8115, www.caravanonexmouth.co.uk). Farringdon tube/rail. **Open** 8am-11.30am, noon-10.30pm Mon-Fri; 10am-4pm, 5-10.30pm Sat; 10am-4pm Sun. **Main courses** £12.50-£15. **Credit** AmEx, MC, V.

In trendy Exmouth Market, the kitchen at fashionable Caravan is run by Kiwi Miles Kirby, who was chef at the Providores & Tapa Room in Marylebone. The all-day menu of small and large plates encapsulates the sort of polygastronomy you find in New Zealand and Australia. The weekend brunch menu focuses on fry-ups, eggs on sourdough toast and fruity porridge. Friands, little Antipodean ground almond cakes, are served with a flawless rhubarb compote. The fresh-roasted coffee is excellent.

Konditor & Cook

30 St Mary Axe, EC3A 8BF (0845 262 3030, www.konditorandcook.co.uk). Liverpool Street tube/rail. **Open** 7.30am-6.30pm Mon-Fri. **Main courses** £3.75-£5.25. **Credit** AmEx, MC, V. **Map** p271 R6.

Larger than most branches of this cake-making café, the Gherkin outlet opened in late 2007. The interior is airy and modern, and filled with suits. Choose from the daily changing hot meals or sandwiches and salads. The cakes, tarts and biscuits are legendary. **Other locations** 22 Cornwall Road, SE1 8TW (7261 0456); 10 Stoney Street, SE1 9AD (7407 5100);

Curzon Soho, 99 Shaftesbury Avenue, W1D 5DY (7292 1684); 46 Gray's Inn Road, WC1X 8LR (7404 6300); 63 Stamford Street, SE1 9NB (7921 9200).

French

Les Trois Garçons

1 Club Row, E1 6JX (7613 1924, www.lestrois garcons.com). Shoreditch High Street rail/8, 388 bus. **Open** 7-10pm Mon-Thur; 7-10.30pm Fri, Sat. **Set meal** £39.50 2 courses; £45.50 3 courses. **Credit** AmEx, DC, MC, V. **Map** p271 S4.

The decor is a happy, flamboyant collision between a taxidermist's and an art installation. Prices are overblown, though the classic French dishes are mostly spot-on. A great place for a proper night out, but not to count the pennies. Dine between Monday and Thursday, and the two-course prix fixe menu is £27. It's on the Shoreditch/Bethnal Green border, so handy if you're hitting the East End clubs.

The best Restaurants

For the food

Bistrot Bruno Loubet (*see p85*); **Clarke's** (*see p98*); **Dehesa** (*see p94*); **Gordon Ramsay** (*see p96*); **Hakkasan** (*see p86*); **Maze** (*see p88*); **Moro** (*see p86*); **Murano** (*see p88*); **Nahm** (*see p96*); **Orrery** (*see p88*); **Providores & Tapa Room** (*see p87*); **Racine** (*see p96*); **Yauatcha** (*see p93*).

For British cuisine

Anchor & Hope (*see p82*); **Great Queen Street** (*see p94*); **Hix** (*see p90*); **National Dining Rooms** (*see p95*); **St John** (*p85*).

For people-watching

Balans (*see p91*); **Bistrotheque** (*see p97*); **The Ivy** (*see p94*); **Momo** (*see p89*); **Zuma** (*see p96*).

For a sense of occasion

Hakkasan (*see p86*); **J Sheekey** (*see p94*); **Nobu** (*see p89*); **Sketch** (*see p88*); **Les Trois Garçons** (*see above*); **The Wolseley** (*see p88*); **Zuma** (*see p96*).

For brunch

Caravan (*see left*); **Inn The Park** (*see p88*); **Ottolenghi** (*see p97*); **Smiths of Smithfield** (*see p86*).

For night owls

Balans (*see p91*); **Bar Italia** (*see p89*).

For vegetarians

First Out (*see p90*); **Food for Thought** (*see p95*); **Gate** (*see p98*); **Mildred's** (*see p94*).

Vegetarian & organic

Vanilla & Black

*17-18 Tooks Court, off Cursitor Street, EC4A 1LB
(7242 2622, www.vanillablack.co.uk). Chancery Lane
tube.* **Open** noon-2.30pm, 6-10pm Mon-Fri; 6-10pm Sat.
Set lunch £23 3 courses. **Set meal** £24 2 courses,
£30 3 courses. **Credit** AmEx, MC, V. **Map** p270 N6.
In London's legal district, Vanilla Black is full of besuited
diners. The vegetarian menu – smoked duck egg and potato croquette, say, or baked sweet potato with saffron risotto – is Modern European with Indian and Japanese touches.

Holborn & Clerkenwell

British

Clerkenwell Kitchen

*27-31 Clerkenwell Close, EC1R 0AT (7101 9959,
www.theclerkenwellkitchen.co.uk). Farringdon tube/rail.*
Open 8am-5pm Mon-Fri. **Main courses** £4.50-£14.
Credit MC, V. **Map** p270 N4.
Delicious, fresh, seasonal food at fair prices. The furnisings
are simple: plenty of wood, windows and white walls, with
architectural seating and lighting. The open kitchen serves
breakfast through to afternoon tea. For lunch, you can pick
up a takeaway (fresh soup, perhaps, or a creamy courgette
and parmesan tart with salad) or eat in.

Medcalf

*38-40 Exmouth Market, EC1R 4QE (7833 3533,
www.medcalfbar.co.uk). Angel tube.* **Open** *Bar* noon-
11pm Mon-Thur, Sat; noon-midnight Fri; noon-4pm
Sun. *Restaurant* noon-3pm, 6-9.45pm Mon-Thur; noon-
3pm, 6-10.20pm Fri, Sat; noon-4pm Sun. **Main courses**
£10.50-£17.50. **Credit** MC, V. **Map** p270 N4.
This former butcher's shop has been a big hit since day
one, its scruffy-chic looks, robust British cooking, relaxed
staff and unpretentious vibe attracting steady custom.
Come for breakfast, lunch, dinner or just a drink and a
snack. The menu features the likes of welsh rarebit, shepherd's pie and pork belly with colcannon.

St John

*26 St John Street, EC1M 4AY (7251 0848, www.
stjohnrestaurant.com). Barbican tube/Farringdon tube/
rail.* **Open** noon-3pm, 6-11pm Mon-Fri; 6-11pm Sat;
1-3pm Sun. **Main courses** £13-£22. **Credit** AmEx,
DC, MC, V. **Map** p270 O5.
Housed in a former smoke house, with whitewashed walls
and steel kitchen counters, the famous St John is a characterful and stylish bar and restaurant. The menu is
renowned for its gore (offal, pigs' tails, brains), but traditional, seasonal British dishes also feature.
Other location St John Bread & Wine, 94-96
Commercial Street, E1 6LZ (7251 0848).

French

Bistro Bruno Loubet

*St John's Square, 86-88 Clerkenwell Road, EC1M
5RJ (7324 4455, www.thezetter.com/en/restaurant).
Farringdon tube/rail.* **Open** 7am-10.30am, noon-
2.30pm, 6-10.30pm Mon-Fri; 7.30am-3pm, 6-10.30pm

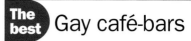

The best Gay café-bars

For digesting the scene
Balans (*see p91*).

For a slab of muscle mary
Box (*see p18*).

For legumes and lesbians
First Out (*see p90*).

For a slice of Soho cool
Edge (*see p20*).

For a taste of Islington
Green (*see p28*).

For pub grub and pretty boys
Rupert Street (*see p24*).

For burgers and beefcake
Profile (*see p23*).

Sat; 7.30am-3pm, 6-10pm Sun. **Main courses**
£12-£18.50. **Credit** AmEx, MC, V. **Map** p270 O4.
In the Zetter hotel, Bruno Loubet's return to the capital
after his years in Oz is a triumph. His interest in French
cuisine de terrior and North African and Asian flavours is
showcased in a menu that satisfies novelty-seekers, without scaring off conservative palates: think confit lamb
shoulder with white beans, preserved lemons and harissa.
Playful desserts are a high point too.

Le Comptoir Gascon

*63 Charterhouse Street, EC1M 6HJ (7608 0851,
www.comptoirgascon.com). Farringdon tube/rail.* **Open**
9am-10pm Tue, Wed, Sat; 9am-11pm Thur, Fri. **Main
courses** £7-£14. **Credit** AmEx, MC, V. **Map** P270 O5.
The bistro offshoot of Club Gascon (57-59 West Smithfield,
EC1A 9DS, 7796 0600, www.clubgascon.com) is a
deservedly popular spot. A small, convivial brick-lined
room that doubles as a deli, it offers refuge on a street lined
with raucous bars. More importantly, the food is great, and
nicely priced. Taste-packed mains of grilled lamb and beef
onglet are excellent; sides are worth ordering, especially
the french fries cooked in duck fat.

Gastropubs

Coach & Horses

*26-28 Ray Street, EC1R 3DJ (7278 8990, www.
thecoachandhorses.com). Farringdon tube/rail.*
Open noon-11pm Mon-Fri; 5-11pm Sat; noon-4pm
Sun. **Meals served** noon-3pm, 6-10pm Mon-Fri;
6-10pm Sat; noon-3pm Sun. **Main courses** £10-
£14. **Credit** AmEx, MC, V. **Map** p270 N4.
A stylish, sophisticated gastropub. The decor is discreet,
the menu is full of tempting, unfussy dishes, and the wine
list is usefully annotated. Sit outside in the summer.

Eagle

159 Farringdon Road, EC1R 3AL (7837 1353).
Farringdon tube/rail. **Open** noon-11pm Mon-Sat;
noon-5pm Sun. **Main courses** £5-£15. **Credit**
MC, V. **Map** p270 N4.
London's first gastropub, the Eagle opened in 1991 and it
still delivers quality food, with an Iberian/Med-influenced
menu and big flavours. It's noisy, crowded and the service
is no-frills, but the mood is convivial.

Modern European

Smiths of Smithfield

*67-77 Charterhouse Street, EC1M 6HJ (7251
7950, www.smithsofsmithfield.co.uk). Barbican tube/
Farringdon tube/rail.* **Open** *Bar* 10am-11pm Mon-
Wed; 10am-12.30am Thur-Sat; noon-10.30pm Sun.
Café 7am-4.30pm Mon; 7am-5pm Tue-Fri; 10am-5pm
Sat; 9.30am-5pm Sun. *Dining Room* noon-3pm, 6-
10.45pm Mon-Fri; 6-10.45pm Sat. **Main courses**
Café £4-£8. *Dining Room* £13-£15. **Credit** AmEx,
DC, MC, V. **Map** p270 O5.
This fashionable eating and drinking emporium is housed
in a converted warehouse. Of the four storeys, the ground
floor serves breakfast and casual fare; the next level up is
a cocktail and champagne bar; the second floor is a lively
brasserie; the third a fine-dining restaurant (Top Floor).

Spanish

Moro

*34-36 Exmouth Market, EC1R 4QE (7833 8336,
www.moro.co.uk). Farringdon tube/rail, or 19, 38 bus.*
Open 12.30-11.45pm Mon-Sat (last entry 10.30pm).
Tapas £3.50-£14.50. **Main courses** £15.50-£19.50.
Credit AmEx, DC, MC, V. **Map** p270 N4.
With constant praise from all sides, three cookbooks and
near-permanently busy tables, Moro has set the style
for restaurants offering an imaginative English take on
Mediterranean food traditions – in this case, from Spain
and North Africa. A tapas bar is to open in late 2010.

Bloomsbury & Fitzrovia

American

Eagle Bar Diner

*3-5 Rathbone Place, W1T 1HJ (7637 1418, www.eagle
bardiner.com). Tottenham Court Road tube.* **Open**
noon-11pm Mon-Wed; noon-1am Thur, Fri; 10.30am-
1am Sat; 11am-6pm Sun. **Main courses** £5-£10.
Credit AmEx, MC, V. **Map** p267 K5.
This trendy eatery is an oasis off the hellish hustle of
Oxford Street. The look is posh diner and the menu is the
same. The juicy hamburgers and milkshakes are a must.

Indian

Rasa Samudra

*5 Charlotte Street, W1T 1RE (7637 0222, www.rasa
restaurants.com). Goodge Street tube.* **Open** noon-
2.30pm, 6-10.45pm Mon-Sat; 6-10.45pm Sun. **Main
courses** £6.50-£12.95. **Set meal** (vegetarian) £22.50;
(seafood) £30. **Credit** AmEx, MC, V. **Map** p266 J5.

A specialist in Keralan cuisine, Rasa Samudra is one of
London's best Indian restaurants. The kitsch interior (pink
walls decorated with saris and wooden sculptures) belies
the quality of the cuisine. What you won't get are the modern Indian flourishes, but what you will get is good service
and excellent food. There's a long list of vegetarian dishes,
but seafood is also a forte.
Other locations throughout the city.

Oriental

Abeno

*47 Museum Street, WC1A 1LY (7405 3211). Holborn
or Tottenham Court Road tube.* **Open** noon-10pm
daily. **Main courses** £8.95-£21.95. **Credit** MC, V.
Map p267 L5.
Japanese 'pancakes' are the speciality here – big and filling ones too. 'Okonomiyaki' ('cooking what you like')
makes a humble but fun meal of vegetables and/or meat
mixed with a flour and egg batter, prepared at your table.
Alternatives include yaki soba and rice dishes.
Other locations Abeno Too, 17-18 Great Newport
Street, WC2H 7JE (7379 1160).

Hakkasan

*8 Hanway Place, W1T 1HD (7927 7000, www.
hakkasan.com). Tottenham Court Road tube.*
Open noon-12.30am Mon-Wed; noon-1.30am
Thur-Sat; noon-midnight Sun. **Dim sum** £4.50-£20.
Main courses £12.50-£58. **Credit** AmEx, MC, V.
Map p267 K5.
Wagamama for movie stars, Hakkasan combines LA glam-
our and eastern serenity. When it opened in 2001, it broke
the Chinatown mould by offering pricey, gourmet Chinese

Sketch. *See p88.*

food and chichi cocktails such as lemongrass martinis. The lunchtime dim sum is unrivalled in London (but you may have to ask for the menu).

Roka

37 Charlotte Street, W1T 1RR (7580 6464, www. rokarestaurant.com). Goodge Street or Tottenham Court Road tube. **Open** noon-2.30pm, 5.30-11.30pm Mon-Fri; 12.30-4pm, 5.30-11.30pm Sat; 12.30-4pm, 5.30-10.30pm Sun. **Main courses** £10.60-£22.60. **Credit** AmEx, DC, MC, V. **Map** p266 J5.
Everything about Roka is enticing: from honey-coloured walls to the aroma of wood burning in the grill. The food – a modern take on traditional Japanese – might rock your budget, but it will rock your taste buds too. The basement lounge is half 21st-century style bar, half feudal Japan. Roka is where to come for restaurant theatre at its best – booking is essential.
Other locations 4 Park Pavilion, 40 Canada Square, E14 5FW (7636 5228).

Spanish

Salt Yard

54 Goodge Street, W1T 4NA (7637 0657, www. saltyard.co.uk). Goodge Street tube. **Open** noon-11pm Mon-Fri; 5-11pm Sat. **Tapas served** noon-3pm, 6-11pm Mon-Fri; 5-11pm Sat. **Tapas** £2-£9. **Credit** AmEx, MC, V. **Map** p266 J5.
The artful menu of Iberian and Italian tapas standards served at this sleek joint is aimed at diners in search of a slow lunch or lightish dinner. Selections of charcuterie and cheese front the frequently changing menu, which features the likes of tuna carpaccio with broad beans, and ham croquettes with manchego.

Marylebone

Cafés, bars & brasseries

La Fromagerie

2-6 Moxon Street, W1U 4EW (7935 0341, www. lafromagerie.co.uk). Baker Street or Bond Street tube. **Open** 8am-7.30pm Mon-Fri; 9am-7pm Sat; 10am-6pm Sun. **Main courses** £6-£14. **Credit** AmEx, MC, V. **Map** p266 G5.
Famed with foodies for its dedicated cheese room, Patricia Michelson's high-end deli also dishes out freshly cooked café food. Its communal tables are often packed with devotees. Fromage-o-philes are spoilt with artisan cheese served with great bread, and a daily changing kitchen menu.
Other locations (shop) 30 Highbury Park, N5 2AA (7359 7440).

Gastropubs

Duke of Wellington

94A Crawford Street, W1H 2HQ (7723 2790, www.thedukew1.co.uk). Marylebone tube/rail. **Open** noon-11pm daily. **Meals served** noon-3pm, 6.30-10pm Mon-Fri; noon-3pm, 7-10pm Sat; 12.30-4.30pm, 7-9pm Sun. **Main courses** £8-£16. **Credit** AmEx, MC, V. **Map** p263 F5.

The Wolsley. *See p88.*

A nouveau pub, the Iron Duke has scrubbed up with sputnik light pendants, fresh lilies and framed Banksy postcards. The bar menu includes crab bisque, say, or chargrilled steak. In the dining room, the slow-roast shoulder of lamb is served with anchovy and garlic, a tower of aubergine and tomato, and lemon-roasted potatoes. Lovely.

Global

Providores & Tapa Room

109 Marylebone High Street, W1U 4RX (7935 6175, www.theprovidores.co.uk). Baker Street or Bond Street tube. **Open** *Providores* noon-2.45pm, 6-10.15pm Mon-Sat; noon-2.45pm, 6-10pm Sun. *Tapa Room* 9-11.30am, noon-10.30pm Mon-Fri; 10am-3pm, 4-10.30pm Sat; 4-10pm Sun. **Main courses** £18-£25. **Tapas** £2-£14. **Credit** AmEx, MC, V. **Map** p266 G4/5.
Welcome to the refined upper reaches of fusion food. The ground-floor Tapa Room is the more casual space; it is open for posh breakfast fry-ups, brunchy snacks and global tapas. Upstairs, the Providores is a serene, clean-lined white room. Here, you can expect globe-trotting influences and ingredients from Asia to the Middle East. Food is adventurous and pleasing.

Modern European

L'Autre Pied

5-7 Blandford Street, W1U 3DB (7486 9696, www. lautrepied.co.uk). Baker Street tube. **Open** noon-2.45pm, 6-10.30pm Mon-Sat; noon-3pm, 6.30-9.30pm Sun. **Meals** courses £21.50-£32.50. **Credit** AmEx, MC, V. **Map** p266 G5.
Sister restaurant to the fabled Pied à Terre – and winner of Time Out's Best New Restaurant gong in 2008 – L'Autre

Gay dining clubs

Champagne Dining Club

7404 0904, www.uniquely4girls.co.uk.
The Champagne Dining Club organises
weekly wine and dine events for gay women
at London's poshest restaurants, often in
Mayfair. This is the glam side of lesbianism,
with nary a sensible shoe in sight. Expect
power dykes aged 30-55, and lots of
exchanging of business cards.

Out & Out Gay Dining Club

8998 8000, www.outandout.co.uk.
London's largest gay male dining club
has been around since 1993 and boasts
hundreds of members. The club attracts
a slick and well-groomed professional crowd
– members apparently range from bankers to
builders, but the former are more in evidence,
especiallyat special events such as trips
to Glyndebourne or theatre evenings. The
regular meetings usually consist of a meal
at a smart restaurant in the West End. Annual
membership costs £169 and meals start from
£45 including drinks.

Pied has talented chef Marcus Eaves at the helm. The cooking is accomplished and precise, with imaginative yet well-considered flavour combinations, and stunning presentation. The oriental-style design is pretty stunning too.

Orrery

55 Marylebone High Street, W1U 5RB (7616 8000, www.danddlondon.com). Baker Street tube. **Open** *Bar* 11am-11pm daily. *Restaurant* noon-2.30pm, 6.30-10.30pm daily. **Main courses** £39-£43. **Set lunch** £24.50 3 courses (£40.50 incl wine). **Set dinner** £55-£59 tasting menu (£100-£104 incl wine). **Credit** AmEx, DC, MC, V. **Map** p266 G4.
This upmarket outfit sets out to offer luxury: from the smiling greeters to the cigar list and vast digestifs trolley. The long space is white, airy and (of course) sleek. The deft haute cuisine is refined, expensive and extremely delicate – just don't let the high prices spoil your appetite.

Mayfair & St James's

British

Inn the Park

St James's Park, SW1A 2BJ (7451 9999, www.inn thepark.com). St James's Park tube. **Open** 8am-9pm Mon-Fri; 9am-9pm Sat, Sun. **Main courses** £14-£23. **Credit** AmEx, MC, V. **Map** p269 K8.
The English class system is alive and well here: self-service customers fight over tables at the back, while the lakefront terrace is reserved for the fatter of wallet. The

forte is local, seasonal ingredients, and rare breeds. Dishes include halibut on samphire in sorrel sauce and a wellington of wild mushrooms, smoked cheese and spinach. But the food struggles to match up to the pretty setting.

Italian

Murano

20-22 Queen Street, W1J 5PP (7592 1222, www. gordonramsay.com/murano). Green Park tube. **Open** noon-2.30pm, 6.30-10.30pm Mon-Sat. **Set lunch** £30 3 courses. **Set meal** £60 3 courses; £75 8-course tasting menu. **Credit** AmEx, MC, V. **Map** p268 H7.
A new Italian restaurant from celebrity chef Angela Harnett. Despite the name, there are no bold chandeliers of Murano glass, no palazzo opulence. The menu and service are urbane and restrained. The food is sensational, from halibut with apple purée and a red wine sauce to vegetarian dishes such as potato gnocchi with globe artichoke and goat's cheese sauce. Good luck getting a table, though.

Modern European

Hibiscus

29 Maddox Street, W1S 2PA (7629 2999, www. hibiscusrestaurant.co.uk). Oxford Circus tube. **Open** noon-2.30pm, 6.30-10pm Tue-Fri; noon-2.30, 6-10pm Sat. **Set meal** £25-£70 3 courses; from £80 tasting menu. **Credit** AmEx, MC, V. **Map** p266 J6.
Tables in this expensive Mayfair dining room are arranged around a large central workstation topped with an extravagant floral display. The crowd is well-heeled. Many stick with the set lunch, on which you might find the moussaka of Elwy Valley mutton with feta and anchovy jus that has become something of a signature dish. For dessert, try clafoutis with almonds and rich pistachio ice-cream.

Maze

10-13 Grosvenor Square, W1K 6JP (7107 0000, www. gordonramsay.com/maze). Bond Street tube. **Open** noon-2.30pm, 6-10.30pm daily. **Main courses** £12.50-£13.50. **Credit** AmEx, DC, MC, V. **Map** p268 G7.
A Ramsay-owned venue with a fun vibe and modern, spacious setting. It's headed by Jason Atherton, who's big on tasting menus and unusual fusions that mix Europe and Asia. Even the simplest dishes are works of art.

Sketch

9 Conduit Street, W1S 2XZ (0870 777 4488, www. sketch.uk.com). Oxford Circus tube. **Open** noon-2.30pm, 7-10.30pm Tue-Fri; 7-10.30pm Sat. **Main courses** £12-£59. **Credit** AmEx, DC, MC, V. **Map** p268 H6.
Of the various elements of Pierre Gagnaire's legendarily expensive Sketch – including the design-led Gallery and the Lecture Room's haute-beyond-haute cuisine – the Glade is the most egalitarian: the menus, while artful, are not unreasonably priced. But nothing can prepare you for the loos, each housed in a gleaming white egg.

The Wolseley

160 Piccadilly, W1J 9EB (7499 6996, www.thewolseley. com). Green Park tube. **Open** 7am-midnight Mon-Fri; 8am-midnight Sat; 8am-11pm Sun. **Main courses** £7-£30. **Credit** AmEx, DC, MC, V. **Map** p268 J7.

The Wolseley shimmers with glamour and excitement. It's always busy, at breakfast, brunch, lunch, tea (*see p93*) or dinner. Staff are warm and professional; tables are laid out with good linen and silverware. Food ranges from humdrum to excellent, but booking is always essential. Joan Rivers' favourite London restaurant.

North African

Momo

25 Heddon Street, W1B 4BH (7434 4040, www.momo resto.com). Piccadilly Circus tube. **Open** 12.30-2.30pm, 6.30-11.30pm Mon-Sat; 6.30-11pm Sun. **Main courses** £13-£23. **Credit** AmEx, DC, MC, V. **Map** p268 J7.
Simply gorgeous, Momo is decked out like Rick's Café Américain (of *Casablanca* fame), staff are kitted out in custom-designed kasbah pop art T-shirts, and the menu supplements the standard tagines and couscous of Morocco with dishes such as baked cod, duck breast and sea bass. The cocktails are great, but pricey, as you'd expect at one of London's hippest restaurants. Still, it has substance to back up the style: it offers some of the best North African food in the city.

Oriental

Nobu

1st floor, The Metropolitan, 19 Old Park Lane, W1K 1LB (7447 4747, www.noburestaurants.com). Hyde Park Corner tube. **Open** noon-2.15pm, 6-10.15pm Mon-Thur; noon-2.15pm, 6-11pm Fri; 12.30-2.30pm,

Gaucho Piccadilly

6-11pm Sat; 12.30-2.30pm, 6-9.30pm Sun. **Main courses** £5.75-£32.75. **Credit** AmEx, DC, MC, V. **Map** p268 G8.
Nobu's tables are small and packed, and the bright lighting and canteen noise levels jar. But the cooking makes up for any such caveats: the fusion of Japanese and Peruvian is no longer novel, but can still inspire surprise and delight. The ceiling windows overlooking Hyde Park lend a touch of romance. This will go down in history as the restaurant where Boris Becker sired a child in a broom cupboard.
Other locations 15 Berkeley Street, W1J 8DY (7290 9222).

Royal China Club

40-42 Baker Street, W1U 7AJ (7486 3898, www. royalchinagroup.co.uk). Baker Street or Marble Arch tube. **Open** noon-11pm Mon-Thur; noon-11.30pm Fri, Sat; noon-10.30pm Sun. **Main courses** £12-£50. **Credit** AmEx, MC, V. **Map** p266 G5.
This sleek chain restaurant is a temple of Cantonese fine dining. Attention to quality and detail is apparent from the first sip of fragrant, premium jasmine tea. Here, the dim sum touches the soul. Traditional and unusual combinations are executed with sublime grace, and service is swift.
Other locations throughout the city.

Steak

Gaucho Piccadilly

25 Swallow Street, W1B 4QR (7734 4040, www. gauchorestaurants.co.uk). Piccadilly Circus tube. **Open** noon-midnight Mon-Sat; noon-11pm Sun. **Main courses** £8-£32. **Credit** AmEx, DC, MC, V. **Map** p268 J7.
Steakhouse chic is what the Gaucho flagship branch is all about – from its well-stocked Cavas wine shop to a pitch-dark cocktail bar and penchant for cowskin wallpaper and pouffes. The steaks? Good, with the bife de lomo (fillet) often outstanding. Service is a touch too slick.
Other locations throughout the city.

Soho

For decadent pastries at **Maison Bertaux** and **Pâtisserie Valerie**, *see p93* **How do you take your tea?**

Cafés, bars & brasseries

Bar Italia

22 Frith Street, W1V 5PS (7437 4520). Leicester Square, Piccadilly Circus or Tottenham Court Road tube. **Open** 24hrs Mon-Sat; 7am-3am Sun. **Main courses** £3.20-£8. **Credit** (7am-11pm only) MC, V. **Map** p267 K6.
Still going strong after more than half a century, Bar Italia is part of the Soho furniture. Sit outside nursing your cappuccino and watch cute boys and girls pass by. Excellent panini; open all night, it's great for a post-clubbing snack.

Fernandez & Wells

73 Beak Street, W1F 9SR (7287 8124, www. fernandezandwells.com). Oxford Circus or Piccadilly Circus tube. **Open** 7.30am-6pm Mon-Fri; 9am-6pm Sat,

Dean Street Townhouse

Other locations 37-63 Southampton Row, WC1B 4DA (7404 7079); 128 Cheapside, EC2V 6BT (7726 8011).

Star Café

22 Great Chapel Street, W1Y 3AQ (7437 8778). Tottenham Court Road tube. **Open** 7am-4pm Mon-Fri. **Main courses** £5-£8. **Credit** MC, V. **Map** p267 K6.
The Star morphs into a lesbian bar (the Star at Night, *see p27*) but in daylight hours feeds hungry locals of all known genders with fry-up or slim-line breakfasts, pasta or salad lunches and mugs of builders' tea.

British

Dean Street Townhouse

69-71 Dean Street, W1D 3SE (7434 1775, www. deanstreettownhouse.com). Tottenham Court Road tube. **Open** *Bar* 7am-1am Mon-Sat; 8am-11pm Sun. *Restaurant* 7am-11.30pm Mon-Thur; 7am-midnight Fri; 8am-midnight Sat; 8am-10.30pm Sun. **Main courses** £11-£33. **Set meal** (5-7pm) £17.50 2 courses, £21.50 3 courses. **Credit** AmEx, DC, MC, V. **Map** p267 K6.
Dean Street Townhouse is a hip hotel with dining room and bar which looks sultry, and also a little burlesque. British cooking used to be ghastly in the 1970s, yet it's fashionable now. And delicious: the mince and tatties here is piquant, properly browned, full-flavoured, and tastes of... childhood. Salt beef is an explosion of flavour; even the brussels sprouts are a pleasure. Comfort food is in, New Austerity the aesthetic. The future is sherry trifle ('to share'), and treacle sponge with custard. Would make any 1970s dinner party host proud.

Hix

66-70 Brewer Street, W1F 9UP (7292 3518, www. hixsoho.co.uk). Piccadilly Circus tube. **Open** noon-11.30pm Mon-Sat; noon-10.30pm Sun. **Main courses** £10.75-£35.50. Set meal (4.30-6.30pm & after 10pm) £15.50 2 courses, £19.50 3 courses. **Credit** AmEx, MC, V. **Map** p268 J7.
A new offering from celebrity chef Mark Hix, formerly of the Ivy. The dark, classic British interior is livened up by bold art by the likes of Tracey Emin and Damien Hirst. There's plenty to amuse and interest on the daily-changing menu that emphasises British and seasonal flavours. Cod's tongues with girolles were cooked perfectly; partridge is served as shredded meat on toast, with piquant elderberries and slivers of water celery. These imaginative combinations sound terrible, but work brilliantly. The kitchen's conscious of fish sustainability. Megrim sole gets the thumbs-up, topped with Morecambe Bay shrimps. Desserts include retro nods such as lemon trifle or cider apple and blackberry jelly with vanilla ice cream.

Diner/burgers

Diner

16-18 Ganton Street, W1F 7BU (7287 8962, www. goodlifediner.com). Oxford Circus or Piccadilly Circus tube. **Open** 10am-midnight Mon-Fri; 9.30am-midnight Sat, Sun. **Main courses** £5-£9. **Credit** AmEx, MC, V. **Map** p266 J6.
A cross between a retro burger joint and a swell cocktail bar. The choice of food here is lengthy, taking in a variety

Sun. **Main courses** £3-£5. **Credit** (over £5) MC, V. **Map** p268 J6.
A great example to all cafés. Its sandwiches aren't cheap, but they are something special, and the coffee is good. At lunchtime, seats are at a premium but worth the wait. Drop by in the morning for, say, a cheese toastie made with sourdough bread, or a breakfast pastry. **Other locations** throughout the city.

First Out

52 St Giles High Street, WC2H 8LH (7240 8042, www.firstoutcafebar.com). Tottenham Court Road tube. **Open** 9am-11pm Mon-Sat; 10am-10.30pm Sun. **Main courses** £4.25-£7.45. **Credit** MC, V. **Map** p267 K6.
On the fringes of Soho, this relaxed café-bar is a gay and lesbian London institution. A filling vegetarian menu offers daily specials – salads, soups, pastas and sandwiches.

Hummus Bros

88 Wardour Street, W1F 0TJ (7734 1311, www.hbros. co.uk). Oxford Circus or Tottenham Court Road tube. **Open** noon-10pm Mon-Wed, Sun; noon-11pm Thur-Sat. **Main courses** £2.80-£7.70. **Credit** AmEx, MC, V. **Map** p267 K6.
The simple and hugely successful formula at this café/takeaway is to serve houmous as a base for a selection of toppings, which you scoop up with excellent, pillowy pitta bread that's toasted while you wait. Sounds too simple? No matter: the food is tasty, filling and great value, whether you eat in or take away.

of fast-food favourites. Breakfasts are a forte: moist, mouth-watering pancakes, hearty omelettes and a broad Mexican spread. Free wireless internet.

Other locations 2 Jamestown Road, NW1 7BY (7485 5223); 128-130 Curtain Road, EC2A 3AQ (7729 4452); 21 Essex Road, N1 2SA (7226 4533); 64 Chamberlayne Road, NW10 3JJ (8968 9033).

Gourmet Burger Kitchen

15 Frith Street, W1D 4RF (7494 9533, www.gbk.co.uk). Tottenham Court Road tube. **Open** noon-11pm Mon-Thur; noon-midnight Fri; 11am-midnight Sat; 11am-10pm Sun. **Main courses** £3.95-£8.95. **Credit** MC, V. **Map** p267 K6.

Gourmet Burger Kitchen's burgers are 100% Aberdeen Angus Scotch beef, shaped into thick patties and cooked to your liking (medium-rare to well done), served in a sour-dough roll topped with sesame. The range of burger varieties – Greek, Thai and Jamaican – is impressive too. Vegetarians opt for the spicy puy lentil burger.

Other locations throughout the city.

Global

Balans

60 Old Compton Street, W1D 4UG (7439 2183, www.balans.co.uk). Leicester Square, Piccadilly Circus or Tottenham Court Road tube. **Open** 8am-5am Mon-Thur; 8am-6am Fri, Sat; 8am-1am Sun. **Main courses** £6.25-£17.95. **Credit** AmEx, MC, V. **Map** p267 K6.

Balans may have its critics, but it's doing something right. The place is always packed, and it's not just celebs like Amy Winehouse who turn up at 3am, tucking into the all-day breakfast. The muscle marys are often out in force too. While the service may sometimes be slow, the waiters are easy on the eye and the range of dishes is well priced and extensive, from generously sized salads to steak and chips and the chef's specials – usually a safe bet.

Other locations 239 Old Brompton Road, SW5 9HP (7244 8838); 187 Kensington High Street, W8 6SH (7376 0115); 214 Chiswick High Road, W4 1PD (8742 1435); 34 Old Compton Street, W1D 4CR (7439 3309); Westfield Shopping Centre, Ariel Way, W12 7GA (8600 3320).

Ice-cream

Gelupo

7 Archer Street, W1D 7AU (7287 5555, www. gelupo.com). Leicester Square or Piccadilly Circus tube. **Open** 11am-11pm Mon-Wed, Sun; 11am-1am Thur-Sat. **Ice cream** £3.50 2 scoops. **Credit** AmEx, MC, V. **Map** p269 K7.

Soho's already got a couple of great ice-cream places, namely Amorino and the new branch of Scoop. But unlike these two, Gelupo's not Italian-run. It's run by people who do Italian food better than many Italians: Jacob Kenedy is a young British chef who cut his teeth at Moro, then opened his own place, Bocca di Lupo, *see p92*. Flavours change on a daily basis, but might include chestnut, watermelon, sour cherry or espresso.

Hix

Consume

Balans. *See p91.*

Indian

Masala Zone

*9 Marshall Street, W1F 7ER (7287 9966, www.
masalazone.com). Oxford Circus tube.* **Open** noon-
3.30pm, 5.30-11pm Mon-Thur; 12.30-4pm, 5.30-11pm
Fri; 12.30-11pm Sat; 12.30-3.30pm, 6-10.30pm Sun.
Main courses £7-£15. **Credit** MC, V. **Map** p266 J6.
Another Soho star, the deservedly popular Masala Zone
has Wagamama-fied Indian dining. The canteen vibe is not
at the expense of authenticity, and the place is good value
for money. The combination thali is a feast.
Other locations throughout the city.

Italian

Bocca di Lupo

*12 Archer Street, W1D 7BB (7734 2223, www.
boccadilupo.com). Piccadilly Circus tube.* **Open**
12.30-3pm, 5.30pm-midnight Mon-Sat; noon-4pm
Sun. **Main courses** £8-£24.50. **Credit** AmEx, MC, V.
Map p269 K7.
This busy, informal Italian has a lively open kitchen and
tapas-style menu of regional specialities. Select one small
dish from several different categories (raw and cured, fried,
pastas and risottos, soups and stews, roasts, and so on) and
you should enjoy a balanced meal; for those who prefer not
to share, large portions of each dish are also offered.

Pulcinella

*37 Old Compton Street, W1D 5JY (7287 3920,
www.pulcinella-soho.co.uk). Piccadilly Circus or
Tottenham Court Road tube.* **Open** noon-midnight
Mon-Wed, Sun; noon-12.45am Thur-Sat. **Main
courses** £5.95-£19.65. **Credit** MC, V. **Map** p267 K6.

If you find yourself hungry in Soho, and the buff boys of
Balans (*see p91*) are too intimidating, try Pulcinella. The
pastas are good, the pizzas even better. But this Italian also
serves traditional meat and fish dishes, plus classics such
as bruschetta napoli, fungi alla milanese and a good old
grappa to round things off. Service is friendly and prices
are reasonable. One word of advice. If the weather is warm,
grab a table outside. It's like a pizza oven in there.

Modern European

Arbutus

*63-64 Frith Street, W1D 3JW (7734 4545,
www.arbutusrestaurant.co.uk). Piccadilly Circus
or Tottenham Court Road tube.* **Open** noon-2.30pm,
5-11pm Mon-Thur; noon-2.30pm, 5-11.30pm Fri, Sat;
noon-3pm, 5-10.30pm Sun. **Main courses** £12-£16.
Credit AmEx, MC, V. **Map** p267 K6.
The menu at this very popular spot is strong on hearty
British fare, accented with continental flavours, and sea-
sonality matters. Arbutus pioneered the 250mL carafe –
not extortionately marked up – for sampling the wines
from a well edited, not endless list.

Quo Vadis

*26-29 Dean Street, W1D 3LL (7437 9585, www.quo
vadissoho.co.uk). Leicester Square, Piccadilly Circus or
Tottenham Court Road tube.* **Open** noon-2.30pm, 5.30-
10.30pm Mon-Sat. **Main courses** £12-£27. **Credit**
AmEx, DC, MC, V. **Map** p267 K6.
This Soho stalwart has recently been reinvented with a
slick hand by the team behind top-quality Spanish eatery
Barrafina (*see p93*). The dishes have a British/Modern
European bent. Dover sole and Colchester oysters vie for
space with grill-restaurant classics including steaks, rack
of lamb and ethically-sound rose veal. Puddings are a high
point, from lemon tart to decadent profiteroles.

Oriental

Bar Shu

*28 Frith Street, W1D 5LF (7287 6688, www.bar-
shu.co.uk). Leicester Square or Tottenham Court Road
tube.* **Open** noon-11pm Mon-Thur, Sun; noon-11.30pm
Fri, Sat. **Main courses** £8.90-£28.90. **Credit** AmEx,
MC, V. **Map** p267 K6.
A shining example of regional Chinese (in this case the
chilli- and pepper-laced cuisine of Sichuan) that hasn't com-
promised on authenticity. Fiery food for the brave.

Busaba Eathai

*106-110 Wardour Street, W1F 0TR (7255 8686,
www.busaba.com). Oxford Circus, Tottenham
Court Road or Leicester Square tube.* **Open** noon-
11pm Mon-Thur; noon-11.30pm Fri, Sat; noon-10pm
Sun. **Main courses** £5-£10. **Credit** AmEx, MC, V.
Map p267 K6.
This high-turnover, canteen-style restaurant was the brainchild of Alan Yau, who also conceived Wagamama (*see
p93*), Hakkasan (*see p86*) and Yauatcha (*see p93*). There
are lots of vegetarian choices among the rice and noodle
dishes, and the green curry is still a must. Popular with
media dykes who only have time for a quick catch-up over
their pad thai and perfumed tea.
Other locations throughout the city.

Cha Cha Moon

15-21 Ganton Street, W1F 9BN (7297 9800, www. chachamoon.com). Oxford Circus tube. **Open** noon-11pm Mon-Fri; noon-11.30pm Sat, Sun. **Main courses** £4-£8.90. **Credit** AmEx, MC, V. **Map** p266 J6.
Alan Yau's Cha Cha Moon offers fast food of pan-Chinese inspiration at low prices, served on long cafeteria-style tables in a sleek room. The main focus is on excellent noodle dishes, hailing from Hong Kong, Shanghai and elsewhere in China, clocking in at around £5.

Wagamama

10A Lexington Street, W1F 0LD (7292 0990, www.wagamama.com). Oxford Circus, Piccadilly Circus or Tottenham Court Road tube. **Open** 11.30am-11pm Mon-Sat; noon-10pm Sun. **Main courses** £6.75-£10.85. **Credit** AmEx, MC, V. **Map** p268 J6.
Everyone's a bit blasé about noodle bars – a high-street staple nowadays – but Wagamama is one of the originals, and it remains a reliable pitstop. Its gleaming, light and airy environment, perky staff and wholesome menu are appealing, though not everyone likes the communal tables and the noisy buzz.
Other locations throughout the city.

Yauatcha

15 Broadwick Street, W1F 0DL (7494 8888). Oxford Circus tube. **Open** noon-11.30pm Mon-Thur; noon-11.45pm Fri, Sat; noon-10.30pm Sun. **Main courses** £7.80-£38. **Credit** AmEx, MC, V. **Map** p266 J6.
Opened to a blaze of publicity, this all-day dim-sum restaurant from innovative restaurateur Alan Yau has a deeply chic design by Christian Liaigre. Located in the basement of Richard Rogers' Ingeni building, the sultry lounge-like den features glowing fish tanks and starry ceiling lights. The dim sum is, as you might expect, exquisite. The kitchen creates magic out of old favourites and new ideas.

Tapas

Barrafina

54 Frith Street, W1D 4SL (7813 8016, www.barrafina. co.uk). Oxford Circus or Tottenham Court Road tube. **Open** noon-3pm, 5-11pm Mon-Sat; 1-3.30pm, 5.30-10.30pm Sun. **Tapas** £1.90-£16.50. **Credit** AmEx, MC, V. **Map** p267 K6.
The toast of the London tapas scene, Barrafina is tiny, popular and doesn't take bookings. The surroundings are slick and the quality of ingredients is impeccable.

Consume

How do you take your tea?

Remember to lift your pinky daintily as you savour a brew that's reminiscent of a more civilised era.

Maison Bertaux

28 Greek Street, W1D 5DQ (7437 6007). Leicester Square, Piccadilly Circus or Tottenham Court Road tube. **Open** 8.30am-11pm Mon-Sat; 8.30am-8pm Sun. **Main courses** £1.50-£4.50. **No credit cards. Map** p267 K6.
Furnished with wonky tables and chairs that have seen better days, this characterful, boho-Soho institution has no menus – what you see is what you get. It's quite a sight, though: French pâtisserie, fresh breads and tip-top savouries.

Pâtisserie Valerie

44 Old Compton Street, W1D 4TY (7437 3466, www. patisserie-valerie.co.uk). Leicester Square, Piccadilly Circus or Tottenham Court Road tube. **Open** 7.30am-8.30pm Mon, Tue; 7.30am-11pm Wed-Sat; 9.30am-8pm Sun. **Main courses** £3.75-£8.25. **Credit** (over £5) AmEx, MC, V. **Map** p267 K6.
This landmark pastry shop and café is more of a special occasion place than Bertaux. The decor is vintage Paris, and the confections hedonistic. The indulgent cakes, marzipans and typically French breads provide a feast for the senses.
Other locations throughout the city.

Postcard Teas

9 Dering Street, W1S 1AG (7629 3654, www. postcardteas.com). Bond Street or Oxford Circus tube. **Open** 10.30am-6.30pm Mon-Sat. **Credit** MC, V. **Map** p266 H6
A simple, Zen-like sanctuary – linger around a communal table and sip fine infusions from around the world. Mop up with a sponge cake.

The Ritz

150 Piccadilly, W1J 9BR (7493 8181, www.theritzhotel.co.uk). Green Park tube. **Tea served** (reserved sittings) 11.30am, 1.30pm, 3.30pm, 5.30pm, 7.30pm daily. **Set tea** £39. **Credit** AmEx, MC, V. **Map** p268 J8.
High tea in a grand setting. Book in advance. Expect dainty sandwiches, melt-in-the-mouth cakes and exotic teas – and tickling of the ivories.

The Wolseley

160 Piccadilly, W1J 9EB (7499 6996, www. thewolseley.com). Green Park tube. **Tea served** 3-6.30pm Mon-Fri; 3.30-5.30pm Sat; 3.30-6.30pm Sun. **Set tea** £9.75-£21. **Credit** AmEx, DC, MC, V. **Map** p268 J8.
Modelled on an elegant *mittel Europa* brasserie. Afternoon tea is £19.50; for a tea-and-scone combo is a bargain at £8.25. *See also p88.*

Dehesa

25 Ganton Street, W1F 9BP (7494 4170). Oxford Circus tube. **Open** noon-11pm Mon-Sat; noon-5pm Sun. **Tapas** £3.50-£8.50. **Credit** AmEx, MC, V. **Map** p266 J6.

A bijou place serving top-rank Spanish-Italian tapas. Expect bicultural bites such as jamón iberico, hand-sliced from a leg on display and intensely flavoured wild boar salami, plus a range of cheeses and charcuterie.

Vegetarian & organic

Mildred's

45 Lexington Street, W1F 9AN (7494 1634, www. mildreds.co.uk). Oxford Circus or Piccadilly Circus tube. **Open** noon-11pm Mon-Sat. **Main courses** £7-£9.20. **Credit** MC, V. **Map** p267 J6.

This gay-friendly veggie favourite is tucked away off the main strip of gay town – and it still isn't big enough for the lunchtime influx of local ladies in search of appetising organic grub, including salads, soups and stir-fries. There's always a vegan and wheat-free option as well as the speciality chips and the naughty-but-nice cake.

Covent Garden

British

Great Queen Street

32 Great Queen Street, WC2B 5AA (7242 0622). Covent Garden or Holborn tube. **Open** noon-2.30pm, 6-10.30pm Mon-Sat; noon-3pm Sun. **Main courses** £9-£18. **Credit** MC, V. **Map** p267 L6.

The pub-style room here hums with bonhomie. Ranging from snacks to shared mains, the classic British menu is designed to tempt and satisfy rather than educate or impress. The emphasis is on local ingredients. Robust highlights include hare ragù and braised Hereford beef with carrots and dumplings. Booking is essential.

Fish/fish & chips

J Sheekey

28-32 St Martin's Court, WC2N 4AL (7240 2565, www.j-sheekey.co.uk). Leicester Square tube. **Open** noon-3pm, 5.30pm-midnight Mon-Sat; noon-3.30pm, 6-11pm Sun. **Main courses** £13-£40. **Credit** AmEx, MC, V. **Map** p269 K7.

Elegant and discreet, with simple but sublime seafood, plus a more upmarket class of celebrity, J Sheekey shares many wonderful things with its sister restaurant, the Ivy (*see below*). Book well in advance.

Rock & Sole Plaice

47 Endell Street, WC2H 9AJ (7836 3785, www. rockandsoleplaice.com). Covent Garden or Holborn tube. **Open** 11.30am-10.30pm Mon-Sat; noon-9.30pm Sun. **Main courses** £10-£13. **Credit** MC, V. **Map** p267 L6.

There has been a chippy on this site since 1871 and, while taramasalata and Efes beer point to the current owners' Turkish heritage, the name of the game is still good old-fashioned British fish and chips.

Modern American/European

The Ivy

1 West Street, WC2H 9NQ (7836 4751, www.theivy. co.uk). Leicester Square tube. **Open** noon-3pm, 5.30pm-midnight Mon-Sat; noon-3.30pm, 5.30-11pm Sun. **Main courses** £9.25-£25.50. **Credit** AmEx, DC, MC, V. **Map** p267 K6.

Yauatcha. *See p93.*

One of the world's most famous restaurants – and notorious for its ages-in-advance booking policy – the Ivy continues to fill its celeb quota, much to the delight of the paparazzi who haunt the street outside. And the quality of the trademark comfort cuisine is as high as ever.

Vegetarian & organic

Food for Thought

31 Neal Street, WC2H 9PR (7836 9072, 7836 0239, www.foodforthought-london.co.uk). Covent Garden tube. **Open** noon-8.30pm Mon-Sat; noon-5pm Sun. **Main courses** £4.80-£7.80. **No credit cards**. **Map** p267 L6.
A cheap, unpretentious vegetarian legend. You normally have to share a table, but it's cheap as chips – which don't feature strongly among the rice, noodles and daily bake.

Westminster & Victoria

British

National Dining Rooms

Sainsbury Wing, National Gallery, Trafalgar Square, WC2N 5DN (7747 2525, www.thenationaldining rooms.co.uk). Charing Cross tube/rail. **Open** 10am-5.30pm Mon-Thur, Sat, Sun; 10am-9pm Fri, Sat. **Main courses** *Bakery* £5.90-£9.50. **Set Meal** £23 2 courses; £26 3 courses. **Set dinner** (Fri only) £17.50 2 courses; £22.50 3 courses. **Credit** MC, V. **Map** p269 K7.
Oliver Peyton's restaurant in the National Gallery offers far better food than museum diners are accustomed to – but at a price. Choose from a bar menu or sample an array of tempting baked goods. But the real attraction remains the main menu of British staples – bacon and pease pudding, say – delivered with skill and efficiency.

Indian

Cinnamon Club

Old Westminster Library, 30-32 Great Smith Street, SW1P 3BU (7222 2555, www.cinnamonclub.com). St James's Park or Westminster tube. **Open** 7.30-9.30am, noon-2.30pm, 6-10.45pm Mon-Sat. **Main courses** £14-£25. **Set meal** £19 2 courses, £22 3 courses. **Credit** AmEx, DC, MC, V. **Map** p269 K9.
One of Britain's best Indian restaurants. Classic dishes are cooked with due diligence, plus the odd unexpected twist. The setting is a conversion of a grand 19th-century library, with cinnamon-hued banquettes and crisp tablecloths.

Oriental

Saké No Hana

23 St James's Street, SW1A 1HA (7925 8988). Green Park tube. **Open** noon-3pm, 6pm-midnight Mon-Sat. **Main courses** £4-£40. **Set meal** £45-£65. **Credit** AmEx, DC, MC, V. **Map** p268 J8.
With a glittering track record (Wagamama, Hakkasan), Alan Yau has done it again with his first Japanese fine-dining restaurant. Discreet, and coolly designed, Japanese-cedar tables sit amid acres of tatami mats; narrow tilted screens add elegance to the wraparound windows. Some of the food is modern and playful, much of it orthodox and simple.

Mildred's

Kensington & Chelsea

Cafés, bars & brasseries

Botanist

7 Sloane Square, SW1W 8EE (7730 0077, www.the botanistonsloanesquare.com). Sloane Square tube. **Open** 8am-10.30pm Mon-Fri; 9am-10.30pm Sat, Sun. **Main courses** £14-£19. **Credit** AmEx, MC, V. **Map** p268 G11.
This beautiful, elegant dining room opened during the Chelsea Flower Show, so the botanical decor is apt. The British menu has Euro flourishes: dinner might be poached gull's egg with chorizo, Alsace bacon and fresh peaches, followed by Scottish Blackface lamb. There are good breakfasts and afternoon teas, and majestic Sunday roasts.

Gallery Mess

Saatchi Gallery, Duke of York's HQ, King's Road, SW3 4LY (7730 8135). Sloane Square tube. **Open** 10am-9.30pm Mon-Sat; 10am-7pm Sun. **Main courses** £9.50-£17. **Credit** AmEx, MC, V. **Map** p265 F11.
The Saatchi Gallery welcomed this fabulous new brasserie in May 2009. You can sit inside surrounded by modern art, but the grounds outside can be a more attractive option in the summer. There's a simple breakfast menu of pastries, eggs and toast or fry-ups served until 11.30am, then lunch and dinner take over, with salads, pastas and burgers joined by more ambitious daily specials. Of the desserts, knickerbocker glory is a triumph.

Tom's Kitchen

27 Cale Street, SW3 3QP (7349 0202, www.toms kitchen.co.uk). Sloane Square or South Kensington tube. **Open** 8-11am, noon-3pm, 6-11pm Mon-Fri; 10am-3pm,

6-11pm Sat, Sun. **Main courses** £14-£29. **Credit** AmEx, MC, V. **Map** p265 E11.
White-tiled walls, vast expanses of marble and a busy open kitchen ensure Tom Aikens' place sounds full even when it isn't. The big draw here is the pancake: almost as big as the serving plate, it's categorically London's best. Lunch and dinner menus make the most of the wood-smoked oven, spit-roast and grill.

French

Bar Boulud

Mandarin Oriental Hyde Park, 66 Knightsbridge, SW1X 7LA (7201 3899, www.barboulud.com). Knightsbridge tube. **Open** *Bar* 11am-1am daily. *Restaurant* noon-3pm, 5.30-11pm daily. **Main courses** £12.50-£23. **Credit** AmEx, DC, MC, V. **Map** p263 F8.
This is no ordinary brasserie. Daniel Boulud, the French chef who is rated as one of the best restaurateurs in New York, has brought Big Apple style and French polish to Knightsbridge. The main dining room has a beautiful seafood and charcuterie bar populated by Americans in dark suits wearing shirts the colour of the FT. So far, so New York. But the menu points to the old world, specifically to Lyon, and the heart of French gastronomy.

Racine

239 Brompton Road, SW3 2EP (7584 4477, www. racine-restaurant.com). Knightsbridge or South Kensington tube/14, 74 bus. **Open** noon-3pm, 6-10.30pm Mon-Sat; 6-10pm Sun. **Main courses** £13.50-£26. **Credit** AmEx, MC, V. **Map** p265 E10.
The essence of a Parisian brasserie. Heavy velvet curtains inside the door allow diners to make a grand entrance into the warm, vibrant, 1930s retro atmosphere. The food is gorgeous French bourgeois cuisine.

Indian

Amaya

19 Motcomb Street, Halkin Arcade, SW1X 8JT (7823 1166, www.realindianfood.com). Knightsbridge tube. **Open** 12.30-2.15pm, 6.30-11.15pm Mon-Sat; 12.45-2.30pm, 6.30-10.15pm Sun. **Main courses** £10-£31. **Credit** AmEx, DC, MC, V. **Map** p268 G9.
Glamorous, stylish and seductive, Amaya is sleekly appointed with sparkly chandeliers, splashes of modern art and a groovy bar. This restaurant's calling card is its sophisticated Indian creations from a menu that cleverly links dressed-up street food with regal specialities.

Modern European

Gordon Ramsay

68-69 Royal Hospital Road, SW3 4HP (7352 4441, www.gordonramsay.com). Sloane Square tube. **Open** noon-2pm, 6.30-11pm Mon-Fri. **Set lunch** £45 3 courses. **Set meal** £90 3 courses; £120 tasting menu. **Credit** AmEx, DC, MC, V. **Map** p265 F12.
You'll need to book at least a month in advance and dig deep into your pockets, but it's worth it. Waiting staff know what they're doing, and the cooking is unimpeachable. The menu has both wide appeal and novelty value. Among the generous, faultless mains, fish dishes are balanced out by

the likes of roasted Welsh lamb or braised pig's cheeks. Also worth trying is Gordon Ramsay at Claridge's (55 Brook Street, 7499 0099), which, apart from the glorious food, also has the benefit of a knockout setting.

Oriental

Nahm

The Halkin, Halkin Street, SW1X 7DJ (7333 1234, www.nahm.como.bz). Hyde Park Corner tube. **Open** noon-2.30pm, 7-10.45pm Mon-Fri; 7-10.45pm Sat; 7-9.45pm Sun. **Main courses** £16.50-£25.50. **Set meal** £60 3 courses. **Credit** AmEx, DC, MC, V. **Map** p268 G9.
Truly exceptional food is produced in this chic Halkin Hotel dining room – but at seriously high prices. The menu features traditional Thai dishes as well as updates on the theme using British ingredients. The best Thai restaurant in London. Visit the website for discount menu offers.

Zuma

5 Raphael Street, SW7 1DL (7584 1010, www.zuma restaurant.com). Knightsbridge tube. **Open** *Bar* noon-11pm Mon-Fri; 12.30-11pm Sat; noon-10.30pm Sun. *Restaurant* noon-2.30pm, 6-11pm Mon-Fri; 12.30-3.15pm, 6-11pm Sat; 12.30-3.15pm, 6-10.30pm Sun. **Main courses** £14.80-£70. **Credit** AmEx, DC, MC, V. **Map** p265 F9.
The pleasures of this Knightsbridge high-flyer don't come cheap, but it is always packed to its designer rafters. Watch star sushi chef Shinji Tani in action; tuck into grilled wagyu beef if you can afford it. The wine list is sophisticated and the saké selection dangerously extensive. Come for lunch to avoid the loud bar scene.

Botanist. *See p95.*

North
Cafés, bars & brasseries

Duke of Cambridge

*30 St Peter's Street, N1 8JT (7359 3066, www.duke
organic.co.uk). Angel tube.* **Open** noon-11pm Mon-
Sat; noon-10.30pm Sun. **Main courses** £12-£20.
Credit MC, V.
The UK's first certified organic gastropub ticks every box
on sustainability, but it's also an appealing pub, with great
organic beers, a handsome open room and a friendly mix
of green-minded folk (from dreadlocked cyclists to City
suits). It's a great place for a beer. As a culinary destination, though, it is a mixed bag.

Ottolenghi

*287 Upper Street, N1 2TZ (7288 1454, www.
ottolenghi.co.uk). Angel tube or Highbury & Islington
tube/rail.* **Open** 8am-10.30pm Mon-Sat; 9am-7pm Sun.
Main courses £6.80-£11.80. **Credit** AmEx, MC, V.
Behind the pastries piled in the window is a deli counter
with lush salads. Diners share long communal tables in the
all-white modernist interior. Service can be slow. Note that
other branches don't have much room to eat-in.
Other locations 13 Motcomb Street, SW1X 8LB (7823
2707); 63 Ledbury Road, W11 2AD (7727 1121);
1 Holland Street, W8 4NA (7937 0003).

Gastropub

Charles Lamb

*16 Elia Street, N1 8DE (7837 5040, www.thecharles
lambpub.com). Angel tube.* **Open** 4-11pm Mon, Tue;
noon-11pm Wed-Sat; noon-10.30pm Sun. **Meals served**
6-9.30pm Mon, Tue; noon-3pm ,6-9.30pm Wed-Sat; noon-
6pm Sun. **Main courses** £9-£11.50. **Cards** MC, V.
Tranquillity reigns in the streets of plush Regency houses
east of Upper Street in N1, and this distinctive pub feels
like a village local. For Sunday lunch, the blackboard menu
sticks to the classics: rare roast beef and roast duck with
all the trimmings hit the right notes. At other times, the
fare on offer might include southern French (merguez
sausages with puy lentils) and British favourites (steak,
mushroom and Guinness pie), but the kitchen is inventive.
No bookings.

East
British

Albion

*2-4 Boundary Street, E2 7DD (7729 1051,
www.albioncaff.co.uk). Shoreditch High Street rail.*
Open 8am-midnight daily. **Main courses** £8-£10.
Credit AmEx, MC, V.
Almost every new London restaurant seems to be mining
the vein of nostalgia for traditional British cuisine, but few
have pulled it off as well as Terence Conran's stand-out
caff. Once you're past the kitsch British products for sale
in the shop (HP sauce, Marmite), you're faced with platters
of cupcakes and doorstop-thick slices of battenberg, baked
on-site. On the main menu, toad in the hole or devilled kid-
neys sit next to a fantastic English breakfast.

Gallery Mess. *See p95.*

Canteen

*2 Crispin Place, off Brushfield Street, E1 6DW (0845
686 1122, www.canteen.co.uk). Liverpool Street tube/
rail.* **Open** 8am-11pm Mon-Fri; 9am-11pm Sat; 9am-
10pm Sun. **Main courses** £7.50-£21.50. **Credit** MC,
V. **Map** p271 R5.
In the new, piazza-like development next to Old Spitalfields
Market, Canteen is clean and modern, with shared blonde
wood tables. Yet the menu is old-school comfort food. You
can eat (own-made) baked beans on toast, or macaroni
cheese. There are more adventurous options too.
Other locations Royal Festival Hall, Belvedere Road,
SE1 8XX (0845 686 1122); 55 Baker Street, W1U 8EW
(0845 686 1122); The Park Pavillion, 40 Canada Square,
E14 5FW (0845 686 1122).

Cafés, bars & brasseries

Brick Lane Beigel Bake

*159 Brick Lane, E1 6SB (7729 0616). Shoreditch
High Street rail.* **Open** 24hrs daily. **No credit cards.**
Map p271 S5.
Banterish Cockneys dole out warm beigels to codgers, cab-
bies and clubbers alike. The classics are salted beef or
smoked salmon with cream cheese. Try the cheesecake too.

French

Bistrotheque

*23-27 Wadeson Street, E2 9DR (8983 7900, www.
bistrotheque.com). Bethnal Green tube/rail or
Cambridge Heath rail or 55 bus.* **Open** Bar 6pm-
midnight Mon-Sat; 6-11pm Sun. **Meals served**
6.30-10.30pm Mon-Thur; 6.30-11pm Fri; 11am-4pm,

6.30-11pm Sat; 11am-4pm, 6.30-10.30pm Sun. **Main courses** £12-£20.50. **Credit** AmEx, MC, V.
Set in an old clothing factory, this modish, gay-friendly bistro boasts two dining rooms, a bar and the Playroom (with cabaret acts). The service is cheery and the menu features retro dishes such as coq au vin and steak tartare.

Global

Eyre Brothers

70 Leonard Street, EC2A 4QX (7613 5346, www.eyre brothers.co.uk). Old Street tube/rail. **Open** noon-2.45pm, 6.30-10.45pm Mon-Fri; 7-11pm Sat. **Main courses** £15-£27.50. **Credit** AmEx, DC, MC, V. **Map** p271 Q4.
Eyre Brothers oozes sophistication. Brothers David and Robert spend as much time crafting the menu as fashioning the decor. Authentic Portuguese dishes reflect the brothers' upbringing in Mozambique, while Spanish and French flavours add range and luxury.

Oriental

Sông Quê

134 Kingsland Road, E2 8DY (7613 3222). Hoxton rail. **Open** noon-3pm, 5.30-11pm Mon-Sat; 12.30pm-11pm Sun. **Main courses** £4.90-£7. **Credit** MC, V.
East London retains its monopoly on the capital's most authentic Vietnamese cafés. And Sông Quê, which was the key pioneer, remains the benchmark. It's an efficient operation to which diners of all types are attracted – be ready to share tables at busy times. Handy for filling up before a big night out in Shoreditch – and if it's packed out, there's a whole row of good Vietnamese places on the same stretch of Kingsland Road.

South

Cafés, bars & brasseries

Bar Estrela

111-115 South Lambeth Road, SW8 1UZ (7793 1051). Stockwell tube or Vauxhall tube/rail. **Open** 8am-11pm Mon-Sat; 10am-11pm Sun. **Main courses** £7-£14. **Tapas** £2.70-£7.80. **Credit** AmEx, MC, V.
Near Vauxhall, this mom-and-pop tapas bar is handy for a pre- or post-club bite. The food is cheap – and good.

SW9

11 Dorrell Place, SW9 8EG (7738 3116). Brixton tube/rail. **Open** 10am-11pm Mon-Thur, Sun; 10am-1.30am Fri, Sat. **Meals served** 10am-8pm daily. **Main courses** £5.50-£12. **Credit** MC, V.
This gay-friendly café-bar has a trendy vibe, gastropubby fare and a unisex bathroom – how modern.

Modern European

Chez Bruce

2 Bellevue Road, SW17 7EG (8672 0114, www. chezbruce.co.uk). Wandsworth Common rail. **Open** noon-2.30pm, 6.30-10pm Mon-Thur; noon-2.30pm, 6.30-10.30pm Fri; noon-3pm, 6.30-10.30pm Sat; noon-3pm,

7-9.30pm Sun. **Set lunch** £25.50-£32.50. **Set dinner** £42.50 3 courses. **Credit** AmEx, DC, MC, V.
This elegant spot is Wandsworth's top venue, but it draws Londoners from far and wide. The bow windows overlook Wandsworth Common; robust dishes have a strong French or Mediterranean influence. Booking is essential.

West

British

Hereford Road

3 Hereford Road, W2 4AB (7727 1144, www. herefordroad.org). Bayswater tube. **Open** noon-3pm, 6-10.30pm Mon-Sat; noon-4pm, 6-10pm Sun. **Main courses** £9-£14. **Credit** AmEx, MC, V. **Map** p262 B6.
Despite having opened just a few years ago, Hereford Road has the assurance of somewhere that's been around much longer. It's an easy place in which to relax, with a mixed crowd and a happy buzz. Starters include the likes of (undyed) smoked haddock with white beans and leeks, while mains might feature mallard with braised chicory and lentils. Wines are keenly priced.

Italian

River Café

Thames Wharf, Rainville Road, W6 9HA (7386 4200, www.rivercafe.co.uk). Hammersmith tube. **Open** 12.30-2.15pm, 7-9.15pm Mon-Sat; 12.30-3pm Sun. **Main courses** £23-£32. **Credit** AmEx, DC, MC, V.
The legendary River Café is known for its produce-based menu, which changes twice daily. The wood-roasted fish might be dover sole with lemon and capers, fine green beans and parsley or wild sea bass with fennel, courgette, swiss chard and aïoli. The seasonal pasta dishes are strong, as is the wine list. The riverside setting is a bonus.

Modern European

Clarke's

124 Kensington Church Street, W8 4BH (7221 9225, www.sallyclarke.com). Notting Hill Gate tube. **Open** 12.30-2pm, 6.30-10pm Tue-Fri; noon-2pm, 6.30-10pm Sat; 12.30-2pm. **Main courses** £16-£21. **Credit** AmEx, MC, V. **Map** p262 B7.
Inspired by her experiences dining at Chez Panisse in California, Sally Clarke brought sunshine and freshness to grey London in the 1980s. From the tender Welsh chargrilled lamb to risotto balls made with buffalo mozzarella, chive and chervil, ingredients are the key. The decor – cane chairs, parquet floor, white tablecloths – is very civilised.

Vegetarian & organic

Gate

51 Queen Caroline Street, W6 9QL (8748 6932, www.thegate.tv). Hammersmith tube. **Open** noon-2.30pm, 6-10.30pm Mon-Fri; 6-11pm Sat. **Main courses** £10.50-£13.75. **Credit** AmEx, MC, V.
There are few dining rooms as immediately pleasing as the Gate's. Lush bamboo soars to the ceiling and there's a feeling of Zen-like calm. A vegetarian restaurant much loved by both vegetarians and meat-eaters.

Shopping

Where to spend your pink pounds.

Shopping, if you believe all the hype about the pink pound and the clichés about the queer sense of style, is practically a gay religion. And London is the ultimate place of worship – a mecca for moneyed Marys. In terms of trends, the relaunch of iconic British labels Biba and Ossie Clark signalled the strength of the retro revival, but London retail exists in a constant state of fashionable flux. One of the world's most exciting and exhaustive shopping centres, it's also one of the most eclectic, spanning multicultural street markets and deluxe department stores, mould-breaking fashion designers and trad tailors, flashy foodshops and dusty antiquarian dens.

You'll also find some of the best places on the planet to buy books, records and second-hand clothes. There are bargains to be had, but pocket the plastic too. We've only the space to cover a fraction of London's shopping here, so we concentrated on British brands and shops.

Most goods – except books, food and children's clothes – are subject to value added tax (VAT) of 17.5 per cent (due to rise to 20 per cent), usually included in the marked price.

For more listings and reviews covering the huge variety of shops in the city, pick up a copy of *Time Out London's Best Shops*.

One-stop shopping

Harrods

87-135 Brompton Road, SW1X 7XL (7730 1234, www.harrods.com). Knightsbridge tube. **Open** 10am-8pm Mon-Sat; noon-6pm Sun. **Credit** AmEx, DC, MC, V. **Map** p265 F9.
Harrods is the mother of all upscale department stores, with floor after floor of designer wares overseen by surprisingly friendly staff. Although the stock is expensive, it costs nothing to soak up the ambience in the ground-floor Room of Luxury, with accessories by the likes of Celine, Gucci, Dior and Hermès; or to linger amid designs by Joseph, Armani, Dolce & Gabbana and more. It's also fun to giggle at the over-the-top glitz that helped make the Harrods name. The enormous cosmetics and skincare section has some affordable options. But for us it's the legendary food halls that are the biggest draw, with mouth-watering meat counters, smelly cheeses, and all manner of luxurious nibbles. The touristy but irresistible marmalades, teas and chocolate will please the relatives.

Harvey Nichols

109-125 Knightsbridge, SW1X 7RJ (7235 5000, www.harveynichols.com). Knightsbridge tube. **Open** *Store* 10am-8pm Mon-Sat; noon-6pm Sun (browsing from 11.30am). *Café* 8am-11pm Mon-Sat; 11.30am-6pm Sun. *Restaurant* noon-3pm, 6-11pm Mon-Thur; noon-4pm, 6-11pm Fri, Sat; noon-4pm Sun. **Credit** AmEx, DC, MC, V. **Map** p265 F9.
It's no coincidence that gay icons Edina and Patsy were mad about Harvey Nicks, and that *Absolutely Fabulous* referred to it endlessly – this London landmark has everything a discerning gay man might need. The store is big, luxurious and enticing. As far as fashion's concerned, there's a great selection of designer labels for men, ranging from John Galliano to Comme des Garçons. When you

Consume

The best Shops

For a one-stop fashion fix
Selfridges (*see p101*).

For pink pages
Gay's the Word (*see p102*).

For Steve McQueen chic
Albam (*see p107*).

For edgy looks
B Store (*see p108*);
No-one (*see p108*).

For designer dreams
Dover Street Market (*see p105*).

For a nostalgia kick
Beyond Retro (*see p113*);
Labour & Wait (*see p117*).

For funky furniture
Twentytwentyone (*see p118*).

For getting the punishment you deserve
RoB London (*see p111* **Buy sexual**).

get hungry or thirsty you can take the weight off your feet in the café or restaurant (both next to the swanky food hall on the fifth floor), or adjourn to the bar, which has a private vodka tasting room.

John Lewis

300 Oxford Street, W1A 1EX (7629 7711, www. johnlewis.co.uk). Bond Street or Oxford Circus tube. **Open** 9.30am-8pm Mon-Wed, Fri; 9.30am-9pm Thur; 9.30am-7pm Sat; noon-6pm Sun (browsing from 11.30am). **Credit** MC, V. **Map** p266 H6.

This is the place to come for all those homely essentials, from bedding to homewares, bathroom accessories to kitchen stuff and, in the vast basement, electrical goods. It will even satisfy all your haberdashery needs. Its famous 'never knowingly undersold' policy gives confidence, although it's at the manager's discretion whether this stretches as far as online prices. Fashion at John Lewis is becoming hipper these days too: it now carries labels such as Day Birger et Mikkelsen and BCBG Max Azria, along with a clutch of respectable classics such as Coast, Jaeger and Fenn Wright Mason. The food hall from Waitrose has speciality food galore, including a walk-in cheese room.

Market forces

For information about the **Columbia Road Flower Market**, *see p118.*

Borough Market

Southwark Street, SE1 1TL (7407 1002, www. boroughmarket.org.uk). London Bridge tube/rail. **Open** 11am-5pm Thur; noon-6pm Fri; 8am-6pm Sat. **Map** p271 P8.
A foodie paradise of organic and artisan goodies. Our favourite stalls are Northfield Farm for rare-breed meat, Furess for fish and game, and the wonderful loaves from Flour Power City Bakery. Don't miss the famous barbecued chorizo and rocket rolls from the Brindisa stand.

Broadway Market

Broadway Market, E8 4PH (www.broadway market.co.uk). London Fields rail or 236, 394 bus. **Open** 8.30am-4.30pm Sat.
Mecca for Hackney's young and trendy, Broadway Market has become a London weekend ritual. Crowds browse the vintage and designer threads and great food stalls – artisan cheeses, luscious cakes (try Claire Cakes) and hot snacks (Ghanian food from Spinach & Agushi is great).

Camden Markets

Camden Market *192-200 Camden High Street, junction with Buck Street, NW1 (7267 3417, www.camdenmarkets.org). Camden Town tube.* **Open** 9.30am-5.30pm daily.
Camden's sprawling collection of markets offers a smörgåsbord of street culture: goths and metalheads, tourists and celebs swarm around myriad vintage clothing shops and stalls touting cheap jeans, customised T-shirts, ethnic crafts, jewellery, bric-a-brac and food.

Portobello Road Market

Portobello Road, W10 & W11 (www.portobello road.co.uk). Ladbroke Grove or Notting Hill Gate tube. **Open** *General* 8am-6pm Mon-Wed, 9am-1pm Thur; 7am-7pm Fri, Sat. *Antiques* 4am-4pm Sat. **Map** p262 A6.

The antiques market starts at the Notting Hill Gate end (between Chepstow Villas and Elgin Crescent); further up are food stalls (between Elgin Crescent and Talbot Road); emerging designer and vintage clothes are found under the Westway flyover and along the walkway to Ladbroke Grove. Fridays are good for sourcing clothes made by young designers; Saturdays are manic but fun. Escape the crowds with a browse in Ledbury Road's boutiques.

Spitalfields Market

Commercial Street, between Lamb Street & Brushfield Street, E1 (7247 8556, www.visit spitalfields.com). Liverpool Street tube/rail. **Open** *General* 10am-4pm Mon-Fri; 9am-5pm Sun. *Antiques* 9am-4pm Thur. *Food* 10am-5pm Wed, Fri, Sun. *Fashion* 10am-4pm Fri. *Records & books* 10am-4pm 1st & 3rd Wed of mth. **Map** p271 R5.
Spitalfields Market comprises the refurbished 1887 covered market and the adjacent modern shopping precinct. Fuel up on global grub from the stallholders around the edge of Old Spitalfields Market and browse creations by up-and-coming designers, vintage clothes, crafts, jewellery and everything from sheepskins to colourful Brazilian flipflops. A record market is held twice a month. Note that Spitalfields is not open on Saturdays (and on Sundays it can be very, very busy).

Sunday (Up)Market

91 Brick Lane, The Old Truman Brewery (entrances on Brick Lane & Hanbury Street), E1 6QL (7770 6028, www.sundayupmarket. co.uk). Shoreditch high Street rail. **Open** 10am-5pm Sun. **Map** p271 S4.
Another good reason to head out east on Sundays – and easily combined with a trip to Brick Lane or Spitalfields markets – the buzzy (Up)Market has 140 stalls touting edgy clothing (by designers fresh from fashion college), vintage gear, gifts, crafts and jewellery. Food stalls offer everything from dainty cupcakes to Japanese noodles, tapas, dim sum and rich Ethiopian coffee. It's more relaxed then Spitalfields and prices are lower.

Other locations Brent Cross Shopping Centre, NW4 3FL (8202 6535); Wood Street, Kingston-upon-Thames, Surrey KT1 1TE (8547 3000); (Peter Jones) Sloane Square, SW1W 8EL (7730 3434).

Liberty

Regent Street, W1B 5AH (7734 1234, www.liberty. co.uk). Oxford Circus tube. **Open** 10am-9pm Mon-Sat; noon-6pm Sun. **Credit** AmEx, DC, MC, V. **Map** p266 J6.
Not really a traditional department store, Liberty is more an emporium of beautiful things. The original 1920s Tudor House on Great Marlborough Street is home to its famous Arts and Crafts prints, available as fabrics or on bags, scarves and notebooks. Fashion covers an eclectic mix of big names, such as Alexander McQueen, Gareth Pugh and PPQ. The new shoe bar on the second floor includes exclusives from Nicholas Kirkwood, Rupert Sanderson and Stella McCartney. Bags are a forte, with exclusives by the likes of Mulberry and Chloé. The home collections, in the basement and on the third floor, are laden with gorgeous oriental rugs and Arts and Crafts-style antiques. Strong points in Regent House on Regent Street include lingerie, menswear and cosmetics (Kiehl's, Miller Harris, Diptyque, Aveda, Laura Mercier and many more).

Selfridges

400 Oxford Street, W1A 1AB (0800 123 400, www.selfridges.com). Bond Street or Marble Arch tube. **Open** 9.30am-8pm Mon-Wed, Fri, Sat; 9.30am-9pm Thur; noon-6pm Sun (browsing from 11.30am). **Credit** AmEx, DC, MC, V. **Map** p266 G6.
Just as it's wise to judge a Chinese restaurant by how many Chinese customers there are, so gay men might be wise to judge a shop by how many like-minded spirits are browsing there. By this criteria, Selfridges is the real deal. Its busy floors have just about everything, from a satisfyingly wide range of underwear to fashion concessions including Paul Smith, John Smedley and Simon Miller Jeans. Sunglasses aficionados will love the selection on the ground floor. In the basement there's a huge electrical goods department, books and all manner of homewares – including stuff by Alessi, Le Creuset and Marco Pierre White for Russell Hobbs – plus a giant food hall. The café on the second floor serves afternoon tea.

Books

The flagship store of the **Waterstone's** chain (203-206 Piccadilly, 7851 2400, www.waterstones. co.uk) has a gay section. For long-running gay bookshop **Gay's the Word**, *see p102*.

Bookmarks

1 Bloomsbury Street, WC1B 3QE (7637 1848, www.bookmarks.uk.com). Tottenham Court Road tube. **Open** noon-7pm Mon; 10am-7pm Tue-Fri; 11am-7pm Sat. **Credit** MC, V. **Map** p267 K5.
London's premier socialist bookshop is refreshingly smart and airy, and stocks a good collection of all the usual suspects – Marx, Trotsky, Marx, Chomsky, Marx and so forth – along with some surprises, such as the carefully chosen film and music titles. It's also home to second-hand books, TUC publications and a considerable number of journals.

Cinema Store

4B Orion House, Upper St Martin's Lane, WC2H 9NY (7379 7838, www.thecinemastore.co.uk). Leicester Square tube. **Open** 10am-6.30pm Mon-Wed; 10am-7pm Thur-Sat; noon-6pm Sun. **Credit** AmEx, MC, V. **Map** p267 L6.
This friendly shop near Leicester Square covers all the silver-screen bases, selling DVDs and posters as well as books. There are specialist manuals on film craft (screenwriting, directing), plus plenty of screenplays and books on specific films, genres, actors and directors.

Daunt Books

83-84 Marylebone High Street, W1U 4QW (7224 2295, www.dauntbooks.com). Baker Street tube. **Open** 9am-7.30pm Mon-Sat; 11am-6pm Sun. **Credit** MC, V. **Map** p266 G5.
A visit to this lovely shop is worthwhile just to marvel at the elegant Edwardian interior, complete with oak balconies and stained glass. The famous travel section at the rear boasts a comprehensive range of specialist travel guides, literature, language books and maps on three separate levels, while the rest houses a commendable selection of general stock, including fine literary fiction, the latest quality hardbacks and political biographies.
Other locations 158-164 Fulham Road, SW10 9PR (7373 4997); 51 South End Road, NW3 2QB (7794 8206); 193 Haverstock Hill, NW3 4QW (7794 4006); 112-114 Holland Park Avenue, W11 4UA (7727 7022).

Forbidden Planet Megastore

179 Shaftesbury Avenue, WC2H 8JR (7420 3666, www.forbiddenplanet.com). Tottenham Court Road tube. **Open** 10am-7pm Mon-Wed; 10am-8pm Thur, Sat; 10am-7.30pm Fri; noon-6pm Sun. **Credit** AmEx, MC, V. **Map** p267 K6.
Heaven for *Dr Who, Star Trek,* Tolkien and Buffy fans, Forbidden Planet is the HMV of the science fiction and cult entertainment world. The colossal selection of books spans the entire spectrum, from sci-fi, fantasy and comic book art to ufology and political titles. All this plus manga and animé books, comics, graphic novels and a mass of action figures, toys and memorabilia.

Foyles

113-119 Charing Cross Road, WC2H 0EB (7437 5660, www.foyles.co.uk). Tottenham Court Road tube. **Open** 9.30am-9pm Mon-Sat; 11.30am-6pm Sun. **Credit** AmEx, DC, MC, V. **Map** p267 K6.
The single most impressive independent bookshop in London, Foyles built its reputation on the sheer volume and breadth of its stock: it has 56 specialist subjects spread out over five floors in this flagship store on Charing Cross Road. The gay section features highbrow fiction, mainstream fiction, gay classics, biographies and art books, not to mention queer theory and sex tips.
Other locations Southbank Centre, Riverside, SE1 8XX (7437 5660); St Pancras International, The Arcade, Pancras Road, NW1 2QP (7437 5660); Westfield London, Ariel Way, W12 7GE (3206 2656).

Freedom Press Bookshop

84B Whitechapel High Street (entrance on Angel Alley), E1 7QX (7247 9249, www.freedompress.org.uk).

Aldgate East tube. **Open** noon-6pm Mon-Sat. **No credit cards. Map** p271 S6.
This bare-boards shop may be physically tiny but, stock-wise, it's the largest anarchist bookshop in Britain, crammed with radical literature, CDs, posters and flyers.

French's Theatre Bookshop

52 Fitzroy Street, W1T 5JR (7387 9373, www.samuel french-london.co.uk). Warren Street tube. **Open** 9.30am-5.30pm Mon-Fri; 11am-5pm Sat. **Credit** AmEx, MC, V. **Map** p266 J4.
As well as a wide selection of scripts and books on the technical aspects of the theatre, you'll also find audio material, biographies, journals, postcards, videos and DVDs.

Gay's the Word

66 Marchmont Street, WC1N 1AB (7278 7654, www.gaystheword.co.uk). Russell Square tube. **Open** 10am-6.30pm Mon-Sat; 2-6pm Sun. **Credit** MC, V. **Map** p267 L4.
Britain's only dedicated gay and lesbian bookshop – established in 1979 – is still hanging on in the face of rising rents and online competition. Stock covers fiction, history and biography, as well as more specialist holdings in queer studies, sex and relationships, children and parenting. There are regular book-signings and author readings (think Adam Mars-Jones, Armistead Maupin, Neil Bartlett, Clare Summerskill), plus weekly lesbian and monthly trans discussion groups.

Gosh!

39 Great Russell Street, WC1B 3NZ (7636 1011, www.goshlondon.com). Tottenham Court Road tube. **Open** 10am-6pm Mon-Wed, Sat, Sun; 10am-7pm Thur, Fri. **Credit** MC, V. **Map** p267 L5.
This welcoming Bloomsbury shop is lined with geek porn – sorry, comic books – featuring all your favourite superheroes. Collectable back issues on the top shelves start at £7.50. Try the basement for Robert Crumb and underground stuff, plus manga books. There's also a great range of Dr Seuss, Charlie Brown, Tintin and Asterix books. Author signings are held regularly.

ICA Bookshop

The Mall, SW1Y 5AH (7766 1452, www.ica.org.uk). Charing Cross tube/rail. **Open** 2.30-9.30pm Wed-Fri; noon-10pm Sat; noon-8.30pm Sun. **Credit** AmEx, DC, MC, V. **Map** p269 K8.
The shop at the Institute of Contemporary Arts reflects the organisation's cutting-edge approach, with a carefully honed selection (many not available elsewhere) of critical titles, cult magazines, DVDs, CDs, cards and gifts.

London Review Bookshop

14 Bury Place, WC1A 2JL (7269 9030, www. lrbshop.co.uk). Holborn tube. **Open** 10am-6.30pm Mon-Sat; noon-6pm Sun. **Credit** AmEx, MC, V. **Map** p267 L5.
Half-owned by the eponymous literary-political journal, this small, smart bookshop opposite the British Museum features an extraordinary range, from Alan Bennett's latest offering and the most recent philosophical tome, to copies of the *New Yorker* and a good selection of cookery and gardening titles. Readings and talks by authors and

members of the intellectual elite take place here regularly, and the adjoining London Review Cake Shop is a delight.

Magma

117-119 Clerkenwell Road, EC1R 5BY (7242 9503, www.magmabooks.com). Chancery Lane tube or Farringdon tube/rail. **Open** 10am-7pm Mon-Sat. **Credit** AmEx, MC, V. **Map** p270 N4.
The first port of call for trendy tomes on art and design, from graphics, typography and illustration to graffiti art, advertising, architecture and photography. There are two branches in Covent Garden, one selling books, the other (at no.16) specialising in design-related products, from quirky T-shirts and arty DVDs to stylish kitchenware.
Other locations 8 Earlham Street, WC2H 9RY (7240 8498); 16 Earlham Street, WC2H 9LN (7240 7571).

Persephone Books

59 Lamb's Conduit Street, WC1N 3NB (7242 9292, www.persephonebooks.co.uk). Holborn or Russell Square tube. **Open** 10am-6pm Mon-Fri; noon-5pm Sat. **Credit** AmEx, MC, V. **Map** p267 M4.
Publisher/bookseller Persephone specialises in forgotten or obscure works by 20th-century (mainly women) writers. Most are novels and short stories, but there are also diaries and cookery manuals. Each book costs £10 (or £27 for three), regardless of size; all have the same dove-grey jacket but different, beautifully patterned endpapers. You can also pick up a free copy of the publisher's literary magazine, *Persephone Biannually.*
Other locations 109 Kensington Church Street, W8 7LN (7221 2201).

CDs & records

For mainstream music, try **HMV** (150 Oxford Street, 0843 221 0289, www.hmv.co.uk).

BM Soho

25 D'Arblay Street, W1F 8EJ (7437 0478, www. bm-soho.com). Oxford Circus tube. **Open** 11am-7pm Mon-Wed, Sat; 11am-8pm Thur, Fri; noon-6pm Sun. **Credit** AmEx, MC, V. **Map** p266 J6.
The focal point of the UK dance vinyl scene, Blackmarket attracts vinyl fanatics from all over the world. It stocks house, minimal and techno, plus new and pre-release drum 'n' bass, dubstep, bassline and UK garage.

Dress Circle

57-59 Monmouth Street, WC2H 9DG (7240 2227, www.dresscircle.co.uk). Covent Garden or Leicester Square tube. **Open** 10am-6.30pm Mon-Sat; noon-5pm. **Credit** AmEx, MC, V. **Map** p267 L6.
This OTT luvvy-magnet and temple to show tunes is still a West End hit after 30 years in business. As well as the staggering collection of CDs and DVDs, there are stage-related books, sheet music, posters and memorabilia.

Harold Moores Records

2 Great Marlborough Street, W1F 7HQ (7437 1576, www.hmrecords.co.uk). Oxford Circus tube. **Open** 10am-6.30pm Mon-Sat. **Credit** AmEx, MC, V. **Map** p266 J6.

This renowned classical music shop is famous for a few things: a marvellous used LP section in the basement, second-hand and deleted CDs, obscure and hard-to-get recordings and a range of historic performances by singers and instrumentalists. Staff know their stuff.

Phonica

51 Poland Street, W1F 7LZ (7025 6070, www.phonica records.co.uk). Oxford Circus or Tottenham Court Road tube. **Open** 11.30am-7.30pm Mon-Wed, Sat; 11.30am-8pm Thur, Fri; noon-6pm Sun. **Credit** MC, V. **Map** p266 J6.

A lively dance vinyl hubbub. Recline on the battered leather sofas and egg-shaped chairs that give the chic space a 1970s gangster feel, or finger the racks of edgy dance music. The cool kids head for the front rack of French electro labels. CDs are displayed on antique tables, boasting the latest alt-indie and electronic releases.

Rough Trade East

Dray Walk, Old Truman Brewery, 91 Brick Lane, E1 6QL (7392 7788, www.roughtrade.com). Liverpool Street tube. **Open** 8am-9pm Mon-Thur; 8am-8pm Fri, Sat; 11am-7pm Sun. **Credit** AmEx, MC, V. **Map** p271 S5.

This temple to indie music has bucked the trend in music retail by opening an emporium. The 5,000sq ft loft-style store, café and gig space offers aural beats and treats for Shoreditch's scenesters. Both the vinyl and CD collections are dizzying in their range, spanning punk, hardcore, American and British indie, reggae, dub, funk, soul, post punk and new wave, with a large row of dance 12-inches. **Other locations** Rough Trade West, 130 Talbot Road, W11 1JA (7229 8541).

Fashion

Concept stores

Anthropologie

158 Regent Street, W1B 5SW (7529 9800, www.anthropologie.co.uk). Piccadilly Circus tube. **Open** 10am-7pm Mon-Wed; 10am-8pm Thur; 10am-7pm Fri, Sat; noon-6pm Sun. **Credit** AmEx, MC, V. **Sells** W. **Map** p268 J6.

Anthropologie, the romantic elder sister to American darling Urban Outfitters, opened its first European store in autumn 2009. Stock is of a feminine bent, with delicate necklaces adorned with puppies and birds, soft knit cardies, craft-edged homewares and blouses with ruffles and bows. London designers such as Eley Kishimoto and Beyond the Valley have collaborated with the label to produce exclusive pieces for the store; but it's the vintage-inspired range of homewares that really inspires. **Other locations** 131-141 King's Road, SW3 4PW (7349 3110).

Aubin & Wills

64-66 Redchurch Street, E2 7DP (3487 0066, www. aubinandwills.com). Shoreditch High Street rail. **Open** 10am-7pm Mon-Sat; 11am-5pm Sun. Credit MC, V. **Sells** M, W. **Map** p271 S4.

Brit brand Aubin & Wills opened this ambitious and rambling boutique, 45-seat cinema and gallery in a hipster apartment block on Redchurch Street in June 2010. The 7,500 square foot space houses its men's, women's and homeware lines in a sort of grown-up collegiate style reminiscent of Aubin's teen labelmate Jack Wills. Upstairs is Brit artist and curator Stuart Semple's Aubin Gallery, and

Anthropologie

Click for protection

Buy high quality low cost condoms & lube online, delivered to your door...

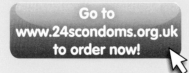

Go to
www.24scondoms.org.uk
to order now!

One 24s bag is
ONLY £7.99
including p+p.
Let us know if you can get it for less!

In each 24s bag you get 24 condoms and a 250ml bottle of lube. A choice of 3 different types of condom is available and you can decide how many of each type you'd like.

24s bags are sent to you in discrete protective packaging. (Deliveries to UK residents only).

West London Gay Men's Project sells condoms and lube at close to cost price via www.24scondoms.org.uk. Any profits made are put back into providing free 24s bags to men who have sex with men in targeted settings.

down in the basement is the Aubin Cinema – a collaboration with neighbour Shoreditch House. The area's rough, hipster edge could be under threat from Aubin's arsenal of blankets, biscuit tins, candles and stylish clothes. **Other locations** throughout the city.

Darkroom

52 Lamb's Conduit Street, WC1N 3LL (7831 7244, www.darkroomlondon.com). Holborn tube. **Open** 11am-7pm Mon-Fri; 11am-7pm Sat. **Credit** AmEx, MC, V. **Map** p267 M5.
Get your mind out of the gutter: Darkroom is not a sleaze pit, but a new concept store. The shop is quite literally dark (the walls and lampshades black), creating a blank canvas for the carefully chosen selection of unisex fashion, accessories and interiors items on sale. Designer items include Borba Margo bags, DMK glassware and Solomia ceramics. The space doubles up as a gallery, with displays intermingling with a range of sculptural jewellery by Florian, Scott Wilson and Maria Francesca Pepe. Each piece begs the question – do I wear it or hang it on the wall?

Designer & boutiques

If your fashion sense and budget are on a par with Posh and Becks, get out your platinum card and head for Bond Street. On New Bond Street, you'll find **Burberry** (nos.21-23, 7839 5222, www.burberry.com), **Calvin Klein** (no.65, 7495 2916, www.calvinklein.com) and **Polo Ralph Lauren** (no.1, 7535 4600, www.polo.com); on Old Bond Street, there's a **Dolce & Gabbana** (nos.6-8, 7659 9000, www.dolcegabbana.it) and a **Prada** (nos.16-18, 7647 5000, www.prada.com). In Chelsea, too, the streets are paved with bling. There's **Gucci** (18 Sloane Street, 7235 6707, www.gucci.com), **Giorgio Armani** (no.37, 7235 6232, www.giorgioarmani.com), **Joseph** (74 Sloane Avenue, 7591 0808, www.joseph.co.uk) and plenty more labels to satisfy designer cravings.

We've noted whether shops sell men's (M), women's (W) or children's (C) clothing.

Alexander McQueen

4-5 Old Bond Street, W1S 4PD (7355 0088, www.alexandermcqueen.com). Green Park tube. **Open** 10am-6pm Mon-Wed, Fri, Sat; 10am-7pm Thur. **Credit** AmEx, DC, MC, V. **Sells** M, W. **Map** p268 J7.
A cross between a spaceship and a gallery, the Alexander McQueen flagship store shows off the late designer's wares sensationally. The ground floor is dedicated to womenswear and accessories; the lower ground floor features wickedly sharp men's tailoring, dapper footwear and manbags. The diffusion line, McQ, is more affordable. Despite McQueen's death, the business is continuing.

Browns

23-27 South Molton Street, W1K 5RD (7514 0038, www.brownsfashion.com). Bond Street tube. **Open** 10am-6.30pm Mon-Wed, Fri, Sat; 10am-7pm Thur. **Credit** AmEx, MC, V. **Sells** M, W. **Map** p266 H6.

Browns was created in 1970 by Joan Burstein, who is credited with discovering such world-class talents as John Galliano, Alexander McQueen, Hussein Chalayan and more. Here, you'll find quality labels such as Chloé, Balenciaga, Dior Homme, Helmut Lang and Issey Miyake. There are rising stars too, such as Christopher Kane, Marios Schwab and Todd Lynn. Not cheap, but a pleasingly elegant experience.

Dover Street Market

17-18 Dover Street, W1S 4LT (7518 0680, www. doverstreetmarket.com). Green Park tube. **Open** 11am-6.30pm Mon-Wed; 11am-7pm Thur-Sat. **Credit** AmEx, MC, V. **Sells** M, W. **Map** p268 H7.
Comme des Garçons designer Rei Kawakubo's groundbreaking six-storey space combines the edgy energy of London's indoor markets – concrete floors, Portaloo dressing rooms – with rarefied labels. All of the Comme collections are here, alongside exclusive lines such as Lanvin, Givenchy and Azzedine Alaia. There's also a Hussein Chalayan area with exclusive pieces, and an area devoted to designer du jour Henry Holland.

Library

268 Brompton Road, SW3 2AS (7589 6569, www. thelibrary1994.com). South Kensington tube. **Open** 10am-6.30pm Mon, Tue, Thur-Sat; 10am-7pm Wed; 12.30-5.30pm Sun. **Credit** AmEx, MC, V. **Sells** M, W. **Map** p265 E10.
This is much more than a clothing emporium that sells books. It's a razor-sharp, one-stop shop for lovers of exquisite purist brands. Buyer Peter Sidell has one of the best eyes in the business for spotting and nurturing hot talent. Stock includes Scaglione knitwear, Martin Margiela, Comme des Garçons and Junya Watanabe, YMC, Dirk Bikkembergs and Maharishi, alongside scents by Creed.

Louis Vuitton Maison

17-20 New Bond Street, W1S 2UE (7399 3856, www. louisvuitton.com). Bond Street tube. **Open** 10am-7pm Mon-Sat; noon-6pm Sun. **Credit** AmEx, DC, MC, V. **Sells** M, W. **Map** p268 H7.
The most luxurious Louis Vuitton store in the world. Designed by New York City's Peter Marino, the Maison is similar to flagships in New York, Paris and Hong Kong, but stocked with the most rare and exclusive of Louis Vuitton finds. Complete with a Men's Club Area, huge changing rooms and a 'Librairie', which sells contemporary British art books, it's a new branded universe. Dog bags priced at £1,000 are just the beginning.

Marc by Marc Jacobs

56 South Audley Street, W1K 2RR (7408 7050, www.marcjacobs.com). Bond Street or Green Park tube. **Open** 11am-7pm Mon-Sat; noon-6pm Sun. **Credit** AmEx, MC, V. **Sells** M, W, C. **Map** p268 G7.
Marc Jacobs' first London shop features rails of fun clothing, rows of Jacobs's signature Wellington boots and a cul-de-sac filled with the perfumes and sunglasses. Head downstairs to 'The Vault' (the building used to be a bank) forshoes and bags. And keep 'em peeled for nude photos of the shop's staff on the walls. They're very well hung... **Other locations** (Marc Jacobs) 24-25 Mount Street, W1K 2RR (7399 1690).

Dover Street Market. *See p105.*

Margaret Howell

34 Wigmore Street, W1U 2RS (7009 9009, www.margarethowell.co.uk). Bond Street tube. **Open** 10am-6pm Mon-Wed, Fri, Sat; 10am-7pm Thur; noon-5pm Sun. **Credit** AmEx, DC, MC, V. **Sells** M, W. **Map** p266 H6.
Margaret Howell's label has become highly desirable as her crisp English aesthetic has reached the height of cool. Her deftly tailored trousers, neatly cropped jackets and crisp white shirts are wardrobe staples for London's fashion insiders, while her timeless classics have a soft, lived-in appeal that improves with age. She also produces a denim line with Japanese label Edwin Jeans, and MHL, a range of sturdy, workwear-inspired clothing.
Other locations 7-8 Duke Street, Richmond, TW9 1HP (8948 5005); 111 Fulham Road, SW3 6RL (7591 2255).

Matches

85 Ledbury Road, W11 2AJ (7221 2334, www.matches.co.uk). Notting Hill Gate tube. **Open** 10am-6pm Mon-Sat; noon-6pm Sun. **Credit** AmEx, MC, V. **Sells** M, W. **Map** p262 A6.
Get tipsy while you shop: this cool designer boutique has a bar to assist that retail therapy. But be careful not to over-do it, or you could splurge on designer names like Bottega Veneta, Burberry, Stella McCartney and Marc Jacobs, and end up with a bad credit-card hangover. Across the road, at Matches Spy, you'll find Acne Jeans, Heidi Klein and Theory.
Other locations 34 High Street, SW19 5BY (8947 8707); 13 Hill Street, Richmond, Surrey TW9 1FX (8332 9733); 60-64 Ledbury Road, W11 2AJ (7221 0255); 87 Marylebone High Street, W1U 4QU, 7487 5400).

Ozwald Boateng

30 Savile Row, W1S 3PQ (7440 5242, www.ozwaldboateng.co.uk). Green Park tube. **Open** 10am-6pm Mon-Wed, Fri, Sat; 10am-7pm Thur. **Credit** AmEx, MC, V. **Sells** M. **Map** p268 J7.
Suits from the store that dresses Anthony Hopkins, Ray Winstone, Lennox Lewis and more. Though prices range from £1,195 for ready-to-wear, or from £3,000 for made-to-measure, the shop is more relaxed than its neighbours.

Paul Smith

40-44 Floral Street, WC2E 9DG (7379 7133, www.paulsmith.co.uk). Covent Garden or Leicester Square tube. **Open** 10.30am-6.30pm Mon-Wed; 10.30am-7pm Thur, Fri; 10am-7pm Sat; 12.30-5.30pm Sun. **Credit** AmEx, DC, MC, V. **Sells** M, W, C. **Map** p267 L6.
The row of Paul Smith shops in Floral Street have entertaining window displays, and similarly enjoyable clothes. At Paul Smith itself, go downstairs for the formal suits, which fit Sir Paul's mantra of 'classic with a twist'. There's also a seemingly unending range of accessories from cufflinks to rings, plus a strong selection of knitwear and shirts. The place is dotted with Sir Paul's collection of art, giving insight into the vision behind his quirky classic tailoring. The sale shop features bargains on casualwear.
Other locations throughout the city.

Casual high street

Muji

6-17 Tottenham Court Road, W1T 9DP (7436 1779, www.muji.co.uk). Tottenham Court Road tube. **Open** 10.30am-8pm Mon; 10am-8pm Tue-Sat; noon-6pm Sun. **Credit** AmEx, DC, MC, V. **Sells** M, W. **Map** p267 K5.
Long favoured as a great place for cheap, understated items, Muji is also worth visiting for its clothing, especially the T-shirts, vests and other basics. Upstairs has homewares.
Other locations throughout the city.

Topman

36-38 Great Castle Street, W1W 8LG (0845 121 4519, www.topman.co.uk). Oxford Circus tube. **Open** 9am-10pm Mon-Fri; 9am-9pm Sat; 11.30am-6pm Sun. **Credit** AmEx, DC, MC, V. **Sells** M. **Map** p266 J6.
From high street also-rans to indispensable fashion outlet, Topman has undergone a resurgence in the past few years (as has sister shop, Topshop, on the same site). A pioneer of 'speed fashion' (inspectors observe buying trends from week to week and alter stock accordingly), the chain has its finger on the pulse of what trendy blokes want to wear. Plenty to choose from at very affordable prices.
Other locations throughout the city.

Uniqlo

311 Oxford Street, W1C 2HP (7290 7701, www.uniqlo.co.uk). Oxford Circus tube. **Open** 10am-8pm Mon-Wed; 10am-9pm Thur-Sat; noon-6pm Sun. **Credit** AmEx, DC, MC, V. **Sells** M, W. **Map** p266 H6.
Uniqlo has recently attempted to rebrand, with celeb envoys such as Chloë Sevigny, a Terry Richardson ad campaign and the opening of two new stores on Oxford Street. The jury's still out as to whether Uniqlo is more than simply a Japanese Gap or not. Highlights are the cut-price pure cashmere and the simple, well-cut selvedge jeans, plus graphic T-shirts and merino wool jumpers.
Other locations throughout the city.

Zara

118 Regent Street, W1B 5SE (7534 9500, www.zara.com). Piccadilly Circus tube. **Open** 10am-8pm Mon-Sat; noon-6pm Sun. **Credit** AmEx, DC, MC, V. **Sells** M, W. **Map** p268 J7.
Can't face Gap, but want something relaxed, affordable and comfortable? Try the Spanish retailer, spreading across Europe as fast as Starbucks. With more of an emphasis on quieter colours and understated looks, the shop has a wide range of delightful clothes, with surprises around every corner. There are plenty of branches, but this one has a large men's section in the basement.
Other locations throughout the city.

Emerging designers

Albam

23 Beak Street, W1F 9RS (3157 7000, www.albamclothing.com). Oxford Circus tube. **Open** noon-7pm Mon-Sat; noon-6pm Sun. **Credit** AmEx, MC, V. **Sells** M. **Map** p268 J6.
Alastair Rae and James Shaw's excellent menswear line, Albam, has jumped off the internet and into its first store on Beak Street. The label's refined yet rather manly aesthetic has won it a loyal fanbase, dressing well-heeled gents, fashion editors and regular guys who appreciate no-nonsense style. With a focus on classic, high-quality design with a subtle retro edge (Steve McQueen has been cited as inspiration), the store is the label's showcase: airy and minimal,

but unselfconsciously warm and friendly. Bestsellers include the Alpine jacket (£315) and Classic T-shirt (£25). **Other locations** 111a Commercial Street, E1 6BG (7247 6254); 286 Upper Street, N1 2TZ (7288 0835).

B Store

24A Savile Row, W1S 3PR (7734 6846, www.bstore london.com). Oxford Circus tube. **Open** 10.30am-6.30pm Mon-Fri; 10am-6pm Sat. **Credit** AmEx, MC, V. **Sells** M, W. **Map** p268 J7.
Possibly London's trendiest clothes shop – where else can you pick up clothes designed by this year's Saint Martins graduates? Choose from emerging and more established designers, including Damir Doma, Opening Ceremony and Peter Jensen. The look is avant-garde – oversized bow ties and caped coats from Mjolk, for example. The emphasis is on men's fashion: the b clothing menswear line is all about high-waisted pleated trousers, worn with bomber jackets and gingham shirts. The edgy shoe collection has styles for men and women, with prices around £160.

Bermondsey 167

167 Bermondsey Street, SE1 3UW (7407 3137, www.bermondsey167.com). London Bridge tube/rail. **Open** 11am-7pm Tue-Sat; noon-4pm Sun. **Credit** AmEx, MC, V. **Sells** M, W.
Former Burberry designer Michael McGrath has poured his heart into Bermondsey 167, a slick and intriguing boutique. The shop's own-label (M2cG) shirts (made in Northern Ireland), fine merino wool sweaters (made in Italy), ties and scarves, and swimwear (from £50) are the main draw, but the unique, commission-only furniture, home accessories, jewellery and coconut-leaf lights are intriguing too; all are sourced from artists and artisans around the world, and particularly in South America. There's also a great range of trendy perspex Toy watches, beloved of celebs and fashionistas.

Folk

49 Lamb's Conduit Street, WC1N 3NG (7404 6458, www.folkclothing.com). Holborn tube. **Open** 11am-7pm Mon-Sat; noon-5pm Sun. **Credit** AmEx, MC, V. **Map** p267 M4
Folk is the label of choice for guys who once dressed like skaters, then progressed to labels such as Silas and are now after more quality, more respectability and less branding. The silhouette and the fabrics are comfortable but hip and slightly dishevelled – in a tasteful rather than grungey way (think stripes, quality knits and casual jackets in bold colours). Sister brand Shofolk offers stylish but comfortable shoes for men and women that have a hand-crafted feel (moccasin styles dominate the collection). For women, this is the place to come for stylish labels Humanoid and Sessùn and a well-edited selection of jeans. **Other location** 11 Dray Walk, E1 6QL (7375 2844).

No-one

1 Kingsland Road, E2 8AA (7613 5314, www.no-one. co.uk). Old Street tube/rail. **Open** 11am-7pm Mon-Sat; noon-6pm Sun. **Credit** AmEx, DC, MC, V. **Sells** M, W.
On the style-setting axis between Old Street and Kingsland Road, this edgy store is a favourite of Shoreditch locals and non-conformist style icons, including Roisin Murphy and Björk. Buyer Teresa Letchford is brilliant at spotting cool new labels, and was the first to champion Swedish denim

Marc by Marc Jacobs. *See p105.*

label Cheap Monday in Britain, which it sells alongside denim by Lee. The stock ranges from the latest Bi La Li womenswear, YMC men's clothing, feminine frocks by Mine (from £70) and kooky clothing by Henrik Vibskov. Shoes are catered for by Opening Ceremony and Bernhard Wilhelm (for women only). Counters brim over with vintage sunglasses, knitted accessories by local label Made With Hands, badges and wittily branded toiletries.

Present

140 Shoreditch High Street, E1 6JE (7033 0500). Old Street tube/rail or Shoreditch High Street rail. **Open** 10.30am-7pm Mon-Fri; 11am-6.30pm Sat; 11am-5pm Sun. **Credit** AmEx, MC, V. **Sells** M.
Store owners Eddie Prendergast and Steve Davies are founders of men's mega-brand Duffer of St George, but don't hold that against them. Present's bright white, clinical interior houses labels from streetwear Billionaire Boys Club and Japanese Haversack to Raf by Raf Simons and the odd polka-dotted pair of socks, as well as Eddie and Steve's collection of knits and T-shirts.

Fetish

The **London Fetish Fair** – held on the second Sunday of every month at Parker McMillan (47 Chiswell Street, EC1Y 4SB) – is brimming with specialist stalls; for further details, visit www.londonfetishfair.co.uk.

Although the shop run by **Babes n Horny** (www.babes-n-horny.com) is now closed, you can still order their artisan-made dildos and the like (in polka dots and other fanciful designs) online or visit their east London studio by appointment. For exclusively gay fetish shops, *see p110* **Buy sexual**.

Fettered Pleasures

90 Holloway Road, N7 8JG (7619 9333, www.fettered pleasures.com). Holloway Road tube. **Open** 11am-7pm Mon-Sat. **Credit** MC, V.
This is hardcore. To enter Fettered Pleasures, you have to be buzzed in. Once inside, you're surrounded by the stuff of nightmares – cleansing enemas, catheters, dungeon devices and gynaecological examining tables. Puppy cages and fisting stools are conveniently sold in flat-pack form: handy for hiding under a bed when the parents come to visit. Chain and rope are sold by the metre. Surplus army gear includes East German tank suits and respiratory masks. We liked the remote control electric shock device. In this light, the love swing seems positively romantic.

Honour

86 Lower Marsh, SE1 7AB (7401 8219, www. honour.co.uk). Waterloo tube/rail. **Open** 10.30am-7pm Mon-Fri; 11.30am-5pm Sat. **Credit** AmEx, MC, V. **Map** p269 M9.
Despite its small size, Honour is thorough. It stocks a strong selection of leather, rubber and PVC clothing. For men, standout PVC items include the boiler suit, trench coat and cycling shorts; in rubber, look out for the skin-tight bermuda shorts. For the ladies, uniforms are a forte, including naughty housemaids, policewomen and nurses. It's also TV/TS friendly, thanks to wigs, hosiery and stilettos. The 'bondage attic' upstairs houses sex toys, DVDs, whips, restraints and more.

House of Harlot

90 Holloway Road, N7 8JG (7700 1441, www.house-of-harlot.com). Highbury & Islington tube/rail. **Open** 10am-6pm Mon-Fri; noon-6pm Sat. **Credit** MC, V.
House of Harlot specialises in haute couture fetishwear, designing classy rubber and leather gear for the likes of Christian Dior and Louis Vuitton. Chances are you've seen its stylish creations in pop promos for Madonna and Marilyn Manson. Clothes range from clubby T-shirts to bespoke ballgowns, men's rubber double-breasted suits and nurses' uniforms. The bumless dresses are pure Leigh Bowery. Clothing can be cut to measure. It's all pricey, but then, this is the sort of stuff you'd see in *Vogue*, not *Hustler*.

Showgirls

64 Holloway Road, N7 8JL (7697 9072, www. showgirlslatexboutique.com). Highbury & Islington tube/rail. **Open** 10.30am-7pm Mon-Sat. **Credit** AmEx, MC, V.
Despite its location on the grotty Holloway Road, Showgirls is known by some as the 'Harvey Nicks of fetish shops'. With its stylish collection of couture fetishwear,

it's definitely more high fashion than down and dirty. Resident designer Atsuko Kudo is famed for her chic rubber dresses and lingerie. Among the more unusual items are avant-garde Leigh Bowery-esque hoods. To complete your ensemble, Showgirls offers a small but striking collection of high heels.

Transformation

52 Eversholt Street, NW1 1DA (7388 0627, www. transformation.co.uk). Euston or King's Cross tube/rail. **Open** 9am-8pm Mon-Sat. **Credit** AmEx, MC, V. **Map** p267 K3.
This shop claims to 'transform men into beautiful women'. Products include 'Born Again' silicone breasts (they require no adhesive), along with fake vaginas, a cream to make your bottom more feminine, and an oestrogen lotion that makes your breasts grow.

Lingerie & underwear

Agent Provocateur

6 Broadwick Street, W1V 1FH (7439 0229, www.agent provocateur.com). Oxford Circus or Tottenham Court Road tube. **Open** 11am-7pm Mon-Wed, Fri, Sat; 11am-8pm Thur; noon-5pm Sun. **Credit** AmEx, DC, MC, V. **Sells** W. **Map** p266 J6.
Since opening this Soho shop nearly 15 years ago, AP has become an international success story, with branches as far afield as New York, Moscow and Dubai. It's the first port of call for the decadent and fashion-forward lingerie fan. The distinctive retro-glamour of the shops' pink and black decor is extended to the staff, who are kitted out in cleavage-enhancing pink nurses' uniforms with lacy black

Albam. *See p107.*

Buy sexual

The following shops flaunt their homosexuality – with an emphasis on the sex – with gay abandon. For a review of the women's sex shop **Sh!**, see p115 **Girls aroused**.

Clone Zone

64 Old Compton Street, W1D 4UQ (7287 1619, www.clonezone.co.uk). Leicester Square tube. **Open** 11am-9pm Mon-Sat; noon-8pm Sun. **Credit** AmEx, MC, V. **Map** p267 K6.
London's original gay superstore. Upstairs you've got your Calvin Klein undies, saucy greeting cards and Glad to be Gay CDs; downstairs things get, ahem, harder amid the skin mags and proctology videos. Fashion includes black leather pants and rubber jeans, sold alongside dildos moulded from the tackle of porn stars such as Aiden Shaw.
Other locations 266 Old Brompton Road, SW5 9HR (7373 0598).

Expectations

75 Great Eastern Street, EC2A 3RY (7739 0292, www.expectations.co.uk). Old Street tube/rail. **Open** 11am-7pm Mon-Fri; 11am-8pm Sat; noon-5pm Sun. **Credit** AmEx, MC, V. **Map** p271 R4.
Clunking down the metal steps to subterranean Expectations, you feel like you're entering a dungeon – how appropriate. Merchandise includes repro gas masks, creepy rubber hoods and City of New York police gear. It caters to just about every fetish going, from Adidas shorts to rubber wading suits. For those who are insecure about their size, rubber pants with a prosthetic penis are sold. Sex toys include dildos so big they hurt to look at.

Freak Fetish

Railway Arch 47B, South Lambeth Road (07956 089748, www.fetishfreak.co.uk). Vauxhall tube/rail. **Open** 1-6.30pm Thur; 1.30-6.30pm, 10pm-2.30am Fri, Sat; 2-6.30pm, 10pm-1.30am Sun. **Credit** MC, V.
Many gay Londoners have suffered the indignity of being turned away from the Hoist nightclub owing to lack of proper leather gear. Now help is at hand. This fetish shop is right next door and just happens to be open late on weekend evenings. So if you are barred by the Hoist's

bras peeping out provocatively (natch). Bras, from 32A to 38F, start at around £60. Corsets, hosiery, nightwear, pasties and perfumes are stocked.
Other locations 305 Westbourne Grove, W11 2QA (7243 1292); 5 Royal Exchange, EC3V 3LL (7623 0229); 16 Pont Street, SW1X 9EN (7235 0229).

Coco de Mer

23 Monmouth Street, WC2H 9DD (7836 8882, www.coco-de-mer.co.uk). Covent Garden tube. **Open** 11am-7pm Mon-Wed, Fri, Sat; 11am-8pm Thur; noon-6pm Sun. **Credit** AmEx, MC, V. **Sells** W. **Map** p267 L6.
Attention, glamorous lesbians. With its sumptuous crimson interior, objet d'art dildos and peep-show changing rooms that allow your partner to 'spy' on you, Coco de Mer is one decadent lingerie shop. Stock has an ethical, artisanled twist; you can be sure your dildo is made from WWF-endorsed wood (owner Sam Roddick clearly inherited her mother Anita's green credentials) or that part of the price includes a charity donation (Bondage for Freedom donates to Burmese charities). It's kinky too, boasting an array of tools, ticklers and restraints: the jewelled nipple clips, jade cock rings and rose-decorated ceramic dildos are intriguing. The flamboyant, feminine own-label lingerie is supplemented by designs by Afterwear, Louise Feuillère, Fifi Chachnil, La Perla, Paul Seville and Ilya Fleet. The female-oriented book range now includes an exclusive rare vintage selection, where you can find 1920s pornography.

Myla

77 Lonsdale Road, W11 2DF (7221 9222, www.myla.com). Notting Hill Gate tube. **Open** 10am-6pm Mon-Sat; noon-5pm Sun. **Credit** AmEx, MC, V. **Sells** W. **Map** p262 A6.
Best known for its saucy lace and freshwater pearl G-string – thanks to a classic Samantha *Sex and the City* scene – Myla is both cute and sexy. Seasonal collections include fashion-forward colours and designs, but the classic options, such as the signature silk and lace couture range (bras £119, knickers £59) are always in stock. For the truly style-obsessed, there's also a range of designer sex toys. Concessions in Harrods, Selfridges and House of Fraser.
Other locations 4 Burlington Gardens, W1S 3ER (7491 8548); 74 Duke of York Square, SW3 4LY (7730 0700); 166 Walton Street, SW3 2LJ (7581 6880); 4A Cabot Place West, E14 4QS (7715 5374).

Tallulah Lingerie

65 Cross Street, N1 2BB (7704 0066, www.tallulah-lingerie.co.uk). Angel tube or Highbury & Islington tube/rail. **Open** 11am-6pm Mon-Fri; 10.30am-6.30pm Sat; 12.30-5pm Sun. **Credit** MC, V. **Sells** W.
Vivid crimson walls, antique furniture and Diana Dors-style feather negligées on display create a boudoir backdrop for labels such as La Perla, Fleur T, Lejaby and Moontide, as well as handmade lingerie by up-and-coming designers. Pretty frilly knickers start at £10, while bras range from £20 to £200.

Shoes

Footwear fans on all budgets are well catered for in London, with excellent choices around town (in the following list, websites are given where doorman, pop in and pick up a pair of leather chaps (£139) or open-crotch shorts (£36) and, poof!, now you may go to the ball.

Prowler

5-7 Brewer Street, W1R 3FN (7734 4031, www. prowlerstores.co.uk). Piccadilly Circus tube. **Open** 11am-10pm Mon-Fri; 10am-10pm Sat; noon-8pm Sun. **Credit** AmEx, MC, V. **Map** p269 K6.
Once billed as a gay department store, Prowler offers a mix of fashion and porn. The front room is full of trendy club gear and tight T-shirts with witty queenie slogans ('I Can't Even Think Straight'), plus Calvin Klein underwear. The books section carries arty (read: nude) coffee table books, gay diva bios and travel guides, plus fiction. Nothing too highbrow, though: this is, after all, a shop that also sells dildos, wank mags and DVDs featuring the men of eastern Europe.

Regulation

17A St Alban's Place, N1 0NX (7226 0665, www.regulation-london.co.uk). Angel tube.

Open 10.30am-6.30pm Mon-Sat; noon-5pm Sun. **Credit** AmEx, MC, V.
Situated down the proverbial back alley, Regulation lives up to its location. It does a brisk trade in rubber gear for clubbers: kilts for gladiators, say, or Frankie-style peaked caps. For the young at heart, there's a range of adult nappies, bibs and dummies. If you think that strait-jackets are boring, try a human-sized vacuum-pack bag – sure to keep your loved one fresh. If all this sound too fancy, there are old-fashioned wooden spoons.

RoB London

24-25 Wells Street, W1T 3PH (3073 1010, www.rob.eu). Oxford Circus tube. **Open** 11am-7pm Mon-Sat; noon-5pm Sun. **Credit** AmEx, MC, V. **Map** p266 J5.
Expanded not too long ago to include a dungeon basement. Where better to showcase its grim products: a sling ergonomically designed to aid fisting, say, or executioners' hoods. Just when you thought the worst was over, you come across a range of catheters, stainless steel ball stretchers and oversized anal probes.

the store has more than one branch). For high-end designer creations, try **Oliver Sweeney** (5 Conduit Street, 7491 9126, www.oliversweeney. com), **Tod's** (35-36 Sloane Street, 7235 1321, www.tods.com), **Georgina Goodman** (12-14 Shepherd Street, 7499 8599, www.georgina goodman.com) and **Rupert Sanderson** (19 Bruton Place, 7491 2220, www.rupert sanderson.com).

There are more affordable yet funky options courtesy of **Camper** (8-11 Royal Arcade, 28 Old Bond Street, 7629 2722, www.camper.com), **Kurt Geiger** (65 South Molton Street, 7758 8020, www.kurtgeiger.com), **Kate Kuba** (22-24 Duke of York Square, King's Road, 7259 0011, www. katekuba.co.uk), and, out in Hackney, **Black Truffle** (4 Broadway Market, 7923 9450, www.blacktruffle.com).

Shoe central is Covent Garden: on Neal Street alone you'll find the **Natural Shoe Store** (no.13, 7836 5254, www.thenaturalshoestore. com), **Birkenstock** (no.70, 7240 2783, www.birkenstock.co.uk) and **Office** (no.57, 7379 1896, www.office.co.uk). Trainerphiles will also be in seventh heaven around here, with **Offspring** (no.60, 7497 2463, www.offspring. co.uk), **RbK** (No.51, 7240 8689) and **Size?** (no.37A, 7836 1404, www.size.co.uk), as well

as the **Adidas Originals Store** (9 Earlham Street, 7379 4042, www.adidas.com/uk).

For trad men's shoes, head to Mayfair's **Russell & Bromley** (24-25 New Bond Street, 7629 6903, www.russellandbromley.co.uk) or **Poste** (10 South Molton Street, 7499 8002). For more unusual shoes, try **House of Harlot** and **Showgirls** (for both, *see p109*).

Street & urban casual

American Classics

20 Endell Street, WC2H 9BD (7831 1210, www. americanclassicslondon.com). Covent Garden, Holborn or Tottenham Court Road tube. **Open** 11am-6.30pm Mon-Sat; 12.30-5.30pm Sun. **Credit** MC, V. **Sells** M. **Map** p267 L6.
A nostalgia fest of retro Americana. Look out for vintage Lee and Levi's jeans, Redwing Boots and Buzz Rickson UCLA sweatshirts, plus checked shirts galore.

Carhartt

15-17 Earlham Street, WC2H 9LL (7836 1551, www.carhartt-europe.com). Covent Garden or Leicester Square tube. **Open** 11am-7pm Mon-Sat; noon-6pm Sun. **Credit** MC, V. **Sells** M, W. **Map** p267 L6.
This workwear label manages to remain a fashion essential season after season. T-shirts – especially with the label emblazoned all over it – cotton shirts and hoodies are the most popular items in the chic, concrete-minimalist store,

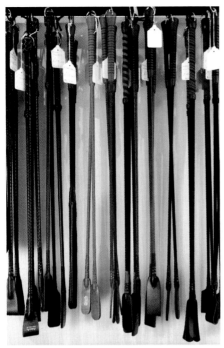

with keenly priced and durable workwear, including belts, trousers and hats, also drawing the eye. For discounted gear, visit the factory store in Hackney.
Other locations 56 Neal Street, WC2H 9LL (7836 5659); 18 Ellingfort Road, off Mare Street, E8 3PA (8986 8875).

Goodhood

41 Coronet Street, N1 6HD (7729 3600, www. goodhoodstore.com). Old Street tube/rail. **Open** 11am-7pm Mon-Fri; 11am-6.30pm Sat. **Credit** AmEx, DC, MC, V. **Sells** M, W.
Stock for this boutique-like store is selected by streetwear obsessives/owners Kyle and Jo, with items weighted towards Japanese independent labels. We like the Gregory Japan rucksacks from Tokyo; these and the Black Dollars Tees are store exclusives. T-shirts from PAM, knits from Australia's Rittenhouse and pieces from Copenhagen's Wood Wood are also popular. A cabinet full of reasonably priced watches and jewellery makes this a great place for pressies for hard-to-please hipster partners.

Interstate

17 Endell Street, WC2H 9BJ (7836 0421). Covent Garden tube. **Open** 11am-6.45pm Mon-Fri; 11am-6.30pm Sat; noon-6pm Sun. **Credit** MC, V. **Sells** M. **Map** p267 L6.
Laid-back and unpretentious compared to some of its Covent Garden competitors, Interstate is a staple for denim, polos and overcoats. There are lots of labels to choose from, with a Stateside slant – such as Carhartt, G-Star, Dickies, Schott, Ringspun, and rucksacks from Eastpak and Manhattan Portage.

Three Threads

47-49 Charlotte Road, EC2A 3QT (7749 0503, www.thethreethreads.com). Old Street tube/rail. **Open** 11am-7pm Mon-Sat; noon-5pm Sun. **Credit** AmEx, MC, V. **Sells** M, W.
Despite its trendy East London address, the Three Threads manages to be both laid-back and friendly. Decent background tunes, sofas, a fridge full of beer and chatty staff create a loungey vibe. Shoes are a forte, from Loakes, an unpretentious British brogue, to Clarks Originals and the largest range of Pointers in town. There's a good choice of T-shirts too, with many of the labels – Tonite, Suburban Bliss or Alakazam (£25-£35) – run by mates of the store. Ultra-practical raincoats from Sweden's Fjall Raven (£100), shirts from Denmark's Won Hundred (£70-£90) and classic Americana-inspired Maiden Noire are further draws.

Suits

If you need to smarten up your act, Mayfair's Savile Row is the place to go: try **Kilgour** (no.8, 7734 6905, www.kilgour.eu) or **Richard James** (no.29, 7434 0605, www.richardjames. co.uk). Over in the East End, **Timothy Everest** (32 Elder Street, E1 6BT, 7377 5770, www.timothy everest.co.uk) is another favourite. Many other shops listed under 'Fashion' (*see p103*) also sell suits, including **Ozwald Boateng** (*see p107*). For shirts, elegant Jermyn Street is the right

Fettered Pleasures. See p109.

address, particularly **Thomas Pink** (no.85, 7930 6364, www.thomaspink.com), where the themed cufflinks make classy and original gifts.

Vintage

Beyond Retro

110-112 Cheshire Street, E2 6EJ (7729 9001, www. beyondretro.com). Liverpool Street tube/rail. **Open** 10am-7pm daily. **Credit** MC, V. **Sells** M, W. **Map** p271 S4.
This East End institution has a loyal following of fancy dress-seekers, hard-up students and offbeat musicians. The vast warehouse is crammed with 10,000 items, helpfully arranged by colour. It's all here: tartan, leopard print, flower power and lace. We saw great Polynesian-print maxi dresses (£16), frou-frou prom dresses for £95 and vintage kimonos (£45). In a raised section you'll find 1930s to '60s dresses (from £50), including old wedding dresses. For men, there are sharp '70s suits, trilbies, waistcoats and a vast array of T-shirts and denim. Not everything is in great nick, but it's priced accordingly.

The Girl Can't Help It

Alfie's Antique Market, 13-25 Church Street, NW8 8DT (7724 8984, www.thegirlcanthelpit.com). Edgware Road tube/Marylebone tube/rail. **Open** 10am-6pm Tue-Sat. **Credit** AmEx, MC, V. **Sells** M, W. **Map** p263 E4.
Named after the Jayne Mansfield film, the Girl Can't Help It is blonde bombshell territory. A cream lace dress worn by Monroe herself is on display – and for sale if you have £5,000 and a 23-in waist. The look is classic Hollywood, personified by co-owner Sparkle Moore, an exuberant New Yorker with a flowing platinum mane and scarlet lips. Always in stock are classic 1940s suits from Lili Ann of California (from £375) and 1950s circle skirts (£100-£350), decorated with everything from kitsch kittens to Mexican-style patterns. There's a range of glam accessories from cute velvet opera hats to straw bags covered in plastic cherries. Suave menswear includes Hawaiian shirts (from £50), gabardine jackets, slick 1940s and '50s suits, pin-up ties and camp accessories, such as tiki-themed bar glasses.

Food

Carluccio's

Garrick Street, WC2E 9BH (7836 0990, www. carluccios.com). Covent Garden tube. **Open** 8am-11.30pm Mon-Fri; 9am-11.30pm Sat; 9am-10.30pm Sun. **Credit** AmEx, MC, V. **Map** p269 L7.
Small, but packed with choice Italian delicacies, Carluccio's is worth visiting when planning a posh dinner party. Wild mushrooms are a highlight, though extremely expensive. There's also own-range pasta, olive oils and ice-cream, plus wine, bread and a delectable deli counter.
Other locations throughout the city.

Fortnum & Mason

181 Piccadilly, W1A 1ER (7734 8040, www.fortnum andmason.co.uk). Green Park or Piccadilly Circus tube. **Open** 10am-8pm Mon-Sat; noon-6pm Sun. **Credit** AmEx, MC, V. **Map** p268 J7.
Dismissed by many Londoners as a tourist trap, Fortnum's food halls are nonetheless a gourmand's fantasy. You could spend hours wandering the aisles of imported antipasti oils

Consume

Coco de Mer. *See p110.*

Beyond Retro.
See p113.

and sauces, biscuits and confectionery; there are also high-quality traiteur dishes and meat and cheese counters. Traditional choices – caviar, smoked salmon, preserves, fine wines and spirits – and lavish hampers are as covetable as ever, as are F&M's famous teas and coffees.

Paul A Young Fine Chocolates

33 Camden Passage, N1 8EA (7424 5750, www. payoung.net). Angel tube. **Open** 11am-6pm Wed, Thur, Sat; 11am-7pm Fri; noon-5pm Sun. **Credit** AmEx, MC, V.
A gorgeous boutique with almost everything – chocolates, cakes, ice-cream – made in the downstairs kitchen and finished in front of customers. Young is a respected pâtissier as well as chocolatier and has an astute chef's palate for flavour-combining. In summer, try the Pimm's cocktail truffles featuring cucumber, strawberry and mint, and white chocolate blondies made with raspberries and blueberries.
Other locations 20 Royal Exchange, EC3V 3LP (7929 7007).

Health & beauty

Cosmetics

For men's spas, *see p144.*

Aveda Lifestyle Institute

174 High Holborn, WC1V 7AA (7759 7355, www. aveda.com). Holborn or Tottenham Court Road tube. **Open** 9am-7pm Mon-Wed; 8am-8pm Thur, Fri; 9am-6.30pm Sat; 11am-5pm Sun. **Credit** AmEx, MC, V. **Map** p267 M5.
The London flagship of the international chain of environmentally friendly beauty products. Bestsellers for men include the shampoo, body bar, grooming clay and aftershave balm. Also look out for 'comforting tea' and Peppymint breath freshener.

Kiehl's

29 Monmouth Street, WC2H 9DD (7240 2411, www. kiehls.com). Covent Garden tube. **Open** 10am-7pm Mon-Sat; noon-5pm Sun. **Credit** AmEx, DC, MC, V. **Map** p267 L6.
Beautiful skin, hair and body products have been sold by New York-based Kiehl's since 1851. Indeed, the discreet and understated packaging makes you feel you've stepped back in time. But the products are anything but outdated, with the All-Sport Everyday shampoo and Hair Thickening Lotion among the most noteworthy. The shop is generous with its free samples, so you can try products before you buy. Which you certainly will.
Other locations 20 Northcote Road, SW11 1NX (7350 2997); 186A King's Road, SW3 5XP (7751 5950); Units 14-15 Royal Exchange, EC3V 3LP (7283 6661).

Space NK

8 Broadwick Street, W1F 8HW (7287 2667, www. spacenk.com). Piccadilly Circus or Tottenham Court Road tube. **Open** 10am-7pm Mon-Fri; 11am-5.30pm Sat. **Credit** AmEx, MC, V. **Map** p266 J6.
A magnet for anyone who's serious about skincare and cosmetics, Space NK has some two dozen shops in

Girls aroused

Sex shop Sh! was conceived in 1992, when the founders visited Soho and discovered that the only type of women made welcome in the sex shops were the inflatable sort. Soon after, the country's first and only store exclusively dedicated to women's sexual pleasure – **Sh! Women's Erotic Emporium** – was born.
Since those early days in the Hoxton hinterland, word of mouth has meant that Sh! is the destination sex shop for everyone from novices to dominatrices. Men are welcome if escorted by a woman, although they're usually a bit nervous. Perhaps it's the leather-clad mistress trying out the six-foot training whip in the street outside.
The stock is amazingly thorough: from clit pleezers to cuffs, satin sheets to strap-ons. And while you can't exactly try out the products there and then, staff will give you the benefit of their sexpertise (sex tips include going down on your partner with a mint in your mouth). With own-brand dildos in over 30 shapes and sizes and the occasional sexology conference, Sh! has really come into its own in recent years. Makes a refreshing change from Ann Summers.

Sh!

57 Hoxton Square, N1 6PB (7613 5458, www.sh-womenstore.com). Old Street tube/ rail. **Open** noon-8pm daily. **Credit** MC, V.

London, and more in the offing. The men's shop in Soho stocks top-end brands such as Kiehl's, the Art of Shaving, MenScience and Acqua di Parma, as well as Space NK own men's line Blue (don't worry, ladies, it sells your favourite stuff too, in the adjoining women's wing). The luxurious treatments on offer include massages, facials, waxing and tinting.
Other locations throughout the city.

Hairdressers

Chains **Toni & Guy** (www.toniandguy.com) and **Vidal Sassoon** (www.sassoon.com) have branches all around town. For spas and male grooming salons where you can also get a haircut, *see p144.*

Brooks & Brooks

13-17 Sicilian Avenue, WC1A 2QH (7405 8111, www.brooksandbrooks.co.uk). Holborn tube. **Open** 9am-7pm Mon, Tue; 9am-8pm Wed-Fri; 9.30am-5.30pm Sat. **Credit** MC, V. **Map** p267 L5.
Jamie and Sally Brooks and their team of stylists have won London Hairdresser of the Year three times in recent years. It's not hard to see why; staff are consummate professionals, specialising in creative, easy-to-manage hairstyles. Prices start at £35 for a ladies' cut and blow-dry.

B:zar

*68 Berwick Street, W1F 8SY (7494 0426, www.
b-zar.com). Oxford Circus or Tottenham Court Road
tube.* **Open** 10am-7pm Mon-Sat. **No credit cards.**
Map p266 J6.
A tiny Soho salon run by an affable team of young
Japanese hairdressers. The vibe is understated cool, but
the attention to detail is impressive, from the hot towels to
the complimentary shiatsu head-and-shoulder massage.
Cuts are £38 for women, £29.50 for men.

Fish

*30 D'Arblay Street, W1F 8ER (7494 2398, www.fish
soho.co.uk). Leicester Square or Piccadilly Circus tube.*
Open 10am-7pm Mon-Wed, Fri; 10am-8pm Thur;
10am-5pm Sat. **Credit** MC, V. **Map** p266 J6.
Equal parts hip hairdresser and chatty barber shop, this
Soho salon – formerly a fishmonger – has been going
strong for 23 years. Cuts are relatively cheap – £41 for a
girl's cut and blow-dry and £34 for gents.

Geo F Trumper

*9 Curzon Street, W1J 5HQ (7499 1850, www.trumpers.
com). Green Park tube.* **Open** 9am-5.30pm Mon-Fri;
9am-1pm Sat. **Credit** AmEx, DC, MC, V. **Map** p268 H8.
An institution since 1875, Trumper is still considered the
finest traditional barber shop in London. The oak-panelled
walls covered with hunting prints, and distinguished old
men reclining on green leather chairs create the vibe of a
gentlemen's club, while red velvet curtains separate each
booth. Morrissey has been known to drop in for a haircut,
and the GQ-reading crowd appreciate the wet shaves.
Other locations 1 Duke of York Street, SW1Y 6JP
(7734 1370).

Murdock

*340 Old Street, EC1V 9DS (7729 2288, www.murdock
london.com). Old Street tube/rail.* **Open** 10am-7pm
Mon-Wed, Fri; 10am-8pm Thur; 10am-5pm Sat.
Credit AmEx, MC, V.
Slap-bang on one of the East End's main arteries,
Murdock is a barber for the Hoxton generation. Expect
decent-value haircuts and luxurious wet shaves by staff
who take their time and know their stuff. There's a selection of hard-to-get colognes and shaving products too,
from the likes of Santa Maria Novella and DR Harris.
Other locations 5B Stafford Street, W1S 4RR
(7495 7310).

Pall Mall Barbers

*27 Whitcomb Street, WC2H 7EP (7930 7787, www.
pallmallbarbers.com). Piccadilly Circus tube.* **Open**
9am-7pm Mon-Fri. **No credit cards. Map** p269 K7.
There's been a barber on this spot since 1896, and much of
the original character – oak panels, old sinks – remains.
Prices are very reasonable: £20.50 for a wash and cut,
£30.50 for a wet shave. A great find, and a hit with everyone from men's magazine editors to local office folk.

Pimps & Pinups

*14 Lamb Street, E1 6EA (7426 2121, www.pimpsand
pinups.com). Liverpool Street tube/rail.* **Open** 10am-
8pm Mon-Fri; 10am-6pm Sat, Sun. **Credit** MC, V.
Map p271 R5.

Pimps & Pinups

Against a cool backdrop of black brick walls, and with theatrical dressing room mirrors, Pimps & Pinups offers 'classic hairdressing with the latest styles': it combines the
decadent styles of the post-war era with the cutting-edge
trends of the Shoreditch set. A simple cut starts at £34 for
men (£40 for women), while the speciality retro hair-up service costs £40 per hour. Amy Winehouse, eat your heart out!

We Are Cuts

*7 Royalty Mews, W1D 3AS (7287 3337, www.
wearecuts.com). Leicester Square or Tottenham Court
Road tube.* **Open** 11-7pm Mon-Fri; 10am-6pm Sat.
No credit cards. Map p267 K6.
This legendary Soho salon, smothered with stickers, flyers, and locals who like to hang out on its beaten-up leather
sofa, is best for guys who need a quick, skilful restyle without the frills (you bend over forwards to wash your hair).
A gents' wet cut with scissors is £32.50, or £28.50 if you
let your stylist loose with clippers, too.

Home

Furniture & home accessories

Aram

*110 Drury Lane, WC2B 5SG (7557 7557, www.aram.
co.uk). Covent Garden or Holborn tube.* **Open** 10am-
6pm Mon-Wed, Fri, Sat; 10am-7pm Thur. **Credit**
AmEx, MC, V. **Map** p267 L6.

Zeev Aram's five-storey shop, in a converted fruit and veg warehouse, houses a mix of furniture and accessories by new names as well as established designers (Ron Arad, Van der Rohe). Expect to find beds, benches, desks, dining tables and chairs, plus lighting, accessories and storage solutions. None of it is cheap, but most of it is desirable.

Aria

Barnsbury Hall, Barnsbury Street, N1 1PN (7704 1999, www.ariashop.co.uk). Angel tube/Highbury & Islington tube/rail. **Open** 10am-6.30pm Mon-Sat; noon-6pm Sun. **Credit** AmEx, DC, MC, V.
This supremely trendy store has moved into an atmospheric space in Islington's Barnsbury Hall. It stocks a greatest-hits medley of fashionable homewares and furniture by big designer names (Alessi, Zack, Ella Doran, Philippe Starck), as well as more unusual items such as Fornasetti's black and white hand-painted wall plates (£99) and the new Bourgie table light by Ferruccio Laviani (£199). This mix, plus accessories, toiletries and a good in-store café, makes Aria a pleasure to visit. A great place for original gift ideas.

Conran Shop

Michelin House, 81 Fulham Road, SW3 6RD (7589 7401, www.conran.com). South Kensington tube. **Open** 10am-6pm Mon, Tue, Fri; 10am-7pm Wed, Thur; 10am-6.30pm Sat; noon-6pm Sun. **Credit** AmEx, MC, V. **Map** p265 E10.
Slick, cosmopolitan and seductive, the Conran Shop is a haven of yuppie porn. Much stock is exclusive and Conran mixes them in among classics to create inspirational room settings on the ground floor. The basement is home to a vast array of lighting, tableware and accessories and a great range of inventive kids' things.
Other locations 55 Marylebone High Street, W1U 5HS (7723 2223).

Habitat

196-199 Tottenham Court Road, W1T 7PJ (08444 991122, www.habitat.co.uk). Goodge Street tube. **Open** 10am-7pm Mon-Wed, Fri; 10am-8pm Thur; 9.30am-7pm Sat; noon-6pm Sun. **Credit** AmEx, MC, V. **Map** p267 K5.
Founded by Terence Conran, and owned by IKEA, Habitat has 'gay' written all over it. Its large ground floor and cavernous basement are filled with style essentials, from rugs to garden chairs, glasses and cutlery to picture frames. But be warned: it's hard to leave without buying something you hadn't even been looking for. An essential destination. **Other locations** throughout the city.

Heal's

196 Tottenham Court Road, W1T 7LQ (7636 1666, www.heals.co.uk). Goodge Street tube. **Open** 10am-6pm Mon-Wed; 10am-8pm Thur; 10am-6.30pm Fri; 9.30am-6.30pm Sat; noon-6pm Sun. **Credit** AmEx, DC, MC, V. **Map** p267 K5.
More upmarket and less frivolous than its neighbour Habitat, Heal's (founded 1810) is crammed with covetable goods. Highlights are the massive sofa and carpet sections, garden furniture and the achingly elegant gifts on the ground floor, including kitchenwares, cookery books, bathroom accessories and top-notch toiletries. The Christmas offerings are always a delight.

Other locations 234 King's Road, SW3 5UA (7349 8411); 49-51 Eden Street, KT1 1BW (8614 5900).

Labour & Wait

18 Cheshire Street, E2 6EH (7729 6253, www.labourandwait.co.uk). Shoreditch High Street rail. **Open** 11am-5pm Wed, Fri; 1-5pm Sat; 10am-5pm Sun. **Credit** AmEx, MC, V. **Map** p271 S4.
If the whole *Darling Buds of May* nostalgic English countryside aesthetic turns you on, this place is a must. Products for both home and garden are of high quality; sturdy garden implements and retro watering cans can be found alongside pastel-coloured enamel jugs and shaving sets. They no longer stock the original Monty duffle coats: these days, vintage French work jackets and Filson hunting jackets are more on trend.

Mar Mar Co

16 Cheshire Street, E2 6EH (7729 1494, www.marmarco.com). Shoreditch High Street rail. **Open** by appt Mon-Wed; 11.30am-5.30pm Thur, Fri; noon-6pm Sat; 11am-5pm Sun. **Credit** MC, V. **Map** p271 S4.
Mar Mar Co seems to have cleverly squeezed the whole world into its tiny space on oh-so-trendy Cheshire Street. This is due entirely to the roving eyes of its owners, Danish Marianne Lumholdt and Brit Mark Bedford, who scour France, Scandanavia, the UK, Holland and the US for contemporary homewares and gifts from emerging new designers. Everything here is functional yet contemporary.

Nicole Farhi Home

17 Clifford Street, W1X 3RQ (7494 9051, www.nicolefarhi.com). Green Park or Piccadilly Circus tube. **Open** 10am-6pm Mon-Wed, Fri, Sat; 10am-7pm Thur. **Credit** AmEx, DC, MC, V. **Map** p268 J7.
Prime hunting ground for celebrities and magazine stylists, this chic store sells gorgeous textiles, ceramics, glassware and furniture. One-off antiques, gathered from Nicole's travels around the world, are also here, as well as raw fabrics in natural hues.

Nina Campbell

9 Walton Street, SW3 2JD (7225 1011, www.ninacampbell.com). Knightsbridge tube. **Open** 10am-6pm Mon-Sat. **Credit** AmEx, MC, V. **Map** p265 F10.
Attention, glamorous gays. Renowned interior designer Nina Campbell sells a sumptuous collection of fabrics, wallpapers, tableware and accessories from this chichi boutique. Among the eclectic selection are paisley silk cushions, hand-painted glass tulip bowls and multi-coloured fish wallpaper. Antiques can also be found.

Reel Poster Gallery

72 Westbourne Grove, W2 5SH (7727 4488, www.reelposter.com). Bayswater or Queensway tube. **Open** 11am-7pm Mon-Fri; noon-6pm Sat. **Credit** AmEx, DC, MC, V. **Map** p262 B6.
Film poster connoisseurs will warm to this airy gallery space. Reel Poster has a great display of original vintage posters, as well as an extensive collection on file. There's an emphasis on classics, European and art films, with attention paid to the designer of the posters. Expect to pay £1,500 for a 1960s Brando poster (*The Wild One)* and around £95 for more recent movies (*The Dark Knight*).

Columbia Road Flower Market

SCP

135-139 Curtain Road, EC2A 3BX (7739 1869, www.scp.co.uk). Old Street tube/rail. **Open** 9.30am-6pm Mon-Sat; 11am-5pm Sun. **Credit** MC, V.

SCP showcases the best in contemporary furniture, lighting and homewares. Sheridan Coakley sources globally and stocks a clutch of respected designers, including Robin Day, Terence Woodgate, Matthew Hilton, James Irvine and Michael Marriott. Furniture and storage solutions are all bold lines and slick minimalism, exemplified by Kay + Stemmer's Foxtrot coffee table in oak (£595) or wenge stain (£615) and Jasper Morrison's Plan modular system of cabinets from Cappellini. Accessories take in everything from the highly decorative to the fun and quirky.

Other locations 87-93 Westbourne Grove, W2 4UL (7229 3612).

Twentytwentyone

274 Upper Street, N1 2UA (7288 1996, www.twenty twentyone.com). Angel tube/Highbury & Islington tube/rail. **Open** 10am-6pm Mon-Sat; 11am-5pm Sun. **Credit** AmEx, MC, V.

Twentytwentyone was recently voted the capital's best furniture and homewares shop by *Time Out*, owing to its mix of vintage originals, reissued classics and contemporary designs. Big-name brands such as Arper, Artek, Cappellini, DePadova, Flos, Swedese and Vitra are stocked, along with young British designers. Eco-issues figure large: Artek's bent bamboo Bambu range looks as good as the vintage pieces stocked. Stock is divided between two locations; the River Street showroom houses most of the larger items, while the Upper Street outpost is good for accessories and gifts – pick up a Yoan David fortune chicken for £15.

Other locations 18C River Street, EC1R 1XN (7837 1900).

Vintage Magazine Store

39-43 Brewer Street, W1F 9UD (7439 8525, www. vinmag.com). Piccadilly Circus tube. **Open** 10am-8pm Mon-Thur; 10am-10pm Fri, Sat; noon-8pm Sun. **Credit** MC, V. **Map** p269 K6.

This is pop culture heaven: think 1980s back issues of *Smash Hits*, vintage editions of *NME* and the *Face*, and '60s issues of *Vogue* and *Playboy*. Although it's most famous for its old magazines, all manner of memorabilia can be found, from rock T-shirts to Che Guevara fridge magnets. As well as original movie posters, there's a huge range of reproductions, most costing £6-£11.

Flowers & plants

Columbia Road Flower Market

Columbia Road, E2 (7364 1717). Hoxton or Shoreditch High Street rail. **Open** 8am-2pm Sun. **Credit** varies.

Oh, come on, you can skip one Saturday night of clubbing so that you get to Columbia Road not feeling like hell on Sunday morning. Actually, if you look around, you'll see plenty of people who've turned up direct from an after-hours club. Bedding plants, cut flowers and pots of every description are available – and at good prices, especially towards the end of trading. The shops lining the street are well worth a gander, offering tableware, clothes, shoes, perfumes and unusual gifts as well as lots of gardening products. Pop into Jones Dairy Café for a coffee and bagel.

Arts & Entertainment

Festivals & Events   **120**

Comedy & Cabaret   **121**

Dance   **122**

Film   **124**
  Porn again   125

Galleries   **127**

Theatre   **129**

Music   **133**

Sport & Fitness   **136**
  Playing away   139
  The swimming pool library   140
  Gonna make you sweat   145

Festivals & Events

Absolutely fabulous.

London Lesbian & Gay Film Festival

BFI Southbank, South Bank, SE1 8XT (7928 3535, www.llgff.org.uk). Embankment tube or Waterloo tube/rail. **Date** late Mar. **Map** p269 M8.
The LLGFF's annual round-up of the world's best lesbian and gay film and video attracts some pretty big names.

London Marathon

Greenwich Park to the Mall, via the Isle of Dogs, Victoria Embankment & St James's Park (7902 0200, www.virginlondonmarathon.com). Blackheath & Maze Hill rail or Charing Cross tube/rail. **Date** Apr.
One of the biggest metropolitan marathons in the world: it attracts 35,000 starters. Arrive early: the front-runners reach the 13-mile mark near the Tower of London by 10am.

Playtex Moonwalk

Start & finish at Hyde Park (01483 741 430, www.walkthewalk.org). **Date** May.
A night walk to raise money for breast cancer research. The 15,000-odd participants wear specially decorated bras (men included) to power-walk the 26.2-mile route.

Chelsea Flower Show

Grounds of Royal Hospital, Royal Hospital Road, SW3 4SR (0845 260 5000, www.rhs.org.uk). Sloane Square tube. **Date** May. **Map** p265 F12.
The hysteria that builds up around this annual flower show has to be seen to be believed. Fight your way past the rich old ladies to get ideas for your own humble plot.

Meltdown

South Bank Centre, Belvedere Road, SE1 8XX (0844 875 0073, www.rfh.org.uk). Embankment tube or Waterloo tube/rail. **Date** June. **Map** p269 M8.
Each year, a different guest curator (Patti Smith, David Bowie, Morrissey) takes over this festival of contemporary culture. Often a good place to see cutting-edge queer artists.

Pride London

Parade from Oxford Street to Victoria Embankment (0844 844 2439, www.pridelondon.org). Hyde Park Corner or Marble Arch tube, or Charing Cross tube/rail. **Date** *Festival* last 2 wks June. *Parade & rally* early July.
Around a million people attended Pride in 2010: the largest number in the event's history. The parade is followed by a rally in Trafalgar Square, and a party in Soho Square. Dance stages, market stalls and a food festival take over the streets, and Leicester Square hosts cabaret. Festival Fortnight – the two weeks before Pride – offers a mix of cultural performances.

Pride London

Walk for Life

Starts at Hyde Park (7539 3895, www.walkforlife.co.uk). Hyde Park Corner or Marble Arch tube. **Date** June.
This 10km sponsored walk, organised by Crusaid, raises huge amounts for HIV and AIDS research.

UK Black Pride

Regent's College, Regent's Park, NW1 (www.ukblack pride.org.uk). Regent's Park tube. **Date** Aug.
A queer alternative to the Notting Hill Carnival.

Notting Hill Carnival

Notting Hill, W10, W11 (www.thenottinghillcarnival. com). Ladbroke Grove, Notting Hill Gate or Westbourne Park tube. **Date** Aug Bank Holiday (Sun, Mon).
Europe's biggest street party attracts hundreds of thousands of revellers, who celebrate Afro-Caribbean culture by drinking beer and listening to reggae at full volume.

UK Ladyboy Competition

Mango Tree restaurant, 46 Grosvenor Place, SW1X 7EQ (7823 1888, www.mangotree.org.uk). Hyde Park Corner tube. **Date** Sept. **Map** p268 G9.
The UK Ladyboy Competition gets bigger with every year. Categories include evening wear and bathing suit.

Arts & Entertainment

Comedy & Cabaret

We're funny that way.

Comedy

Black Cap

171 Camden High Street, NW1 7JY (7485 0538, www.theblackcap.com). Camden Town tube. **Shows** midnight Thur-Sat; 10.30pm Sun. **Admission** £2-£5. **Credit** AmEx, MC, V.
This ancient gay pub has long been the home of 'traditional comedy drag mime', ie lip-synching and dick jokes.

Comedy Camp

Barcode, 3-4 Archer Street, W1D 7AP (7483 2960, 08444 771 000 tickets, www.comedycamp.co.uk). Leicester Square tube. **Shows** 8.30pm Tue. **Admission** £10 (includes membership); £8 members. **Credit** (bar) MC, V. **Map** p269 K7.
A 'straight-friendly' gay comedy club. Some top-notch acts appear here, including Graham Norton. Book in advance.

Leicester Square Theatre

6 Leicester Place, WC2H 7BX (7534 1740, 0844 847 2475 tickets, www.leicestersquaretheatre.com). Leicester Square tube. **Shows** varies. **Admission** £10-£20. **Credit** MC, V. **Map** p269 K7.
This cosy venue opened in 2008 with a Joan Rivers play. And the first annual Big Joke festival (September) featured the queen of trash talk, Roseanne Barr.

99 Club Oxford Circus

Wheatsheaf, 25 Rathbone Place, W1T 1DG (07760 488 119, www.the99comedyclub.com). Tottenham Court Road tube. **Shows** *Winter* 7.30pm, 9.30pm Sat. *Summer* 9.30pm Sat. **Admission** £10. **No credit cards. Map** p267 K5.
Paul Foot hosts this night of comedy for 'the gay, the gayish and the beautiful of Soho'.

Soho Theatre

21 Dean Street, W1D 3NE (7819 9539, www.soho theatre.com). Leicester Square tube. **Admission** £8-£20. **Credit** MC, V. **Map** p267 K6.
Past performers have included cabaret terrorists Kiki & Herb, 'air hostess from hell' Pam Ann and the gloriously offensive American Scott Capurro.

Two Brewers

114 Clapham High Street, SW4 7UJ (7836 7395, www.the2brewers.com). Clapham Common tube. **Open** 5pm-2am Mon-Thur, Sun; 5pm-4am Fri, Sat. **Shows** varies. **Admission** free-£6. **Credit** AmEx, MC, V.
Old-school drag: the ubiquitous Sandra, the hilarious Dave Lynn and Kandi Kane, a truly creative American artist.

RVT

Cabaret

Bistrotheque

23-27 Wadeson Street, E2 9DR (8983 7900, www. bistrotheque.com). Bethnal Green tube/rail/Cambridge Heath rail/55 bus. **Open** 6pm-midnight Mon-Fri; 11am-midnight Sat, Sun. **Shows** varies. **Admission** £7-£12. **Credit** AmEx, MC, V.
Regulars include the Lip Sinkers, who turn miming pop into a twisted art, and drag terrorist Jonny Woo.

Madame JoJo's

8-10 Brewer Street, W1F 0SE (7734 3040, www. madamejojos.com). Piccadilly Circus tube. **Shows** from 7pm Sat; 7-9.30pm Sun. **Admission** £8-£20 (£40 seated Sat). **Credit** MC, V. **Map** p269 K6.
Vegas glitz reigns supreme on Saturday at Kitsch Cabaret, featuring music, dinner, dancing and comedy. On Sunday, the line-up veers towards burlesque and vaudeville.

RVT (Royal Vauxhall Tavern)

372 Kennington Lane, SE11 5HY (7820 1222, www. rvt.org.uk). Vauxhall tube/rail. **Open** 7pm-midnight Mon, Wed, Thur; 6pm-midnight Tue; 7pm-2am Fri; 9pm-2am Sat; 2pm-midnight Sun. **Shows** see website for details. **Admission** £5-£7. **Credit** MC, V. **Map** p25.
There's usually some strange comedy or cabaret on stage in this old boozer on any given weekday evening. Regulars pile in on Sunday afternoons to see the genius that is the Dame Edna Experience. *See also p44* **An urban legend.**

Dance

All the right moves.

The biggest festival on London's dance calendar is the world-class **Dance Umbrella** (Sept-Nov, www.danceumbrella.co.uk), offering troupes and performers from home and abroad, working in a huge variety of styles.

Major venues

Barbican Centre

Silk Street, EC2Y 8DS (7638 8891, www.barbican. org.uk). Barbican tube or Moorgate tube/rail. **Box office** 9am-8pm Mon-sat; 11am-8pm Sun. **Tickets** £10-£35. **Credit** AmEx, MC, V. **Map** p270 P5.
The Barbican International Theatre Event (BITE) has turned this arts centre into a major player on the dance scene. You'll find an eclectic mix of dance, drama, opera and circus, with the boundaries between genres often blurred. The Barbican frequently co-commissions works in collaboration with both continental and American theatre and dance companies.

Place

17 Duke's Road, WC1H 9PY (7121 1100, www.the place.org.uk). Euston tube/rail. **Box office** noon-6pm Mon-Sat; noon-8pm on performance days.**Tickets** £5-£15. **Credit** MC, V. **Map** p267 K3.
This internationally recognised dance venue provides top-notch professional training as well as classes in all genres for all levels. The 300-seat theatre presents innovative contemporary dance from around the globe. Note that seating is first come, first served.

Royal Opera House

Covent Garden, WC2E 9DD (7304 4000, www.roh. org.uk). Covent Garden tube. **Box office** 10am-8pm Mon-Sat. **Tickets** £6-£210. **Credit** AmEx, MC, V. **Map** p269 L6.
This magnificent theatre's main stage is home to the Royal Ballet, where you can see superstars of the calibre of Carlos Acosta, Alina Cojocaru and Sylvie Guillem. The Linbury Studio Theatre and Clore Studio Upstairs present edgier fare. The Vilar Floral Hall, one of London's most handsome public spaces, holds afternoon tea dances, usually twice a month. A 90-minute backstage tour is available most days.

Sadler's Wells

Rosebery Avenue, EC1R 4TN (0844 412 4300, www.sadlerswells.com). Angel tube. **Box office** *In person* 9am-8.30pm Mon-Sat. *By phone* 24hrs daily. **Tickets** £8-£58. **Credit** AmEx, MC, V.

One of the premier dance venues in the world, with the most exciting line-up in town. Expect top companies, from Pina Bausch and William Forsythe, to notable British troupes such as Birmingham Royal Ballet and Rambert Dance Company. A major new initiative has brought several important British dancemakers into the theatre. Tickets are often much cheaper than any West End theatre, although the most popular companies sell out fast. Dance is best viewed from the stalls; even restricted view at this level is preferable to sitting in the upper circle. A specially chartered bus departs after each performance to Farringdon, Victoria and Waterloo stations.

Siobhan Davies Dance Studios

85 St George's Road, SE1 6ER (7091 9650, www.siobhandavies.com). Elephant & Castle tube. **Box office** 9am-9pm Mon-Fri; 10am-2pm Sat, Sun. **Tickets** £3-£18. **Credit** AmEx, MC, V.
Opened in 2006, this award-winning studio was designed in consultation with dancers, ensuring that the building meets their needs. Davies, who founded her own company in 1988, often explores different spaces beyond this beautiful theatre, so be sure to check with the venue for her performances before setting out.

Southbank Centre

Belvedere Road, SE1 8XX (0871 663 2501 information, 0844 847 9910 tickets, www.southbank centre.co.uk).Embankment tube or Waterloo tube/rail. **Box office** *In person* 10am-8pm daily. *By phone* 9am-8pm daily. **Tickets** £7-£75. **Credit** AmEx, MC, V. **Map** p269 M8.
The refurbishment of the Royal Festival Hall has led to a revival in the dance programme at the Southbank Centre. The Centre hosts the inaugural Dance Union, a celebration of European dance that draws works from some 23 countries; Dance Umbrella also visits each year. Outside festival seasons, companies such as CandoCo often take over the mammoth RFH, the medium-sized Queen Elizabeth Hall, the intimate Purcell Room or the riverside terrace outside.

Other venues

Circus Space

Coronet Street, N1 6HD (7613 4141, www.thecircus space.co.uk). Old Street tube/rail. **Open** 9am-10pm Mon-Thur; 9am-9pm Fri; 10am-6pm Sat, Sun. **Classes** phone for details. **Credit** MC, V.
Courses and workshops in all types of circus arts, such as trapeze, juggling and live-wire walking. The impressive space (a former power station) also hosts cabaret-style performances (Medium Rare).

Royal Opera House

Jacksons Lane is a community theatre and platform for young choreographers. The intimate space has a warm and friendly vibe and offers a variety of dance classes, including the lesbian-oriented Waltzing with Hilda (*see p58*).

Laban Centre

Creekside, Deptford, SE8 3DZ (8691 8600 information, 8469 9500 tickets, www.laban.org). Cutty Sark or Deptford Bridge DLR, or Greenwich DLR/rail. **Open** 10am-6pm Mon-Sat. **Tickets** £6-15; £3-£8 reductions. **Credit** MC, V.
The home of Transitions Dance Company, this beautiful independent conservatoire for dance training is renowned as the home of Rudolf Laban, founder and creator of a unique and enduring discipline for movement. The stunning premises, including the 300-seat auditorium, were designed by Herzog & de Meuron (the architects of Tate Modern). The centre also runs undergraduate and post-grad courses. International companies also appear.

Dance classes

For dance classes for gay men and lesbians, *see also p137*. For dance club nights, *see p52* **You shall go to the ball.**

Cecil Sharp House

2 Regent's Park Road, NW1 7AY (7485 2206, www. efdss.org). Camden Town tube. **Open** *Phone enquiries* 9.30am-5.30pm Mon-Fri. **Classes** vary; check website for details. **Credit** (during office hours) MC, V.
The home of the English Folk Dance & Song Society holds classes and workshops in numerous dance styles. Pitch up for the barn dances and ceilidhs or try something new, from Cajun to flamenco.

Danceworks

16 Balderton Street, W1K 6TN (7629 6183, www. danceworks.net). Bond Street tube. **Open** 9am-10pm Mon-Fri; 9.30am-6pm Sat, Sun. **Classes** £4-£10. **Membership** £2-£5/day; £45/mth; £123/yr. **Credit** AmEx, MC, V. **Map** p266 G6.
Danceworks offers a wide selection of dance and fitness classes in an intimate setting. The studio is located just off Oxford Street, so shopaholics can fall straight out of class and into Selfridges for some serious designer shopping.

Drill Hall

16 Chenies Street, WC1E 7EX (7307 5060, www.drillhall. co.uk). Goodge Street tube. **Open** 10am-10pm Mon-Sat; 10am-6pm Sun. **Credit** AmEx, MC, V. **Map** p267 K5.
Long-standing performance space with a strong lesbian and gay presence. *See also p131.*

Greenwich Dance Agency

Borough Hall, SE10 8RE (8293 9741, www.greenwich dance.org.uk). Greenwich DLR/rail. **Box office** 9.30am-5.30pm Mon-Fri. **Classes** *Drop-in* £6; £4.40 reductions. *6wk course* £45; £39 reductions. **Tickets** £7-£15. **Credit** MC, V.
Several of the country's best young companies and dance artists reside in this large art deco venue, where a variety of classes and workshops are complemented by an inventive programme of shows.

Jacksons Lane

269A Archway Road, N6 5AA (8341 4421, www. jacksonslane.org.uk). Highgate tube. **Open** 10am-10pm Tue-Sat; 10am-5pm Sun. **Classes** £6-£8. **Tickets** £5-£13. **Credit** MC, V.

Pineapple Dance Studios

7 Langley Street, WC2H 9JA (7836 4004, www. pineapple.uk.com). Covent Garden tube. **Open** 9am-10pm Mon-Fri; 9am-7pm Sat; 10am-6pm Sun. **Classes** £6-£8. **Membership** £2/day; £4/evening; £25/mth; £65/qtr; £140/yr. **Credit** AmEx, MC, V. **Map** p267 L6.
Covent Garden's famous Pineapple Dance Studios is more than 30 years old and still kicking, the recent Sky1 TV documentary series (and the outrageous Louie) having raised its profile hugely. Whatever your level – from total beginner to professional – there is a class for you. Styles include ballet, jazz, street locking and hip hop. The fusion class (yoga/ballet/Pilates), taught by David Olton, is popular. This is also where pop stars' backing dancers and would-be starlets come to tone up and hone their moves. You don't have to book a course: just turn up and pay on the day.

Screen legends.

Somerset House

West End

In this day and age, gay cinema is spilling into the mainstream, as Hollywood tries to to cash in on the pink pound. Although the quality of the output is debatable (remember *The Birdcage*, the patronisingly limp-wristed remake of *La Cage aux Folles*?), the recent successes of *A Single Man*, *Capote*, *Brokeback Mountain* and *Transamerica* are a hopeful sign.

Unsurprisingly, the venues dotted around the West End, such as the **Prince Charles**, the **Curzon Soho** (which occasionally hosts seasons of gay films on Sundays) and **Odeon Wardour Street**, are the most receptive to screening gay films that do not belong in the same category as, well, *The Birdcage*. The **Renoir** is another good bet for alternative or foreign films.

In the summer, keep an eye out for outdoor screens that pop up across the capital. **Somerset House Summer Screen** (www.somersethouse.org.uk/film) shows first-runs and old classics in its Georgian courtyard, and **Park Nights** at the Serpentine Gallery (*see p204*) shows films in the architectural splendour of the gallery's annual summer pavilion. For details on the mainstream multiplexes, check the websites www.odeon.co.uk, www.myvue.com and www.cineworld.co.uk. Pick up a copy of the weekly *Time Out* magazine for the latest listings or visit www.timeout.com.

Curzon Soho

99 Shaftesbury Avenue, W1D 5DY (7292 7686 information, 0871 703 3988, www.curzoncinemas. com). Leicester Square tube. **Screens** 3. **Tickets** £7-£12.50. **Credit** MC, V. **Map** p269 K6.
Expect a superb range of shorts, rarities, double bills and seasons alongside new international releases. The buzzing, gay-friendly basement bar is great for dates and chat. **Other locations** Curzon Chelsea, 206 King's Road, SW3 5XP (7351 3742); Curzon Mayfair, 38 Curzon Street, W1J 7TY (7495 0500).

Prince Charles

7 Leicester Place, Leicester Square, WC2H 7BY (0870 811 2559, www.princecharlescinema.com). Leicester Square tube. **Screens** 2. **Tickets** £5.50-£10. **Credit** MC, V. **Map** p269 K7.
In addition to cut-price films, the Prince Charles also hosts regular 'Sing-a-Long-a' screenings, including the gloriously camp *The Sound of Music*.

Renoir

Brunswick Square, WC1N 1AW (0871 7033 991, www. curzoncinemas.com). Russell Square tube. **Screens** 2. **Tickets** £5-£10.50. **Credit** MC, V. **Map** p267 L4.

Arts & Entertainment

Around London

There are good alternatives outside the West End. The **Rio** in Dalston is renowned for its progressive programming policy, while the storeyed **Ritzy** in Brixton – an elegantly faded movie house – is similarly artsy and located in a vibrant part of London. Those living westwards can look to the **Riverside Studios** for queer celluloid solace. The riverside location is lovely too. There's also **Ciné Lumière** at the Institut Français in South Kensington; its seasons have included directors like François Ozon (*Sitcom*, *8 Women*) and the most complete retrospective ever put together in the UK of the work of Italian gay saint Pier Paolo Pasolini.

Barbican

Silk Street, EC2Y 8DS (7382 7006, www.barbican. org.uk). Barbican tube or Moorgate tube/rail. **Screens** 1. **Tickets** £5.50-£9.50; £5.50 Mon. **Credit** AmEx, MC, V. **Map** p270 P5.
The three screens at the concrete behemoth show new releases of world and independent cinema alongside an inventive range of seasons, including the Bad Film Club (as in, 'so bad it's good') and the always excellent Directorspective strand, featuring the likes of Werner Herzog and Jacques Tati.

BFI IMAX

1 Charlie Chaplin Walk, South Bank, SE1 8XR (0870 787 2525, www.bfi.org.uk/imax). Waterloo tube/rail. **Screens** 1. **Tickets** £13.50-£15. **Credit** AmEx, MC, V. Map p269 M8.
Experience the biggest screen in the UK at the BFI's gigantic state-of-the-art IMAX. The films are a mix of made-for-IMAX fare – the New York Metropolitan Opera

Prince Charles

Porn again

Soho sleaze has returned. And porn being such a staple of queer cinematic pleasure, we couldn't leave it out. Those who get bored of watching screen sex in the solitude of their bedrooms – and who yearn nostalgically for the days of shifty men in dirty macs – should join the **Soho Gay Cinemas**. The self-proclaimed 'only gay hardcore cinema in London' boasts two 50-seat cinemas and several new hardcore flicks every week.

Soho Gay Cinemas

7-12 Walkers Court, W1T 0BY (7439 0835). Leicester Square or Piccadilly Circus tube. **Open** 10am-11pm Mon-Thur; noon-1am Fri, Sat; noon-10pm Sun. **Admission** (with free membership) £14/day. **Map** p269 K6.

in HD, *Lions of the Kalahari* – and the odd mainstream blockbuster like *Alien*, *Dark Knight* or *300*. But be warned: the steeply raked seats enhance the special effects and those of a sensitive disposition should stay away!

BFI Southbank

South Bank, SE1 8XT (7928 3535 information, 7928 3232 tickets, www.bfi.org.uk/nft). Embankment tube or Waterloo tube/rail. **Screens** 3. **Tickets** £9. **Credit** AmEx, MC, V. **Map** p269 M8.
Something of a year-round festival in its own right, the BFI regularly features films that are of interest to gay audiences (for instance, a season called the History of Lesbian Cinema). Its mixture of oldies, retrospectives, special events and contemporary films is particularly enticing. As far as queer reclamation of classics goes, the NFT is a treasure trove for vintage aficionados.

Ciné Lumière

Institut Français, 17 Queensberry Place, SW7 2DT (7073 1350, www.institut-francais.org.uk). South Kensington tube. **Screens** 1. **Tickets** £7-£9. **Credit** MC, V. **Map** p265 D1

Electric Cinema

191 Portobello Road, W11 2ED (7908 9696, www. electriccinema.co.uk). Ladbroke Grove or Notting Hill Gate tube. **Screens** 1. **Tickets** £7.50-£15; £7.50-£10 Mon. **Credit** AmEx, MC, V.
A legend among London filmgoers, the Electric is one of the city's oldest cinemas. It's gone from fleapit to luxury with leather seats and sofas, footstools and a bar inside the auditorium. It also has a fashionable brasserie.

ICA Cinema

The Mall, SW1Y 5AH (7930 6393 information, 7930 3647 tickets, www.ica.org.uk). Piccadilly Circus tube or Charing Cross tube/rail. **Screens** 2. **Tickets** £9-£12. **Credit** MC, V. **Map** p269 K8.

Arts & Entertainment

Another venue to be reckoned with when it comes to alternative cinema. With an art gallery, theatre, cinema, bookshop and late-night bar all rolled into one, the ICA is a reference point for queer and alternative audiences.

Rio Cinema

107 Kingsland High Street, E8 2PB (7241 9410, www. riocinema.org.uk). Dalston Kingsland rail. **Screens** 1. **Tickets** £6.50-£8.50. **Credit** AmEx, MC, V.

Ritzy Picturehouse

Brixton Oval, Coldharbour Lane, SW2 1JG (0871 902 5739, www.picturehouses.co.uk). Brixton tube/rail. **Screens** 5. **Tickets** £7-£9. **Credit** MC, V.

Riverside Studios

Crisp Road, W6 9RL (8237 1111, www.riverside studios.co.uk). Hammersmith tube. **Screens** 1. **Tickets** £7.50. **Credit** MC, V.

Festivals

The **London Lesbian & Gay Film Festival** (www.llgff.org.uk; *see also p120*), the largest event of its kind in Europe. Organised by the British Film Institute (www.bfi.org.uk), it takes place yearly at BFI Southbank on the South Bank and other venues in the West End, usually around late March and April. Booking early is advised, as tickets tend to sell out fast. The alternative **Raindance Film Festival** (7287

3833, www.raindance.co.uk) and the underground **Exploding Cinema** (www.explodingcinema.org), an open access platform that exhibits all films submitted, are other happenings to keep an eye out for. Another excellent, uncompromising alternative is the **Portobello Film Festival** (8960 0996, www.portobellofilmfestival.com), which takes place in August in Notting Hill, and offers a rich, irreverent and politicised line-up.

Galleries & museums

Galleries and museums often show films that are of interest to a gay and lesbian audience. **Tate Modern** (*see p165*) has an excellent, artsy film programme. The **Whitechapel Art Gallery** (*see p212*) also has a queer-friendly programming policy, and the **South London Gallery** (*see p128*) is worth checking out.

Alternative

Horse Hospital

Colonnade, WC1N 1HX (7833 3644, www.thehorse hospital.com). Russell Square tube. **Screens** 1. **Tickets** vary; phone for details. **No credit cards.** **Map** p267 L4.
Dubbed 'the Chamber of Pop Culture', this multimedia venue lies outside the mainstream of contemporary arts. The venue is redolent of the days of 'happenings', with a strong countercultural appeal; film is a major component.

BFI Southbank. *See p125.*

Galleries

Picture this.

The galleries featured below are only a sample of what's on offer. Bigger spaces are listed in the Around Town chapters, including the **Barbican** (*see p169*), the **Courtauld Gallery** (*see p172*), the **Design Museum** (*see p166*), **Dulwich Picture Gallery** (*see p224*), the **Hayward Gallery** (*see p163*), the **ICA** (*see p199*), the **National Gallery** (*see p198*), **Royal Academy of Arts** (*see p184*), **Saatchi Gallery** (*see p206*), **Tate Britain** (*see p201*), **Tate Modern** (*see p165*), the **V&A** (*see p202*) and **Whitechapel Art Gallery** (*see p212*).

Central

Alison Jacques Gallery

16-18 Berners Street, W1T 3LN (7631 4720, www. alisonjacquesgallery.com). Goodge Street, Oxford Circus or Tottenham Court Road tube. **Open** 10am-6pm Tue-Sat. **No credit cards**. **Map** p266 J5.
This elegant space shows work from emerging contemporary art centres such as Berlin. Past names have include the likes of Jon Pylypchuk and André Butzer, plus icons such as Robert Mapplethorpe and Hannah Wilke.

Gagosian

6-24 Britannia Street, WC1X 9JD (7841 9960, www. gagosian.com). King's Cross tube/rail. **Open** 10am-6pm Tue-Sat. **No credit cards**. **Map** p267 M3.
American super-dealer Larry Gagosian ('Go-Go' to his friends) shows a wealth of big names, among them Andy Warhol, Roy Lichtenstein, Jasper Johns, Cy Twombly, Howard Hodkin and Franceso Clemente. When the big names aren't there, Gagosian features a second tier of fashionable artists from the US and Europe, including Carsten Höller and Cecily Brown.
Other locations 17-19 Davies Street, W1K 3DE (7493 3020).

Haunch of Venison

6 Haunch of Venison Yard, W1K 5ES (7495 5050, www.haunchofvenison.com). Bond Street tube. **Open** 10am-6pm Mon-Fri; 10am-5pm Sat. **Credit** AmEx, DC, MC, V. **Map** p266 H6.
This high-ceilinged converted Georgian townhouse, formerly home to Lord Nelson, has lent itself to large-scale installations and exhibitions by big names such as Turner Prize-winners Rachel Whiteread, Keith Tyson and Richard Long, as well as some mid-career and emerging artists (Diana Thater, Zarina Bhimji). The gallery is now owned by Christie's, so expect more big shows.

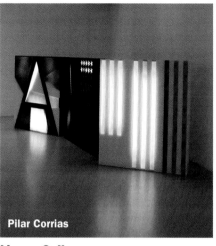

Pilar Corrias

Lisson Gallery

52-54 Bell Street, NW1 5DA (7724 2739, www.lisson. co.uk). Edgware Road tube. **Open** 10am-6pm Mon-Fri; 11am-5pm Sat. **Credit** MC, V. **Map** p263 E5.
One of London's more established contemporary galleries, the Lisson is a platform for Douglas Gordon, Tony Oursler, Julian Opie and the 'Lisson Sculptors': Anish Kapoor, Tony Cragg, Richard Wentworth and Richard Deacon.
Other location 29 Bell Street, NW1 5BY (7535 7350).

Pilar Corrias

54 Eastcastle Street, W1W 8EF (7323 7000, www. pilarcorrias.com). Oxford Circus tube. **Open** 10am-6pm Mon-Fri; 11am-6pm Sat. **No credit cards**. **Map** p266 J6.
Formerly a director at the Lisson and Haunch of Venison, Corrias opened this Rem Koolhaas-designed art gallery in October 2008 with a giant aluminium Christmas tree by Philippe Parreno. Look out for works by Tala Madani, Keren Cytter and Francis Alÿs.

Photographers' Gallery

16-18 Ramillies Street, W1F 7LW (0845 262 1618, www.photonet.org.uk). Oxford Circus tube. **Open** 11am-6pm Tue-Wed, Sat; 11am-8pm Thur, Fri; noon-6pm Sun. **Credit** AmEx, DC, MC, V. **Map** p266 J6.
A giant among photography galleries, this space hosts a great range of diverse shows each year, including the Deutsche Börse Photography Prize – an important event.

Note: after 37 years on the edge of Covent Garden, the gallery has moved to premises in Soho. A new six-storey building will open on the same site in 2011.

Royal Institute of British Architects

66 Portland Place, W1B 1AD (7580 5533, www. architecture.com). Great Portland Street or Regent's Park tube. **Open** 10am-5pm Mon-Sat. **Credit** MC, V. **Map** p266 H4/5.
Based in a monumental edifice built by Grey Wornum in 1934, the RIBA gallery celebrates the profession's great and good and checks emerging architecture from around the world. The café has a lovely outdoor terrace.

Timothy Taylor Gallery

15 Carlos Place, W1K 2EX (7409 3344, www.timothy taylorgallery.com). Bond Street tube. **Open** 10am-6pm Mon-Fri; 10am-2pm Sat. **Credit** MC, V. **Map** p268 H7.
Among the high-profile artists shown here are Lucian Freud, Sean Scully, Richard Patterson and Martin Maloney.

North

176

176 Prince of Wales Road, NW5 3PT (7428 8940, www.projectspace176.com). Chalk Farm tube/ Kentish Town West rail. **Open** noon-6pm Thur-Sun. **Credit** MC, V.
Opened in autumn 2007, this former Methodist chapel – a remarkable neoclassical building – holds three shows a year, enabling artists to create experimental new work and curators to build exhibitions around the Zabludowicz Collection of global emerging art in all media.

East

Approach E2

Approach Tavern, 1st floor, 47 Approach Road, E2 9LY (8983 3878, www.theapproach.co.uk). Bethnal Green tube. **Open** noon-6pm Wed-Sun; also by appointment. **No credit cards.**
Occupying a converted function room above the Approach Tavern, this gallery is a great venue for combining an exhibition with a Sunday pub lunch and a pint or two. It has a deserved reputation for showing both emerging and more established artists such as Michael Raedecker and Gary Webb.

Chisenhale Gallery

64 Chisenhale Road, E3 5QZ (8981 4518, www. chisenhale.org.uk). Bethnal Green or Mile End tube, or 8, 277, D6 bus. **Open** 1-6pm Wed-Sun. **No credit cards.**
With a reputation for recognising new talent, Chisenhale Gallery ommissions work by emerging artists. Rachel Whiteread's *Ghost* and Cornelia Parker's exploded shed *Cold Dark Matter* were both Chisenhale commissions.

Flowers East

82 Kingsland Road, E2 8DP (7920 7777, www. flowerseast.com). Hoxton rail. **Open** 10am-6pm Tue-Sat. **Credit** AmEx, MC, V.

Angela Flowers is one of the original champions of YBAs. Some, like Patrick Hughes and Derek Hirst, are still with the gallery 35 years on, creating a good age mix. **Other locations** Flowers Central, 21 Cork Street, W1S 3LZ (7439 7766).

Matt's Gallery

42-44 Copperfield Road, E3 4RR (8983 1771, www. mattsgallery.org). Mile End tube. **Open** 10am-6pm Wed-Sun; also by appointment. **No credit cards.**
Few galleries in town are as well respected as Matt's. Characterised by ambitious pieces, the gallery has commissioned works such as Richard Wilson's sump oil installation *20:50* and Mike Nelson's *Coral Reef.*

Maureen Paley

21 Herald Street, E2 6JT (7729 4112, www.maureen paley.com). Bethnal Green tube. **Open** 11am-6pm Wed-Sun; also by appointment. **No credit cards.**
Here since 1999, Maureen Paley represents Turner Prize-winners Wolfgang Tillmans and Gillian Wearing, Paul Noble and sculptor Rebecca Warren.

Victoria Miro Gallery

16 Wharf Road, N1 7RW (7336 8109, www.victoria-miro.com). Angel tube or Old Street tube/rail. **Open** 10am-6pm Tue-Sat. **Credit** MC, V.
A beautifully converted ex-Victorian furniture factory, showing high-calibre artists like Chris Ofili, Peter Doig, Chantal Joffe and William Eggleston.

White Cube Hoxton Square

48 Hoxton Square, N1 6PB (7930 5373, www.white cube.com). Old Street tube/rail. **Open** 10am-6pm Tue-Sat. **Credit** AmEx, MC, V.
White Cube buzzes with A-list Young British Artists, among them Tracey Emin, Damien Hirst, Jake and Dinos Chapman and Sam Taylor-Wood. **Other locations** 25-26 St Mason's Yard, SW1 6BU (7930 5373).

South

South London Gallery

65 Peckham Road, SE5 8UH (7703 6120, www. southlondongallery.org). Oval tube then 36, 436 bus, or Elephant & Castle tube/rail then 12, 171 bus. **Open** 11am-6pm Tue, Thur-Sun; 11am-9pm Sun. **Credit** MC, V.
Built in 1891, this cathedral-like space is a showcase for British emerging artists. Past exhibitors include Tom Friedman, Steve McQueen and Saskia Olde Wolbers.

West

Adonis Art

1B Coleherne Road, SW10 9BS (3417 0238, www.adonisartgallery.com). Earl's Court tube. **Open** 11am-5.45pm Mon-Fri; 10.30am-5pm Sat. **Credit** AmEx, MC, V. **Map** p264 B11.
In the old gay neighbourhood of Earl's Court, Adonis Art pays homage to the male nude. Works include oil paintings, watercolours, bronze figures and photography. Not for the faint of heart – or for those with subtle taste.

Theatre

Calling all drama queens.

London is never short of theatre, and London theatres are never short of homosexuals. Whether acting, writing, directing or smiling at you from the box office, it can sometimes feel like, as the title of Ivor Novello's 1950 musical had it, *Gay's the Word* – front and backstage. There is dispute about whether the proportion of same-sex oriented professionals is actually greater in the theatre than in other London institutions – Parliament, London Transport or the John Lewis Partnership, for example. But you'd have to work pretty hard to spend a few nights at the theatre in London entirely in the twilight world of the heterosexual. Even if there aren't overtly lesbian or gay stories, characters or interpretations, it's likely that some of that indefinable 'sensibility' might have wafted in during rehearsal.

That said, if you're one of those who likes your gay experiences up there on the stage, you'll find it in London: *History Boys* is the most prominent example of a recent flurry of gay theatre. Alan Bennett's portrait of a gay middle-aged teacher, and his intense relationship with his teenage pupils, had West End runs in 2004 and 2007.

But before you book your tickets to any show, beware of a few things: tribute shows (except *Mamma Mia!*); titles ending in exclamation marks (except *Mamma Mia!*); shows where you already know all the songs (but you'll go anyway, won't you?). And be especially wary of posters featuring clearly defined pectoral muscles; if that's the best thing about the show, you can find it elsewhere – and not be forced to sit through a mediocre play.

If you've got your heart set on a show, book in advance. For same-day, discounted tickets, go to the **tkts booth** on the south side of Leicester Square. For all the latest developments, reviews and practical information, check the theatre section of *Time Out* magazine. The Society of London Theatre's website, www.officiallondon theatre.co.uk, also has some useful links.

West End

You can divide London Theatreland into three camps: the West End, the subsidised camp and the fringe. The West End consists of a huddle of venues that straddle Shaftesbury Avenue as it enters Piccadilly. This is traditional Theatreland. (For a map of where the venues in Theatreland are located, *see p187.*) There are 20-odd West End theatres: grand dames decorated in tarty red velvet and gilt trim. At the top end, these theatres survive on top-of-the-range star vehicles and musicals; at the bottom, expect musical tribute shows and bottom-of-the-barrel tosh with superannuated sitcom veterans.

West End theatres are huge: the more you pay the closer you get to the stage. In some of the barn-like venues, that matters, but a truly thrilling show makes you tingle even if you're sitting in the 'gods'. Top twinkle venue for stars remains the genuinely classy **Theatre Royal Haymarket** (Haymarket, 0845 481 1870, www.trh.co.uk).

THE SUBSIDISED CAMP

London's subsidised theatres may not have red velvet and chandeliers, but they usually offer the most new and interesting productions. The **Donmar Warehouse** in Covent Garden, led by artistic director Michael Grandage, was the first of the new West End mini-venues, joined in 2004 by the **Trafalgar Studios** (Whitehall, 0844 871 7627, www.ambassador tickets.com.co.uk). These provide a space for West End transfers of midscale shows from companies like the **Young Vic** (66 The Cut, 7922 2922, www.youngvic.org, artistic director David Lan) or the **Royal Shakespeare Company**. The Donmar and Islington's **Almeida** are also popular with movie stars coming back to what they will always claim is their real love – live adulation night after night. But one Hollywood star has gone behind the scenes: Kevin Spacey is the current artistic director of the **Old Vic** (Waterloo Road, 0844 871 7628, www.oldvictheatre.com), which has staged classic theatre for nearly 200 years.

Long-runners

The big shows usually perform from Monday to Saturday nights, with matinées taking place on Saturdays and one weekday.

Billy Elliot the Musical

*Victoria Palace Theatre, Victoria Street, SW1E 5EA
(0844 811 0055, www.billyelliotthemusical.com).
Victoria tube/rail.* **Shows** 7.30pm Mon-Sat. *Matinée*
2.30pm Thur, Sat. **Tickets** £19.50-£65. **Credit**
AmEx, MC, V. **Map** p268 H10.
The musical version of that film about the straight boy
with the gay friend who just wants to dance his way out
of the mines. Elton John ('Billy's story reminded me of my
own life') does the music, Stephen Daldry directs.

Chicago

*Cambridge Theatre, Earlham Street, WC2H 9HU
(0871 297 0777, www.cambridgetheatre.co.uk). Covent
Garden tube.* **Shows** 8pm Mon-Sat. *Matinée* 5pm Fri;
3pm Sat. **Tickets** £15-£57.50. **Credit** AmEx, MC, V.
Map p267 L7.
The 1975 murder-musical from John Kander and the late
Fred Ebb has proved even more popular in this sleek
cabaret-style revival. The staging is robust enough to
survive periodic recasts, and the publicity campaign with
its fishnets and tits razzle-dazzles everyone.

Grease

*Piccadilly Theatre, Denman Street, W1D 7DY (0844
412 6666, www.greasethemusical.co.uk). Piccadilly
Circus tube.* **Shows** 7.30pm Mon-Thur, Sat; 8.30pm
Fri. *Matinée* 5.30pm Fri; 3pm Sat. **Tickets** £15-£55.
Credit AmEx, MC, V. **Map** p268 J7.
Danny and Sandy are still electrifyin' audiences decades
after *Grease* made its Broadway debut. As this guide went
to press, Jimmy Osmond was set to play the Teen Angel
and Noel Sullivan from Hear'Say was to be Danny.

Jersey Boys

*Prince Edward Theatre, 28 Old Compton Street,
W1D 4HS (0844 482 5151, www.jerseyboyslondon.
com). Leicester Square or Piccadilly Circus tube.*
Shows 7.30pm Tue-Sat. *Matinée* 3pm Tue, Sat, Sun.
Tickets £20-£65. **Credit** AmEx, MC, V. **Map** p268 K7.
You may not recognise the name of the band, but you will
recognise the songs. This is the rags-to-riches story of
Frankie Valli and the Four Seasons, featuring sing-a-long
standards 'Big Girls Don't Cry' and 'Oh, What a Night!'

The Lion King

*Lyceum Theatre, Wellington Street, WC2E 7RQ
(0844 844 0005). Covent Garden tube/Charing Cross
tube/rail.* **Shows** 7.30pm Tue-Sat. *Matinée* 2pm Wed,
Sat; 3pm Sun. **Tickets** £21-£62.50. **Credit** AmEx,
MC, V. **Map** p269 L7.
Disney extravaganza about an orphaned young lion cub
struggling to grow up and find his place on the savannah.

Mamma Mia!

*Prince of Wales Theatre, Coventry Street, W1V 6AS
(0844 482 5115, www.mamma-mia.com). Piccadilly
Circus tube.* **Shows** 7.30pm Mon-Thur, Sat; 8.30pm Fri.
Matinée 5pm Fri; 3pm Sat. **Tickets** £20-£85. **Credit**
AmEx, MC, V. **Map** p269 K7.
It may be all about a wedding, but the West End doesn't
get any gayer than this, the only tribute show you can
admit to watching without shame.

Les Misérables

*Queens Theatre, Shaftesbury Avenue, W1D 6BA (0844
482 5160, www.lesmis.com). Leicester Square tube.*
Shows 7.30pm Mon-Sat. *Matinée* 3pm Tue; 4pm Sat.
Tickets £15-£59. **Credit** AmEx, MC, V. **Map** p269 K7.
These French waifs have kept the tills rolling for Cameron
Mackintosh and the RSC for more than two decades.

The Mousetrap

*St Martin's Theatre, West Street, WC2H 9NZ (0844
499 1515, www.the-mousetrap.co.uk). Leicester Square
tube.* **Shows** 7.30pm Mon-Sat. *Matinée* 2.45pm Tue;
5pm Sat. **Tickets** £15-£39.50. **Credit** AmEx, MC, V.
Map p267 K6.
The world's longest-running show. When it opened, 'gay'
either meant the life and soul of the party or a course of
electric shock therapy.

Phantom of the Opera

*Her Majesty's Theatre, Haymarket, SW1Y 4QR
(0844 412 2707, www.thephantomoftheopera.com).
Piccadilly Circus tube.* **Shows** 7.30pm Mon-Sat. *Matinée*
2.30pm Tue, Sat. **Tickets** £20-£59. **Credit** AmEx,
MC, V. **Map** p269 K7.
Once upon a time, if you threw a stone on Shaftesbury
Avenue you'd hit an Andrew Lloyd Webber musical. The
millionaire knight has fewer lights in the West End these
days, but *Phantom* remains a beacon to those in search of
madness, Gothic tragedy, lavish sets and great love songs
with loads of vibrato. Is there anybody who hasn't seen this?

Priscilla Queen of the Desert

*Palace Theatre, Cambridge Circus, Shaftesbury
Avenue, W1V 8AY (0844 755 0016, www.priscilla
themusical.com). Leicester Square of Tottenham Court
Road tube.* **Shows** 7.30pm Mon-Sat. *Matinée* 2.30pm
Thur, Sat. **Tickets** £20-£65. **Credit** AmEx, MC, V.
Map p267 K6.

Arts & Entertainment

The stage version of the 1994 cult film is the gayest musical in London. An extravaganza of drag and camp; the Abba songs have been replaced by a Kylie medley.

We Will Rock You

Dominion Theatre, Tottenham Court Road, W1P 0AG (0844 847 1775, www.wewillrockyou.co.uk). Tottenham Court Road tube. **Shows** 7.30pm Mon-Sat. *Matinée* 2.30pm Sat. **Tickets** £28-£60. **Credit** AmEx, MC, V. **Map** p267 K5.
All your favourite Queen hits, stitched together by a feeble Ben Elton plot. Freddie would've hated it.

Wicked

Apollo Victoria Theatre, Wilton Road, SW1V 1LG (0844 826 8000, www.wickedthemusical.co.uk). Victoria tube/rail. **Shows** 7.30pm Mon-Sat. *Matinée* 2.30pm Wed, Sat. **Tickets** £15-£62.50. **Credit** AmEx, MC, V. **Map** p268 H10.
Prequel to *The Wizard of Oz* telling the story of Glinda the Good Witch and the Wicked Witch of the West before they were famous. 'Defying Gravity' is a showstopper.

Alternative

Drill Hall

16 Chenies Street, WC1E 7EX (7307 5060, www. drillhall.co.uk). Goodge Street tube. **Box office** 10am-9.30pm Mon-Fri; 10am-6pm Sat, Sun. **Credit** AmEx, MC, V. **Map** p267 K5.
Built in 1882 for the Bloomsbury Rifles, the Drill Hall has since provided a space for those a tad lighter on their feet – Nijinsky rehearsed here back in the early 1900s. Today, it's at the forefront of experimental and gay theatre. Queer performers have particularly benefited from the policy to nurture new, left-field work. Michelle Shocked and the Ridiculous Theatrical Company both made their UK debuts here. Other projects have included the first stage adaptation of Armistead Maupin's *Babycakes*, and Out & Proud's *Giovanni's Room* and *The Nualas*.

Royal Court. *See p132.*

Leicester Square Theatre

5 Leicester Place, WC2H 7BP (0844 847 2475, www.leicestersquaretheatre.com). Leicester Square tube. **Box office** *In person* 2.30-8pm Mon-Sat (performance nights). *By phone* 24hrs daily. **Credit** AmEx, MC, V. **Map** p269 K7.
A Leicester Square curiosity, this former dance hall is handy for Soho. As the Venue, it opened with the Boy George, musical *Taboo*. In 2008, it re-opened with Joan Rivers's one-woman play, so you know it's gay-friendly.

The subsidised camp

Public subsidy projects keep London theatre alive in a kind of co-dependent relationship with the red-blooded capitalism of the West End. Taxpayers, via Arts Council England, support big operations as well as more experimental and innovative work. When a smaller show transfers to the West End, there is a big financial boost to the original subsidised theatres, as well as a boost to their credibility. Some of the West End's solid bankers were created in the state sector: *Les Misérables* (from the Royal Shakespeare Company) being the most prominent and profitable. Shows such as *Shopping and Fucking*, Mark Ravenhill's exploration of rimming and Western capitalism (from Out of Joint and Royal Court) or gory music-theatre *Shockheaded Peter* (Lyric Hammersmith and Cultural Industry) found huge audiences 'in town', despite being not at all 'West Endy'. One of the most respected venues for new plays is the **Hampstead Theatre** (Eton Avenue, NW3 3EU, 7722 9301, www.hampsteadtheatre.com).

Almeida

Almeida Street, N1 1TA (7359 4404, www.almeida. co.uk). Angel tube. **Box office** *In person* 10am-7.30pm Mon-Sat. **Credit** AmEx, MC, V.
The Almeida turns out thoughtfully crafted theatre for grown-ups. Under artistic director Michael Attenborough, it has drawn top directors such as Howard Davies and Richard Eyre, and staged premières from the likes of Stephen Adly Guirgis. Expect new plays, European translations, classic revivals and a summer opera season. Slightly precious, always chic.

Donmar Warehouse

41 Earlham Street, WC2H 9LX (0844 871 7624, www.donmarwarehouse.com). Covent Garden tube. **Box office** *In person* 10am-7.30pm Mon-Sat. *By phone* 9am-10pm Mon-Sat; 10am-8pm Sun. **Credit** AmEx, MC, V. **Map** p267 L6.
The Donmar is less a warehouse than an intimate chamber. Artistic director Michael Grandage has kept the venue on a fresh, intelligent path since 2008. The combination of artistic integrity and intimate space is hard to resist, which is perhaps why so many high-profile film actors have returned to their stage roots (or discovered them) here, including Gwyneth Paltrow (*Proof*) and Nicole Kidman (*The Blue Room*). A bit more tarty and West End than the Almeida, it does classic plays and the odd starry musical.

Arts & Entertainment

National Theatre

by artistic director Nicholas Hytner. You can try queuing up in the morning for day seats if shows are sold out.

Royal Court

Sloane Square, SW1W 8AS (7565 5000, www.royal courttheatre.com). Sloane Square tube. **Box office** 10am-6pm Mon-Fri; 10am-6pm Sat (performance days only). **Credit** AmEx, MC, V. **Map** p265 F11.
This handsome Sloane Square veteran has retained its reputation as London's flagship theatre for new plays.

Royal Shakespeare Company (RSC)

01789 403 444, 0844 800 1110 box office, www. rsc.org.uk. **Box office** *By phone* 9am-8pm Mon-Sat. **Credit** AmEx, MC, V.
The stage-hopping RSC can now look forward to a stable London home: it recently signed a deal to take up a five-year residency at the newly renovated Novello Theatre.

Shakespeare's Globe

21 New Globe Walk, SE1 9DT (7401 9919, www. shakespeares-globe.org). London Bridge tube/rail. **Box office** *May-Oct* 10am-6pm Mon-Sat; 10am-5pm Sun. *Nov-Apr* 10am-5pm Mon-Fri. **Credit** AmEx, MC, V. **Map** p270 O7.
More than just a heritage site, this is one of the most atmospheric venues in the city. A sure bet for girl-on-girl action, as seen regularly in its all-female Shakespeare productions.

Soho Theatre

21 Dean Street, W1D 3NE (7478 0100, www. sohotheatre.com). Tottenham Court Road tube. **Box office** 10am-7pm Mon-Sat; 10am-2hrs before start of performance (performance days only). **Credit** AmEx, MC, V. **Map** p267 K6.
The Soho is brilliant for cabaret and comedy, but its theatre can be hit and miss. Occasionally, they stage a gem, such as *How to Lose Friends and Alienate People* and *Julie Burchill is Away*.

Lyric Hammersmith

Lyric Square, King Street, W6 0QL (0871 221 1729, www.lyric.co.uk). Hammersmith tube. **Box office** 9.30am-5.30pm Mon-Sat (non-performance days only); 9.30am-15min after performance start (performance days only). **Credit** MC, V.
The Lyric has a knack for vibrant, offbeat plays, overseen by artistic director Sean Holmes.

National Theatre

South Bank, SE1 9PX (7452 3000, www.national theatre.org.uk). Embankment tube or Waterloo tube/rail. **Box office** 9.30am-8pm Mon-Sat. **Credit** AmEx, MC, V. **Map** p269 M7/8.
With three theatres to choose from, there's always something going on at this South Bank concrete palace, led

Soho Theatre

Music

Get into the groove.

Royal Albert Hall. *See p134.*

London is a great place for music lovers, gay or straight. Sure, there's plenty to keep all the stereotypes happy, from opera queens to show-tune fanatics. But music is music, whatever your bent: just as Judy Garland has straight fans (there must be a few), why shouldn't gay visitors check out a rock club or a church recital?

Classical & opera

Many London churches are atmospheric settings for classical concerts. The elegant 18th-century **St John's, Smith Square** (Smith Square, 7222 1061, www.sjss.org.uk), in Westminster, hosts a nightly programme (except in summer) of chamber and orchestral concerts, and Wren's **St James's Piccadilly** (197 Piccadilly, 7734 4511, www. sjpconcerts.org) presents free lunchtime recitals (Mon, Wed, Fri) and a less regular programme of evening concerts. Just across from Trafalgar Square, **St Martin-in-the-Fields** (7766 1100, www.stmartin-in-the-fields.org) hosts candlelit evening concerts (days vary), while its free lunchtime recitals (Mon, Tue, Fri) are frequently wonderful. The London Symphony Orchestra (LSO) recently converted the Hawksmoor-designed **St Luke's** (161 Old Street, 7490 3939, http://lso.co.uk) into a concert hall.

Barbican Centre

Silk Street, EC2Y 8DS (7638 8891, www.barbican. org.uk). Barbican tube or Moorgate tube/rail. **Box office** 9am-8pm Mon-Sat; 11am-8pm Sun. **Tickets** £10-£35. **Credit** AmEx, MC, V. **Map** p270 P5.
Europe's largest multi-arts complex is the home of the London Symphony Orchestra, the richest, if not the best, of the capital's international orchestras. It plays some 90 concerts a year here, tours the world and records prolifically for both film and audio formats. Its rival, the BBC Symphony Orchestra, also performs here. The modern music programming, taking in jazz, rock, world and country, continues to find ever larger audiences.

KOKO

Cadogan Hall

*5 Sloane Terrace, SW1X 9DQ (7730 4500, www.
cadoganhall.com). Sloane Square tube.* **Box office**
10am-8pm Mon-Sat; 3-8pm Sun. **Tickets** £10-£35.
Credit MC, V. **Map** p268 G10.
Built a century ago as a Christian Science church, this
austere building was transformed into a light and airy
auditorium in 2004. It would be hard to imagine how the
renovations could have been bettered: the 905-capacity hall
is comfortable and the acoustics excellent.

Kings Place

*90 York Way, N1 9AG (0844 264 0321, www.kings
place.co.uk). Kings Cross tube/rail.* **Box office** noon-
8pm Mon-Sat; noon-7pm Sun (performance days only).
Tickets £6.50-£34.50. **Credit** MC, V. **Map** p267 L2.
Part of a complex that also includes an art gallery and the
offices of the *Guardian* and *Observer* newspapers, this 420-
seat auditorium opened in 2008 with an excellent series of
concerts. In the long run, Kings Place will provide a home
for both the London Sinfonietta and the Orchestra of the
Age of Enlightenment, but there's also jazz, folk and rock.

Royal Albert Hall

*Kensington Gore, SW7 2AP (7589 3203 information,
7589 8212 box office, www.royalalberthall.com).
South Kensington tube or 9, 10, 52 bus.* **Box office**
9am-9pm daily. **Tickets** £4-£150. **Credit** AmEx,
MC, V. **Map** p265 D9.

This grand 5,200-seat rotunda is the home of the BBC
Proms (mid July-mid Sept), the world's finest orchestral
music festival, with 70 or so concerts of both staple repertoire and newly commissioned works. For more information, visit www.bbc.co.uk/proms; to book tickets, call 0845
401 5040. Otherwise, the hall, built as a memorial to Queen
Victoria's husband, is a venue for all forms of music
including opera, rock and awards ceremonies.

Southbank Centre

*Belvedere Road, SE1 8XX (0871 663 2501 information,
0871 847 9910 tickets, www.southbankcentre.co.uk).
Embankment tube or Waterloo tube/rail.* **Box office**
In person 10am-8pm daily. *By phone* 9am-8pm
daily. **Tickets** £7-£75. **Credit** AmEx, MC, V.
Map p269 M8.
The Southbank Centre has three concert halls: the 3,000-
seat Royal Festival Hall for major orchestral concerts, the
slightly smaller Queen Elizabeth Hall for piano recitals and
the little Purcell Room for chamber groups and contemporary music. The RFH is home to six classical music
ensembles, including the London Philharmonic Orchestra.

Wigmore Hall

*36 Wigmore Street, W1U 2BP (7935 2141 box office,
www.wigmore-hall.org.uk). Bond Street tube.* **Box
office** *In person* 10am-8.30pm daily (performance days
only). *By phone* 10am-7pm daily. **Tickets** £5-£75.
Credit AmEx, DC, MC, V. **Map** p266 H5.

With its perfect acoustics, discreet art nouveau decor and excellent basement restaurant, this remains one of the world's top concert venues for chamber music and song.

Opera companies

There are also performances at **Sadler's Wells** (0844 412 4300, www.sadlerswells.com).

English National Opera

The Coliseum, St Martin's Lane, WC2N 4ES (0871 911 0200 tickets, www.eno.org). Leicester Square tube or Charing Cross tube/rail. **Box office** *In person* from 10am-6pm Mon-Sat. *By phone* 24hrs daily. **Tickets** £20-£90. **Credit** AmEx, MC, V. **Map** p269 L7.
Recently refurbished for £80 million, this magnificent venue near Trafalgar Square has been home to the ENO, the premier company for opera in English, since 1968.

Royal Opera

Royal Opera House, WC2E 9DD (7304 4000, www. roh.org.uk). Covent Garden tube. **Box office** 10am-8pm Mon-Sat. **Tickets** £8-£210. **Credit** AmEx, MC, V. **Map** p269 L6.
One of the great opera houses of the world. The conversion of Floral Hall into a restaurant and bar was a stroke of genius – it is one of London's most atmospheric settings. The air-conditioned auditorium and comfortable seating make a night out at the opera a positive prospect.

Rock & jazz

There are always live pop acts on Saturday nights at **G-A-Y** (*see p40*). Performers range from boybands-du-jour to gay pop icons (Madonna, Kylie, Cyndi Lauper and Boy George).

HMV Hammersmith Apollo

Queen Caroline Street, W6 9QH (0844 844 4748 tickets, 8563 3800 information, www.hammersmith apollo.net). Hammersmith tube. **Box office** *In person* 4pm-8pm performance days. *By phone* 24hrs daily. **Tickets** £5-£30. **Credit** MC, V.
This '30s cinema is now a 5,000-capacity concert space, hosting everyone from Kenny Rogers to Deacon Blue.

ICA

The Mall, SW1Y 5AH (7930 0493 information, 7930 3647 tickets, www.ica.org.uk). Piccadilly Circus tube/Charing Cross tube/rail. **Box office** noon-9.15pm Wed-Sun. **Tickets** £2-£20. **Credit** AmEx, DC, MC, V. **Map** p269 K8.
The Institute of Contemporary Arts' music programme is generally interesting, fashionable and alternative.

Jazz Café

5 Parkway, NW1 7PG (7688 8899 information, 0844 847 2514 tickets, www.jazzcafe.co.uk). Camden Town tube. **Box office** *In person* 10.30am-5.30pm Mon-Sat. *By phone* 24hrs daily. **Admission** £10-£30. **Credit** MC, V.

The name doesn't tell the whole story: jazz is a mere piece in the jigsaw of events here, which also takes in funk, hip hop, soul, R&B, singer-songwriters and more besides.

KOKO

1A Camden High Street, NW1 7JE (0870 432 5527 information, 0870 847 2258 tickets, www.koko.uk. com). Mornington Crescent tube. **Box office** *In person* 1-5pm Mon-Fri (perfromance days only). *By phone* 24hrs daily. **Tickets** £3-£25. **Credit** AmEx MC, V.
Opened in 1900 as a music hall, the former Camden Palace scrubbed up nicely during a 2004 refit. The 1,500-capacity auditorium stages club nights alongside indie gigs.

100 Club

100 Oxford Street, W1D 1LL (7636 0933, www. the100club.co.uk). Oxford Circus tube. **Open** *Shows* 7.30pm-midnight Mon; 7.30-11.30pm Tue-Thur; 7.30pm-12.30am Fri; 7.30pm-1am Sat; 7.30-11pm Sun. **Tickets** £8-£20. **Credit** MC, V. **Map** p266 J6.
Established 60 years ago, when Glenn Miller was a regular. In the 1950s, it became a leading jazz joint, in the '60s a blues and R&B hangout, and in the '70s it was the home of punk. These days, it's a mix of indie and jazz/swing.

O2 Arena

Millennium Way, SE10 0BB (8463 2000 information, 0844 856 0202 tickets, www.theo2.co.uk). North Greenwich tube. **Box office** *In person* noon-7pm daily; noon-9pm (performance days only). *By phone* 24hrs daily. **Tickets** £10-£100. **Credit** AmEx, MC, V.
Since its launch in 2007, the former Millennium Dome has been a successful concert venue. It's now a state-of-the-art, 23,000-capacity enormodome with good acoustics and sightlines, hosting big acts (the likes of Celine Dion, Pet Shop Boys, Prince, Justin Timberlake and Kylie).

Pizza Express Jazz Club

10 Dean Street, W1D 3RW (0845 602 7017, www. pizzaexpresslive.com). Tottenham Court Road tube. **Shows** hrs vary. **Admission** £15-£25. **Credit** AmEx, MC, V. **Map** p267 K6.
The food takes second billing in the basement of this eaterie: this is all about contemporary mainstream jazz.

Ronnie Scott's

47 Frith Street, W1D 4HT (7439 0747, www.ronnie scotts.co.uk). Leicester Square or Tottenham Court Road tube. **Shows** 7.30pm daily. **Admission** (non-members) £15-£100. **Credit** AmEx, DC, MC, V. **Map** p267 K6.
Scott died in 1996 after running one of the world's most famous jazz clubs for four decades. It remains an atmospheric Soho fixture, though it's not as jazzy as it once was.

12 Bar Club

22-23 Denmark Place, WC2H 8NL (7240 2622, www.12barclub.com). Tottenham Court Road tube. **Open** *Café* 11am-7pm Mon-Fri; noon-7pm Sat, Sun. *Bar* 7pm-3am Mon-Sat; 6-10.30pm Sun. **Shows** from 7.30pm; nights vary. **Admission** £5-£15. **No credit cards. Map** p267 K6.
The tiny 12 Bar Club, an acoustic venue, is popular with visiting US singer-songwriters.

Sport & Fitness

Work that body.

Back in the dark days of the closet, one of the predominant gay stereotypes was that of a limp-wristed weakling, who, as a child, was always picked last for the team. There may be some truth in stereotypes – many gays would still rather listen to Judy Garland than pump iron – but times are changing.

These days, many gay men have chiselled torsos that make straight guys look like Pee Wee Herman. As for lesbians, the butch cliché holds true when it comes to team sports, but surely this is a good thing if you're an athletically inclined woman. And judging from the wealth of gay sports teams in London, from footie to cricket to rugby, it seems that queers have finally discovered their inner athletic prowess.

For general information about the scene, visit the websites of the **European Gay & Lesbian Sports Foundation** (www.gaysport.org) or **Out for Sport** (www.outforsport.org).

Clubs & societies

Badminton

Fit Women Badminton

Britannia Leisure Centre, 40 Hyde Road, N1 5JU (fitwomenfw@yahoo.co.uk, www.fitwomen.org.uk). Old Street tube/rail or Hoxton rail. **Meetings** 7-9pm Mon. **Admission** £5 for 2hrs.
A social club open to women of all ages and ability. Drinks in the pub often follow meetings, and there are occasional camping and walking weekends. Members compete in the annual Goslings International Badminton Tournament, and travel to the World Out Games.

Goslings Lesbian & Gay Badminton Club

www.goslingssportsclub.com. **Meetings** 7-10pm Mon, Tue; 7.30-10pm Thur. **Membership** £6/yr. **Admission** £7-£8; £5-£6 members; £3-£4 reductions.
This social badminton club welcomes all standards of players. Sessions take place at Finsbury Leisure Centre, EC1 (Old Street tube/rail); Kensington Sports Centre, W11 (Ladbroke Grove tube); and Talacre Community Sports Centre, NW5 (Kentish Town tube/rail). They usually culminate with a few drinks at a nearby pub. The club also runs a social swim night (*see p142*).

St Gabriel's Badminton Club

Church Hall, Glasgow Terrace, Churchill Gardens, off Lupus Street, SW1V 3AA (07967 655 515, www.stgabriels.org.uk). Pimlico tube. **Meetings** 6.30-10.30pm Wed, Fri. **Membership** £100/yr. **Admission** £8; £5 members.
Suited to more experienced players, this is a mostly male club, but all are welcome. The two teams play in the local London league on Sundays and also compete in international gay tournaments. There are social events too. To arrange a trial, email info@stgabriels.org.uk.

Basketball

London Cruisers Basketball Team

Women *Bethnal Green Technical College, 8 Gosset Road, E2 6NW (contact: Hannah 07800 647 271).* Bethnal Green tube. **Training** 7-9pm Thur. **Membership** phone for details.
Men *Britannia Leisure Centre, 40 Hyde Road, N1 5JU (contact: Kasper 07881 996 617). Haggerston rail.* **Training** 7-9pm Fri. **Membership** £90/6 mths. **Both** *www.cruisers.org.uk.*
Ten years ago, the Cruisers formed a women's team to play in the Gay Games in Amsterdam. Now they have four teams, including two for men, which participate in league games. Experienced players are always welcome.

Bowling

Bowling Bears

Queens, 17 Queensway, W2 4QP (contact: Adam Cook 07092 292 695, www.bowlingbears.com). Bayswater tube. **Meetings** 4.30pm last Sun of mth. **Admission** £10. **Map** p262 C7.
This friendly group is open to gay men looking for a fun, sociable bowling experience (is there any other kind?). Members meet around the bar for a drink before taking to the alleys. Call first or email info@bowlingbears.com to confirm your attendance. The venue occasionally changes.

Cricket

Grace's Cricket Club

Contact: Duncan Irvine 7278 3294, www.gaycricket.org.uk.
This gay cricket group plays about 25 matches during the summer; training begins in April at the prestigious Lords Cricket Ground. There are opportunities for overseas tours as well. It's open to all ages and the membership fee is dependent on income.

Salsa Rosada Gay Salsa Classes

Cycling

Cycleout

Contact: Peter 8747 4640, www.cycleout.org.uk.
Covering the greenbelt surrounding London, Cycleout's
weekend rides vary from gentle Sunday spins to more
serious racing. Membership costs £4-£6 per year; a list
of upcoming events can be found on the website.

Cycleout is open to gay men only; email info@cycle-
out.org.uk to join. Lesbians wishing to participate are
referred to the sister group Dykes on Bikes.

Dykes on Bikes

www.dobs.org.uk.
The sister group of Cycleout, Dykes on Bikes organises a
similar calendar of events for lesbian cycling enthusiasts.

Dance

For more dance classes, *see p123*. For dance club
nights, *see p52* **You shall go to the ball**.

Dance Out Loud

Central YMCA, 112 Great Russell Street,
WC1B 3NQ (Contact: Bodhi 07971 465 290,
www.5rhythms.webs.com). Tottenham Court Road
tube. **Classes** 7.30-9.30pm Fri. **Admission** £10;
£8 reductions. **Map** p267 K5.
Anything goes at this free-form dance class. The clientele
is predominantly gay and lesbian.

Salsa Rosada Gay Salsa Classes

The Welsh Centre, 157-163 Gray's Inn Road, WC1X
8UE (7813 4831, www.salsa-rosada.co.uk). Chancery
Lane or Russell Square tube/King's Cross tube/rail.
Classes *Beginners* 7-8pm Wed. *Intermediate* 8-9pm
Wed. **Admission** £6 1 class, £9 2 classes. **No credit
cards**. **Map** p267 M4.
Salsa Rosada has been teaching gay men and women to
salsa since 1994. Beginners can attend the first class of the
evening, followed by intermediates at 8pm.

Studio LaDanza

89 Holloway Road, N7 8LT (7700 3770, www.
studioladanza.co.uk). Highbury & Islington tube/rail.
Workshops 7-8.30pm Wed. **Social dancing**
8.30-10.30pm Wed. **Admission** social only £6;
workshops £38/4wks (incl entrance to social dance).
No credit cards.
The large dancefloor provides plenty of room for ballroom
and Latin workshops or socials, which take place from
8.30pm onwards (bring your own refreshments).
Individual lessons cost £42 for 55mins. There are also residential weekends in Paris and the annual gay and lesbian
black-tie ball in January.

Football

Club Leftfooters

www.leftfooters.org.uk, info@leftfooters.org.uk.
The Leftfooters meet for friendly kickabouts in Regent's
Park every Sunday from 2pm. As the name would suggest,

players of all – or no – ability are welcome. Although most of the play is recreational, the Leftfooters do take part in the GFSN Football League. Membership is free.

Gay Football Supporters Network

www.gfsn.org.uk.
In the largely straight world of football, the GFSN aims to bring together like-minded footie supporters. There are newsletters, socials, tournaments and an annual knees-up.

Hackney Women's Football Club

Contact: Amanda 07867 946 614, www. intheteam.com/ hackneywfc. **Training** *Summer* (Clissold Park, N16) 6-8pm Wed. *Winter* (St Thomas Moore School, N22) 7.30-9.30pm Wed. **Membership** £60/yr; £40 reductions.
For further details and confirmation of training times, check the website. *See right* **Playing away**.

International Gay & Lesbian Football Association (IGLFA)

www.iglfa.org.
International association with online magazine, team pictures and advice for gay and lesbian football enthusiasts.

Joybabe WFC

Contact: Catherine 07764 752 731, www.joybabe.com. **Membership** £100/season; £50 reductions.
Based in north London, the Joybabes are a team of experienced players who like to play for the fun of the game, meeting for matches or indoor five-a-sides rather than training sessions. The team play in the Greater London Regional Women's League, Division 2.

London Lesbian Kickabouts

Contact: Andrea 07773 928 434, www.lesbianfootball.com.

As the name suggests, this is a football group for lesbians looking for a friendly kickabout. Games are held in Camden on Tuesdays, and Regent's Park on Sundays, and are usually rounded off with a drink at a pub. Everyone can take part regardless of ability; come as little or as often as you like. Email info@lesbianfootball.com for times or check details on the website.

South London Studs

Contact: Gillian southlondonstuds@hotmail.com.
This lesbian team has participated in the Greater London League for more than a decade and regularly attends gay tournaments in the UK and abroad. That said, all standards are welcome. Training (7.30-9pm Thur) takes place in Norbury. Matches are played Burrbage Road, Dulwich, usually 2pm on Sundays. Fees: £3 for training, £5 for matches.

Stonewall Football Club

07896 620 513, www.stonewallfc.com.
Stonewall is a well-established club that plays a first and a reserve team with weekly Saturday fixtures in the Middlesex County Football League. In addition, there are various overseas tours and social events. Two separate training sessions take place on Thursday evenings; one is just for casual players. Email stonewallfc@hotmail.com if you're interested.

Golf

Irons Golf Society

www.ironsgolf.co.uk.
Irons play at least one Sunday a month during the summer at courses in and around London. Tours abroad in the past have included such destinations as France and Thailand, and there are knockout tournaments and golf weeks organised around Britain. Open to all lesbian and gay golfers with at least some experience of the sport.

Remnants Hockey Club

Hockey

Remnants Hockey Club

Eltham College, Marvels Lane, Grove Park,
SE12 9PH (contact: Phil 07870 690 794,
www.remnantshockey.org.uk). Grove Park rail.
Training 8pm Thur. **Membership** £100/yr.
One of the only openly gay women's hockey clubs in the
United Kingdom, Remnants Hockey Club has two teams,
with a mix of abilities and skill levels. During the regular hockey match season, games are held every Saturday
at various south London venues.

Kickboxing

KB Kickboxing

7681 0114, 07881 957 977, www.kbkickboxing.co.uk.
Admission £45/mth 5-6 classes (1 discipline);
£89/mth unlimited classes.
Kelly Bunyan's kickboxing school is a great success, with
more than 30 classes a week to choose from at various
venues in central London. Kung fu, judo, self-defence and
Pilates are also taught.

Martial arts

Ishigaki Ju-Jitsu Club

Contact: Simon 07740 857 261, www.ishigaki.org.uk.
Training 7.30-9.30pm Mon, Tue, Thur; 3.30-5.30pm
Sat. **Membership** £25-£30/yr. **Admission**
£8/session.
Ideal for those wishing to learn self-defence, the Ishigaki
Ju-Jitsu Club welcomes a diverse crowd of gay men and
women. Beginners are encouraged to watch a session
(at a location in central London) and then join the group
at the pub afterwards. Check the website for more information about the club.

Kung Fu

American Church, Tottenham Court Road, W1T 4TD
(7681 0114, www.kbfitness.co.uk). Goodge Street tube.
Map p267 K5. **Admission** £45/mth 5-6 classes.
Run by the KB Kickboxing crowd, this gay-friendly class
welcomes everyone. Confirm class times on the website.

Motorcycling

Gay Bikers Motorcycle Club

www.gaybikers.co.uk.
With over 150 members, the Gay Bikers Motorcycle Club
is the largest organisation of its type for gay and lesbian
riders in Europe. Email info@gaybikers.co.uk for details.

Women's International Motorcycle Association

www.wimagb.co.uk.
The UK sector of this international outfit welcomes all
female bikers, gay or straight. Members are encouraged to
organise rides and meetings in their local area, and attend
regional meetings (there are also national UK rallies and
international events). You can print a membership form
from the website.

Playing away

Hackney Women's Football Club (*see left*),
London's most infamous women's football
team, has been running around in short trousers
since 1986. They're a thoroughly right-on team:
they were the first squad to instigate a 'fair play'
policy, ensuring that all women are encouraged
to play competitive football regardless of their
skills, age, ethnic origin or sexual orientation.
Visiting players are welcome to join in, as are
newcomers to the beautiful game. As well as
pub visits after training and matches, there are
gatherings to go ten-pin bowling or to the dogs –
and friends are welcome to tag along. The whole
club ethos is to work as a team, have fun and
get exercise. And that's just the supporters.

Sure, the team's song might give the
impression these girls aren't all that serious.
The lyrics, sung to the tune of 'These Boots
Are Made for Walking', go like this: 'You keep
playing where you shouldn't be playing/You
keep losing when you oughta win/You keep
raving when you oughta be a saving/And you
keep playing when you're out of your skin.'
But don't be fooled by the fun: with two teams –
a first and a reserve – Hackney Women's
Football Club is a highly respected competitor
in the Greater London Women's Football
League, having played in the Premier League
after winning the Division 1 championships
in 2005, and having won the 2009 GLWFL
League Cup. That said, the girls are anything
but respectable at their post-match soirées,
which are when they really let their hair down.

Rugby

Visit www.rfu.com, the website of the **Rugby
Football Union**, the official body for both men's
and women's rugby, for the game's history, news
and team contact info.

Kings Cross Steelers RFC

*East London RFC, Holland Road, E15 3BP (07767 232
909, www.kxsrfc.com). West Ham tube.* **Training** 7-9pm
Mon, Wed. **Membership** £75/season; £35 reductions.
The world's first gay/bisexual rugby team was founded in
1995 and has since been accepted as a full member of the
English Rugby Football Union. The first team play in the
Essex League Division 2. The benefits of playing at this
reputable club include the professional coaching, regular
social events and access to Six Nations and other international tickets from Twickenham. The club welcomes both
inexperienced and competitive rugby players.

Rosslyn Park Slingbacks

*Rosslyn Park FC, Priory Lane, Upper Richmond Road,
SW15 5JH (Contact: Lizzie 07788 651 637, www.rosslyn
park.co.uk). Barnes rail.* **Training** 7-9pm Mon, Wed.

Arts & Entertainment

The swimming pool library

Chilly, grey London isn't exactly synonymous with swimming pools. But getting wet in the capital doesn't always mean reaching for your umbrella. In fact, although London's weather is far from tropical, there are a couple of Riviera-style lidos, and an outdoor pool where – believe it or not – swimming in January is commonplace. What's more, public bathing spots are, ahem, a good place to pull, as writer Alan Hollinghurst pointed out in his 1998 novel, *The Swimming Pool Library*, in which the swimming took a back seat to sex.

The **Oasis Sports Centre** (*see p144*) is ground zero for gay swimmers. This rooftop pool, located in the heart of the capital, is open all year – rain or shine. For those who can't brave the winter chill, there's an indoor pool. But the outside pool is the star of the show; potted palm trees lend an exotic air, and, in the winter months, steam rises off the warm blue waters. Inside, the men's showers get steamy too, with all the ogling and posing that goes on. In summer, the sundeck is also a prime cruising ground.

For swimming in style, south London has a pair of deliciously retro lidos. On a sunny day, **Brockwell Park Lido** (Dulwich Road, SE24 0PA, 7274 3088, closed Oct-May) and **Tooting Bec Lido** (Tooting Bec Common, SW16, 8871 7198,

www.slsc.org.uk, closed Sept-April) evoke Miami Beach circa 1950, with their colourful art deco touches, sunbeds, palm trees and gaudy blue waters. Both pools attract a considerable gay constituency, though be warned: screaming kiddies are also out in full force. Likewise, in north London, **Parliament Hill Lido** (Hampstead Heath, Gordon House Road, NW5 1QR, 7485 3873) and **Finchley Lido** (Great North Leisure Park, High Road, N12 0GL, 8343 9830) offer similar poolside pleasures, as does the glorious, restored **London Fields Lido** (London Fields Westside, E8 3EU, 7254 9038, www.gll.org), which stays open all year.

For a taste of genteel homoeroticism, the **Porchester Centre** (*see p146*) has an indoor swimming pool and a nicely refined air, though the gay vibe here is more of an undercurrent than anything overt. The most luxurious hotel swimming pool is the shimmering underground beauty at **One Aldwych** (*see p73*), which pipes classical music underwater in dimly lit surroundings. Annual or day memberships are available for both health clubs.

But London's most atmospheric swimming spots are not actually pools. The **Hampstead**

This women's team plays in Premier 2 of the national league and welcome new players at any level. Having a good night out also figures high on the agenda; the Slingbacks often cross paths with the Rosslyn men's team on socials. Contact the club for details about joining and membership prices.

Running

London Frontrunners

07092 346 340, www.londonfrontrunners.org.
Runs 7pm Mon (South Bank); 7pm Wed (Regent's Park); 10am Sat (Hyde Park). **Membership** £25/yr.
A diverse group of lesbians and gay men who simply love to run. Meeting three times a week, the Frontrunners attract a mixed crowd, from those wishing to improve their fitness levels to those training to run marathons. Runs are often followed by drinks. Email info@londonfrontrunners.org or see the website for more details.

Sailing

Sailing & Cruising Association

Downstairs, Kudos, 10 Adelaide Street, WC2N 4HZ (www.gaysailing.org.uk). Charing Cross tube/rail.
Meetings 8pm 2nd Tue of mth. **Membership** £15 single; £20 couple. **Map** p269 L7.
No experience is required to join this group of 350 gay men and women, who enjoy cruises (the sailing kind) during the summer and meet up in the Kudos bar in the West End all year round. If you don't own a boat, you can still come and crew. Summer dinghy sailing in London (in the Docks or on the Thames) is also popular.

Softball

London Raiders

Wandsworth Common, Bellevue Road, SW12 (www.londonraiders.co.uk). Wandsworth Common rail. **Training** *Mar-Sept* times vary; check website for deatils. **Membership** £55.
This gay softball group welcomes new players, regardless of experience – the emphasis is on having fun. Games usually take place on Wandsworth Common.

Squash

4play Squash Club

www.4playsquash.org. **Training** 10am-noon, 4-6pm Sat; 5.20-7.20pm, 6.30-8pm Sun.
Admission £3-£6.
A squash group for gay people and their friends, which holds regular social outings. All standards are welcome as long as you own a racquet; an optional annual tournament is held in May each year.

Swimming

Gay London Swimmers

Camberwell Leisure Centre, Artichoke Place, SE5 8TS (contact: Roger, evenings 8591 3508). Bus 12, 36, 176.
Meetings 8.15pm-9.15pm Fri. **Membership** £5/yr.
Admission £2.50-£3.50.

Heath Ponds (*see p209*) are dreamy, bucolic oases. Surrounded by lush woodland, the secluded lakes are magical enclaves, and the stuff of midsummer nights' dreams. The men's bathing pond is not exclusively gay, but it is very homoerotic: after all, this is Hampstead Heath, the city's number-one cruising ground (*see p208* **Fast love**); a sheltered concrete sundeck allows nude sunbathing; and the changing rooms are full of smouldering glances. The ladies' pond has a similarly sapphic appeal.

For more swimming in the great outdoors, try the **Serpentine Swimming Club** (www.serpentine swimmingclub.com) in Hyde Park. Running since 1864, this club of hardy souls assembles every Saturday morning on the lake's banks at 8am – all year round (in winter, swimmers will even break holes in the ice to get their fix). For a less bracing experience, the **Serpentine Lido** (7706 3422, closed mid Sept-May), a buoyed-off area of the lake, is open to casual swimmers between June and September, with a veranda for fair-weather frolics.

For information about other swimming pools, *see p143* **Gyms, saunas & spas**.

Arts & Entertainment

The 30 or so members of this club swim *au naturel* every week at Camberwell Leisure Centre. Those who don't or can't swim can turn up and learn – or just play beach ball.

Soho Gym. *See p144.*

Goslings Swimming

Oasis Sports Centre, 32 Endell Street, WC2H 9AG (07814 258 055, www.goslingssportsclub.com). Covent Garden, Holborn or Tottenham Court Road tube. **Meetings** 5.30-6.30pm Mon; 8.30-9.30pm Thur. **Admission** £3.60-£4. **Map** p267 L6.
Operating for more than 20 years, the friendly Goslings organise badminton (*see p136*) and swimming sessions – usually followed by drinks at a pub. Open to all levels; new swimmers welcome. Contact goslings@hotmail.com.

Hampstead Heath Ponds

Millfield Lane, N6 (7485 4491,www.cityoflondon.gov.uk/ openspaces). Archway tube/Gospel Oak rail. **Open** dawn-dusk daily (times may vary). **Admission** £2; £1 reductions. *Season ticket* £149/yr; £82/yr reductions.
The men's and women's ponds are open every day of the year; the mixed pond is May-Sept only. *See also p140* **The swimming pool library**.

Out to Swim

www.outtoswim.org.
Aimed at gay swimmers who are confident in at least two different strokes and fit enough to swim for an hour, swims take place most evenings in various London sports centres. After Thursday sessions, women often go to the Star at Night (*see p55*) or First Out (*see p53*). There are various membership options, the cheapest starts with an initial £25, then £3.50 per session.

Tennis

Many parks around the city have council-run outdoor courts that cost little or nothing to use. For lessons, try the **Regent's Park Tennis Centre** (7486 4216, www.tennisinthepark.co.uk). For grass courts, phone the **Lawn Tennis Association**'s information department (8487 7000, www.lta.org.uk). The **Islington Tennis Centre** (7700 1370, www.aquaterra.org) has indoor as well as outdoor courts, as does the **Westway Sports Centre** (8969 0992, www.westway.org).

London Gay Tennis Club

Islington Tennis Centre, Market Road, N7 9PL (contact: Derek 8445 3641, Garrey 8673 3351). Caledonian Road tube. **Meetings** 11am-1pm Sun. **Admission** £4-£6/session.
A pay-and-play session for confident gay and lesbian tennis players.

Tennis London International

Westway Indoor Tennis Centre, Crowthorne Road, W10 6RP (www.tennislondon.com). Latimer Road tube. **Meetings** 5-9 pm Sun. **Membership** £30/yr; £15/yr reductions. **Admission** *Members* £10; £5 reductions. *Non-members* £15; £8 reductions.

Every Sunday evening, between 30 and 50 members meet up to play short doubles sets and engage in 'light banter and heavy gossip', according to the website. The club also runs the Tennis London International Championships. Lessons for beginners and those needing a refresher course are also held on Sundays; check the website, or email info@tennislondon.com for details.

Volleyball

Dynamo Dykes Volleyball Club

www.dynamodykes.org.uk.
London's premier lesbian volleyball team takes part in league matches and international tournaments. They practise twice weekly – beginners on Thursdays at Brixton Recreation Centre, Brixton Station Road, SW9 (Brixton tube/rail) and intermediate and advanced players on Wednesdays at Bethnal Green Sports Centre, Gosset Street, E2 (Bethnal Green tube) – during the volleyball season (Sept-May). During the summer, the action moves to Hyde Park. Contact dynamoteam@hotmail.com for details of membership prices and to join up.

London Spikers Volleyball Club

Bethnal Green Sports Centre, Gosset Street,
E2 6NW (www.londonspikers.org). Bethnal Green tube.
Training *Sept-Apr* noon-4pm Sun.
Spikers, a gay men's volleyball team, offers a welcoming atmosphere for beginners and a chance for pros to prove their talents at league matches and European tournaments. In addition to Sundays, there are individual team sessions during the week. In summer, team training is moved to Hyde Park, near Speakers' Corner. They won the London Premier League title in 2010. Contact info@londonspikers.org for details of membership prices and to join up.

Walking

Gay Outdoors Club London

www.goc.org.uk.
These day walks, held on the second Sunday of each month, attract groups of between 12 and 20 people from a variety of backgrounds and ages. The walks are usually eight to 12 miles long, and start and finish at a rural railway station (about an hour from London). Lunch is often eaten in a pub; alternatively, bring a packed one. From May to September, there are also evening walks in London, rounded off by a meal or pub visit. Visitors to London are welcome, as are non-members who want to give the Gay Outdoors Club a try.

Gay Sunday Walking Group (GSWG)

GSWG, PO Box 63976, SW15 6BW (contact: John
7701 1013, www.gswg.org.uk).
Walks generally take place in London or out in the rolling countryside of the Home Counties – with clearly set out train times and meeting points – and the 30-odd ramblers usually end up in a pub. Membership is only £5/year and application forms to join the group can be printed from the website. For details of walks, send an SAE to the PO Box address above to receive a list of dates.

Yoga

Yoga For Gay Men

Yoga Base, 255-257 Liverpool Road, N1 1LX
(contact: David Tierney 7625 4521, www.gayyoga.
gn.apc.org). **Classes** 6.45pm Fri; 7pm Sun.
Admission £10.
David Tierney's popular yoga classes are limited to 16 people, so you need to book in advance. Lessons for beginners are held on Sundays.

Gyms, saunas & spas

For gay saunas, *see p49.*

Central YMCA

112 Great Russell Street, WC1B 3NQ (7343 1700,
www.ymca.co.uk). Tottenham Court Road tube. **Open**
6.30am-10pm Mon-Fri; 10am-8pm Sat; 10am-6.30pm Sun. **Membership** (varies depending on age) £53/wk; £182-£255/3 mths; £467-£552/yr. **Joining fee** £30. **Admission** (non-members) £15/day. **Credit** MC, V. **Map** p267 K5.
As the Village People song suggests, this YMCA attracts its fair share of gay men. It's hard to beat the unpretentious atmosphere, reasonable prices and broad curriculum. At its core is a large hall, with facilities for circuit training, badminton, table tennis and basketball; or you can run, cycle or ski in front of a bank of screens. You'll also find a free-weights room, a squash court, a treadmill and step-machine area, and studios for step, spinning, toning and firming, Pilates and yoga. Balconies overlooking the main sports hall are lined with a full range of CV and resistance weights machines. The large 25m pool is divided for lane swimming. Numerous classes are run throughout the week, and there's also a chapel, sunbeds and a good café.

Fitness First

6 Bedford Street, WC2E 9HD (7240 8411, www.
fitnessfirst.com). Covent Garden tube. **Open** 6.30am-9pm Mon-Fri; 10am-5pm Sat, Sun. **Membership** varies; phone for details. **Credit** MC, V. **Map** p269 L7.
Another gay favourite, probably due to the Covent Garden location, Fitness First has a good selection of gym equipment, including CV and resistance machines, free weights and a studio. There are also classes, sunbeds and a sauna. **Other locations** throughout the city.

Jubilee Sports Centre

Caird Street, W10 4RR (8960 9629, www.courtneys.
co.uk). Westbourne Park tube/Queen's Park tube/rail.
Open 6.30am-10pm Mon-Fri; 8am-8pm Sat, Sun. **Membership** £30-£48/mth. **Induction fee** (non-members) £37.60. **Admission** (non-members) *Gym* £8.45; £2.75 reductions (off-peak). *Pool only* £4.55; free reductions. **Credit** MC, V.
The Jubilee Centre announces itself to passers-by with huge floor-length windows by the pavement, so you can be a street-side spectator of the swimmers inside. The 25m pool is of the lovely serene type, clean with wide lanes and never too busy. The two gyms separate the CV theatre from the free weights, so you can work out without feeling weedy in front of muscle men. Other highlights include a sauna and steam room, plus classes in martial arts, boxercise and yoga.

Arts & Entertainment

Oasis Sports Centre

32 Endell Street, WC2H 9AG (7831 1804, www.gll.org). Holborn tube. **Open** 6.30am-10pm Mon-Fri; 9.30am-6pm Sat, Sun. **Membership** £46/mth; £460/yr. **Admission** *Pool only* £4. **Credit** MC, V. **Map** p267 L6.

The Oasis Sports Centre, a long-standing gay favourite in Covent Garden, is renowned for its palm-fringed sun terrace and outdoor heated swimming pool – a haven for sun-seekers and sturdy winter dippers alike. If you're less ballsy, try the adjacent indoor pool, which has swimming and aqua fitness classes (*see also p140* **The swimming pool library**). The gym is spacious, well equipped and buzzing, with friendly staff on hand to offer advice; the quantity of CV machines also means that queuing is rare. There's also a wide choice of group classes, from aero-biking to Pilates, circuits to yoga. The changing facilities are clean and spacious.

Paris Gym

73 Goding Street, SE11 5AW (7735 8989, www.paris gym.com). Vauxhall tube/rail. **Open** 6.30am-11pm Mon-Fri; 9am-10pm Sat; 9am-8pm Sun. **Membership** £39-£46/mth; £390-£460/yr. **Admission** (non-members) £10. **Credit** AmEx, MC, V.

London's only exclusively gay, all-male gym is tucked under the railway arches in the shadow of the MI6 head-quarters, a few doors down from the gay clubs. Pectoral muscles and tight T-shirts abound inside: the place is reminiscent of the sultry film version of *A Streetcar Named Desire*. The gym itself is well equipped, mostly with weights and cardio machines. Staff are friendly, but this place is meant to be more exercise and less cruise, as the website states: 'Although we do have a sauna, we strongly recommend you look elsewhere if you are hoping for that "other sort" of workout.' Personal trainers can be booked; other perks include a nutrition bar, stand-up sunbed, free internet and a hairdresser on Fridays.

Queen Mother Sports Centre

223 Vauxhall Bridge Road, SW1V 1EL (7630 5522, www.courtneys.co.uk). Victoria tube/rail. **Open** 6.30am-10pm Mon-Fri; 8am-8pm Sat, Sun. **Membership** £30/mth (pool only); £49/mth (gym). **Induction fee** (non-members) £37.65. **Admission** (non-members) £8.65. **Credit** MC, V. **Map** p268 J10.

The 25m pool, with its new tiles, roof and slide, is superb. Yet even without the pool, the QM is still one of the best no-nonsense fitness centres in the area, with a huge CV room, two spring-floored studios, separate male and female sessions in the steam room and sauna – and plenty more besides. The sports hall is situated towards the back of the centre, and is often busy with all kinds of court sports, from basketball to volleyball, not to mention the popular five-a-side football and occasional cricket nets.

Slim Jim's Health Club

1 Finsbury Avenue, EC2M 2PF (7247 9982, www.slim-jims.co.uk). Liverpool Street or Moorgate tube/rail. **Open** 6am-10pm Mon-Thur; 6am-8pm Fri. **Membership** £49-£63/mth. **Credit** MC, V. **Map** p271 Q5.

SJ's has something of the gentlemen's club about it: deep leather sofas and mahogany tables sit stolidly beneath the war portraits on the walls. The gym itself is large and modern, with a perimeter of fitness bikes and treadmills overlooking the resistance machines below. Classes cover everything from spinning to crewing.

Soho Gym

12 Macklin Street, WC2B 5NF (7242 1290, www.soho gyms.com). Holborn tube. **Open** 7am-10pm Mon-Fri; 8am-8pm Sat; noon-6pm Sun. **Membership** from £43/mth. **Admission** (non-members) £10. **Credit** MC, V. **Map** p267 L6.

This mostly male club, decked out in cool blue and silver, is a voyeur's heaven. There are mirrors everywhere (even tactically placed ones in the showers), enabling the largely gay clientele to admire themselves (and one another) unrestrainedly. In the spacious gym, all the usual CV machinery is lined up in rows. The studio, although on the small side, offers a variety of classes dedicated to the body beautiful. The club also has a café and two sunbeds, plus physio and massage facilities.

Other locations 193 Camden High Street, NW1 7JY (7482 4524); 95-97 Clapham High Street, SW4 7TB (7720 0321); 254 Earl's Court Road, SW5 9AD (7370 1402); 11-15 Brad Street, SE1 8TG (0845 270 9270); Empire Square, Tabard Street, SE1 4NL (0845 677 8890).

Sweatbox Soho

Ramillies House, 1-2 Ramillies Street, W1F 7LN (3214 6014, www.sweatboxsoho.com). Oxford Circus tube. **Open** noon-2am Mon-Thur; 24hrs Fri-Sun. **Membership** £39/mth; £349/yr. **Admission** (non-members) £15 24hr pass; £15 spa only; £10 under-25s. **Map** p266 J6.

See right **Gonna make you sweat**.

Spas

For hairdressers and barbers, *see pp115-116*.

Gentlemen's Tonic

31A Bruton Place, W1J 6NN (7297 4343, www. gentlemenstonic.com). Green Park tube. **Open** 10am-7pm Mon, Fri; 10am-8pm Tue, Wed; 10am-9pm Thur; 10am-6pm Sat. **Credit** AmEx, MC, V. **Map** p268 H7.

Gentlemen's Tonic offers an extensive array of male grooming services, from hand and facial treatments to Swedish massage. Our chosen 'tonic' could only be the wet shave (£34). The enthusiastic master barber, Mark Nimki, leads the way into his old-world-meets-modern booth. After a brief chat, the barber's chair is reclined to horizontal. Any thoughts of Sweeney Todd vanish as almond oil is applied to soften the bristles, followed by a hot towel and a cream-lathered badger-hair brush. Then the master goes to work with his cut-throat razor. A visit here is a must.

Other locations Selfridge's, 400 Oxford Street, W1A 1AB (7318 3709).

Jason Shankey

19 Jerdan Place, SW6 1BE (7386 3900, www.jason shankey.com). Fulham Broadway tube. **Open** 10am-7pm Mon, Tue, Fri; 11am-8pm Wed, Thur; 10am-6pm Sat; 11am-4pm Sun. **Credit** AmEx, MC, V.

Jason Shankey is a barber's shop with a difference. Although half of the business comprises straightforward haircuts (a shampoo, cut and rinse costs £25), waxing, massage and facials are offered in three treatment rooms on the first floor. Situated in an old Fulham townhouse, the salon has a friendly feel that is unintimidating and

Gonna make you sweat

Described as 'the world's sexiest gay gym and sauna', **Sweatbox Soho** (*see left*) is aimed squarely at the gay male market. And it looks more like a nightclub than a typical gymnasium. The sleek red and black design can appear intimidating, but the staff are friendly and soon put you at ease.

Though small, the space is well laid out, with the multi-gym on the ground floor and the free weights room below. The gym includes five state-of-the-art Body Shaker machines, which were developed for astronauts and enable you to maximise the effect of your workout while minimising the time you spend exercising. The machines can be used for practically every muscle group,

from chest to legs, and work by literally shaking the body so the muscles are forced to contract at many times the normal speed.

After the first session, regular gym users often wake up in some discomfort – a sure sign that a routine is working. If pain isn't your thing, rest assured that there are qualified masseurs on hand, offering a range of treatments from deep-tissue massage to the 'Full Body LA Stone Special', which uses hot stones to ease away tensions in tired muscles. Massages cost £45-£90 – if you book a massage, admission is free. And if that doesn't do the trick, or the reason you've come is to do a trick, there's always the sauna (*see p49*) downstairs.

masculine without being overtly blokeish. You're free to help yourself to a beer from the fridge in the tiny lounge, but this is more *GQ* reader than lager lout territory.

Nickel Spa

27 Shorts Gardens, WC2H 9AP (7240 4048, www. nickelspalondon.co.uk). Covent Garden tube. **Open** noon-6pm Mon; 10am-7pm Tue, Wed, Sat; 10am-8pm Thur, Fri; noon-5pm Sun. **Credit** AmEx, MC, V. **Map** p267 L6.
Nickel is a mini haven in Covent Garden. The staff are knowledgeable and do everything in their power to make you feel at ease. The list of treatments available is extensive and reasonably priced: expect to pay £35 for a standard facial, £20 for a manicure, £25 for a pedicure and £60 for a back, crack and sack waxing. The five treatment rooms, situated in the basement, ring to a soundtrack of pan pipes – which is surprisingly relaxing. The deep tissue massage (£60 for 60mins) is pleasurable and professional; what more could a boy ask for? You can also pick up plenty of products in the reception area, from morning-after rescue gel to Silicon Valley anti-ageing cream. It's a popular place, so book ahead.

Porchester Centre

Queensway, W2 5HS (7792 2919, www.courtneys. co.uk). Bayswater, Queensway or Royal Oak tube. **Open** 6.30am-10pm Mon-Fri; 8am-8pm Sat, Sun. **Membership** from £30/mth. **Induction fee** (non-members) £15. **Admission** (non-members) £8.60. *Pool only* £5; free reductions. **Credit** AmEx, MC, V. **Map** p262 C6.
Housed in a marvellously ornate Victorian building, the Porchester Centre is split into sports activities and the Porchester Spa. The gym is always busy – as befits its central location – and the spa offers a host of luxury treatments in surroundings of sheer opulence. Only the pool, with its scuffed edges, lets the side down a little.

Spa London

Refinery

60 Brook Street, W1K 5DU (7409 2001, www.the-refinery.com). Bond Street tube. **Open** 10am-7pm Mon, Tue; 10am-9pm Wed-Fri; 9am-6pm Sat; 11am-5pm Sun. **Credit** AmEx, MC, V. **Map** p266 H6.
One of the first male grooming salons, and still thriving. The vibe is old-school gentlemen's club – indeed, the *Independent* quipped 'You come out feeling like Cary Grant'. Treatments range from manicures and massages to waxing and wet shaves. New treatments include micro-dermabrasion facials and 'intimate' waxing (£45-£120). **Other locations** Harrods, 87-135 Brompton Road, SW1X 7XL (7893 8332).

Spa London

York Hall Leisure Centre, Old Ford Road, E2 9PJ (8709 5845, www.spa-london.org). Bethnal Green tube/rail. **Open** *Men* 11am-9.30pm Mon; 10am-9.30pm Thur. *Women* 10am-9.30pm Tue, Fri; 10am-4.30pm Wed; 9am-7.30pm Sat. *Mixed* 5-9.30pm Wed; 9am-7.30pm Sun. **Membership** £600/yr. **Credit** MC, V.
Located inside historic York Hall, this leisure centre is known for its Turkish baths, hammam and plunge pool. The baths used to attract a lot of gay men and curious straight men, with plenty of amateur masseurs in tow. Now that the centre is more upmarket and more mainstream, the homoeroticism is less obvious, though there are same-sex days for men and women.

Ice rinks

In addition to the skating rinks listed below (of which only Broadgate is outdoors), the courtyard of **Somerset House** (*see p171*) has a delightful outside rink for two months over the Christmas period (7845 4600, www.somerset-house.org.uk). Over the past few years numerous other seasonal rinks have popped up at attractions around the capital, including Marble Arch, Hampstead Heath, Hampton Court Palace, the Tower of London, the Old Royal Naval College, Kew Gardens and the Natural History Museum.

Alexandra Palace Ice Rink
Alexandra Palace Way, N22 7AY (8365 4386, www.alexandrapalace.com). Wood Green tube then W3 bus. **Open** Phone for details. **Admission** (incl skate hire) £6-£9.

Broadgate Ice Rink
Broadgate Circle, EC2M 2QT (7505 4068, www.broadgatelive.co.uk). Liverpool Street tube/rail. **Open** Nov-Feb. Phone for details. **Admission** £8; £5 reductions; £2 skate hire. **Map** p271 Q5.

Queens
17 Queensway, W2 4QP (7229 0172, www.queens iceandbowl.co.uk). Bayswater or Queensway tube. **Open** 10am-11pm daily. **Admission** (incl skate hire) £12.50. **Map** p262 C6.

Streatham Ice Arena
386 Streatham High Road, SW16 6HT (8769 7771, www.streathamicearena.co.uk). Brixton tube/rail then 109 bus, or Streatham rail. **Open** Phone for details. **Admission** (incl skate hire) £5-£8.

Around Town

History   **148**
  Queeny kings   151
  An affair to remember   154

Getting started   **159**
  The best Sights   159

South Bank & Bankside   **160**

The City   **167**

Holborn & Clerkenwell   **171**

Bloomsbury & Fitzrovia   **174**

Marylebone & Oxford Street   **179**

Mayfair & St James's   **182**

Soho   **186**
  Map Soho   187
  My favourite things Jonny Woo   191

Covent Garden   **194**

Westminster & Victoria   **198**

Kensington & Chelsea   **202**

North London   **207**
  Fast love   208

East London   **211**

South London   **217**

West London   **225**

Brighton   **229**
  Proud marys   232

History

Tales of the city.

London might truly be called the Modern Sodom. A century ago, that was the view of French anthropologist Dr Jacobus X, who rated London as the world's homosexual capital and the English 'perhaps the chief pederasts in the world'.

That was 1904, and the city has kept its end up, as far as sodomy goes, ever since. Except we don't use the 'S' word any more. Lesbian, gay, homosexual, bisexual, transgendered, trisexual, queer… the shifting flow of terms is as fluid as the scene. How times have changed since homosexuality was referred to as 'the love that dare not speak its name' in London's Central Criminal Court, the Old Bailey, on 3 April 1895 during Oscar Wilde's trials.

And just as today's commentators debate the existence of a 'gay community', some historians argue that a 'gay history' of London is impossible. Indeed, some critics say the catamites and 'ingles' (younger male lovers) of Shakespeare's London, the mollies and sapphists of Georgian London, the Victorian city's Uranians and inverts and today's LGBTs are just too diverse to lump together. But there is a definite line connecting today's gay experience to yesterday's queer.

COCKY CELTS AND RANDY ROMANS

The history of gay London, like the history of London itself, starts by the river. Stand in Battersea Park and imagine Julius Caesar trying to subdue the Catuvellani, a Celtic tribe that once dominated southern Britain. Though Caesar's 54 BC expedition failed to establish a permanent base here, it was London's first touch of what we might call 'that old Roman camp', as Christopher Isherwood put it. True, there is no record of the Roman leader trying any bedtime homo tactics with Cunobelinus, the king of the Catuvellani (who was memorably portrayed in Shakespeare's *Cymbeline*). But there are rumours that Caesar had previously conquered Bithynia (Turkey) by seducing the homosexual king, Nicomedes, in 79 BC. What's more, homosexuality was said to have flourished among the Celts. Picture it: tattooed warrior lads fellating each other and priestesses worshipping labial lesbian goddesses.

Caesar may or may not have bedded any Celts. But the Romans certainly brought some buggery to Britain, according to the National Theatre's 1980 production of Howard Brenton's play *The Romans in Britain*, which sparked controversy during its run at the Southbank. A scene set north of the Thames, in which a Roman soldier rapes a Celtic druid, raised a few gay eyebrows. But this was nothing compared to the reaction of someone who never saw the play – Mary Whitehouse, the self-appointed moral guardian of Britain. The campaigner's decision to prosecute the (straight) director of the play for 'procuring an act of gross indecency' aligned her with the far-right protesters who threw fireworks and bags of flour at the actors, shouting 'Get poofs off the stage!' Whitehouse abandoned her prosecution mid-trial and was made to pay costs.

Those curious about what else the Romans might have got up to in Britain should go to the British Museum (*see p175*) and look at the Warren Cup in Room 70. This is not a prize for athletic achievement, but a prize piece of ancient gay smut. It's a silver drinking cup, probably made in the reign of Nero, carefully decorated with two scenes of mattress-sharing males.

MEDIEVAL MARYS

Things went rather quiet during the Middle Ages. That's partly because records are sparse, although the period marked the beginning of the Church's continuing struggle to sort out what to do about non-procreative sex. During the seventh century, London Bishop Theodore (later a saint) set out a penitential – a list of sins and punishments – which classified seven-year penances for the *sodomita* (insertive) and *mollis* (receptive) partners in anal intercourse. Lesbians got three years, but punishment was even more severe for oral sex.

The homosexual trail goes cold until the 11th century. But under King William Rufus (1087- 1100), son of the Norman Conqueror, London was a queer old place. William's court was derided for its swishy ways, long haircuts and fancy footwear, according to the Victorian historian EA Freeman: 'The day they passed in sleep, the night in revellings, dicing and vain talk. Vices before unknown, the vices of the East, the special sin… were rife among them… deepest of all in guilt was the King himself.' Some irony, as the authorities prosecuted homosexuality ruthlessly in the courts of Westminster Hall, which the monarch built as an extension to his palace. Here, an endless parade of sodomites, cross-dressing women and the like were dragged to judgement.

Westminster Hall's queer connections don't stop with King William Rufus. It was also the scene of King Edward II's abdication in 1327. Arguments continue over whether Edward II's reputation as a monarch was fatally undermined by his love for other men. Or was sodomy simply a convenient stick with which to beat a failed ruler? (*See p151* **Queeny kings**.)

RENAISSANCE MEN

With the Renaissance, notions of gay love started to corrupt the innocent minds of London students. Dodgy teachers have always been a target of the press, but the tabloids weren't around to cover the charges against Desiderius Erasmus. A twentysomething Dutch monk and philosopher, Erasmus was accused of seducing his young English pupil Thomas Grey, while tutoring him in Paris. The charges didn't stick. And, in actual fact, the great love of Erasmus's life seems to have been a strapping chap called Servatius Roger, with whom he continued to correspond once he moved to England in 1499. Staying with Thomas More, the author and Catholic martyr, in Bucklersbury (near Mansion House) and Cheyne Walk, Erasmus wrote some yearning gay love letters: 'Farewell my soul, and if there is anything human in you, return the love of him who loves you.' There's a carving of Erasmus at 15 Cheyne Walk (*see p205*).

'Henry VIII's death penalty for gay sex was still on the statute books for much of the 19th century.'

Concerns about tutors and their pupils continued in 16th-century London. In the 1599 satire *The Scourge of Villainy*, John Marston worried that: 'some pedant Tutor… in his bed/Should use my fry, like Phrygian Ganymede.' (In Greek myth, Phrygian Ganymede, a shepherd boy, was kidnapped by Zeus, who was besotted with him.) Given the climate of paranoia, you would assume that if, for example, a headmaster was convicted of buggering his pupils, it would be bad for his career. Yet that is not what happened in the 16th century to Nicholas Udall, a teacher and translator of Erasmus – and friend of queens.

In 1541, Udall, the headmaster of Eton was brought before the courts concerning a robbery that had been committed by an Eton boy, Thomas Cheyney. Udall confessed 'that he did commit buggery with the said Cheyney, sundry times heretofore and of late the sixth day of this present month in the present year.' Unsurprisingly, Udall was sent straight to the Marshalsea prison in Southwark (now demolished). Yet he was out the following year, back at work, and being paid the arrears on his Eton salary. Far from losing favour, there soon followed a royal injunction to keep Udall's Erasmus translation in every church in the country. Furthermore, King Edward VI made Udall canon of Windsor ten years later. This is irony indeed, considering the king was the son of Henry VIII, who had enacted England's uncompromising sodomy law in 1533 ('If any person shall commit the detestable sin of buggery with mankind or beast etc, it is felony… and he lose his clergy').

Eton, meanwhile, continues to teach the country's poshest young males. Those humming the *Eton Boating Song* ('Jolly boating weather/ And a hay harvest breeze… Swing, swing together/ With your backs between your knees') are quite likely unaware it was penned by the Victorian poet William Johnson, who changed his name to Cory after being dismissed from the school for committing the same dodgy practices Udall got into trouble for. Presumably he didn't have friends in high places.

BEHIND THE STAGE DOOR

Away from the boarding schools, there were plenty of queer goings-on in 16th-century London. Francis Bacon – the famous thinker, essayist and statesman (1561-1626) – was no stranger to strange love. Neither was his brother Anthony. The boys knew their way around London's loucher quarters, to their mother's consternation. Lady Bacon warned them to steer clear of Bishopsgate: 'A place haunted with such pernicious and obscene plays and theatres is able to poison the very godly.' If but a fraction of what the period's satirists said about Shakespeare's London was true, she was right.

Theatregoers, according to Thomas Middleton's *Father Hubbard's Tales* (1604), would 'see a nest of boys able to ravish a man' at the Blackfriars Playhouse. The puritan Philip Stubbes also noted homosexual behaviour in theatreland: 'Mark the flocking and running to theatres and curtains…

Around Town

these goodly pageants being done, every mate sorts to his mate, every one brings another homeward of their way very friendly, and in their secret conclaves they play the Sodomites, or worse.' Ben Jonson referred to sodomites seducing boy actors. And one Edward Guilpin railed against the theatregoer 'who is at every play and every night Sups with his ingles'. ('Ingle' refers to a sodomite's younger male companion, with an implication of prostitution or some kind of financial dependence: ie, rent boys, house boys or toy boys.)

But it's hardly surprising male theatregoers were tempted to 'sup with ingles'. On the Elizabethan and Jacobean stage, young men played female roles. There were dire warnings that, for a young man attending the theatre, the sight of boys in costume would be enough to inflame lust. (Those who wish to experiment with this should go to an all-male or all-female production at the Globe Theatre; *see p132*.)

It's no wonder that Lady Bacon was worried about her sons mingling with stage folk. It turns out that Francis Bacon was besotted with the younger Tobie Matthew, who appeared on stage at Gray's Inn as a youth. There are extensive affectionate letters between Matthew and Bacon.

In fact, it is said that Matthew inspired Bacon's influential essay 'On Friendship', which includes the observation that, 'If a man have not a friend, he may quit the stage.' Diarist John Aubrey was more concise on the subject of Francis Bacon: 'He was a pederast.' And Puritan moralist Sir Simonds D'Ewes (Bacon's fellow member of parliament) wrote in his autobiography of Bacon's love for his Welsh servants, in particular an 'effeminate-faced youth' whom he called 'his catamite and bed-fellow'. Meanwhile, brother Anthony couldn't keep his hands off his servants either, according to Daphne Du Maurier's biography of the Bacon brothers, *Golden Lads*. He was charged with sodomy in 1586: apparently 'all the world knew Monsieur Bacon was a bugger.'

Funnily enough, the Bacon family home, York House (Strand), was located near a current gay landmark: the nightclub Heaven. But Bacon was forced to relinquish his house to another man's man, George Villiers, who was the apple of King James I's queer eye (Villiers Street is named after him). Bacon, meanwhile, is commemorated on the side of Islington Central Library (2 Fieldway Crescent), which is also a gay landmark for other reasons: it was here that playwright Joe Orton and lover Kenneth Halliwell mutilated books

Joe Orton

Queeny kings

Edward II is England's most notorious man-loving king (at least until James I). His father, Edward I, wanted sodomites burned to death. Having introduced young Edward to the Gascon youth Piers Gaveston, he soon regretted it and banished Gaveston. But after the old king's death, and Edward II's 1308 coronation in Westminster Abbey, Gaveston was back with a vengeance. Rumour had it that Gaveston was given the pick of Queen Isabella's wedding presents. And Gaveston was apparently so fancily dressed 'he more resembled the god Mars, than an ordinary mortal', according to one account.

No surprise, then, that the royal marriage wasn't a happy one. Things got so bad that, in 1326, Edward's disgruntled wife, aided by her lover Roger Mortimer, raised an army in France and invaded London. Edward was forced to flee – which puts the Charles and Diana feud into perspective. After abdicating (his son Edward III took over the royal duties), Edward was imprisoned in Berkeley Castle in Gloucestershire. In 1327, the king was reportedly murdered when Mortimer's stooges shoved a red-hot poker in his rectum.

In the 1590s, Christopher Marlowe revived interest in Edward's story. In his play *Edward II*, Queen Isabella complains that her husband is more interested in his friend's cheeks than her: 'For now my lord the king regards me not/But dotes upon the love of Gaveston/He claps his cheeks and hangs about his neck/Smiles in his face and whispers in his ears/And, when I come, he frowns.' This was written hundreds of years after anyone saw Edward and Gaveston together, but it's intriguingly similar – as gay historian Alan Bray pointed out – to a description of Scottish lad Robert Carr getting cosy with his king, James VI of Scotland, both Marlowe's contemporaries.

When James came down to London and became James I of England, the gossips made a great deal of the king's favourites. Before Carr, who had started as a pageboy, James had been pressed by his nobles to banish an older favourite, Esmé Stuart, from the Scottish court. Then came gorgeous George Villiers, whom one observer felt the king kissed so enthusiastically in public, one could only wonder what they got up to alone: 'In wanton looks and wanton gestures they exceeded any part of womankind.'

James wrote to Villiers, whom he had made Duke of Buckingham: 'I desire only to live in the world for your sake, and I had rather live banished in any part of the world with you, than live a sorrowful widow-life without you.' When admirer of masculine beauty Francis Bacon (*see p149*) fell out of favour with the king, Villiers got his residence, York House. When Villiers' son sold it for development, it was on condition that his name be remembered in all the new streets: hence George Court, Villiers Street, Duke Street, Buckingham Street and York Place. The only remaining trace of York House is the Water Gate, located at the bottom of Villiers Street in the Victoria Embankment Gardens. Fittingly, this park was a popular wartime cruising spot, and Villiers Street became the home of London's first gay superclub, Heaven (now G-A-Y; *see p40*).

in the 1960s – they drew a picture of a naked man on a John Betjeman poetry book – an offence for which they were imprisoned.

Incidentally, the other gay Francis Bacon (1909-92), whose carcass-like depictions of his lover George Dyer and others are among the most extraordinary paintings of the 20th century, worked at 7 Reece Mews, in South Kensington, for over 30 years.

WOMEN BEHAVING BADLY

Men didn't have a monopoly on queer behaviour during the Renaissance. An anonymous book entitled *The Life and Death of Mrs Mary Frith* tells the tale of a female gender-bender. Frith, the daughter of a shoemaker, grew up in the 1580s in the Barbican area of the City. She was a notorious tomboy who 'delighted and sported only on boys' play and pastime, not minding or companying with the girls… she could not endure the sedentary life of sewing or stitching, a sampler was as grievous as a winding-sheet, her needle, bodkin and thimble, she could not think on quietly, wishing them changed into a sword or dagger for a bout at cudgels… She would fight with boys and courageously beat them, run, jump, leap or hop with any of them, or any other play whatsoever.'

Frith, aka Moll Cutpurse, became a stage actress who specialised in tough historical women, such as Mary Ambree, the butch heroine who fought the Spanish at the 1584 Siege of Ghent. But it was her clothing that brought her the most notoriety. For while male transvestism on stage was ubiquitous, cross-dressing in the other direction was taboo. For a woman to dress as a man was perversion itself: Venetian law banned it as 'a kind of sodomy'. Frith appeared in ecclesiastical court on 27 January 1612 on charges of immorality: 'she had long frequented… the disorderly and licentious places in this City… usually in the habit of a man.' Frith did not deny dressing in men's clothes, but claimed not to have 'drawn other women to lewdness'. Her

Around Town

punishment was to do public penance at Paul's Cross next to St Paul's Cathedral on 9 February 1612, where she entertained the crowd more than the preacher appointed to discipline her.

POETIC LICENTIOUSNESS

In addition to the queer theatrical types, gay writers were causing a stir in Renaissance London. At Stationers Hall (Ludgate Hill), for instance, there is a plane tree in the rear courtyard, marking a spot where seditious books were burnt on 4 June 1599. The books included satires of queer streetlife in London. In one, the young poet John Marston described a fancily made-up man and his rent boy: 'His clothes perfumed, his fusty mouth is aired/His chin new swept, his very cheeks are glazed/But ho, what Ganymede is that doth grace/The gallant's heels? One, who for two days space/Is closely hired.' In a far from subtle pun, Marston dubbed the prancing dandy 'an open Ass'.

Other London poets wrote classically modelled lyrics panting over handsome boys. Shakespeare's sonnets are full of homoeroticism. But Barnabe Barnes described caressing a flirtatious boy like a Caravaggio Cupid: 'He bare about him a long dart… And had a pile of steel… Said I, "Will this pile wound a heart?"/"Touch it!" quoth he, "and feel!"'

But Richard Barnfield was London's leading Renaissance same-sex lyricist. One of his lyrics decorates a monument to Renaissance composer John Dowland in Wren's church of St Andrew-by-the-Wardrobe. But his most homoerotic verse has had less public circulation: 'Sometimes I wish that I his pillow were/So might I steal a kiss… His lips ripe strawberries, his tongue a honeycomb, his teeth pure pearl.'

Amid all the man-on-man murmurings at the turn of the 17th century, a few women's voices started to be heard expressing their passion for each other. The poet Katharine Phillips was one of them. Married at 16 to a man of 54, Phillips was an early feminist of sorts, forming the all-female Society of Friendship and christening herself 'the Matchless Orinda'. Her sensual poems espoused love between women and, today, open many a lesbian anthology: 'Come, My Lucasia… To the dull, angry world let's prove/There's a religion in our love.'

Anne Killigrew, another lesbian favourite, lived a short life. She was born off St Martin's Lane around 1660 and died at 25 from smallpox. But she found time to pen some wonderful poetry. One classic was the suggestively erotic, 'On the Soft and Gentle Motions of Eudora'. There's a monument to Killigrew in the Savoy Chapel (Savoy Street, WC2), later a popular spot for illegal marriages.

As the 17th century ended, passionate women weren't just writing private verses. London-born playwright and philosopher Catharine Trotter entertained the town with her play *Love at a Loss* (1701), which embraced same-sex comradeship and featured a character named Lesbia. *Agnes de Castro* (1696), a previous work, had similar sapphic elements; both pieces were dedicated to Trotter's intimate friend Sarah Piers.

THE KING WHO WOULD BE QUEEN

While the sapphic poets penned their sensuous verse, a queer king was busy conquering the British Isles. After defeating James II in England, King William III (1689-1702) repeated his victory in Ireland, defeating the Catholics and establishing a Protestant stronghold in Ulster. King William III, to this day, is championed by Northern Ireland loyalists, who decorate their banners and walls with his face. Which is ironic, because Northern Ireland is one of the UK's more homophobic parts. During the early 1980s, for instance, preacher and politician Rev Ian Paisley led a 'Save Ulster from Sodomy' campaign in response to Westminster's bill to decriminalise homosexuality in Northern Ireland. The north of Ireland hadn't been included in the 1967 act decriminalising homosexuality in England – and Paisley liked it that way. Though the bill was passed, Paisley's gay anxieties still loom large in Ulster. But Paisley and the unionists should read a bit deeper into their history books. Their beloved King Billy enjoyed some 'infamous pleasures'. Take William Bentinck – as the king did. This Dutch lad joined William's household as a 15-year-old pageboy, and ended up – following William's takeover of Britain in the 1688 Revolution – Earl of Portland, one of the richest men in the country. A nice reward for life as a royal catamite.

'In 1952 alone, 3,087 men were convicted of attempted sodomy.'

Life was not so easy for those who did not have the king's ear – or any other part of his anatomy. In 1694, Westminster Hall witnessed the trial of a 'young woman in man's apparel, or that personated a man, who was found guilty of marrying a young maid'. The woman's lesbian love letters were read out in court, 'which occasioned much laughter'. And that humiliation was not enough: the trouser-wearer was taken to Bridewell Prison (now destroyed) 'to be well whipped and kept to hard labour'.

Other records of lesbianism in the early 18th century include several attempts in which two women sought to get married. In 1720, one Sarah Ketson was found guilty of having tried to marry Ann Hutchinson (as 'John'), and was sent to Fleet Prison. Mary East was luckier. She was reported to have run a pub in Poplar, east London, between 1730 and 1766 with another woman 'as man and wife'.

One place of pilgrimage for those interested in the developing awareness of passionate female friendship is Dr Johnson's House (*see p167*), which contains the memorabilia of 18th-century writer Elizabeth Carter. Johnson, no great feminist, grudgingly allowed that Carter 'could make a pudding as well as translate Epictetus from the Greek'. In her translation, if not her pudding-making, Carter was encouraged by her passionate

Vita Sackville-West. *See p156.*

Around Town

An affair to remember

It was a classic British sex scandal. Take a Tory peer, a *Daily Mail* hack, a gay 'orgy', and you've got a queer version of the Profumo affair. But the 1954 trial of Peter Wildeblood and Lord Montagu of Beaulieu was also a turning point for gay rights.

In post-war Britain, homosexuality was still illegal and synonymous with Cold War paranoia. Like the McCarthy witchhunts in the US, the British government equated homosexuality with communism: Guy Burgess and Donald Maclean, the two foreign diplomats who had defected to Moscow in 1951, were gay.

Sir David Maxwell Fyfe, then home secretary, gave the police carte blanche to launch a 'new drive against male vice' to 'rid England of this plague' (the British Medical Association regarded homosexuality as a contagious disease). To increase convictions, police acted as agents provocateurs in public toilets. In the 1950s, 1,000 British men a year were jailed for gay offences. The act of buggery carried a maximum sentence of life in prison.

Amid this climate of hysteria, Peter Wildeblood, then 28, met Edward McNally, 23, on a rainy night in 1952 outside Piccadilly tube station and took him back to his flat. Solidly middle class, Wildeblood was the royal correspondent for the *Daily Mail* with a degree from Oxford. In his job, Wildeblood moved in heady circles and had befriended Lord Montagu of Beaulieu, Britain's youngest peer. McNally, by contrast, was a working-class Scot and a corporal in the RAF. He hated toffs. Yet this odd couple had an affair that would shake the British establishment and change history.

In July 1952, Lord Montagu, who was bisexual, invited Wildeblood and McNally for a holiday at his beach hut on his Hampshire estate. One night, they threw a party that 'achieved more notoriety than any other since the days of Nero', Wildeblood later recalled. 'It was, in fact, extremely dull... The airmen sampled the contents of every bottle in sight and became slightly obnoxious... But there [were] no activities which could be described as improper.'

However, two years later, Peter Wildeblood and Lord Montagu were both convicted of homosexual offences and sent to prison; McNally got off scot-free.

The trouble started when RAF snoops found love letters from Wildeblood in McNally's kit. Police offered to grant McNally immunity if he testified against Wildeblood and Lord Montagu, and he sang like a bird. The defendants were targeted for their class as much as for their crime. Such influential men 'posed security risks' and threatened the social order by consorting with the working class.

And though homosexuality was scandalous enough, it was the notion of love between men that was beyond the pale. 'If my interest in McNally had been merely physical, I should never have gone to prison,' said Wildeblood. 'It was [my] letters expressing a deep emotional attachment which turned the scales against me.' Indeed, the judge called the letters 'nauseating'.

Leaving court at Winchester Assizes one evening, Wildeblood felt the fury of Middle England. 'A woman spat at me. She was a respectable looking, middle-aged tweedy person wearing a sensible felt hat... like the country gentlewomen with whom my mother [took] coffee... But what did I look like to her? Evidently, I was a monster.'

Though Lord Montagu denied all charges, Wildeblood admitted in court that he was a homosexual. It was a defining moment – one that sealed his conviction, but ultimately set him free. 'In a world of hypocrites, I would at least be honest.' Wildeblood got 18 months, Lord Montagu a year. Yet Wildeblood was surprised by the degree of public support. A baying mob jeered at McNally, but cheered Wildeblood and Lord Montagu as they were bundled into a police van.

After his release from Wormwood Scrubs in 1955, Wildeblood ran a Soho bar, immortalised in his quasi-autobiography (*A Way of Life*) and wrote several plays, including *The Crooked Mile* (1959). But his book about his ordeal, Against the Law (1956), was his greatest achievement; an eloquent defence of his sexuality, it spurred the government to reform. The 1957 Wolfenden Report, with contributions from Wildeblood, recommended that homosexuality be decriminalised, which it was, in 1967.

After Lord Montagu was released from prison, he opened the famous National Motor Museum in Beaulieu, Hampshire. Now in his eighties, and openly bisexual, Lord Montagu has married twice and fathered three children. Wildeblood emigrated to Canada in 1971, where he worked in television. In June 1994, he suffered from a stroke that left him paralysed; he died in 1999, aged 76, a forgotten figure. But as gay Londoners bask in the luxury of the scene and enjoy their new-found rights and freedoms, he deserves to be remembered. Simply by standing up in court and saying the unsayable – 'I am homosexual' – he changed everything.

Critics called him an attention-seeker. But *Times* journalist Matthew Parris summed it up best when he wrote in a new foreword to Against the Law: 'Attention-seeking is... an often unlikeable quality, but I wonder where many just causes would be without it. I prefer to remember the courage which accompanied the self-advertisement. Everyone counselled silence, and he chose noise.'

friend Catherine Talbot, whom she loved for 30 years. As she grew older, Carter became a grande dame of the new 'bluestocking' salons, where London's intellectual women gathered.

ROUND THE MOLLY HOUSES

During the late 18th and early 19th centuries, Londoners became aware of an identifiable 'gay scene'. In 1709, journalist Ned Ward wrote a feature exposing the 'Molly' scene, a network of private and public locations where men interested in sex with other men could meet. 'There are a particular gang of Sodomitical wretches in this Town, who call themselves the Mollies… affecting to speak, walk, tattle, curtsey, cry, scold, and to mimic all manner of Effeminacy.'

In case that's not clear enough, Ward claimed that they practised 'odious bestialities, that ought forever to be without a name… at a certain Tavern in the City, whose sign I shall not mention.' Around that time, a *Times* journalist referred to 'the Master Pollys and Master Jennys of Bond Street and Cheapside'.

Perhaps the most celebrated Molly House was Margaret Clap's in Field Lane, off Saffron Hill, near Farringdon. There, according to the statement of morality spy Samuel Stevens, 'I found between 40 and 50 men making love to one another, as they called it. Sometimes they would sit in one another's laps, kissing in a lewd manner and using their hands indecently. Then they would get up, dance and make curtsies, and mimic the voices of women… Then they would hug, and play, and toy, and go out by couples into an other room on the same floor to be married, as they called it.' This seminal (in every way) location in London's gay male history was brought to life in Mark Ravenhill's 2001 play *Mother Clap's Molly House*.

This developing commercial scene had its drawbacks. If sodomites could find one another, so could the authorities. Taliban-style penalties were still in force – Henry VIII's death penalty for gay sex was still on the statute books for much of the 19th century. Those lucky enough to live might still be locked up, mounted for public display and pelted by the London public with mud, potatoes, rotten eggs, blood, offal, animal corpses and dung.

Fear of exposure was understandably terrifying. In 1822, Lord Castlereagh, the foreign secretary and leader of the House of Commons, killed himself. Many despised him for his ruthless suppression of a reform demonstration – the 1819 Peterloo Massacre, but his angst was likely fuelled by his double life. The last straw seems to have come when he rushed to see the king at the opulent (and now demolished) Carlton House

in Pall Mall over a gay scandal: Castlereagh claimed he was being blackmailed by an accuser for having had sex with a man. Despite what is supposed to have been George IV's sympathetic response, Castlereagh killed himself with his own penknife a few days later.

Around this time, revolutionary queer Victorian writers like John Addington Symonds and Edward Carpenter emerged. They bravely explored how a better world might recognise the existence, and the ideals, of 'Greek' or 'homogenic' love. Though they wrote about Greek love, they generally stayed away from the fleshpots of London.

And it was just as well. With the passing of the Labouchere Amendment in 1885, sex in private between consenting male adults was formally criminalised. (Anal sex had been illegal since the time of Henry VIII, but Labouchere's law extended punishment to 'any act of gross indecency' in public or in private.) During the next 80 years, thousands of lives were ruined by an ill-considered bit of legislation passed on a sparse night in the House of Commons. The 1895 trials of Oscar Wilde – in which the writer was convicted of gross indecency and sentenced to two years' hard labour – were its most infamous manifestation.

TWENTIETH-CENTURY FOXES

Although, at the end of the 20th century, there was excitement at the first public decorations to be awarded to openly gay men – the actor Ian McKellen was knighted in 1990 – it was not the first time queers had received official recognition. In 1922, the redoubtable lesbian composer and suffragette Ethyl Smyth was awarded a DBE. And in 1930, Smyth unveiled the statue of women's suffrage campaigner Emmeline Pankhurst, in Victoria Tower Gardens between Parliament and Lambeth Bridge, to the sound of a police band playing her feminist anthem, 'March of Women'.

In contrast to the militant sexual dissidence of Smyth and the suffragettes, a discreet form of upper-middle-class homosexuality was taking shape in Bloomsbury. Located around the British Museum, Bloomsbury's boundaries remain slightly vague – like the sexual preferences of its celebrated group. The writer Lytton Strachey lived in Gordon Square. His house, where fellow gay writer André Gide came to stay, is marked with a blue plaque. Painter Duncan Grant was Strachey's cousin (and, briefly, lover). He later moved into the square with a new love, Britain's leading interwar economist John Maynard Keynes – who had also been Strachey's lover. Meanwhile, at 52 Tavistock Square, Virginia Woolf was wooed by Vita Sackville-West, rather more successfully than she was by Ethel Smyth (who had an unrequited crush on the novelist).

EM Forster was part of the Bloomsbury set, but he kept his distance, living round the corner in Brunswick Square (when he wasn't staying with his policeman lover). His novel *Maurice* (which he kept from publication until after he died) portrayed the sense of the ambivalence with which these middle- and upper-class homosexuals tried to live after the shocks of the Wilde trials.

'In 1988, a group of lesbian protesters abseiled into the House of Lords.'

Others found London's fog of hypocrisy suffocating. Poet WH Auden had tasted freedom in 1920s Berlin. So had novelist Christopher Isherwood, whose tales of decadent Germany were immortalised in his book *Goodbye to Berlin*, and the musical and movie *Cabaret*. As World War II loomed, Berlin wasn't an option. But neither did Auden and Isherwood want to stay in London. The pair left the capital, and what Auden called the 'great batshadow of home', and headed

A Terence Higgins Trust poster

to the US. They were accompanied by composer Benjamin Britten and pacifist singer Peter Pears (Britten and Pears returned to England in 1942).

This exodus wasn't admired as part of the war effort. Neither, however, was the stay-at-home Ivor Novello, the gorgeous Welsh star of the interwar West End, whose flat above the Strand Theatre in Aldwych hosted many theatrical gatherings, costumed or otherwise. Novello entertained the troops with the same vigour as other gay men did during the blackout. He was nabbed with dodgy petrol coupons and imprisoned in Wormwood Scrubs, but bounced back with the wryly titled 1950s musical *Gay's the Word* – a name adopted by London's veteran gay bookstore (*see p102*).

VICTIMS OF LOVE

Those London homosexuals who had fought in the war were rewarded afterwards with a massive rise in prosecutions for same-sex activity. In 1952 alone, there were 670 prosecutions in England for sodomy; 3,087 prosecutions for attempted sodomy or indecent assault; and 1,686 prosecutions for gross indecency. Punishments for these offences ranged from small fines to life imprisonment. Medical regimens, such as aversion therapy and hormone treatments, were often forced on gay men as conditions for parole. Cold War hysteria – fanned by the 1951 defections to Moscow of gay spies Guy Burgess and Donald Maclean – fostered an environment in which hundreds of lives were ruined by police harassment and legal humiliation. Actor John Gielgud, choreographer John Cranko, MP Ian Harvey and Lord Montagu of Beaulieu were the public faces of this 1950s witch hunt (*see p154* **An affair to remember**).

As with the Molly Houses, press reports of the venues in which men were being arrested helped homosexuals to devise a gay map of London, augmented by gossip and hints as he (or indeed she) sought out this twilight world. This was the era of Chelsea lesbian bar the Gateways Club (just off the King's Road, now closed) with its stairway to a basement full of regulars, which featured in Maureen Duffy's 1962 novel, *The Microcosm*, and in the 1968 film *The Killing of Sister George*. In Covent Garden, meanwhile, the Victorian splendour of the Salisbury (89 St Martin's Lane) was the backdrop for plenty of shifty male glances – and featured in the 1961 classic gay film, *Victim*, starring Dirk Bogarde (it is now a straight pub).

Despite the persecution, times were changing in the capital. A burgeoning movement was starting to question whether homosexuality should be classified as a criminal activity. A breakthrough in 1957 was the publication of the Wolfenden

Peter Tatchell and Clause 28 protesters

Report, a government paper that recommended homosexuality should be decriminalised. And it finally was in 1967. That legal breakthrough was followed by the radicalism of the 1970s.

GLAD TO BE GAY

During the late 20th century, gay London came into its own, thanks to the decriminalisation of homosexuality in 1967. The capital developed a staggering collection of gay venues and services. The London Gay Liberation Front was formed in 1971; that same year, the first gay march through London was held, culminating in a rally in Trafalgar Square. The following year, *Gay News*, the UK's first homosexual newspaper, was launched; the Lesbian & Gay Switchboard, a helpline, followed two years later. In the pop charts, meanwhile, Tom Robinson hit the top with 'Glad to Be Gay' in 1976. And in 1980, Heaven, London's first gay superclub (now G-A-Y; *see p40*), opened.

But just as the push for visibility reached new heights, disaster struck. On 26 November 1982, London's gay newspaper *Capital Gay* ran a story with the headline: 'US Disease Hits London'. AIDS wasn't an American disease, of course, but its impact was as devastating here as it was across the pond. Gay activists had to fight even harder in the face of the new epidemic and the subsequent homophobia. As a result, a host of community services sprang up. In 1982, the HIV charity Terence Higgins Trust was founded, named after the first UK man thought to have died of AIDS.

The commercial scene too was forced to become more professional, and, in the process, gay business became a viable proposition. So did gay pop stars: ironically, the Conservative 1980s ushered in an era when homosexuality became positively mainstream, with queer acts such as Boy George, Frankie Goes to Hollywood, Marc Almond, Bronski Beat, Dead or Alive, Erasure and Pet Shop Boys topping the charts. Politicians also started opening up about their sexuality: Chris Smith, a Labour MP for Islington, came out in 1984 – the first MP to do so while in office.

But progress was hindered by politics. As AIDS took its toll, Margaret Thatcher rubbed salt into the wound: the passing of Clause 28 of the local government bill made it clear which side the Tories were on. The legislation was a knee-jerk reaction to the progressive policies of London local authorities – particularly the Greater London Council, which Thatcher abolished – who were derided by the tabloids for their 'gays on the rates' mentality.

The passing of Clause 28 brought gay protesters on to London's streets – and some more unlikely places. In 1988, for instance, a team of lesbian activists abseiled into the House of Lords; the same year, they disrupted a live broadcast of the BBC *Six O'Clock News* in protest. The next year, activist groups Stonewall and Act-Up were founded, followed by OutRage! in 1990.

At the forefront of this radicalism was Peter Tatchell, a former Labour politician, who, after being outed by the tabloid press in a 1983 London by-election, became an outspoken gay rights

Elton John and David Furnish

campaigner. Famous for his publicity stunts, Tatchell threatened to out closeted Church of England bishops and interrupted the Archbishop of Canterbury's Easter sermon in 1998 in protest at the Church's bigotry; then in 2001, he made headlines when he tried to make a citizen's arrest on Robert Mugabe – in London, then in Brussels – but was beaten up by his bodyguards. His recent projects include waging war on homophobic ragga music (*see p11* **The bravest man in Britain?**).

As politicians and pop stars started coming out, so too did gay pubs. The gay scene had previously consisted of a few seedy pubs in Earl's Court, but, in the early 1990s, glossy, glass-fronted gay bars such as the Village (*see p27*) proudly opened their doors in the centre of town. Before long, Soho was London's official gay village (*see pp186-193*).

But not all was smooth sailing. In April 1999, three people were killed when a nail bomb tore through the Admiral Duncan, a Soho gay pub. It was the work of right-wing extremist David Copeland, who had also targeted blacks and Asians with bombs in Brixton and Brick Lane. The Duncan's bar manager, 34-year-old David Morley, survived the bombing, only to be beaten to death by a homophobic gang in 2004. And bashings continue. In 2005, 24-year-old barman Jody Dobrowski was beaten to death while cruising Clapham Common; in October 2008, a 21-year-old gay man was stabbed by a gang in Shoreditch; he is now paralysed. The story was ignored by the mainstream press. In September 2009, tragedy struck again when

Ian Baynham, 62, was beaten to death on a Friday night in Trafalgar Square as passersby looked on; three teenagers, including two girls, were charged with manslaughter, and the jury had not reached a verdict as this guide went to press.

Still, there has been progress on the legal front. Between 1999 and 2008, almost every homophobic law in Britain was repealed. In 2005, civil partnerships for gay couples – which grant them the same legal rights as heterosexual couples – were passed into law. Elton John and David Furnish got hitched and made headlines, even though civil partnerships are still not recognised by the Church. And there was a legal setback in 2008, when Lillian Ladele, a marriage registrar for Islington council, won the right not to perform civil partnerships between gay people because they offend her religious views.

Triumphs and tragedies will continue to leave their mark on the capital, often in the shadows. Indeed, the history of gay London is one of fragments, of discoveries on the margins. Roam the streets and ponder the legacy of London's gay residents, even those who just stayed a short time: Greek poet Constantine Cavafy (who lived at Queensborough Terrace, Bayswater, during his childhood); the French poets Arthur Rimbaud and Paul Verlaine (there's a plaque to the latter at 8 Royal College Street, Camden); and America's first lady of lesbian letters, Gertrude Stein (who briefly lived at 40 Bloomsbury Square). None was a long-term resident of London, but all made a big splash or were vastly influenced by the capital. And you?

Getting Started

Have a gay old time.

What's the difference between ordinary sightseeing and gay sightseeing? On the surface, not much. But there can be a queer context to the sights of London. The British Museum, for instance, used to be frequented by closeted gay men who ogled its nude Greek statuary in the days before homosexuality was legalised; the Caravaggios at the National Gallery might also hold an extra significance to gay eyes. Some gays might prefer to cruise Hyde Park than smell the roses, while a walk on Hampstead Heath may be less about the trees than the totty. The Changing of the Guard too might hold special resonance for those who like a man in uniform. As for Kensington Palace, the former home of Princess Diana, a gay icon of the 20th century… enough said. Finally, gay visitors might like to fit in sightseeing with a drink at a gay pub; we've tried to highlight these where relevant.

PRACTICALITIES

For general tourist info, see www.visitlondon. com. For the hardcore sightseer, a **London Pass** (0870 242 9988, www.londonpass.com) gives you pre-paid access to more than 50 sights and costs from £40, or £48 with a travelcard thrown in. For bus tours, try the **Big Bus Company** (7233 9533, www.bigbus.co.uk) or the **Original London Sightseeing Tour** (8877 1722, www.theoriginal tour.com). For river tours try **City Cruises** (7740 0400, www.citycruises.com), which pick up at Westminster, Waterloo, Tower and Greenwich piers. If you don't embarrass easily, climb aboard an amphibious yellow vehicle courtesy of **London Duck Tours** (7928 3132, www.londonducktours. co.uk). For a classic London experience, try **Black Taxi Tours of London** (7935 9363, www.black taxitours.co.uk, rates £100-£110), which give tailored two-hour tours for up to five people. For gay tours, a new company called **Urban Gentry** (8149 6253, www.urbangentry.com) runs a queer-themed tour of the East End, along with tours based on fashion, design and shopping.

Central London neighbourhoods are clearly delineated on the colour-coded map on pages 260-261, and detailed street maps of the main sightseeing areas are on pages 262-271.

The best Sights

For queens who love queens
Buckingham Palace (*see p183*); Hampton Court (*see p222*); Kensington Palace (*see p204*).

For ancient homoerotica
British Museum (*see p175*).

For drama queens
Shakespeare's Globe (*see p164*).

For design enthusiasts
Design Museum (*see p166*); Eltham Palace (*see p224*); Geffrye Museum (*see p213*); Victoria & Albert Museum (*see p202*).

For flâneurs
The villagey streets of Hampstead (*see p209*); Spitalfields area at the weekend (*see p212*).

For pilgrims
Bloomsbury Group HQ (*see p174*); Diana, Princess of Wales Memorial Fountain (*see p203*); Judy Garland's bed at the Gore (*see p74*); Marc Bolan memorial (*see p219*); Oscar Wilde statue (*see p194*); Radclyffe Hall's tomb in Highgate Cemetery (*see p210*).

For romantic views
London Eye (*see p162*); Greenwich Park (*see p223*); Primrose Hill (*see p208*); Royal Botanic Gardens (Kew Gardens) (*see p219*).

For art on the edge
ICA (*see p199*); Tate Modern (*see p165*); Whitechapel Art Gallery (*see p212*).

For cruising grounds
Clapham Common (*see p219*); Hampstead Heath (*see p209*); Hyde Park (*see p203*).

For the fetish crowd
London Dungeon (*see p166*).

Around Town

South Bank & Bankside

Take me to the water.

South Bank

Gay culture vultures should certainly familiarise themselves with the South Bank. With its massive observation wheel, concrete concert halls, national theatres, cinemas and contemporary art galleries, the south side of the river has become the arts and entertainment showpiece of the capital. In fact, the South Bank and Bankside are the places that Londoners have always gone to be entertained – the only change is in the level of refinement. Art, music, theatre, film, books and food today; prostitutes, bears and bards in centuries past. This is an area that has long lived on the margins – not just of the river, but of the city and society itself.

The transformation of this stretch of river over the last 50 years or so has been steady but laborious. The Festival of Britain in 1951 opened the way for the Royal Festival Hall and subsequent later buildings (in a monumental brutalist style) that make up the **Southbank Centre**. The biggest and most expensive party, however, was the one to celebrate the arrival of the 21st century, marked by the erection of the **London Eye** and the 'blade of light' shooting across the river to St Paul's Cathedral, the **Millennium Bridge**. The equally lovely Hungerford footbridges, linking the South Bank to Embankment on the north side, are another reason to start a walking tour here.

With its riverside walkways, frequent festivals, outdoor cafés and restaurants, and fine views across the Thames, the South Bank is eminently strollable. Another way to explore is to hop on the RV1 bus, which links riverside attractions between Covent Garden and Tower Gateway.

Gay venues include **G-A-Y** (*see p40*) and the **Retro Bar** (*see p24*); both are actually on the north bank across Hungerford Bridge; on the south side are the saunas **Chariots Waterloo** (*see p49*) and **Pleasuredrome** (*see p49*).

Lambeth Bridge to Hungerford Bridge

Map p269

Embankment or Westminster tube/Waterloo tube/rail. Lambeth Bridge is adorned with carved pineapples as a tribute to the father of British gardening (John Tradescant, whose plant-hunting habit brought the exotic fruit here in the 16th century). On its southern side, **Lambeth Palace**, official residence of the Archbishop of Canterbury since the 12th century, opens to the public on high days and holidays, notably during London Open House (www.londonopenhouse.org).

Walking west along the Albert Embankment and under Westminster Bridge, you arrive at London's major tourist zone. The **London Eye** packs in the crowds, while the grand **County Hall** (the former residence of the London government) attracts families to the **London Aquarium**.

Florence Nightingale Museum

St Thomas's Hospital, 2 Lambeth Palace Road, SE1 7EW (7620 0374, www.florence-nightingale.co.uk). Westminster tube or Waterloo tube/rail. **Open** 10am-5pm daily. **Admission** £5.80; £4.80 reductions. **Credit** AmEx, MC, V. **Map** p269 M9.
The nursing skills and campaigning zeal that made Florence Nightingale's Crimean War work the stuff of legend are honoured at the museum, with a tour through her remarkable life. On returning from the battlefields, she opened her own nursing school here in St Thomas's.

Garden Museum

Lambeth Palace Road, SE1 7LB (7401 8865, www.gardenmuseum.org.uk). Lambeth North tube or Waterloo tube/rail. **Open** 10.30am-5pm Mon-Fri, Sun; 10.30am-4pm Sat; closed 1st Mon of mth. **Admission** £6; £5 reductions. **Credit** AmEx, MC, V. **Map** p269 L10.
Intrepid plant hunter and gardener to Charles I, John Tradescant is buried here at the world's first museum of gardening. A replica of a 17th-century knot garden has been created in his honour. Topiary and box hedging, old roses, herbaceous perennials and bulbs give interest all year. A sarcophagus in the graveyard garden contains

London Eye. *See p162*.

the remains of Captain Bligh of *Mutiny on the Bounty* fame. Inside the museum are displays of ancient tools, exhibitions about horticulture, a shop and a café.

London Aquarium

County Hall, Riverside Building, off Belvedere Road, SE1 7PB (7967 8000, 7967 8007 tours, www.sealife. co.uk/london). Westminster tube or Waterloo tube/rail. **Open** 10am-7pm Mon-Thur, Sun; 10am-8pm Fri, Sat. **Admission** £17.50; £12.50-£16 reductions. **Credit** MC, V. **Map** p269 M9.

The aquarium, one of Europe's largest, is set up according to geographical origin: the tanks' denizens vary from bright fish from the Indian Ocean to temperate freshwater fish from the rivers of Europe and North America. There are also tanks devoted to sharks, jellyfish, octopuses and piranhas.

London Eye

Riverside Building, next to County Hall, off Belvedere Road, SE1 7PB (0871 781 3000, www.londoneye.com). Westminster tube or Waterloo tube/rail. **Open** *Oct-Mar* 10am-8pm daily. *Apr, Sept* 10am-9pm daily. *May, June* 10am-9pm Mon-Thur, Sun; 10am-9.30pm Fri, Sat. *July, Aug* 10am-9.30pm daily. **Admission** £17.88; £9.50-£14.30 reductions (only applicable Mon-Fri Sept-June). **Credit** AmEx, MC, V. **Map** p269 M8.

Such is its impact on the London skyline, it's hard to believe that this giant wheel was originally intended to turn majestically over the Thames for only five years. It's so popular that it's now scheduled to keep spinning for another 20 years. The 450ft monster, whose 32 glass capsules each hold 25 people, commands superb views over London. A 'flight' takes half an hour; you can buy a guide (£3) to identify the landmarks. Many visitors book in advance, but you can turn up and queue for a ticket on the day – though the lines can be long in summer.

London Film Museum

County Hall, Riverside Building, SE1 7PB (7202 7040, www.londonfilmmuseum.com). Westminster tube or Waterloo tube/rail. **Open** 10am-5pm Mon-Fri; 10am-6pm Sat, Sun. **Admission** £12; £8-£10 reductions. **Credit** MC, V. **Map** p269 L9.

Dedicated to British film since the 1950s (films made in Britain, that is, so blockbusters like *Star Wars* can sneak in), the London Film Museum is focused more on fun than detailed history – although the story of Pinewood Studios is told. Among thousands of artefacts, you can see the sets from *Star Wars*, while techniques from the *Superman* films allow visitors to take part in one of more than 200 films.

BFI Southbank

Hungerford Bridge to Blackfriars Bridge

Maps p269 & p270

Embankment tube/Blackfriars or Waterloo tube/rail.
When the riverside warehouses were cleared to make way for the **Southbank Centre** in the 1960s, the big concrete complex, containing the Royal Festival Hall, Purcell Room and Queen Elizabeth Hall, was hailed as a daring testament to modern architecture. Together with the National Theatre and Hayward Gallery,

Royal Festival Hall

it remains one of the largest and most popular arts centres in the world. The centrepiece, Sir Leslie Martin's **Royal Festival Hall** – built for the Festival of Britain – has been given a £75 million overhaul: the improvement of its Thames frontage is largely complete, with the arrival of retail outlets and restaurants on the riverside level.

The **Hayward Gallery** next door is a landmark of brutalist architecture. Film buffs should check the schedule at the **BFI Southbank** (*see p125*). Squatting underneath Waterloo Bridge, it's a fantastic venue for old classics and art films, and one of the venues of the **Lesbian & Gay Film Festival** (*see p120*). The second-hand book stalls and semi-official skate park add to the atmosphere. Next up is the **National Theatre** (*see p132*), which has free open-air performances next to the river in summer.

Beyond the concrete mass of the Southbank Centre, the mellow red bricks of the **Oxo Tower Wharf** come as light relief. The warehouse building's art deco tower incorporates covert advertising for the stock cube company that bought it. It also provides affordable housing, interesting designer shops and galleries, and a rooftop restaurant, bar and bistro with wonderful views. Nearby, the bustling cafés and shops of **Gabriel's Wharf** are another hotspot.

Hayward Gallery

Belvedere Road, SE1 8XX (7921 0813, 0844 875 0073 box office, www.haywardgallery.org.uk). Embankment tube or Waterloo tube/rail. **Open** 10am-6pm Mon-Thur, Sat, Sun; 10am-10pm Fri. **Admission** check website for details. **Credit** AmEx, MC, V. **Map** p269 M8.

Casual visitors to the Hayward can hang out in the new industrial-look café downstairs (which becomes a bar at night), aptly called Concrete, before visiting the free contemporary exhibitions at the inspired Hayward Project Space. The gallery itself has an excellent programme of challenging modern shows loaned from around the world.

Around Waterloo

Map p269

Waterloo tube/rail.
Waterloo Station is still busy with scurrying commuters, though the Eurostar trains to Paris and Brussels now operate from St Pancras. The jury's still out on the stonking great **BFI IMAX** cinema (7199 6000) plonked down in the middle of the roundabout. Another place of interest is the street market on **Lower Marsh**. On the corner of Waterloo Road and the Cut is the restored Victorian façade of the **Old Vic Theatre**. Known in Victorian times as the 'Bucket of Blood' for its penchant for melodrama, it is now in the hands of Hollywood actor Kevin Spacey. Further down the Cut is the revamped home of the **Young Vic**, a hotbed of youthful theatrical talent.

Bankside

Blackfriars Bridge to London Bridge

Maps p270 & p271

Borough or Southwark tube/London Bridge tube/rail.
Bankside, the area around the river between Blackfriars Bridge and London Bridge, was the epicentre of bawdy Southwark in Shakespeare's day. As well as playhouses such as the Globe and

the Rose stirring up all sorts of trouble among the groundlings, there were the famous 'stewes' (brothels), seedy inns and other dens of iniquity where decent folk could be led astray.

Presiding over all this depravity were the Bishops of Winchester, who made a tidy income from the fines they levied on prostitutes and other lost souls. All that's left of the grand Palace of Winchester, home of successive bishops, is the rose window of the Great Hall on Clink Street, a short walk from the river, next to the site of the Clink prison (now the **Clink Prison Museum**).

The parish church at this time was St Saviour's, now (since 1905) the Anglican **Southwark Cathedral**. Shakespeare's brother Edmund was buried in the graveyard here and there's a monument to the playwright inside. You have to walk back down Clink Street, past **Vinopolis**, the wine attraction, to reach **Shakespeare's Globe**. Built on the site of the original playhouse, this reproduction in wattle and daub is separated from its neighbour, **Tate Modern**, by a wonky terrace of houses, where Sir Christopher Wren stayed when building St Paul's across the water. The Tate's repository of modern art was a power station designed by Sir Giles Gilbert Scott.

Bankside Gallery

48 Hopton Street, SE1 9JH (7928 7521, www. banksidegallery.com). Southwark tube or London Bridge tube/rail. **Open** 11am-6pm daily. **Admission** free; donations appreciated. **Credit** MC, V. **Map** p270 O7.
Crouching beside Tate Modern, this little gallery is the home of the Royal Watercolour Society and the Royal Society of Painter-Printmakers. Its changing exhibitions reflect established and experimental practices.

Clink Prison Museum

1 Clink Street, SE1 9DG (7403 0900, www.clink.co.uk). London Bridge tube/rail. **Open** *Summer* 10am-9pm daily. *Winter* 10am-6pm Mon-Fri; 10am-7.30pm Sat, Sun. **Admission** £5; £3.50 reductions. **Credit** MC, V. **Map** p270 P8.
A fetishist's paradise, this small, grisly exhibition looks behind the bars of the hellish prison 'The Clink', which operated between the 12th and 18th centuries. Thieves, prostitutes and debtors served their sentences within its walls. On display are torture devices and the fetters whose clanking gave the prison its name.

Golden Hinde

St Mary Overie Dock, Cathedral Street, SE1 9DE (0870 011 8700, www.goldenhinde.com). Monument tube or London Bridge tube/rail. **Open** 10am-5.30pm daily. **Admission** £6; £4.50 reductions. **Credit** MC, V. **Map** p271 P8.
Turned on by Russell Crowe in *Master and Commander*? Then visit this re-created ship for a close-up vision of olde worlde testosterone on the high seas. The *Golden Hinde* is a reconstruction of Sir Francis Drake's 16th-century flagship, on which he circumnavigated the globe in 1577.

Shakespeare's Globe

21 New Globe Walk, SE1 9DT (7401 9919, www. shakespeares-globe.org). Mansion House or Southwark tube, or London Bridge tube/rail. **Open** *Exhibition* 10am-5pm daily. *Globe Theatre tours Oct-Apr* 10am-5pm daily. *May-Sept* 9.30am-12.30pm Mon-Sat; 9.30-11.30am Sun. *Rose Theatre tours May-Sept* 1-5pm Mon-Sat; noon-5pm Sun. **Tours** every 30mins. **Admission** £10.50; £6.50-£8.50 reductions. **Credit** AmEx, MC, V. **Map** p270 O7.
The historians are still battling it out over whether William Shakespeare was gay, but we'd like to claim him for his gender-bending ways (*Measure for Measure*) and coded gay lines ('God has given you one face, and you make yourself another'). The original Globe Theatre, where many of Shakespeare's plays were first staged and which he co-owned, burned down in 1613 during a performance of *Henry VIII*. Nearly 400 years later, it was rebuilt in the style of the original. A fine exhibition tells the story. You can tour the theatre itself except during afternoons in the May to early October season, when performances are staged (*see p132*). When matinees are on, there's a substitute tour of the Rose Theatre site (www.rosetheatre.org.uk). Bankside's first playhouse, it was operational from 1587 until 1606; both Christopher Marlowe and Ben Johnson worked there.

Southwark Cathedral

London Bridge, SE1 9DA (7367 6700, 7367 6734 tours, http://cathedral.southwark.anglican.org). London Bridge tube/rail. **Open** 8am-6pm daily (closing times vary on religious holidays). *Services* 8am, 8.15am, 12.30pm, 12.45pm, 5.30pm Mon-Fri; 9am, 9.15am, 4pm Sat; 8.45am, 9am, 11am, 3pm, 6.30pm Sun.

Borough Market

Old Operating Theatre. *See p166.*

Choral Evensong 5.30pm Tue (boys & men), Fri (men only); 5.30pm Mon, Thur (girls). **Admission** £4. **Credit** AmEx, MC, V. **Map** p271 P8.
The oldest bits of the building are more than 800 years old. The trials of several Protestant martyrs took place in the retro choir during the reign of Mary Tudor. After the Reformation, the church fell into disrepair and parts of it became a bakery and a pigsty. In 1905 it became a cathedral. An interactive museum called the Long View of London, a refectory and a lovely garden are highlights.

Tate Modern

Bankside, SE1 9TG (7887 8888, www.tate.org.uk/ modern). Southwark tube or London Bridge tube/rail. **Open** 10am-6pm Mon-Thur, Sun; 10am-10pm Fri, Sat. *Tours* 11am, noon, 2pm, 3pm daily. **Admission** free. *Temporary exhibitions* prices vary. **Map** p270 O7.
A powerhouse of modern art, Tate Modern's imposing architecture – it's housed in the converted Bankside power station – is awe-inspiring even before you see the art. Galleries are centred on four main genres: Cubism, Futurism and Vorticism; Surrealism and Surrealist Tendencies; Abstract Expressionism and European Informal Art; and Minimalism. If you don't know where to start, take a guided tour. The temporary exhibitions are also worth a look – though non-members have to pay for those. Leave time for the cafés and the shop. The Tate to Tate boat service (decor courtesy of Damien Hirst) links the Tates every 40 minutes.

Vinopolis

1 Bank End, SE1 9BU (7940 8300, www.vinopolis. co.uk). London Bridge tube/rail. **Open** *Jan-Nov* noon-10pm Thur-Sat; noon-6pm Sun. *Dec* noon-6pm daily. Last entry 2hrs before closing. **Admission** £19.50-£37.50. **Credit** AmEx, MC, V. **Map** p270 P8.

Calling all lushes. This wine experience, aimed more at amateurs than oenophiles, teaches you about different varieties of grape. Visitors are furnished with a wine glass and an audio guide. Exhibits are set out by country, with opportunities to taste champagne or wine from different regions. Gin crashes the party thanks to Bombay Sapphire, and there are whisky-tastings and a microbrewery.

Borough

Maps p270 & p271

Borough or Southwark tube/London Bridge tube/rail.
Just by Southwark Cathedral is **Borough Market** (www.boroughmarket.org.uk; 11am-5pm Thur, noon-6pm Fri, 8am-5pm Sat), a busy food market that dates back to the 13th century. In its current incarnation, it's a foodie's paradise, and a great stop-off for a snack on a riverside walk.

Around London Bridge Station, a number of tourist attractions clamour for attention. Blood-curdling shrieks emanate from the entrance of the **London Dungeon**, while next door the dulcet tones of Vera Lynn attempt to lure travellers to **Winston Churchill's Britain at War Experience**. Across Tooley Street stands a half-hearted shopping mall called **Hay's Galleria**, once an enclosed dock. If you exit on the riverside, you can walk east past the great grey hulk of **HMS Belfast** toward City Hall and Tower Bridge.

Gay nightlife in the neighbourhood includes the popular bear club **XXL** (*see p47*), located in three arches near London Bridge.

HMS Belfast

Morgan's Lane, Tooley Street, SE1 2JH (7940 6300, www.iwm.org.uk). London Bridge tube/rail. **Open** *Mar-Oct* 10am-6pm daily. *Nov-Feb* 10am-5pm daily. **Admission** £12.95; £6.50-£10.40 reductions. **Credit** MC, V. **Map** p271 R8.

Hello, sailor. Soak up a whiff of navy life in this 11,500-ton battlecruiser, now a floating museum. You can live out your macho fantasies in the boiler and engine rooms, get your hands on deck or take in some history. Built in 1938, HMS *Belfast* played a leading role in the Normandy Landings and supported UN forces in Korea.

London Dungeon

28-34 Tooley Street, SE1 2SZ (7403 7221, www.the dungeons.com). London Bridge tube/rail. **Open** times vary. **Admission** £22.50; £16.50-£20.50 reductions. **Credit** AmEx, MC, V. **Map** p271 Q8.

Warm up for a fetish club with a visit to the London Dungeon. Tucked away under the Victorian arches of London Bridge, this disturbing world of torture, death and disease attracts hordes of ghoulish visitors. Expect dry-ice fog, gravestones and hideously rotting corpses. The Great Plague exhibition features an actor-led medley of corpses, boils and projectile vomiting. Then there are the Wicked Women: Boudicca, Anne Boleyn, Queen Elizabeth I – and, a new addition, Anne Robinson.

London Fire Brigade Museum

94A Southwark Bridge Road, SE1 0EG (8555 1200, www.london-fire.gov.uk/ourmuseum.asp). Borough tube. **Open** *Tours* 10.30am, 2pm Mon-Fri by appt only. **Admission** £3; £2 reductions. **Credit** MC, V. **Map** p270 O9.

We love a man in uniform. You need to book ahead for this small museum, which traces the history of firefighting from the Great Fire of London in 1666 to the present. It has plenty of hunky outfits – too bad there aren't any well-oiled firemen to go with them. Exhibits include medals, equipment and paintings by firemen-artists of their Blitz experiences.

Old Operating Theatre, Museum & Herb Garret

9A St Thomas's Street, SE1 9RY (7188 2679, www.thegarret.org.uk). London Bridge tube/rail. **Open** 10.30am-5pm daily. **Admission** £5.80; £3.25-£4.80 reductions. **No credit cards**. **Map** p271 Q8.

This Victorian operating theatre displays surgical equipment that resembles implements of torture (pity the poor women faced with the cervical dilators). Items include strangulated hernias, leech jars and amputation knives.

Winston Churchill's Britain at War Experience

64-66 Tooley Street, SE1 2TF (7403 3171, www. britainatwar.co.uk). London Bridge tube/rail. **Open** *Apr-Oct* 10am-5pm daily. *Nov-Mar* 10am-4.30pm daily. **Admission** £12.95; £5.50-£6.50 reductions. **Credit** AmEx, MC, V. **Map** p271 Q8.

An authentically drab and dusty exhibition about the privations endured by the British people during World War II. There's plenty about London during the Blitz, including displays of real bombs; the exhibits on rationing, food production and Land Girls are fascinating.

Tower Bridge & Bermondsey

Map p271

Bermondsey tube/London Bridge tube/rail.

Next to the Thames, just before you reach Tower Bridge, are the pristine environs of **City Hall**, the home of the current London government. Designed by Norman Foster (who was also responsible for the Millennium Bridge), the rotund glass structure leans squiffily away from the river. It uses just a quarter of the energy of a normal office building because of its simple water-cooling system (there's no air-conditioning). The building has a café on the lower ground floor and a pleasant outdoor amphitheatre.

Just near **Tower Bridge** (*see p170*) a noticeboard announces when the bridge will next open (which it does about 500 times a year for tall ships to pass through). The bridge is one of the lowest crossings over the Thames, which is why it incorporates twin lifting sections (bascules), designed by architect Horace Jones and engineer John Wolfe Barry.

Further east, upscale riverside dining is mainly what **Butler's Wharf** is about: a series of restaurants founded by Terence Conran overlook the river. **Shad Thames** is the main thoroughfare behind the wharves; in days gone by dockworkers unloaded tea, coffee and spices to be stored in the huge warehouses (now apartments, offices and the **Design Museum**).

Past the museum, across Jamaica Road and down Tanner Street, is historic Bermondsey Street, site of Zandra Rhodes's labour of love, the **Fashion & Textile Museum** (83 Bermondsey Street, 7407 8664, www.ftm london.org). It's just one sign of the area's booming popularity with artists and designers. Further south, around **Bermondsey Square**, it's all Starbucks and delis, new cobbles and hanging baskets. The Friday antiques market here is lovely (6am-1pm).

Design Museum

28 Shad Thames, SE1 2YD (7403 6933, www. designmuseum.org). Tower Hill tube or London Bridge tube/rail. **Open** 10am-5.45pm daily. **Admission** £8.50; £5-£6.50 reductions. **Credit** AmEx, MC, V. **Map** p271 S9.

Formerly a warehouse, this white, 1930s-style building is now an acclaimed shrine to design. It's hard to ignore the shop's glossy design books and chic household accessories, but remember you're here for the exhibitions. The space has frequently changing temporary shows, covering all kinds of design, from furniture to fashion, illustration to industrial products. On the first floor, the Blueprint Café (with a smart Modern European menu) has a balcony overlooking the Thames and Tower Bridge; the ground-floor café is run by the estimable Konditor & Cook.

The City

Strike it rich.

The Square Mile is the economic heart of the capital. And it certainly feels that way when you see the phalanxes of besuited business people striding purposefully along. But visit it at the weekend and it's quiet – though getting busier every year thanks to new developments such as One New Change, the modern shopping complex opposite St Paul's designed by Jean Nouvel.

The City of London was built nearly 2,000 years ago as an outpost of the Roman Empire. In around AD 200, the Romans built a defensive wall arcing north from the riverbank between the present-day Tower Bridge and Blackfriars Bridge; the area enclosed by it – 300 acres – is the bulk of what is known as the City. The Romans stayed for four centuries, but after they departed the Anglo-Saxons ignored the place. When the French moved in after the Norman invasion, they marked their arrival by building the **Tower of London**.

In the medieval period, the City's first mayor was elected in 1397: Dick Whittington, who famously believed the streets were paved with gold. And, in a sense, they were: merchants moved in and did a roaring trade. The Plague of 1665 and the Great Fire of 1666 halted progress, but only briefly. The destruction wrought by the latter provided an opportunity to rebuild London as the most modern city in the world. Despite serious damage caused by World War II bombings, many 17th-century buildings remain, including **Mansion House**, the façade of the **Guildhall**, and **St Paul's Cathedral**, completed in 1710. Gradually, as shipping declined, the merchants turned to the money markets – with great success.

Although the City is a vast temple to money, there's no shortage of spiritual retreats. There are 40-odd churches (many designed by Sir Christopher Wren) in the area. Pop into any of them for details of opening times (usually Monday to Friday only). Most have pleasant gardens.

City Information Centre

St Paul's Churchyard, EC4M 8BX (7332 1456). St Paul's tube. **Open** 9.30am-5.30pm Mon-Sat; 10am-4pm Sun. **No credit cards. Map** p270 O6. Come here for information on all manner of subjects – sights, events, walks and talks – relating to the Square Mile.

Along Fleet Street
Map p270

Chancery Lane tube/Blackfriars tube/rail.
Designed to link Whitehall Palace to the City (and the monarch to the money), Fleet Street is synonymous with the British press. The history of journalism on Fleet Street dates back to 1702, when the first issue of the *Daily Courant* rolled off the presses. All the newspapers have moved out, but traces remain in the buildings that housed the *Daily Telegraph* (no.135) and the art deco *Daily Express* (nos.121-128, known as the Black Lubianka after its glossy black glass façade), and in the pubs and bars where hacks once drank: El Vino (no.47), the Punch Tavern (no.99, where satirical magazine *Punch* was founded in 1841) and Ye Olde Cheshire Cheese (no.145).

Dr Johnson's House

17 Gough Square, off Fleet Street, EC4A 3DE (7353 3745, www.drjohnsonshouse.org). Chancery Lane or Temple tube, or Blackfriars tube/rail. **Open** *May-Sept* 11am-5.30pm Mon-Sat. *Oct-Apr* 11am-5pm Mon-Sat. **Admission** £4.50; £1.50-£3.50 reductions. **No credit cards. Map** p270 N6.
The writer Samuel Johnson (1704-84) lived in this Georgian townhouse while working on his *Dictionary of the English Language*. Deeply atmospheric, the museum has creaky floorboards, Queen Anne furniture and authentic sash windows. You can almost feel the old wit's presence.

Around St Paul's
Map p270

St Paul's tube.
Is there a finer sight in London than **St Paul's Cathedral**, rising majestically above the City skyline? There has been a cathedral dedicated to St Paul here for 14 centuries. After one incarnation was destroyed in the Great Fire of 1666, Sir Christopher Wren designed the present structure.

North of the cathedral sits **Paternoster Square**, centred on a 75ft-high Corinthian column. The oft-moved **Temple Bar**, the 1672 gateway to the City from the Strand, was installed here in 2004 with the original statues reinstated. There's also a fine modern bronze by Elisabeth

Around Town

St Paul's Cathedral

Frink, *Shepherd and Sheep*. The square is a buzzy spot, even at the weekend, thanks to the lively mix of cafés, bars and restaurants.

To the east, **Bow Lane** is a cosy alleyway with a quaint row of shops, bistros and champagne bars. It's bookended by **St Mary-le-Bow**, whose peals once defined a true Cockney. West of St Paul's is the most famous court in the land, the **Old Bailey**.

Old Bailey (Central Criminal Court)

Corner of Newgate Street & Old Bailey, EC4M 7EH (7248 3277). St Paul's tube. **Open** *Public gallery* 10am-1pm, 2-5pm Mon-Fri. **Admission** free. **Map** p270 O6.
It is a mark of success in the criminal world to be tried at the Old Bailey. Built in 1907, the courthouse has hosted some notorious trials, including those of Oscar Wilde. It is also famous for its copper dome and golden statue of justice. The public is welcome to visit the courts and watch justice in action; a notice by the door provides details of the day's trials. Join the queue but note: you will not be allowed in with food, large bags, cameras or mobile phones (no storage facilities are provided).

St Paul's Cathedral

Ludgate Hill, EC4M 8AD (7236 4128, www.stpauls. co.uk). St Paul's tube. **Open** 8.30am-4pm Mon-Sat. *Galleries, crypt & ambulatory* 9.30am-4.15pm Mon-Sat. Hours may changedue to special events; check first. *Tours of cathedral & crypt* 10.45am, 11.15am, 1.30pm,

2pm Mon-Sat. **Admission** *Cathedral, crypt & gallery* £12.50; £4.50-£11.50 reductions. *Tours* £3; £1-£2.50 reductions. **Credit** (shop) AmEx, MC, V. **Map** p270 O6.
Sir Christopher Wren had to fight to get his plans for this most famous of cathedrals approved. However, be glad he persisted: St Paul's is an impressive sight, both by day and, illuminated, at night. After a massive refurbishment for its 300th anniversary St Paul's glows with renewed health.

Of the millions who visit each year, many come as much for the views as anything: it's a 530-step, 280ft climb to the open-air Golden Gallery. The Whispering Gallery is 259 steps up, runs around the dome's interior and takes its name from its marvellous acoustics: if you whisper along the dome's wall, someone at the other side of the gallery can hear you perfectly. Less well known is the Triforium tour visiting the library, the Dean's amazing spiral staircase and Wren's 'Great Model' (11.30am, 2pm Mon, Tue; 2pm Fri – pre-book on 7246 8357, £17.50 with admission).

Monuments include one to the Americans who died in Britain during World War II, and another to poet John Donne (1572-1631) in the south aisle. The most eye-catching tombs in the crypt belong to the Duke of Wellington and Horatio Nelson. Notable figures from the arts buried here are Henry Moore, JMW Turner, Joshua Reynolds, Max Beerbohm, Arthur Sullivan – and Wren himself, whose small, plain tombstone is inscribed with the epitaph: 'Reader, if you seek a monument, look around you.'

North to Smithfield

Barbican or St Paul's tube.
From St Paul's, a short walk across Cheapside takes you to Foster Lane, and another Wren church, **St Vedast-alias-Foster**. Fans claim its delicately phased tower is the prettiest in town.

To the west, **St Bartholomew-the-Great** (West Smithfield, 7606 5171, www.greatstbarts. com), is the capital's oldest parish church. Nearby, a memorial to William Wallace marks the spot of his execution in 1305.

Behind St Bart's is the vast **Smithfield Market**, built by Horace Jones in 1868. Until World War II, this was the main food market in the City, but today only the meat market survives. Early risers should visit at first light, when the corridors bustle with carcass-hauling porters and jovial butchers. It's also ideal for a post-pub snack – there are lots of all-night caffs. However, the area is being gentrified and slick bars and brasseries are springing up. Even the **Fox & Anchor** pub (115 Charterhouse Street, 7250 1300, www.foxandanchor.com), has been taken over by Malmaison and now has six rooms and posh British food, though the beer is as good as ever.

Around Bank

Map p271

Mansion House tube/Bank tube/DLR.
Made from the finest Portland stone, a triumvirate of imposing buildings – the Bank of England, the Royal Exchange and Mansion House – is arguably

the symbolic heart of the Square Mile. The **Bank of England** was founded in 1694 to fund William III's war against the French. Most of what you see today was the work of Sir Herbert Baker in the 1920s; Sir John Soane's original building was demolished to make room for it.

The Lord Mayor of London's official residence, the grand **Mansion House** was designed by George Dance and completed in 1753. It's the only private residence in the UK to have its own court of justice, complete with 11 prison cells. The current **Royal Exchange**, the third on the site, was opened by Queen Victoria in 1844. The only trading that takes place now is in the classy shops in the arcades around the central court.

Off to the west you'll find the centre of the City's civic life: the **Guildhall**, the ancient base of the Corporation of London. To the east lie a couple of modern architectural marvels: Richard Rogers' high-tech **Lloyd's of London Building**, which wears its mechanical services (ductwork, stairwells) on the exterior. It's in marked contrast to rival architect Norman Foster's sleek, banded **Swiss Re** tower – known by all as the Gherkin – facing off against it at 30 St Mary Axe.

Bank of England Museum

Entrance on Bartholomew Lane, EC2R 8AH (7601 5545, www.bankofengland.co.uk/museum). Bank tube/DLR. **Open** 10am-5pm Mon-Fri. **Admission** free. **Map** p271 Q6.
The life story of the national bank – complete with coins and banknotes – unfolds amusingly in these elegant rooms. Those with strong forearms can lift a real gold bar worth around £98,000 (depending on the bullion market rate). Entry costs nothing; there are no free samples.

Guildhall

Gresham Street, EC2P 2EJ (7606 3030, www.city oflondon.gov.uk). St Paul's tube or Bank tube/DLR. **Open** *May-Sept* 10am-5pm daily. *Oct-Apr* 10am-5pm Mon-Sat. Closes for functions, call ahead. **Admission** free. **Map** p270 P6.
The centre of the City's government for more than 800 years, the Guildhall oozes history. The cathedral-like Great Hall is adorned with shields of livery companies and memorials to national heroes. Many famous trials have taken place here over the centuries, including the treason trial of Lady Jane Grey, 'the nine days queen', in 1553. But possibly the most interesting aspect of the Guildhall is the Clockmakers' Museum (Guildhall Library, 7732 1868, www.clockmakers.org, closed Sun), where hundreds of ticking, chiming clocks and watches are displayed.

Guildhall Art Gallery

Guildhall Yard, off Gresham Street, EC2P 2EJ (7332 3700, www.cityoflondon.gov.uk). St Paul's tube or Bank tube/DLR. **Open** 10am-5pm Mon-Sat; noon-4pm Sun. **Admission** £2.50; £1 reductions. Free after 3.30pm daily, all day Fri. **Credit** (over £5) MC, V. **Map** p270 P6.

The largest exhibit at the Guildhall Art Gallery is not a work of art, but the ruins of London's Roman amphitheatre. Elsewhere, the Pre-Raphaelites are exquisite, the Egyptian scenes exotic, the bust of Clytie positively sensuous. The contemporary paintings are of mixed quality.

North to the Barbican

Barbican tube/Moorgate tube/rail.
London Wall follows the northerly course of the old Roman fortifications to the **Museum of London**. Running along the same route is a signposted 1.75-mile walk. The best bits are just north of the Tower of London and to the east of the Museum of London. North of here is the **Barbican**, a vast, post-war concrete estate of flats and an arts complex (box office 7638 8891, www.barbican.org.uk). The architecture may be austere, but the arts centre is fantastic.

Barbican Art Gallery

Barbican Centre, Silk Street, EC2Y 8DS (7638 8891 box office, 7382 7006, www.barbican.org.uk). Barbican tube or Moorgate tube/rail. **Open** 11am-8pm Mon, Fri-Sun; 11am-6pm Tue, Wed; 11am-10pm Thur. **Admission** £10; £8 reductions. **Credit** (shop) AmEx, MC, V. **Map** p270 P5.
It's not quite as 'out there' as it would like you to think, but the exhibitions on design, architecture and pop culture are

Barbican

usually diverting. On the ground floor, the Curve is a free exhibition space (and, yes, it is actually curved) for specially commissioned works and contemporary art shows.

Museum of London

150 London Wall, EC2Y 5HN (0870 444 3851, www. museumoflondon.org.uk). Barbican or St Paul's tube. **Open** 10am-6pm daily. **Admission** free. **Credit** (shop) MC, V. **Map** p270 P5.

This great museum traces the history of London in fascinating style. Detailed, engaging displays begin with 300,000-year-old flint tools found near Piccadilly. Among the highlights are the Great Fire Experience, the walk-through Victorian street scene, and the central garden, which presents a curious botanical history of the City. From Elizabethan and Jacobean London, heyday of the

Monument

Globe Theatre, comes the Cheapside Hoard, an astonishing cache of jewellery unearthed in 1912. The recently remodelled downstairs galleries are a delight, the new space freeing up room for everything from an unexploded World War II bomb to a multimedia display on the Brixton riots and an outfit by the late Alexander McQueen. Don't miss the recreated Georgian pleasure gardens with mannequins sporting Philip Treacy masks and hats.

Around the Tower of London

Map p271

Tower Hill tube/Tower Gateway DLR.

Unlike certain other attractions, the **Tower of London** delivers plenty of entertainment, but get here early to beat the crowds. Close by, **Tower Bridge** is the capital's most distinctive (some would say ugliest) bridge. Between the Tower and Liverpool Street Station to the north sit many churches, including **St Helen Bishopsgate**, the City's equivalent of Westminster Abbey.

Monument

Monument Street, EC3R 8AH (7626 2717, www.the monument.info). Monument tube. **Open** 9.30am-5.30pm daily. **Admission** £3; £1-£2 reductions. **No credit cards. Map** p271 Q7.

The Monument, built in the 1670s by Sir Christopher Wren and Robert Hooke to commemorate the Great Fire of 1666, comprises a 311-step spiral staircase enclosed within a 202ft Doric column with views over the City.

Tower Bridge Exhibition

Tower Bridge, SE1 2UP (7403 3761, www.tower bridge.org.uk). Tower Hill tube or Tower Gateway DLR. **Open** *Apr-Sept* 10am-6.30pm daily. *Oct-Mar* 9.30am-6pm daily. **Admission** £7; £3-£5 reductions. **Credit** AmEx, MC, V. **Map** p271 R8.

You're paying mainly for the spectacular bird's-eye views of the Thames, though films and displays cover the design of the bridge, an ambitious feat of engineering in its day.

Tower of London

Tower Hill, EC3N 4AB (0844 482 7777, www.hrp. org.uk). Tower Hill tube or Tower Gateway DLR. **Open** *Mar-Oct* 10am-5.30pm Mon, Sun; 9am-5.30pm Tue-Sat. *Nov-Feb* 10am-4.30pm Mon, Sun; 9am-4.30pm Tue-Sat. **Admission** £17; £9.50-£14 reductions. **Credit** AmEx, MC, V. **Map** p271 R7.

A key tourist destination, the history-saturated Tower, which has served as a fortress, palace, prison and royal execution site over its 900-year history, doesn't disappoint. On the contrary, the tales it tells are grimly fascinating. The best way to see the Tower is on a free hour-long tour led by one of the 40 Yeoman Warders (Beefeaters), cheery red-coated ex-soldiers resident within the grounds. Of permanent, haunting fascination is the chopping block on Tower Green. The Crown Jewels are in the Jewel House; the Armoury, meanwhile, is in the White Tower; here you can admire Henry VIII's enormous codpiece.

Holborn &
Clerkenwell

Gowns and wigs – but not a drag queen in sight.

Holborn

Maps p267 & p270

Chancery Lane, Holborn or Temple tube.
The Saxons chose Holborn as their London home, and where they led, the lawyers followed. The area became the heart of the British justice system and, unlike Fleet Street (*see p167*) vis-à-vis journalists, it has remained so. The four Inns of Court, where English common law first developed during the Middle Ages, still provide working space for myriad barristers and their acolytes. The inns were founded in medieval times and were originally public houses where barristers gathered to do business, lodge and eat – hence the name. They eventually became formal institutions where barristers could be trained. Every barrister is aligned to one of them. Today their narrow alleys, courtyards and lawns are wonderful, archaic places to wander.

Aldwych

Maps p267, p269 & p270

Holborn or Temple tube.
The wide sweep of Kingsway points straight to Bush House (home to the BBC's World Service), the centrepiece of a trio of imperial buildings (the others are India House and Australia House) along the curve of semi-circular Aldwych. The revered **London School of Economics**, just off Aldwych on Houghton Street, was the origin of the gay rights movement in Britain.

If you walk east along the Strand you will pass the **Royal Courts of Justice** before the thoroughfare becomes Fleet Street. Tucked away south of here are **Middle Temple** (Middle Temple Lane, 7427 4800) and **Inner Temple** (Inner Temple Treasury Office, 7797 8250). The names derive from the Knights Templar, who owned the site for 150 years. Built around a maze of courtyards, these Inns have a villagey feel and

are especially atmospheric when gas-lit after dark. The **Middle Temple Hall**, built in 1573, has a huge table made from a single oak tree donated by Queen Elizabeth I, and a smaller table made from the hatch of Drake's ship, the *Golden Hinde*. The Inner Temple has several fine buildings, and its lawns are a beautiful spot for picnics. Of special note is **Temple Church** (Fleet Street, 7353 8559, www.templechurch.com); consecrated in 1185, it is London's only surviving round church. Part of Dan Brown's *The Da Vinci Code* is set here.

Royal Courts of Justice

Strand, WC2A 2LL (7947 6000, www.hmcourts-service.co.uk). Temple tube. **Open** 9am-4.30pm Mon-Fri. **Admission** free. **Map** p270 M6.
If you want to see British justice in action, then pay a visit to these splendid Gothic buildings. Anyone is free to take a pew in one of the 76 courts, where the High Court presides over serious civil trials. Cameras are not permitted. Two-hour tours of the building are usually given on the first and third Tuesday of each month at 11am or 2pm. They cost £10 per person and must be booked in advance on 7947 7684 or rcjtours@talktalk.net.

Somerset House

Strand, WC2R 1LA (7845 4600, www.somersethouse.org.uk). Temple tube or Charing Cross tube/rail. **Open** 10am-6pm (last entry 5.30pm) daily. *Tours* phone for details. **Admission** *Courtyard & terrace* free. *Courtauld Gallery* £5; £4 reductions. *Embankment Gallery* £5; £4 reductions. Free students & under-18s daily. *Courtauld Gallery* free 10am-2pm Mon. *Tours* phone for details. **Credit** (shop) MC, V. **Map** p269 M7.
The original Somerset House was a Tudor palace commissioned by the Duke of Somerset in 1547. In 1775 it was demolished to make way for an entirely new building, effectively the first purpose-built office block in the world. The architect Sir William Chambers spent the last 20 years of his life working on the vast neoclassical edifice that now overlooks the Thames at Waterloo Bridge. It was built to accommodate learned societies such as the Royal Academy, but today it houses the formidable Courtauld art gallery, a new site for temporary exhibitions, the beautiful fountain court, a little café and a classy restaurant. The courtyard is used for outdoor concerts and, in winter, a very popular ice rink.

Somerset House. *See p171.*

Courtauld Gallery

7872 0220, www.courtauld.ac.uk/gallery.
The Courtauld has one of the country's greatest collections of paintings, and it contains several works of world importance. Although there are some outstanding works from earlier periods (don't miss the wonderful Adam & Eve by Lucas Cranach), the collection's strongest suit is its holdings of Impressionist and post-Impressionist paintings. There are some popular masterpieces: Manet's astonishing *A Bar at the Folies-Bergère* is undoubtedly the centrepiece, alongside plenty of superb Monets and Cézannes, important Gauguins (including *Nevermore*), and some excellent Van Goghs and Seurats. On the top floor, the 20th century is represented by a selection of gorgeous Fauvist works, a lovely room of Kandinskys and plenty more besides. An essential stop if you have any interest in art. The little café, hidden downstairs, is a joy.

Embankment Galleries

7845 4600, www.somersethouse.org.uk.
The new Embankment Galleries replace the old Hermitage Rooms and Gilbert Collection. The sparkling gewgaws and objects from the latter can now be seen at the Victoria & Albert Museum and the former – an outpost of the Hermitage in St Petersburg – has shut for good owing to lack of funds. The new galleries place an emphasis on contemporary art, fashion, architecture and graphics.

Lincoln's Inn

Map p267

Chancery Lane or Holborn tube.
A stone's throw from the West End lies the verdant tranquillity of **Lincoln's Inn Fields**, the largest public square in London, flanked by a series of

historic buildings. On the north side is the splendid **Sir John Soane's Museum**; south-west on Portsmouth Street is the **Old Curiosity Shop**, supposedly the oldest extant shop in London (now selling shoes); to the south is the Royal College of Surgeons, whose **Hunterian Museum** reopened in 2005 after extensive renovation; and south-east is **Lincoln's Inn** (7405 1393, www.lincolnsinn. org.uk), the Inn of Court from which the fields take their name. You can relive scenes from *Bleak House*, Dickens's ferocious attack on the legal system, as virtually nothing has changed in hundreds of years. The Inn's various buildings are a historical catalogue of architecture including Gothic, Tudor and Palladian; its Old Hall was built well over 500 years ago.

Opposite Chancery Lane tube, the half-timbered **Staple Inn** (which features in *Bleak House*) is one of the few buildings to have survived the Great Fire of London, and one of the only remaining Tudor structures in the capital. On Chancery Lane itself, visit the underground **London Silver Vaults** (7242 3844, www.thesilvervaults.com), opened in 1876, where the goods of over 30 dealers constitute the world's largest 'collection' of antique silver.

Hunterian Museum

Royal College of Surgeons, 35-43 Lincoln's Inn Fields, WC2A 3PE (7869 6560, www.rcseng.ac.uk/museums). Holborn tube. **Open** 10am-5pm Tue-Sat. **Admission** free. **Map** p267 M6.

John Hunter (1728-1793), a pioneering anatomist and surgeon to George III, amassed a huge collection of medical specimens. There is nothing that gory about the exhibits, but it's not for the squeamish: the brain of 19th-century mathematician Charles Babbage and Winston Churchill's dentures are among the displays. There's also a collection of (non-medical) paintings that Hunter amassed.

Sir John Soane's Museum

13 Lincoln's Inn Fields, WC2A 3BP (7405 2107, www.soane.org). Holborn tube. **Open** 10am-5pm Tue-Sat; 10am-5pm, 6-9pm 1st Tue of mth. *Tours* 11am Sat. **Admission** free. *Tours* £5; free reductions. **No credit cards. Map** p267 M5.
Sir John Soane (1753-1837) was one of the leading architects and most obsessive collectors of his day. He acquired a huge raft of treasures before turning his house into a museum, one of London's most idiosyncratic. Surfaces are covered with sculptures, paintings, architectural models, furniture, antiquities and jewellery. Highlights include Hogarth's *Rake's Progress*, the sarcophagus of an Egyptian pharaoh and hundreds of plaster casts of Greek statues, plus many of Soane's architectural designs. Tickets for the Saturday tours go on sale at 2pm on a first come, first served basis – you may need to queue.

Clerkenwell

Map p270

Farringdon tube/rail.
Modern-day Clerkenwell epitomised the Cool Britannia trend of the 1990s: in the 1880s it was a slum; a century later it was full of abandoned factories and office space. Then artists began moving into empty warehouses and converting them into lofts. By the next decade, property developers had seen the area's potential, and nightclubs and restaurants followed.

The neighbourhood's enduring destinations include the pioneering modern British restaurant **St John** (26 St John Street, 7251 4090), gastropub the **Eagle** (159 Farringdon Road, 7837 1353) and the brilliant artisan food shops, fashion boutiques, restaurants and bohemian bars strung along Exmouth Market. All are frequented by denizens of local creative and media companies. If you care more about history than fashion, pop into the **Crown Tavern** (43 Clerkenwell Green, 7253 4973), where Lenin and Stalin had a drink together in 1903. No wonder: the office of *Iskra*, the Russian socialist newspaper, was next door at 37A; it is now the **Marx Memorial Library** (7253 1485, www.marx-memorial-library.org).

Clerkenwell means the clerks' well, which drew water from the River Fleet, but fell out of use and was covered over (probably because in its lower reaches the Fleet had become more of a sewer than a river). In 1924 builders chanced upon the old well, and it can now be seen through a window at 14-16 Farringdon Lane. A monastic

community flourished here as early as the 11th century, when the Order of St John of Jerusalem set up its priory; all that remains is **St John's Gate** (1504), now home to the **Museum & Library of the Order of St John**, and the priory's Norman crypt.

During industrialisation, new trades took root here on the fringes of the City, and many factories and workshops were constructed on the open spaces of Clerkenwell. Most of these trades have long since departed, though the area is still London's jewellery-making epicentre, with countless craftsmen and shops, especially in **Hatton Garden**, London's diamond capital, which lies north of Holborn.

Museum & Library of the Order of St John

St John's Gate, St John's Lane, EC1M 4DA (7324 4005, www.sja.org.uk/museum). Farringdon tube/rail. **Open** 10am-5pm Mon-Sat. *Tours* 11am & 2.30pm Tue, Fri, Sat. **Admission** free. *Tours* free. Suggested donation £5; £4 reductions. **Map** p270 O4.
Today, the Order of St John is best known for its provision of ambulance services, but it dates back to the Crusades. This museum charts the evolution of the medieval Order of Hospitaller Knights and there are fascinating collections of objects and artworks relating to this varied history, which visits Jerusalem, Malta and the Ottoman Empire. At the time this guide went to press, the museum was closed for refurbishment, but scheduled to reopen imminently.

Old Curiosity Shop

Around Town

Bloomsbury & Fitzrovia

Live and learn.

Bloomsbury

Map p267

Chancery Lane, Holborn or Tottenham Court Road tube.
The attraction of Bloomsbury cannot be pinned down to one thing alone, like the British Museum, say, or those elegant squares and Georgian terraces so redolent of the area's literary past. Instead, its charm lies more in the sum of its parts, in an afternoon spent wandering through leafy, open spaces, peering into museum display cabinets and losing yourself in the throng of a student café.

But for all its intellectual cachet, Bloomsbury hasn't always been a refuge for the high-minded: back in 1086, for instance, the neighbourhood was a breeding ground for pigs. What's more, its pretty floral name also has humdrum origins: it's taken from 'Blemondisberi', or 'the manor of William Blemond', who acquired the area in the early 13th century. It remained rural until the 1660s, when the fourth Earl of Southampton built Bloomsbury Square around his house, though today none of the original architecture remains. The Southamptons intermarried with the Russells (the Dukes of Bedford), and both families developed the area as one of London's first planned suburbs. During subsequent centuries, they built a series of grand squares and streets, laid out in the classic Georgian grid style: check out **Bedford Square** (1775-80), the capital's only complete Georgian square, and huge **Russell Square**, now an attractive public park (and formerly a cruising ground; no longer after the council cracked down). **Gower Street** is also an uninterrupted stream of classic Georgian terraced houses.

Things are not so posh now (witness the aforementioned students), but the area's shabby grandeur is undeniably charming. And the streets are speckled with blue plaques, reading like a Who's Who of English literature: William Butler Yeats once lived at 5 Upper Woburn Place; Edgar Allan Poe lived at 83 Southampton Row;

Mary Wollstonecraft lived on Store Street, the birthplace of Anthony Trollope (he was born at no.6). Then there's **Charles Dickens Museum**, at 48 Doughty Street, where the author once lived. As for the famous – and famously bisexual – Bloomsbury Group, its headquarters were at 50 Gordon Square, where EM Forster, Lytton Strachey, John Maynard Keynes, Clive and Vanessa Bell and Duncan Grant would discuss literature, art and politics. Virginia and Leonard Woolf lived at 52 Tavistock Square.

But the real academia is clustered around Bloomsbury's western borders. Here, Malet Street, Gordon Street and Gower Street are dominated by the University of London. The most notable building is **University College**, on Gower Street, founded in 1826 and built in the Greek Revival style by William Wilkins, the architect responsible for the National Gallery. Inside lies one of the strangest exhibits in London: the preserved remains of philosopher Jeremy Bentham, who introduced the world to utilitarianism. The massive **Senate House**, on Malet Street, holds the university's biggest library. It was a particular favourite of Hitler's: had Germany won the war, he planned to make his headquarters here. South of the university lies the fabled **British Museum**.

Such grand institutions may have put Bloomsbury on the map, but aficionados claim that the area's real delights lie in hidden pockets. **Sicilian Place**, a pedestrianised stretch of colonnaded shops that links Bloomsbury Way with Southampton Row, is one such gem. **St George's Bloomsbury** (Bloomsbury Way, 7242 1979, www.stgeorgesbloomsbury.org.uk), Hawksmoor church, has recently reopened following a lavish £10 million restoration project. North-east of here is **Lamb's Conduit Street**, a convivial area with a good selection of old-fashioned pubs, stylish restaurants and independent shops. At the top of this street lies

British Museum

wonderful **Coram's Fields**, a children's park (adults are only admitted if accompanied by a child) built on the former grounds of Thomas Coram's Foundling Hospital, which provided for abandoned children. The legacy of the Coram family is now commemorated in the beautiful **Foundling Museum**. Tucked away behind student-land is Mecklenburgh Square, and to the north-west lie budget hotel-land and Cartwright Gardens.

It's not all Georgian grandeur. Take the **Brunswick Centre** opposite Russell Square tube station. When it was built in 1973, Patrick Hodgkinson's brutalist concrete jungle was hailed as the future for community living: a complex of shopping centre, flats, the arty **Renoir Cinema** (0871 703 3991, www.curzoncinemas.com) and an underground car park. These days, modernism's young dream still divides opinion. But after a makeover – and the addition of several smart shops and cafés – the centre is now more distinguished than depressing.

A flurry of small, distinguished bookshops are dotted around the area, including Bookmarks for left-wing tomes, and the excellent London Review Bookshop – not forgetting queer mecca **Gay's the Word** (*see p102*). And for comic fans, the **Cartoon Museum** (35 Little Russell Street, 7580 8155, www.cartoon museum.org) provides respite from the area's more highbrow museums, featuring doodles spanning the centuries from 18th-century high-society caricatures to *Rupert the Bear* and the works of Gerald Scarfe.

British Museum

Great Russell Street, WC1B 3DG (7323 8299, www. britishmuseum.org). Russell Square or Tottenham Court Road tube. **Open** *Galleries* 10am-5.30pm Mon-Wed, Sat, Sun; 10am-8.30pm Thur, Fri. *Great Court* 9am-6pm Mon-Wed, Sun; 9am-11pm Thur-Sat. *Eye Opener tours* (30-40mins) phone for details. **Admission** free; donations appreciated. *Temporary exhibitions* prices vary. *Eye Opener tours* free. **Credit** (shop) AmEx, DC, MC, V. **Map** p267 K/L5.

Britain's most popular tourist attraction, the museum attracts six million visitors annually. The architecture is part of the draw: the building is a neoclassical marvel built in 1847 by Robert Smirke, one of the pioneers of the Greek Revival style. Also impressive is Lord Foster's glass-roofed Great Court, the largest covered space in Europe. This £100m landmark surrounds the domed Reading Room, where Marx, Lenin, Thackeray, Dickens, Hardy and Yeats once worked (it's now home to an information centre).

But the form does not overshadow the museum's extra-ordinary contents. Star exhibits include Ancient Egyptian artefacts – the Rosetta Stone, statues of the pharaohs, mummies – and Greek antiquities, such as the marble friezes from the Parthenon (aka the Elgin Marbles). The Celts Gallery has the Lindow Man, killed in 300 BC and preserved in peat, while the Wellcome Gallery of Ethnography has an Easter Island statue and regalia from Captain Cook's travels.

Gay visitors should look out for the Warren Cup in Room 70. This silver drinking cup, probably made in the reign of Nero, is decorated with scenes of Roman men going at it – as the museum says, it's 'notable for its exceptional scenes of homosexual love-making.' We'll say. Before 1967, when homosexuality was legalised in Britain, gay men used to make a beeline for the room of Greek statuary, where they could admire the nude male physique without fear of being arrested. The bronze Roman statue featuring two phalluses, and the priapic wind chime, are also eye openers. In the Reading Room, meanwhile, you'll find a bust of Antinous, the Emperor Hadrian's younger lover.

The finest neoclassical space in London, King's Library is home to 'Enlightenment: Discovering the World in the 18th Century', a 5,000-piece collection devoted to the formative period of the museum. It covers physics, archaeology and the natural world, and contains objects as diverse as 18th-century Indonesian puppets and a beautiful orrery.

You won't be able to see everything in a day, so buy a guide (£6) and pick out the showstoppers, or join a 40-minute Eye Opener tour focusing on specific aspects of the collection.

Charles Dickens Museum

48 Doughty Street, WC1N 2LX (7405 2127, www.dickensmuseum.com). Chancery Lane or Russell Square tube. **Open** 10am-5pm Mon-Sat; 11am-5pm Sun. *Tours* by arrangement. **Admission** £6; £3-£4.50 reductions. **Credit** (shop) AmEx, DC, MC, V. **Map** p267 M4.
London is scattered with plaques marking the many addresses where Charles Dickens lived, including Devonshire Terrace near Paddington and Camden's Bayham Street, but this is the only one of the author's many London homes that is still standing. Dickens lived here for three years between 1837 and 1840 while he wrote *Nicholas Nickleby* and *Oliver Twist*. Restored to its former condition, the house is packed with Dickens ephemera. There are personal letters, all sorts of manuscripts and his writing desk.

Foundling Museum

40 Brunswick Square, WC1N 1AZ (7841 3600, www.foundlingmuseum.org.uk). Russell Square tube. **Open** 10am-5pm Tue-Sat; 11am-5pm Sun. **Admission** £7.50; £5 reductions. **Credit** MC, V. **Map** p267 L4.
British society's sentimental attitude toward its pampered young is nothing new: the idealisation of innocent babes was all the rage in fashionable Georgian society. This museum recalls the social history of the Foundling Hospital, set up by compassionate shipwright and sailor Thomas Coram in 1739 in response to the epidemic of orphaned street children. Many artists, including Reynolds, Gainsborough and Wilson, donated works to the hospital; some of these still hang here, including the Hogarth series

featuring the poverty-stricken Gin Lane. Handel also gave performances of his *Messiah* at the hospital chapel; today, the museum's top floor consists of cases of Handeliana.

Petrie Museum of Archaeology

University College London, Malet Place, WC1E 6BT (7679 2884, www.petrie.ucl.ac.uk). Euston Square or Warren Street tube. **Open** 1-5pm Tue-Sat. **Admission** free. **Map** p267 K4.
Where the British Museum's Egyptology collection is strong on the big stuff, the Petrie focuses on the minutiae of ancient life. Its aged wooden cabinets are full of pottery shards and primitive tools. Among the oddities are a 4,000-year-old skeleton of a man who was buried in an earthenware pot. The gloomy interior and 1950s wooden display cabinets give it all a kind of 'Indiana Jones on home leave' vibe, and some of the labelling is professorial (read: dry). But the girly bits are fun: make-up pots, grooming tools, jewellery and a dress dating back to 2800 BC. Check out the coiffured head of a mummy with eyebrows and lashes intact. The Petrie is hard to find (the entrance is via the UCL Science Library), but museum buffs should try.

St Pancras New Church

Euston Road, corner of Upper Woburn Place, NW1 2BA (7388 1461, www.stpancraschurch.org). *Euston tube/rail.* **Open** 10am-2pm Mon; 10am-1pm Tue; 12.45-2pm Wed; noon-2pm Thur; 10.30am-noon Fri; 9.15-11am Sat; 7.45am-noon, 5.30-7.15pm Sun. *Services* 8am, 10am, 6pm Sun; 1.15pm Mon, Wed. *Recitals* 1.15pm Thur. **Admission** free. **Map** p267 K3.
Built in 1822, this church is a spectacular example of the Greek Revivalist style. At the time of its construction it was, at £89,296, the most expensive church to be built in London apart from St Paul's. Inspired by the Erechtheion in Athens, its most notable feature is its Caryatid porches, entrances to the burial vaults. The interior is more restrained, but has beautiful 19th-century stained-glass windows. Free lunchtime concerts (1.15pm Thur) feature performances by violinists, pianists and sopranos.

St Pancras Station

British Library

King's Cross

Map p267

Euston or King's Cross tube/rail.
Occupying an unlovely stretch of the Euston Road, King's Cross looks humdrum, and gained notoriety in the 20th century as a haven for prostitutes, drug dealers and runaways, immortalised in Neil Jordan's 1987 film *Mona Lisa*, and the Pet Shop Boys' eerie 1987 track 'King's Cross'. But the grit may soon be replaced by glamour, as the area is on its way to becoming a major European transport hub, thanks to a £500m makeover and the opening of its glorious centrepiece, the renovated and restored **St Pancras Station**. Welcoming the high-speed Eurostar train from Paris and Brussels is William Barlow's gorgeous Victorian glass-and-iron train shed, which for many years had the largest clear-span enclosure in the world. Sir George Gilbert Scott's magnificent neo-gothic hotel building, which fronts the station – and was the set for the Spice Girls' first video, 'Wannabe' – will also reopen in 2011 as a five-star hotel, the Renaissance St Pancras. In fact, St Pancras International has become somewhere to linger, with the longest champagne bar in Europe, shops, and an inviting gastropub. For details of its ongoing development, see www.stpancras.com.

Once all the building work is done, the badlands to the north of St Pancras and King's Cross stations will have been transformed into a mixed-use nucleus called King's Cross Central. **Kings Place** (*see p134*) a new arts centre and classical music hub, is a promising sign of things to come.

The area has a few gay venues, including the down and dirty **Central Station** (*see p28*).

British Library

96 Euston Road, NW1 2DB (7412 7332, www.bl.uk). Euston or King's Cross tube/rail. **Open** 9.30am-6pm Mon, Wed-Fri; 9.30am-8pm Tue; 9.30am-5pm Sat; 11am-5pm Sun. **Admission** free. **Map** p267 K3.
Dubbed 'one of the ugliest buildings in the world' by a parliamentary committee, the British Library has been mired in controversy since it opened in 1997. The project went over budget by £350 million and took 20 years to complete (longer than St Paul's and 15 years behind schedule). When it finally opened, architecture critics ripped it to shreds.

But don't judge a book by its cover: the interior is spectacular, all white marble, glass and light. In the piazza sits Antony Gormley's sculpture *Planets*. The focal point of the building is the King's Library, a six-storey glass-walled tower that houses George III's collection. But the library's treasures are displayed in the John Ritblat Gallery: the Magna Carta, the Lindisfarne Gospels and original manuscripts from Chaucer. There's fun stuff, too: Beatles lyric sheets and archive recordings of everyone from James Joyce to Bob Geldof (of particular gay interest is a recording of Joe Orton, taken the week before he was murdered, and Tennessee Williams ranting and raving about the critics. You can also see Charlotte Brontë's manuscript of *Jane Eyre* and Jane Austen's writing desk. The 80,000-strong stamp collection is world famous.

In short, this is one of the greatest libraries in the world, with 150 million items. Each year, it receives a copy of every publication produced in the UK and Ireland.

St Pancras Old Church & Gardens

St Pancras Road, NW1 1UL (7387 4193, 7424 0724, www.posp.co.uk). Mornington Crescent tube or King's Cross tube/rail. **Open** *Gardens* 7am-dusk daily. *Services* 9am Mon-Fri; 7pm Tue; 9.30am Sun. **Admission** free. **Map** p267 K2.
Its site dates back to the fourth century, but the Old Church has been rebuilt many times. The current structure is handsome, but it's the churchyard that delights. Among those buried here are writer William Godwin and his wife, Mary Wollstonecraft; over this grave, daughter Mary Godwin

(author of *Frankenstein*) declared her love for poet Percy Bysshe Shelley. The tomb of Sir John Soane is a listed monument; its dome influenced Sir Giles Gilbert Scott's design of the classic British phone box.

Wellcome Collection

183 Euston Road, NW1 2BE (7611 2222, www. wellcomecollection.org). Euston Square tube or Euston tube/rail. **Open** 10am-6pm Tue, Wed, Fri, Sat; 10am-10pm Thur; 11am-6pm Sun. *Library* 10am-6pm Mon-Wed, Fri; 10am-8pm Thur; 10am-4pm Sat. **Admission** free. **Map** p266 J4.

Founder Sir Henry Wellcome, a pioneering 19th-century pharmacist and entrepreneur, amassed a vast and idiosyncratic collection of implements and curios relating to the medical trade, which is now displayed in this swanky little new museum. In addition to these fascinating and often grisly items – delicate ivory carvings of pregnant women, used guillotine blades, a viciously bladed torture chair, Napoleon's toothbrush – there are several serious (and sometimes disturbing) works of modern art, most of them on display in a smaller room to one side of the main chamber of curiosities.

Fitzrovia

Map p266

Tottenham Court Road or Goodge Street tube.

Fitzrovia may not be as famous as Bloomsbury, but its history is just as rich. Squeezed in between Gower Street, Oxford Street, Great Portland Street and Euston Road, it only became known as Fitzrovia during the 20th century. The origins of its name are hazy: some say it comes from Fitzroy Square, named after Henry Fitzroy, the son of Charles II. Others insist it was named after the **Fitzroy Tavern** (7580 3714) at 16 Charlotte Street, a centre of London bohemia for much of the 20th century. Once a favourite with radicals and artists, regulars included Dylan Thomas, George Orwell, Aleister Crowley and England's most famous stately homo, Quentin Crisp.

Fitzrovia's radical roots go deep. In 1792 Thomas Paine lived at 154 New Cavendish Street – the same year he published *The Rights of Man* and incurred governmental wrath. His friend Edmund Burke lived at 18 Charlotte Street. During the 19th century, the district became a hotbed of Chartist activity and working men's clubs. Later, Karl Marx attended Communist meetings here.

During the 1880s, 19 Cleveland Street was a male brothel. Clients included, so rumour has it, Prince Eddy, the eldest son of the Prince of Wales and presumed future King of England. Eddy died soon after the brothel was exposed in July 1889, and any mention of his involvement was kept out of the British press. The police targeted the house because many of its 'renters' – a term for male prostitutes that later became 'rent boy' – earned a fortune while holding down menial jobs.

More recently, Fitzrovia went pop. In the 1960s, the Stones played gigs at the **100 Club** (*see p135*). A young Bob Dylan made his British debut singing at the **King & Queen** pub (1 Foley Street) in 1962. Concert scenes for the Beatles' *A Hard Day's Night* were filmed at the Scala Theatre, then at 21-25 Tottenham Street. Pink Floyd and Jimi Hendrix were regulars at the Speakeasy at 50 Margaret Street. As flower power declined, punk took over. Regular performers at the 100 Club included the Sex Pistols, Siouxsie and the Banshees, the Damned and the Clash. At this time, Fitzrovia was descended upon by squatters. Boy George lived in squats on Great Titchfield Street, Warren Street and Carburton Street.

In the 1980s, its raffish image was transformed when ITN and Channel 4 moved in. Meanwhile, the BBC's pared-down **Broadcasting House** had been on the western fringe of the area – at 2-8 Portland Place – since 1922. Prominent among its carvings is a statue of Shakespeare's Prospero and Ariel. The statue caused controversy due to the flattering size of the sprite's manhood; artist Eric Gill was recalled and asked to make it more modest.

The district's icon is the 1964 **BT Tower**, first known as the Post Office Tower. It was open to the public until the IRA exploded a bomb there in 1971; the revolving restaurant is now only open for the benefit of corporate functions.

For olde worlde Fitzrovia, drop into the cosy **Newman Arms** (23 Rathbone Street, 7636 1127), where Michael Powell's *Peeping Tom* was filmed. For bohemian scruff, try seedy **Hanway Street**, lined with late Spanish bars. **Charlotte Street** is the place to go for smart restaurants and bars.

Gay venues include **Vault 139** (*see p27*), an underground cruise bar with regular naked nights, and **RoB London** (*see p111*), a gay fetish shop.

All Saints

7 Margaret Street, W1W 8JG (7636 1788, www. allsaintsmargaretstreet.org.uk). Oxford Circus tube. **Open** 7am-7pm daily. *Services* 7.30am, 8am, 1.10pm, 6pm, 6.30pm Mon-Fri; 7.30am, 8am, 6pm, 6.30pm Sat; 8am, 10.20am, 11am, 5.15pm, 6pm Sun. **Admission** free. **Map** p266 J5.

This 1850s church was designed by William Butterfield, one of the great Gothic Revivalists. Notable for its soaring architecture, lofty spire and lavish marble interior.

Pollock's Toy Museum

1 Scala Street (entrance on Whitfield Street), W1T 2HL (7636 3452, www.pollockstoymuseum.com). Goodge Street tube. **Open** 10am-5pm Mon-Sat. **Admission** £5; £2-£4 reductions. **Credit** (shop) MC, V. **Map** p266 J5.

Housed in a creaky Georgian townhouse, and crammed with vintage toys, Pollock's is a respite from the PlayStation era. It should raise a nostalgic smile from adults and a resentful stare from the Ritalin generation. Famed for its toy theatres.

Marylebone & Oxford Street

Go ape, wax lyrical and shop till you drop.

Marylebone

Maps p263 & p266

Baker Street, Bond Street, Edgware Road, Great Portland Street, Marble Arch or Oxford Circus tube/ Marylebone tube/rail.

Not too long ago, Marylebone – a quiet, affluent neighbourhood – was considered rather boring. Apart from **Madame Tussauds**, there was little to lure the tourist; Londoners only came to see the highbrow specialists on **Harley Street**, or passed through on their way to Regent's Park. But during the past decade this area – bordered by heaving Oxford Street to the south and thundering Marylebone Road to the north – has become downright fashionable. Curving **Marylebone High Street** is now the heart of what has been rebranded 'Marylebone Village'. Its character is still evolving, but the current mix of low-key restaurants, lively bars, tasteful chain shops and independents is luring visitors and locals.

And while there's certainly no gay 'scene' to speak of, the **Quebec** (*see p24*) is a thoroughly congenial gay pub/club; it attracts a friendly, older crowd – you might even get some decent conversation. Gay-friendly hotels in Marylebone include the **Edward Lear** (*see p61*) and **Lincoln House Hotel** (*see p62*), both housed in elegant townhouses. The area has not always been so genteel, though. In the 14th century, it was a violent place: a plaque on the traffic island at Marble Arch marks the site of the notorious Tyburn gallows, operational until 1783.

After the original parish church was demolished in 1400, a new one was built near the top of what is now Marylebone High Street. Called St Mary by the Bourne, its name soon covered the entire village, and was shortened to Marylebone by 1626. Although nothing remains of the first two parish churches, the foundations of the third were preserved as the Memorial Garden of Rest. The fourth church, on Marylebone Road, was built to accommodate a rapidly growing population in 1817. It was here that Elizabeth Barrett of 50 Wimpole Street secretly married fellow poet Robert Browning in 1846. Dickens, who lived next door at 1 Devonshire Terrace (demolished in 1959), had his son baptised in the church.

In the 16th century, the northern half of Marylebone – now **Regent's Park** – became a royal hunting ground, while the southern section was bought up by the Portman family. Two centuries later, the Portmans developed many of the elegant streets and squares that lend the locale its dignified air; gems include Bryanston Square and Montagu Square. One of the squares, laid out in 1761, still bears the Portman name; another, 1776's Manchester Square, is the home of the **Wallace Collection** of art.

Running parallel to Harley and Wimpole Streets, **Portland Place** was the glory of 18th-century London. At its southern end, Langham Place, where it links with John Nash's handsome Regent Street, is the BBC's HQ, **Broadcasting House**. Next door is Nash's only remaining church, **All Souls** (1822-24), which daringly combines a Gothic spire and classical rotunda. Over the road is the **Langham Hotel**, the first of London's grand hotels (1865); further north is the **Royal Institute of British Architects** (RIBA; 7580 5533, www.riba.org), which has exhibitions, a bookshop and a café with a lovely rooftop terrace. A few blocks to the west, by York Gate, the **Royal Academy of Music**, another Nash design, founded in 1822, has a small museum (7873 7373, www.ram.ac.uk).

Further west, opposite Marylebone railway station, is the **Landmark Hotel**, the last significant Victorian hotel to be built in the golden age of steam (1899). Closed in 1939, the building was redeveloped as a hotel again in 1986.

North of Marylebone Road, it's worth taking a detour to Bell Street for the cutting-edge **Lisson Gallery** (Nos.52-54, 7724 2739, www.lisson.co.uk).

Regent's Park

Church Street is a popular local food and general market that is rapidly gentrifying at its eastern end, thanks to Alfie's Antiques Market (Nos.13-25, 7723 6066, www.alfiesantiques.com).

Around Marylebone High Street

This picturesque shopping street really does have a genuine 'village' feel, maintaining a delicate balance between independent shops and chains. Some of the most interesting shops are at the north end of **Marylebone High Street**, including the super-stylish Conran Shop (no.55, 7723 2223, www.conranshop.co.uk). Daunt Books (no.83, 7224 2295, www.dauntbooks.co.uk), with its beautiful Edwardian interior, is known for its extensive travel section. On the home front, the Skandium flagship (no.86, 7935 2077, www.skandium.com) showcases the best of Scandinavian design. Nearby, the natural American skincare company Fresh opened its first stand-alone store at no.92 (7486 4100, www.fresh.com). Gourmets will salivate over the high street's pâtisseries, and chocolatier Rococo (no.45, 7935 7780, www.rococochocolates.com). There's also a clutch of gourmet shops here – such as La Fromagerie (nos.2-6, 7935 0341,

www.lafromagerie.co.uk) – on tiny offshoot **Moxon Street**, which leads to the site of the weekly farmers' market (in the Cramer Street car park behind Waitrose, 10am-2pm Sun).

Quainter still is winding **Marylebone Lane**, home to shoe designer Tracey Neuls (no.29, 7935 0039, www.tn29.com) and womenswear boutique KJ's Laundry (no.74, 7486 7855, www.kjslaundry.com), as well as an atmospheric corner pub, the Golden Eagle (no.59, 7935 3228), which hosts regular old-style piano singalongs (Tue, Thur, Fri). The 106-year-old lunchroom/deli Paul Rothe & Son (no.35, 7935 6783) is presided over by the original Rothe's grandson and great-grandson. Hemmed in between buildings behind Spanish Place, **St James's** church (22 George Street) has a surprisingly soaring Gothic interior (1890); Vivien Leigh wed barrister Leigh Holman here in 1932. A more interesting example of ecclesiastical architecture lies to the west, on Crawford Street: **St Mary's, Wyndham Place** (completed in 1824), designed by British Museum architect Sir Robert Smirke, is a dramatic example of the Greek Revival style.

Wallace Collection

Hertford House, Manchester Square, W1U 3BN (7563 9500, www.wallacecollection.org). Bond Street tube. **Open** 10am-5pm daily. **Admission** free. **Credit** (shop) AmEx, MC, V. **Map** p266 G5.
Presiding over leafy Manchester Square, this handsomely restored late 18th-century house contains a collection of furniture, paintings, armour and objets d'art. It all belonged to Sir Richard Wallace, who, as the illegitimate offspring of the fourth Marquess of Hertford, inherited his father's treasures. There's room after room of Louis XIV and XV furnishings and Sèvres porcelain, galleries of lush paintings by Titian, Velázquez, Boucher, Gainsborough and Reynolds – Franz Hals's *Laughing Cavalier* is one of the best-known masterpieces. The Wallace, Oliver Peyton's new French restaurant in the courtyard conservatory, ranks among the London's top museum eateries.

Regent's Park

With its varied landscape, from formal flowerbeds to extensive, recently renovated playing fields, Regent's Park (open 5am to dusk daily) is one of London's most treasured green spaces. But it wasn't created for public pleasure; indeed, the masses weren't allowed in until 1845. Originally Henry VIII's 'chase', the park was designed in 1811 by John Nash, Crown Architect and friend of the Prince Regent, as a private residential estate to raise royal revenue. The Regency terraces of the **Outer Circle**, the road running around the park, are still Crown property, but of the 56 villas planned, only eight were built. Development of the Royal Park, with its botanic and zoological gardens, took almost two more decades. As well as the famous **London Zoo**, it has a boating lake (home to many unusual wildfowl species), tennis courts, several cafés and an open-air theatre. To the west of the park is the **London Central Mosque**, built in 1978.

Just south of the park is **Madame Tussauds**. Nearby Baker Street is forever associated with a certain fictional detective. The **Sherlock Holmes Museum** at no.221B (7224 3688, www.sherlock-holmes.co.uk) occupies the fictional detective's address and contains atmospheric room sets, but serious Sherlockians may want to check out the Sherlock Holmes Collection of books, journals, photos and film scripts around the corner at **Marylebone Library** (7641 1300).

London Zoo

Regent's Park, NW1 4RY (7722 3333, www.zsl.org). Baker Street or Camden Town tube then 274, C2 bus. **Open** *Mar-June, Sept, Oct* 10am-5.30pm daily. *July, Aug* 10am-6pm daily. *Nov-Feb* 10am-4pm daily. Last entry 1hr before closing **Admission** (including £1.70 voluntary contribution) £19.80; £16-£18.30 reductions. **Credit** AmEx, MC, V. **Map** p266 G2.

A zoo in Amsterdam famously offers a gay-themed tour: the same-sex action between animals is supposed to show visitors that homosexuality is just a twist of mother nature. Unfortunately, London Zoo only offers the straight version. But watch closely: the female chimps, apparently, routinely engage in lesbian acts. The zoo is also, as zoos go, a pretty right-on place: opened in 1828, it was the world's first scientific zoo, and today it stresses its commitment to worldwide conservation; part of the admission price goes towards its animal protection projects around the world.

The zoo's habitats keep pace with the times: the elephants have been given room to roam at sister site Whipsnade Wild Animal Park in Bedfordshire, and the penguins have been moved from Lubetkin's famous modernist pool after it was deemed uncomfortable for the birds. Recent additions include a butterfly tunnel and the 'Meet the Monkeys' attraction. The latter allows visitors to walk through an enclosure that recreates the natural habitat of black-capped Bolivian squirrel monkeys, while personal encounters of the avian kind can be had in the Blackburn Pavilion. Gorilla Kingdom and the Clore Rainforest Lookout are typical of the zoo's new approach of 'bringing down the bars' between animals and visitors. The reptile house delights and horrifies in equal measure.

Madame Tussauds

Marylebone Road, NW1 (0870 400 3000, www. madame-tussauds.com). Baker Street tube. **Open** 9.30am-5.30pm Mon-Fri; 9.30am-6pm Sat, Sun. Times vary during holiday periods. **Admission** £28; £24 reductions. **Credit** AmEx, MC, V. **Map** p266 G4.

They may have removed Boy George, but there are still plenty of gay icons in London's famous waxwork museum (and campest tourist attraction – it hosted its first gay wedding in 2006). Marilyn has been there since day one, but most gay men make a beeline for Kylie (who's always being recast, as is Madonna). Amy Winehouse, as always, causes a stir; this time by virtue of how healthy she looks. Angelina and Brad receive A-lister adulation, and Tom Cruise is a favourite with gay visitors; other hunks include Robert Pattinson and Daniel Craig. Visitors are encouraged to touch the figures; you can tousle Prince Harry's hair or pinch David Beckham's cheeks (do restrain yourself; this is a family attraction).

Other rooms contain public figures past and present, from Henry and his six wives to Tony Blair and Barack Obama, by way of the Fab Four circa 1964. Waxworks are constantly being added to keep up with new celebrities, movies and TV shows – and removed when a star's popularity fades. Below stairs, the Chamber of Horrors surrounds you with hanging corpses. A different kind of star is projected onto the domed ceiling of the adjacent planetarium, a landmark since the 1950s.

South to Oxford Street

Heading south, Marylebone High Street turns into Thayer Street, then Mandeville Place. Across Wigmore Street, narrow shop-lined pedestrian alleyway **St Christopher's Place** widens to a fountain courtyard, which in summer is filled with tables from the surrounding cafés. Carrying on after it contracts – to even narrower alley Gees Court – will take you to **Oxford Street**.

The western stretch of the Oxford Street, near Marble Arch, is more salubrious than the tourist tat at its eastern end. It is punctuated with large department stores: **John Lewis** (no.300, 7629 7711), **Debenhams** (nos.334-348, 08445 616161) and **Selfridges** (no.400, 0800 123 400). The last of these, opened in 1909, is especially grand, with much of the building completed in the art deco heyday of the 1920s.

Marble Arch, another Nash creation, marks Oxford Street's western extent. This unremarkable monument was intended to be the entrance to Buckingham Palace but, discovered to be too puny, was moved to this site in 1851. Only members of the Royal Family and some military types are allowed by law to walk through the central portal.

London Zoo

Around Town

Mayfair & St James's

Posh shops and a palace fit for a queen.

Mayfair

Map p268

Bond Street, Green Park, Hyde Park Corner, Marble Arch, Oxford Circus or Piccadilly Circus tube.

It may sport one of the prettiest names in London (deriving from the fair that used to take place here each May), but Mayfair – the area between Oxford Street, Regent Street, Piccadilly and Park Lane – is austere, important and untouristy. When it was all rolling green fields at the edge of London town, it belonged to the Grosvenor ('Grove-ner') and Berkeley families, who developed the pastures into a posh new neighbourhood in the 1700s. In particular they built a series of squares surrounded by elegant houses – although the three biggest squares, Hanover, Berkeley and the immense Grosvenor, are ringed by offices and embassies these days.

The most famous of these, **Grosvenor Square**, is where you'll find the drab US Embassy. Finished in 1960, it takes up one whole side of the square and its only decoration is a fierce-looking eagle, a lot of protective fencing and some heavily armed police. Out front, a big statue of President Eisenhower takes pride of place, although there's also a grand statue of President Franklin D Roosevelt standing nobly in the square nearby. When in London, Eisenhower stayed at **Claridge's** (*see p66*), located a block away on Brook Street. American troops stationed in London during World War II went to Sunday services at the **Grosvenor Chapel** on South Audley Street. It's still popular with Americans, and part of the attraction could be the beautiful **Mount Street Gardens** behind it. The gardens lead to the peaceful, neo-Gothic **Church of the Immaculate Conception**, on Farm Street, where the Jesuits have run things since the 19th century.

The tone of the neighbourhood remains genteel. It has always been smart: the Duke of Wellington is its most distinguished former resident; he briefly lived at 4 Hamilton Place, before moving to **Apsley House** – but he has stiff competition from Admiral Lord Nelson (147 New Bond Street), Benjamin Disraeli (29 Park Lane), Florence Nightingale (10 South Street) and Sir Robert Peel (16 Upper Grosvenor Street). Brook Street has its musicians: GF Handel lived at no.25 and Jimi Hendrix briefly next door at no.23. These adjacent buildings have been combined into a museum dedicated to Handel's memory.

Crowded, noisy **Oxford Street** to the north is less typical of Mayfair's consumer facilities. Other than a handful of good department stores, it's a chain-store rat race. More representative are **New Bond Street**, the designer drag, and **Cork Street**, gallery row. On Albemarle Street, you'll find the Royal Institution, home to the **Faraday Museum** (no.21, 7409 2992, www.rigb.org), the old laboratory of physicist Michael Faraday.

The most famous Mayfair shopping street is **Savile Row**, the land of made-to-measure suits of the highest quality. At no.15 is the estimable Henry Poole & Co, which, over the years, has cut suits for Napoleon Bonaparte, Charles Dickens, Winston Churchill and Charles de Gaulle. No.3 was the home of Apple Records, the Beatles' recording studio. The boys famously played their last gig in February 1969 on the roof.

Savile Row leads on to the equally salubrious **Conduit Street**, where fashion shocker Vivienne Westwood (no.44) faces the more staid Rigby & Peller (no.22A), corsetières to the Queen. From here you can follow St George Street to **Hanover Square**, where you'll find **St George's Church**, built in the 1720s. Among the luminaries who took their vows at the altar were George Eliot and Teddy Roosevelt. Handel, who married nobody – nudge, nudge, wink, wink – attended services here.

The area around **Shepherd Market** – where the raucous May Fair was held in the 17th century – is a pleasant, upscale area with a couple of fine pubs (Ye Grapes at 16 Shepherd Market and the

Eros. *See p185*.

Shepherd's Tavern at 50 Hertford Street) and some decent pavement dining. That said, you'll still see prostitutes working from tatty apartment blocks.

Handel House Museum

25 Brook Street, W1K 4HB (7399 1953, www.handel house.org). Bond Street tube. **Open** 10am-6pm Tue, Wed, Fri, Sat; 10am-8pm Thur; noon-6pm Sun. **Admission** £5; £2-£4.50 reductions. **Credit** MC, V. **Map** p268 J7. George Frideric Handel moved to Britain from his native Germany aged 25. The confirmed bachelor settled in this Mayfair house 12 years later, remaining until his death in 1759. The house has been beautifully restored with period furnishings, paintings and some of the composer's scores.

Piccadilly & Green Park

Maps p268 & p269

Grandiose **Piccadilly** links the traffic-strewn bear pit of Hyde Park Corner with the pickpocket heaven of Piccadilly Circus. Its charming name comes from the fancy suit collars ('picadils') favoured by the posh gentlemen who once paraded down its length. It's not really classy any more, but you can still see remnants of its glossy past in the historic shopping arcades, designed to protect shoppers from mud and horse manure. One of the nicest is the Burlington Arcade. Just next door, the **Royal Academy of Arts** lures with innovative art exhibitions. Across the road, it's virtually impossible to pass the wonderfully overwrought, mint green veneer of department store **Fortnum & Mason** without stepping in. Recently revamped, it looks stunning, with a new

basement food hall, five restaurants and an ice-cream parlour. Just to the east, the simple-looking church at no.197 is **St James's**, the personal favourite of its architect Sir Christopher Wren.

Back to the west along Piccadilly, the **Wolseley** restaurant looks like it has been there for ever, while a few doors down, the old-fashioned uniforms sported by the doormen and the 1950s-style glitzy sign leave no doubt that you've reached the **Ritz** hotel (*see p70*). The simple green expanse just beyond the Ritz is the aptly named **Green Park**. It may not match the grandeur of Regent's Park or the sheer scale of Hyde Park, but it has its charms, most evident in the spring, when its gentle slopes are covered in bright daffodils (there are no planted flower beds here, hence the name). Continuing down Piccadilly, you'll reach the Duke of Wellington's old homestead, **Apsley House**, and **Wellington Arch**, both at Hyde Park Corner.

The arch now marks the end of Constitution Hill, which separates Green Park from **Buckingham Palace** and its extensive gardens, and ends at the Queen Victoria Memorial. She gazes down the Mall, where, to the south, **St James's Park**, with its lovely views and exotic birdlife, is even prettier than Green Park. Originally a royal deer park for St James's Palace, its pastoral landscape owes its influence to John Nash, who redesigned it in the early 19th century under the orders of George IV. The view of Buckingham Palace from the bridge over the lake is wonderful, especially at night when the palace is floodlit. The lake is a sanctuary for wildfowl such as pelicans (fed at 3pm daily) and Australian black swans.

Apsley House: The Wellington Museum

149 Piccadilly, W1J 7NT (7499 5676, www.english-heritage.org.uk). Hyde Park Corner tube. **Open** *Nov-Mar* 11am-4pm Wed-Sun. *Apr-Oct* 11am-5pm Wed-Sun. *Tours* by arrangement. **Admission** £6; £3-£5.10 reductions. *Joint ticket with Wellington Arch* £7.40; £3.70-£6.30 reductions. **Credit** MC, V. **Map** p268 G8. Built by Robert Adam in the 1770s, Apsley House was the Duke of Wellington's London residence from 1817 until his death in 1852. Though his descendants still live here, some rooms are open to the public and contain interesting trinkets, including extravagant porcelain dinnerware and plates – the Portuguese Service is a 26ft-long silver fantasy. The magnificent Waterloo gallery houses Goya's portrait of Wellington, ornately framed paintings by Van Dyck, Rubens and Caravaggio, and Canova's nude statue of Napoleon.

Buckingham Palace & Royal Mews

The Mall, SW1A 1AA (7766 7300 Palace, 7766 7301 Queen's Gallery, 7766 7302 Royal Mews, www.royal collection.org.uk). Green Park or Victoria tube/rail. **Open** *State Rooms* mid July-Sept 9.45am-6pm daily (last entry 3.45pm). *Queen's Gallery* 10am-5.30pm daily (last entry 4.30pm). *Royal Mews* Mar-July, Oct 11am-4pm

Savile Row. See p182.

Mon-Thur, Sat, Sun (last entry 3.15pm). Aug, Sept 10am-5pm daily (last entry 4.15pm). **Admission** *Palace, Queen's Gallery & Royal Mews* £30.50; £17.50-£27.50; reducitons. *Palace only* £17; £9.75-£15.50 reductions. *Queen's Gallery only* £8.75; £4.50-£7.75 reductions. *Royal Mews only* £7.75; £5-£7 reductions. **Credit** AmEx, MC, V. **Map** p268 H9.

The world's most famous palace, built in 1703, was originally intended as a house for the Duke of Buckingham, but George III liked it so much he bought it for his young bride, Charlotte. His son, George IV, hired John Nash to convert it into a palace. Thus construction on the 600-room palace began, but the project was a disaster. Nash was fired after George IV's death – he was too flighty, apparently – and the reliable but unimaginative Edward Blore was hired to finish the job. After critics saw the final result, they dubbed him 'Blore the Bore'. Queen Victoria, the first royal to live here, hated the place, calling it 'a disgrace to the country'.

Judge for yourself. In summer, while the Windsors are off on their holidays, the State Rooms – used for banquets and investitures – are open to the public. After the initial thrill of being inside Buckingham Palace, it's not all that interesting, save for the Queen's Gallery, which is open year round, and contains highlights of Liz's decorative and fine art collection: Old Masters, Sèvres porcelain, ornately inlaid cabinets and the Diamond Diadem (familiar from millions of postage stamps) and other glittering baubles. Further along Buckingham Palace Road, the Royal Mews holds those royal carriages that are rolled out for the royals to wag their hands from on very important occasions. Best in Show award goes to Her Majesty's State Coach, a breathtaking, double-gilded affair built in 1761.

The famous Changing of the Guard ceremony, a tourist favourite, also takes place at the Palace. In it, one of the regiments of Foot Guards, in their scarlet coats and bearskin hats, march around the palace forecourt (May-July 11.30am daily, Sept-March alternate days).

Royal Academy of Arts

Burlington House, Piccadilly, W1J 0BD (7300 8000, 0870 848 8484 bookings, www.royalacademy.org.uk). Green Park or Piccadilly Circus tube. **Open** 10am-6pm Mon-Thur, Sat, Sun; 10am-10pm Fri. **Admission** free. *Special exhibitions* varies. **Credit** AmEx, MC, V. **Map** p268 J7.

Britain's first art school was founded in 1768 and moved to the extravagantly Palladian Burlington House a century later. It's best known for its galleries, which stage a roster of populist exhibitions. The Academy's biggest event is the Summer Exhibition (mid June-mid Aug), which for more than two centuries has drawn from works entered by the public. Some 12,000 pieces are submitted each year, with 10% making it past the judges. Artworks in the John Madejski Fine Rooms are drawn from the RA's holdings – ranging from Constable to Hockney – and are free.

St James's Church Piccadilly

197 Piccadilly, W1J 9LL (7734 4511, www.st-james-piccadilly.org). Piccadilly Circus tube. **Open** 8am-6.30pm daily. **Admission** free. **Map** p268 J7.

Consecrated in 1684, St James's was Sir Christopher Wren's favourite creation. It's a calming building without architectural airs or graces, but not lacking in charm. It was bombed to within an inch of its life in World War II, but was painstakingly reconstructed. This is a busy church: along with its inclusive ministry, it runs a counselling service, stages regular classical concerts, provides a home for the William Blake Society (the poet was baptised here) and hosts markets in its churchyard: antiques on Tuesday, arts and crafts from Wednesday to Saturday.

Wellington Arch

Hyde Park Corner, W1J 7JZ (7930 2726, www.english-heritage.org.uk). Hyde Park Corner tube. **Open** *Apr-Oct* 10am-5pm Wed-Sun. *Nov-Mar* 10am-4pm Wed-Sun. **Admission** £3.70; £1.90-£3.10 reductions. *Joint ticket with Apsley House* £7.40; £3.70-£6.30 reductions. **Credit** MC, V. **Map** p268 G8.

Built in the 1820s to mark Britain's triumph over Napoleonic France, Decimus Burton's Wellington Arch was shifted from its original location to accommodate traffic at Hyde Park Corner in 1882. It was initially topped by a statue of Wellington, but since 1912, Captain Adrian Jones's *Peace Descending on the Quadriga of War* has finished it with a flourish. Inside, three floors of displays tell the history of the arch. From the balcony, you can just see the Houses of Parliament and Buckingham Palace.

Piccadilly Circus & Regent Street

The **Piccadilly Circus** of today, an uneasy mix of the tawdry and the grandiose, is not what the original architect John Nash would have envisaged. His original 1820s design for the intersection of two of the West End's most elegant streets was an elegant circle of curved frontages. Sixty years later, Shaftesbury Avenue muscled its way in, to create the present lopsided effect; in an attempt to compensate, a delicate statue in honour of child-labour abolitionist Earl Shaftesbury was installed. Its subject was the Angel of Christian Charity, but it looks like **Eros** and so now is thus known. His unseeing eyes have gazed on further indignities: the arrival of the billboards in 1910, the junkie culture of the 1980s and the continual invasion of tourist tack: overpriced pizza and drab arcades.

Connecting Piccadilly Circus to Oxford Circus to the north and Pall Mall to the south, **Regent Street** is a broad, curving boulevard designed by Nash in the early 1800s to separate the wealthy of Mayfair from the working classes of Soho. The grandeur of the sweeping road is impressive, as are the shops, including the famous toy emporium Hamleys, the landmark Liberty department store and the sleek Apple Store.

St James's

Maps p268 & p269

Green Park or Piccadilly Circus tube.
One of central London's quieter parts, St James's does not get many visitors. Bordered by Piccadilly, Haymarket, the Mall and Green Park, it's even

Fortnum & Mason. *See p183.*

posher than Mayfair, its comrade-in-swank north of Piccadilly. The material needs of the venerable gents of St James's are met by the anachronistic shops and restaurants of **Jermyn Street** and **St James's Street**, among them cigar retailer James J Fox (19 St James's Street, 7930 3787, www.jjfox.co.uk) and upmarket cobbler John Lobb (no.88, 7930 8089, www.johnlobb.com). To stroll around the alleys is to step back in time, and up in class.

Around the corner from St James's Street is the Queen Mother's old gaff, **Clarence House**. Nearby, **St James's Palace** was originally built as a residence for Henry VIII in 1532. It has remained the official residence of the sovereign throughout the centuries, despite the fact that since 1837 the monarchs have all actually lived at Buckingham Palace. Today, St James's Palace is used by the Princess Royal and various minor royals. Although the palace is closed to the public, you can attend Sunday services at its **Chapel Royal** (Oct-Good Friday; 8.30am, 11.15am).

Across Marlborough Road lies the **Queen's Chapel**, which was the first classical church to be built in England. Designed by Inigo Jones in the 1620s, the chapel now stands in the grounds of **Marlborough House** and is only open to the public during Sunday services (Easter to July; 8.30am, 11.15am). The house itself was built by Sir Christopher Wren. Overlooking Green Park, on St James's Place, is the beautiful, 18th-century **Spencer House** (no.27, 7499 8620, www.spencerhouse.co.uk), one of the capital's finest Palladian mansions and ancestral townhouse of the late Princess Diana's family; it's open some Sundays as a museum and art gallery.

Reached from the west via King Street or the Mall, **St James's Square** was the most fashionable address in London for the 50 years after it was laid out in the 1670s: some seven dukes and seven earls were residents by the 1720s. Further east, overlooking the Mall, is **Carlton House Terrace**.

Clarence House

SW1A 1AA (7766 7303, www.royal.gov.uk). Green Park or St James's Park tube. **Open** *Aug* 10am-4pm Mon-Fri (last entry 3pm); 10am-5.30pm Sat, Sun (last admission 4.30pm). **Admission** £8.50; £4.50-£8.50 reductions. *Tours* pre-booked tickets only. **Credit** AmEx, MC, V. **Map** p268 J8.
Though built for Prince William Henry, Duke of Clarence, in 1827, and designed by John Nash, Clarence House is best known as the former residence of the Queen Mother. After she died in 2002, Prince Charles and his two sons moved in (joined later by Camilla), but parts of the house are open to the public in summer: five receiving rooms and the small but significant art collection, strong in 20th-century British art, accumulated by the Queen Mother. Among the art on display is work by Noël Coward, John Piper, WS Sickert and Augustus John. Tickets often sell out by late August.

Around Town

Soho

Otherwise known as So-homo.

Soho Square

Soho is officially London's gay mecca, having replaced Earl's Court as the heart of homo life in the early 1990s. But the neighbourhood – bounded by the four Circuses (Oxford, Piccadilly, Cambridge and St Giles's) – has had many different characters during its long and fruitful life, alternately wealthy and poor, cultured and seedy. That diversity continues today: queer revellers share their village with businessmen, hookers, market traders, tourists, immigrants, media types and old-timers. They all cosy up in what is London's spiciest quarter, characterised by skinny avenues and buzzing streetlife.

Soho's recorded history begins in the Middle Ages, when the area was a rural idyll used as a hunting ground by London's aristocracy. It was after the Great Fire of 1666 that Soho became residential, when thousands of people were forced to relocate to the area. Around this time, Soho also got its first wave of immigrants: Greek Christians (hence Greek Street) fleeing Ottoman persecution, and French Protestants (Huguenots) forced out

of France by Louis XIV. Soon, the only trace of the neighbourhood's pastoral roots was its name: the huntsmen who once rode the fields here used to cry 'So-ho!' when they spotted their prey.

As immigrants poured into Soho, the wealthy moved out. Architect John Nash encouraged this social apartheid in 1813, when he designed Regent Street to provide 'a complete separation between the Streets occupied by the Nobility and Gentry [Mayfair], and the narrower Streets and meaner houses occupied by mechanics and the trading part of the community'. With Nash's kind of thinking ruling the day, Soho became one of Britain's worst slums during the 19th century. Grinding poverty forced scores of women on to the game. At one time, an estimated 80,000 prostitutes worked here.

During the early 20th century, Soho became synonymous with prostitutes and showgirls, but it was not altogether seedy: most of the madams were French, they kept immaculate brothels and drank champagne in the French House (*see p26* **Straight up**). The bohemian vibe attracted artists galore. In the 1950s, painter Francis Bacon and photographer John Deakin lunched and boozed their way around the area; Britain's earliest rock singers congregated at the long-since-closed 2 i's coffee bar at 59 Old Compton Street. In 1962, Georgie Fame started his sweat-soaked residency at the Flamingo Club (33-37 Wardour Street); the nearby Marquee (then at 90 Wardour Street, now in Leicester Square) hosted early gigs by Jimi Hendrix and Pink Floyd.

In 1959, Soho changed immeasurably when the Street Offences Act was passed, forcing hookers off the streets. The pimps took over, luring men into massage parlours and strip clubs, where a rendezvous could be arranged. In the 1960s, after censorship laws were relaxed in Scandinavia, Soho was flooded with porn cinemas and seedy magazine shops. Though pockets of sleaze remain, the gay community moved in to replace them in the 1990s: pubs such as the Golden Lion on Dean Street had long been the haunt of gay servicemen (as well as writer Noël Coward), but in the early '90s Old Compton Street became a sea of gay

bars. It was around this time that activist group OutRage! staged a noisy party on Old Compton Street, and renamed it 'Queer Street'.

The future? As ever, it's impossible to speculate. In many places, there are already tell-tale signs of homogenisation: an identikit bar here, and a supermarket chain there. And with the sky-high rents showing no signs of dropping, it could get worse. That said, it would be a fool who'd bet on this most characterful, gutsy neighbourhood going the way of Covent Garden. Soho has – and always has had – a resilient nature.

Old Compton Street & around

Maps p266 & p267

Leicester Square or Tottenham Court Road tube.
The heart of boys' town is **Old Compton Street**. All human life hangs out here: either in the bars, shops, cafés (try the venerable

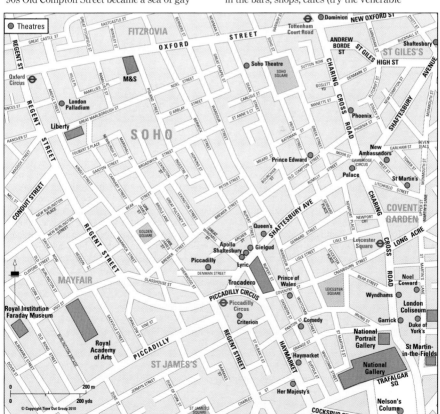

saturdays
every saturday until 1am

bcs
barcode soho
3-4 archer st soho w1d 7ep barcode.co.uk fb: bar-code

Compton's

Pâtisserie Valerie – *see p93* **How do you take your tea?**) and restaurants, or just passing through en route to somewhere else. On Fridays and Saturdays, the atmosphere resembles a street party. Gangs of tight-shirted, close-cropped gays rub shoulders with herds of tight-shirted, close-cropped straights. But while the uniforms are the same, the accessories are not: the straight guys are the ones carrying the half-drunk lager pints, the queens the ones with the gym-built bodies.

The place buzzes; if not quite 24/7, then certainly 18/7. Popular gay venues along here include the legendary **Admiral Duncan** pub (*see p18*), **Compton's** (*see p20*), teenybopper fave **G-A-Y Bar** (*see p21*), and the gay sex emporium **Clone Zone** (*see p110* **Buy sexual**). Gay café/restaurant **Balans** (*see p91*) is filled with pretty boys in tight T-shirts munching on burgers. Also joining the fray on Old Compton are gaggles of girls out on the razzle, lairy stag parties down from the north, illegal minicab drivers touting for work (don't even think about it), elderly jazz buffs en route to the local jazz club, and confused tourists either heading to or leaving the immensely popular production of *Jersey Boys* (*see p130*) at the Prince Edward Theatre. At dawn, club-goers wander distractedly along the traffic-free street, the homeless finally settle down to sleep in doorways and the street cleaners move in to begin mopping up in preparation for the locals to do it all over again the following day.

A couple of stones' throws north of Old Compton Street, **Soho Square** marks the neighbourhood's

northern gateway. This tree-lined quadrangle was initially called King Square, and a weather-beaten statue of Charles II stands in the centre. It's held up pretty well: not as grand as it once was (traffic cruises around it all day and night, waiting for a parking meter), but still popular with local workers, who pack the grass in good weather. On a summer evening, the square is full of gay

Around Town

Maison Bertaux

Old Compton Street

men shooting the breeze before hitting the bars. Jackie Leven and Kirsty MacColl wrote songs about the square; the latter, who died in 2000, has a bench dedicated to her on the south side. And Marianne Faithfull slobbed out here during her 1970s heroin period. Two churches provide spiritual nourishment, but the area is dominated by the advertising and film industries: the British Board of Film Classification and 20th Century Fox both have their offices here.

The two streets that link Old Compton with Soho Square are rich with history. Casanova and Thomas de Quincey once lodged on **Greek Street**, though the street is now notable mainly for its gloriously old-fashioned Hungarian restaurant, the **Gay Hussar** (no.2, 7437 0973, www.gayhussar.co.uk) and the swish gay bar **Green Carnation** (*see p23*). Further south, the **Coach & Horses** (no.29, 7437 5920, www.coachandhorsessoho.co.uk), though not a gay pub, is a legendary louche and literary hangout. Nearby pâtisserie **Maison Bertaux** (*see p93* **How do you take your tea?**) and champagne bar **Kettners** (29 Romilly Street, 7734 6112, www.kettners.com) add a touch of class and have been around longer than most their customers can remember – the latter was frequented by Oscar Wilde.

Neighbouring **Frith Street**, formerly home to Constable, Mozart and William Hazlitt, is livelier, thanks to the presence of jazz club **Ronnie Scott's** (*see p135*) and similarly mythologised all-night café **Bar Italia** (*see p89*). The latter – a narrow slice of nostalgia in chrome – feels like the centre of the world on busy nights, with the whole of London revolving around its overworked espresso machine. **Barrafina** (*see p93*), is another slice of Euro cool, this one a slick tapas bar.

Dean Street, just west of Frith Street, has an equally colourful history, mostly composed of the bohemian characters who got drunk in its pubs. Dylan Thomas – surprise, surprise – held

marathon drinking sessions at the York Minster (south of Old Compton Street at no.49), then nicknamed 'the French Pub' for its association with Charles de Gaulle and the Free French resistance movement; later, it became a favourite with painters Lucian Freud and Francis Bacon. It's now called the **French House**, and still retains its louche charm. Also along here is the members-only **Groucho Club** (no.44), a media industry haunt, and the Sunset Strip (no.30), the sole remaining legitimate strip club in Soho (in contrast to the unlicensed places further west, the prices are reasonable and the girls actually take their clothes off). Hard to believe that Karl Marx, who lived at both no.28 and no.44 for a time, would have approved of either.

Further north is the **Soho Theatre** (*see p132*), which has fast cemented a reputation for its programme of new plays, comedy and gay-friendly material, and the **Crown & Two Chairmen** (no.31, 7437 8192, www.thecrown andtwochairmenw1.co.uk), a straight – but great – old-school pub. One of the best Indian restaurants in town, the **Red Fort** (no.77, 7437 2525, www. redfort.co.uk) is a big draw, as is its downstairs cocktail bar, Akbar.

Wardour Street, the next street along, is less interesting, its buildings housing an assortment of film and TV production companies. But it is home to a number of gay watering holes, including the **Village** (*see p27*), which, in the early 1990s, was the first trendy gay bar to open in Soho, setting the stage for a queer invasion, and **Profile** (*see p23*), a bar and club run by the people behind Gaydar. Just to the south of Old Compton Street is the churchyard of **St Anne's**, a gay-friendly Anglican church with literary links (Dorothy L Sayers was once the church warden); bombed during the Blitz, only the 19th-century tower remains (note: the entrance is at 55 Dean Street, 7437 8039, www.stannes-soho.org.uk).

Those with a keen eye and an expansive record collection will recognise the next street along from the cover of the Oasis album *(What's the Story) Morning Glory*? Indeed, **Berwick Street** (four streets west of Greek Street) was once awash with independent record stores. But many have gone or are selling off stock fast. **Sister Ray** (nos.34-35, 7734 3297, www.sisterray.co.uk) remains a mecca for beat obsessives and fans of vinyl (it stocks more than 20,000 records). **Vinyl Junkies** (no.94, 7439 2923, www.vinyl-junkies.com) also does a steady trade.

The music retailers are joined on Berwick Street by two other cottage industries: the fruit and veg salesmen who make up the bulk of the street market (come late in the afternoon for

My favourite things
Jonny Woo
drag queen & performance artist

Gay men who are fed up with being surrounded by lots of young chickens love my **Gay Bingo** nights (www.myspace.com/gay_bingo or www.facebook.com/jonnywoouk), held every few months at various venues around town, including **Carpet Burn** (*see p37*) and **Dalston Superstore** (*see p39*). It's one of the only times attractive gay men over 30 get to meet each other in this city. The gorgeous John Sizzle does the music, Ma Butcher generates the numbers and there's lots of ranting and terrorising of the public.

Soho Theatre (*see p121 and p132*) is a great place to see new drag acts – it's probably the only theatre venue that actually takes inspiration from London's club scene. They've had late shows with some really top alternative performers like Justin Bond and Varla Jean Merman.

Another good place to spot new talent is **Gutterslut** (*see p40*), a disco night at various venues, usually in the East End. It's an electro party and there's a bit of pole-dancing going on. They get a really mixed crowd: a few regular trannies, the local gay fags, the electro crowd and a few fetish people from Torture Garden. It gets ram-packed.

There are still a lot of hot drag acts that are emerging at **Bistrotheque** (*see p121*). They have an ongoing season of events two or three times a year, running for eight weeks and called Under Construction, which showcases new work.

After dancing the night away, I'll go to the **Nelson's Head** (32 Horatio Street, E2 7SB, 7739 6054), a little gay pub just off Columbia Road. It has a market licence, which means it opens at 7am on Sundays. If you're still up, it's a great place to go for a pint to take the edge off your night.

the bargains), and the prostitutes who conduct their trade at the top of a number of scruffy stairwells; doorways are adorned with handwritten signs that read 'Busty Model 1st Floor'. At the southern end of Berwick Street, what remains of the Soho sex industry is at its most visible. Tiny **Walker's Court** (linking Berwick and Brewer Streets) and even smaller **Tisbury Court** (joining Wardour and Rupert Streets) are lined with insalubrious strip joints that lure punters with the promise of untold bodily riches and then send them away again with a bar bill running to several hundred pounds and nary a tit in sight. Gay bars have also brought
some class to **Rupert Street**. Though it's home to several strip joints that perform cash-guzzling services on the young, dumb and desperate, it's also the site of fashionable gay bar **Rupert Street** (*see p24*) and the popular courtyard bar the **Yard** (*see p27*).

Rupert Street intersects with **Brewer Street**, the western continuation of Old Compton Street. Here you'll find **Prowler** (*see p111* **Buy sexual**), a gay 'lifestyle' boutique (with the obligatory porn section in the back) and a chic gay cocktail bar, the **Shadow Lounge** (*see p25*).

At the top end of Berwick Street, **Broadwick Street** is famous for a couple of reasons: it was the birthplace of William Blake, and the epicentre of a severe cholera outbreak in 1854. Local doctor John Snow became convinced that the disease was transmitted by polluted water and had the street's water pump closed. Snow's hypothesis proved correct, leading to a breakthrough in epidemiology. The doctor is commemorated by a replica water pump and in the name of the street's pub.

West Soho

Maps p266 & p269

Piccadilly Circus tube.

West of Berwick Street, Soho grows noticeably quieter; there are fewer bars and almost no restaurants around here. Brewer Street has a few interesting stores, including the **Vintage Magazine Store** (*see p118*), which sells everything from 1980s issues of *Smash Hits* and *NME* to pre-war issues of *Vogue*.

The roads that spout off Brewer Street don't offer a great deal of note, either, but **Great Windmill Street**, which runs south of Brewer Street, offers the perfect illustration of Soho's changing mores. In 1932 the Windmill Theatre embarked on its now-legendary 'revuedeville' shows with erotic 'tableaux', which were adapted to comply with a law that dictated that such shows, if they existed at all, could feature only

Leicester Square

is the 1891 **Palace Theatre** on Cambridge Circus, which has showed mostly musicals: *Sound of Music* in 1961, *Jesus Christ Superstar* in 1972 and *Les Misérables* from 1985 to 2004. Shaftesbury Avenue marks the north edge of **Chinatown**, a district that extends to Leicester Square.

Soho has always attracted immigrants, but the Chinese were relative latecomers: most arrived in the 1950s from Hong Kong. Migrating west from their original location in Limehouse, and attracted by the cheap rents along Gerrard and Lisle Streets, thousands of Chinese moved in. The ersatz oriental gates, stone lions and pagoda-topped phone boxes suggest a Chinese theme park, but in reality this is a close-knit residential and working enclave. **Gerrard Street** is the glitziest spot, crammed with restaurants and twinkly lights.

South of here is the tourist trap of **Leicester Square**, which, in the 17th and 18th centuries, was one of London's most exclusive addresses. By the 19th century, as Soho became a slum, the aristos fled. Today, it's still no fun: Londoners tend to avoid the cheap fast fooderies, pricey cinemas and loud buskers, and so should you – on weekend evenings, scantily clad, inebriated and aggressive suburbanites descend here for a night on the town. The horror, the horror.

However, it's not all bad news. The south side of the square is where you'll find cheap theatre tickets to that day's shows at the **tkts booth,** which is operated by the Society of London Theatres. (The other ticket shops in or near the square are unofficial, but also offer deals.) And north, in Leicester Place, is the **Prince Charles Cinema** (*see p124*), which screens an eclectic mix of recent movies and cult films at low prices as well as 'Sing-a-Long-a' screenings of camp classics like *The Sound of Music*. Next door, the French Catholic church of **Notre Dame de France** contains a selection of murals by Jean Cocteau; below, the **Leicester Square Theatre** (0207 534 1740, www.leicestersquare theatre.com) is a particularly gay-friendly venue (icons ranging from Boy George and Joan Rivers to Debbie Reynolds and Sandra Bernhard have performed here; it opened in 2002 as the venue for the Boy's musical, *Taboo*).

The **Hippodrome**, on the corner of Leicester Square and Charing Cross Road, is an impressive red-brick edifice designed by the prolific theatre architect Frank Matcham. It became famous as the 'Talk of the Town' cabaret venue in the 1960s, featuring the likes of Shirley Bassey and Judy Garland. Recently refurbished, it now hosts corporate events and the occasional theatre production in the variety show mould.

stationary naked girls. Some 70 years later, it's now a lap-dancing joint, the premises around it filled with sleazy, unlicensed clip joints. North of Brewer Street, things grow calmer for a while, with Golden Square now home to some of the area's grandest residential buildings.

Just north of this area is **Carnaby Street**: four decades ago, this was the epitome of swinging London, and it's recently undergone a revival of sorts. On Carnaby Street and Newburgh Street, there are a mix of independent and familiar shops trading happily and, in some cases, lucratively off the area's colourful history. The sole reason to stray up diminutive Argyll Street, which runs north to Oxford Street, is to visit the grand old **London Palladium** theatre.

Chinatown & Leicester Square

Map p269

Leicester Square tube.
Shaftesbury Avenue, which wends its way down from New Oxford Street to Piccadilly Circus, is the heart of Theatreland. During the late Victorian era, seven grand theatres were built here – six remain. The most impressive

Covent Garden

Stage struck.

Covent Garden

Maps p267 & p269

Covent Garden or Leicester Square tube.
Covent Garden is Soho's next-door neighbour.
And a pretty gay place it is too. For one thing,
it's the heart of Theatreland, with more show
tunes in the air than a gay piano bar – this is
the place where Henry Higgins discovered Eliza
Doolittle in *My Fair Lady* – and plenty of light-
footed actors swishing the boards to boot.

It's also prime shopping territory; the boutiques
around Neal, Monmouth and Earlham Streets are
thronging with gay shopaholics. And there are
glamorous hotels such as **St Martins Lane** and
the **Covent Garden Hotel** (for both, *see p71*).

There's a sprinkling of gay watering holes
in the area, including **Kudos** (*see p23*), next
to *A Conversation with Oscar Wilde*, a sculpture
by lesbian Maggi Hambling: the dandy gazes
up at the heavens from the pedestrianised bit
of Adelaide Street (behind St Martin-in-the-Fields).
There's also gym-queen favourite the **Box** (*see p18*)
and **Halfway to Heaven** (*see p23*). Active types
might want to check out the cruisey gay-friendly
pool at the **Oasis** (*see p144*).

As colourful as Covent Garden is today,
the neighbourhood's name has straightforward
origins. Covent Garden belonged to the Convent
of St Peter at Westminster. After the dissolution
of the monasteries, Covent Garden lost its
ecclesiastical connection: the land was granted
by the Crown to John Russell, first Earl of Bedford.
It was the fourth earl, Francis Russell, who set
the area on its way, building houses 'fitt for the
habitacions of Gentlemen and men of ability'.

Russell hired Inigo Jones, the most fashionable
architect in the land. Taking inspiration from the
Palladian designs he had studied in Italy, Jones
built an open square, flanked by St Paul's Church
and terraced houses. In 1639, affluent Londoners
flocked to live in the designer's stylish houses.
The square's status as a fashionable residence
waned as market traders began hawking their
wares here; recognising the potential, the fifth
Earl of Bedford obtained in 1670 a royal charter

for a market selling flowers, fruit, roots and herbs
in Covent Garden. The air grew thick with the
smell of roasting java as coffee houses sprang
up, catering for the literary and theatrical folk –
Henry Fielding, James Boswell, Alexander Pope –
who patronised the area's theatres, gambling
dens and brothels. A count in 1722 tallied 22
gambling houses, and the magistrate Sir John
Fielding remarked: 'One would imagine that
all the prostitutes in the kingdom had picked
upon the rendezvous.' The market, London's
pre-eminent fruit and veg wholesaler, thrived
for three centuries, employing 1,000 porters.

In 1974, when the market moved to Vauxhall,
property developers pegged the area for office
blocks, and it was only through mass protests
that it was saved. Today, though the piazza itself
is eschewed by Londoners, the area as a whole,
especially to the north, is an example of planning
gone right: a thriving residential community

Royal Opera House

Around Town

Covent Garden Market

with an interesting mix of shops and small businesses, along with various cultural venues. All in all, then, pleasant wandering territory.

Covent Garden Piazza

Little remains of Jones's original piazza, but it's nonetheless a handsome galleried square, with lots of outdoor restaurant seating in summer and no cars allowed. Tourists flock here for a combination of gentrified shopping and less predictable street performances. The majority of the latter take place under the portico of **St Paul's**. Shoppers favour the old covered market (7240 5781, www.coventgardenlondonuk.com), now a collection of small stores, many of them with a twee, touristy appeal. The **Apple Market**, in the North Hall, has arts and crafts stalls every Tuesday to Sunday, and antiques on Monday.

Across the road, the cheaper, tackier **Jubilee Market** deals mostly in novelty T-shirts and unofficial calendars, although it too is filled with antiques on Monday, and crafts at the weekend.

London Transport Museum

Covent Garden Piazza, WC2E 7BB (7379 6344, www.ltmuseum.co.uk). Covent Garden tube. **Open** 10am-6pm Mon-Thur, Sat, Sun (last admission 5.15pm); 11am-6pm Fri (last admission 5.15pm). **Admission** £10; £6-£8 reductions. **Credit** AmEx, DC, MC, V. **Map** p269 L7.

Re-opened in 2007 after a massive overhaul, London's Transport Museum is now more spacious and better organised. The renovations also show off the setting: a magnificent old flower market building with great arched windows and soaring iron columns. But the star of the show is the superb array of preserved buses, trams and trains. The museum traces the city's transport history from the horse age to the present day, beginning with the

Victorian gallery, where a replica of Shillibeer's first horse-drawn bus service in 1829 takes pride of place. Another gallery is dedicated to an impressive collection of poster art associated with London transport through the ages.

Royal Opera House

Bow Street, WC2E 9DD (7304 4000, www.royalopera house.org). Covent Garden tube. **Open** 10am-3pm Mon-Sat. **Admission** free. *Stage tours* £10; £9 reductions. **Credit** AmEx, DC, MC, V. **Map** p269 L7.

Opera and homosexuality go hand in hand. And the Royal Opera House has certainly witnessed its share of drama, both real and theatrical. Founded in 1732, it has burned to the ground twice – the existing structure dates back to 1858. And frenzied opera-lovers twice rioted against rising ticket prices: in 1763, the baying mob almost destroyed the galleries; in 1809, the protests lasted for 61 nights. On the artistic side, between 1735 and 1759 Handel premièred Samson, Judas Maccabaeus and Solomon here. Today, there are organised tours, taking in the main auditorium, the costume workshops and sometimes even a rehearsal. Certain parts of the building are also open to the general public, including the glass-roofed Floral Hall, the Crush Bar (so named because in Victorian times the only thing served during intermissions was orange and lemon crush) and the Amphitheatre Café Bar, with its terrace overlooking the Piazza.

St Paul's Covent Garden

Bedford Street, WC2E 9ED (7836 5221, www.actors church.org). Covent Garden tube or Charing Cross tube/rail. **Open** 8.30am-5pm Mon-Fri; times vary Sat; 9am-1pm Sun. *Services* 1.10pm Tue, Wed; 6pm Thur; 11am Sun. *Choral Evensong* 4pm 2nd Sun of mth. **Admission** free. **Map** p269 L7.

Theatre is a religion for many gays, and this is the church for worshipping the stars. Also known as the Actors' Church, it has a long association with Covent Garden's Theatreland. It boasts memorial plaques to the likes of Boris Karloff and Ivor Novello, Vivien Leigh and Noël Coward. George Bernard Shaw set the first scene of *Pygmalion* under the church's portico, and the ashes of Dame Ellen Terry rest here. On a more sombre note, the first victim of the plague, Margaret Ponteous, is buried in the churchyard. The architecture is also noteworthy: the plain Tuscan pastiche was erected by Inigo Jones in 1633.

Elsewhere in Covent Garden

The area around St Martin's Lane is nothing if not a mixture, from the trendy – Ian Schrager's St Martins Lane hotel – to the trad: the opulent **Salisbury** (90 St Martin's Lane, 7836 5863), a former gay pub from the dark closeted days, and the **Coliseum** (7836 0111, www.eno.org), the home of the English National Opera.

Meanwhile, neighbouring alleys in the shadow of the Wyndham and Albany theatres exude an overpowering old-world charm; from the nook-and-cranny antique bookshops of Cecil Court to the clockwork-operated gas lighting of Goodwin's Court, which nightly illuminates a row of handsome bow-fronted 17th-century housing.

Closer to the piazza, most of the older, more unusual shops have been superseded by a homogeneous mass of cafés and by the time you reach the end of King Street, Covent Garden offers only token gestures towards its colourful history. High-profile fashion designers and chain stores have all but domesticated Floral Street, Long Acre and, most noticeably, **Neal Street**, but more interesting shopping experiences await on **Monmouth** and **Earlham Streets**. The latter is lined with streetwear labels, as well as bookstores such as the **Dover Bookshop** (no.18, 7836 2111), which has a good range of art volumes, and **Magma** (see p102), one of the best sources of art, film and fashion literature in London. **Dress Circle** (see p102) is a must for theatre fans seeking CDs, tapes and records of their favourite musicals. Back on Neal Street, venerable **Food for Thought** (see p95) is one of London's most famous vegetarian cafés – it's probably best to grab a takeaway as seating is sparse.

Halfway along Earlham Street is the **Seven Dials** roundabout, which was named after both the number of sundials incorporated into the central monument (the seventh being formed by the pillar itself) and streets branching off it. A stone's throw from Seven Dials, the bohemian enclave of **Neal's Yard** – one of the district's best-kept secrets – is known for its co-operative cafés, herbalists, head shops and wholefoods.

Towards Holborn, Covent Garden becomes less distinguished. Endell Street is perhaps most noticeable for the queues leading to the ace chippie **Rock & Sole Plaice** (see p94). These days, Drury Lane is largely ignored even by theatre-goers: the current **Theatre Royal** (the first was built

there in 1663) opens on to Catherine Street, with its excess of restaurants vying for the attention of pre- and post-performance diners. Meanwhile, the historical depravity of the area is remembered at the **Bow Street Magistrates Court**, home to author and one-time magistrate Henry Fielding's Bow Street Runners (the original precursors to the Metropolitan Police), as well as the site of Oscar Wilde's detention, in 1895, for committing 'indecent acts'.

That this is a residential neighbourhood is evident in peaceful Ching Court, off Shelton Street, and the beautiful **Phoenix Garden** (21 Stacey Street), where willow trees, fruit trees and honeysuckle attract birds and lunchtime dreamers.

Strand & Embankment

Map p269

Embankment tube/Charing Cross tube/rail.
As its name suggests, the **Strand** – which connects Westminster to the City in a narrow, unbroken thread – once ran directly beside the Thames. In the 14th century, the street was lined with waterside homes and gardens for the well-to-do. But by the 19th century it was a notorious blackspot for poverty and prostitution. Then Sir Christopher Wren suggested the creation of a reclaimed embankment to ease congestion and house the main sewer. By 1891, things were looking up. Richard D'Oyly Carte's Savoy Theatre, created in the 1880s to host Gilbert and Sullivan operas, coupled with the Savoy hotel (1888) indicates how its fortunes changed after the reinforced concrete **Embankment** was completed. Just south of the Strand, on George Court, is the excellent alternative gay pub, the **Retro Bar** (see p24).

The Embankment itself can be approached down Villiers Street, named after George Villiers, paramour of James I. Along the way, you'll pass **G-A-Y** (see p40), a mainstream gay superclub, which was scheduled to take over the Heaven club as this guide went to press.

On the Embankment itself, there are several boat tours available. A couple of boats also feature as entertainment: the **Bateaux London** restaurant (7695 1800, www.bateauxlondon.com) and the jolly **Queen Mary** floating nightclub (7240 9404, www.caniseethat.co.uk/QueenMary).

On dry land stands **Cleopatra's Needle**, a stone obelisk first erected in Egypt under Pharaoh Tothmes III in 1500 BC, and repositioned on the Thames in 1878. **Embankment Gardens**, which sits on the opposite side of the road, is a tranquil park with an annual programme of free summer music played out on its small stage.

Benjamin Franklin House

36 Craven Street, WC2N 5NF (7839 2006, www. benjaminfranklinhouse.org). Charing Cross tube/ rail. **Open** *Box office* 10.30am-5pm Wed-Sun. *Tours* pre-book by phone or online. **Admission** £7; £5 reductions. **Credit** AmEx, MC, V. **Map** p269 L7.
Restoration of the Georgian house where Benjamin Franklin – scientist, philosopher, diplomat, inventor and Founding Father of the United States – lived between 1757 and 1775 was completed in 2006. It is now open to the public as a centre for academic research on Franklin. The house can be explored on well-run, pre-booked 'experiences' lasting a short but intense 45 minutes (at noon, 1pm, 2pm, 3.15pm and 4.15pm from Wednesday to Sunday). These are led by an actress in character as Franklin's landlady Margaret Stevenson, who conjures up the world and times in which he lived. More straightforward 20-minute tours are provided by house interns on Mondays (at the same times as above), and cost £3.50.

St Giles's

Map p267

Tottenham Court Road tube.
Immortalised unfavourably in Hogarth's *Gin Lane*, and described with venom by Charles Dickens, this once-squalid area has improved significantly in recent years, despite being overshadowed by the controversial **Centrepoint** office tower. Indeed, the acres of predominantly Irish slums were dispersed in 1847 with the construction of New Oxford Street. All that remains of those bad old days is the original church of **St Giles in the Fields**, located just behind Centrepoint on the High Street; it dates back to the early 1700s. Just along the road, a pub known to Elizabethans as the Bowl mercifully offered last pints to condemned men on their walk from Newgate to the gibbet at Tyburn. Don't be put off, however: the **Angel** (61 St Giles High Street, 7240 2876), which now stands in its place, is a great pub. Lesbians are familiar with the area owing to the popular **First Out** (*see p90*), a veggie-friendly café and bar. There's also a clutch of good and cheap Korean restaurants along here.

Beyond this, St Giles's is probably best known for the musical heritage of **Denmark Street**, affectionately known as Tin Pan Alley, and once home to Regents Sound Studios, where the Stones recorded 'Not Fade Away' and the Kinks cut their first demo. The Small Faces were signed at the Giaconda Café, where Bowie met his first band, and the Sex Pistols wrote 'Anarchy in the UK' in what is now a guitar shop at no.6. These days, instrument sales and repairs are what Denmark Street does best, although the **12 Bar Club** (*see p135*) remains the city's most intimate songwriters' venue.

Charing Cross Road is big on books. Our favourite is the still traditional if now more efficient **Foyles** (*see p101*), which also boasts a good gay section. Still, the real gems are to be found in the smaller, specialised and second-hand stores such as Henry Pordes Books (arts and humanities; nos.58-60, 7836 9031, www.henrypoardesbooks.com).

Around Town

Neal's Yard

Westminster & Victoria

The power and the glory.

Westminster

Map p269

This is the London you've seen on postcards: the Houses of Parliament, Westminster Abbey, Big Ben, Trafalgar Square. Westminster has been at the heart of the Church and monarchy for almost 1,000 years, since Edward the Confessor built his 'West Minster' and palace on marshy Thorney Island in the 11th century. Politics came to the fore in the 14th century, when the first Parliament met in the abbey. Today, the splendid Houses of Parliament provide an iconic backdrop for holiday photos: go on, pose in front of Big Ben.

Trafalgar Square

Embankment or Leicester Square tube/Charing Cross tube/rail.

The centrepiece of London was conceived by the Prince Regent, later George IV, who wanted a monument to imperial Britain. He commissioned John Nash to create a grand square to pay homage to Britain's naval power. It was laid out in 1840. The focal point is **Nelson's Column**, a tribute to the heroic Horatio, who died during the Battle of Trafalgar in 1805. This Corinthian column, designed by William Railton, is topped by a 17-foot high sandstone statue of Nelson. Hitler was so impressed by the monument that he ordered bombers not to touch it, as he hoped to move it to Berlin. The granite fountains were added in 1845 (then redesigned by Lutyens in 1939); and the bronze lions – the work of Edwin Landseer – in 1868. Statues of George IV and a couple of Victorian military heroes anchor three of the square's corners. Neoclassical buildings overlook the square: James Gibbs's **St Martin-in-the-Fields**, and the **National Gallery**.

National Gallery

Trafalgar Square, WC2N 5DN (7747 2885, www. nationalgallery.org.uk). Leicester Square tube or Charing Cross tube/rail. **Open** 10am-6pm Mon-Thur, Sat, Sun; 10am-9pm Fri. *Tours* 11.30am, 2.30pm Mon-Thur, Sat, Sun; 11.30am, 2.30pm, 7pm Fri. **Admission** free. *Special exhibitions* prices vary. **Credit** (shop) MC, V. **Map** p269 K7.

Founded in 1824, this gallery is a national treasure. With more than 2,000 western European paintings, it has masterpieces from virtually every school of art, starting with 13th-century religious works and culminating in Van Gogh. You name it, they're here: da Vinci, Raphael, Rubens, Rembrandt, Caravaggio, Gainsborough, Monet, Picasso...

The Sainsbury Wing concentrates on the early Renaissance period, with an emphasis on Italian and Dutch painters. In the North Wing, look out for masterpieces by Rubens, Rembrandt and Vermeer. The East Wing has a strong collection of English paintings, including Constable's *The Hay Wain*, Turner's romantic watercolours and works by Gainsborough, Reynolds and Hogarth. The real big-ticket items, however, are the Impressionist paintings, and the blockbuster temporary exhibitions are often a sell-out. Oliver Peyton's two restaurants are a bonus.

National Portrait Gallery

2 St Martin's Place, WC2H 0HE (7306 0055, www. npg.org.uk). Leicester Square tube or Charing Cross tube/rail. **Open** 10am-6pm Mon-Wed, Sat, Sun; 10am-9pm Thur, Fri. **Admission** free. *Special exhibitions* prices vary. **Credit** AmEx, MC, V. **Map** p269 K7.

The National Portrait Gallery contains everything from oil paintings of Tudor royals to photos of current celebrities. The portraits are organised chronologically from top to bottom. One of the gallery's most prized possessions is the only known portrait of William Shakespeare. It's also a fascinating 'who's who' of medieval monarchy. Dickens, Darwin and Disraeli are among those on the first floor, while more recent figures include union leader Arthur Scargill and his nemesis Margaret Thatcher, photographed by Helmut Newton. Newer additions include footballer David Beckham and novelist Margaret Drabble. The other high point is the restaurant, located on the top floor.

St Martin-in-the-Fields

Trafalgar Square, WC2N 4JJ (7766 1100, 7766 1122 Brass Rubbing Centre, www.smitf.org). Leicester Square tube or Charing Cross tube/rail. **Open** *Church* 8am-6pm daily. *Services* 8am, 1.15pm, 6pm Mon, Tue, Thur, Fri; 8am, 1pm, 5pm, 6.15pm Wed; 8am, 10am, 1pm (in Mandarin), 2.15pm (in Cantonese), 5pm, 6.30pm Sun. *Brass Rubbing Centre* 10am-6pm Mon-Wed; 10am-8pm Thur-Sat; 11.30am-5pm Sun. **Admission** free. *Brass rubbing* £4.50. *Evening concerts* prices vary. **Credit** MC, V. **Map** p269 L7.

A church has stood on this site since the 13th century, when it really was surrounded by fields; this one, built in 1726 by James Gibbs, is a curious mix of neoclassical and baroque styles. This is the parish church for Buckingham Palace (note the royal box to the left of the gallery), but it is known for its classical concerts, café and brass rubbing. Reynolds and Hogarth are buried in the churchyard.

Trafalgar Square

Around the Mall

Embankment tube/Charing Cross tube/rail.
From Trafalgar Square, the grand processional route of the Mall passes beneath Aston Webb's 1910 Admiralty Arch to the Victoria Memorial.

As you walk along the Mall, look out on the right for **Carlton House Terrace**, the last project completed by John Nash before his death. It was built on the site of Carlton House, which was George IV's home until he built Buckingham Palace to replace it. Part of the terrace now houses the multidisciplinary **Institute of Contemporary Arts** (ICA). On the south side of St James's Park the Wellington Barracks, home of the Foot Guards, contains the **Guards' Museum**.

Guards' Museum

Wellington Barracks, Birdcage Walk, SW1E 6HQ (7414 3428, www.theguardsmuseum.com). St James's Park tube. **Open** 10am-4pm daily. **Admission** £4; £1-£2 reductions. **Credit** (shop) AmEx, MC, V. **Map** p268 J9.
The Changing of the Guard is one of the capital's great spectacles (*see p183* **Buckingham Palace**). This small museum, founded in the 17th century under Charles II, tells the history of the British Army's five Guards regiments using flamboyant uniforms and other memorabilia.

Institute of Contemporary Arts

The Mall, SW1Y 5AH (7930 0493, 7930 3647 box office, www.ica.org.uk). Piccadilly Circus tube or Charing Cross tube/rail. **Open** *Galleries* if exhibition noon-7pm Wed, Fri-Sun; noon-9pm Thur. **Admission** free. **Credit** AmEx, DC, MC, V. **Map** p269 K8.
Founded in 1948 by the anarchist Herbert Read, the ICA still challenges traditional notions of art. Many mavericks have held key exhibitions here: Henry Moore, Picasso and Damien Hirst, to name a few. The ICA's cinema shows arty films, its theatre stages performance art and indie gigs and its art exhibitions are always talking points. The annual Beck's Futures exhibition (mid Mar-mid May) features the best of contemporary art in myriad forms.

Whitehall to Parliament Square

Embankment or Westminster tube/ Charing Cross tube/rail.
You're in civil servant territory now. Lined with faux-imperial government buildings, the long, gentle curve of **Whitehall** is named after Henry VIII's magnificent palace, which burned down in 1698. The street is still home to the Ministry of Defence, the Foreign Office and the Treasury. Halfway down the street, the Horse Guards building faces the Italianate **Banqueting House**.

Nearby is Edwin Lutyens' plain memorial to the dead of both world wars, the **Cenotaph**, and, on **Downing Street** (closed off by iron gates), the equally plain homes of the prime minister and chancellor, at nos.10 and 11.

Near the Cenotaph stands John Mills' huge bronze memorial to the women of World War II, which commemorates their efforts with 17 sets of work clothes hanging on pegs.

At the end of Whitehall, **Parliament Square** has architecture on an appropriately grand scale. Constructed in 1868, it features the fantastical, neo-Gothic **Middlesex Guildhall** (1906-13) on the west side. Just behind that is **Westminster Central Hall** with its great black dome, used for conferences (the first assembly of the United Nations was held here in 1946) and Methodist church services. The buildings overlook the shady square with its statues of British politicians, such as Disraeli and Churchill, and one outsider, Abraham Lincoln, who sits sombrely to one side.

Close by, **Westminster Abbey** is the most venerable ancient building in central London.

Few buildings in London genuinely dazzle, but the extravagant **Houses of Parliament** are an exception. One note: **Big Ben** is actually the name of the bell, not the clock tower. In its shadow, at the end of Westminster Bridge, stands a statue of the warrior Boudicca and her daughters.

National Portrait Gallery. See p198.

See p198.

Banqueting House

Whitehall, SW1A 2ER (0844 482 7777, www.hrp.
org.uk). Westminster tube or Charing Cross tube/rail.
Open 10am-5pm Mon-Sat. **Admission** £4.80;
£4 reductions. **Credit** MC, V. **Map** p269 L8.
Designed by the great neoclassicist Inigo Jones in 1622,
this was one of London's first Palladian buildings. It is also
the only surviving part of Henry VIII's Whitehall Palace,
which burned down in 1698. The simple exterior belies the
sumptuous ceiling inside, painted by Rubens. Charles I
commissioned the Flemish artist to glorify his father James
I, 'the wisest fool in Christendom', and the divine right of
Stuart kings. Call to check the hall is open.

Churchill War Rooms

Clive Steps, King Charles Street, SW1A 2AQ
(7930 6961, www.iwm.org.uk). St James's Park
or Westminster tube. **Open** 9.30am-6pm daily.
Admission £14.95; £12 reductions. **Credit** MC, V.
Map p269 K9.
An informative blast from the past, this small underground
set of rooms was Churchill's war bunker. Almost nothing
has changed since it was closed on 16 August 1945: every
book, chart and pin in the map room remains in place, as
does the BBC microphone he used when addressing the
nation. The statesman's bedroom displays a chamber pot
and nightshirt. The audio guide's sound effects – wailing
sirens, Churchill's wartime speeches – add to the nostalgia.
The museum features displays about Churchill's life.

Houses of Parliament

Parliament Square, SW1A 0AA (7219 4272
Commons information, 7219 3107 Lords information,
0870 906 3773 tours information, www.parliament.
uk). Westminster tube. **Open** (when in session)
House of Commons Visitors' Gallery 2.30-10.30pm
Mon, Tue; 11.30am-7.30pm Wed; 10.30am-6.30pm
Thur; 9.30am-3pm Fri. *House of Lords Visitors'*
Gallery 2.30-10.30pm Mon, Tue; 3-10pm Wed; 11am-
7.30pm Thur; from 10am Fri. **Tours** summer recess
only; phone for details. **Admission** *Visitors' Gallery*
free. *Tours* £12; £5-£8 reductions. **Credit** MC, V.
Map p269 L9.
This neo-Gothic extravaganza reflects Victorian confidence,
even if its style is medieval. Completed in 1860, it was
designed by Charles Barry, who was replacing the original
Houses of Parliament, which burned down in 1834. Barry
was assisted on the interiors by Augustus Pugin. The original palace was home to Henry VIII, until he upped sticks
to Whitehall in 1532. The first parliament was held here in
1275, but Westminster did not become its permanent home
until Henry moved out. The only remnants of the original
palace are the Jewel Tower and Westminster Hall, one of
Europe's great medieval buildings.
 The buildings are not usually open to the public, but you
can watch the Commons or Lords in session from the galleries. Most debates are dry, though the odd fox-hunting
protesters or abseiling lesbians (activists invaded the Lords
in 1988) spice things up. Visitors queue at St Stephen's
Entrance and, in high season, may wait a couple of hours.
The best spectacle is Prime Minister's Question Time at
noon on Wednesday, but you need to book tickets through
your MP or embassy. Parliament goes into recess in the
summer, when tours of the main ceremonial rooms are
available to the general public.

Jewel Tower

Abingdon Street, SW1P 3JX (7222 2219, www.
english-heritage.org.uk). Westminster tube. **Open**
Mar-Oct 10am-5pm daily. *Nov-Mar* 10am-4pm daily.
Admission £3.30; £2.70 reductions. **Credit** MC, V.
Map p269 L9.
Emphatically not the home of the Crown Jewels, this easy
to overlook stone tower was built in 1365 to house
Edward III's gold and silver plate. It's still worth a look,
though, because, along with Westminster Hall, it is the
only surviving part of the medieval Palace of
Westminster. It contains an exhibition on Parliament and
a ninth-century Rhenish sword.

St Margaret's Church

Parliament Square, SW1P 3JX (7654 4840,
www.westminster-abbey.org). St James's Park
or Westminster tube. **Open** 9.30am-3.30pm Mon-
Fri; 9.30am-1.30pm Sat; 2-5pm Sun (times may change
at short notice due to services). *Services* 11am Sun;
phone to check for other days. **Admission** free.
Map p269 K9.
For impressive pre-Reformation stained glass, this is the
place to visit. The east window (1509) commemorates the
marriage of Henry VIII and Catherine of Aragon. Later
windows celebrate explorer Sir Walter Raleigh, executed
in Old Palace Yard, and writer John Milton (1608-74), who
was married here. Founded in the 12th century, the church
was rebuilt in 1523. Above the door is a bust of Charles I,
looking at a statue of his old adversary, Cromwell.

Westminster Abbey

20 Dean's Yard, SW1P 3PA (7222 5152, 7654 4832 tours, www.westminster-abbey.org). St James's Park or Westminster tube. **Open** *Summer* 9.30am-3.30pm Mon, Tue, Thur, Fri; 9.30am-6pm Wed; 9.30am-3.30pm Sat. *Winter* 9.30-3.30pm Mon, Tue, Thur, Fri; 9.30am-6pm Wed; 9.30am-1.30pm Sat. *Abbey Museum & Chapter House* 10am-4pm Mon-Sat. *College Garden* 10am-4pm Tue, Wed, Thur. *Tours* phone for details. **Admission** £15; £12 reductions. *Tours* £3. **Credit** AmEx, MC, V. **Map** p269 K9.

Known to the masses as the site of Princess Diana's funeral, Westminster Abbey has been synonymous with British royalty since 1066, when Edward the Confessor built a church on the site just in time for his own funeral: it was consecrated eight days before he died. Since then, a 'who's who' of monarchy have been buried here and, with two exceptions (Edwards V and VIII), every English monarch since William the Conqueror (1066) has been crowned in the abbey. Of the original abbey, only the Pyx Chamber and the Norman undercroft remain. The Gothic nave and choir were rebuilt in the 13th century; the Henry VII Chapel was added in 1503-12; Nicholas Hawksmoor's west towers completed the building in 1745. The interior is cluttered with monuments to statesmen, scientists, musicians and poets. Poets' Corner contains the graves of Dryden, Samuel Johnson, Browning and Tennyson.

Millbank

Pimlico or Westminster tube/Vauxhall tube/rail.
Millbank runs along the river from Parliament to Vauxhall Bridge. By the river, the **Victoria Tower Gardens** contain a statue of suffragette leader Emmeline Pankhurst, and the Buxton Drinking Fountain, which commemorates the emancipation of slaves. Opposite, Dean Stanley Street leads to Smith Square, home to the architecturally striking **St John's, Smith Square**, built as a church in grand baroque style.

Tate Britain

Millbank, SW1P 4RG (7887 8888, www.tate.org.uk). Pimlico tube. **Open** 10am-6pm daily; 10am-10pm 1st Fri of mth. *Tours* 11am, noon, 2pm, 3pm Mon-

Guards' Museum. *See p199.*

Fri; noon, 3pm Sat, Sun. **Admission** free. *Special exhibitions* prices vary. **Credit** MC, V. **Map** p269 K11.
Tate Modern, its younger, sexier sibling, seems to get all the attention, but don't forget the Britain, founded by sugar magnate Sir Henry Tate: it contains London's second great collection of art, after the National Gallery. With the opening of Tate Modern, oodles of space was freed up to accommodate the holdings of British art from the 16th century to the present day.

Spanning five centuries, the collection takes in works by artists such as Hogarth, the Blakes (William and Peter), Gainsborough, Constable (who gets three rooms all to himself), Reynolds, Bacon and Moore. Turner is particularly well represented, even more so since 2003 when the gallery recovered two classics – *Shade and Darkness: The Evening of the Deluge* and *Light and Colour (Goethe's Theory)* – that were stolen in 1994. And Tate Modern doesn't have a monopoly on modern artists: there are works here by Howard Hodgkin, Lucian Freud, Francis Bacon and David Hockney. The gallery also hosts the controversy-courting annual Turner Prize exhibition (Oct-Jan). The shop is well stocked with posters and art books, and the restaurant is highly regarded.

You can also have the best of both art worlds, thanks to the Tate to Tate boat service (*see p165* **Tate Modern**).

Victoria & Pimlico

Map p268

Pimlico tube/Victoria tube/rail.
Victoria Street, stretching from Parliament Square to Victoria Station, links political London with a rather colourful, chaotic backpackers' London. Victoria Coach Station is a short distance away in Buckingham Palace Road; Belgrave Road provides an unbroken line of cheap and fairly grim hotels.

Westminster Cathedral

42 Francis Street, SW1P 1QW (7798 9055, www. westminstercathedral.org.uk). Victoria tube/rail. **Open** 7am-6pm Mon-Fri; 8am-6.30pm Sat; 8am-7.30pm Sun. *Bell tower* 9.30am-5pm Mon-Fri; 10am-4.30pm Sat, Sun. *Exhibition* 9.30am-5pm Mon-Fri; 9.30am-6pm Sat, Sun. *Services* 7am, 8am, 10.30am, 12.30pm, 1.05pm, 5.30pm Mon-Fri; 8am, 9am, 10.30am, 12.30pm, 6pm Sat; 8am, 9am, 10.30am, noon, 5.30pm, 7pm Sun. **Admission** free; donations appreciated. *Bell tower or exhibition* £5; £2.50 reductions. *Both* £8; £4 reductions. **Credit** MC, V. **Map** p268 J10.
Westminster Abbey might be more famous, but Westminster Cathedral is spectacular in its own bizarre way. Part wedding cake, part sweet stick, this neo-Byzantine confection is Britain's premier Catholic cathedral, built in 1895-1903 by John Francis Bentley, who was inspired by the Hagia Sophia in Istanbul. With such a festive exterior, you'd expect an ornate interior. Not so: the inside has yet to be finished. Even so, there are magnificent columns and mosaics (made from more than 100 kinds of marble). Eric Gill's sculptures of the *Stations of the Cross* (1914-18) are world renowned. Westminster Cathedral's nave is the broadest in England, and the view from the 273ft bell tower is superb; it's got a lift too. A new permanent exhibition, 'Treasures of the Cathedral', displays vestments and precious artefacts.

Around Town

Kensington & Chelsea

Brilliant minds and shopping finds.

South Kensington

Map p265

Gloucester Road or South Kensington tube.
For gay visitors who have come to London for culture, not clubs, South Kensington is far more interesting than Soho. The capital's intellectual hub, it is brimming with august museums and lofty institutes. This situation owes much to Queen Victoria's husband Prince Albert – he of pierced penis fame (*see p204* **Albert Memorial**) – who was one of the leading lights behind the establishment of cultural and academic institutions in South Kensington, using the profits of 1851's Great Exhibition. Consequently, the **Natural History Museum**, with its dinosaurs and volcanoes, sits cheek by jowl with the technology-stuffed **Science Museum** and the endlessly aesthetic **Victoria & Albert Museum**.

The area is also known for its elegant Victorian terraced houses, and the **Royal Albert Hall** (*see p134*), which hosts the Proms and other big concerts; to the south, the **Royal College of Music** (Prince Consort Road, 7589 3643, www.rcm.ac.uk) offers concerts and a museum containing 800 instruments from 1480 to the present (open 11.30am-4.30pm Tue-Fri, free).

Natural History Museum

Cromwell Road, SW7 5BD (7942 5000, www. nhm.ac.uk). South Kensington tube. **Open** 10am-5.50pm daily. **Admission** free; charges apply for special exhibitions. *Tours* free. **Credit** (shop) MC, V. **Map** p265 D10.
This stunning museum thrills from the moment you enter its impressive doorway. The Diplodocus skeleton puts *Jurassic Park* to shame, but it isn't the biggest creature here: that honour belongs to the 90ft blue whale in the Mammals room. Nearby, kids queue to see the animatronic dinosaurs. Other star exhibits are the cross-section through a Giant Sequoia tree and an amazing array of stuffed birds. The Geological Museum is reached via an escalator ride through a giant globe complete with twinkling stars. A popular exhibition called Restless Surface has a mock-up of a Kobe supermarket, where the floor shakes to video coverage of the 1995 earthquake. Earth's Treasury shows off precious metals, gems and crystals. Many of the museum's 22 million insect and plant specimens are housed in the Darwin Centre. Outside, the Wildlife Garden (open Apr-Oct only) is the Natural History Museum's living exhibition, with a range of British lowland habitats including a Bee Tree, a hollow tree trunk that opens up to reveal a busy hive.

Science Museum

Exhibition Road, SW7 2DD (0870 870 4868, www. sciencemuseum.org.uk). South Kensington tube. **Open** 10am-6pm daily. **Admission** free; charges apply for special exhibitions. **Credit** MC, V. **Map** p265 D9/10.
There are enough buttons, flashing lights and interactive gizmos in this museum to please a gay clubber with a short attention span. Indeed, this marvellous institution achieves a rare feat: it makes science interesting. On the ground floor, the shop sells whizzy and wacky toys. The Energy Hall showcases an array of 18th-century steam engines. Beyond, in Exploring Space, rocket science and the lunar landings are illustrated by dramatically lit mock-ups and models. In Making the Modern World, you can see the *Apollo 10* command module and stacks of classic cars. Beyond is the Wellcome Wing, bathed in an eerie blue light, celebrating new discoveries in the biomedical sciences. The Who Am I? gallery on the first floor explores discoveries in genetics, brain science and psychology. Other highlights include displays on computing, marine engineering and mathematics and flight.

Victoria & Albert Museum

Cromwell Road, SW7 2RL (7942 2000, www.vam. ac.uk). South Kensington tube. **Open** 10am-6pm Mon-Thur, Sat, Sun; 10am-10pm Fri. *Tours* 10.30am-3.30pm daily. **Admission** free; charges apply for special exhibitions. **Credit** MC, V. **Map** p265 E10.
The V&A parades a world-beating array of decorative arts, with around four million pieces of furniture, textiles, ceramics, fashion, sculpture, paintings, posters, jewellery and metalwork. The sheer scale is daunting, so it's best to wander idly and ponder the connections between, say, a cone-breasted Gaultier catsuit and Italian Renaissance sculpture. (The V&A's collection of the latter is the finest outside Italy.) Other highlights include the seven Raphael Cartoons painted in 1515 as tapestry designs for the Sistine Chapel; the Gloucester candlestick, an elaborate Romanesque object that would make Liberace drool; Canova's sensuous *Three Graces* sculpture (owned jointly with the National Gallery of Scotland); and the Ardabil carpet, the world's oldest and most splendid floor covering, in the new Jameel Gallery of Islamic Art. The Fashion galleries range from 18th-century court dress to a contemporary chiffon numbers. The Architecture gallery and the famous Photography collection are also big draws. The new William and Judith Bollinger Gallery is dedicated to the history of European jewellery. Among the 3,500 items are diamonds worn by Catherine the Great of Russia, and the Beauharnais Emeralds, which were a gift from Napoleon to his adopted daughter.

Victoria & Albert Museum

Around Town

Hyde Park & Kensington Gardens

Maps p262 & p263

*Hyde Park Corner, Knightsbridge, Lancaster Gate
or Queensway tube.*

If the parks are the lungs of London, then massive
Hyde Park does most of the breathing. Residents
and visitors in their thousands come here to walk,
picnic, play sport, take a rowing boat out, listen
to brass bands, admire art in the **Serpentine
Gallery**, go horse riding (7723 2813), or cruise
for sex. The park gets busy in summer, but there's
always space for those seeking peace. The Rose
Garden is a popular spot for frisky gay men.

Snatched from the monks of Westminster Abbey
by Henry VIII for hunting grounds, the parks were
first opened to the public in the reign of James I
in the early 17th century, although they were only
frequented by the cream of society. At the end of
the 17th century, William III, suffering from asthma
and averse to the dank air of Whitehall Palace,
relocated to the village of Kensington and made his
home in **Kensington Palace**. A corner of Hyde
Park was sectioned off to make grounds for it, and
though today the two merge, Kensington Gardens
was closed to the public until King George II
opened it on Sundays to those in formal dress only
– soldiers, sailors and servants were not welcome.

These days, soldiers have an integral role
in the park's life: at 10.30am each day (9.30am
on Sundays), after a warm-up in the park, the
Household Cavalry leaves its barracks near the
Prince of Wales Gate and trots in full ceremonial
dress to Whitehall for the Changing of the Guard.

There are plenty of less formal attractions in
Hyde Park, however, not least of which is the
Serpentine boating lake. Hyde Park is also a
focus for freedom of speech. It became a hotspot
for mass demonstrations in the 19th century and
remains so today – a march against the war in
Iraq in 2003 was the largest in its history. The
legalisation of public assembly in the park led
to the establishment of **Speakers' Corner** in
1872, where ranters both sane and bonkers have
the floor. This isn't the place to come for balanced,
political debate, but Marx, Engels, Lenin, Orwell
and the Pankhursts have all attended.

Princess Diana devotees should head to the
controversial **Diana, Princess of Wales
Memorial Fountain**, an oval slab of Cornish
granite, part of a commemorative seven-mile walk
designed in her memory. Created by American
architect Kathryn Gustafson, the fountain was
supposed to reflect the personality of the princess:
inclusive, elegant and child-friendly. But its
cruellest critics have likened it to a storm drain.

Albert Memorial

Kensington Gardens, opposite Royal Albert Hall, SW7 (tours 7495 0916). South Kensington tube. **Tours** 2pm, 3pm 1st Sun of mth. **Admission** £5; £4.50 reductions. **No credit cards. Map** p263 D8.

'It would upset my equanimity to be permanently ridiculed and laughed at in effigy,' suggested Prince Albert in 1851. Thankfully his wishes were ignored because the Albert Memorial is one of the great sculptural achievements of the Victorian period. Created by Sir George Gilbert Scott and unveiled in 1876 – 15 years after Albert's death from typhoid – the Prince is surrounded on all sides by marble statues of famous poets and painters. Overhead, the dramatic 180ft spire is inlaid with semi-precious stones. Incidentally, the slang term 'Prince Albert', which means pierced penis, comes from a rumour that Queen Victoria's husband wore a ring down below strapped to his thigh – allegedly to prevent him getting an erection in public.

Kensington Palace

Kensington Gardens, W8 4PX (0844 482 7777, www.hrp.org.uk). Bayswater, High Street Kensington or Queensway tube. **Open** *Mar-Oct* 10am-5pm daily. *Nov-Feb* 10am-4pm daily. **Admission** £12.50; £11 reductions. **Credit** MC, V. **Map** p262 B/C8.

Princess Diana's legions of gay fans are among the hordes of tourists who pay a pilgrimage to her former residence, built in the 1661 as a Jacobean mansion and transformed into a palace by Sir Christopher Wren in 1689. But like the People's Princess, Kensington is far more warm and intimate than other, more regal palaces. A series of Diana's dresses, including the blue silk number in which she danced with John Travolta at the White House, are permanently displayed alongside the Royal Ceremonial Dress

Albert Memorial

Collection, an exhibition of royal and court dress dating from the 18th century. The King's Gallery, meanwhile, is filled with portraits of the first glamorous royals to live here. Those preferring to avoid the entry fees to the State Apartments (the palace itself is closed to visitors) can walk around the sunken gardens or take tea in the Orangery.

Serpentine Gallery

Kensington Gardens, near Albert Memorial, W2 3XA (7402 6075, www.serpentinegallery.org). Lancaster Gate or South Kensington tube. **Open** 10am-6pm daily. **Admission** free; donations appreciated. **Credit** AmEx, MC, V. **Map** p263 D8.

Tucked away in the middle of the park, the Serpentine Gallery comes as a surprise. The delicate exterior – a 1930s tea pavilion – belies the challenging art inside: the gallery regularly courts controversy with provocative exhibitions by modern artists. Past exhibitions include work by the likes of queer icons Cindy Sherman and Gilbert and George or *enfants terribles* such as Banksy and Tracey Emin. Each year, a famous architect – Zaha Hadid, Rem Koolhaas, Frank Gehry – designs an outdoor pavilion.

Knightsbridge

Map p265

Knightsbridge or South Kensington tube.

Knightsbridge is a shopper's paradise. The vogueish **Harvey Nichols** still holds sway over the top end of **Sloane Street**, where urban princesses graze with shopping bags. Expensive brands dominate, with the likes of Gucci, Chanel and Christian Dior letting you know you're in a moneyed neighbourhood. More understated is **Beauchamp Place**, a peaceful road with good restaurants. But the neighbourhood's chief claim to fame is **Harrods**. From its tan bricks to its olive-green awning and green-coated doormen, it's an instantly recognisable retail legend.

Brompton and **Belgravia** serve primarily as residential catchment areas for wealthy families who imagine they couldn't survive at all without Harrods' dog-grooming service on their doorstep. So it's perhaps not surprising to find a pillar of penitence like the **Brompton Oratory Catholic Church** amid the excess. There's not much else in Brompton to fire the imagination, however, bar Arne Jacobsen's **Danish Embassy** building (55 Sloane Street). Belgravia has a few nice pubs tucked away behind its serious marble parades: the Nag's Head (52 Kinnerton Street, 7235 1135) and the Grenadier on (18 Wilton Row, 7235 3074) are worth seeking out.

Brompton Oratory Catholic Church

Thurloe Place, Brompton Road, SW7 2RP (7808 0900, www.bromptonoratory.com). South Kensington tube. **Open** 6.30am-8pm daily. *Services* 7am, 10am, 12.30pm, 6pm Mon-Sat; 7am, 8am, 9am, 10am, 11am, 12.30pm, 4.30pm, 7pm Sun. **Admission** free. **Map** p265 E10.

The second-biggest Catholic church in Britain, after Westminster Cathedral, the mighty Brompton Oratory was built in 1884. It feels older, however, partly because of its baroque Italianate style, but also because many of its florid marbles, mosaics and statuary pre-date the structure.

Chelsea

Map p265

Sloane Square tube.
Once famous for its painters, poets and punks, today Chelsea is more about beautiful bodies and bursting bank accounts. The heart of both 1960s swinging London and 1970s punk London, in the 21st century Chelsea epitomises café society.

Sloane Square, at the end of the King's Road closest to the tube station, gets its name from Sir Hans Sloane (1660-1753), a physician and canny entrepreneur who bought the Manor of Chelsea and saved the famously restorative **Chelsea Physic Garden** from decline. The **Royal Court Theatre** (*see p132*), with its reputation for avant-garde performances, looks imperiously over the square towards the King's Road, past **Peter Jones**, the polished department store beloved of lunching ladies from the Shires.

Once the trendiest street in the city, the **King's Road** still has a few independent boutiques, but its glory days are largely over. Back in the swinging '60s, it became a focal point for designers such as Mary Quant (whose shop, Bazaar, stood at no.138), who dared the city to wear their creations. In the 1970s, it became the bedrock of the punk movement, when Vivienne Westwood's shop, Sex, made headlines with its outlandish approach to style. It was there that Malcolm McLaren famously met John Lydon and Sid Vicious, and from that shop that the Sex Pistols reportedly got their name. Westwood still has a boutique there (World's End, no.430), but the fashions within don't shock like they used to. Indeed, it's all very tasteful now. Restaurants include Bluebird (no.350, 7559 1000, www.danddlondon.com), a swanky Chelsea landmark housed in the 1923 garage of the record-breaking car. Still, certain gay traditions live on: the **Queen's Head** (*see p36*), an old-school, cosy homosexual boozer just north of the King's Road, is still serving after all these years.

Between the King's Road and Chelsea Embankment, the grounds of the **Royal Hospital** are best known these days as the site of the flashy, posh celebrity-magnet that is the **Chelsea Flower Show** (*see p120*) – which takes place in late May the hospital's old Ranelagh Gardens – but for the other 51 weeks of the year, the district is quiet and peaceful, as befits a place of sanctuary for retired soldiers.

Chelsea Physic Garden. *See p206.*

Riverside Chelsea

Continuing down Royal Hospital Road toward the **Chelsea Physic Garden**, you pass Tite Street, where Whistler once had a studio, and where Oscar Wilde lived (at no.34) before his arrest for gross indecency at the Cadogan hotel. The heart of the original Chelsea village is **Chelsea Old Church** (www.chelseaoldchurch.org.uk), where the saint and statesman Thomas More once sang in the choir; though bombed heavily in 1941, it dates back to the 13th century.

The artists' and writers' community was centred at the western end of the Chelsea Embankment, on **Cheyne Walk**, where the fashionable houses have changed little. Blue plaques abound: George Eliot at no.4; Pre-Raphaelite painter DG Rossetti at no.16; James McNeill Whistler at no.96; JMW Turner at no.119.

At the turn of the 20th century – several centuries after the queer philosopher Erasmus lived here – Cheyne Walk played host to a number of key homosocial figures. The houses of family man Charles Robert Ashbee – an enthusiast for Edward Carpenter's ideas of Uranian love and its brew of socialism and sex between men of different classes, made equal by love and hard work – still stand at nos.38 and 39. The movement inspired the setting up of the Guild of Handicrafts, responsible for some of the great works of the Arts and Crafts movement.

Henry James, meanwhile, who never married but nursed Erasmus-like passions for men, lived in Carlyle Mansions. Painter Glyn Philpot, the famous portraitist of interwar London, had his first studio in Cheyne Row around the corner. While at Cheyne Row, Philpot met artists Charles Ricketts and Charles Shannon, arguably London's first 'out' gay couple. The pair lived together from their art school days as teenagers in Lambeth until Ricketts died 50 years later. Max Beerbohm, the Edwardian writer, satirist and dandy, described the pair as 'the Sisters of the Vale' after their house in the Vale nearby.

Carlyle's House

24 Cheyne Row, SW3 5HL (7352 7087, www.national trust.org.uk). Sloane Square tube or 11, 19, 22, 49, 211, 239, 319 bus. **Open** *mid Mar-Oct* 2-5pm Wed-Fri; 11am-5pm Sat, Sun. **Admission** £5.10. **Credit** MC, V. **Map** p265 E12.

This house witnessed some very lively discussions when the prim scholar lived here from 1834 with his wife, Jane, their days filled with visits from the Victorian glitterati: Dickens, Tennyson, Browning, Darwin, Trollope. Visitors can see the original decor, furniture, books and pictures, and the 'sound-proofed' study where the writer spent 13 years slaving over *The History of Frederick the Great*.

Chelsea Physic Garden

66 Royal Hospital Road, entrance on Swan Walk, SW3 4HS (7352 5646, www.chelseaphysicgarden.co.uk). Sloane Square tube or 11, 19, 239 bus. **Open** *Apr-Oct* noon-5pm Wed-Fri; noon-6pm Sun. *Tours* times vary; phone to check. **Admission** £8; £5 reductions. *Tours* free. **Credit** (shop) AmEx, MC, V. **Map** p265 F12.

This therapeutic garden was founded in 1673 by the Worshipful Society of the Apothecaries of London, and remains a draw today. The garden's objective was to provide medical students with the means to study plants used in healing, and Sir Hans Sloane helped to develop it in the early 18th century. Free tours conducted by entertaining volunteers trace the history of the medicinal beds, where mandrake, yew, feverfew and other herbs are still grown.

National Army Museum

Royal Hospital Road, SW3 4HT (7730 0717, www.national-army-museum.ac.uk). Sloane Square tube or 11, 19, 239 bus. **Open** 10am-5.30pm daily. **Admission** free. **Map** p265 F12.

If you love a man in uniform, have we got a museum for you. Historians dressed as soldiers explain the ups and downs of army life. Galleries include the 'Road to Waterloo', with an enormous model of the battle employing 70,000 model soldiers, and a skeleton that is supposedly Napoleon's favourite horse, Marengo. There's also a trench mock-up in 'World at War 1914-1946' and a Tudor cannon in the section on the army's early years.

Saatchi Gallery

Duke of York's HQ, off King's Road, SW3 4SQ (7823 2363, www.saatchi-gallery.co.uk). Sloane Square tube. **Open** 10am-6pm daily. **Admission** free. **Map** p265 F11.

Back in the 1990s, Charles Saatchi expended considerable energies promoting figures who became known as the Young British Artists (Damien Hirst, Tracey Emin et al). It will surprise many, then, that Saatchi's new gallery – housed in magnificent former military barracks – launched with a display of new Chinese art, followed by exhibitions featuring US and Indian artists. And Saatchi continues to push the envelope with provocative exhibitions from the next wave of YBAs: come here to spot the next Tracey Emin before the rest of the world does. Admission is free.

Saatchi Gallery

North London

Market trade and babes in the wood.

Primrose Hill. *See p209.*

Camden

Camden Town or Chalk Farm tube/Camden Road rail.
Although it's one of London's most fashionable
addresses, Camden Town has had a long
association with lowlife. Cheap lodging houses
dominated the area when the **Regent's Canal**
was laid out in 1816, and it was still a rough place
in Victorian times, too – at least according to
Charles Dickens, who grew up in Bayham Street.
In later decades, Irish and Greek immigrants
followed and, by the 1960s, the neighbourhood
had developed a raffish character.

Around this time, arty types, including gay writer
Alan Bennett, saw the potential of its tall elegant
houses. White-collar professionals followed, and
today Camden has a middle-class flavour. Yet the
area retains an edge: at night, Camden Town tube
is garlanded with exotica – punks and goths in full
regalia and less photogenic junkies. Students and
teens love **Camden Market**, once an alternative
hangout but now a crowded tourist attraction.

Camden is let down by a dearth of good eateries,
but Italian ice-cream parlour/restaurant **Marine**
Ices (8 Haverstock Hill, 7482 9003, www.marine
ices.co.uk) is a local institution. For gay venues,
the **Black Cap** (*see p28*) is a legendary north
London pub/club with a long tradition of cabaret.

Camden Market

192-200 Camden High Street, NW1 (7267 3417,
www.camdenmarkets.org). **Open** 9am-5.30pm daily.
Camden Lock *Camden Lock Place, off Chalk Farm*
Road, NW1 8AF (7485 7963, www.camdenlock
market.com). **Open** 10am-6pm Mon-Thur, Sun;
10am-6.30pm Fri, Sat.
Camden Market *Camden High Street, junction*
with Buck Street, NW1 (www.camdenmarkets.org).
Open 9.30am-6pm daily.
Inverness Street Market *Inverness Street, NW1*
(www.camdenlock.net). **Open** 8.30am-5pm daily.
Stables Market *off Chalk Farm Road, opposite*
junction with Hartland Road, NW1 (7485 5511,
www.stablesmarket.com). **Open** 10.30am-6pm daily.
All *Camden Town or Chalk Farm tube/*
Camden Road rail.
Camden's collection of markets offers a smörgåsbord of
street culture and urban fashion. It's quieter during the week,
but weekends are better for variety and atmosphere – pass
loitering goths and scowling punks to join crowds of tourists

and locals bustling around 700 shops and stalls. The Stables area comprises a combination of fashion and food, with an art and exhibition space. Find stalls selling antiques and bric-a-brac at the Horse Tunnel Market. Camden Lock sells everything from corsets and vintage to Japanese tableware and delicious food. Head to Camden (Buck Street) Market for cheapo jeans, sunglasses, T-shirts and accessories.

Jewish Museum

Raymond Burton House, 129-131 Albert Street, NW1 7NB (7284 7384, www.jewishmuseum.org.uk). Camden Town tube. **Open** 10am-5pm Mon-Wed; 10am-9pm Thur; 10am-2pm Fri; 10am-5pm Sun; (last admission 30mins before closing). **Admission** £7; £3-£6 reductions; £17 family; free under-5s. **Credit** MC, V.

The Jewish Museum provides a fascinating insight into one of Britain's oldest immigrant communities. Different aspects of six centuries of Jewish life are illustrated through oil paintings, artefacts, photographs and ceremonial art. Galleries include one devoted to the Holocaust and another devoted to Jewish rituals. A multimedia gallery features interviews with concentration camp survivors, a smoked salmon tycoon and a London cabbie who fought in the Yom Kippur war. It recently reopened after a £10m refurbishment.

Around Camden

Primrose Hill, to the west of Camden, is as pretty as the actors and pop stars who frequent the gastropubs and quaint cafés along Regent's

Fast love

London is the cruising capital of the world: just ask George Michael. The pop star's exploits on Hampstead Heath – a nocturnal playground for woodland fairies – have been well publicised.

But cruising is not necessarily a by-product of our highly sexualised modern society. On the contrary, cruising was common as early as the 1700s in public gardens, where 'mollies' would wave white hankies as part of a secret code. Police paid agents provocateurs to trap men on 'Sodomites' Walk', a marshy area in Moorfields, during the 19th century. And in 1810, the home secretary even proposed locking the gates of Hyde Park and St James's Park at night to prevent the practice. But the Victorian boom in building public lavatories provided fertile ground for hanky-panky to flourish indoors – a practice known as cottaging.

Sad closet cases and married men – that's the old cliché about cruising. But an NHS survey revealed that 75 per cent of those who seek sex in public loos and parks are openly gay men who also frequent gay pubs. It seems there are deeper psychological reasons for cruising than just sowing your wild oats. Take the case of serial cruiser Joe Orton. 'It wasn't just the cheap sex: Joe liked to be a fly on the wall,' said his sister Leoni Orton-Barnett. 'You don't get to know what life is really like by knocking about with BBC directors and Oxford dons. The crudity and sparseness of life is to be found in public lavatories.'

Among them were the 105-year-old toilets in South End Green, Hampstead, as featured in Orton biopic *Prick Up Your Ears*; if you believe Orton's diaries, a visit to the urinal could quickly turn into an orgy. The toilets of Brockwell Park were the subject of a 2001 TV documentary, *The Truth about Gay Sex*, which introduced the Great British Public to the curious 'glory holes' in cubicle partitions. Who said romance was dead?

Speaking of romance, **Hampstead Heath** (*see right*) is arguably London's dreamiest cruising ground: on a hot summer night, silent men pose like statues along moonlit, wooded paths. Derek Jarman's diary entries document the carnal

pleasures – and the feeling of camaraderie. To get there, head for the parking lot behind Jack Straw's Castle, a block of flats about a ten-minute walk north of the tube station. But the action isn't confined to Hampstead: London is one giant cruising ground. Just check out the cruising guide at the subtly named www.squirt.org, or www. pinkuk.com or www.gaytoz.com: there's Epping Forest car park ('sound action most nights'); Streatham Common ('heaving after dark'); Hyde Park (the rose garden); even Brompton Cemetery – really, guys, is nowhere sacred? In south London, you'll find London's second most famous cruising ground, **Clapham Common** (*see p219*), where MP Ron Davies had 'a moment of madness' in 1998. The action takes place on the southern border of the park, in a thicket of woods, though it's not as safe as Hampstead Heath.

If you're not brave enough to venture outside, stay indoors and cruise online, like half of London seems to. Gaydar (www.gaydar.co.uk) is the *ne plus ultra* of online lust: every gay man in London eventually seems to succumb and post a profile.

But wherever you do it, cruising can be a risky business. HIV is still a problem and old nemeses hepatitis B and syphilis are on the rise in London. Muggings, assaults and murders still occur. In 2005, 24-year-old gay bar manager Jody Dobrowski was savagely beaten to death on Clapham Common and, in 2008, a 21-year-old gay man was left paralysed after an attack in Shoreditch.

Thankfully, the police are less of a problem. According to the 2003 Sex Offences Act, having sex outdoors is no longer illegal as long as it's done in a private place – and in many cases 'private place' extends to the remote corners of parks and commons under the cover of darkness. Unless you make a spectacle of yourself, you should be OK. Sex in a public toilet, though, is technically still against the law, and the law occasionally cracks down in random places – be careful, for instance, who you flash your bits to in the toilets at Liverpool Street Station. Or at least, be more careful than George Michael.

Park Road and Gloucester Avenue. On sunny Sunday mornings, there's no better spot to read the papers than the pavement tables in front of Ukrainian café **Trojka** (101 Regents Park Road, 7483 3765, www.trojka.co.uk). Other favourite hangouts include the long-established **Primrose Pâtisserie** (no.136, 7722 7848), upmarket Greek bistro **Lemonia** (no.89, 7586 7454) and chic Modern European eatery **Odette's** (no.130, 7586 8569, www.odettesprimrosehill.com). For a filling gastropub meal, head to Gloucester Avenue to the **Engineer** (no.65, 7722 0950, www.the-engineer.com) or the **Lansdowne** (no.90, 7483 0409, www.thelansdownepub.co.uk). For a romantic view of the city, climb to the top of Primrose Hill itself.

Hampstead

Golders Green or Hampstead tube/Hampstead Heath or Gospel Oak rail.

Like many rural villages on the fringes of the city, Hampstead was a popular retreat in times of plague. Its undulating thoroughfares and protected heath ensured that urbanisation never happened and the village remains exclusive to this day. For centuries, it has been the favoured roosting place for literary and artistic bigwigs; Keats and Constable called it home in the 19th century, while modernist and surrealist artists such as Barbara Hepworth and Henry Moore lived the village London idyll here in the 1930s. Today it's home to a couple of gay pop icons named George: Boy and Michael.

Hampstead tube station stands at the top of the steep High Street, home to the villagey and traditional gay pub **KW4 (King William IV)** (*see p29*), where cruisers often stock up on Dutch courage before heading out into the wilderness. The twin lines of the higgledy-piggledy terraces that make up Church Row, one of Hampstead's most beautiful streets, lead down to **St John at Hampstead** (7794 5808, www.hampsteadparishchurch.org.uk), which has a bucolic cemetery. Constable is buried here.

East of Heath Street, a maze of quaint streets shelters **Burgh House** on New End Square, a Queen Anne house that contains a small museum, and modernist gem **2 Willow Road**. Nearby is **Keats House**, where the poet did his best work.

Hampstead Heath, the inspiration for CS Lewis's Narnia, is the city's countryside. Its charming contours and woodlands conspire to make it feel far larger than it is (something over a mile in each direction). The views of London from the top of **Parliament Hill** are stunning; on hot days, the murky bathing ponds are a godsend (the men's and women's ponds are

Ottolenghi. *See p210.*

open daily all year, the mixed pond is seasonal). There's also a great lido at Gospel Oak (for all, *see p140* **The swimming pool library**). Maps are displayed at information points on the heath. At the north end of the park is **Kenwood House**. To try your luck in the famous cruising grounds (*see left* **Fast love**), go to the western edge of the park north of the tube station and behind Jack Straw's Castle (once a pub, now luxury flats).

Freud Museum

20 Maresfield Gardens, NW3 5SX (7435 2002, www.freud.org.uk). Finchley Road tube. **Open** noon-5pm Wed-Sun. **Admission** £6; £3-£4.50 reductions. **Credit** MC, V.

Homosexuality is caused by a combination of overbearing mothers, absent, meek fathers and the child's failure to master the Oedipus complex. So said Sigmund Freud, who lived here with his daugher Anna. You can see the analyst's study, complete with couch, cigars and vast library.

Keats House

Keats Grove, NW3 2RR (7332 3868, www.keats house.org.uk). Hampstead tube, Hampstead Heath rail or 24, 46, 168 bus. **Open** 1-5pm Fri-Sun. **Admission** from £5; £3 reductions. **Credit** MC, V.

The Romantic poet made his home here from 1818 to 1820, when he left for Rome (where he died of tuberculosis the following year, aged 25). As well as mooching through the rooms, you can see a display on Keats's sweetheart, Fanny Brawne, who lived next door. For a romantic reverie, wander in the garden where he wrote 'Ode to a Nightingale'.

Around Town

Kenwood House/Iveagh Bequest

Hampstead Lane, NW3 7JR (8348 1286, www.english-heritage.org.uk). Hampstead tube or Golders Green tube then 210 bus. **Open** 11.30am-4pm daily. **Admission** free. **Credit** AmEx, MC, V.

Built in 1616, this manor house was later the residence of the first Earl of Mansfield, who banned slavery in England in 1772. Brewing magnate Edward Guinness bought the house in 1924 and filled it with his art collection. Now English Heritage is in charge of the elegant interiors. Art includes works by Vermeer, Rembrandt, Van Dyck and Gainsborough. Outside, Humphrey Repton's 1793 landscape – gardens, terraces and lake – is bucolic. There's a good café; in summer, there are concerts on the lawn.

2 Willow Road

2 Willow Road, NW3 1TH (7435 6166, www.national trust.org.uk). Hampstead tube or Hampstead Heath rail. **Open** *mid-Mar-Oct* noon-5pm Thur-Sun. *Nov-Oct* noon-5pm Sat, Sun. *Tours* noon, 1pm, 2pm Thur-Sat. **Admission** £5.50. **No credit cards**.

This strange and atmospheric 1939 house is a striking example of international modernism. James Bond author Ian Fleming was so annoyed by its architect, Hungarian Ernö Goldfinger – also responsible for some brutalist flats – that he named a villain after him. The atmospheric building also contains works by Max Ernst and Henry Moore.

Highgate

Archway or Highgate tube.

Highgate Cemetery

Swains Lane, N6 6PJ (8340 1834, www.highgate-cemetery.org). Archway tube or 143, 210, 271 bus. **Open** *East Cemetery* Mar-Oct 10am-4.30pm Mon-Fri; 11am-4.30pm Sat, Sun. Nov-Feb 10am-3.30pm Mon-Fri; 11am-3.30pm Sat, Sun. *West Cemetery* by tour only. *Tours* Mar-Oct 2pm Mon-Fri; hourly 11am-4pm Sat, Sun. Nov-Mar hourly 11am-3pm Sat, Sun. Closed during burials. **Admission** £3; £2 reductions. *Tours* £7 (incl camera permit). No video cameras. **No credit cards**.

Highgate Cemetery is London's most famous graveyard, marked by its dramatic tombs of towering angels and curling roses. Celebrity spotters seek out the Karl Marx and George Eliot memorials in the East Cemetery, but the West Cemetery (accessible only on guided tours) is the highlight. It is a breathtaking place: long pathways wind through tall tombs, gloomy catacombs and elaborate funerary architecture. Ask to see Lebanon Circle, where Radclyffe Hall is interred in the same vault as her lover Mabel Batten.

Islington

Angel tube/Highbury & Islington tube/rail.

In Victorian times, Islington was an industrial slum, but its Georgian squares and Victorian terraces have been gentrified in recent decades. Despite pockets of poverty, this is a middle-class area, as is clear when you walk along **Upper Street**, past countless shops, Camden Passage antiques market and trendy eateries. On the way along Upper Street, pop into yummy minimalist **Ottolenghi** café (*see p97*), then take a detour to Canonbury Square, once home to George Orwell (no.27) and Evelyn Waugh (no.17A). At 25 Noel Road, outrageous playwright Joe Orton was bludgeoned to death by his partner Kenneth Halliwell in 1967. You can read more about Orton at the new **Islington Museum** (245 St John Street, 7527 3235, www.islington.gov.uk, closed Wed, Sun), which has displays about playwright and feminist pioneer Mary Wollstonecraft.

Islington is home to a few gay watering holes, such as cruisy pub **King Edward VI** (*see p29*) and the trendier **Green** (*see p28*).

Estorick Collection of Modern Italian Art

39A Canonbury Square, N1 2AN (7704 9522, www.estorickcollection.com). Highbury & Islington tube/rail or 271 bus. **Open** 11am-6pm Wed, Fri, Sat; 11am-8pm Thur; noon-5pm Sun. **Admission** £5; £3.50. **Credit** AmEx, MC, V.

Eric Estorick was a US political scientist and art collector whose interest in the Futurists began in the 1950s. On show are Balla's *Hand of the Violinist*, Boccioni's *Modern Idol* and pieces by Carra, Marinetti, Russolo and Severini. There's also a library, shop and small café.

Estorick Collection of Modern Italian Art

East London

The rough with the smooth.

Whitechapel Art Gallery. *See p212.*

Whitechapel & Spitalfields

Map p271

Aldgate, Aldgate East or Whitechapel tube/ Liverpool Street tube/rail.

With its gritty appearance and reputation for gangsters and hard men, the East End might not seem like an obvious gay neighbourhood. But think again: some gays love a bit of rough (though gentrification is setting in).

Whitechapel and Spitalfields form the beating heart of the East End, but don't expect cockney patois on every corner. Centuries of immigration have made this one of the most multicultural parts of London. First to arrive were French Huguenots (Protestant refugees) in the 18th century, followed by the Irish and Germans in the 19th century and Jewish refugees from eastern Europe at the start of the 20th. As the Jews prospered and headed to north London, Bangladeshis and Indians moved in.

Now City Man is making his mark and the area is going upmarket. Bars, cafés and trendy shops are springing up on every corner, particularly around **Brick Lane** and **Spitalfields Market**. For a blast from the past, take an Original London Walk (www.walks.com): the Jack the Ripper option remains perenially popular.

Whitechapel

Named after a vanished chapel, this area of wholesale clothing shops and curry houses draws bargain-hunters to the street markets on Wentworth Street and Whitechapel Road for cheap clothes and imported 'fancy goods'. On Sundays, the famous **Petticoat Lane Market** takes up most of the streets behind Aldgate East tube station. For a taste of the old East End, pick up a tub of cockles from the Tubby Isaacs seafood stall on the corner of Whitechapel High Street and Goulston Street, and stroll east, past the art nouveau **Whitechapel Art Gallery**, along Whitechapel Road, to the **Whitechapel**

Bell Foundry (nos.32-34, 7247 2599, www. whitechapelbellfoundry.co.uk), which has been churning out bells since 1570, including Big Ben and the Liberty Bell. You can tour by arrangement, or visit the free museum on weekdays.

While Jack the Ripper terrorised Whitechapel in the 1880s, this honour passed to the Kray twins in the 1960s. The Krays have often been associated with homosexuality: Ronnie was known to be gay, while Reggie attracted a fair amount of gay gossip. Maybe this explains why he was idolised by Morrissey in 'Last of the International Playboys'. Ronnie Kray was finally arrested after shooting George Cornell dead at the Blind Beggar pub (337 Whitechapel Road) in March 1966. (For more about London's gay gangsters, read Jake Arnott's acclaimed novel *The Long Firm*.)

Of interest to lesbians is the **Women's Library** (25 Old Castle Street, 7320 2222, www.thewomens library.ac.uk), which offers challenging exhibits devoted to women's history and suffrage.

Whitechapel Art Gallery

77-82 Whitechapel High Street, E1 7QX (7522 7888, www.whitechapel.org). Aldgate East tube. **Open** 11am-6pm Tue, Wed, Fri-Sun; 11am-9pm Thur. **Admission** free. **Map** p271 S6.
Whitechapel Art Gallery has been exposing East Enders to contemporary art for more than a century. After a £13m expansion into the former library next door, the gallery reopened in spring 2009. The surroundings might be new, but the edgy spirit remains: the Whitechapel has

a reputation for championing avant-gardes and over the years the gallery has supported the careers of artists such as Lucian Freud, Barbara Hepworth, David Hockney, Gilbert and George and Bridget Riley.

Spitalfields

For most Londoners, Spitalfields is synonymous with the historic covered **(Old) Spitalfields Market** (www.visitspitalfields.com) on Commercial Street. Originally a fruit and veg market, it is now dominated by a quality mixture of food, fashion, furniture and music. The market is open every day except Saturday, but the best day to visit is Sunday.

Outside, along Brushfield Street, the shops look quaint and Dickensian, but with more modern offerings: the deli **Verde & Co** (no.40, 7247 1924, www.verde-and-company-ltd.co.uk) was opened by lesbian author Jeanette Winterson, inspired by the local food shops she found in France.

Directly opposite Spitalfields Market is the dramatic **Christ Church Spitalfields** (Commercial Street, 7859 3035, www.christchurch spitalfields.org). Built in 1729 by baroque architect Nicholas Hawksmoor, it is one of London's finest churches, to rival Wren's.

Lesser-known attractions are peppered around the surrounding streets. Turn into Fournier Street (home to artists Gilbert and George) for a trip back in time; the street is lined with tall and distinctive shuttered Huguenot houses.

Rivington Place. *See p214.*

Dennis Severs' House

18 Folgate Street, E1 6BX (7247 4013, www.dennis severshouse.co.uk). Liverpool Street tube/rail or Shoreditch High Street rail. **Open** noon-4pm Sun; noon-2pm Mon following 1st & 3rd Sun of mth; times vary Mon evenings. **Admission** £8 Sun; £5 noon-2pm Mon; £12 Mon evenings. **Credit** V. **Map** p271 R5.

One block north of Spitalfields Market, this splendid Huguenot home contains one of the East End's more unusual attractions. This curious 'still-life drama' was the brainchild of eccentric American artist Dennis Severs, and each room in the house is set up to re-create the sights, sounds and smells of a different period.

Brick Lane

The building that houses the **Jamme Masjid Mosque**, at the south end of Brick Lane, symbolises the street's multiculturalism: it began life as a Huguenot chapel and was later used as a synagogue before being converted, in 1976, into a mosque. A lasting trace of the Jewish heritage is the unmissable 24-hour Beigel Bake further north at no.159, whose cheap salt beef bagels are legendary across town. However, it's the Bangladeshi influence that's ubiquitous – though, despite the innumerable curry restaurants, there are much better places to eat curry in the capital.

Brick Lane earned its name from the brick factories that once operated here alongside clothesmakers and the **Old Truman Brewery**, which is now an artistic and creative hub. North of the brewery, the street is dotted with quirky cafés and fashion, crafts, vintage and antiques shops. Brick Lane has now become a bustling, trendy nightspot, and many old factories also house spacious bars such as 93 Feet East (no.150).

Shoreditch & Hoxton

Old Street tube/rail.

Originally two distinct but neighbouring hamlets: **Shoreditch**, at the junction of the Roman roads Old Street and Kingsland Road, and **Hoxton**, just north of Old Street. Nowadays, both names are buzzwords for the trendy, bohemian district that has risen from the ashes of an area left derelict after the war. First adopted as a cheap hangout by a new generation of British artists (such as Tracey Emin and Damien Hirst) in the mid 1990s, it is now one of London's most vibrant and dynamic social centres; enduring creative energy is visible at the **White Cube** gallery (48 Hoxton Square, 7930 5373, www.whitecube.com).

DJ bars and clubs dominate Shoreditch High Street, Curtain Road, Old Street and **Hoxton Square**. In recent years, a local gay scene with an arty bent has sprung up around club nights such as **Gutterslut** (*see p40*), where drag artist

Brick Lane

Jonny Woo lures flamboyantly dressed kids. Other gay hotspots include the **George & Dragon** (*see p31*) and the **Joiners Arms** (*see p32*), a lively gay boozer. Interior design historians, meanwhile, will be impressed by the **Geffrye Museum**.

Geffrye Museum

136 Kingsland Road, E2 8EA (7739 8543, www. geffrye-museum.org.uk). Hoxton rail. **Open** *Museum* 10am-5pm Tue-Sat; noon-5pm Sun. *Almshouse tours* 1st Sat of mth, 1st & 3rd Wed of mth; phone for times. **Admission** *Museum* free. *Almshouse tours* £2. **Credit** (shop) MC, V.

Gay designers will lap up this superb museum of interior design. Housed in a close of Georgian almshouses, it offers a chronological sequence of room interiors from the 1600s to the present day. Fans of retro furniture will love the chintzy 1930s and '60s living rooms. There is also an airy restaurant and a fragrant herb garden.

Around Town

Broadway Market

Rivington Place

Rivington Place, EC2A 3BA (7729 9616, www. rivingtonplace.org). Old Street tube/rail. **Open** 11am-6pm Tue, Wed, Fri; 11am-9pm Thur; noon-6pm Sat. **Admission** free. **Credit** (shop) MC, V.
One of Shoreditch's more exciting recent additions, this public space champions culturally diverse visual arts. Designed by David Adjaye as a lattice-like structure of glass and dark concrete, this striking building provides a platform for British and international work.

Bethnal Green, Hackney & Mile End

Bethnal Green/Mile End tube/Dalston Kingsland or Hackney Central rail.
The terraced streets of **Bethnal Green** were used as a location for the movie *The Krays*, but the twins – one of whom was gay, allegedly – were actually born down the road in Hoxton's Stean Street. This used to be a slum – the 1960s tower blocks are still pretty grim – but the remaining Victorian terraces have become desirable real estate for City workers.

A short walk away is **Columbia Road**, which erupts into a riot of colour every Sunday for the flower market. Famous boxing venue York Hall (5-15 Old Ford Road) is the site of gay pop history: Boy George sashayed around the swimming pool in the video for 'Do You Really Want to Hurt Me?'. The building's old Turkish baths have been smartened up and now form part of **Spa London** (8709 5845, www.spa-london.org).

North of Bethnal Green, the London borough of **Hackney** is a shabby but artsy neighbourhood, known for its gloriously restored **Hackney Empire** theatre, art deco town hall on Mare Street and the bucolic London Fields park. The district's trendy epicentre is **Broadway Market**, a vital artery that successfully mixes pie and mash with an influx of artisan cheeses and designer coffees, most apparent during the Saturday farmers' market.

Like Hackney, **Mile End** – east of Bethnal Green – is rough and ready but coming up. Though bombed heavily in World War II, it has pockets of impressive architecture: **Tredegar Square**, in particular, is one of London's finest Georgian squares. Its neighbouring watering hole, the **Morgan Arms** (43 Morgan Street, 8980 6389), is a stylish gastropub. Despite Mile End's bleak reputation, it's blessed with a gorgeous green space: the avant-garde **Mile End Park**, which also has a tiny art gallery (7364 4147) and a romantic canalside walk to the splendid and unsung **Victoria Park** to the north.

V&A Museum of Childhood

Cambridge Heath Road, E2 9PA (8983 4200, www.museumofchildhood.org.uk). Bethnal Green tube or Cambridge Heath tube/rail. **Open** 10am-5.45pm daily. **Admission** free. **Credit** MC, V.
For a fun nostalgia kick, this quirky museum is a must – it has been collecting children's toys since 1872. It's hard not to fall for the old board games, 1970s puppets and Barbie in her many phases. Upstairs, you'll find an astounding collection of dolls' houses.

Walthamstow

Walthamstow tube/rail.
With its bustling street market full of cheeky barrow boys, fruit and veg and cheap gear, this corner of London is *EastEnders* come to life.

William Morris Gallery

Lloyd Park, Forest Road, E17 4PP (8496 4390, www. lbwf.gov.uk/wmg). Walthamstow Central tube/rail or 34, 97 bus. **Open** 10am-5pm Wed-Sun. *Tours* phone for details. **Admission** free. **Credit** (shop) MC, V.
Artist, socialist and wallpaper mogul William Morris lived in this house until 1856, so it's appropriate that it was chosen to house the only gallery in London highlighting his work. You don't have to be an Arts and Crafts buff to appreciate the wonderful wallpaper, fabric, stained glass and ceramics produced by Morris and his colleagues.

Docklands

Various stops on the Docklands Light Railway (DLR).
For many, Docklands is a living memorial to the values of Thatcher's Britain. During the 1980s, working-class neighbourhoods along the river were bulldozed to make way for high-rise office buildings and lofts. Modern Docklands is London's answer to Manhattan, a towering cityscape of skyscrapers and coffee franchises.

The redevelopment was inevitable. Labour unrest, the decline of Empire and the development of deep-draught container ships hastened the docks' closure in the 1960s. Today, close to 100,000 people commute to work at Canary Wharf.

Thames Clippers (7001 2222, www. thamesclippers.com) provides daily ferry connections between various jetties in Docklands and through central London. The **Thames Path** (www.nationaltrail.co.uk/thamespath) provides excellent insights into riverside development.

The Isle of Dogs is not an island but the land contained in a prominent loop in the Thames. Many of the docks here played a pivotal role in the development of the British Empire, most notably the **East** and **West India Docks**, which unloaded spices, sugar, tea, rum, coconut fibre and timber from India and the Caribbean well into the 20th century. The area took a pounding during World War II. The story is told at the **Museum of London Docklands** on West India Quay. But it was the development of modern container ships that ultimately spelled doom for the Port of London. By the 1980s the area was so run-down that Stanley Kubrick chose it as a stand-in for war-torn Vietnam in his movie *Full Metal Jacket*.

After two decades of development, the area has been reinvented as a futuristic metropolis, with Japanese-style gardens, perky apartment complexes and subterranean shopping malls

and the elevated DLR snaking through the skyscrapers. The grandest structure here is still Cesar Pelli's **Canary Wharf Tower**, officially known as One Canada Square: at 800 feet, it's been the tallest building in the UK since 1991.

Heading south down the Isle of Dogs, **Island Gardens** offers a gorgeous view across the Thames towards Greenwich. Nearby, you'll find one end of the Victorian **foot tunnel** (lift service 7am-7pm Mon-Sat, 10am-5.30pm Sun) that surfaces beside the *Cutty Sark* on the south bank.

Museum of London Docklands

No.1 Warehouse, West India Quay, Hertsmere Road, E14 4AL (7001 9844, www.museumindocklands. org.uk). Canary Wharf tube/DLR or West India Quay DLR. **Open** 10am-6pm daily. **Admission** free. **Credit** MC, V.
Housed in a 19th-century storehouse, this huge museum explores the complex history of London's docklands over two millennia. Displays take you from the arrival of the Romans all the way to the docks' 1980s closure and the area's subsequent redevelopment. The 'Docklands at War' section is very moving, while a haunting new permanent exhibition sheds light on the dark side of London's rise as a centre for finance and commerce, exploring the city's involvement in the transatlantic slave trade. Allow plenty of time to explore or visit often; tickets are valid for a year.

Museum of London Docklands

Around Town

saturdays

every saturday until 6am

SCV

bcv
barcode vauxhall

69 albert embankment sell bar-code.co.uk fb bar-code

South London

Village people and palace intrigue.

Vauxhall, Stockwell & Brixton

Stockwell tube/Brixton or Vauxhall tube/rail.
Vauxhall has a hedonistic history. Back in the 18th century, the Vauxhall Pleasure Gardens were London's number one playground. With their Chinese pavilion, fountains and lamp-lit lovers' walks, they attracted pleasure-seekers from all walks of life (indeed, Thackeray said they attracted 'loose characters'). The gardens were closed in 1859, but Vauxhall's hedonistic origins live on: in recent years, it has become one of the capital's gay hotspots. Some have christened it London's 'gay village', but this seems a bit of a stretch: it has a handful of gay clubs and bars, but Soho it ain't. That said, if you walk around here on a weekend evening, the streets are almost paved with gay men.

The crumbling **Royal Vauxhall Tavern** (372 Kennington Lane, 7820 1222, www. theroyalvauxhalltavern.co.uk) is the grande dame of the scene, and feels the most villagey; elsewhere it's mostly cavernous megaclubs that don't get going until the wee hours. Behind the tavern lie the paltry remains of the old Pleasure Gardens – a drab park called **Spring Gardens**. Much of the action lies on the other side of the arches, over on Albert Embankment: a new branch of **BarCode** (Arch 69) adds a bit of glam; then there's superclub **Area** (Arch 67) and an outpost of the **Chariots** sauna chain (Arch 63). (For more on Vauxhall bars and clubs, *see p24* **The village people**.) For a glimpse of old Vauxhall, walk south on to lovely, leafy **Bonnington Square**, a bohemian enclave with a café and lavender garden.

Up by the river, MI6's futuristic-looking cream and emerald headquarters dominates the riverbank, as do the green tower blocks at the adjacent St George's Wharf – a glitzy apartment complex justifiably nicknamed the 'five ugly sisters'.

South of Vauxhall, **Stockwell** is commuter land, and there's not much to lure a visitor to its busy main streets, which hold a grim stretch of housing estates (its back streets are lined with Victorian gems). It's also home to **Little Portugal**, a string of shops and tapas bars along South Lambeth Road.

South of Stockwell, you can sense you're approaching **Brixton** before you reach it: the boom-boom-boom of the music, the funky street vibrations – this is as cool as south London gets. It's an interesting, unpredictable district, with late-night clubs and a vibrant Afro-Caribbean community.

Start your Brixton wandering near the chaotic mess of Brixton Station: turn a corner and you're in the noisy craze of the long, colourful **Brixton Market**, which sells everything from kebabs to jewellery and bright African garb.

Be on your guard: there is a lot of drug-related crime here. (Watch your bag as you stroll – purse snatchers and pickpockets are a problem – and take a cab home at night, as homophobia and muggings are not unheard of here.) Despite this, the mood is upbeat, and there is an artsy vibe and a sprinkling of gay people.

For gay action, Brixton may be on the wane, but there is still a gay-friendly bar and café, **SW9** (*see p34*). The **Brixton Academy** is one of London's premier rock venues. For old-school Brixton, check out the splendid 1911 cinema, **Ritzy Picturehouse** (*see p126*).

Kennington

Kennington or Oval tube/Elephant & Castle tube/rail.
Kennington Park is the remains of a common where, during the 18th and 19th centuries, John Wesley and other preachers addressed large audiences. During the summer, the park itself is filled with local gay men sunning themselves – especially at the weekend, when many of them come straight from the after-hours clubs in nearby Vauxhall; a gay couple manage the cute café in the middle of the park. Off Kennington Lane are elegant streets: Cardigan Street and Courtenay Square all have lovely neo-Georgian terraced houses.

Like nearby Oval, Kennington is a popular gay neighbourhood, due in part to it being a short walk from Vauxhall clubland. The **Locker Room** (*see p49*) is a small gay sauna located on a pretty Victorian street here.

Imperial War Museum

Lambeth Road, SE1 6HZ (7416 5000, www.iwm.org.uk).
Lambeth North tube or Elephant & Castle tube/rail.
Open 10am-6pm daily. **Admission** free. **Credit** MC, V.
This heavyweight museum shows off its military might in
the lobby: tanks, planes, submarines and jeeps all salvaged
from past world wars. Beyond the hardware, the awful-
ness of war is exposed. On the lower ground floor, you're
plunged into World War I with its smelly 'Trench
Experience'; World War II features a teeth-chattering 'Blitz
Experience'. The haunting 'Holocaust Exhibition' on the
third floor traces the history of anti-Semitism and the rise
of Hitler; it also includes mention of the gay victims of
the Nazis. On the fourth floor, 'Crimes Against Humanity'
covers genocide and ethnic violence.

Clapham

Clapham Common tube.
Once a hub for the 'Clapham Sect,' a 19th-century
sect of hardcore Christians, today leafy Clapham
is one of south London's most desirable addresses,
although the High Street can be a bit raucous.
Shopping areas include **Abbeville Road** and
Clapham Old Town.

The heart of the neighbourhood is the green
and pleasant **Clapham Common**, an oasis of
peace surrounded by the roar of traffic. During
the summer, the common switches into music
festival mode, attracting thousands to a series
of high-profile events. On sunny days, it's packed
with joggers, footballers and sunbathers; at night,
gay cruisers hit the woods (*see p208* **Fast love**).
However, a spate of violent homophobic attacks
on the Common in recent years, including a
murder, darkened the atmosphere somewhat.

Popular gay watering holes in the Clapham area
include the legendary **Two Brewers** (*see p34*)
and **Kazbar** (*see p34*).

South-west London

Barnes & Kew

Kew Gardens tube/rail/Barnes, Barnes Bridge
or Kew Bridge rail.
The upmarket, riverside village of **Barnes** feels
worlds away from London. The **WWT Wetland
Centre** lies on the other side of **Barnes Common**.
The main road across the expanse, Queen's Ride,
humpbacks over the railway line below. It was
here, on 16 September 1977, that singer Gloria
Jones drove her Mini off the road, killing her
passenger, T-Rex singer Marc Bolan. The slim
trunk of the sycamore tree hit by the car is now
covered with notes, poems and declarations
of love. Steps lead to a bronze bust of the star.

Further west, **Kew**'s leafy streets and rarefied
air is as much a draw as its gardens (properly
known as the **Royal Botanic Gardens**).

Royal Botanic Gardens

Royal Botanic Gardens (Kew Gardens)

Kew, Richmond, Surrey TW9 3AB (8332 5655, www.
kew.org). Kew Gardens tube/rail or Kew Bridge rail/
riverboat to Kew Pier. **Open** *Apr-Aug* 9.30am-6.30pm
Mon-Fri; 9.30am-7.30pm Sat, Sun. *Sept-Oct* 9.30am-6pm
daily. *Late Oct-early Feb* 9.30am-4.15pm daily. *Early
Feb-late Mar* 9.30am-5.30pm daily. **Admission** £13.50;
£11.50 reductions. **Credit** AmEx, MC, V.
Lush Kew Gardens represents the pinnacle of English gardening. Designed in the 1770s by Lancelot 'Capability'
Brown, it was originally a garden for a pair of royal residences: White House and Richmond Lodge, home to
George II and Queen Caroline during the 18th century.
These days, it has several claims to fame: it's got the
world's biggest plant collection, oldest potted palm tree
and largest collection of orchids.

For the most flamboyant floral displays, come in the
spring. In April/May, look out for blossoming lilacs, cherries, crab apples and magnolias or the carpets of bluebells
by Queen Charlotte's cottage; in May/June, the rhododendrons and azaleas are at their peak. The Rose Garden and
Woodland Garden are the stuff of fairy tales. The sultry
Palm House hosts a greatest hits medley of the tropics. The
Temperate House, meanwhile, features the giant pendicu-
lata sanderina, the Holy Grail for orchid hunters. Visit the
Waterlily House (open Apr-Oct) to marvel at the giant
waterlily; its pads can grow to over 8ft in diameter. The
must-see new attraction is the soaring Xstrata Treetop
Walkway: careful if you have vertigo. For an interesting
perspective on 17th-century life, head to Kew Palace
(www.hrp.org.uk/kewpalace, open Apr-Sept, £5, £4.50
reductions) – the smallest royal palace in Britain.

The Kew Explorer train from Victoria Gate offers riders
a 35-minute overview of the gardens. For sustenance, there
are several tea rooms, including the elegant Orangery.

Around Town

Make the most of London life

WWT Wetland Centre

Queen Elizabeth's Walk, SW13 9WT (8409 4400, www.wwt.org.uk). Hammersmith tube then 209, 283 bus, Barnes rail or 33, 72 bus. **Open** *Mar-Oct* 9.30am-6pm daily (last entry 5pm). *Nov-Feb* 9.30am-5pm daily (last entry 4pm). **Admission** £9.95; £7.40 reductions. **Credit** MC, V.

A mere four miles from central London, the WWT Wetland Centre feels worlds away. This marshy oasis – ponds, rushes, rustling reeds and wildflower gardens – is an avian five-star hotel. Inhabiting old reservoirs, the teeming bird life (150 species at last count) sends twitchers into fits of ecstasy. Botanists ponder its 27,000 trees and 300,000 plants; naturalists swoon at the butterflies, dragonflies and frogs. The visitors' centre has a waterside café.

Battersea

Clapham Junction rail.

Once a small Saxon farming settlement, Battersea is now home to a large yuppie population. The most distinctive piece of industrial architecture is **Battersea Power Station**, Sir Giles Gilbert Scott's iconic 1933 structure, long derelict, though there have been plans to develop it. **Battersea Park** was re-landscaped to match its Victorian splendour. Today, the riverside promenades, Peace Pagoda, boating lake and fountains all look lovely. There's a small art gallery too (Pumphouse Gallery, 7350 0523, www.pumphousegallery.org.uk).

Wimbledon

Wimbledon tube/rail.

The main attractions in this sleepy, leafy suburb are a string of posh boutiques in **Wimbledon Village**, the wild green expanse of **Wimbledon Common** and the **Wimbledon Lawn Tennis Museum** at the All England Club. The famous annual tennis championships take place during the last week of June and the first week of July.

Wimbledon Lawn Tennis Museum

Museum Building, All England Lawn Tennis Club, Church Road, SW19 5AE (8946 6131, www.wimbledon. org/museum). Southfields tube or 39, 493 bus. **Open** 10.30am-5pm daily; ticket holders only during championships. **Admission** (incl tour) £18; £15.75. **Credit** MC, V.

Highlights at this museum on the history of tennis include a 200° cinema screen that allows you to find out what it's like to play on Centre Court and a re-creation of a 1980s men's dressing room, complete with a 'ghost' of John McEnroe. Visitors can get to grips with rackets, check changing fashions and take a behind-the-scenes tour.

Richmond

Richmond tube/rail.

Despite the constant roar of planes overhead, Richmond retains much of its villagey charm. From the high street, antiquated alleyways (such as Brewer's Lane) filled with tiny boutiques lead to **Richmond Green**, bordered by ancient pubs and the elegant **Richmond Theatre**.

The riverside promenade is very pretty. It's dotted with pubs, but Richmond's pièce de résistance is the ruggedly beautiful **Richmond Park**. The largest park in London, it's one of the last vestiges of the magnificent oak woodland that once encircled the city, and is a great place for rambling and cycling. Buildings include the Palladian splendour of White Lodge; Isabella

Battersea Power Station

Greenwich Park

Plantation offers a winding walk through its landscaped gardens, full of rhododendrons and azaleas (May is the month to visit).

Ham House

Ham, Richmond, Surrey TW10 7RS (8940 1950, www.nationaltrust.org.uk/hamhouse). Richmond tube/ rail then 371 bus. **Open** *Gardens* Jan 11am-4pm Sat, Sun. mid Feb-Oct 11am-5pm Mon-Wed, Sat, Sun. Nov, Dec 11am-5pm Sat, Sun. *House* mid Mar-Oct noon-4pm Mon-Wed, Sat, Sun. **Admission** *House & gardens* £10.40. *Gardens only* £3.50. **Credit** MC, V.
Built in 1610 for one of James I's courtiers, this lavish red-brick mansion is one of the most outstanding Stuart properties in the country. The grand interior is filled with period furnishings such as rococo mirrors and ornate tapestries. The formal grounds, featuring a trellised cherry garden and a statue of Bacchus, attract the most attention.

Further south-west

Hampton Court Palace

East Molesey, Surrey KT8 9AU (0844 482 7777, www.hrp.org.uk). Hampton Court rail, or riverboat from Westminster or Richmond to Hampton Court Pier (Apr-Oct). **Open** *Palace* Apr-Oct 10am-6pm daily. Nov-Mar 10am-4.30pm daily. *Park* dawn-dusk daily. **Admission** *Palace, courtyard, cloister & maze* £14; £11.50. *Maze only* £3.50. *Gardens only* Apr-Oct £4.60; £4 reductions. Nov-Feb free. **Credit** AmEx, MC, V.
Remembered for chopping off Anne Boleyn's head, having six wives and bringing about the English Reformation, Henry VIII is one of English history's most unforgettable monarchs. And this Tudor palace – nicknamed 'Magnificence-upon-Thames' – is a suitably spectacular monument to the king. Built in 1514, it still dazzles five

centuries later. But its vast size can be daunting, so take advantage of the audio guides. A good place to start is Henry VIII's State Apartments, which include the Great Hall with its fine hammer-beam roof and stained glass windows. The King's Apartments, added in 1689 by Sir Christopher Wren, are notable for a splendid mural of Alexander the Great, painted by Antonio Verrio. The Queen's Apartments and Georgian Rooms feature similarly elaborate paintings, chandeliers and tapestries. The Tudor Kitchens are great fun, with their giant cauldrons and fake pies. But the palace's most spectacular sights are the exquisitely landscaped gardens (and the famous maze). In summer there's a music festival and a flower show; in winter check out the ice-skating rink.

Marble Hill House

Richmond Road, Twickenham, Middx TW1 2NL (8892 5115, www.english-heritage.org.uk). Richmond tube/rail, St Margaret's rail or 33, 90, 490, H22, R70 bus. **Open** *Apr-Oct* 10am-2pm Sat; 10am-5pm Sun; group visits Mon-Fri by request. *Nov-Mar* by request. **Admission** £5; £4.30 reductions. **Credit** MC, V.
King George II built this perfect Palladian house (1724) for his lover Henrietta Howard. The likes of Alexander Pope, Jonathan Swift and Horace Walpole were entertained in its opulent rooms. A seasonal foot/bike ferry regularly crosses the river to Ham House.

World Rugby Museum/ Twickenham Stadium

Twickenham Rugby Stadium, Rugby Road, Twickenham, Middx TW1 1DZ (8892 8877, www.rfu.com). Hounslow East tube then 281 bus or Twickenham rail. **Open** *Museum* 10am-5pm Tue-Sat; 11am-5pm Sun. *Tours* 10.30am, noon, 1.30pm, 3pm Tue-Sat; 1pm, 3pm Sun. **Admission** £14; £8 reductions. **Credit** AmEx, MC, V.

Tours of the stadium, the home of English rugby union, take in the dressing room ('sights, sounds and smells'), so you can indulge your Lawrence 'Thighs' Dallaglio fantasies. The museum charts the game's development.

South-east London

Greenwich

Cutty Sark DLR/Greenwich DLR/rail.

With its handsome Georgian and Regency architecture, Greenwich earned its smart reputation when it was a playground for Tudor royalty. Henry VIII and his daughters Mary I and Elizabeth I were all born here – Greenwich Palace was Henry's favourite residence. The palace fell into disrepair under Cromwell, later became the Royal Naval Hospital, and is now the Old Royal Naval College.

If you take a riverboat to Greenwich, you will disembark at the pier. It is beside the tarp-covered work-in-progress that is, sadly, the *Cutty Sark* (www.cuttysark.org.uk). This historic vessel, the fastest sailing tea clipper ever to ride the ocean wave, was devastated by fire in 2007, but it is being restored for 2011. The **Greenwich Foot Tunnel**, which takes you under the Thames to Island Gardens and Docklands, is also here. The **Greenwich Visitor Centre** (0870 608 2000) is based in the Pepys Building at the Old Royal Naval College and is a useful first port of call.

Busy **Greenwich Market** pulls in the tourists at weekends, but the area's loveliest parts are away from the centre, either along the pub-dotted riverside walk or around expansive **Greenwich Park**, with the Wren-designed **Royal Observatory** at the top of the hill and the **National Maritime Museum** and **Queen's House** at the bottom. Greenwich doesn't really have a gay scene, but it does boast a gay pub – the **George & Dragon** (*see p33*), not to be confused with the fashionable Shoreditch watering hole – and a gay guesthouse, **St Alfeges** (*see p62*).

National Maritime Museum

Romney Road, SE10 9NF (8858 4422, 8312 6565 information, 8312 6608 tours, www.nmm.ac.uk). Cutty Sark DLR or Greenwich DLR/rail. **Open** 10am-5pm daily. *Tours* phone for details. **Admission** free; donations appreciated. **Credit** (shop) MC, V.

The world's largest maritime museum opened in 1937. It contains a huge store of maritime art, cartography, models and regalia. Ground-level galleries include 'Passengers', an exploration of the 20th-century fashion for cruise travel, as well as the story of mass emigration by sea. 'Explorers' covers the great sea expeditions since medieval times. 'Maritime London' concentrates on the city as a port. Upstairs, 'Your Ocean' reveals our dependence on the health of the world's oceans, while 'Nelson's Navy' exhibits more than 250 objects of naval memorabilia from this period.

Old Royal Naval College

Greenwich, SE10 9LW (8269 4747, 8269 4791 group tours, www.oldroyalnavalcollege.org.uk). Cutty Sark DLR or Greenwich DLR/rail. **Open** 10am-5pm daily. *Tours* by arrangement. **Admission** free. **Credit** MC, V.

Designed by Sir Christopher Wren in 1694, with Hawksmoor and Vanbrugh helping to complete the project, this superb collection of buildings was originally a hospital for the relief and support of seamen and their dependants. The complex of buildings became the Royal Naval College in 1873, until the Navy left in 1998. Now the neoclassical buildings house part of the University of Greenwich and Trinity College of Music. The public are allowed into the rococo chapel, where there are free organ recitals, and the lavish Painted Hall. In the Pepys building – now the visitor centre – the £10m Discover Greenwich museum opened in March 2010, with exhibitions about Henry VIII's life in Greenwich, a history of the Royal Navy and architectural displays featuring Inigo Jones, Nicholas Hawksmoor and Christopher Wren.

Queen's House

Romney Road, SE10 9NF (8312 6565, www.nmm.ac.uk). Cutty Sark DLR or Greenwich DLR/rail. **Open** 10am-5pm daily. *Tours* noon, 2.30pm. **Admission** free; occasional charge for temporary exhibitions. *Tours* free. **Credit** (over £5) MC, V.

The National Maritime Museum's art collection is displayed in this house, once the summer villa for Charles I's queen, Henrietta Maria. It was completed in 1638 by Inigo Jones and its interior is as impressive as the paintings. It has a stunning 1635 marble floor and the first centrally unsupported spiral stair in Britain (called the tulip stair). The art collection includes portraits of famous maritime figures and works by Hogarth and Gainsborough.

Dulwich Picture Gallery. *See p224.*

Around Town

Ranger's House

Chesterfield Walk, SE10 8QX (8853 0035, www. english-heritage.org.uk). Blackheath rail or Cutty Sark DLR/53 bus. **Open** *Apr-Sept* 10am-4.30pm Mon-Wed, Sun. *Oct-Dec* group bookings only. **Admission** £6; £5.10 reductions. **Credit** MC, V.

The house of the 'Ranger of Greenwich Park', a post held by George III's niece, Princess Sophia Matilda, from 1815, now contains the collection of treasure amassed by German diamond magnate Julius Wernher. He collected medieval and Renaissance art, including jewellery, bronzes, tapestries, furniture, porcelain and paintings. It's all displayed in 12 lovely rooms in this Georgian villa, whose back garden is the Greenwich Park rose collection.

Royal Observatory & Planetarium

Greenwich Park, SE10 9NF (8312 6565, www.rog. nmm.ac.uk). Cutty Sark DLR or Greenwich DLR/rail. **Open** 10am-5pm daily. *Tours* phone for details. **Admission** *Observatory* free. *Planetarium* £6.50; £4.50 reductions. **Credit** MC, V.

Built for Charles II by Wren in 1675, this observatory examines the life of Royal Astronomer John Flamsteed, with a series of set-piece rooms evoking his household. In the courtyard is the Prime Meridian Line – star of a billion snaps of tourists with a foot in each hemisphere. There are clocks and watches, from hourglasses to an atomic clock, in the new Time Galleries. Shows in the planetarium (see website for details) include 'Black Holes: The Other Side of Infinity', narrated by hunk of burning love Liam Neeson, and 'Starlife', which looks at the birth and death of stars.

Woolwich

Charlton or Woolwich Dockyard rail/Woolwich Arsenal DLR/rail.

Firepower

Royal Arsenal, SE18 6ST (8855 7755, www.firepower. org.uk). Woolwich Arsenal DLR/rail. **Open** 10.30am-5pm Wed-Sun. **Admission** £5; £4.50 reductions. **Credit** MC, V.

The Royal Artillery Museum is a must-see for devotees of military hardware. Exhibits trace the evolution of artillery from primitive catapults to nuclear warheads. Galleries include the Gunnery Hall (howitzers and tanks), the Real Weapons gallery and the Cold War gallery.

Thames Barrier Information & Learning Centre

1 Unity Way, SE18 5NJ (8305 4188, www. environment-agency.gov.uk/thamesbarrier). North Greenwich tube, Charlton rail or 180 bus. **Open** *Apr-Sept* 10.30am-4.30pm daily. *Oct-Mar* 11am-3.30pm daily. **Admission** *Exhibition* £3.50; £3 reductions. **Credit** MC, V.

The world's largest adjustable dam was completed in 1982 at a cost of £535m. It's quite a sight: the nine shiny metal piers, which resemble a cross between sharks' fins and the Sydney Opera House, anchor massive steel gates that can be raised to protect London from surge tides. The visitors' centre shows how the barrier works and the bits of London that would be submerged if it didn't. The best way to see the barrier is by boat: Thames River Services (7930 4097) runs trips from Greenwich (Mar-Oct only).

Dulwich & Crystal Palace

Crystal Palace, East Dulwich, Herne Hill, North Dulwich or West Dulwich rail.

Comfortable Dulwich Village is home to a boys' public school, a lovely park and the **Dulwich Picture Gallery**. South of here, leafy **Crystal Palace Park** no longer has its crystal palace – it burned down in 1936 – but its Victorian-era dinosaurs still sit around the landscaped lakes. In nearby Forest Hill, the astonishing **Horniman Museum** (100 London Road, 8699 1872, www. horniman.co.uk) is crammed with curiosities collected by a Victorian traveller, with an emphasis on natural history, anthropology and musical instruments. Further south-east, in commuter land, suburban Bexleyheath is where the founder of the Arts and Crafts movement, William Morris, settled in the **Red House**. Eltham, where gay icons Boy George and Frankie Howerd grew up, boasts magnificent **Eltham Palace**.

Dulwich Picture Gallery

Gallery Road, SE21 7AD (8693 5254, www. dulwichpicturegallery.org.uk). North Dulwich or West Dulwich rail. **Open** 10am-5pm Tue-Fri; 11am-5pm Sat, Sun. **Admission** £5; £4 reductions; free students. **Credit** MC, V.

Sir John Soane's neoclassical building was the first public art gallery. Inside is a roll-call of greats: Rubens, Van Dyck, Cuyp, Poussin, Raphael and Reynolds.

Eltham Palace

Court Yard, SE9 5QE (8294 2548, www.english-heritage.org.uk). Eltham rail. **Open** *Apr-Oct* 10am-5pm Mon-Wed, Sun. *Nov-Dec, Feb-Mar* 11am-4pm Mon-Wed, Sun. Closed Jan. **Admission** *House & grounds* (incl audio tour) £8.70; £7.40 reductions. *Grounds only* £5.60; £4.80 reductions. **Credit** MC, V.

Built in the 13th century, the original palace was a royal residence until Henry VIII's heyday. But it soon fell into disrepair. In 1931, it came back under public gaze, thanks to Stephen and Virginia Courtauld, who built a luxurious art deco house to stand among the ruins of the old palace. The Great Hall, with its stained glass and hammer-beam roof, is all that's left of the original. The new house is a stunning example of 1930s, high-society glamour, with its deco furniture and accents.

Red House

13 Red House Lane, Bexleyheath, Kent DA6 8JF (booking line 8304 9878, www.nationaltrust.org.uk). Bexleyheath rail then 15min walk or taxi from station. **Open** *Mar-Nov* 11am-5pm Wed-Sun. *Dec* 11am-4.45pm Fri-Sun. *Tours* phone for details. **Admission** *Tour* £7.60. *Garden only* 50p. **Credit** MC, V.

This handsome red-brick house was built (by Philip Webb) in 1859 for William Morris, whose Society for the Protection of Ancient Buildings gave rise to the National Trust. When furnishing it, Morris combined his taste for Gothic romanticism with the need for practical domesticity. Beautifully detailed stained glass, tiling, paintings and items of furniture remain in the house.

West London

West side story.

Regent's Canal. *See p226.*

Around Town

Back in the 1970s, west London – more specifically, Earl's Court – was the centre of London's gay universe. The gay village has since migrated east to Soho, but the area still retains a queer vibe. The rest of west London, however, is a tad sedate. Because, for all the talk about the north–south divide (London's most touted psycho-geographical distinction), the east–west one is more telling. London's west is perceived as less 'happening' than the east: more metropolitan but less urban; fashionable rather than cool.

Paddington, Maida Vale & Bayswater

Maps p262 & p263

Bayswater, Lancaster Gate, Queensway, Maida Vale or Warwick Avenue tube/Paddington tube/rail.
The fact that a certain small, Peruvian bear who immortalised **Paddington** was an émigré is appropriate, given that the area has long served as a home to refugees and immigrants.

But the district owes its name to an Anglo-Saxon chieftain named Padda. For centuries just a rural backwater, the neighbourhood's identity changed with the building of Paddington Station in 1838 (the original station was replaced in 1851 by the magnificent structure designed by Isambard Kingdom Brunel). The area soon descended into seediness, plagued by overcrowding and poverty in Victorian times. The grim situation prevailed throughout the 20th century, but today, those behind the massive Paddington Waterside project, one of the most high-profile urban regeneration projects in Europe, are giving the area a major facelift. Just east of the station, in the Alexander Fleming Laboratory Museum in **St Mary's Hospital** (Praed Street, 7886 6528, www.imperial.nhs.uk), you can explore the room where penicillin was discovered in 1928.

Running north-west from Marble Arch, the undeviating progress of **Edgware Road** gives a clue to its provenance: yes, the Romans laid it. The road's southernmost end – up to Praed Street – is interesting for its colourful collection of Middle

Eastern businesses, including excellent kebab shops. Further north, it changes its name, first to **Maida Vale** and then Kilburn High Road. It's affluent round here, and prettified immensely by the canal-fronted area known as **Little Venice**. From here, you can walk or take a waterbus down **Regent's Canal** to London Zoo (*see p181*).

To the south and west of Paddington, **Bayswater** was fashionable during Victorian times when the well-to-do snapped up its smart houses on pretty squares. These days the area is a mishmash of grubby hotels and touristy shops and restaurants, centred on the main drag, **Queensway**. It's a great place for skaters: for ice there's Queens Ice Bowl; for rollerblading in Hyde Park, you can rent a pair at London Skate Centre (27 Leinster Terrace, 7706 8769, www.lonskate.com). At the southern edge runs Bayswater Road, a tree-lined street facing Hyde Park. A blue plaque to Sir James Barrie, of *Peter Pan* fame, adorns no.100.

At the top of Queensway, a right turn leads to the 1929 **Porchester Spa** (7792 3980, www.courtneys.co.uk), one of the few surviving examples of the Victorian Turkish baths that once proliferated in Britain. This art deco spa is not gay, but there can be homoerotic undercurrents on male-only days: Monday, Wednesday and Saturday. Or head left for trendy **Westbourne Grove**, where a number of reliable Middle Eastern restaurants give way to more varied options at the Notting Hill end.

Portobello Market

Notting Hill

Map p262

Ladbroke Grove, Notting Hill Gate or Westbourne Park tube.
Initially farmland, old Knottynghull has gone from gracious (18th century), via poor working class (1950s) and bohemian (1960s-'80s), to astronomically expensive (no thanks to the blockbuster film *Notting Hill*).

From Notting Hill Gate, follow Pembridge Road to **Portobello Road**, a narrow winding street that's home to cafés, bars, restaurants, delis and shops, the **Electric Cinema** (no.191, 7908 9696, www.electriccinema.co.uk) and, towards the northern end on Fridays and Saturdays, a flea market with hip vintage clothes and accessories. Some of the area's best shops are just off Portobello Road. At its northern end, for instance, Golborne Road has fine antiques shops and Portuguese pâtisseries such as the **Lisboa** (no.57, 8968 5242).

Just to the east, the posh end of **Westbourne Grove** has a good selection of boutiques, antiques shops and galleries, organic haven Fresh & Wild and, particularly on **Ledbury Road**, chic clothes shops. There's also the unique **Museum of Brands, Packaging & Advertising** (2 Colville Mews, Lonsdale Road, 7908 0880, www.museumofbrands.com), which aims to show how people's lives have changed over the past 200 years through the evolution of consumer brands.

Besides the film, Notting Hill is most famous for the annual **Notting Hill Carnival**, usually held on the last weekend in August. The event was introduced in 1959 as a celebration of the newly arrived West Indian immigrants (though most of said immigrants have been priced out of the area).

Rather quieter is the famously spooky **Kensal Green Cemetery** (Harrow Road, 8969 0152, www.kensalgreen.co.uk), at the top end of Ladbroke Grove. It's the final resting place for Thackeray, Trollope and Wilkie Collins.

The **Westbourne Park** area is scruffy but hip, particularly the quirky little boutiques clustered around All Saints Road.

Kensington & Holland Park

Maps p262 & p264

High Street Kensington or Holland Park tube.
From rich farmland listed in the *Domesday Book* of 1086, to the description by one historian in 1705 as a place 'inhabited by gentry and persons of note', **Kensington** is as smart today as it's always been.

Kensington High Street offers a decent mix of shops, while the surrounding streets and squares are lined by imposing townhouses. The most famous square, Kensington Square, sports plaques for such distinguished former residents as Thackeray (no.16) and John Stuart Mill (no.18). Nearby, there's a plaque to camp comedian Frankie Howerd at 27 Edwardes Square.

Kensington Church Street is peppered with shops selling antique furniture. St Mary Abbots, at the bottom of the street, is a superb Victorian neo-Gothic church built by Sir George Gilbert Scott in 1869-72. It has the tallest spire in London (250 feet), as well as fine stained-glass windows.

Further west is romantic Holland Park; its woods and formal gardens surround the reconstructed Jacobean Holland House, named after an early owner, Sir Henry, Earl of Holland. The house suffered serious bomb damage during World War II; the restored east wing contains the most dramatically sited youth hostel (see p81) in the capital, and the summer ballroom has been converted into a restaurant. Open-air operas are staged in the park under a canopy during the summer. Three beautiful formal gardens are located close to the house; a bit further away is the Japanese-style Kyoto Garden, with huge koi carp and a charming bridge at the foot of a waterfall. Among the noteworthy historic houses close by are Leighton House and Linley Sambourne House.

18 Stafford Terrace

18 Stafford Terrace, W8 7BH (7471 9160 Mon-Fri, 7938 1295 Sat, Sun, www.rbkc.gov.uk/subsites/museums.aspx). High Street Kensington tube. Open Sept-June by appointment only. Admission £6; £4 reductions. Credit MC, V. Map p264 A9.
The Italianate home of cartoonist Edward Linley Sambourne was built in the 1870s and all of its fashionable period fittings and furniture are original. Tours must be booked in advance; they last one and a half hours, with weekend tours led by an actor in period costume.

Leighton House

12 Holland Park Road, W14 8LZ (7602 3316, www.rbkc.gov.uk/leightonhousemuseum). High Street Kensington tube. Open 10am-5.30pm Mon, Wed-Sun. *Tours* 3pm Wed. Admission £5; £1 reductions. *Tours* £8. Credit MC, V. Map p264 A9.
This gorgeous Victorian house was originally the residence and studio of Victorian artist Frederic, Lord Leighton (1830-96). From without, it presents a sternly Victorian façade of red-brick respectability. But inside it's like a scene from the Arabian Nights, complete with tinkling fountain, exotic mosaics and golden friezes. These highly decorative rooms and halls are adorned with his paintings and drawings, including The Death of Brunelleschi. Other works of art are by contemporaries such as John Everett Millais and Edward Burne-Jones.

Roof Gardens

99 Kensington High Street, W8 5SA (7937 7994, www.roofgardens.virgin.com). High Street Kensington tube. Open phone for details. Admission free. Map p264 B9.
A rooftop oasis in West London, the Roof Gardens are one of London's best-kept secrets. Established in 1936 on the roof of the old Derry & Tom's department store, they are now used mostly for corporate entertaining, but (as long as they're not booked for an event; call ahead to check) they are open to all: simply take the lift up and emerge to find water gurgling into a brook. Follow the stream through a woodland garden, complete with trees rooted 100ft above the ground, past pools and over bridges. To complete the exotic scene, a pair of Lesser Chilean flamingos sieve for crustaceans alongside various ducks.

Earl's Court & Fulham

Map p264

Earl's Court, Fulham Broadway tube/West Brompton tube/rail.
Once a gay mecca, Earl's Court has gone a bit straight – not to mention Australian (the place is nicknamed Kangaroo Court because of all the Aussie backpackers who congregate in the cheap hotels and hostels). The closure of two gay bars in recent years, the iconic Coleherne and Brompton's, hasn't helped. But there's still a fair number of people for whom this will always be 'Girls Court', as local trolley dollies are given to saying. On Old Brompton Road, for instance, there are still a couple of gay haunts: Clone Zone (see p110 Buy sexual) and a branch of Balans restaurant. Around the corner, Adonis Art (1b Coleherne Road, 3417 0238, www.adonisartgallery.com) sells in-your-face oil paintings of nude men.

Nearby Brompton Cemetery, just south-east of Earl's Court Station, is a popular, if ghoulish, cruising ground – and apparently subject to police sting operations (they've even trimmed back the bushes to reduce opportunities for hanky panky). If you're more interested in stonemasonry

Around Town

than sex, this huge Victorian burial ground features grand funereal architecture. It's also the final resting place of suffragette Emmeline Pankhurst. Speaking of icons, Earl's Court was once home to a gay legend: Queen's Freddie Mercury lived in Logan Place before moving to Stafford Terrace in the 1980s. But the area's regal associations go back much further: it was once owned by the earls of Warwick and Holland, who built a courthouse here, hence the name.

Grand landowners notwithstanding, the area was a mere hamlet until the 1860s, when the Metropolitan Railway purchased farmland to build Earl's Court Station. A fairground was built in 1887, including the country's first – and the world's largest – Ferris wheel. Today, the site hosts the gigantic **Earl's Court Exhibition Centre**, site of numerous trade fairs.

During the early 1900s, many of Earl's Court's residential properties were turned into flats, drawing a large immigrant population to the area. Back then, rents were cheap. But, as any urban planner will tell you, once gays colonise a neighbourhood it becomes gentrified – sure enough, Earl's Court is no longer the real-estate bargain it once was (though there's still a good clutch of decently priced hotels; *see pp79-80*).

Nearby neighbourhoods **Parsons Green** and **Fulham** are both affluent. The former is centred around a small green that once supported, well,

a parsonage, as long ago as 1391. Nearby is the **Queen's Club**, where the pre-Wimbledon Stella Artois tennis tournament is held. Also in the area is **Fulham Palace**, which is inside pretty **Bishop's Park**, adjacent to the Thames.

Fulham Palace & Museum

Bishop's Avenue, off Fulham Palace Road, SW6 6EA (7736 8140, www.fulhampalace.org). Putney Bridge tube or 14, 74, 220, 414, 430 bus. **Open** *Museum* 1-4pm Mon-Wed, Sat, Sun. *Gallery varies; phone for details. Gardens dawn-dusk daily. Tours* 2pm 2nd & 4th Sun of mth; 2pm 3rd Thur of mth. **Admission** free. Tours £5. **No credit cards**.

The foundations of Fulham Palace can be traced back to 704. But the present building was built in Tudor times (try out the echo in the courtyard), with later significant Georgian and Victorian additions. It would be more accurate to call it a manor house than a palace, but it gives a fine glimpse into the changing lifestyles and architecture of nearly 500 years from the Tudor hall to the Victorian chapel (the building served as the episcopal retreat for the Bishops of London from the Middle Ages until 1975). There's also access to a glorious stretch of riverside walk, and the overgrown botanic gardens will soon be restored. Overlooking a secluded and beautiful expanse of grass and mature trees, Oliver Peyton's new Lawn restaurant is a beauty. Best of all, these delights remain undiscovered by the majority of Londoners.

Shepherd's Bush & Hammersmith

Goldhawk Road, Hammersmith or Shepherd's Bush Market tube/Shepherd's Bush tube/rail.

BBC Television Centre Tours

TV Centre, Wood Lane, W12 7RJ (0370 603 0304, www.bbc.co.uk/tours). White City or Wood Lane tube. **Tours** by appointment only Mon-Sat. **Admission** £9.95; £8.95 reductions; £7.50 students. **Credit** MC, V.

Tours of the BBC include visits to the news desk, the TV studios and the Weather Centre and more, though you must book ahead to secure a place. To be part of a TV audience when a show is being recorded for TV or radio, log on to www.bbc.co.uk/tickets.

Chiswick

Turnham Green tube/Chiswick rail.

Chiswick House

Burlington Lane, W4 2RP (8995 0508, www.chgt. org.uk). Hammersmith tube/rail then 190 bus, or Chiswick rail. **Open** *Apr* 10am-5pm daily. *May-Oct* 10am-5pm Mon-Wed, Sun. **Admission** £5; £4.30 reduction. **Credit** MC, V.

The cream of artistic society – Pope, Swift, Handel – hung out at this lovely Palladian villa, designed by the third Earl of Burlington in 1725. The gorgeous reception rooms connect with a magnificent, domed central salon.

Leighton House. *See p227.*

Brighton

A gay getaway beside the seaside.

Brighton is a seaside city with a reputation that far exceeds its size. It's known as 'the gay capital of the UK', and 'London by the sea'. Both seem apt. It has a huge lesbian and gay population. But this is not something that exists in a vacuum. Brightonians pride themselves on being liberal, easy-going and ever-so alternative: thus it came as little surprise that it was the constituency of Brighton Pavilion that elected Britain's first Green Party MP, Caroline Lucas, in the 2010 General Election.

Many gay men who now live here say they once came down on a visit, realised this was a place that was unlike any other in otherwise uptight old England, and decided they wanted to stay.

One of its main attractions is that it is most definitely not a 'gay ghetto'. Lesbians and gay men will invariably be out to their workmates, friends and neighbours. Most bars and clubs, certainly in the centre of town, are neither gay nor straight, just healthily mixed. Nor is Brighton's 'gay village', centred around St James's Street, a gay enclave; as they are in, say, Manchester or Birmingham. It's a rather ordinary-looking shopping street dotted with rather a lot of gay bars, clubs and shops.

The reasons why Brighton became such a gay magnet are hazy. Were gay men drawn to its most iconic building, the Royal Pavilion? This delightfully bizarre piece of orientalist kitsch was built in the late 18th century by Prince George (later King George IV), a notorious womaniser and bon viveur. George may have set the 'anything goes' tone of the town that grew up around it. Tellingly, the prudish Queen Victoria literally disowned the Pavilion after George died, and sold the building to the townspeople.

British gay men have often gravitated to seaside resorts. But unlike Bournemouth or Blackpool, Brighton's proximity to London has always given it a sophisticated air. When foreign holidays became popular and affordable in the '60s and '70s, the tourist trade subsided. But it was still a popular destination for 'dirty weekends'. The novelist Keith Waterhouse famously wrote: 'The beautiful thing about Brighton is that you can buy your lover a pair of knickers at

Royal Pavillion.
See p230.

Victoria station and have them off again at the Grand Hotel in less than two hours.'

In 1961, Sussex University opened. Once a hotbed of radical activism, it later gave birth to Sussex Gay Liberation Front, one of the first such groups outside London. The town of Brighton was then somewhat down at heel – and cheap to live in. Much of **North Laine**, just south of the station, was squats. This bohemian legacy can still be felt in this bustling pedestrianised area, with its vegan cafés and New Agey shops; some call this 'Glastonbury by the sea'. It's also now home to a number of idiosyncratic shops selling everything from handmade suits to funky retro second-hand clothes, plus all kinds of knowing kitsch, rare records and dusty books.

Its near namesake, **the Lanes**, is a network of narrow cobbled alleyways, containing a wealth of jewellery and antique shops, but also some dreadful tourist tat.

Out of Town

Brighton Pier

If you're keen on ticking off the tourist sites, a few places stand out: **Brighton Pier**, a noisy clutter of hotdog stands, karaoke, candyfloss and fairground rides; the aforementioned **Royal Pavilion** (4-5 Pavilion Buildings, BN1 1EE, 03000 290 900, www.royalpavilion.org.uk); and the **Sea Life Centre** (Marine Parade, BN2 1TB, 0871 423 2110, www.sealife.co.uk), a Victorian aquarium. For a bit of culture, stop by the **Brighton Museum & Art Gallery** (4-5 Pavilion Buildings, BN1 1EE, 03000 290 900). Its permanent exhibitions on the history of the town integrate lesbian and gay life deftly.

The beach is probably the city's biggest draw, even if it is pebbly, and packed on sunny weekends. Brightonians like to mock the 'DFLs' (Down From Londons) – the straight lads who come down in summer, plonk themselves on the first bit of beach they see, and drink endless pints of strong lager while the sun turns them as pink as a lobster. It's easy to avoid them, just walk five minutes away in either direction from the Pier.

The seven miles of uninterrupted coastline, flanked by a promenade, are a prime spot for walking, reflecting – and cruising. The eastern edge of the beach, near the rather tacky Marina, is officially nude, but invariably empty. The winding paths of the hillside behind it form Brighton's most famous cruising ground, Duke's Mound. Known as 'the Bushes', it's busy for pick-ups during the day and much wilder after dark, with strangers writhing in the undergrowth. But be careful, as gay-friendly as Brighton is, gay-bashings are not uncommon, and most of them seem to take place here. On the opposite side of town is the nocturnal takeaway; Hove Lawns, which is just west of what's left of the West Pier. If you haven't pulled in the clubs, roam the seafront here until you meet a kindred spirit.

For indoor games, try the saunas: the **Amsterdam** (*see right*), **Bright & Beautiful** (9 St Margaret's Place, 01273 328 330), or **TBS2 Sauna** (86 Denmark Villas, Hove, 01273 723 733, www.tbs2.com). Though all are smallish; oddly, saunas don't seem to be that big in Brighton.

For less clandestine liaisons, **Pride in Brighton & Hove** (*see p232* **Proud Marys**) takes place on the first Saturday in August, and attracts more than 100,000 revellers, who seem to have the time of their lives. It could be the biggest Pride event in the country, and is possibly the best loved. The whole city comes to a halt to cheer, to take part and to party, as if it's this city's own 'national holiday'. Which, for Brighton – the gay capital of the UK – seems touchingly appropriate.

For tourist information, contact the **Tourist Information Centre** (Royal Pavilion Shop,

4-5 Pavilion Buildings, BN1 1EE, 0300 300 0088, www.visitbrighton.com) or visit www.realbrighton.com; be sure to pick up a free 'Gay Brighton Map'.

Where to stay

Wherever you stay, book well ahead. The Tourist Information Centre (*see above*) operates a reservation service. Most hotels in Brighton are gay-friendly (they have to be). But for gay-owned hotels, visit www.gaydealsbrighton.co.uk, which offers discounts for midweek stays.

There are a huge number of smaller hotels on the streets around the St James's Street gay village, with cheap B&Bs nestling next to swanky boutique hotels. One good gay-owned hotel is the **New Steine** (12A New Steine, BN2 1PB, 01273 681 546, www.newsteinehotel.com, doubles £49-£105), a cosy, eclectic guesthouse in a rather grand Georgian townhouse. For sceney hotels, the **Amsterdam** (11-12 Marine Parade, BN2 1TL, 01273 688 825, www.amsterdam.uk.com, doubles £70-£180) is at the heart of all the action, with a sauna in the basement and a terrace bar; the **Legends Hotel** (31-34 Marine Parade, BN2 1TR, 01273 624 462, www.legendsbrighton.com, doubles from £75) is another destination for scene queens, with a late bar and a popular club in the basement. If you crave – and can afford – old-fashioned luxury, book the **Grand** (97-99 King's Road, BN1 2FW, 01273 224 300, www.grandbrighton.co.uk, doubles £165-£305), where Maggie Thatcher almost met her maker in the 1984 Brighton bombing. The **Royal Albion** (35 Old Steine, BN1 1NT, 01273 329 202, www.royal-albion-hotel.co.uk, doubles £45-£220) is a huge Regency hotel where Oscar Wilde used to stay with Bosie. At the other end of the scale, try one of the **Grapevine**'s two locations (75-76 Middle Street, BN1 1AL, 01273 777 717, and 29-30 North Road, BN1 1YB, 01273 703 985, www.grapevinewebsite.co.uk, dorm £12.50-£15).

Blanch House
17 Atlingworth Street, BN2 1PL (01273 603 504, www.blanchhouse.co.uk). **Rates** £130-£230 double. **Rooms** 12. **Credit** AmEx, MC, V.
The epitome of Brighton hip, this designer hotel also has a sleek bar and restaurant. Its stylish themed rooms (all en suite) zip across eras, places and styles, from rococo to Renaissance, India to Morocco, suburbia to snowstorms.

Brightonwave Hotel
10 Madeira Place, BN2 1TN (01273 676 794, www.brightonwave.com). **Rooms** 8. **Credit** AmEx, MC, V.
This gay-owned guesthouse is chic and attractive, but unpretentious. Set in the gay village, it is decorated in a minimalist style, with splashes of colour and stunning modern art. Late breakfasts, and checkouts, can be arranged for the club crowd. There are flatscreen TVs and DVD players, and the hotel is no-smoking throughout.

Claremont
Second Avenue, Hove, BN3 2LL (01273 735 161, www.theclaremont.eu). **Rates** £95-£185 double. **Rooms** 11. **Credit** MC, V.
This friendly, gay-owned boutique hotel is an appealing mix of trad and contemporary, with local artwork adorning the walls. It's located in genteel Hove, west of the main gay hub, but within walking distance of the sea and scene.

Drakes
43-44 Marine Parade, BN2 1PE (01273 696 934, www.drakesofbrighton.com). **Rates** £105-£325 double. **Rooms** 20. **Credit** AmEx, MC, V.
This design hotel has got the required lobby lounge bar, black-clad staff and a sophisticated restaurant, Gingerman. But it's the bedrooms that sparkle: all beautiful ash wood walls, bamboo flooring and sensuous, curvy cornices. There are also open bathtubs in the rooms.

George IV
34 Regency Square, BN1 2FJ (01273 321 196, www.georgeivbrighton.co.uk). **Rates** £65-£150 double. **Rooms** 8. **Credit** AmEx, DC, MC, V.
This period townhouse conversion is surely the best bargain with a sea view in Brighton. Set in one of the city's grandest squares, Sue and Steve's welcoming George IV comprises seven rooms, four with fabulous views of the West Pier and surrounding waves. The triple comes with an expansive balcony, ideal for a leisurely room-service breakfast; the solitary single is surprisingly roomy considering its shoebox price. Board games, books and a jukebox provide pastime pleasure in the lounge, and DVDs and videos can be borrowed from reception, but you're just a short stroll from the seafront, clubs and the Regency Tavern – a flamboyant, gay-friendly pub.

Hotel du Vin
2-6 Ship Street, BN1 1AD (01273 718 588, www.hotelduvin.com). **Rates** £180-£480 double. **Rooms** 49. **Credit** AmEx, DC, MC, V.
This is one stylish joint. The elegant bar is buzzy, and the bistro-style restaurant is good – both are gay magnets. Bedrooms are luxurious, with deluxe mattresses, Egyptian linen and deep bathtubs. Spa treatments pamper too.

Hotel Pelirocco
10 Regency Square, BN1 2FG (01273 327 055, www.hotelpelirocco.co.uk). **Rates** £90-£300 double. **Rooms** 19. **Credit** AmEx, MC, V.
An unbelievably cool, stylish, and downright funky rock 'n' roll hotel, renowned for its themed pop culture rooms, including a shrine to Leigh Bowery, and the Play Room, where they promise guests 'the ultimate dirty weekend'.

myhotel Brighton
17 Jubilee Street, BN1 1GE (01273 900 300, www.myhotels.com). **Rates** £84-£140 double. **Rooms** 80. **Credit** AmEx, MC, V.

Proud marys

Pity the organisers of anyone involved in the organisation of Pride events that aren't **Brighton Pride** (www.brightonpride.org). The others provoke all kinds of complaints, but Brighton Pride never attracts criticism. Every year, thousands of gay and lesbian Londoners decamp to the south coast for a parade by the beach and a party in Preston Park, and every year they return full of the joys of lesbian folk singers, traditional drag, Wild Fruit and kiss-me-quick hats. Hazell Dean has even been known to make an appearance, and still nobody raises any objections. Try that in London.

Then again, one of the reasons Brighton Pride is so popular is because it isn't in London. Soho may have its charms, but it doesn't have a beach; you can enjoy a Sea Breeze, but you can't enjoy those cooling sea breezes. Whereas at Brighton Pride you can do both. The fact that you can do so while dressed in drag or a fetching pair of leather shorts is simply an added bonus.

Plus, of course, Brighton Pride is free. The same is true of London Pride and Soho Pride, but these days they don't usually involve a party in a park. It's also cheaper to stage an event in Brighton than in London; what the organisers save here they can spend on other attractions like the funfair, the big tops and, er, Hazell Dean.

For many gay Londoners, Brighton Pride is a chance to experience Pride the way it used to be, before the marketing men moved in to promote

endless line-ups of boy bands and pop wannabes
who 'love their gay fans'. For many, it was the
sidelining of gay artists in favour of opportunistic
pop acts that contributed to Pride's demise
in the late 1990s. Even today, people go misty-
eyed at the memory of Holly Johnson singing 'The
Power of Love' at the last free Pride on Clapham
Common. You didn't get that with Atomic Kitten.

There's something refreshingly old-fashioned
about a Pride event that boasts more drag queens
than you'll find on Gran Canaria. Not everyone
loves drag queens, but they have done their bit for
the gay cause. Lest we forget, it was drag queens
who fought against the police at the Stonewall
Riots. It was drag queens who led the fundraising
efforts for AIDS. And it is drag queens who are
photographed at Pride events around the world.
What's more, they do it in high heels, on every
kind of terrain. Respect, as they say, is due.

A recent Brighton Pride had a 'Carry On'
theme. Unashamedly nostalgic and defiantly naff,
it harked back to a time before the gay scene was
overrun with drugs and muscle marys without an
ounce of fat or a joyous bone in their bodies. It's
more than 30 years since the first Brighton Pride
march, and it is still the largest free LGBT event
in the country – so give generously on the day.

Out of Town

This offshoot of the two myhotels in London opened in 2008. From the ground-floor cocktail bar/Italian restaurant to the rootop penthouse complete with a vintage carousel horse, it's a stylish mix of feng shui design principles (curving walls everywhere) and 21st-century mod cons (free Wi-Fi, flatscreen TVs).

Nineteen

19 Broad Street, BN2 1TJ (01273 675 529, www.hotelnineteen.co.uk). **Rates** £80-£250 double. **Rooms** 8. **Credit** AmEx, MC, V.
Nineteen is a fashionable, minimalist hotel located right near the city's gay nightlife. Beds sit on illuminated glass bricks; rooms are stocked with CD/DVD players, flatscreen TVs and fresh flowers.

Oriental Brighton

9 Oriental Place, BN1 2LJ (01273 205 050, www.orientalbrighton.co.uk). **Rates** £79-£200 double. **Rooms** 9. **Credit** AmEx, MC, V.
The Oriental is a resolutely contemporary boutique hotel – complete with crisp white bedding – complemented by nostalgic touches such as chaise longues, faux leather desks and Indian-style wardrobes.

Sea Spray

25-26 New Steine, BN2 1PD (01273 680 332, www.seaspraybrighton.co.uk). **Rates** £65-£145 double. **Rooms** 15. **Credit** AmEx, MC, V.
The gimmick of this themed boutique hotel is the chance to share your bedroom with Elvis, Salvador Dali or Andy Warhol – but this doesn't detract from the comfort. Standard 'budget' doubles are also themed (Indian or

Japanese) and all are equipped with CD players; there are flatscreen TVs in the luxury doubles and suites (£99-£210). There's also a chic bar and a late check-out option.

Square

4 New Steine, BN2 1PB (01273 691 777, www.squarebrighton.com). **Rates** £110-£175 double. **Rooms** 9. **Credit** AmEx, MC, V.
This trendy boutique, in the heart of gayville, has the textbook cool lobby bar, plus swish bedrooms, with fake fur throws and trendy retro furnishings. Square, it ain't.

Where to eat & drink

It's said that Brighton has more restaurants per head of population than anywhere else in Britain. Although there is little at the high end of the culinary scale, everyone else is well catered for. Preston Street – in the centre of town, off Western Road – is known as 'restaurant row', and has a dizzying selection of cheap and cheerful eateries, from Chinese and Indian to Thai and Tex-Mex. In the gay village around St James's Street, most places are cafés or 'pizza and pasta' brasseries. Better to step over the Old Steine to the Lanes, where most of the best restaurants are to be found.

Unsurprisingly for a seaside town, fish and chip shops abound, and traditional, no-frills fishy fare is perhaps best sampled at the **Regency** (131 King's Road, BN1 2HH, 01273 325 014, www.theregency restaurant.co.uk). Vegetarians are extremely well

catered for in Brighton. In North Laine, it's hard to find somewhere with a menu that isn't vegetarian/vegan, organic and fairtrade. Recommended are **Wai Kika Moo Kau** (11A Kensington Gardens, BN1 4AL, 01273 671 117), fast-food joint **Red Veg** (21 Gardner Street, BN1 1UP, 01273 679 910, www.redveg.com), and the **Prince George** (5 Trafalgar Street, BN1 4EQ, 01273 681 055), a charming veggie/vegan pub. **Food for Friends** (17-18 Prince Albert Street, BN1 1HF, 01273 202 310, www.foodforfriends.com) is a long-standing local favourite over in the Lanes. **The Sanctuary Café** (51-55 Brunswick Street East, BN3 1AU, 01273 770 002, www.sanctuarycafe.co.uk) is a hip Hove hangout, serving vegetarian and fish dishes; bands play upstairs.

In the gay village, the **Tin Drum** (43 St James's Street, BN1 1RG, 01273 624 777, www.tindrum.co.uk) is a popular bar and restaurant that serves decent, gastropub-style fare. Note that **Blanch House**, **Drakes** and **Hotel du Vin** (for all, *see p231*) operate classy, contemporary restaurants.

La Capannina

15 Madeira Place, BN2 1TN (01273 680 839). **Meals served** noon-2.30pm, 6-11pm Mon-Thur, Sun; noon-2.30pm, 6-11.30pm Fri, Sat. **Main courses** £6.95-£16.95. **Credit** AmEx, MC, V.
This is hands down the best Italian restaurant in town. La Capannina is a cosy, family-run place with a wooden,

North Laine. *See p229.*

rustic feel. It is, however, the food – and the decent prices – that keep the regulars coming back (its lively clientele includes a fair share of Kemptown drag queens). There are plenty of antipasti to choose from, as well as soups, stone-baked pizzas and pasta.

Due South

139 King's Road Arches, BN1 2NF (01273 821 218, www.duesouth.co.uk). **Meals served** noon-3.30pm, 6-9.45pm daily. **Main courses** £11.50-£18.50. **Credit** AmEx, DC, MC, V.
Multi-award winning contemporary British restaurant with a sea view. From jugged hare to wild mushrooms on toasted brioche, and pedigree Sussex steak, food is organically and locally sourced.

English's of Brighton

29-31 East Street, BN1 1HL (01273 327 980, www.englishs.co.uk). **Open** noon-10pm Mon-Sat; 12.30-9.30pm Sun. **Main courses** £9.95-£29.95. **Credit** AmEx, DC, MC, V.
This labyrinthine old restaurant has five little dining rooms, including an oyster bar. It serves locally caught seafood: crab, dover sole, lobster and scallops. It's a popular celebrity hangout, so booking is recommended.

Terre à Terre

71 East Street, BN1 1HQ (01273 729 051, www.terreaterre.co.uk). **Meals served** noon-10.30pm Mon-Fri; noon-11pm Sat; noon-10pm Sun. **Main courses** £11.50-£14.50. **Credit** AmEx, DC, MC, V.
One of Britain's most famous – and lauded – vegetarian restaurants. The innovative dishes are gourmet and good enough to convert carnivores. Booking recommended.

Nightlife

Most of Brighton's gay venues are clustered on or around St James's Street in Kemptown, or the seafront strip directly in front of it. But it's worth travelling outside this bubble to visit some of the city's less frenetic and more mixed pubs.

For more information, check out the local gay magazines, *G-Scene* and *3Sixty*. The gay scene website www.realbrighton.com features a day-by-day what's on guide, along with reviews, news and photo galleries.

Pubs & bars

There's a cluster of more-relaxed spots to the west of the pier, near the border of Brighton and Hove. Located down a side alley, the **Regency Tavern** (32 Russell Square, BN1 2EF, 01273 325 652) is a secret gem – what used to be called a 'theatrical pub'. The music is as likely to be show tunes as pop, and the decor, all gilt mirrors and gold cherubs, is over the top. Taking a long Sunday lunch here is a local tradition. Around the corner is the **Queensbury Arms** (Queensbury Mews, BN1 2FE, 01273 328 159), a tiny hole in the wall, frequented by older gay men. Another cosy mixed pub nearby is the **Bedford Tavern** (30 Western Street, BN1 2PG, 01273 739 495).

Kemptown, the heart of the gay village, is teeming with pubs and clubs. **The Zone** (33 St James's Street, BN2 1RF, 01273 682 249) is unmissable for its huge glass frontage, where there's usually a giant drag act on display. It's frequented by those who like cheap drinks and singing along. A little further down, the **Bulldog Tavern** (no.31, BN2 1RF, 01273 696 996, www.bulldogbrighton.com) is cruisey and dark, but friendly, and often stays open for the entire weekend. Round the corner, the cosy **Queen's Arms** (7 George Street, BN2 1RH, 01273 696 873, www.queensarmsbrighton) attracts lesbians and gay men, with karaoke and drag most evenings. It also lures a young pre-club crowd at weekends.

The **Aquarium** (6 Steine Street, BN2 1TE, 01273 605 525, www.the-aquarium-theatre-bar. co.uk), the **Marine Tavern** (13 Broad Street, BN2 1TJ, 01273 681 284, www.marinetavern.co.uk) and the **Camelford Arms** (30-31 Camelford Street, BN2 1TQ, www.camelfordarms.com) are traditional gay pubs tucked away on side streets. They all have loyal regulars, but may not be the best starting point for visitors. The **Star Inn** (7-9 Manchester Street, BN2 1TF, 01273 601 450, www.starinnbrighton.com) is a popular bear bar, with quizzes and sports nights during the week. At weekends, customers spill out on to the street. A short walk away, by the Pavilion, the **Marlborough** (4 Princes Street, BN2 1RD, 01273 570 028) is the main lesbian venue: part quiet pub, part pool hall.

Along the seafront there are a host of bars of more vintage, mainly catering for younger gay men. **Charles Street Bar** (8-9 Marine Parade, BN2 1RD, 01273 624 091, www.charles-street.com) is Brighton's biggest gay bar – and rumoured to be the most profitable in the UK. People often meet here in the afternoon for a chat and a meal; it gets busy in the evening, especially at weekends. The pumping dance music, and the stylish and beautiful boys that pack it out, lend it a clubby feel. Its next-door rival, **R-Bar** (5-7 Marine Parade, BN2 1TA, 01273 608 133) is a less frenetic version. Like **Vavoom** (31 Old Steine, BN1 1EL, 01273 603 010, www.vavoom.co.uk), it's really a feeder bar for **Revenge** (*see below*).

Walk east along the front and you'll come to the **Amsterdam Hotel** (*see p231*). It has a bar with big video screens, and glass-fronted windows overlooking the sea; its outdoor terrace is the place to be on sunny summer days. Further along, the bar at **Legends Hotel** (*see p231*), is almost as big as Charles Street, but more relaxed. Outside,

there's another sun terrace; inside, the walls are adorned with Pop Art prints of the usual gay icons (Madonna, Audrey Hepburn). It gets very busy after midnight when the other bars start to close.

Clubs

Clubland has expanded considerably in recent years. It also has a few quirks: Thursdays are busy, with clubs offering drinks deals; and, ironically for a seaside town, there is a slight lull in the summer months – spring and autumn are busier. While the rough straight clubs on West Street are best avoided, the cooler clubs on the seafront – most notably the **Honey Club** (214 King's Road Arches, BN1 1NB, 01273 202 807, www.thehoneyclub.co.uk) and **Audio** (10 Marine Parade, BN1 1NB, 01273 606 906, www.audio brighton.com) – have a gay presence. Most Brightonians won't bat an eyelid if two men snog.

Revenge (32-34 Old Steine, BN1 1EL, 01273 606 064, www.revenge.co.uk) is Brighton's biggest gay club, attracting a varied crowd: young and old, students and bears, lesbians and gay men. It has two floors, with strippers and PAs during the week. The main dancefloor downstairs plays pop, disco and chart dance, upstairs is harder. Its main competitor is the **Basement Club**, beneath the Legends Hotel bar. Entry is usually free during the week; at weekends, the bar turns into a second – and very sociable – floor of the club. If you want to meet and chat to people, this is your best bet.

The **Charles Street Club** above the Charles Street Bar (*see left*) gets busiest in the week when cheap drinks are offered, or at weekends on House nights, Religion and GBH. **Wild Fruit** (Tru, 78 West Street, 01273 327 083, www.aeon events.co.uk) is Brighton – and the entire south coast's – big night out. It's held in a mega club once a month, usually on the last Sunday (most of Brighton book the following Monday off work). Nights usually have a dressy-up theme and feature big-name DJs, including Brighton's favourite son, Fatboy Slim. The Wild Fruit team run several other nights for hardcore clubbers, often in the wee hours or on a Sunday. Check the Wild Fruit website for details.

Following the recent demise of alternative legend Dynamite Boogaloo, a camp and trashy club night, host Boogaloo Stu (www.boogaloo stu.com) has returned with two new kitsch offerings: **Pop Kraft Saturday Special** (Brighton Ballroom, St George's Road, Brighton BN2, 01273 605 789, www.brightonballroom.com), to start the month, and **Stu and Dolly's Big Boogaloo Ball** held mid-month on a Tuesday at Revenge (*see above*).

Directory

Getting Around   **238**

Resources A-Z   **242**
Night owls   246

Further Reference   **249**

Index   **251**

Advertisers' Index   **257**

Maps   **258**
London Overview   258
Central London by Area   260
Street Maps   262
London Underground   272

Directory

GETTING AROUND

Arriving & leaving

By air

Gatwick Airport

0844 335 1802, www.gatwickairport. com. About 30 miles south of central London, off the M23.
Of the three rail services that link Gatwick to London, the quickest is the **Gatwick Express** (0845 850 1530, www.gatwickexpress.com) to Victoria; it takes 30mins and runs 3.30am-12.30am daily. Tickets cost £16.90 single or £28.70 for an open return (valid for 30 days). Under-15s pay £8.45 for a single and £11.50 for returns; under-5s go free.
Southern (0845 748 4950, www. southernrailway.com) also runs a rail service between Gatwick and Victoria, with trains every 5-10mins (every 30mins between 1am and 4am). It takes about 35 mins, and costs £11.30 for a single, £11.40 for a day return (after 9.30am).
If you're staying in King's Cross or Bloomsbury, consider trains run by **Thameslink** (0845 748 4950, www. firstcapitalconnect.co.uk) to St Pancras. Tickets cost £8.90 single, £9.50 day return (after 9.32am).
A **taxi** to the centre costs about £100 and takes a bit over an hour.

Heathrow Airport

0844 335 1801, www.heathrowairport. com. About 15 miles west of central London, off the M4.
The **Heathrow Express** train (0845 600 1515, www.heathrowexpress.co.uk) runs to Paddington every 15mins (5.10am-11.25pm daily), and takes 15-20mins. The train can be boarded at the tube station that serves Terminals 1, 2 and 3 (aka Heathrow Central; Terminal 2 is currently closed for rebuilding), or the separate station serving the new Terminal 5; passengers travelling to or from Terminal 4 can connect with a free shuttle train at Heathrow Central. Tickets cost £16.50 single or £32 return (£1 less if purchased online, £2 more if you buy on board); under-16s go half-price. Many airlines have check-in desks at Paddington.

Heathrow Connect (0845 678 6975, www.heathrowconnect.com) is a stopping service to Paddington. Trains run every half-hour, serving Heathrow Central for Terminals 1 and 3; a free rail shuttle (every 15mins) links Heathrow Central to Terminals 4 and 5. A single to or from Paddington is £7.90.
The journey by tube into central London is longer but cheaper. The 50-60min **Piccadilly Line** ride into central London costs £4.50 one way. Trains run every few minutes from about 5am to 11.57pm daily (6am-11pm Sun).
National Express (0871 781 8181, www.nationalexpress.com) runs daily coach services to London Victoria (90mins, 5am-9.35pm daily), leaving Heathrow Central bus terminal every 20-30mins. It's £5 for a single, £9 for a return.
A **taxi** into town will cost £45-£65 and take 30-60mins.

London City Airport

7646 0000, www.londoncityairport.com. About 9 miles east of central London.
The journey on the **DLR** to Bank station in the City takes around 20mins, and trains run 5.30am-12.30am Mon-Sat or 7.30am-11.30pm Sun. By road, a taxi costs around £30 to central London; less to the City or to Canary Wharf.

Luton Airport

01582 405100, www.london-luton.com. About 30 miles north of central London, J10 off the M1.
It's a short bus ride from the airport to Luton Airport Parkway station. From here, the **Thameslink** rail service (*see left*) calls at many stations (St Pancras International and City among them); journey time is 35-45mins. Trains leave every 15mins or so and cost £13.50 single one-way and £23 return, or £14.50 for a cheap day return (after 9.30am Mon-Fri, all day weekends). Trains between Luton and St Pancras run at least hourly all night.
By coach, the Luton to Victoria journey takes 60-90mins. **Green Line** (0870 608 7261, www.greenline.co.uk) runs a 24-hour service. A single is £14 and returns cost £19.
A **taxi** to London costs £70-£80.

Stansted Airport

0844 335 1803, www.stanstedairport. com. About 35 miles north-east of central London, J8 off the M11.

The **Stansted Express** train (0845 748 4950, www.stanstedexpress.com) runs to and from Liverpool Street station; the journey time is 40-45mins. Trains leave every 15mins, and tickets cost £19.80 single, £28.70 return.
Several companies run coaches to central London. The **Airbus** (0871 781 8181, www.nationalexpress.com) coach service from Stansted to Victoria takes at least 80mins. Coaches run roughly every 30mins (24hrs daily), more frequently at peak times. A single is £10, return is £17.
A **taxi** into the centre of London costs around £100.

By coach

Coaches run by **National Express** (0871 781 8181, www.nationalexpress. com), the biggest coach company in the UK, arrive at Victoria Coach Station (164 Buckingham Palace Road, SW1W 9TP, 0843 222 1234, www.tfl.gov.uk), a good 10 minutes' walk from Victoria tube station. This is also where companies such as **Eurolines** (01582 404511, www.eurolines. com) dock their European services.

By rail

Trains from mainland Europe run by **Eurostar** (0843 218 6186, www.eurostar. com) arrive at **St Pancras International** (7843 7688, www.stpancras.com).

Public transport

Getting around London on public transport is easy but expensive.

Information

Timetables and other travel information are provided by **Transport for London** (0843 222 1234, www.tfl.gov.uk). Complaints or comments on most public transport can also be taken up with **London TravelWatch** (7505 9000, www.londontravelwatch.org.uk).

Travel Information Centres

TfL's Travel Information Centres provide help with the tube, buses and other public transport. You can find them in Camden Town Hall, opposite St Pancras (9am-5pm Mon-Fri), and in the stations below. Call 0843 222 1234 for more information.

Euston station 7.15am-9.15pm Mon-Fri; 7.15am-6.15pm Sat; 8.15am-6.15pm Sun.
Heathrow Terminals 1, 2 & 3 tube station 6.30am-9pm daily.
Liverpool Street tube station 7.15am-9.15pm Mon-Sat; 8.15am-8pm Sun.
Piccadilly Circus tube station 9.15am-7pm daily.
Victoria station 7.15am-9.15pm Mon-Sat; 8.15am-8.15pm Sun.

Fares & tickets

Tube and DLR fares are based on a system of six zones, stretching 12 miles out from the centre of London. A flat cash fare of £4 per journey applies across zones 1-4 on the tube, and £4.50 for zones 1-6; customers save up to £2.50 per journey with a pre-pay Oyster card. Anyone caught without a ticket or Oyster card is subject to a £50 on-the-spot fine (reduced to £25 if you pay within three weeks).

Oyster cards A pre-paid smart-card, Oyster is the cheapest way of getting around on buses, tubes and the DLR. You can charge up standard Oyster cards at tube stations, Travel Information Centres (*see above*), some rail stations and newsagents. There is a £3 deposit payable on each card.

In addition to standard Oyster cards, new **Visitor Oyster cards** (which come pre-loaded with money) are available from Gatwick Express outlets, National Express coaches, Superbreak, visitlondon.com, visitbritaindirect.com, Oxford Tube coach service and on Eurostar services.

A tube journey in zone 1 using Oyster pay-as-you-go costs £1.80, compared to the cash fare of £4. A single tube ride within zones 2, 3, 4, 5 or 6 costs £1.30; single journeys from zone 1 to 6 using Oyster are £4.20 (7am-7pm Mon-Fri) or £2.40 (all other times).

If you make a number of journeys using Oyster pay-as-you-go in a day, the total deducted will always be capped at the price of an equivalent Day Travelcard.

Day Travelcards If you're only using the tube, DLR and buses, using Oyster to pay as you go will always be capped at the same price as a Day Travelcard. However, if you're also using National Rail services, Oyster may not be accepted: opt instead for a Day Travelcard, a standard ticket with a coded stripe that allows travel across all networks.

Anytime Day Travelcards can be used all day. They cost from £7.20 for zones 1-2, up to £14.80 for zones 1-6. Tickets are valid for journeys started by 4.30am the next day. The cheaper **Off-Peak Day Travelcard** allows travel after 9.30am Mon-Fri and all day at weekends and public holidays. It costs from £5.60 for zones 1-2 up to £7.50 for zones 1-6.

London Underground

Delays are fairly common, with lines closing at weekends for engineering works. Trains are hot and crowded in rush hour (8-9.30am and 4.30-7pm Mon-Fri). Even so, the 12 colour-coded lines of the underground rail system – also known as 'the tube' – remain the quickest way to get around London. Comments or complaints are dealt with by **LU Customer Services** on 0845 330 9880 (8am-8pm daily); for lost property, *see p247*.

Supplementing the tube, and also accepting Oyster, are **Tramlink** services in South London, **London Overground** (*see below*) and **Docklands Light Railway** (DLR; 7363 9700, www.tfl.gov.uk/dlr). DLR trains run east from both Bank and Tower Gateway stations and then branch out to serve Canary Wharf, Greenwich, Stratford and other destinations, operating 5.30am-12.30am daily.

Using the system You can get Oyster cards (*see left*) from www.tfl.gov.uk/oyster, by calling 0845 330 9876, at tube stations, Travel Information Centres, some rail stations and newsagents. Single or day tickets can be bought from ticket offices or machines. You can buy most tickets and top up Oyster cards at self-service machines. Some ticket offices close early (around 7.30pm); carry a charged-up Oyster card to avoid being stranded.

Timetables Tube trains run daily from around 5am (except Sunday, when they start an hour or so later depending on the line, and Christmas Day, when there's no service). You shouldn't have to wait more than ten minutes for a train; during peak times, services should run every two or three minutes. Times of last trains vary; they're usually around 12.30am daily (11.30pm on Sun). The tubes run all night only on New Year's Eve; otherwise, you're limited to night buses (*see right*).

National Rail & London Overground services

Independent commuter services coordinated by **National Rail** (0845 748 4950, www.national rail.co.uk) leave from the city's main rail stations. Visitors heading to south London,

or to more remote destinations such as Hampton Court Palace, will likely need to use these rail services. Travelcards are valid on these services within the right zones, but not all routes accept Oyster pay-as-you-go; check before you travel.

London Overground services operate in essentially the same way as the tube, providing a semi-orbital rail service around London. They're particularly handy for Dalston and Shoreditch. The trains run about every 20mins (every 30mins on Sun).

Buses

You must have a ticket or valid pass before boarding any bus in zone 1, and before boarding any articulated bus ('bendy buses') anywhere in the city. You can buy a ticket (or a 1-Day Bus Pass) from machines at bus stops, although they're often not working; better to travel with an Oyster card or some other pass (*see left*). Inspectors patrol buses at random; if you don't have a ticket or pass, you may be fined £50.

All buses are now low-floor vehicles that are accessible to wheelchair-users. The only exceptions are Heritage routes 9 and 15, which are served by the world-famous open-platform Routemaster buses. For lost property, *see p247*.

Fares Using Oyster pay-as-you-go costs £1.20 a trip; your total daily payment, regardless of how many journeys you take, will be capped at £3.90. Paying with cash at the time of travel costs £2 for a single trip. A 1-Day Bus Pass gives unlimited bus and tram travel for £3.90.

Night buses Many bus routes operate 24 hours a day, seven days a week. There are also special night buses with an 'N' prefix, which run from about midnight to 6am. Most night services run every 15-30mins, but busier routes run a service around every 10mins. Fares are the same as for daytime buses; Bus Passes and Travelcards can be used at no extra fare until 4.30am of the morning after they expire.

Green Line buses Green Line buses (0844 801 7261, www.greenline.co.uk) serve

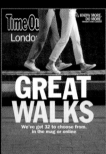

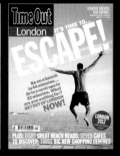

the suburbs within 40 miles of London. Its office is opposite **Victoria Coach Station** (*see p238*); services run 24 hours.

Water transport

Most river services operate every 20-60mins between 10.30am and 5pm, and may run more often and later in summer. Timetables, plus a full list of leisure operators and which piers are served by each, are on www.tfl.gov.uk.

Thames Clippers (0870 781 5049, www.thamesclippers.com) runs a commuter service between Embankment Pier and Royal Arsenal Woolwich Pier; a standard day roamer ticket (valid 10am-5pm) costs £12, while a single from Embankment to Greenwich is £5.30, or £4.80 for Oyster cardholders. **Thames Executive Charters** (www.thamesexecutive charters.com) also offers travelcard discounts (£3 instead of the £4.50 standard single) on its River Taxi between Putney and Blackfriars. **Westminster Passenger Service Assocation** (7930 2062, www.wpsa. co.uk) runs daily from Westminster Pier to Kew, Richmond and Hampton Court from April to October. At around £12 for a single, it's not cheap, but it is a lovely way to see the city (discounts of 30%-50% for Travelcard holders). **Thames River Services** (www.westminsterpier. co.uk) operates from the same pier, with trips to Greenwich, Tower Pier and the Thames Barrier. A trip to Greenwich costs £9.50, though £13 buys you a Rivercard, which allows you to hop on and off at will. Travelcard holders get a third off.

Taxis

Black cabs

The licensed London taxi, aka 'black cab' (though they come in many colours), is a much-loved feature of London life. Drivers must pass a test called 'the Knowledge' to prove they know every street in central London. If a taxi's orange 'For Hire' sign is lit, it can be hailed. If a taxi stops, the cabbie must take you to your destination if it's within seven miles. It can be hard to find an empty cab, especially just after the pubs close. Fares rise after 8pm on weekdays and at weekends.

You can book black cabs from the 24hr **Taxi One-Number** (0871 871 8710, a £2 booking fee applies, plus 12.5% if you pay by credit card), **Radio Taxis** (7272 0272)

and **Dial-a-Cab** (7253 5000; credit cards only, with a booking fee of £2). Comments or complaints about black cabs should be made to the **Public Carriage Office** (0845 602 7000, www.tfl.gov.uk/pco). Note the cab's badge number, which should be displayed in the rear of the cab and on its back bumper. For lost property, *see p247*.

Minicabs

Minicabs (saloon cars) are generally cheaper than black cabs, but can be less reliable. Only use licensed firms (look for a disc in the front and rear windows), and avoid those who illegally tout for business in the street: drivers may be unlicensed, uninsured and dangerous.

Trustworthy and fully licensed firms include **Addison Lee** (7387 8888), which will text you when the car arrives, and **Lady Cabs** (7272 3300), **Ladybirds** (8295 0101) and **Ladycars** (8558 9511), which employ only women drivers. Otherwise, text HOME to 60835 ('60tfl'). Transport for London will then text you the numbers of the two nearest licensed minicab operators and the number for Taxi One-Number, which provides licensed black taxis in London. The service costs 35p plus standard call rate. No matter who you choose, always ask the price when you book and confirm it with the driver.

Driving

London's roads are often clogged with traffic and roadworks, and parking (*see below*) is a nightmare. Walking or using public transport are better options. But if you do hire a car, you can use any valid licence from outside the EU for up to a year after arrival. Speed limits in the city are generally 20 or 30mph on most roads. Don't use a mobile phone (unless it's hands-free) while driving or you risk a £1,000 fine.

Congestion charge Drivers coming into central London between 7am and 6pm Monday to Friday have to pay £8, a fee known as the congestion charge. The area within this zone is shown on the map on pp260-261, however Mayor Boris Johnson had campaigned on a platform that included removing the charge in the areas west of Park Lane (as this guide went to press, the issue had not been resolved). In any event, you'll know when you're about to drive into the charging zone from the

red 'C' signs on the road. You can also enter the postcode of your destination at www.tfl.gov.uk/roadusers to discover if it's within the charging zone.

The scheme is enforced by numberplate recognition from CCTV cameras. Passes can be bought from some newsagents, garages and NCP car parks; you can also pay online at www.cclondon.com, by phone on 0845 900 1234 or by SMS (if you pre-register online). You can pay any time during the day; payments are also accepted until midnight on the next charging day, although the fee is £10 if you pay then. Expect a fine of £50 if you fail to pay, rising to £100 if you delay payment.

Parking Central London is scattered with parking meters, but free spots are rare. Meters cost £1.10 for 15mins, and are limited to two hours. Parking on a single or double yellow line, a red line or in residents' parking areas during the day is illegal, and you may end up being fined, clamped or towed.

However, in the evening and at various times at weekends, parking on single yellow lines is legal and free. If you find a clear spot on a single yellow line during the evening, look for a sign giving the local regulations. Parking on double yellow lines and red routes is illegal at all times.

NCP 24-hour car parks (0845 050 7080, www.ncp.co.uk) are numerous but pricey (£2-£7.20 for two hours). Central ones include Arlington House, Arlington Street, St James's, W1; Snowsfields, Southwark, SE1; and 4-5 Denman Street, Soho, W1.

The immobilising of illegally parked vehicles with a clamp is commonplace in London. There will be a label on the car telling you which payment centre you need to phone or visit. If your car has disappeared, it's either been stolen or, if it was parked illegally, towed to a car pound by the local authorities. To find out how to retrieve your car, call the **Trace Service** hotline (7747 4747).

Cycling

London isn't the friendliest of towns for cyclists, but the **London Cycle Network** (www.londoncyclenetwork. org.uk) and **London Cycling Campaign** (7234 9310, www. lcc.org.uk) help make it better.

Barclays Cycle Hire Mayor Boris Johnson has put a lot of weight behind developing cycling. The Barclays Cycle Hire scheme ('Boris Bikes') launched in summer 2010, with up to 6,000 bikes available for quick and easy rental from one of 400 self-service docking stations around central London. Users rent bikes with a credit card, and are charged a fee based on the length of time before parking the bike at another docking station. For details of the City Hall-sponsored bike rental scheme and a printable route-finder, see www.tfl.gov.uk/cycling.

Directory

RESOURCES A-Z

Addresses

A London postcode takes a point of the compass – N, E, SE, SW, W and NW, plus EC (East Central) and WC (West Central) – and then a number; for example, N1, WC2, SE23. Other than those numbered 1 (which denote the areas nearest the centre), the numbers bear no relation to geography.

Age restrictions

You must be 17 or older to drive in the UK, and 18 to buy alcohol (to be safe, carry photo ID if you're under 22 or look young). For homosexuals (and heterosexuals), the age of consent is 16.

Counselling & help

See also p245 **STDs, HIV & AIDS.**

Al-Anon (Lesbian & Gay Friendly)

Basement of Hinde Street Methodist Church, Hinde Street, W1U 2AY (7403 0888, www.al-anonuk.org.uk). Bond Street tube. **Meetings** 7.30pm Thur. **Map** p266 G5.

Albany Trust

8767 1827, www.albanytrust.org. Short and long-term psychotherapy for lesbian, gay and bisexual people, or anyone with issues around sexuality.

Antidote

Turning Point, 32A Wardour Street, W1D 6QR (7437 4669). Piccadilly Circus tube. **Open** 6-8.30pm Thur. **Map** p269 K7.
Drop-in service for gay, transgender and bisexual men and women who want to change their drug/alcohol use.

British Homeopathic Association

01582 408 675, www.british homeopathic.org. **Open** *Phone enquiries* 9am-5pm Mon-Fri.
The BHA will indicate your nearest homeopathic chemist and/or doctor.

Drug & Alcohol Service for London

Capital House, 134-138 Romford Road, E15 4LD (8257 3068, www.dasl.org.uk). **Open** 9am-9pm Mon-Thur; 9am-5pm Fri; 9am-1pm Sat pre-booked counselling sessions only.
Free and confidential services.

Healing Circle

116 Judd Street, WC1H 9NS (7713 7120, www.helioshealth.org.uk). King's Cross tube/rail. **Meetings** 7.15-9.15pm Tue. **Admission** free, donations appreciated. **Map** p267 L3.
Holistic affirmations and empowerment for gay men and women.

London Friend

7837 3337, www.londonfriend.org.uk. **Open** 7.30-9.30pm Tue, Wed, Fri.
Counselling services for lesbians, gays, bisexuals and the undecided.

Metronet Mental Health Drop-in

Metro Centre, Norman House, 110-114 Norman Road, SE10 9QJ (8305 5000, www.metrocentreonline.org). Greenwich rail/DLR. **Open** 1-4pm Thur.

NHS Direct

0845 4647, www.nhsdirect.nhs.uk. **Open** 24hrs daily.
NHS Direct is a free, first-stop service for medical advice on all subjects.

Nicotine Anonymous

6-8 Ogle Stret, W1W 6HS (7976 0076, www.nicotine-anonymous.org). Goodge Street tube. **Meetings** 6.45pm Wed. **Map** p266 J5.
Friendly, mixed support group, open to all, regardless of sexuality.

PACE

7700 1323, www.pacehealth.org.uk. **Open** 10am-1pm, 2-5pm Mon-Fri.
PACE provides counselling, employment and family services for lesbians, gay men, bisexuals and transgendered people.

Queer Love Quest

Info pack: David Parker 7388 3109.
Counselling and therapy for co-dependent behaviour, and alcohol, drug and sex abuse.

Rape & Sexual Abuse Support Centre

8683 3300. **Open** noon-2.30pm, 7-9.30pm daily.
Support for victims and families.

Samaritans

08457 909090, www.samaritans.org.uk. **Open** 24hrs daily.
The Samaritans listen to anyone with emotional problems.

Stonewall Housing

7359 6242, 7359 5767 advice, www.stonewallhousing.org. **Open** *Phone advice* 10am-1pm Mon, Thur, Fri; 2-5pm Tue, Wed. *Drop-in services* London Friend, 86 Caledonian Road, N1 2-3.30pm Mon; Contemporary Urban Centre, Great Chapel Street, W1 10-11.30am Wed; Lighthouse South London, 14-15 Lower Marsh, SE1 2-3.30pm Thur.
Provides housing advice and supported housing for gays and lesbians.

Terrence Higgins Trust

0845 1221 200, www.tht.org.uk. **Open** *Phone enquiries* 9.30am-5.30pm Mon-Fri.
Confidential support for talking about sexual health, sexuality, relationships and HIV.

Turning Point

London Friend, 86 Caledonian Road, N1 9DN (7837 1674, www.london friend.org.uk). King's Cross tube/rail. **Meetings** 7-8.30pm 2nd & 4th Wed of mth. **Map** p267 M2.
Coming-out group for gay men and those who think they may be.

Victim Support

0845 303 0900, www.victimsupport.com. **Open** *Support line* 9am-9pm Mon-Fri; 9am-7pm Sat, Sun.
Victims of crime are put in touch with a volunteer who provides emotional and practical support, including information and advice on legal procedures. Interpreters can be arranged.

Customs

Citizens entering the UK from outside the EU must adhere to the following duty-free import limits:

● 200 cigarettes or 100 cigarillos or 50 cigars or 250g of tobacco
● 2 litres still table wine plus either 1 litre spirits or strong liqueurs (above 22% abv) or 2 litres fortified wine (under 22% abv), sparkling wine or other liqueurs
● 60cc/ml perfume
● 250cc/ml toilet water
● other goods to the value of no more than £145

The import of meat, poultry, fruit, plants, flowers and protected animals is restricted or forbidden; there are no restrictions on the import or export of currency.

People over the age of 17 arriving from an EU country are able to import unlimited goods for their own personal use, if bought tax-paid (so not duty-free).

For more details about Customs, see www.hmrc.gov.uk.

Disabled

Many of the capital's sights have disabled access, but transport can be a problem. For information on tube access, pick up a copy of the 'Access to the Underground' booklet, available from ticket offices, or call 7222 1234.

Artsline

www.artslineonline.com.
Information on disabled access to arts and entertainment venues in London.

Can Be Done

11 Woodcock Hill, Harrow, Middlesex HA3 0XP (8907 2400, www. canbedone.co.uk). Kenton tube/rail. **Open** 9.30am-5pm Mon-Fri. Disabled-adapted worldwide holidays.

Interactive

Unit 2B07, London South Bank University, 90 London Road, SE1 6LN (7717 1699, www.london sportsforum.org.uk). **Open** *Helpline* 9am-5pm Mon-Fri. Campaigns for disabled sports facilities.

Royal Association for Disability & Rehabilitation

12 City Forum, 250 City Road, EC1V 8AF (7250 3222, 7250 4119 textphone, www.radar.org.uk). Old Street tube/rail. **Open** 9am-5pm Mon-Fri. Campaigns for the disabled.

Tourism for All UK

0845 124 9971, www.tourism forall.org.uk. **Open** *Helpline* 9am-5pm Mon-Fri. Advice on disabled accommodation.

Wheelchair Travel & Access Mini Buses

1 Johnston Green, Guildford, Surrey GU2 9XS (01483 233 640, www.wheelchair-travel.co.uk). **Open** 9am-6pm Mon-Fri. Hires out converted vehicles, including adapted minibuses (with or without driver), plus cars with hand controls.

Embassies & consulates

For more addresses, see the *Yellow Pages.*

American Embassy

24 Grosvenor Square, W1A 2LQ (7499 9000, london.usembassy.gov). Bond Street or Marble Arch tube. **Open** 8am-9pm Mon-Fri; 9am-4pm Sat. **Map** p268 G7.

Australian High Commission

Australia House, Strand, WC2B 4LA (7379 4334, www.uk.embassy.gov.au). Holborn or Temple tube. **Open** 9am-5pm Mon-Fri. **Map** p269 M7.

Canadian High Commission

1 Grosvenor Square, W1K 4AB (7258 6600, www.canada.org.uk). Bond Street or Oxford Circus tube. **Open** 8-4pm Mon-Fri. **Map** p268 H7.

Embassy of Ireland

17 Grosvenor Place, SW1X 7HR (7235 2171, www.embassyofireland.co.uk). Hyde Park Corner tube. **Open** 9.30am-noon, 2.30-5pm Mon-Fri. **Map** p268 H7.

New Zealand High Commission

New Zealand House, 80 Haymarket, SW1Y 4TQ (7930 8422, www.nzembassy .com/uk). Piccadilly Circus tube. **Open** 9am-5pm Mon-Fri. **Map** p269 K7.

South African High Commission

South Africa House, Trafalgar Square, WC2N 5DP (7451 7299, www.south africahouse.com). Charing Cross tube/rail. **Open** 8.45am-12.45pm Mon-Fri. **Map** p269 K7.

Emergencies

In the event of a serious accident, fire or incident, call 999 – free from any phone, including payphones – and specify whether you require ambulance, fire service or police. For addresses of Accident & Emergency departments in London hospitals, *see right*; for helplines, *see p242.*

Health

Free emergency medical treatment under the National Health Service (NHS) is available to the following:

● European Union nationals, plus those of Iceland, Norway and Liechtenstein. They are also entitled to specific treatment for a non-emergency condition on production of a European Health Insurance Card (EHIC).
● Nationals (on production of a passport) of New Zealand, Russia, most former Soviet Union states and the former Yugoslavia.

● Residents, irrespective of nationality, of Anguilla, Australia, Barbados, the British Virgin Islands, the Channel Islands, the Falkland Islands, Iceland, the Isle of Man, Montserrat, Poland, Romania, St Helena and the Turks & Caicos Islands.
● Anyone who has been in the UK for the previous 12 months.
● Anyone who has come to the UK to take up permanent residence.
● Students and trainees whose courses require more than 12 weeks in employment during the first year. Others living in the UK for more than six months may also not have to pay.
● Refugees.
● Anyone formally detained by the immigration authorities.
● People with HIV/AIDS at a special clinic for the treatment of sexually transmitted diseases. The treatment covered is limited to a diagnostic test and counselling associated with that test.

There are no NHS charges for the following services:

● Treatment in Accident & Emergency departments.
● Certain district nursing, midwifery or health visiting.
● Emergency ambulance transport to a hospital.
● Diagnosis and treatment of certain communicable diseases, including STDs.
● Family planning services.
● Compulsory psychiatric treatment.

Accident & emergency

Below are listed most of the central London hospitals that have 24-hour Accident & Emergency departments.

Charing Cross Hospital *Fulham Palace Road, W6 8RF (8846 1234). Barons Court or Hammersmith tube.*
Chelsea & Westminster Hospital *369 Fulham Road, SW10 9NH (8746 8000). South Kensington tube.* **Map** p264 C12.
Guy's Hospital *St Thomas Street, SE1 9RT (7188 7188). London Bridge tube/rail.* **Map** p271 Q8.
Homerton Hospital *Homerton Row, E9 6SR (8510 5555). Homerton rail.*
Royal Free Hospital *Pond Street, NW3 2QG (7794 0500). Belsize Park tube or Hampstead Heath rail.*
Royal London Hospital *Whitechapel Road, E1 1BB (7377 7000). Whitechapel tube.*
St Mary's Hospital *Praed Street, W2 1NY (3312 6666). Paddington tube/rail.* **Map** p263 D5.
St Thomas's Hospital *Lambeth Palace Road, SE1 7EH (7188 7188). Westminster tube or Waterloo tube/rail.* **Map** p271 L9.
University College Hospital *235 Euston Road, NW1 2BU (0845 155 5000). Euston Square or Warren Street tube.* **Map** p266 J4.

Directory

A City Law Firm

They advise individuals and companies alike in the following areas:

If I am in a civil partnership, why do I need a Will?

The majority of your assets will automatically pass to your partner. However, you may want to make a Will to provide for others or substitute beneficiaries should your partner predecease you. Inheritance tax is also an important consideration.

What effect does dissolution of my partnership have on my Will?

The law treats your former partner as having passed away, so any gifts made to your partner will usually fall back into the residue of your estate.

In a gay relationship, how are legal parental rights over children acquired?

A lesbian couple can have both names placed on the birth certificate immediately if the biological father consents to this before the child is born or they use a sperm bank.

If a gay male couple wish to have sole parental rights over the child the only way is through adoption. However, you can now have a new birth certificate with both your names recorded.

Being in a civil partnership will be a factor that is taken into consideration when granting the Adoption Order in your favour. While not being in a civil partnership will not prevent an order being made, it will certainly be harder to persuade the local authority that adoption is in the child's best interests.

Pre-Civil Partnership Agreements

Although not strictly legally binding these agreements can be highly persuasive to the court. It is often helpful in determining how your finances and assets will be divided. They will govern the assets owned prior to the civil partnership as well as those made subsequently.

How do I end my partnership?

They are ended by dissolution in much the same way marriages are. There is only one ground and that is that the relationship has irretrievably broken down. You cannot rely on the grounds of adultery. If your partner will not consent to the dissolution you must have either lived apart for 5 years in order to apply or you have been deserted for more than 2 years or they have acted unreasonably and you can no longer be expected to reside with them.

I am receiving continuous calls and texts from my ex-partner who I used to live with. Can I legally stop this?

Yes, by applying to the Court for a Non-Molestation Order.

You have the right not to be subject to harassment from anyone with whom you used to live. Harassment is defined broadly and does include pestering, for example persistent unwanted phone calls and text messages.

If your application is successful the Order can be indefinite but will normally last three to six months.

- **Family:**
  Civil partnership & cohabitation agreements or separations & divorce;

- **Children:**
  Such as fertility, adoption or surrogacy advice, residence orders, parental rights or maintenance;

- **Employment:**
  Discrimination, drafting contracts, disciplinary, unfair dismissal or redundancy

- **Litigation:**
  Equality Act, Property or contract disputes; debt recovery; cross border claims;

- **Private Client:**
  Wills, trust deeds & powers of attorney;

- **Start-up business:**
  Fixed fees for the first year (comprehensive advice and reduced rates to help your business develop).

A City Law Firm

2 Devonshire Square,
London EC2M 4UJ
T: 020 7426 0382
E: enquiries@acitylawfirm.com
www.acitylawfirm.com

Dentists

Dental care is free for resident students, under-18s and people on benefits. NHS-eligible patients pay on a subsidised scale. To find an NHS dentist, contact the local Health Authority or a Citizens' Advice Bureau (*see p247*).

Dental Emergency Care Service
Guy's Hospital, St Thomas Street, Bankside, SE1 9RT (7188 0511). London Bridge tube/rail. **Open** *8.30am-3.30pm Mon-Fri.* **Map** *p271 Q8.*
Queues start forming at 8am, so arrive early to be seen at all.

Doctors

If you're a British citizen or working in the UK, you can go to any general practitioner (GP). People ordinarily resident in the UK, including overseas students, are also permitted to register with an NHS doctor.

Hospitals

For a list of hospitals with Accident & Emergency departments, *see p243*. For other hospitals, consult the *Yellow Pages*.

Pharmacies

For late-night pharmacies, *see p246* **Night owls**.

STDs, HIV & AIDS

NHS Genito-Urinary Clinics are affiliated to hospitals. They provide free, confidential treatment of STDs and other problems, such as thrush and cystitis; offer counselling about HIV and other STDs; and can conduct HIV blood tests.

The 24-hour **Sexual Healthline** (0800 567 123, www.nhs.uk/choices) is free and confidential.

After 5 Clinic

Lloyd Clinic, 2nd floor, Southwark Wing, Guy's Hospital, St Thomas Street, SE1 9RT (7188 2664, www.gsttsexualhealth.org.uk). London Bridge tube/rail. **Open** *8.10am-6pm*

Mon, Fri; 8.10am-3.30pm Tue; 8.50am-6pm Thur. **Map** *p271 Q8.*
Confidential sexual health clinic for lesbians, gay men and bisexuals.

Ambrose King Centre

Royal London Hospital, Whitechapel Road, E1 1BB (7377 7306, www.barts andthelondon.nhs.uk). Whitechapel tube. **Open** *9am-6pm Mon; 9am-3pm Tue, Fri; noon-4pm Wed; 9am-4pm Thur.*
The centre provides a specialist gay health clinic, East One, 5.15-8pm Thursday – for details, call 7377 7313. Walk-in Hep B vaccination for men. You don't need an appointment.

Centre for Sexual Health

Jefferiss Wing, St Mary's Hospital, Praed Street, W2 1NY (7886 1697). Paddington tube/rail. **Open** *Walk-in 8.45am-6.15pm Mon, Tue, Thur; 11.45am-6.15pm Wed; 8.45am-3.15pm Fri.* **Map** *p263 D5.*
A free and confidential walk-in clinic.

56 Dean Street

56 Dean Street, W1D 6AQ (8846 6699, www.56deanstreet.nhs.uk). Leicester Square or Piccadilly Circus tube. **Open** *Appointments 8am-6pm Mon-Fri (from 10am Wed). Walk-in noon-7pm Mon, Thur; 9am-4pm Tue, Fri; noon-4pm Wed; 11am-4pm Sat.* **Map** *p267 K6.*
Soho sexual health clinic providing walk-in service for Hep B vaccinations and free one-hour HIV tests. Most other services by appointment only.

Mortimer Market Centre for Sexual Health

Mortimer Market, off Capper Street, WC1E 6JB (7530 5050 appointments). Goodge Street or Warren Street tube. **Open** *9am-6pm Mon, Thur; 9am-7pm Tue; 1-6pm Wed; 8.30am-3pm Fri.* **Map** *p266 J4.*
Confidential clinic for all men under-24 (3.45-6pm Mon). No appointment needed.

Pitstop

Metro Centre, Norman House, 110-114 Norman Road, SE10 9QJ (8305 5000, www.metrocentreonline.org). Greenwich rail/DLR. **Open** *6.30-8.30pm Wed; 11am-1pm Sat.*
Confidential sexual health service for gay and bisexual men of all ages. No appointment necessary.

Rainbow Clinic

Caldecot Centre, 15-22 Caldecot Road, SE5 9RL (3299 3448). Loughborough Junction rail. **Open** *By appt 5-8pm Wed.*
Confidential sexual health clinic for gay and bisexual men. By appointment only.

Sorted City

Barts Sexual Health Centre, St Bartholomew's Hospital, EC1A 7BE (7601 8090). St Paul's tube or Farringdon tube/rail. **Open** *noon-3pm Mon-Wed; 9am-4pm Thur; 9am-3pm Fri.* **Map** *p270 O4.*
Walk-in Hep A and B vaccination for gay men.

Terrence Higgins Trust Lighthouse

314-320 Gray's Inn Road, WC1X 8DP (7812 1600 office, 0845 122 1200 helpline, www.tht.org.uk). King's Cross tube/rail. **Open** *Office 9.30am-5.30pm Mon-Fri. Helpline 10am-10pm Mon-Fri; noon-6pm Sat, Sun.* **Map** *p267 M4.*
This long-standing charity advises and counsels those with HIV/AIDS, and their loved ones.

Gay groups

Since many gay social groups are informally run, contact details, venues and meeting times may be subject to change, so it's best to phone ahead to check details.

Choirs

Diversity Lesbian & Gay Choir

www.diversitychoir.co.uk.
Check website for details of rehearsals and concerts.

London Gay Men's Chorus

Hampstead Town Hall Centre, 213 Haverstock Hill, NW3 4QP (0845 838 2059, www.lgmc.org.uk). Belsize Park tube.
From classical to Abba, London's best-known gay choir covers all the bases, and gives concerts too. No audition required.

Pink Singers

07020 934 678, www.pinksingers.co.uk.
Tenors/sopranos required. No formal audition. Varied repertoire.

Social

Champagne Dining Club

www.uniquely4girls.co.uk. **Meetings** Dinner Sat or lunch Sun, drinks parties & theatre trips. **Membership** £75/yr. **Admission** £35-£70 (depending on venue).
Weekly wine and dine with gay professional women at London's finest restaurants.

Changes

London Friend, 86 Caledonian Road, N1 9DN (7837 3337, www.londonfriend.org.uk). King's Cross tube/rail. **Meetings** 6.45-8pm 2nd & 4th Mon of mth (not bank hols). **Helpline** 7.30-10pm daily.
Support and social for women of all ages and backgrounds.

Shine

Metro Centre, Norman House, 110-114 Norman Road, SE10 9QJ (8305 5000, www.metrocentreonline.org). Greenwich rail/DLR. **Meetings** 2-5pm Sun. Weekly social for LGBs aged 16-26 in Greenwich.

Citypink Network for Gay Women Professionals

Adam Street Club, 9 Adam Street, WC2N 6AA (www.citypink.co.uk). Charing Cross tube/rail. **Meetings** check website for dates and changes to venue. **Admission** £10.

Club Mellow Men

Elop, 56-60 Grove Road, E17 9BN (8509 3898). Walthamstow Central tube/rail. **Meetings** 6.30-9.30pm last Mon of mth. **Admission** £2. Gay men's group.

Club Mellow Women

Elop, 56-60 Grove Road, E17 9BN (8509 3898). Walthamstow Central tube/rail. **Meetings** 6.30-9.30pm Tue. **Admission** £2. Social group for lesbian and bi women in a friendly space.

Gay Gordons

Unity Church Hall, 279 Upper Street, N1 2TZ (07752 617 708, www.thegaygordons.org). Angel tube. **Meetings** 7-9pm Mon; 7-9pm Thur. **Admission** £5-£7. Scottish country dance for gay people and friends.

Gay's the Word

66 Marchmont Street, WC1N 1AB (7278 7654, www.gaystheword.co.uk). Russell Square tube. **Meetings** 8-9pm Wed. Lesbian discussion group held in the famous bookshop.

Girl Diva

7700 1323, www.outzone.org. **Meetings** 6.30-9.30pm Wed.

North London-based youth group; social and support events for lesbians and bi women under 26.

Hiking Dykes

www.hikingdykes.co.uk. Lesbian walking group.

Mosaic Youth

07931 336 668, www.mosaicyouth. org.uk. **Meetings** 6.30-9pm Wed (phone to confirm venue). Weekly group for LGBT youth under 25.

North West London Lesbian & Gay Social Group

07941 707 884, www.nwlgay.com. **Meetings** 8.30-11pm Mon. Social events at the Tenterden Sports Clubhouse and licensed bar. All welcome.

NRG

7803 1684. **Meetings** 6.30-9pm Wed. Social weekly in Waterloo for LGB under-21s. Call for further details.

Out & Out Gay Dining Club

8998 8000, www.outandout.co.uk. **Membership** £169/1st yr; £99 renewals. **Events** £45-£59. Dining and social club for professional gay men.

Outzone

7700 1323, www.outzone.org. **Meetings** 6.30-9.30pm Fri. North London-based youth group; social and support events for gay and bi men under 26.

Over-50s Social Group

Metro Centre, Norman House, 110-114 Norman Road, SE10 9QJ (8305 5000, www.metrocentreonline.org). Greenwich rail/DLR. **Meetings** 2-4pm last Tue of mth.

South London Gays

1st Floor, Bread & Roses, 68 Clapham Manor Street, SW4 6DZ (8674 5191, 8672 5268, www.slago.org.uk). Clapham North tube. **Meetings** 8pm 2nd Tue of mth. Social group with occasional speakers.

Step Forward

234 Bethnal Green Road, E2 0AA (7739 3082, www.stepforward-web.org). Bethnal Green tube/rail. **Meetings** 5-8pm Tue. LGB group for under-26s.

West London Gay Bridge Club

Upstairs at the Victoria, 10A Strathearn Place, W2 2NH (contact: Andy 7537 2481, www.wlgbc.co.uk). Lancaster Gate tube. **Meetings** 7.30-11pm Mon. **Admission** £3 (table money).

Zest

Metro Centre, Norman House, 110-114 Norman Road, SE10 9QJ (8305 5000, www.metrocentreonline.org). Greenwich rail/DLR. **Meetings** 4.30-6.30pm 2nd & 4th Fri of mth. Group for under-16 LGBs.

Spiritual

Kensington Unitarians

112 Palace Gardens, W8 4RT (7221 6514, www.kensington-unitarians.org.uk). Notting Hill Gate tube. **Meetings** 11am Sun. **Map** p262 B7. Affirming, inclusive spiritual community.

Lesbian & Gay Christians

Oxford House, Derbyshire Street, E2 6HG (7739 1249, www.lgcm.org.uk). **Open** *Phone* 10am-6pm Mon-Fri. A society for gay and lesbian Christians.

Metropolitan Community Church of North London Trinity

URC, Buck Street, NW1 8NJ (0844 335 0507, www.mccnorthlondon.org). Camden Town tube. **Services** 7pm Sun. Spiritual uplift for LGBTs.

Roman Catholic Mass

The Church of Our Lady of the Assumption, Warwick Street, W1B 5NB (8986 0807, www.sohomasses.com) Piccadilly Circus tube. **Services** 5pm 1st & 3rd Sun of mth. **Map** p267 K6. Services for LGBT Catholics, their families and friends.

St Anne's Soho

55 Dean Street, W1D 6AF (7437 8039, www.stannes-soho.org.uk). Piccadilly Circus tube. **Services** 11am Sun. **Map** p267 K6. Church of England services for LGBT and their friends at this community stronghold. Stay for coffee and tea after the service.

Night owls

The following pharmacies and convenience stores are open 24 hours (except Bliss) and take MasterCard and Visa.

Bliss Pharmacy

5-6 Marble Arch, W1H 7EL (7723 6116). Marble Arch tube. **Map** p263 F6. Bliss Pharmacy is open every day from 9am until midnight.

Riteway Supermarket

57 Edgware Road, W2 2HZ (7402 5491). Marble Arch or Edgware Road tube. **Map** p263 F6.

Spar

33 The Strand, WC2N 5HZ (7930 7814). Charing Cross tube/rail. **Map** p269 L7. *56 Haymarket, SW1Y 4RN (7930 2522). Piccadilly Circus tube.* **Map** p269 K7.

Zafash Pharmacy

233-235 Old Brompton Road, SW5 0EA (7373 2798, www. zafash.com). Earl's Court tube. **Map** p264 B11.

Directory

Internet

Internet access

Many hotels and cafés have wireless internet access, either free of charge or for a fee.

Cybergate

3 Leigh Street, WC1H 9EW (7387 3210, www.c-gate.com). Russell Square tube. **Open** 8.30am-9pm Mon-Sat; noon-8pm Sun. **Net access** £1/30mins. **Terminals** 24. **Map** p267 L3.

Internet cruising

For more gay-related websites, *see p250.*

www.fitlads.co.uk
www.gay.co.uk
www.gaydar.co.uk
www.gayromeo.com
www.gaytoz.com
www.outintheuk.com
www.rainbownetwork.com
www.squirt.org

Left luggage

Airports

Gatwick Airport *01293 502 014 South Terminal, 01293 569 900 North Terminal.* **Heathrow Airport** *8745 5301 Terminal 1, 8759 3344 T3, 8897 6874 T4, 8283 5073 T5.* **London City Airport** *7646 0162.* **Stansted Airport** *01279 663 213.*

Rail & bus stations

The threat of terrorism means that London rail and bus stations tend to have left-luggage desks rather than lockers; to find out whether a station offers this facility, call 08457 484 950.

Legal help

Those in difficulties can visit a Citizens' Advice Bureau or contact the groups below.

For more information, try the **Legal Services Commission** (0845 345 4345, www.legal services.gov.uk).

Citizens' Advice Bureau

www.adviceguide.org.uk.
The council-run CABs offer free legal, financial and personal advice. Check the website for your nearest branch.

Rights of Women

7251 6577, www.rightsofwomen.org.uk. **Open** *Helpline* 2-4pm, 7-9pm Tue-Thur; noon-2pm Fri. Times may vary. Legal advice for women.

Libraries

Unless you're a London resident, you won't be able to sign out books from a lending library. Only the exhibition areas of the British Library are open to non-members.

Barbican Library

Barbican Centre, Silk Street, EC2Y 8DS (7638 0569, www.cityoflondon.gov.uk/ barbicanlibrary). Barbican tube/Moorgate tube/rail. **Open** 9.30am-5.30pm Mon, Wed; 9.30am-7.30pm Tue, Thur; 9.30am-2pm Fri; 9.30am-4pm Sat. **Map** p271 P5.

British Library

96 Euston Road, NW1 2DB (7412 7000, www.bl.uk). King's Cross tube/rail. **Open** *Reading room* 10am-8pm Mon; 9.30am-8pm Tue-Thur; 9.30am-5pm Fri, Sat. *Admissions office* 9.30am-5.45pm Mon, Wed, Thur; 9.30am-7.45pm Tue; 9.30am-4.15pm Fri, Sat. **Map** p267 K3.

Victoria Library

160 Buckingham Palace Road, SW1W 9UD (7641 4258, www. westminster.gov.uk/libraries). Victoria tube/rail. **Open** 9.30am-8pm Mon; 9.30am-7pm Tue, Thur, Fri; 10am-7pm Wed; 9.30am-5pm Sat. *Music library* 11am-7pm Mon-Fri; 10am-5pm Sat. **Map** p268 H10.

Lost property

Inform the police if you lose anything, if only to validate insurance claims. See the *Yellow Pages* for the nearest police station. Only dial 999 if violence has occurred. Report lost passports to police and to your embassy (*see p243*).

Airports

For property lost on the plane, contact the relevant airline. For items lost in an airport, contact:

Gatwick Airport *01293 503 162.* **Heathrow Airport** *8745 7727.* **London City Airport** *7646 0000.* **Luton Airport** *01582 405 100.* **Stansted Airport** *01279 663 293.*

Public transport

If you've lost property in an overground station or on a train, call **0870 000 5151**. For any property lost on the tube or a bus or a registered black cab, contact:

Transport for London

Lost Property Office, 200 Baker Street, Marylebone, NW1 5RZ (0845 330 9882, www.tfl.gov.uk). Baker Street tube. **Open** 8.30am-4pm Mon-Fri. **Map** p266 G5.
Allow three working days from the time of loss. If you lose something on a bus, call 7222 1234. For items lost on the tube, get a lost property form from any station.

Media

Attitude Glossy pop culture monthly with celebrity interviews and features.
Bent Monthly northern-based glossy.
Boyz Weekly freebie; club listings.
Diva Lesbian glossy monthly.
Gay Times Monthly, strong arts/news.
g3 Free monthly glossy for lesbians; club listings.
Homovision TV Gay video news for London and the world available at www.homovision.tv
Out in the City Free glossy monthly from the former editor of *Boyz*.
Pink Paper Free weekly newspaper.
QX International Weekly club freebie.
reFRESH Monthly gay lifestyle mag.

Money

Britain's currency is the pound sterling (£). One pound equals 100 pence (p). Coins are copper (1p, 2p), silver (round: 5p, 10p; seven-sided: 20p, 50p), yellowy-gold (£1) or silver in the centre with a yellowy-gold edge (£2). Paper notes are blue (£5), orange (£10), purple (£20) or red (£50).

You can exchange foreign currency at banks, bureaux de change and post offices, where there's no commission charge.

If you want to open a bank or building society account, you'll need a passport and probably a reference from your home bank.

Western Union

0800 833833, www.westernunion.co.uk.
The old standby for bailing cash-challenged travellers out of trouble.

Directory

ATMs

Other than inside and outside banks themselves, cash machines can be found in certain shops and supermarkets and in larger tube and rail stations. The vast majority accept withdrawals on major credit cards, and most also allow withdrawals using the Maestro/Cirrus debit system.

Banks

Minimum banking hours are 9.30am to 3.30pm Monday to Friday, but most branches close at 4.30pm (some stay open until 5pm). Commission is sometimes charged for cashing travellers' cheques in foreign currencies, but not for sterling travellers' cheques, provided you cash the cheques at a bank affiliated to the issuing bank (get a list when you buy your cheques); it's also charged if you change cash into another currency. You always need ID, such as a passport, to exchange travellers' cheques.

Credit cards

Visa and MasterCard are the most widely accepted cards, American Express and Diners Club less so. Report lost/stolen credit cards immediately to both the police and the 24-hour services below, and inform your bank by phone and in writing.

American Express
01273 696 933.
Diners Club
01252 513 500.
MasterCard/Eurocard
0800 964 767.
Visa/Connect
0800 895 082.

Tax

With the exception of food, books, newspapers and a few other items, UK purchases are subject to VAT – aka sales tax – of 17.5 per cent (due to rise to 20 per cent). Unlike in the US, this is included in prices quoted in shops (a price tag of £10 means you pay £10, not £11.75). In hotels, check that the room rate quoted includes tax.

Travel
Holidays

Amro Holidays
01462 434 663, www.amroholidays.com.
Phone enquires 10am-6pm Mon-Fri.
Gay package holidays to destinations around the world, featuring tours, cruises and women-only holidays.

International Gay & Lesbian Travel Association
www.iglta.org.
The world's leading gay travel trade organisation.

Mantrav
0845 026 6906, www.mantrav.co.uk.
Phone enquires 10am-6pm Mon-Fri; 11am-4pm Sat.
International specialist in gay and lesbian travel.

Home exchange & accommodation

www.homearoundtheworld.com
Website facilitating gay home exchanges around the world.
www.oneworldonefamily.com
US-based organisation offering free listings for home exchanges.
www.gayhometrade.com
International home exchange listings.
www.gaytravel.co.uk
The UK Gay Hotel & Travel guide will help you find gay-owned/gay-friendly hotels in the UK and worldwide.

Travel insurance

For online insurers offering HIV cover on travel insurance, try **www.gaytravelinsurance. com**. They have preferential couple's rates and policies that recognise lesbian/gay families.

Useful gay contacts

Gay to Z Online Directory
www.gaytoz.com.
The UK's gay phonebook.

London Lesbian & Gay Switchboard
7837 7324, www.queery.org.uk.
A 24hr advice and information service, with textphone facility for deaf people.

Outlet
32 Old Compton Street, W1D 4TP (7287 4244, www.outlet4homes.com).
Tottenham Court Road tube. **Open** 9am-7pm Mon-Fri; 11am-4pm Sat.
Map p267 K6.
Gay and lesbian accommodation agency based in the heart of Soho. *See also p74*
Homo is where the heart is.

OutRage!
PO Box 17816, SW14 8WT (8240 0222, info@outrage.org.uk).
Gay rights direct-action group synonymous with Peter Tatchell (www.petertatchell.net). *See also p11*
The bravest man in Britain?

Schools Out
Contact: Tony 01582 451 424, Sue 7635 0476, www.schools-out.org.uk.
Campaigns for lesbian, gay, bisexual and transperson equality in education.

Stonewall
Tower Building, York Road, SE1 7NX (0800 050 2020, www.stonewall.org.uk). **Phone enquiries** 9.30am-5.30pm Mon-Fri.
Gay rights lobby group founded in 1989.

Walking tours & other activities

Phone or check websites for times and dates. For walking groups, *see p143*.

Gay Tours London
7737 1800, www.gaytourslondon.com.
Cost £170/half day; £250/day.
Blue Badge guides giving personalised tours for groups of 1-30.

Oscar Wilde's West End Walk
07720 715 295, www.silvercane tours.com. **Cost** £8; £5 reductions.

Suffragettes/Women Behaving Badly Tour
07720 715 295, www.silvercanetours. com. **Cost** £8; £5 reductions.

Urban Gentry
8149 6253, www.urbangentry.com.
Cost £149-£269/group of 4. *Custom tours* £300.
Off-the-shelf and tailor-made tours of London. Themes include design, hidden architectural gems, markets, galleries and, of special interest to gay visitors, a Gay East End tour.

Directory

FURTHER REFERENCE

Books

Fiction

JR Ackerley *We Think the World of You* (1963). Gay love and the English class system.
Peter Ackroyd *Hawksmoor* (1985), *The House of Doctor Dee* (1993), *Great Fire of London* (1982). Fictional studies of arcane London by gay author.
Jake Arnott *He Kills Coppers* (2001), *The Long Firm* (1999). Critically acclaimed West End gangster/geezer homoeroticism by gay author.
EF Benson *The Freaks of Mayfair* (1916). British society during World War I, featuring gays, snobs and social climbers.
Paul Burston *Shameless* (2001). Biting comedy about pill-popping and relationships on the London gay scene. *The Gay Divorcee* (2009). Comedy of manners about a gay London bar owner planning his civil partnership.
William Corlett *Now and Then* (1996). A middle-aged London book editor waxes nostalgic about unrequited love at an English boarding school.
Harry Daley *This Small Cloud* (1986). Gay policeman, a friend of EM Forster, reminisces on the seediness of Soho and Hammersmith in the 1930s.
Charles Dickens *Our Mutual Friend* (1864-65). Classic Victorian novel much analysed by queer theorists.
Maureen Duffy *The Microcosm* (1962). The lives of London lesbians in the 1960s. *Wounds* (1969), *Capital* (1975), *Londoners: An Elegy* (1983). This trilogy features more gay and lesbian lives in London, written with a broader political context.
EM Forster *Howards End* (1910). Queer undertones abound in this classic tale of class conflict and troubled relationships in Edwardian London. *Maurice* (1913). Classic Edwardian gay romance; final scenes set in London.
Gillian Freeman *The Leather Boys* (1961). Married London couple drift apart.
Radclyffe Hall *The Well of Loneliness* (1928). The classic English lesbian novel.
Alan Hollinghurst *Line of Beauty* (2004). Booker prize-winning novel about gay life in London in the Thatcher era. *The Swimming Pool Library* (1988). Literary tale of young English aristocrat buggering his way around London before the onset of AIDS. *The Spell* (1995). Foreign office man becomes obsessed with younger lover, discovers hedonistic world of gay nightlife.
Hanif Kureishi *Buddha of Suburbia* (1990). Busy, colourful tale of a young boy growing up in south London in the 1970s. *My Beautiful Laundrette* (1996). Asian boy finds gay love in 1980s London.
David Leavitt *While England Sleeps* (1996). Gay romance set during the time of the Spanish Civil War.
Colin MacInnes *Absolute Beginners* (1980). Sex, drugs, rock and racial tension in Notting Hill, circa 1958.
Armistead Maupin *Babycakes* (1984). Michael Tolliver comes to London.

Mary Renault *The Charioteer* (1973). The lives of gays during World War II.
Rupert Smith *I Must Confess* (1998). Thirty years of British pop culture, mercilessly satirised with a queer twist. *Fly on the Wall* (2002). The tale of a reality TV show set in Elephant & Castle, populated by a transsexual, rent boy and two old queens.
William Sutcliffe *New Boy* (1998). Comedy about teenage boy who develops a crush on friend at a London boys' school.
Colm Toibin *The Master* (2004). Critically praised, fictionalised biography of Henry James.
Sarah Waters *Affinity* (1999). Dark, lesbian-themed novel set in a London women's prison in Victorian times. *Tipping the Velvet* (1998). Small-town girl follows a Victorian music-hall star to London; steamy lesbian scenes ensue. *The Night Watch* (2006). Lesbians and young gay men in World War II London.
Evelyn Waugh *Brideshead Revisited* (1944). Oxbridge, class and a teddy bear.
Oscar Wilde *The Picture of Dorian Gray* (circa 1891). Beauty at all costs.
Jeanette Winterson *Sexing the Cherry* (1989). Magical realism tale set in Restoration London by lesbian author who plays with gender boundaries.
Virginia Woolf *Orlando* (1928). Woolf's time-travelling, gender-bending classic.

Non-fiction

JR Ackerley *My Father and Myself* (1971). Memoir of gay author.
Peter Ackroyd *London* (2000). The definitive biography of the city written by the acclaimed historian, who is gay.
Marc Almond *Tainted Life* (1999). Warts-and-all biography of the Soft Cell frontman and electro torch singer.
Paul Bailey *The Stately Homo: A Celebration of the Life of Quentin Crisp* (2000).
Mark Barrett *Ian McKellen: An Unofficial Biography* (2005).
Neil Bartlett *Who Was That Man?: Present for Mr Oscar Wilde* (1988). Arty meditation on Oscar Wilde, comparing 1980s gay London with Victorian times.
Cecil Beaton *The Unexpurgated Beaton: The Cecil Beaton Diaries as He Wrote Them, 1970-1980* (2003). Bitchy diaries of high society photographer.
Boy George *Take it Like a Man* (1995), *Straight* (2005). No-holds-barred, bitchy autobiographies by the gender-bending pop star.
Paul Burston *Gutterheart – Marc Almond 1981-1996* (1997). Career retrospective of the gay singer. *Queen's Country* (1998). A witty tour of gay Britain. *What Are You Looking At? Queer Sex, Style and Cinema* (1995). Provocative essays on gay pop culture by *Time Out* journalist.
Simon Callow *Charles Laughton: A Difficult Actor* (1990).
Quentin Crisp *The Naked Civil Servant* (1968). England's stateliest homo wittily

tells his tale of coming out in London, long before gay liberation.
Daniel Farson *Gilbert & George: A Portrait* (1999). Profile of the enfants terribles of British art. *The Gilded Gutter Life of Francis Bacon: The Authorised Biography* (1994). Portrait of the gay artist. *Never a Normal Man* (1998). Autobiography of one of the great Soho characters of the 1950s.
Daniel Farson, George Melly *Soho in the Fifties* (1993). The Soho boho scene.
Stephen Fry *Moab is My Washpot* (1997). Autobiography of the gay actor.
Fergus Greer *Leigh Bowery Looks* (2002). Visual biography of the club legend.
Chris Heath *Literally* (1990). Fly-on-the-wall literary documentary about the Pet Shop Boys, following their 1989 tour.
John Gielgud *Sir John Gielgud: A Life in Letters* (2004).
Philip Hoare *Noël Coward: A Biography* (1995).
Henry James *The Complete Notebooks* (1987).
Derek Jarman *Dancing Ledge* (1986). Diaries about homophobia and AIDS in Thatcher's Britain. *Kicking the Pricks* (1987). Diaries, interviews, scripts and articles about being gay in Britain. *At Your Own Risk* (1992). Autobiographical musings on queer politics in 1990s London. *Modern Nature* (1994). The gay film-maker's journals, 1989-90. *Smiling in Slow Motion* (2000). The final diaries of Jarman, concluding just before his death.
Holly Johnson *Bone in My Flute* (1994). Autobiography of the Frankie Goes to Hollywood singer.
John Lahr *Prick Up Your Ears* (1986). Biography of Joe Orton.
Neil McKenna *The Secret Life of Oscar Wilde* (2003).
Carl Miller *Stages of Desire: Gay Theatre's Hidden History* (1996).
Sheridan Morley *Sir John Gielgud: the Authorised Biography* (2002).
Graham Norton *So Me* (2004). Autobiography of the gay comedian.
Rictor Norton *Mother Clap's Molly House: Gay Subculture in England, 1700-1830*. Queer goings-on in 18th-century London.
Joe Orton *Diaries* (1986). Provocative diaries of the mischievous playwright.
Tony Parsons *Bare* (1990). Sanitised biography of George Michael.
Matthew Parris *Chance Witness* (2002). Gay journalist and former Tory MP writes about cruising, coming out and working for Maggie Thatcher.
Graham Payn, Barry Day *My Life with Noël Coward* (1994).
Mark Simpson *It's a Queer World* (1996). Spiky essays on queer pop culture.
Alan Sinfield *The Wilde Century: Oscar Wilde, Effeminacy and the Queer Movement* (2000).
Steve Strange *Blitzed* (2002). The life and times of one of the original New Romantics.
Judith Summers *Soho: A History of London's Most Colourful Neighbourhood* (1989).

Sue Tilley *Leigh Bowery: the Life and Times of an Icon* (1997). Biography of the London club icon.
Sylvia Townsend Warner *Diaries* (1995). Memoirs of the lesbian poet and author.
Denton Welch *In Youth is Pleasure* (1944). Gay man goes on a walking tour of England.
Oscar Wilde *The Wit and Wisdom of Oscar Wilde* (1960).
Kenneth Williams *Diaries* (1993). The *Carry On* star on showbiz and sex.

Plays

Neil Bartlett *A Vision of Love Revealed in Sleep* (1989). Explores the life of gay artist Simeon Solomon.
Alan Bennett *A Question of Attribution* (1991). Recreates the later life of gay spy Anthony Blunt.
Alan Bennett *History Boys* (2004). Drama about gay teacher and his pupils.
Noël Coward *Blithe Spirit* (1942), *Hay Fever* (1925), *Private Lives* (1930).
Kevin Elyot *My Night with Reg* (1994). Comedy about men coping with AIDS.
Peter Gill *Mean Tears* (1987). Romantic drama about lost friendship and betrayal.
Simon Gray *Butley* (1971). Drama about a gay teacher whose life falls apart.
Noel Greig *Poppies* (1983). Radical gay take on militarism and the nuclear threat.
Jonathan Harvey *Beautiful Thing* (1993). Moving coming-of-age gay love story set on a London council estate.
Frank Marcus *The Killing of Sister George* (1965). Lesbian classic set in 1960s London.
Joe Orton *Entertaining Mr Sloane* (1964), *Loot* (1967), *What the Butler Saw* (1969). Scandalous, salacious satires laced with Orton's subversive queer themes.
Philip Osment *This Island's Mine* (1988). A gay man and lesbian are forced into a marriage of convenience.
Mark Ravenhill *Mother Clap's Molly House* (2002). Cross-dressing and bordellos in ye olde London, with a contemporary twist. *Shopping and Fucking* (1996). Scathing satire on the commercialisation of gay culture.
Oscar Wilde *The Importance of Being Earnest, An Ideal Husband* (circa 1899).
Patrick Wilde *What's Wrong With Angry?* (2000). Coming-of-age gay drama.
Chay Yew *Porcelain* (1989). A Chinese gay man faces bigotry in London.

Film & TV

Absolute Beginners (1986). *Directed by Julien Temple.* Film version of the MacInnes book, starring David Bowie.
Beautiful Thing (1996). *Directed by Hettie Macdonald.* Romantic film version of the Jonathan Harvey play.
Bedrooms and Hallways (1998) *Directed by Rose Troche.* Comedy about a male bonding group with a gay twist.
Brideshead Revisited (1981). *Directed by Michael Lindsay-Hogg.* Acclaimed TV mini-series of the Waugh classic, starring Jeremy Iron. A film version, directed by Julian Jarrold, came out in 2008.

Buddha of Suburbia (1993). *Directed by Roger Michell.* TV version of the Hanif Kureishi novel.
Butley (1973). *Directed by Harold Pinter.* A gay teacher gets dumped – and bitter.
The Crying Game (1992). *Directed by Neil Jordan.* Gender-bending love meets the IRA in 1990s London.
Darling (1965). *Directed by John Schlesinger.* Starring Dirk Bogarde and Julie Christie.
Four Weddings and a Funeral (1993). *Directed by Mike Newell.* Rom-com with a gay sub-plot featuring Simon Callow.
The Hours (2002). *Directed by Stephen Daldry.* Lesbian tales through the ages, featuring Virginia Woolf in 1923 London.
An Ideal Husband (1998). *Directed by Oliver Parker.* Starring Rupert Everett.
Jubilee (1978). *Directed by Derek Jarman.* Elizabeth I is transported forward in time to witness the queering of her kingdom.
The Killing of Sister George *Directed by Robert Aldrich* (1968). Beryl Reid as lesbian soap star in meltdown.
The Krays (1990). *Directed by Peter Medak.* Homoerotic biopic of Ron and Reg Kray, the 1960s East End gangsters, starring Gary and Martin Kemp.
Leather Boys (1964). *Directed by Sidney J Furie.* South London couple drift apart after husband meets a cyclist.
Lost Language of the Cranes (1991). David Leavitt's novel, moved to London.
Love is the Devil: Study for a Portrait of Francis Bacon (1998). *Directed by John Maybury.* The artist's stormy love life. With Daniel Craig (nude!)
Maurice (1987). *Directed by James Ivory.* Film version of the Forster novel. See Hugh Grant kiss another man.
My Beautiful Laundrette (1985) *Directed by Stephen Frears.* Film version of the Kureishi novel. See Daniel Day Lewis kiss another man.
The Naked Civil Servant (1975). *Directed by Jack Gold.* TV film of Quentin Crisp's autobiography, with John Hurt.
Orlando (1992). *Directed by Sally Potter.* A historical pageant of 400 years of English history, based on Woolf's novel. Featuring Jimmy Somerville, and Quentin Crisp as Queen Elizabeth I.
Prick Up Your Ears (1987). *Directed by Stephen Frears.* Biopic of Joe Orton, starring Gary Oldman.
A Question of Attribution (1991). *Directed by John Schlesinger.* Film version of Alan Bennett's play about gay spy Anthony Blunt, art advisor to the Queen.
The Servant (1963). *Directed by Joseph Losey.* Starring Dirk Bogarde; screenplay by Harold Pinter.
Sunday Bloody Sunday (1971). *Directed by John Schlesinger.* Murray Head stars as the detached lover of both Peter Finch and Glenda Jackson.
Theatre of Blood (1973). *Directed by Douglas Hickox.* Eight theatre critics meet a grisly end in this comedy horror.
The Trials of Oscar Wilde (1960). *Directed by Ken Hughes.* With Peter Finch.
Victim (1961). *Directed by Basil Dearden.* Dirk Bogarde plays a homosexual barrister who is being blackmailed.
Wilde (1997). *Directed by Brian Gilbert.* Biopic with Stephen Fry and Jude Law.
Young Soul Rebels (1991). *Directed by Isaac Julien.* London in the summer of 1977.

Music

Albums

David Bowie *Space Oddity* (1969), *The Man Who Sold the World* (1970), *Hunky Dory* (1971), *Ziggy Stardust* (1972).
Boy George *U Can Never Be 2 Straight* (2002), *Taboo Original Soundtrack* (2002).
Bronski Beat *Age of Consent* (1984).
Culture Club *Colour by Numbers* (1983), *Greatest Moments* (1998).
Dead or Alive *Evolution* (2003).
Erasure *Pop* (1992).
The Feeling *Twelve Stops and Home* (2006), *Join with Us* (2008).
Frankie Goes to Hollywood *Welcome to the Pleasure Dome* (1984).
Jesus Loves You *The Martyr Mantras* (1991)
George Michael *Ladies and Gentlemen* (1998), *Patience* (2004).
Morrissey *Bona Drag* (1990), *Vauxhall and I* (1994), *You are the Quarry* (2003).
Pet Shop Boys *Please* (1985), *Actually* (1987), *Introspective* (1988), *Behaviour* (1990), *Very* (1993), *Nightlife* (1999), *Closer to Heaven* (2001), *Release* (2002).
Soft Cell *Non-stop Erotic Cabaret* (1981), *The Very Best of Soft Cell* (2002).
Jimmy Somerville *The Singles Collection 1984-1990* (1990).
Suede *Suede* (1993), *Dog Man Star* (1994).

Songs

David Bowie 'London Boys', 'Boys Keep Swinging'.
Boy George 'Mr Strange', 'She Was Never He', 'Ich Bin Kunst', 'Satan's Butterfly Ball', 'No Clause 28'.
Bronski Beat 'Smalltown Boy'.
Noël Coward 'London Pride'.
Culture Club 'Cold Shoulder'.
Judy Garland '(A Foggy Day) in) London Town'.
Holly Johnson 'Legendary Children'.
McAlmont & Butler 'Yes'.
George Michael 'Outside', 'Fast Love'.
Morrissey 'Come Back to Camden', 'Dagenham Dave', 'Hairdresser on Fire', 'Piccadilly Palare'.
Pet Shop Boys 'London', 'West End Girls', 'King's Cross', 'Being Boring', 'To Speak is a Sin', 'In Denial'.
Soft Cell 'Bedsitter', 'Seedy Films'.
Suede 'Animal Nitrate'.

Websites

See also p247 **Internet cruising.**

www.boyz.co.uk
www.gaybritain.co.uk
www.gaydar.co.uk
www.gaydarnation.com
www.gayguide.co.uk
www.gaytoz.com
www.homovision.tv
www.outuk.com
www.pinkuk.com/tourism
www.timeout.com

Index

Page numbers in **bold** indicate chapters or sections giving key information on a place or topic; *italics* indicate photographs.

A

accident & emergency 243
accommodation 60-81
  apartment rental 80
  the best 61
  by price:
    budget 61, 65, 67, 76, 77, 79
    deluxe 63, 69, 70, 71, 74
    expensive 63, 65, 70, 71, 73, 75, 77
    moderate 61, 63, 66, 67, 73, 76, 77, 79
  gay-friendly hotels 60-62
  staying with locals 80
  university residences 80
  YMCAs 81
  youth hostels 80
Act-Up 157
Addington Symonds, John 155
addresses 242
Admiral Duncan, bombing of 158
Adonis Art **128**, 227
Against the Law 154
Agnes de Castro 152
age restrictions 242
AIDS & HIV 12, 45, 157, 208, 245
air, arriving & leaving by 238
Albam 99, **107**, *109*
Albert Memorial 202, **204**, *204*
Aldwych 171
Alison Jacques Gallery 127
All Saints 178
All Souls 179
Almeida 129, **131**
apartment rental 80
Anthropologie **103**, *103*
Apple Market 195
Approach E2 128
Apsley House: The Wellington Museum 182, **183**
Arnott, Jake 212
Ashbee, Charles Robert 206
ATMs 248
Aubrey, John 150
Auden, WH 156

B

Bacon, Francis (1561-1626) 149, 187, 191
Bacon, Francis (1909-92) 151
badminton 136
Baker, Sir Herbert 169
Bank of England 168
Bank of England Museum 169
banks 248
Bankside *see* South Bank & Bankside
Bankside Gallery 164
Banqueting House 199, **200**
Barbican Art Gallery 127, **169**
Barbican Centre 122, 125, 133, 169, *169*
Barnes 219
Barnes Common 219
Barnfield, Richard 152
Barrett, Elizabeth 179
Barry, John Wolfe 166
bars *see* nightlife
basketball 136
Battersea 221
Battersea Park 221
Battersea Power Station 221, *221*
Baynham, Ian 158

Bayswater 226
BBC Television Centre Tours 228
Beatles, the 178
Bedford Square 174
Beerbohm, Max
Belgravia 204
Benjamin Franklin House 197
Bennett, Alan 207
Bentham, Jeremy 174
Bentinck, William 152
Bermondsey 166
Bermondsey Square 166
Berwick Street 191
Bethnal Green 214
Beyond Retro 99, **113**, *114*
BFI IMAX **125**, 163
BFI Southbank 63, **125**, *126*, *162*, 163
Big Ben 199, 211
Bishop's Park 228
Blackfriars Bridge 163, 167
Blake, William 192
Bleak House 172
Bloomsbury & Fitzrovia 174-178
  accommodation 65-67
  restaurants & cafés 86-87
Bloomsbury Group HQ 159, **174**
Bolan, Marc 159, **219**
Bonnington Square 217
books 249
bookshops 101-102
Borough 165
Borough Market **100**, *164*, 165
Bow Street Magistrates Court 196
Bow Street Runners 196
bowling 136
Boy George 209, 224
Brick Lane 211, **213**, *213*
Brighton 229-236
  accommodation 231-234
  pubs & bars 235-236
  restaurants & cafés 234-235
  saunas 230
Brighton Museum & Art Gallery 230
Brighton Pier 230, *230*
British Library **177**, *177*
British Museum 159, 174, **175**, *175*
Brixton 217
Brixton Academy 217
Brixton Market 217
Broadcasting House 178, 179
Broadway Market **100**, 214, *214*
Brompton 204
Brompton Cemetery 227
Brompton Oratory Catholic Church 204
Brown, Dan 171
Browning, Robert 179
Brunel, Isambard Kingdom 225
Brunswick Centre 175
BT Tower 178
Buckingham Palace & Royal Mews 159, **183**
Burgh House 209
Burston, Paul 42, **46**
buses 239
Butler's Wharf 166

C

cabaret 121
Cadogan Hall 134
Caesar, Julius 148
cafés *see* restaurants & cafés
Camden 207
Camden Market **100**, 207
Cameron, Rhona 57

Canary Wharf 215
Canary Wharf Tower 215
Carlton House Terrace 199
Carlyle's House 206
Carnaby Street 193
Carpenter, Edward 155
Carter, Elizabeth 153
Cartoon Museum 175
Castlereagh, Lord 155
casual high street fashion shops 107
CD & record shops 102-103
Cenotaph 199
Centrepoint 197
Chapel Royal 185
Charing Cross Road 197
Chariots (saunas) 25, **49**, 63, 160, 217
Charles Dickens Museum 174, **176**
Charles II, King 178, 189
Chelsea *see* Kensington & Chelsea
Chelsea Flower Show **120**, 205
Chelsea Old Church 205
Chelsea Physic Garden 205, *205*, **206**
Cheyne Walk 149, 205
Chinatown 193
Chisenhale Gallery 128
Chiswick 228
Chiswick House 228
choirs 245
Christ Church Spitalfields 212
Churchill War Rooms 200
Church of the Immaculate Conception 182
Church Street 180
Ciné Lumière 125
cinemas *see* film
City, the 167-170
  accommodation 63
  restaurants & cafés 83-85
City Hall 166
City Information Centre 167
civil partnerships 158
Clapham 219
Clapham Common 159, 208, **219**
Clarence House 185
Clause 28 157
Cleopatra's Needle 196
Clerkenwell *see* Holborn & Clerkenwell
Clink Prison Museum 164
Clone Zone 189, 227
Closet Case 46
clubs *see* nightlife
Coco de Mer **110**, *113*
Coliseum 196
Columbia Road 214
Columbia Road Flower Market **118**, *118*
comedy & cabaret 121
Comedy Store 57
concept fashion stores 103
congestion charge 241
consulates 243
contacts 248
Copeland, David 158
Coram's Fields 714
Cornell, George 212
cosmetics shops 115
counselling & help 242
County Hall 160
Courtauld Gallery 127, **172**
Covent Garden 194-197
  accommodation 71-73
  restaurants & cafés 94-95
Covent Garden Market *195*
Covent Garden Piazza 195
credit cards 248
cricket 136

Index

cruising 159, 203, **208**, 209, 219, 227, 247
Crystal Palace 224
Crystal Palace Park 224
Curzon Soho 57, **124**
customs 242
cycling 137, 241

D

D'Ewes, Sir Simonds 150
Da Vinci Code, The 171
dance 122-123, 137
   classes 123
   venues 122
Dance, George 169
Dance Umbrella 122
Danish Embassy 204
Deakin, John 187
Dean Street 190
Debenhams 181
Denmark Street 197
Dennis Severs' House 213
dentists 245
department stores 99
Design Museum 127, 159, **166**
designer & boutique fashion shops 105-106
Diana, Princess 185, 203
Diana, Princess of Wales Memorial Fountain 159, 203
Dickens, Charles 197, 207
directory 238-250
disabled 243
Dobrowski, Jody 158, 208
Docklands 215
Dr Johnson's House 153, **167**
doctors 245
Donmar Warehouse 129, **131**
Dover Bookshop 196
Dover Street Market 99, **105**, *106*
Downing Street 199
drag scene 38
Dress Circle 196
Drill Hall 37, 53, **131**
driving 241
Du Maurier, Daphne 150
Duke of Wellington 182
Dulwich 224
Dulwich Picture Gallery 127, *223*, **224**
Dyer, George 150
Dylan, Bob 178

E

Earl of Holland, Sir Henry 227
Earl's Court 225, **227**
Earl's Court Exhibition Centre 228
East India Docks 215
East London 211-215
   accommodation 76
   pubs & bars 30-33
   restaurants & cafés 97
East, Mary 153
Edgware Road 225
Edward I, King 151
Edward II, King 149, 151
Edward III, King 151
Edward VI, King 149
18 Stafford Terrace 227
Eisenhower, President 182
Electric Cinema **125**, 226
Elizabeth I, Queen 171, 223
Eltham 224
Eltham Palace 159, **224**
Embankment 196
Embankment Galleries 172
Embankment Gardens 196
embassies 243
emergencies 243
emerging designer fashion shops 107
Emin, Tracey 213
English National Opera 135
Erasmus, Desiderius 149, 205
Eros 183
Estorick Collection of Modern Italian Art 210, *210*

Eton 149
European Gay & Lesbian Sports Foundation 136
Eurostar 177, 238
events 120
Exploding Cinema 126

F

Faithfull, Marianne 190
Fame, Georgie 187
Faraday, Michael 182
Faraday Museum 182
Fashion & Textile Museum 166
fashion 103
Father Hubbard's Tales 149
festivals & events 120
fetish shops 108
Fettered Pleasures **109**, *109*
Fielding, Henry 194, 196
Fielding, Sir John 195
film 124-125
   alternative 126
   festivals & events 126
   further reference 249
   in galleries & museums 126
   porn 125
   venues 124
Firepower 224
fitness *see* sport & fitness
Fitzrovia 178
Fitzroy, Henry 18
Fleet Street 167
Fleming, Alexander 225
Florence Nightingale Museum 160
flower & plant shops 118
Flowers East 128
food shops 113-115
football 137-138
Forster, EM 156
Fortnum & Mason 183, *185*
Foster, Norman 166, 169
Foundling Museum 174, **176**
Foyles 47, **101**, 197
Frankie Goes to Hollywood 8
Freeman, EA 148
Freud Museum 209
Frink, Elisabeth 168
Frith, Mary 15
Frith Street 190
Fulham 228
Fulham Palace & Museum 228
Full Metal Jacket 215
Furnish, David 158, *158*
furniture & home accessory shops 116-118

G

Gabriel's Wharf 163
Gagosian 127
galleries 127-128
Garden Museum 160
Garland, Judy 133, 193
Gatwick Airport 238
Gaveston, Piers 151
Gay Bingo 191
gay groups 245
Gay News 157
Gay's the Word 46, 65, 99, **102**, 175
Gay's the Word 129, 156
Geffrye Museum 159, **213**
George II, King 203
George IV, King 198, 199, 229
GHB 12, 24
Gherkin *see* Swiss Re tower
Gillespie Sells, Dan 19
Gin Lane 197
Golden Hinde 164
Golden Lads 150
golf 138
Gower Street 174
Grant, Duncan 155
Great Fire of 1666 167, 187
Greek Street 190
Green Park 183

Greenwich 223
Greenwich foot tunnel 223
Greenwich Market 17, 223
Greenwich Park 159, *222*, **223**
Greenwich Visitor Centr e 223
Grey, Thomas 149
Grosvenor Chapel 182
Grosvenor Square 182
Groucho Club 191
Guards' Museum 199, *201*
Guildhall 167, **169**
Guildhall Art Gallery 169
Guilpin, Edward 150
gyms & saunas 143

H

Hackney 214
Hackney Empire 214
Hackney Women's Football Club 139
hairdressers 115-116
Halliwell, Kenneth 150
Ham House 222
Hambling, Maggi 37, 194
Hammersmith 228
Hampstead 159, **209**
Hampstead Heath 57, 159, 208, **209**
Hampstead Heath Ponds 140
Hampstead Theatre 131
Hampton Court Palace 159, **222**
Handel House Museum 183
A Hard Day's Night 178
Harley Street 179
Harrods **99**, 204
Harsh, Jodie 38
Harvey Nichols 46, **99**, 204
Haunch of Venison 127
Hawksmoor, Nicholas 133, 212
Hay's Galleria 165
Hayward Gallery 127, **163**
health 243
Heathrow Airport 238
Henry VIII, King 149, 180, 185, 199, 203, 223
Highgate Cemetery 159, **210**
Hippodrome 193
Hirst, Damien 213
historic houses *see under* museums & galleries
history 148-158
History Boys, The 129
HMS Belfast 165, **166**
HMV Hammersmith Apollo 135
hockey 139
Hodgkinson, Patrick 175
Holborn & Clerkenwell 171-173
   accommodation 63-65
   restaurants & cafés 85-86
Holland House 227
Holland Park 227
Horniman Museum 224
Horse Hospital 126
hospitals 245
hotels *see* accommodation
House of Homosexual Culture 42
Houses of Parliament 199, **200**
Hoxton 213
Hoxton Square 213
Hoyle, David 37
Hungerford Bridge 160
Hunterian Museum 172
Hyde Park 159, **203**

I

ICA 127, 159, **135**, 199
ICA Cinema 125
ice rinks 146
Imperial War Museum 219
Inner Temple 171
Institute of Contemporary Arts (ICA) 199
internet 247
IRA 178
Isabella, Queen 151
Isherwood, Christopher 148, 156
Island Gardens 215
Islington 210

Index

J

Jack the Ripper 211, 212
James I, King 150, 196, 203
James, Henry 206
Jamme Masjid Mosque 213
Jazz Café 135
jazz music 135
Jersey Boys **130**, 189
Jewel Tower 200
Jewish Museum 208
John, Elton 158, *158*
John Lewis **100**, 181
Johnson, Boris 8
Johnson, William 149
Jonson, Ben 150
Jones, Gloria 219
Jones, Horace 166
Jones, Inigo 185, 194
Jordan, Neil 177
Jubilee Market 195

K

Keats House 209
Kennington 217
Kennington Park 217
Kensal Green Cemetery 226
Kensington & Chelsea 202-206, 226
   accommodation 74-76
   restaurants & cafés 95-96
Kensington Gardens 203
Kensington High Street 227
Kensington Palace 159, 203, **204**
Kenwood House/Iveagh Bequest 57, 209, **210**
Ketson, Sarah 153
Kew 219
Kew Gardens *see* Royal Botanic Gardens
kickboxing 139
Killigrew, Anne 152
King's Cross 177
Kings Place 134, 177
King's Road 205
Knightsbridge 204
KOKO *134*, **135**
Krays, the 212
Krays, The 214
Kubrick, Stanley 215

L

Labouchere Amendment 155
Ladele, Lillian 158
Lamb's Conduit Street 174
Lambeth Bridge 160
Lambeth Palace 160
Landseer, Edwin 198
Lassco 17
legal help 247
Leicester Square *192*, **193**
Leicester Square Theatre 121, **131**, 193
Leighton House **227**, *228*
Lesbian & Gay Film Festival **120**, **126**, 163
Liberty 101
libraries 247
Life and Death of Mrs Mary Frith, The 151
Lincoln's Inn 172
Lincoln's Inn Fields 172
lingerie & underwear shops 109-110
Linley Sambourne House 227
Lisson Gallery **127**, 179
Little Portugal 217
Little Venice 226
Lloyd's of London Building 169
Locker Room **47**, 219
London Aquarium 160, **162**
London Bridge 163
London Central Mosque 180
London City Airport 238
London Dungeon 159, 165, **166**
London Eye 159, 160, *161*, **162**
London Film Museum 162
London Fire Brigade Museum 166
London Gay Liberation Front 157
London Marathon 120

London Palladium 193
London School of Economics 171
London Silver Vaults 172
London Transport Museum 195
London Wall 169
London Zoo 181, *181*
Long Firm, The 212
lost property 247
Love at a Loss 152
Lucas, Caroline 229
luggage, left 247
Luton Airport 238
Lutyen, Edwin 199
Lyric Hammersmith 132

M

MacColl, Kirsty 190
Madame JoJo's 121
Madame Tussauds 179, **181**
Magma 196
Maida Vale 226
Mall 199
Mansion House 167, 169
Marble Arch **181**, 225
Marble Hill House 222
Marc by Marc Jacobs **105**, *108*
Marlborough House 185
Marston, John 149, 152
martial arts 139
Martin, Leslie 163
Marx Memorial Library 173
Mary I, Queen 223
Marylebone & Oxford Street 179-181
   accommodation 67
   restaurants & cafés 87-88
Marylebone High Street 179, **180**
Marylebone Library 181
Matthew, Tobie 150
Matt's Gallery 128
Maureen Paley 128
Maurice 156
Maxwell Fyfe, Sir David 154
Mayfair & St James's 182-185
   accommodation 69-70
   restaurants & cafés 88-89
Maynard Keynes, John 155
McKellen, Ian 155
McNally, Edward 154
media 247
Meltdown 120
Mercury, Freddie 228
Michael, George 208, 209
Middle Temple 171
Middle Temple Hall 171
Middlesex Guildhall 199
Middleton, Thomas 149
Mile End 214
Mile End Park 214
Millbank 201
Millennium Bridge 160
Mills, John 199
'Molly' scene 155
Mona Lisa 177
money 247
Montagu of Beaulieu, Lord 154
Monument **170**, *170*
More, Thomas 149, 205
Morley, David 158
Morris, William 224
Mother Clap's Molly House 155
motorcycling 139
Mount Street Gardens 182
Mugabe, Robert 158
Museum of Brands, Packaging
   & Advertising 225, *227*
Museum and Library of the Order
   of St John 173
Museum of London 169, **170**
Museum of London Docklands **215**, *215*
museums & galleries
   advertising: Museum of Brands, Packaging
      & Advertising 225, *227*
   applied arts: Victoria & Albert Museum
      127, 159, **201**, *202*

   archaeology: Petrie Museum of
      Archaeology 176
   art: Bankside Gallery 164; Barbican Art
      Gallery 169; Courtauld Gallery 127, **172**;
      Dulwich Picture Gallery 127, *223*, **224**;
      Embankment Galleries 172; Estorick
      Collection of Modern Italian Art 210,
      210; Guildhall Art Gallery 169; Hayward
      Gallery 127, **163**; Lisson Gallery 179;
      National Gallery 127, **198**; National
      Portrait Gallery 198, *200*; Royal
      Academy of Arts 127, 183, **184**; Saatchi
      Gallery 127, **206**, *206*; Serpentine
      Gallery 203, **204**; South London Gallery
      126, **128**; Tate Britain 127, **201**; Tate
      Modern 63, 126, 127, 159, **165**; Wallace
      Collection 67, 179, **180**; White Cube
      Gallery 213; Whitechapel Art Gallery
      126, 127, 159, 211, **212**
   arts & crafts: William Morris Gallery 215
   cartoons: Cartoon Museum 175
   children: Foundling Museum 176; Pollock's
      Toy Museum 178; V&A Museum of
      Childhood 214
   collectors: Sir John Soane's Museum
      172, **173**
   design: Design Museum 127, 159, **166**
   ethnology: British Museum 159, 174, **175**,
      175; Horniman Museum 224
   fashion: Fashion & Textile Museum 166
   fire fighting: London Fire Brigade
      Museum 166
   gardens: Garden Museum 160
   historic houses & palaces: Apsley House:
      The Wellington Museum 182, **183**;
      Burgh House 209; Chiswick House 228;
      Clarence House 185; Dennis Severs'
      House 213; Eltham Palace 224; Fulham
      Palace & Museum 228; Hampton Court
      Palace 222; Keats House 209; Kenwood
      House/Iveagh Bequest 57, 209, **210**;
      Lambeth Palace 160; Linley Sambourne
      House 227; Marlborough House 185;
      Queen's House 223; Ranger's House 224;
      Red House 224; Spencer House 185; 2
      Willow Road 209, **210**
   interior design: Geffrye Museum 213
   literature: Carlyle's House 206; Charles
      Dickens Museum 174, **176**; Dr Johnson's
      House 153, **167**
   local: Brighton Museum & Art Gallery 230
   London: Museum of London 170; Museum
      of London Docklands **215**, *215*; Tower
      Bridge Exhibition 170
   maritime: National Maritime Museum 223
   medicine: Florence Nightingale Museum
      160; Freud Museum 209; Hunterian
      Museum 172; Old Operating Theatre,
      Museum & Herb Garret *165*, **166**;
      Wellcome Collection 178
   military: Firepower 224; Guards' Museum
      199, *201*; National Army Museum 206
   money: Bank of England Museum 169
   music: Handel House Museum 183;
      Horniman Museum 224
   natural history: Horniman Museum 224;
      Natural History Museum 202
   prison: Clink Prison Museum 164
   religion: Jewish Museum 208; Museum &
      Library of the Order of St John 173
   science: Faraday Museum 182; Science
      Museum 202
   sport: Wimbledon Lawn Tennis
      Museum 221; World Rugby
      Museum/Twickenham Stadium 222
   transport: London Transport Museum 195
   waxworks: Madame Tussauds 181
   war: Churchill War Rooms 200; Imperial
      War Museum 219; Winston Churchill's
      Britain at War Experience 165, **166**
   see also galleries
music 133-135
   classical & opera 133-134
   opera companies 135
   further reference 250
   rock & jazz 135

N

Nash, John 180, 183, 184, 186, 198, 199
National Army Museum 206
National Gallery 127, **198**
National Maritime Museum 223
National Portrait Gallery 198, *200*
National Theatre **132**, *132*, 163
Natural History Museum 202
Neal Street 196
Neal's Yard 196, *197*
Nelson's Column 198
nightlife (gay) 15-49
  the best 18
  in Brighton 235-236
  clubs 37-47
  culture nights 42
  pubs & bars 18-36
    Central 18-27
    East 30-33
    North 28-30
    South 33-34
    'Vauxhall Gay Village' 24-25
    West 36
  saunas 49
  straight bars 26
nightlife (lesbian) 50-58
  ballroom dancing 52-53
  the best clubs 50
  in Brighton 235-236
  clubs 55-58
  pubs & bars 50-55
  straight bars 26
North Laine, Brighton 229, *235*
North London 207-210
  accommodation 76
  pubs & bars 28-30
  restaurants & cafés 97
Notre Dame de France 193
Notting Hill 226
Notting Hill Carnival **120**, 226
Novello, Ivor 129, 156

O

O2 Arena 135
Oasis Sports Centre 71, **144**, 194
Odeon Wardour Street 124
Old Bailey (Central Criminal Court) 168
Old Compton Street 187, *190*
Old Curiosity Shop *172*, *173*
Old Operating Theatre, Museum & Herb Garret *165*, **166**
Old Royal Naval College 223
Old Truman Brewery 213
Old Vic Theatre 129, 163
176 128
100 Club **135**, 178
Orton, Joe 150, *150*, 208
Outlet 60, 61, 70, **74**
OutRage! 157, 187
Oval House Theatre 37
Oxford Street **181**, 182
Oxo Tower Wharf 163
Oyster card 239

P

Paddington 225
Paine, Thomas 178
Paisley, Rev Ian 152
Palace Theatre 193
palaces *see under* museums & galleries
Pankhurst, Emmeline 155, 201, 228
Park Nights 124
parking 241
Parliament Hill 209
Parliament Square 199
Parris, Matthew 154
Parsons Green 228
Paternoster Square 167
Peeping Tom 178
Pelli, Cesar 215
Pet Shop Boys 177

Peter Jones 205
Petrie Museum of Archaeology 176
Petticoat Lane Market 211
pharmacies 245
Phillips, Katherine 152
Philpot, Glyn 206
Phoenix Garden 196
Photographers' Gallery 127
Piccadilly 183
Piccadilly Circus 184
Pilar Corrias 127, *127*
Pimlico 201
Pimps & Pinups **116**, *116*
Pizza Express Jazz Club 135
Place, The 122
Plague of 1665 167
plays 250
Playtex Moonwalk 120
Pleasuredome **49**, 63, 160
Pollock's Toy Museum 178
Porchester Centre/Spa 146
Portland Place 179
Portobello Film Festival 126
Portobello Road Market 17, 100, *226*
Prick Up Your Ears 208
Pride in Brighton & Hove 232-233
Pride London 120
Primrose Hill 159, **208**, *207*
Prince Albert 202
Prince Charles Cinema **124**, *125*, 193
Prowler 46, 192
public transport 238
pubs *see* nightlife

Q

Quant, Mary 205
Queen's Chapel 185
Queen's Club 228
Queen's House 223

R

rail
  arriving & leaving by 238
  getting around by 239
Railton, William 198
Raindance Film Festival 126
Ranger's House 224
Ravenhill, Mark 37, 155
Red House 224
reference, further 249-250
Regent Street 185
Regent's Canal 207, 226, *225*
Regent's Park 179, **180**, *180*
Remnants Hockey Club **138**, **139**
Renoir cinema 65, **124**, 175
resources A-Z 242-248
restaurants & cafés 82-98
  the best gay café-bars 85
  the best restaurants 83
  in Brighton 234-235
  by cuisine/type
    American 86
    British 82, 85, 88, 90, 94, 95, 97, 98
    cafés, bars & brasseries 83, 87, 89, 95, 97, 98
    diner/burgers 90
    fish/fish & chips 94
    French 83, 85, 96, 97
    gastropubs 82, 85, 87, 97
    global 82, 87, 91, 98
    ice-cream 91
    Indian 86, 92, 95, 96
    Italian 83, 88, 92, 98
    Modern American/European 86, 87, 88, 92, 94, 96, 98
    North African 89
    oriental 86, 89, 92, 95, 96, 98
    Spanish 86, 87
    steak 89
    tapas 93
    vegetarian & organic 85, 94, 95, 98
  gay dining clubs 88
  tea 93

Richards, Vicky Lee 38
Richmond 221
Richmond Green 221
Richmond Park 221
Richmond Theatre 221
Ricketts, Charles 206
Rights of Man, The 178
Rio Cinema 125, **126**
Ritzy Picturehouse Brixton 125, **126**, 217
Riverside Studios 125, **126**
Rivington Place *212*, **214**
Robinson, Tom 157
RoB London **111**, 178
rock music 135
Rogers, Richard 169
Romans in Britain 148
Ronnie Scott's **135**, 190
Roof Gardens 227
Royal Academy of Arts 127, 183, **184**
Royal Academy of Music 179
Royal Albert Hall *133*, **134**, 202
Royal Botanic Gardens (Kew Gardens) 159, **219**, *219*
Royal College of Music 202
Royal Court Theatre *131*, **132**, 205
Royal Courts of Justice 171
Royal Exchange 169
Royal Festival Hall 37, 163, *163*
Royal Hospital 205
Royal Institute of British Architects (RIBA) **128**, 179
Royal Observatory & Planetarium 223, **224**
Royal Opera 135
Royal Opera House 122, *123*, **194**, **194**
Royal Pavilion, Brighton *229*, 230
Royal Shakespeare Company (RSC) 129, **132**
rugby 139
running 141
Russell Square 174

S

Saatchi Gallery 127, **206**, *206*
Sackville-West, Vita *153*, 156
Sadler's Wells **122**, 135
sailing 141
St Anne's 191
St Bartholomew-the-Great 168
St Christopher's Place 181
St George's Bloomsbury 174
St George's Church 182
St Giles in the Field 197
St Giles's 197
St Helen Bishopsgate 170
St James's *see* Mayfair & St James's
St James's Church, Marylebone 180
St James's Palace 185
St James's Park 183
St James's Church Piccadilly 133, 183, **184**
St James's Square 185
St John's Gate 173
St John at Hampstead 209
St John's, Smith Square 133, 201
St Luke's 133
St Margaret's Church 200
St Martin-in-the-Fields 133, **198**
St Mary Abbots 227
St Mary-le-Bow 168
St Mary's Hospital 225
St Mary's, Wyndham Place 180
St Pancras New Church 176
St Pancras Old Church & Gardens 177
St Pancras Station *176*, 177
St Paul's Cathedral 167, **168**, *168*
St Paul's, Covent Garden 195
St Vedast-alias-Foster 168
saunas 49
Savage, Lily 44
Savile Row 182, *184*
Science Museum 202
Scott, Sir George Gilbert 164, 177, 221, 227
Scourge of Villainy, The 149
Sea Life Centre, Brighton 230
Selfridges 46, 99, **101**, 181
Senate House 174
Serpentine 203

Serpentine Gallery 203, **204**
Seven Dials 196
Severs, Dennis 213
Sex Pistols 197, 205
Sh! Women's Erotic Emporium 115
Shad Thames 166
Shaftesbury Avenue 185, 193
Shakespeare's Globe 132, 159, **164**
Shannon, Charles 206
Shepherd and Sheep 168
Shepherd Market 182
Shepherd's Bush 228
Sherlock Holmes Museum 181
shoe shops 110-111
shopping 99-118
  the best shops 99
Shoreditch 213
Sicilian Place 174
sightseeing 159-236
  the best sights 159
Siobhan Davies Dance Studios 122
Sir John Soane's Museum 172, **173**
Sister Ray 191
Sloane Square 205
Sloane Street 204
Smirke, Sir Robert 180
Smith, Chris 157
Smithfield Market 168
Smith, Rupert 6
Smyth, Ethyl 155
Soane, Sir John 169
softball 141
Soho 186-193
  accommodation 70
  restaurants & cafés 89-94
Soho Gay Cinemas 125
Soho Gym *142*, **144**
Soho Square *186*, 189
Soho Theatre 121, **132**, *132*, 191
Somerset House *124*, **171**, *172*
Somerset House Summer Screen 124
South Bank & Bankside 57, 160-166
  accommodation 63
  restaurants & cafés 82
Southbank Centre 63, 122, 134, 160, 162
South Kensington 202
South London 217-224
  accommodation 77
  pubs & bars 33-36
  restaurants & cafés 98
South London Gallery 126, **128**
Southwark Cathedral 164
Spa London **146**, *146*, 214
spas 144
Speakers' Corner 203
Spencer House 185
spiritual groups 246
Spitalfields 159, **212**
Spitalfields Market 100, 211, 212
sport & fitness 136-146
  clubs & societies 136-143
Spring Gardens 217
squash 141
Stansted Airport 238
Staple Inn 172
Stevens, Samuel 155
Stockwell 217
Stonewall 157
Strachey, Lytton 155
Strand 196
street & urban casual fashion shops 111-112
Stubbes, Philip 149
suit shops 112
Sunday (Up)Market 100
Sussex Gay Liberation Front 229
Sweatbox Soho 144, **145**
swimming 141
Swimming Pool Library, The 140
Swiss Re tower 169

T

Tatchell, Peter **11**, 157, *157*,
Tate Britain 127, **201**
Tate Modern 63, 126, 127, 159, **165**
tax 248

taxis 241
Temple Bar 167
Temple Church 171
tennis 142
Terence Higgins Trust *156*, 157
Thames Barrier Information & Learning
  Centre 224
Thames Path 215
Thatcher, Margaret 215
theatre 129-132
Theatre 503 37
Theatre Royal 196
Theatre Royal Haymarket 129
Theatre Royal Stratford East 37
Theodore, Bishop 148
Thomas, Dylan 178, 190
Timothy Taylor Gallery 128
Tisbury Court 192
tkts booth **129**, 193
tours of London 248
Tower Bridge 167, *166*, **170**
Tower Bridge Exhibition 170
Tower of London 167, **170**
Tradescant, John 160
Trafalgar Square **198**, *199*
Trafalgar Studios 129
transvestites *see* drag scene
travel 248
travelcards 239
Tredegar Square 214
The Truth about Gay Sex 208
12 Bar Club **135**, 197
2 Willow Road 209, **210**

U

Udall, Nicholas 149
UK Black Pride 120
UK Ladyboy Competition 120
underground 239
University College 174
university residences 80

V

V&A Museum of Childhood 214
Vauxhall 217
Verde & Co 212
Victoria *see* Westminster & Victoria
Victoria, Queen 169, 202, 229
Victoria & Albert Museum 127, 159,
  201, *202*
Victoria Miro Gallery 128
Victoria Park 214
Victoria Tower Gardens 201
Villiers, George 150, 196
Vinopolis 164, **165**
vintage fashion shops 113
Vintage Magazine Store **118**, 192
Vinyl Junkies 191
volleyball 143

W

Walk for Life 120
Walker's Court 192
walking 143
  tours 248
Wallace Collection 67, 179, **180**
Wallace, William 168
Walthamstow 215
Ward, Ned 155
Wardour Street 191
Warren Cup 148
water transport 241
Waterhouse, Keith 229
Waterloo 163
websites 250
Wellcome Collection 178
Wellington Arch 183, **184**
West India Docks 215
West London 225-228
  accommodation 77-80
  pubs & bars 36
  restaurants & cafés 98

Westbourne Grove 226
Westbourne Park 226
Westminster & Victoria 198-201
  accommodation 73
  restaurants & cafés 95
Westminster Abbey 199, **201**
Westminster Cathedral 201
Westminster Central Hall 199
Westwood, Vivienne 182, 205
We Will Rock You 130
White Cube Gallery **128**, 213
Whitechapel 211
Whitechapel Art Gallery 126, 127, 159,
  211, **212**
Whitechapel Bell Foundry 211
Whitehall 199
Whitehouse, Mary 148
Whittington, Dick 167
Wigmore Hall 134
Wilde, Oscar 37, 148, 155, 159, 190, **194**,
  196, 205
Wildeblood, Peter 154
Wilkins, William 174
William III, King 152, 169, 203
William Morris Gallery 215
William Rufus, King 148, 149
Wimbledon 221
Wimbledon Common 221
Wimbledon Lawn Tennis Museum 221
Windmill Theatre 192
Winston Churchill's Britain at War
  Experience 165, **166**
Winterson, Jeanette 212
Wolfenden Report 154, 156
Women's Library 212
Woo, Jonny **30**, 38, 191
Woolf, Virginia 155, 174
Woolwich 224
World Rugby Museum/Twickenham
  Stadium 222
World War II 44, 167, 168, 199, 214, 227
Wren, Sir Christopher 133, 165, 167, 185,
  196, 223
WWT Wetland Centre 219, **221**

Y

YMCAs 81
yoga 143
Young, Will 17
Young Vic Theatre 129, 163
Youth hostels 80

Pubs, bars & clubs/club nights

Admiral Duncan *15*, **18**, 189
A:M 25, **37**
Anchor & Hope 82, 83
Angel 197
Backstreet 30
Bar Italia 19, 83, **89**, 190
Bar Wotever **37**, 45, 50, *54*, **55**
BarCode Soho **18**, 46
BarCode Vauxhall **33**, 217
Beyond 25, **37**
Bird Club 55
BJ's White Swan 17, **30**, 52
Black Cap **28**, 121, 207
Blind Beggar 212
Bootylicious 18, **37**, 50, **55**
Box **18**, 71, 85, 194
Candy Bar **50**, *51*
Carpet Burn 30, **37**, 18, *35*, 46, 191
Central Station 18, **28**, **52**, 61
Champagne Bar 26
Chapel Bar 28
Circus 39
City Pink 56
Claridges Bar 17, 26, 61, **69**, 182
Club Kali 18, **39**, 50, **56**
Coach & Horses **85**, 190
Coburg Bar at the Connaught 26
Cockabilly 39
Code 56
Comedy Camp 121
Commercial Tavern 19
Compton's of Soho *16*, **20**, 189, *189*
Crown Tavern 173
Crown & Two Chairmen 191
Dalston Superstore 18, **31**, *36*, **39**, 46, 191
Dirtyconverse Disco 39
Duckie 17, 18, 24, 37, **39**, 45, **56**, *56*
Duke of Cambridge 97
Duke of Wellington Marylebone 87
Duke of Wellington Soho 20
Eagle 46, **86**, 173
Eagle London 18, 25, **33**
Edge **20**, *23*, 82
Escape Bar 20
Exilio Latino 18, **40**, 52
First Out **21**, 50, **53**, 71, 82, 83, 85, **90**, 197
Fitladz 40
Floridita 26
Fort 18, **33**
Fox & Anchor 25, 168
Freedom Bar *20*, **21**
French House 26, 186, 191
Friendly Society 19, **21**, **54**
G-A-Y 17, 18, **40**, 63, 135, 160, 196
G-A-Y Bar **21**, 189
G-A-Y Camp Attack 18, **40**
Galvin at Windows 26
Gay Gordons 53
George & Dragon, Greenwich **33**, 223
George & Dragon, Hoxton 18, 19, **31**, 213
Girls Go Down 54
Gravity 40
Green **28**, 50, **54**, 82, 85
Green Carnation **23**, 190
G Spot Girl Bar 54
Gutterslut 18, **40**, 191, 213
Habibi 40
Hakkasan 26, 82, 83, **86**
Halfway to Heaven **23**, 194
Hard On 40
Heaven 17, 150, 151, 157, 196
Hoist 17, **34**
Horse Meat Disco 17, 18, 19, 25, **40**, *43*, 46
Jacky's Jukebox 53
Joiners Arms 17, *31*, **33**, 213
Kazbar **34**, 219
Kensington Dance Studio 53
King & Queen pub 178
Kings Arms 18, **23**
King Edward VI 29
Klub Fukk 42, 56

Ku 23
Kudos **23**, 71, 194
KW4 (King William IV) 17, **29**, **54**, 209
Lamb & Flag 26
Later 18, 25, **42**
Little Apple 34
Lounge 57
Loungelover 26
Lower the Tone **43**, 50, **57**
Morgan Arms 214
Nelson's Head **33**, 191
Newman Arms 178
99 Club Oxford Circus 121
93 Feet East 213
Oak Bar **30**, 50, **54**
Old Ship 33
100% Babe 50, **55**
Onyx 43
Orange 18, 25, **43**
O-Zone 43
Pink Jukebox 53
Pink Punters 39
Play Pit 30
Polari 17, 42, **43**, 46
Popcorn 43
Popstarz 17, 18, **43**, *47*, **58**
Portobello Gold 17
Profile **23**, *27*, 82, 85, 191
Quebec 18, **24**, 29, 179
Queen Mary 196
Queen's Head **36**, 74, 205
Retro Bar 18, **24**, **54**, 71, 160, 196
Richmond Arms 36
Rose & Crown 34
Ruby Tuesdays 58
Rudeboiz 43
RuMoUrS 58
Rupert Street **24**, 82, 85
RVT (Royal Vauxhall Tavern) 17, 24, **34**, 44, 121, *121*, 217
Salisbury 196
Salsa Rosada 53, *137*
Seven Stars 26
79 CXR 25
Shadow Lounge 17, **25**, *28*, 46, 192
Shinky Shonky 18, **43**
S.L.A.G.S 46
Stag **36**, 73
Star at Night **27**, 50, **55**, *55*
Star of Bethnal Green 33
Studio LaDanza 53
Stunners 39
SuperMartXé 18, **46**
SW9 **34**, 217
Tart 42
Ted's Place 18, **36**
Trade 46
Trader Vic's 26
Trailer Happiness 26
Trannyshack 17, 18, 38, **47**
Twat Boutique 58, *58*
Two Brewers **34**, 121, 219
Vault 139 **27**, 178
Vauxhall Griffin 34
Vauxhall Tavern Chill-Out 47
Village **27**, 191
Waltzing with Hilda 53, **58**
WayOut Club 18, 38, **47**
West 5 36
Wig Out 47
Windsor Castle 26
Wish 50, **58**
Work! 47
Yard **27**, 192
XXL 18, **47**, 165
in Brighton 235-236

Accommodation

Amsterdam Hotel 61
Andaz Liverpool Street 63
Arosfa 67
Aster House 76
B&B Belgravia 60, 61, **73**
Baglioni 61, **74**
Base2Stay *77*, **79**
Blakes 74
Central Station 52, **61**, 177
Charlotte Street Hotel 65
Church Street Hotel 61, *62*
City Inn Westminster 73
Claridges 17, 26, 61, **69**, 182
Clink Hostel 65
Comfort Inn, Vauxhall 60, 61, **77**
Connaught *66*, 69
Covent Garden Hotel *70*, **71**, 194
Dorchester 69
easyHotel 79
Edward Lear **61**, 179
Garth Hotel 61
George 62
Gore 61, **74**, 159
Guesthouse West 79
Halkin *71*, **75**
Hampstead Village Guesthouse 76
Harlingford Hotel 66
Haymarket Hotel 61, *67*, **69**
Hazlitt's 61, **70**
Hoxton Hotel 60, 61, *75*, **76**
Jenkins Hotel 67
Landmark Hotel 179
Lanesborough 75
Langham Hotel 179
Lincoln House Hotel **62**, 179
Lynton Hotel 62
Malmaison 61, **63**
Mayflower Hotel 60, **80**
Metropolitan 69
Milestone Hotel & Apartments 75
Morgan 67
myhotel Bloomsbury 66
New Linden 61, **79**
No.5 Maddox Street 70
Number Sixteen 75
One Aldwych 26, **73**
Pavilion 61, *78*, **80**
Portobello Hotel *76*, **77**
Premier Inn London County Hall 63
Ritz, the **70**, 93, 183
Rockwell 79
Rookery 61, **65**, *65*
St Alfeges **62**, 223
St Martins Lane Hotel **71**, 194
Sanderson 26, **66**
Savoy, the 196
Soho Hotel 61, **70**
Southwark Rose 63
Stylotel 80, *81*
Sumner 67
Threadneedles 63
Trafalgar 73
Twenty Nevern Square 60, **79**
22 York Street 61, **67**
Vancouver Studios 61, **79**
Vicarage Hotel 76
Windermere Hotel 73
Windmill on the Common 61, **77**
York & Albany 76
Zetter 61, **65**
in Brighton 231-234

Index

Restaurants & cafés

Abeno 86
Albion 97
Amaya 96
Arbutus 92
L'Autre Pied 87
Balans 82, 85, **91**, *92*, 189, 227
Baltic 82
Bar Boulud 96
Bar Estrela 98
Bar Italia 83, **89**
Bar Shu 92
Barrafina **93**, 190
Batueux London 196
Bistrot Bruno Loubet 83, **85**
Bistrotheque 30, 83, **97**, 121, 191
Bluebird 205
Bocca di Lupo 92
Botanist 95, *96*
Box 85
Brick Lane Beigel Bake 97
Busaba Eathai 92
Café Below 83
Canteen 97
Caravan 83
Cha Cha Moon 93
Champagne Dining Club 52, **88**
Charles Lamb 97
Chez Bruce 98
Cinnamon Club 95
Clarke's 83, **98**
Clerkenwell Kitchen 85
Le Comptoir Gascon 85
Dean Street Townhouse **90**, *90*
Dehesa 83, **94**
Diner 90
Duke of Cambridge 97
Eagle Bar Diner 86
Edge **20**, *23*, 82

Engineer 209
Eyre Brothers 98
Fernandez & Wells 89
First Out **21**, 50, **53**, 71, 82, 83, 85, 90, 197
Food for Thought 83, **95**, 196
La Fromagerie 87
Gallery Mess 95, *97*
Gate 83, **98**
Gaucho Piccadilly **89**, *89*
Gay Hussar 190
Gelupo 91
Gordon Ramsay 83, **96**
Gourmet Burger Kitchen 91
Great Queen Street 82, 83, **94**
Green **28**, 50, **54**, 82, 85
Hakkasan 26, 82, 83, **86**
Hereford Road 98
Hibiscus 88
Hix 82, 83, **90**, *91*
Hummus Bros 90
Inn the Park 83, **88**
Ivy, the 57, 83, **94**
Joe Allen 57
J Sheekey 83, **94**
Kettners 190
Konditor & Cook 83
Lansdowne 209
Lemonia 209
Lisboa 226
Maison Bertaux 93, *189*, 190
Marine Ices 207
Masala Zone 92
Maze 83, **88**
Medcalf 85
Mildred's 83, **94**, *95*
Momo 83, **89**
Moro 83, **86**
Murano 83, **88**
Nahm 82, 83, **96**
National Dining Rooms 82, 83, **95**

Nobu 83, **89**
Odette's 209
Orrery 83, **88**
Ottolenghi 83, **97**, *209*, 210
Out & Out Gay Dining Club 88
Pâtisserie Valerie **93**, 189
Postcard Teas 93
Primrose Pâtisserie 209
Providores & Tapa Room 83, **87**
Pulcinella 92
Quo Vadis 92
Racine 83, **96**
Rasa Samudra 86
Rebato's 46
Red Fort 191
Ritz, the **70**, 93, 183
River Café 98
Roast 82
Rock & Sole Plaice **94**, 196
Roka 26, **87**
Royal China Club 89
Rupert Street **24**, 82, 85
St John 83, **85**, 173
Saké No Hana 95
Salt Yard 87
Sketch 83, **88**
Smiths of Smithfield 83, **86**
Sông Quê 98
Star Café 90
SW9 98
Tom's Kitchen 95
Trattoria Nuraghe 57
Les Trois Garçons 83
Trojka 209
Vanilla & Black 85
Wagamama 93
Wolseley, the 83, *87*, **88**, 93
Yauatcha 83, **93**, *94*
Zucca *82*, **83**
Zuma 83, **96**
in Brighton 234-235

Advertisers' Index

Please refer to relevant sections for addresses/telephone numbers

Gaydar	**OBC**
Maleforce	**IBC**
The Lion King	**IFC**

Early

Gaydar	**9**

Nightlife

Tonker	**14**
Saunabar	**19**
Horse Meat Disco	**22**
The Retro Bar	**32**
Ku Bar	**41**
Cutting Edge Bars	**48**

Where to stay

Ultimate Guide Company	**64**
Gaydar Girls	**68**
Central Station	**72**

Restaurants & Cafés

Attitude	**84**

Shopping

West London Gay Men's Project	**104**

Around Town

Barcode Soho	**188**
Barcode Vauxhall	**216**
Carpet Burn	**218**

Directory

A City Law Firm	**244**

Index

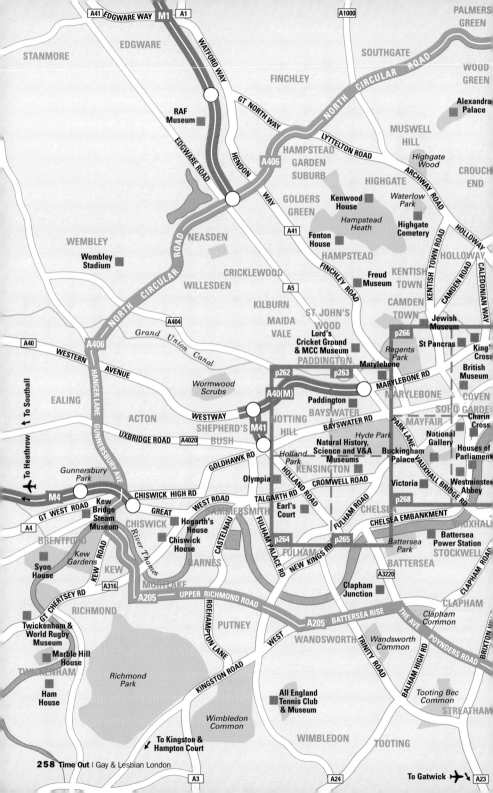

STANMORE

A41 EDGWARE WAY **M1** A1

EDGWARE

WATFORD WAY

A1000

PALMERS GREEN

SOUTHGATE

WOOD GREEN

EDGWARE ROAD

RAF Museum

GT. NORTH WAY

HENDON WAY

A406

HAMPSTEAD GARDEN SUBURB

LYTTELTON ROAD

FINCHLEY

MUSWELL HILL

Alexandra Palace

NORTH CIRCULAR ROAD

ARCHWAY ROAD

Highgate Wood

HIGHGATE

CROUCH END

WEMBLEY

Wembley Stadium

NEASDEN

A41

Kenwood House

Waterlow Park

HOLLOWAY

CRICKLEWOOD

WILLESDEN

Fenton House

Hampstead Heath

Highgate Cemetery

KENTISH TOWN ROAD

CAMDEN ROAD

HOLLOWAY

CALEDONIAN WAY

NORTH CIRCULAR ROAD

KILBURN

A5

HAMPSTEAD

Freud Museum

KENTISH TOWN

MAIDA VALE

ST JOHN'S WOOD

FINCHLEY ROAD

CAMDEN TOWN

A404

Grand Union Canal

Lord's Cricket Ground & MCC Museum

Regents Park

Jewish Museum

St Pancras

King's Cross

A40

WESTERN AVENUE

A406

HANGER LANE

GUNNERSBURY AVE.

Wormwood Scrubs

PADDINGTON

Marylebone

p266

British Museum

To Southall

EALING

ACTON

UXBRIDGE ROAD

WESTWAY

SHEPHERD'S BUSH

A4020

p262

A40(M)

M41

p263

Paddington

MARYLEBONE RD

MARYLEBONE

PARK LANE

COVENT GARDEN

SOHO

To Heathrow

GOLDHAWK RD

NOTTING HILL

BAYSWATER

BAYSWATER RD

Hyde Park

MAYFAIR

Charing Cross

National Gallery

Gunnersbury Park

M4

Kew Bridge Steam Museum

CHISWICK HIGH RD

WEST ROAD

GREAT

Olympia

Holland Park

Natural History, Science and V&A Museums

Buckingham Palace

VAUXHALL BRIDGE RD

Houses of Parliament

Westminster Abbey

GT WEST ROAD

A4

BRENTFORD

Kew Gardens

Hogarth's House

Chiswick House

CHISWICK

River Thames

HAMMERSMITH

CASTELNAU

Talgarth RD

Earl's Court

HOLLAND ROAD

CROMWELL ROAD

KENSINGTON

FULHAM ROAD

Victoria

CHELSEA

p268

Syon House

Kew Gardens

KEW

A316

MORTLAKE

BARNES

FULHAM PALACE RD

p264

FULHAM

NEW KINGS RD

p265

CHELSEA EMBANKMENT

Battersea Park

Battersea Power Station

VAUXHALL

GT CHERTSEY RD

A205

UPPER RICHMOND ROAD

ROEHAMPTON LANE

A205

BATTERSEA RISE

STOCKWELL

BATTERSEA

CLAPHAM HIGH RD

CLAPHAM ROAD

Twickenham & World Rugby Museum

RICHMOND

Clapham Junction

THE AVE.

Clapham Common

A3220

Marble Hill House

Richmond Park

KINGSTON ROAD

PUTNEY

WEST

WANDSWORTH

Wandsworth Common

TRINITY ROAD

BALHAM HIGH RD

POYNDERS ROAD

BRIXTON ROAD

CLAPHAM

TWICKENHAM

Ham House

Wimbledon Common

All England Tennis Club & Museum

Tooting Bec Common

STREATHAM

To Kingston & Hampton Court

WIMBLEDON

TOOTING

A3

A24

To Gatwick

A23

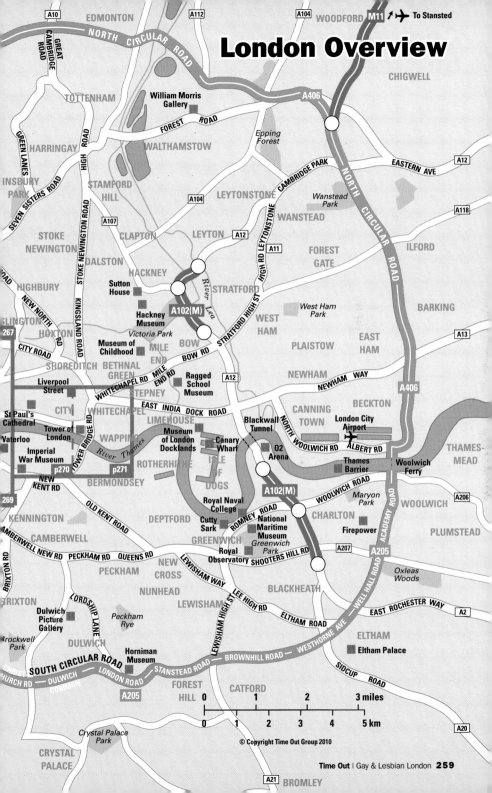

London Overview

A10 EDMONTON
A112
A104 WOODFORD M11 ✈ To Stansted

NORTH CIRCULAR ROAD

GREAT CAMBRIDGE ROAD

CHIGWELL

TOTTENHAM

A406

William Morris Gallery

FOREST ROAD

Epping Forest

EASTERN AVE A12

HARRINGAY

GREEN LANES

WALTHAMSTOW

STAMFORD HILL

CAMBRIDGE PARK

A104 LEYTONSTONE

Wanstead Park

A118

FINSBURY PARK

SEVEN SISTERS ROAD

HIGH ROAD

A107

WANSTEAD

NORTH CIRCULAR ROAD

ILFORD

STOKE NEWINGTON

CLAPTON

LEYTON A12

FOREST GATE

BARKING

STOKE NEWINGTON ROAD

HIGHBURY

DALSTON

HACKNEY

Sutton House

River Lea

STRATFORD

STRATFORD HIGH ST

HIGH RD LEYTONSTONE

A11

A102(M)

WEST HAM PARK

EAST HAM

A13

NEW NORTH

ISLINGTON

KINGSLAND ROAD

Hackney Museum

Victoria Park

BOW

WEST HAM

PLAISTOW

267

CITY ROAD

HOXTON

Museum of Childhood

MILE END

BOW RD

A12

NEWHAM WAY

A406

SHOREDITCH

BETHNAL GREEN

MILE END RD

Ragged School Museum

NEWHAM

BECKTON

Liverpool Street

WHITECHAPEL RD

STEPNEY

EAST INDIA DOCK ROAD

CANNING TOWN

London City Airport

THAMES-MEAD

St Paul's Cathedral

CITY

WHITECHAPEL

LIMEHOUSE

Museum of London Docklands

Blackwall Tunnel

NORTH WOOLWICH RD

ALBERT RD

Tower of London

TOWER BRIDGE RD

WAPPING

Canary Wharf

O2 Arena

Thames Barrier

Woolwich Ferry

Vaterloo

Imperial War Museum

River Thames

ROTHERHITHE

ISLE OF DOGS

A102(M)

WOOLWICH ROAD

Maryon Park

ACADEMY ROAD

WOOLWICH

A206

p270

p271

NEW KENT RD

BERMONDSEY

Royal Naval College

ROMNEY ROAD

CHARLTON

Firepower

PLUMSTEAD

269

KENNINGTON

OLD KENT ROAD

DEPTFORD

Cutty Sark

National Maritime Museum

A207

A205

WELL HALL ROAD

Oxleas Woods

CAMBERWELL

CAMBERWELL NEW RD

PECKHAM RD

QUEENS RD

GREENWICH

Greenwich Park

Royal Observatory

SHOOTERS HILL RD

EAST ROCHESTER WAY

A2

BRIXTON

PECKHAM

NEW CROSS

LEWISHAM WAY

ELTHAM ROAD

WESTHORNE AVE

ELTHAM

BRIXTON

LORDSHIP LANE

Peckham Rye

NUNHEAD

LEE HIGH RD

BLACKHEATH

Eltham Palace

Dulwich Picture Gallery

LEWISHAM HIGH ST

SIDCUP ROAD

Brockwell Park

DULWICH

Horniman Museum

BROWNHILL ROAD

SOUTH CIRCULAR ROAD

LONDON ROAD

STANSTEAD ROAD

FOREST HILL

CATFORD

CHRIST CHURCH RD

DULWICH COMMON

A205

0 1 2 3 miles

0 1 2 3 4 5 km

A20

Crystal Palace Park

© Copyright Time Out Group 2010

CRYSTAL PALACE

A21 BROMLEY

Central London
by Area

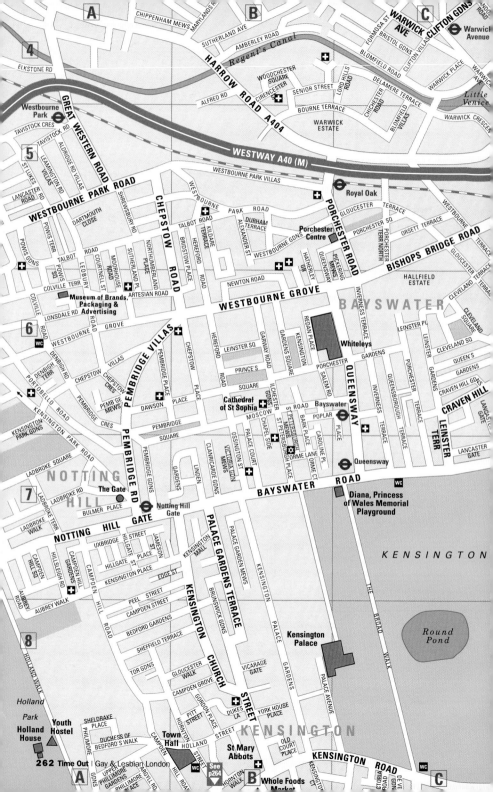

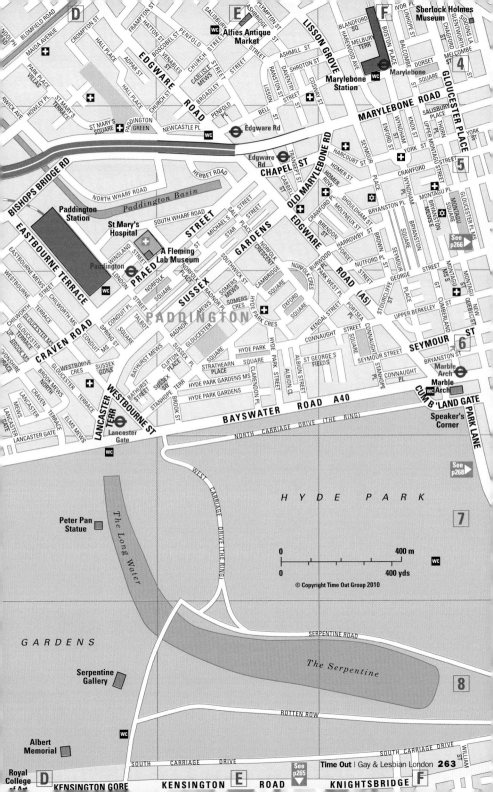

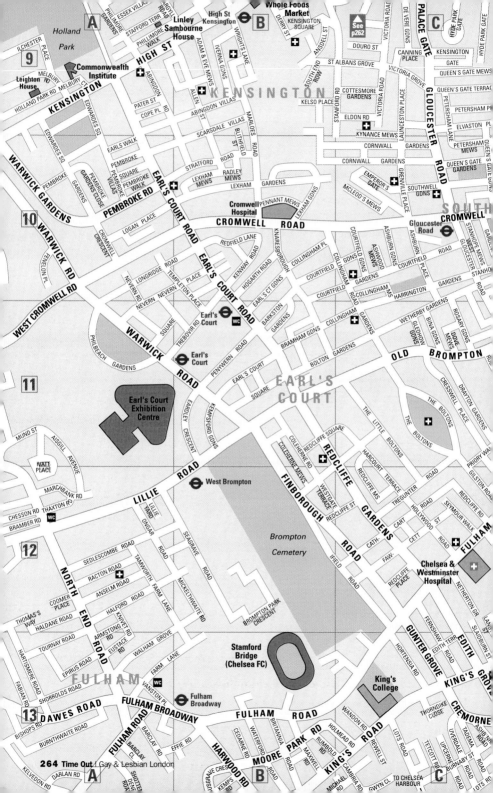

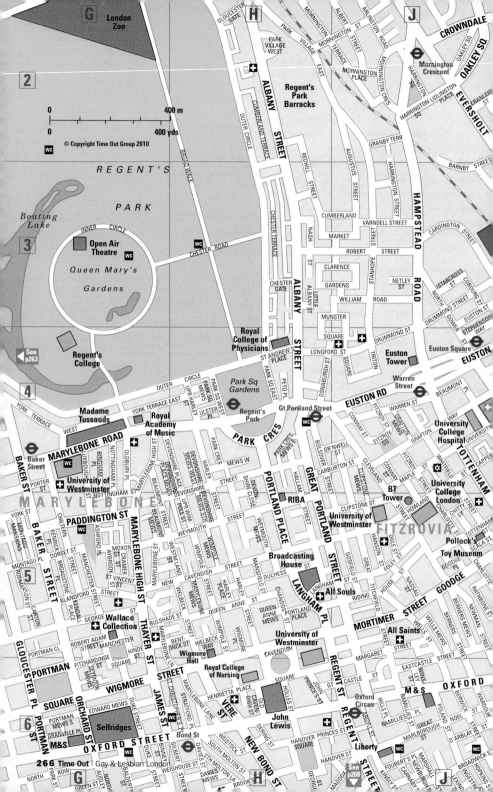

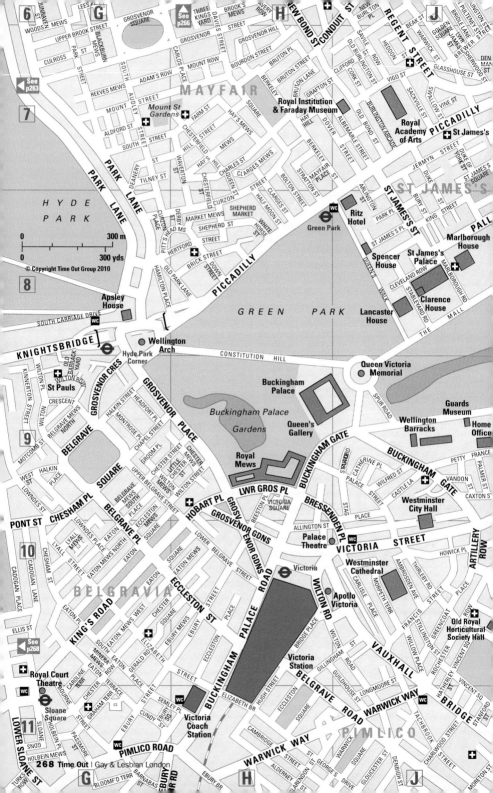

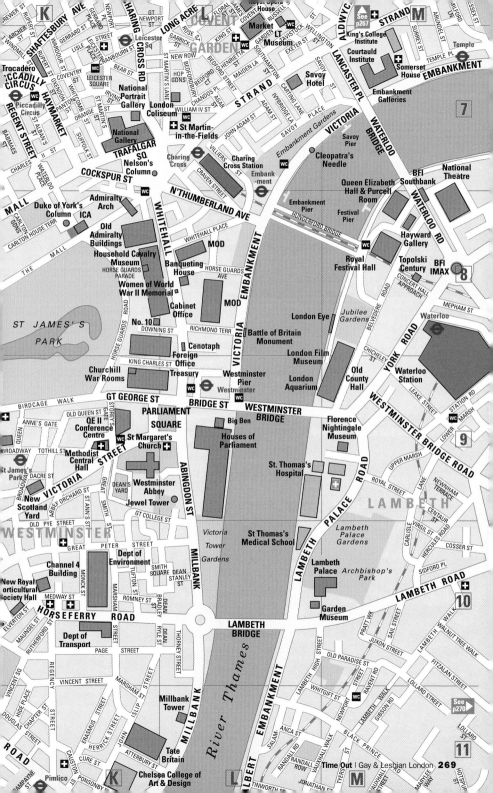

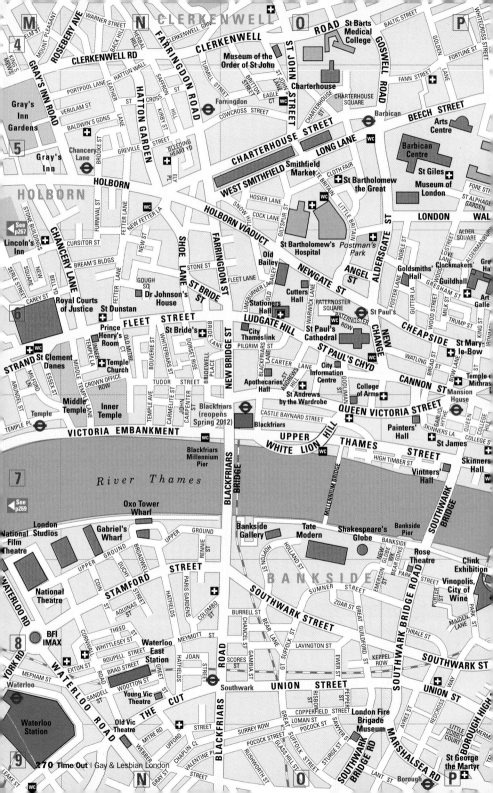

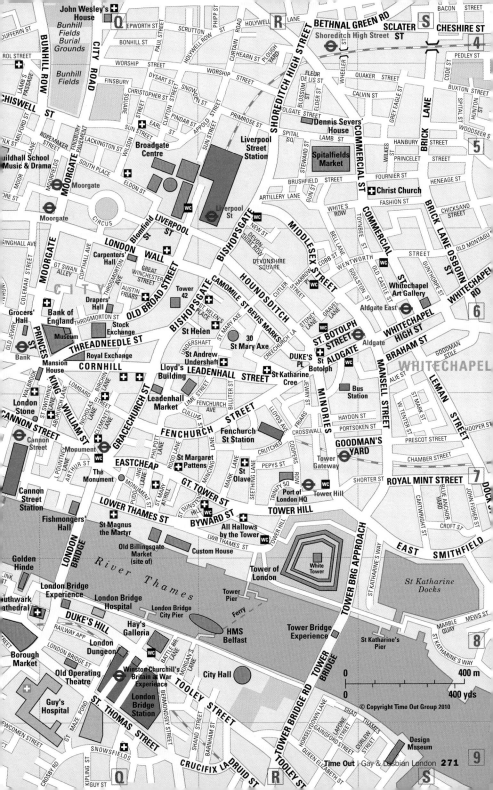

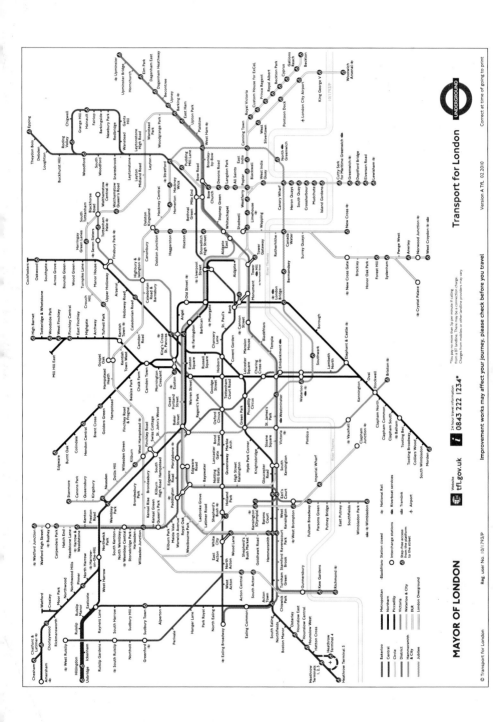